Tolkien's Lost Chaucer

Tolkien's Lost Chaucer

JOHN M. BOWERS

OXFORD
UNIVERSITY PRESS

OXFORD
UNIVERSITY PRESS

Great Clarendon Street, Oxford, OX2 6DP,
United Kingdom

Oxford University Press is a department of the University of Oxford.
It furthers the University's objective of excellence in research, scholarship,
and education by publishing worldwide. Oxford is a registered trade mark of
Oxford University Press in the UK and in certain other countries

© John M. Bowers 2019

The moral rights of the author have been asserted

First Edition published in 2019

Impression: 1

All rights reserved. No part of this publication may be reproduced, stored in
a retrieval system, or transmitted, in any form or by any means, without the
prior permission in writing of Oxford University Press, or as expressly permitted
by law, by licence or under terms agreed with the appropriate reprographics
rights organization. Enquiries concerning reproduction outside the scope of the
above should be sent to the Rights Department, Oxford University Press, at the
address above

You must not circulate this work in any other form
and you must impose this same condition on any acquirer

Published in the United States of America by Oxford University Press
198 Madison Avenue, New York, NY 10016, United States of America

British Library Cataloguing in Publication Data

Data available

Library of Congress Control Number: 2019941406

ISBN 978-0-19-884267-5

DOI: 10.1093/oso/9780198842675.001.0001

Printed and bound by
CPI Group (UK) Ltd, Croydon, CR0 4YY

Links to third party websites are provided by Oxford in good faith and
for information only. Oxford disclaims any responsibility for the materials
contained in any third party website referenced in this work.

Acknowledgements

No scholar works in a vacuum, especially one like myself coming late to a major author, and a number of Tolkien experts made the research more accurate as well as more enjoyable. Many of their names appear in subsequent pages but deserve mentioning here. Oxford medievalists Helen Barr and Simon Horobin referred me to local authorities who in turn referred me to other authorities. Peter Gilliver at the Dictionary Department of Oxford University Press made initial investigations, experienced as he was with the author's handwriting from his work on Tolkien as an *OED* lexicographer, and he introduced me to the other Dictionary staffers Jonathan Dent, Bethan Tovey, and Edmund Weiner who have been liberal with time and knowledge. Charlotte Brewer shared overlapping interests in Skeat's editorial work and the *OED*'s history. Gilliver further connected me with Verlyn Flieger, Michael Drout, John Rateliff, and Jane Chance. Stuart Lee and Elizabeth Solopova added to the camaraderie of Oxford's medievalists turned Tolkien specialists. Christopher Stray kindly sent his forthcoming entry for Kenneth Sisam in *ODNB*. Kathy Lavezzo tracked down information on the independent scholar Mary Edith Thomas. Thomas Honegger was astonishingly eagle-eyed at spotting errors and suggesting improvements in an early draft. It was my very good fortune that UNLV's Black Mountain Institute hosted John Garth as Visiting Humanities Fellow in Las Vegas for the academic year 2015–16, with an office across the hallway from my own, and he shared unstintingly his great store of knowledge on Tolkien's life and works.

Archivists are often the unsung heroes of research projects, and huge credit goes to Martin Maw of Oxford University Press, his OUP predecessor Peter Foden, Robin Darwall-Smith of Magdalen College (who also provided many helpful comments on an early draft), Julian Reid of Merton College, and particularly Catherine McIlwaine of the Bodleian Library's Special Collections. My gratitude to librarians begins with Kyle Felker of UNLV's Lied Library for arousing an interest in Tolkien before I knew that I had one. Colin Harris and his staff assisted gallantly under difficult conditions when the Special Collections Reading Room was exiled to the basement of the Radcliffe Science Library. James Fishwick of Magdalen College Library unearthed publications by George Gordon. Other rare volumes by Gordon were provided by Susan Usher, English Subject Librarian at Oxford's English Faculty Library; she also provided me with a scan of catalogue cards for Tolkien's 'Celtic Library' donated upon his retirement in 1959 and transferred in 2015 to the Bodleian's Weston Library where it is now part of the Tolkien Archive. Michael Spurling and his staff at the Oxford University Press

Library were unfailingly helpful and good-humoured during my two summers in their midst.

Merton College made this venture possible by hosting me grandly during the summers of 2013 and 2014. My thanks go to the Warden Sir Martin Taylor and the Fellows, particularly Richard McCabe, Steven Gunn, Stuart Lee, Julia Walworth, and Domestic Bursar Douglas J. Bamber.

Early overviews of this project were presented at biennial congresses of the New Chaucer Society in Portland in July 2012 and in Reykjavik in July 2014. Tony Edwards is always astonishing for how much he knows and generously shares, notably as a commentator on this entire book in draft form. Bruce Holsinger invited a talk for the Medieval Colloquium at the University of Virginia in October 2014 during my much-appreciated sabbatical from the University of Nevada Las Vegas. In attendance was A. C. Spearing who had met Tolkien when he came to Cambridge in 1964 for the election of a successor to C. S. Lewis's professorship. I wish to express my thanks to Professor Spearing and others who shared their remembrances of Tolkien: John Burrow, Anne Hudson, Peter Dronke, Prosser Gifford, Carter Revard, Derek Brewer, Derek Pearsall, and Roger Highfield. Celia Sisam in retirement on the Scilly Isles kindly read the manuscript and found nothing obviously wrong about her father Kenneth Sisam. V. A. Kolve not only shared his recollections of Tolkien as a teacher in the 1950s but also read an early draft of this book with the same careful attention as when supervising my doctoral dissertation. More times than I can count, my graduate research assistant Peter Steffensen kept me from blunders of citation and quotation.

Cathleen Blackburn of Maier Blackburn granted permission on behalf of the Tolkien Estate for having photocopies of Clarendon Chaucer materials and for using quotations in this book from Tolkien's previously unpublished writings. I am grateful for her quick and generous attentions. Letters from OUP's 'Clarendon Chaucer' file for the years 1922–60 are quoted by permission of the Secretary to the Delegates of Oxford University Press.

When reproducing manuscript quotations, I have followed Christopher Tolkien's lead for expanding abbreviations and applying better punctuation and more consistent capitalization.[1] I share everyone's sense of challenge with handwriting sometimes impossible to read with certainty, and I occasionally make my own best guesses without cluttering the text with brackets to signal conjectures. Tolkien's typewriter produced italics; when he underlined in his handwritten drafts, these were intended as italics and have been reproduced as such. I make reference to *The Lord of the Rings* by volumes, books, and chapters (e.g. *FR* II/2) since these have not changed over several different editions whereas page-numbers have. Every fact, date, and piece of background information not otherwise noted can be

---

[1] See Christopher Tolkien's 'Foreword' to his father's *The Book of Lost Tales: Part I* (1983; New York: Ballantine Books, 1992), pp. xix–xx.

assumed to come from Christina Scull and Wayne G. Hammond's magisterial three-volume *J. R. R. Tolkien Companion and Guide*, the value of which cannot be overestimated. Lastly, I want to thank OUP's copyeditor Dorothy McCarthy for the final stage of improvements; if Tolkien suspected that Chaucer's scribes changed his spellings to fifteenth-century norms, she has changed my spellings to the British usages which would surely have pleased Tolkien.

Contents

List of Illustrations	xi
List of Abbreviations	xiii
1. Prologue: Concerning Chaucer	1
2. Unexpected Journeys	13
3. Four Chaucerians: Walter W. Skeat, Kenneth Sisam, George S. Gordon, C. S. Lewis	41
4. Tolkien as Editor: Text and Glossary	79
5. The Chaucerian Incubus: The Notes	105
6. Tolkien as a Chaucerian: *The Reeve's Tale*	187
7. Chaucer in Middle-earth	223
8. Coda: Fathers and Sons	269
Appendix I	279
Appendix II	283
Works Cited	285
Index	303

List of Illustrations

1. Tolkien's letter of 8 June 1951 to OUP's Dan Davin. By permission of the Secretary to the Delegates of Oxford University Press. © The Tolkien Estate Ltd 2019. — 19
2. Walter W. Skeat. Portrait by Charles Edmund Brock. With kind permission from the Master and Fellows of Christ's College, Cambridge. — 42
3. Kenneth Sisam standing on Middle Carn, the outcrop of rock from which his retirement house on the Scilly Isles took its name. Photograph with permission of Celia Sisam. — 53
4. George S. Gordon. Official portrait with the permission of the President and Fellows of Magdalen College, Oxford. — 61
5. C. S. Lewis. Photograph copyright of Arthur Strong provided by Camera Press, London. — 68
6. Title-page and Tolkien's handwritten table of contents for Proof 1, Copy 1 of *Selections from Chaucer's Poetry and Prose* (Oxford, Bodleian Library, MS Tolkien A 39/1, fol. 1). © The Tolkien Estate Ltd 2019. — 83
7. Tolkien's 'working copy' of the first page-proofs of the *Canterbury Tales* (Oxford, Bodleian Library, MS Tolkien A 39/1, fol. 232). © The Tolkien Estate Ltd 2019. — 91
8. Galley long-sheet of Glossary corrected by Tolkien (Oxford, Bodleian Library, MS Tolkien A 39/3, fol. 10). © The Tolkien Estate Ltd 2019. — 98
9. Tolkien's typed commentary on Chaucer's *Romaunt* (Oxford, Bodleian Library, MS Tolkien A 39/2/1, fol. 6). © The Tolkien Estate Ltd 2019. — 110
10. Handwritten notes on Chaucer's *The Former Age* (Oxford, Bodleian Library, MS Tolkien A 39/2/1, fol. 23). © The Tolkien Estate Ltd 2019. — 130
11. Rewritten commentary on Chaucer's *Boece* (Oxford, Bodleian Library, MS Tolkien A 39/2/1, fol. 37). © The Tolkien Estate Ltd 2019. — 144
12. Handwritten introduction to *Canterbury Tales* (Oxford, Bodleian Library, MS Tolkien A 39/2/2, fol. 83). © The Tolkien Estate Ltd 2019. — 163
13. Introduction to the *Reeve's Tale* with reference in margin to his 1934 "Chaucer as a Philologist." (Oxford, Bodleian Library, MS Tolkien A 39/2/2, fol. 132). © The Tolkien Estate Ltd 2019. — 190
14. Tolkien's 1939 programme edition of *The Reeve's Tale*—last page of introduction and first page of text (Oxford, Bodleian Library, MS Tolkien A 39/3, fols. 28v–29r). © The Tolkien Estate Ltd 1939, 2019. — 191
15. Tolkien's opening page of his lecture series *The Pardoner's Tale: The Story and its Form* (Oxford, Bodleian Library, MS Tolkien A 13/2, fol. 39). © The Tolkien Estate Ltd 2019. — 258

List of Abbreviations

AI	Harold Bloom, *The Anxiety of Influence*. New York: Oxford University Press, 1973.
Biography	Humphrey Carpenter, *J. R. R. Tolkien: A Biography*. 1977; Boston and New York: Houghton Mifflin, 2000.
DNB	*Dictionary of National Biography: 1912–1921*. Ed. H. W. C. Davis and J. R. H. Weaver. London: Oxford University Press, 1927.
EETS	Early English Text Society
Essays	J. R. R. Tolkien, *The Monsters and the Critics and Other Essays*. Ed. Christopher Tolkien. 1983; London: HarperCollins, 2006.
FR	J. R. R. Tolkien, *The Fellowship of the Ring*. 1954; Boston and New York: Houghton Mifflin, 1988.
Hobbit	J. R. R. Tolkien, *The Annotated Hobbit: Revised and Expanded Edition*. Ed. Douglas A. Anderson. Boston and New York: Houghton Mifflin, 2002.
Inklings	Humphrey Carpenter, *The Inklings: C. S. Lewis, J. R. R. Tolkien, Charles Williams and Their Friends*. 1978; London: HarperCollins, 2006.
Letters	*The Letters of J. R. R. Tolkien*. Ed. Humphrey Carpenter and Christopher Tolkien. 1981; Boston and New York: Houghton Mifflin, 2000.
ODNB	*Oxford Dictionary of National Biography*
OED	*Oxford English Dictionary*
OUP	Oxford University Press
RES	*Review of English Studies*
RK	J. R. R. Tolkien, *The Return of the King*. 1955; Boston and New York: Houghton Mifflin, 1988.
SAC	*Studies in the Age of Chaucer*
SH	Christina Scull and Wayne G. Hammond, *J. R. R. Tolkien Companion and Guide: Revised and Expanded Edition*. London: HarperCollins, 2017: Vol. 1: *Chronology*; Vol. 2: *Reader's Guide, Part I: A–M*; Vol. 3. *Reader's Guide, Part II: N–Z*.
Sil	J. R. R. Tolkien, *The Silmarillion*. Ed. Christopher Tolkien. 1977; London: HarperCollins, 2008.
Skeat	Walter W. Skeat, ed. *The Complete Works of Geoffrey Chaucer*. 6 vols. Oxford: Clarendon Press, 1894.
TE	*J. R. R. Tolkien Encyclopedia: Scholarship and Critical Assessment*. Ed. Michael D. C. Drout. New York and London: Routledge, 2007.
TLOR	J. R. R. Tolkien, *The Lord of the Rings*. 1954–5; Boston and New York: Houghton Mifflin, 1988.
TLS	*Times Literary Supplement (London)*
TT	J. R. R. Tolkien, *The Two Towers*. 1954; Boston and New York: Houghton Mifflin, 1988.
UT	J. R. R. Tolkien, *Unfinished Tales of Númenor and Middle-earth*. Ed. Christopher Tolkien. Boston and New York: Houghton Mifflin, 1980.

Tolkien knows more about Chaucer than any living man.

John Masefield
Poet Laureate, 1930–67

1
Prologue: Concerning Chaucer

J. R. R. Tolkien was a specialist in early Germanic languages haunted by how much had disappeared, regretting especially the lost mythology of pre-Christian England and the lost poetry of the Anglo-Saxons.[1] Races as well as languages had gone missing, and archaeological sites not far from his Oxford home bore witness to those long-vanished peoples like his own prehistoric race which left behind its monuments at Dunharrow: 'Their name was lost and no song or legend remembered it.'[2] Personally he had suffered the early loss of both parents and the deaths of close friends during the First World War, and his pessimism showed itself in what his biographer Humphrey Carpenter called his 'deep sense of impending loss. Nothing was safe. Nothing would last.'[3] He found in *Beowulf* this ancient theme that all men and all their works must die. Titles like *The Lost Road*, *The Cottage of Lost Play*, and *The Book of Lost Tales* bear witness to this abiding sense of doom, and his *Silmarillion* grew to become a vast chronicle of loss upon loss. Even when tracing an etymology to a word's earliest roots, he faced the sad reality that 'there is always a lost past'.[4] It is therefore fitting that one of his most widely quoted lines has become 'Not all those who wander are lost.'[5]

Tolkien's Lost Chaucer picks up this theme by exploring his Clarendon edition *Selections from Chaucer's Poetry and Prose* begun in 1922 but left unfinished in 1928, abandoned among so many other dropped projects, and finally lost to Tolkien himself when obliged to return his materials to Oxford University Press in 1951.[6] In contrast with his other unfinished book *'Beowulf' and the Critics*, his Clarendon Chaucer had advanced much farther toward publication, its text and

---

[1] Christina Scull and Wayne G. Hammond, *J. R. R. Tolkien Companion and Guide: Revised and Expanded Edition* (London: HarperCollines, 2017), on 'Loss' 2:740–4. See J. R. R. Tolkien, 'Sigelwara Land', *Medium Ævum* 1 (1932), 183–96: 'In *Sigelhearwan* is preserved at least a name, if no more, from the vanished native mythology' (p. 192).

[2] J. R. R. Tolkien, *The Return of the King* (1956; Boston and New York: Houghton Mifflin, 1988), V/3.

[3] Humphrey Carpenter, *J. R. R. Tolkien: A Biography* (1977; Boston and New York: Houghton Mifflin, 2000), 39.

[4] *The Letters of J. R. R. Tolkien*, ed. Humphrey Carpenter and Christopher Tolkien (1981; Boston and New York: Houghton Mifflin, 2000), 268.

[5] *FR* I/10. 'Alas the lost lore!' he would exclaim about the vanished sources of Virgil's epic (*Essays* 27); see also W. A. Senior, 'Loss Eternal in J. R. R. Tolkien's Middle-earth', in *J. R. R. Tolkien and His Literary Resonances: Views of Middle-earth*, ed. George Clark and Daniel Timmons (Westport and London: Greenwood Press, 2000), 173–82.

[6] See SH 3:1029 for Tolkien's dealings with Oxford University Press.

glossary typeset and meticulously corrected in galleys. Largely as a result of these editorial papers disappearing into OUP's cellar—and disappearing, too, from the biographical record—readers have lost an important sense of Tolkien as a Chaucerian with a deep debt to the fourteenth-century author. When he was elected Oxford's Professor of Anglo-Saxon in 1925, he had become officially an Old English scholar remembered for his bard-like readings from *Beowulf* by students such as W. H. Auden.[7] Tom Shippey's groundbreaking study *The Road to Middle-earth* showed how much Tolkien's training as a medievalist matters for understanding his imaginative writings, and yet Chaucer's name did not appear in his section 'Tolkien's Sources: The True Tradition'.[8] Now with characteristic generosity, Shippey has been the first to herald news of the recovery of the Clarendon Chaucer.[9]

Shippey's previous oversight is hardly surprising since Tolkien lectured on Old English and Icelandic during his first two decades as an Oxford professor and delivered his landmark lecture '*Beowulf*: The Monsters and the Critics' in 1936. His 1934 study 'Chaucer as a Philologist: *The Reeve's Tale*', though routinely cited by the shrinking company of language specialists, has always looked like an accidental detour.[10] Now this substantial article can be seen as an outgrowth of his editorial work on the Reeve's Tale for his Clarendon edition. Though Tolkien had taught Chaucer during his later years at Oxford—when his lectures on the Pardoner's Tale spanned all three terms during 1955–6—his remarks on Chaucer in his 'Valedictory Address' must have sounded unexpected to an audience that did not know how much toil, tears, and sweat he had expended on his Clarendon edition during the 1920s.[11]

Discovery of these materials brings into better focus his professional engagements with the fourteenth-century poet throughout his career. As a schoolboy, he came to medieval literature by way of the *Canterbury Tales* (*Biography*, 36), and as an undergraduate, he took copious notes on Sir Walter Raleigh's Chaucer lectures and wrote essays on topics such as 'Chaucer's Dialect' for his tutor Kenneth Sisam. During his first academic appointment at Leeds, he lectured on the General

---

[7] W. H. Auden, 'A Short Ode to a Philologist' (1962), in *Collected Poems*, ed. Edward Mendelson (New York: Random House, 1976), 566–7.

[8] Tom Shippey, *The Road to Middle-earth*, rev. edn (Boston and New York: Houghton Mifflin, 2003), 343–52. Shippey reasserts the value of this approach in 'Introduction: Why Source Criticism?' in Jason Fisher, ed., *Tolkien and the Study of His Sources: Critical Essays* (Jefferson, NC and London: McFarland & Co., 2011), 7–16.

[9] Tom Shippey, 'Tolkien as Editor', in *A Companion to J. R. R. Tolkien*, ed. Stuart D. Lee (Oxford: Wiley Blackwell, 2014), 41–55 at p. 44: 'thanks to the persistence of John M. Bowers, all Tolkien's materials for this project have been rediscovered.' See also Jane Chance, *J. R. R. Tolkien, Self and Other: 'That Queer Creature'* (New York: Palgrave Macmillan, 2016), 146–7, for discussion of this discovery.

[10] J. R. R. Tolkien, 'Chaucer as a Philologist: *The Reeve's Tale*', *Transactions of the Philological Society* (1934), 1–70. Tom Shippey, 'Tolkien's Academic Reputation Now', in *Roots and Branches: Selected Papers on Tolkien* (Zurich and Jena: Walking Tree Publishers, 2007), 203–12 at pp. 207–8, notes the article's negligible impact on the profession.

[11] *Essays* 233–4; see SH 3:1373–4 on his '*Valedictory Address*'.

Prologue as well as Chaucer's Language. Begun under pressure for scholarly publications as a young academic, the Clarendon Chaucer drew his attention to the dialect humour in the Reeve's Tale and resulted in 'Chaucer as a Philologist', originally delivered in 1931 as the lecture 'Chaucer's Use of Dialects'. Later in this decade, at the invitation of the Poet Laureate John Masefield, Tolkien actually dressed up as Chaucer and recited from memory the Nun's Priest's Tale in 1938 and the Reeve's Tale in 1939. For this second performance, he edited the text for the printed programme in a daring attempt at re-creating the poet's original language, and he probably used this pamphlet later as a teaching text for cadets during the Second World War. Though usually overlooked, the Chaucerian word *losenger* formed the subject of his last scholarly article in 1953.[12] Chaucer was part of Tolkien's mental furniture, so to speak, that he spent a lifetime rearranging.

When he became Oxford's Merton Professor of Language and Literature in 1945, he returned to lecturing on Chaucer after a twenty-year hiatus. The Pardoner's Tale was a set text in the Literature course and the Clerk's Tale for the Language course, the latter replaced by the *Parlement of Foules* in 1948. Chaucerian influences naturally followed during these years when he was completing *The Lord of the Rings*, although the fourteenth-century author had never been far from his thoughts. To follow just one strand with Chaucer's Clerk of Oxford, Tolkien's 1923 review of Furnivall's *Hali Meidenhad* highlighted the female virtue 'most widely familiar in the Clerk's Tale', but he judged that the treatise's discussion was 'more repulsive to modern feeling than anything in Chaucer's tale'.[13] The title of his 1925 poem 'Light as Leaf on Lind' came from the Clerk's Tale where wives were advised to be 'light as leef on lynde',[14] and the phrase went on to survive as 'light as linden-leaves' in Aragorn's lay of Beren and Lúthien (*FR* I/11). When in 1956 he admitted his *Silmarillion* was full of 'all that "heigh stile" (as Chaucer might say)' (*Letters*, 238), he was remembering a phrase from the Clerk's Prologue.

His Chaucerian expertise was most fully displayed in the 160 pages of annotations which he drafted for his *Selections*. Although critics have not explored fully the notes actually published in his *Gawain* and *Pearl* editions, produced in

---

[12] J. R. R. Tolkien, 'Middle English "Losenger": Sketch of an Etymological and Semantic Enquiry', *Essais de Philologie Moderne (1951)* (Paris: Société d'Édition Les Belles Lettres, 1953), 63–76.

[13] Tolkien's unsigned review of *Hali Meidenhad: An Alliterative Prose Homily of the Thirteenth Century*, ed. F. J. Furnivall, EETS Original Series 18 (1922), appeared in *TLS* 26 April 1923, p. 281; it was reprinted in *TLS* 30 June 2017, p. 34. His review copy went with other books donated to Oxford's English Faculty Library, now in the Bodleian's Tolkien Archive. His close reading of this edition brought to Tolkien's attention the word *eaueres* which led to his article 'The Devil's Coach-Horses', *RES* 1/3 (July 1925), 331–6. Half of his article 'Some Contributions to Middle-English Lexicography', *RES* 1 (1925), 210–15, was devoted to the glossary of Furnivall's EETS edition.

[14] Joe R. Christopher, 'Tolkien's Lyric Poetry', *Tolkien's 'Legendarium'*, ed. Flieger and Hostetter, 143–60 at p. 150. The lyric 'Light as Leaf on Linden' was embedded in 'The Lay of the Children of Húrin' in Tolkien's *The Lays of Beleriand*, ed. Christopher Tolkien (1985; New York: Ballantine Books, 1994), 128–31, with commentary on poem's evolution, pp. 142–7.

collaboration with E. V. Gordon, his unpublished annotations for the Clarendon Chaucer, produced on his own, represent a goldmine for appreciating his literary and linguistic interests at the start of his career. His 1939 lecture 'On Fairy–Stories' dedicated a major section to 'Recovery'—by which Tolkien meant 'a re-gaining—regaining of a clear view'.[15] Regaining that clear view of Chaucer's importance for Tolkien's career as scholar and storyteller is the purpose of this book.

'Chapter 2: Unexpected Journeys' recounts how Tolkien laboured on this project during the 1920s, how he bemoaned its standstill during the 1930s, and how he complained bitterly about returning his materials to OUP in 1951. The chapter then recounts how Tolkien's lost book was unearthed in the Press archives where I began studying the materials during summer 2013 and making sense of the documents in light of the correspondence. Early in 2014, these materials were transferred to the Bodleian Library's Special Collection where archivist Catherine McIlwaine has carefully arranged the batches into folders, paginated them, and granted them the safeguards afforded to other Tolkien papers. My second research visit during autumn 2014 allowed additional study of Tolkien's lectures on the Pardoner's Tale from the 1950s to reveal a deepening engagement with Chaucer at the same time as publishing *The Lord of the Rings*.

But what to do with the long-lost Chaucer edition? A doctoral thesis could follow the details of the evolving project during the 1920s, and *Selections from Chaucer's Poetry and Prose* could be published as a hefty volume representing exactly what Tolkien did accomplish. Such editions have a noble pedigree. Frederick J. Furnivall and his Early English Text Society editors often reproduced manuscripts almost as facsimiles in print.[16] The method endured into the twentieth century with Tolkien's own EETS edition of the *Ancrene Wisse*. But Michael Drout's heroic struggles with Tolkien's unfinished *'Beowulf' and the Critics* demonstrate how this undertaking would not be easy for an editor or attractive for readers. Here is how Drout's text ends as the legibility of Tolkien's handwriting trails off: 'It is slow laborious, compact and often taken ???? but full of feeling. ??? ??? what the ???? same time is large and ??????'[17] Straining over Tolkien's draft manuscripts, a researcher often feels like Gandalf puzzling over the slashed, stabbed, and partly burned Book of Mazarbul.

Tolkien's review of Furnivall's posthumous *Hali Meidenhad* explains why he would have objected to having his own unfinished edition published in this fashion: 'It may be doubted whether, even though it has been done out of great respect for a great name, the best service has been rendered to that name, or to English scholarship, by publishing work that might have been revised and

---

[15] *Essays* 146; see also SH 3:1064–6 'Recovery'.
[16] Donald C. Baker, 'Frederick James Furnivall (1825–1910)' in *Editing Chaucer*, ed. Ruggiers, 157–69.
[17] J. R. R. Tolkien, *'Beowulf' and the Critics*, ed. Michael D. C. Drout (Tempe: Arizona Center for Medieval and Renaissance Studies, 2002), 78.

supplemented.' Still on the threshold of a career not yet littered with unfinished works, Tolkien regretted that the indefatigable pioneer of Middle English studies had not lived to complete an edition printed by EETS without alteration as he left it.

My approach takes into respectful account what Tolkien *did* accomplish in his edited text, glossary, and notes, drawing into discussion his ancillary publication 'Chaucer as a Philologist' and highlighting this editorial project's contributions to his career as a fiction-writer as well as a scholar and teacher. As much as possible, I quote from these pages to let him speak in his own voice when sharing thoughts about Chaucer, Middle English language, and storytelling in general. He wrote in 1951 to the Press Secretary Dan Davin that his materials represented 'much that is fresh, and a prodigious amount of labour' (Fig. 1). It is only right that the fruits of these labours should not be entirely lost but preserved, like Christopher Tolkien's edition of his father's undergraduate *Beowulf* lectures, 'in words of his own, hitherto unpublished'.[18]

'Chapter 3: Four Chaucerians' discusses Tolkien's editorial collaborator George S. Gordon (not to be confused with E. V. Gordon, his co-editor for *Gawain*) as well as Walter W. Skeat, Kenneth Sisam, and C. S. Lewis and reviews the various roles they played in the project's genesis and the complications that arose. The names of Gordon and Sisam will have become familiar from the survey of OUP correspondence in Chapter 2, but more about their personalities and Oxford careers will help for understanding the fate of the Clarendon Chaucer. Tolkien's practice in scholarly studies like '*Beowulf*: The Monsters and the Critics' was to dismiss prior critical efforts to clear ground for his own views, but the colossal presence of Skeat's *Complete Works of Geoffrey Chaucer* could not be so handily discharged.[19] Though somewhat hackneyed after more than forty years, Harold Bloom's *anxiety of influence* proves remarkably applicable to Tolkien's various responses as he laboured in the shadow of Skeat's monumental six-volume edition. By tracing the transmissions from older writers to new ones, Bloom offered a different kind of the source criticism useful for understanding how Tolkien sorted out Chaucer's literary sources while himself wrestling with Skeat as his principal scholarly source.[20] No description of Tolkien's Oxford life would be complete without considering the role of C. S. Lewis, and so I conclude this chapter by wondering why Lewis, always so effective at encouraging his friend

---

[18] J. R. R. Tolkien, *Beowulf: A Translation and Commentary*, ed. Christopher Tolkien (Boston and New York: Houghton Mifflin, 2014), p. xiii. Most publications refer to Christopher Tolkien by first name as shorthand for distinguishing him from his father.

[19] *The Complete Works of Geoffrey Chaucer*, ed. Walter W. Skeat, 6 vols. (Oxford: Clarendon Press, 1894).

[20] E. L. Risden, 'Source Criticism: Background and Applications', in Fisher, ed., *Tolkien and the Study of His Sources*, 17–28, at pp. 21 and 24 for the usefulness of Bloom's *Anxiety of Influence*. See also SH 3:1245–50 'Source Criticism'.

to finish other books, did not nudge him ahead to complete this seemingly straightforward editorial project.

The next chapter, 'Tolkien as Editor: Text and Glossary', examines the printed materials passed back and forth in various states of correction, revision, abbreviation, and re-typesetting during the mid-1920s when the edition moved haltingly forward. It is hardly an exciting subject even for specialists, but Tolkien invested considerable effort in these dry-as-dust details. Like other survivors of the Great War, he dedicated himself anew to rescuing Europe's cultural artefacts, even when these legacies resided in the tiniest details of a canonic author's spelling and pronunciation. What he learned from close acquaintance with Chaucer—for example, the poet's indebtedness to the Alliterative tradition—anticipated discoveries by subsequent scholars and marked the course of Tolkien's own endeavours as philologist and poet.

The fifth chapter, 'The Chaucerian Incubus: The Notes', looks all out of proportion because Tolkien's annotations themselves far exceeded the modest scale of a student edition. Despite demands from his OUP overseer Kenneth Sisam for only twenty pages, Tolkien by 1928 had drafted some 160 pages delving into etymologies, Classical and Continental sources, and historical contexts at far greater length than financially feasible. Ironically Tolkien had praised the self-restraint of a fellow scholar in 1927: 'Knowing how these little lexicographical chases open vista after vista and one complication after another, we can well believe that much self-denial was practiced to keep the notes down to thirteen pages.'[21] But he found it easier to praise than imitate this self-denial as he struggled under the burden of Skeat's achievements, walking in his predecessor's footsteps but (to switch metaphors) knowing at every pace that he was not filling his shoes. Though these excesses doomed the project, Tolkien's annotations now hold considerable value for the insights they provide into his own philological and literary interests.

The sixth chapter, 'Tolkien as a Chaucerian: *The Reeve's Tale*', discusses what has always seemed like a mysterious outlier in Tolkien's career. Just when he should have been making headway on his *Beowulf* book in the 1930s, he marshalled an immense amount of detailed evidence for his landmark study 'Chaucer as a Philologist' published in *Transactions of the Philological Society*. When viewed in light of the Clarendon edition, however, this language study emerges as a logical extension of the investigations incomplete on paper but not in the editor's mind. His ongoing fascination with Chaucer's mastery of Northern dialect then led Tolkien to edit anew the Reeve's Tale in the printed programme for the Oxford Summer Diversions in 1939. And in the 1940s, when teaching the Reeve's Tale to cadets heading off to the battlefield, he had clearly in mind the two young men

---

[21] J. R. R. Tolkien, 'Philology: General Works', *Year's Work in English Studies*, 6 (1927), 32–66 at p. 35. See SH 3:1453–4 '*Year's Work in English Studies*'.

John and Alain's fight with the miller Simkin and—I shall argue—he drew upon this core-story when imagining how the young hobbits Merry and Pippin join the attack upon the mill-master Saruman.[22] Malicious millers were already prominent in the Chaucerian legacy—from the violent, vulgar Miller of the General Prologue to the devious, dangerous miller of the Reeve's Tale—and Tolkien extended this tradition in his own fiction beginning with Hobbiton's unsavoury millers Sandyman and his son Ted.[23]

The next to last chapter, 'Chaucer in Middle-earth', follows Tolkien's involvements with the fourteenth-century author even after his collaborator George Gordon's death in 1942 when it was clear their edition would never see completion. He had learned many things that he found useful, as he said in his last letter to OUP's Dan Davin, and the creative legacy of Chaucer's other works such as *Troilus and Criseyde* proved crucial, for example, when writing his account of Faramir's love and courtship of Éowyn. Tolkien well understood how his stories grew 'out of all that has been seen or thought or read, that has long ago been forgotten, descending into the deeps' (SH 2:370), and Chaucer provided a great deal of this deep-buried remembrance, his influence palpable to the very end of Tolkien's fiction-writing in works such as *Smith of Wootton Major*. His *Beowulf* lecture may have mocked source-hunters more interested in the tower's building-blocks than the lofty construction, and he lamented this pursuit to the end of his life when writing that 'the search for the sources of *The Lord of the Rings* is going to occupy academics for a generation or two' (*Letters*, 418). But he was perfectly capable of launching upon his own quest for sources when it suited his purposes. This happened in his late Oxford lectures on the Pardoner's Tale when he recognized, probably to his own great surprise, that Chaucer's core-story of three men fighting to the death over a gold treasure was also his core-story in *The Lord of the Rings*.

But why a whole book on Tolkien's unfinished student edition of Chaucer? Let me put this question another way. What if researchers discovered Shakespeare's heavily annotated copy of Stowe's 1561 Chaucer edition which he had used when writing *A Midsummer Night's Dream* and *Troilus and Cressida*?[24] It would be front-page news, a facsimile would be announced, and multiple scholars would begin work at teasing out the Bard's reader-responses. This is exactly the storm of

---

[22] J. R. R. Tolkien, *The Treason of Isengard: The History of 'The Lord of the Rings': Part Two*, ed. Christopher Tolkien (Boston and New York: Houghton Mifflin, 1989), 437, shows this was his plan early in the 1940s: 'Then relate the battle from Merry and Pippin's point of view.'

[23] Lee Patterson, *Chaucer and the Subject of History* (Madison: University of Wisconsin Press, 1991), 'The Miller's Tale and the Politics of Laughter', pp. 244–79, traces the roots of Chaucer's hostility to the role played by millers in the Peasants' Revolt of 1381; Tolkien's hostility was based more upon mills as dirty, violent machines that required fuel from the felling of trees.

[24] Nevill Coghill, 'Shakespeare's Reading in Chaucer', *Elizabethan and Jacobean Studies Presented to F. P. Wilson*, ed. Herbert Davis and Helen Gardner (Oxford: Oxford University Press, 1959), 86–99.

publicity that surrounded the recent discovery of a previously unknown source for Shakespeare.[25] And if Jane Austen had written a long, thoughtful commentary on Thomas Tyrwhitt's 1775 edition of the *Canterbury Tales*, wouldn't we want to know what she had to say about her great predecessor in comic irony? Here in the twenty-first century, in terms of readership, book sales, number of translations, and success of film adaptations, Tolkien has come to occupy a position in English literature just as conspicuous as Shakespeare and Jane Austen—whether the dons like it or not. A 2003 poll in the United Kingdom found that *The Lord of the Rings* had edged out *Pride and Prejudice* to become the nation's favourite novel. Therefore a book-length study of Tolkien's Chaucer edition has value for appreciating what he thought about the Father of English Literature in the 1920s when he had not yet begun his own career as one of the most widely read authors of all times.[26]

It is even possible to speculate (somewhat recklessly) that Tolkien would never have become a published novelist without the Clarendon Chaucer project. It is generally acknowledged that his co-editor George Gordon manoeuvred behind the scenes to secure Tolkien's 1925 election as Professor of Anglo-Saxon at Oxford. His motives for this string-pulling have always seemed murky, but now we may have a specific reason, if only one among many, why Gordon wanted him in Oxford. By 1924 Tolkien was causing delays by re-editing instead of simply reprinting from Skeat. And instead of sending a twenty-page glossary as assigned, he compiled thirty-eight pages before he was forced to reduce it. Next he experienced even greater difficulty with keeping his explanatory notes to a manageable length. Tolkien had worked successfully on his *Gawain* edition because elbow-to-elbow with his collaborator E. V. Gordon in Leeds.[27] Clearly he required on-site supervision and later admitted as much when trying to complete *The Silmarillion*: 'It needs the actual *presence* of a friend and adviser at one's side' (*Letters*, 366). Though Tolkien had certainly proven himself a brilliant linguist and programme-builder at Leeds, George Gordon had reason to believe that bringing him to Oxford would also allow direct oversight for completing their Chaucer edition. There were certainly many contributing factors, including the fact that the best-qualified candidate withdrew, but finishing the Clarendon

---

[25] A front-page article in the *New York Times* (8 February 2018) heralded publication of Dennis McCarthy and June Schlueter, '*A Brief Discourse of Rebellion and Rebels' by George North: A Newly Uncovered Manuscript Source for Shakespeare's Plays* (Cambridge: D. S. Brewer, 2018).

[26] T. A. Shippey, *J. R. R. Tolkien: Author of the Century* (Boston and New York: Houghton Mifflin, 2001), pp. xvii–xxvi, makes the case for Tolkien exercising tremendous influence on the literary world even prior to the upsurge in popular readership in the wake of Peter Jackson's film adaptations. My book *Chaucer and Langland: The Antagonistic Tradition* (Notre Dame: University of Notre Dame Press, 2007) has as its central question why Chaucer was established as the Father of English Literature.

[27] Douglas A. Anderson, '"An Industrious Little Devil": E. V. Gordon as Friend and Collaborator with Tolkien', *Tolkien the Medievalist*, ed. Jane Chance (London: Routledge, 2003), 15–25; see also SH 2:464–6.

Chaucer might certainly be added to Gordon's motives for securing Tolkien's Oxford professorship.

Had Gordon not pulled strings behind the scenes, an alternative history can be imagined for Tolkien's career—and not a happy one for fans of *The Lord of the Rings*. Without his move to Oxford, Tolkien might well have spent the rest of his academic life at Leeds where he was already promoted to Professor of English Language in 1924, but where he probably would not have flourished to the same degree as a fiction-writer. Not working in Oxford would have deprived him of the encouragement from C. S. Lewis to complete *The Hobbit*. Without Oxford as a prestigious base, he would not have benefited from the fortuitous connection with the London publishing house of Allen & Unwin. Without robust sales of *The Hobbit* boosted by Lewis's rave reviews in *TLS* and *The Times*, Stanley Unwin would not have encouraged him to write a second hobbit book. And even if he had started a sequel, Tolkien would not have completed his book during the difficult 1940s except for the support of his Inklings friends, particularly Lewis. Tolkien admitted as much: 'But for his interest and unceasing eagerness for more, I should never have brought *The Lord of the Rings* to a conclusion' (*Letters*, 362).

Tolkien's masterpiece came into being and changed the literary landscape, in short, because George Gordon finagled successfully to hire Tolkien at Oxford in some measure for the sake of completing their stalled Chaucer edition. Thus this humble-looking textbook, albeit never finished and published, became a fateful link in the chain of events. If not for *Selections from Chaucer's Poetry and Prose*, it is just possible that we would never have heard of Bilbo, Frodo, and Gandalf the Grey.

Journey in the Dark

Everyone has his own Tolkien story, and mine almost disqualifies me from writing this book. I never read *The Hobbit* in high school or *The Lord of the Rings* at university because I was put off by the Tolkien cult whose members wore FRODO LIVES! T-shirts. Reading the Harvard Lampoon's *Bored of the Rings* did not motivate me to tackle the original work. And when I arrived as a student at Oxford in 1973, I sensed the lingering resentment toward Tolkien as a professor who published bestsellers about fairies instead of scholarly books about *Beowulf*. So I remained a holdout.

On the other hand, a medievalist is potentially Tolkien's best-equipped reader. As a graduate student, I studied *Sir Gawain and the Green Knight* in his Clarendon edition and *Pearl* in the edition which he helped to complete. I had read his *Beowulf* lecture with admiration, recommending its concluding paragraph as a model of bravura rhetoric to my first-year students at the University of Virginia, and I happened upon 'Chaucer as a Philologist' early in my graduate training, wondering even then why Tolkien wrote at length about one of the cruder fabliaux from the *Canterbury Tales*. My first book on *Piers Plowman* discussed Langland's use of the word *fairye* by quoting Tolkien's 'On Fairy-Stories' without at the time knowing anything about Legolas, Elrond, or Galadriel.[28]

Events nonetheless conspired to put me in the right places. When I first arrived in Oxford in 1972 for a summer programme at Exeter College—unbeknownst to me at the time Tolkien's undergraduate college—I happened to witness the scarlet-gowned academics processing into the Sheldonian Theatre without knowing that Professor Tolkien was among them being awarded an honorary Doctor of Letters. So just as Ovid wrote with regret, 'I only saw Virgil',[29] I too can say that I only saw Tolkien—but without knowing until many years afterwards that I had actually seen him.

When I returned to Oxford as a Rhodes Scholar for Michaelmas Term 1973, I would discover that all my teachers had been Tolkien's students. My thesis supervisor Rosemary Woolf had been assigned Tolkien as her thesis examiner in 1949 and later contributed her chapter 'Moral Chaucer and Kindly Gower' to the memorial volume *J. R. R. Tolkien, Scholar and Storyteller*. I attended a class on Old Norse taught by Ursula Dronke whose thesis *An Edition of Þorgils and Haflið* had been supervised by Tolkien. My B.Phil. examiner Celia Sisam, daughter of Kenneth Sisam, had been assigned Tolkien as her B.Litt. adviser. My college supervisor Norman Davis, also my teacher for History of the English Language, was Tolkien's former student and successor as Merton Professor of Language and Literature.[30] Douglas Gray, my tutor for Scottish Chaucerians, would become the first J. R. R. Tolkien Professor of English Literature and Language at Oxford. And my Chaucer tutor John Burrow attended Tolkien's Chaucer lectures in the mid-1950s as did his future wife Diana Wynne Jones. 'We both heard Tolkien lecture (inaudibly), and Diana found him interesting on plots', Professor Burrow wrote me. 'An impressive, handsome man—but not a public performer like C. S. Lewis.'[31]

Even my American doctoral adviser V. A. Kolve figures in this story as one of Tolkien's last probationer B.Litt. students in 1958. He well remembers the ritual for relieving shyness on both sides when he arrived for these sessions at eleven o'clock and Tolkien would ask, 'Do you think it's too early for gin?' Two glasses, neither very clean but each with a splash of gin, relaxed them both and moved the

---

[28] John M. Bowers, *The Crisis of Will in 'Piers Plowman'* (Washington, DC: Catholic University of America Press, 1986), 138.

[29] Ovid, *Tristia ex Ponto*, ed. and trans. Arthur Leslie Wheeler (Cambridge: Loeb Classics, Harvard University Press, 1965), IV, x, 51: 'Vergilium vidi tantum' (p. 200).

[30] In his *Letters*, pp. 322–3, Tolkien mentions the surprise Festschrift for his seventieth birthday: 'A plot hatched and carried out by Rayner Unwin & Norman Davis (my successor) of which I knew nothing.' Davis also earned good mention in Carpenter's *Biography* for driving the Tolkiens for weekly luncheons at country inns; see SH 2:296.

[31] Private correspondence, 19 June 2006, by permission.

conversation forward. All these years later Professor Kolve recalls Tolkien's kindness in giving him rolls of handwritten notes, stored in pigeon-holes along the wall of his Merton rooms, and saying on each occasion, 'Here. Take these and see if you find them useful.' Thus Tolkien's drawbacks as a lecturer found compensation: 'one-on-one, in the intimate setting of a supervision, he was generous and could be quite wonderful.'[32]

As a member of Merton College, I often walked to our squash courts past the house at 3 Manor Road where Tolkien completed *The Lord of the Rings*. My student digs at 3 Holywell Street faced across to 99 Holywell where Tolkien lived when compiling the Appendices.[33] But matriculating in October 1973 meant that I arrived too late to meet the man himself, who had returned to college accommodations at 21 Merton Street, but had died in Bournemouth a month before my coming up. I had arrived in time only to attend his memorial service in Merton Chapel. After the ceremonies Professor Davis introduced me to someone important, but whether Christopher Tolkien or Rayner Unwin, I cannot recall after more than forty-five years. I did, however, keep the ticket of admission and sometimes wonder what it might fetch on eBay's online auction.

My neglect of Tolkien's fiction lasted until 2001 when Peter Jackson's film adaption of *The Fellowship of the Ring* was released and my sister gave me a boxed set of the trilogy for Christmas.[34] Immediately I was hooked as a 'film-firster' who saw the movies before reading the books.[35] Soon I was teaching a Tolkien course for undergraduates, and not long afterwards I published a piece in *Tolkien Studies*. In a sense this article, 'Tolkien's Goldberry and *The Maid of the Moor*', set the model for this book, first looking at a medieval text which Tolkien had closely studied and then following its influences into his imaginative writings.[36] My late-career enthusiasm led me during the fall semester 2011 to reading straight through Scull and Hammond's *Chronology* where I began spotting references to the Clarendon Chaucer—and my unexpected journey began.

---

[32] Private email, 8 October 2012, by permission. John D. Rateliff, *The Story of The Hobbit* (London: HarperCollins, 2013), 3–4, cited other instances of Tolkien giving away manuscript materials, and Professor Kolve laments that his handwritten pages went missing during the move to his first job at Stanford University. In summer 1973 when I served as Kolve's research assistant in Oxford, we too ended our work days with tumblers of gin.
[33] In Tolkien's *Lays of Beleriand*, 394, Christopher dates the revision of *Lay of Leithian* because on one of the pages 'my father drew a floor-plan of part of the house 99 Holywell Street, Oxford, to which he removed in 1950'.
[34] Tolkien never approved of this term. See *Letters*, 221: 'The book is *not* of course a "trilogy". That and the titles of the volumes was a fudge thought necessary for publication, owing to length and cost.'
[35] Shippey, 'Another Road to Middle-earth: Jackson's Movie Trilogy', *Roots and Branches*, 365–86, reckons that film-watchers outnumber readers of *The Lord of the Rings*; for many, the trilogy means the movies, not the books.
[36] John M. Bowers, 'Tolkien's Goldberry and *The Maid of the Moor*', *Tolkien Studies* 8 (2011), 23–36; he had studied closely this dance-song when compiling the glossary for Kenneth Sisam's *Fourteenth Century Verse and Prose* (Oxford: Clarendon Press, 1921), 167.

So it is not entirely accurate that I was the least likely person to make this discovery and appreciate its value. I had established myself as a Chaucerian by publishing sixteen articles as well as my book *Chaucer and Langland*, where I proposed Chaucer's son Thomas as the person responsible for posthumous publication of his father's unfinished *Canterbury Tales*—much as Christopher took charge of publishing his father's *Silmarillion*.[37] My two books *The Politics of 'Pearl'* and *Introduction to the 'Gawain' Poet* broke new ground with the other fourteenth-century poet on whom Tolkien laboured steadily over the years.[38] I also published on Middle English textual theory and edited my own collection of fifteenth-century Chaucerian poems.[39] By the time I chanced upon Scull and Hammond's references to Tolkien's unpublished Clarendon edition, in short, I had unwittingly positioned myself for this undertaking. I knew Chaucer, and I knew editing. With my long-time Merton College connections, tracing Professor Tolkien's Chaucerian legacy in *The Hobbit* and *The Lord of the Rings* felt almost like an act of collegiate piety.

---

[37] Bowers, *Chaucer and Langland*, 'The House of Chaucer & Son', 183–90.
[38] John M. Bowers, *The Politics of 'Pearl': Court Poetry in the Age of Richard II* (Cambridge: D. S. Brewer, 2001), and *An Introduction to the 'Gawain' Poet* (Gainesville: University Press of Florida, 2012).
[39] John M. Bowers, 'Hoccleve's Two Copies of *Lerne to Dye*: Implications for Textual Critics', *Papers of the Bibliographical Society of America* 83 (1989), 437–72, and *The Canterbury Tales: Fifteenth-Century Continuations and Additions* (Kalamazoo: Western Michigan University TEAMS Medieval Institute Publication; 2nd edn rev. 1999).

2
Unexpected Journeys

J. R. R. Tolkien would have become Geoffrey Chaucer's most famous editor if he had completed his *Selections from Chaucer's Poetry and Prose*. This is not because his textbook would have superseded Walter W. Skeat's editions or prevented F. N. Robinson's *Riverside Chaucer* from becoming the standard text for teaching and scholarly citation in the twentieth century—it would not have done so—but because readers of *The Lord of the Rings* are forever curious about any book with his name on the title-page and the trilogy's readers are legion. Tolkien did make discoveries and provided brilliant insights, but the volume on its own merits would likely have sunk without trace if published as planned in 1925.[1] As things turned out, not only was his Chaucer edition left unfinished and unpublished, but it was also wholly unknown as a scholarly project until the twenty-first century.[2] Although Tolkien's life has been as thoroughly documented as any writer who ever lived, his Clarendon Chaucer was not mentioned in Humphrey Carpenter's authorized biography, his companion volume *The Inklings*, or his edition of Tolkien's letters.[3] Not even C. S. Lewis referred to his friend's edition in his diaries for the period 1922–7 when Tolkien completed as much work as he ever completed.[4]

When donating manuscripts to the Bodleian Library in 1985, Christopher noted that his father's unfinished *'Beowulf' and the Critics* was entirely unknown,[5] but at least the book was known *about* in the 1930s when Tolkien distilled its content in his British Academy lecture 'The Monsters and the Critics'. His father worked on so many projects at the same time, however, that even Christopher missed out on works like the 2,000-line *Lay of the Children of Húrin*: 'I do not

---

[1] Shippey, 'Tolkien's Academic Reputation Now', concludes that his overall scholarly impact was minimal except for the *Beowulf* lecture, *Gawain* edition, and glossary for Sisam's *Fourteenth Century Verse and Prose*.

[2] *Who's Who in Literature* for 1925 was easy to miss; even his name was not spelled correctly: 'TOLKIEN, John Ronal Reuel, M.A. B. 1892. Au. of *A Middle English Vocabulary* (Clar. Pr.), 1922; *Sir Gawain and the Green Knight* (do.), 1924; *Selections from Chaucer* (do.), 1925...'.

[3] Carpenter, *J. R. R. Tolkien: A Biography* (1977); *The Inklings* (1978; London: HarperCollins, 2006); and *The Letters of J. R. R. Tolkien*, ed. Humphrey Carpenter and Christopher Tolkien (1981; Boston and New York: Houghton Mifflin, 2000).

[4] *All My Road Before Me: The Diary of C. S. Lewis 1922-1927*, ed. Walter Hooper (San Diego: Harcourt Brace Jovanovich, 1991), 392–3, recounts his first meeting with Tolkien in May 1926, two years before he quit drafting the Clarendon Chaucer's notes.

[5] Tolkien, *'Beowulf' and the Critics*, ed. Drout, p. xv.

Tolkien's Lost Chaucer. John M. Bowers, Oxford University Press (2019). © John M. Bowers.
DOI: 10.1093/oso/9780198842675.001.0001

recollect his ever speaking of it.'[6] Because Tolkien conceived of his professional duties largely in terms of editing,[7] some mystery remains why no mention of the Clarendon Chaucer surfaced until Scull and Hammond's *Companion and Guide* in 2006.[8] These two assiduous researchers studied the OUP correspondence in order to chronicle the editorial project from 1922 when Tolkien joined as co-editor until 1951 when he returned the materials to the Press Secretary. When I came across these references in their *Chronology* volume, curiosity prompted some long-distance sleuthing. It was never my intention to launch a major research project, but Scull and Hammond provided tantalizing hints that made discovering what materials he surrendered in 1951 into a worthwhile quest. As Jane Chance has observed, what Tolkien read and studied 'opens a door into understanding how he uniquely interpreted and repurposed the medieval in constructing fantasy'.[9] The more we know about this editorial project, in short, the more Chaucer's contributions to his other scholarly and fictional writings come into focus.

The story of his Chaucer edition is a long one because delays extended over many years. Tolkien's letters are famously filled with health complaints as excuses, not all of them fancied. C. S. Lewis's brother Warren wrote about their accident-prone friend: 'Of all the men I have ever met, poor Tolkien is the most unfortunate.'[10] In addition to ailments and domestic disruptions, Tolkien was easily distracted by side projects at Leeds and Oxford throughout the 1920s. For example, his three 'Philology' chapters for *The Year's Work in English Studies* (1923–5) required him to review long dense books, often in German, with very short deadlines for publication. Overall, though, he was a perfectionist and by his own admission a niggler prone to chasing down details interesting mostly to himself, indulging over the course of his career in extravagant ambitions realized only in *The Lord of the Rings*. During the search for an editor for the *OED* Supplement in 1922, R. W. Chapman proved

---

[6] *Lays of Beleriand*, p. vii; see also J. R. R. Tolkien, *The Legend of Sigurd and Gudrún*, ed. Christopher Tolkien (Boston and New York: Houghton Mifflin Harcourt, 2009), 4–5 and 13–15.

[7] Shippey, 'Tolkien as Editor', identifies eleven editorial projects with only *Gawain* completed on time according to expectations.

[8] SH 2:220–3. Concurrent with Scull and Hammond's 2006 edition was Peter Gilliver's conference paper on the Clarendon Chaucer subsequently published with colleagues Edmund Weiner and Jeremy Marshall as 'The Word as Leaf: Perspectives on Tolkien as Lexicographer and Philologist', in *Tolkien's 'The Lord of the Rings': Sources of Inspiration*, ed. Stratford Caldecott and Thomas Honegger (Zollikofen, Switzerland: Walking Tree Publishers, 2008), 57–83; Gilliver's Part I, pp. 59–70, discusses Tolkien's eight surviving letters in OUP's Clarendon Chaucer file (CP57/1041).

[9] Chance, *Tolkien, Self and Other*, p. xii; she herself now connects the Clarendon Chaucer with Tolkien's imagining of his hobbits, especially the fabliaux's influence on the rusticity of the Shire (p. 139).

[10] *Brothers and Friends: The Diaries of Major Warren Hamilton Lewis*, ed. Clyde S. Kilby and Marjorie Lamp Mead (San Francisco: Harper & Row, 1982), 173. See SH 2:483–7 'Health' and 2:302–4 'Domestic Duties'.

prescient when writing to the Vice-Chancellor: 'Tolkien hasn't (yet) enough driving power.'[11]

First of all, it is worth clarifying what a Clarendon edition was—and why Tolkien was chosen to work upon one. Central to this story is Kenneth Sisam about whom much will be said in Chapter 3. After serving as lexicographer at *OED* during 1915–16, Sisam joined OUP as Junior Assistant Secretary in 1923 and became Assistant Secretary to the Delegates in 1925.[12] He believed the Clarendon imprint should be reserved for books produced only at Oxford, not London, though marketed to the widest possible readership.[13] Sisam himself became instrumental in this move toward inexpensive textbooks for a growing educational market after young men returned from the Great War. Even before Sisam joined the Press, however, George Gordon had spotted an opening and proposed a new edition of Chaucer.

It would not be unfair to say the Clarendon Chaucer started with miscalculations and ended as a mess. When Sisam took charge, he made his first mistake by approving George Gordon as senior co-editor. Gordon had arrived in Oxford to become Merton Professor of Literature in 1922, and although a popular lecturer and expert organizer, he was not a Chaucer specialist. He accepted the assignment of writing the Introduction and Testimonials—the latter essentially a reception history—during that bygone era when it was assumed any English don could write intelligently about any English author. Gordon did produce brief biographies of later writers such as Francis Bacon and Sir Thomas Browne, enough of them to collect in a book after his death,[14] but for some reason the fourteenth-century Chaucer stymied him. It has been noted that Tolkien needed a collaborator to push him along,[15] but the Clarendon Chaucer needed a collaborator more expert on medieval literature as well as more steadily focused than George Gordon.

And why Tolkien as junior co-editor? When working at the *OED* in 1919, the young lexicographer performed so capably that his former tutor Sisam commissioned him to compile the glossary for his own Clarendon textbook *Fourteenth Century Verse and Prose*. Sisam was a stickler for punctuality; his planning and oversight would figure in the successful completion of major projects like the *OED* and its Supplement. When Tolkien was tardy delivering his assignment

---

[11] Peter Gilliver, *The Making of the Oxford English Dictionary* (Oxford: Oxford University Press, 2016), 360.
[12] Ibid. 331.
[13] *The History of Oxford University Press*, gen. ed. Simon Eliot: *Volume II: 1780–1896*, ed. Simon Eliot; *Volume III: 1896–1970*, ed. Wm. Roger Louis (Oxford: Oxford University Press, 2013), 3:394–5.
[14] George S. Gordon, *The Lives of Authors* (London: Chatto & Windus, 1950).
[15] Carpenter, *Biography*, 145, attributed problems with the *Pearl* edition to the fact that his collaborator E. V. Gordon moved to Manchester and could not provide the steady encouragement which Tolkien required.

(a harbinger of things to come) Sisam forged ahead with publication of his portion in October 1921.[16] As a result, Tolkien's glossary initially appeared in May 1922 as a separate volume entitled *A Middle English Vocabulary*, his first published book. When combined with Sisam's edition in June of that year, the double-column glossary bulked large, taking up 168 of the total 460 pages. Tolkien himself admitted to his old tutor Joseph Wright's wife how arduous the project had been: 'I certainly lavished an amount of time on it which is terrible to recall' (*Letters*, 11). Yet it earned acclaim in *The Year's Work in English Studies* as 'a piece of work which can hardly be praised too highly'[17]—just when Gordon was looking for a co-editor to handle the glossary for his Clarendon Chaucer.

Gordon already knew Tolkien well after recruiting the younger scholar to Leeds, and years later Tolkien acknowledged this debt when recalling 'my prime feeling and first thoughts of him are always of personal gratitude' (*Letters*, 56). In all fairness, Tolkien had missed Sisam's deadline for *Fourteenth Century Verse and Prose* not because he was dilatory and unmethodical, as C. S. Lewis later described him,[18] but rather because he made a great deal more of the project than necessary. This glossary has recently been described as unequalled in its thoroughness, concision, and accuracy—Tolkien readily admitting 'I am a pedant devoted to accuracy even in what may appear to others unimportant matters'—but this diligence greatly exceeded any undergraduate's practical needs.[19] Shippey guesses that during the anthology's many decades of use, a great many of Tolkien's thousands of references have never been glanced at once.[20] Gordon, however, may have felt that such meticulousness would compensate for his own lack of expertise.

While still working at the *OED*, Tolkien had already gained some standing as a Chaucerian when, in June 1920, he received two guineas for a 'report on Thomas' Predecessors to Chaucer'.[21] The Press paid many individuals for reviewing book submissions, and while Tolkien's report does not survive, it must have been negative because OUP never published such a volume. Thirty years later, however, the independent scholar Mary Edith Thomas did publish a book with *Chaucer and His Immediate Predecessors* in its subtitle, and the reasons for Tolkien's unfavourable response can be suspected in the book's main title—*Medieval*

---

[16] Kenneth Sisam, ed., *Fourteenth Century Verse and Prose* (Oxford: Clarendon Press, 1921). Long a classroom classic, the textbook has been reprinted as Kenneth Sisam and J. R. R. Tolkien, *A Middle English Reader and Vocabulary, 1921–22* (Mineola: Dover, 2005) with Tolkien's name now on the front cover.

[17] SH 2:783–6 at p. 786 quote the reviewer Margaret L. Lee. Elizabeth Solopova, 'Middle English', in *Companion*, ed. Lee, 230–43, places this achievement in context of a career not exclusively devoted to Old English.

[18] Quoted in Carpenter's *Biography*, 203.

[19] *Letters*, 372; see Peter Gilliver, Jeremy Marshall, and Edmund Weiner, *The Ring of Words: Tolkien and the 'Oxford English Dictionary'* (Oxford: Oxford University Press, 2006), 35–7.

[20] Shippey, 'Tolkien as Editor', 44.

[21] I am grateful to Peter Gilliver for this reference in Publishing Business Cash Book No. 6 in the OUP archives.

Skepticism and Chaucer.[22] Her 'Acknowledgements' helps tracking a project begun as doctoral research at Columbia University under Roger Sherman Loomis, who had been a Rhodes Scholar in the same class as Kenneth Sisam and probably recommended that his student submit her thesis to him at OUP. Loomis was an Arthurian scholar whose early work was cited by Tolkien and E. V. Gordon in their *Gawain* edition (p. xii), but he gained later notoriety for his articles 'Was Chaucer a Laodicean?' (1940)—a lukewarm Christian—and 'Was Chaucer a Free Thinker?' (1961). Thomas had established the backgrounds for these radical propositions which would go far toward accounting for Tolkien's adverse reaction.

His later annotations for the Clarendon Chaucer showed him ready to accept a writer critical of corruption in religious institutions, but Tolkien could not imagine his author questioning the basic tenets of the Christian faith. His Chaucer was not perplexed, disbelieving, or rebellious. His Chaucer did not doubt the very existence of Heaven and Hell. If the poet felt any scepticism—and Gordon would include a section on 'Chaucer's Scepticism' in his draft Introduction—it was restricted to the existence of fairies and the dubious sciences of astrology and alchemy.[23] Hence Tolkien's commentaries never mentioned that John of Gaunt was patron of both Chaucer and John Wyclif—or that the poet's friends included the courtiers dubbed 'Lollard knights' by his Oxford colleague Bruce McFarlane— or that his particular friend Sir Lewis Clifford was forced to recant heretical views on infant baptism.[24] It would await Anne Hudson's researches into Lollardy for assessing Chaucer's engagements with this increasingly unorthodox movement.[25] In a telling anecdote, an American Fulbright student came to Oxford in the early 1950s with the intention of writing a thesis on Chaucer and Lollardy, she was assigned Tolkien as her supervisor, and at their first meeting he announced curtly, 'Chaucer and the Lollards. Nothing to that!' They did not have another meeting.[26]

Though Tolkien already had some credibility as a Chaucerian before 1922, Sisam made his second mistake by assigning him responsibility for the notes as well as the text and glossary. After Tolkien became Reader in English Language at Leeds, he started working jointly on three different Clarendon editions: *Sir Gawain and the Green Knight* with E. V. Gordon, *Pearl* also with E. V. Gordon, and *Selections from Chaucer's Poetry and Prose* with George Gordon. Each project

---

[22] Mary Edith Thomas, *Medieval Skepticism and Chaucer: An Evaluation of the Skepticism of the 13th and 14th Centuries of Geoffrey Chaucer and His Immediate Predecessors—An Era That Looked Back on an Age of Faith and Forward to an Age of Reason* (1950; rpt. New York: Cooper Square Publishers, 1971).

[23] Richard Firth Green, *Elf Queens and Holy Friars: Fairy Beliefs and the Medieval Church* (Philadelphia: University Pennsylvania Press, 2016), 197–205, makes large claims for Chaucer's *Canterbury Tales* encouraging scepticism regarding superstitious beliefs in fairies.

[24] K. B. McFarlane, *Lancastrian Kings and Lollard Knights* (Oxford: Clarendon, 1972), 212–13, for the account of Clifford's recantation. See SH 2:760 'McFarlane'.

[25] Anne Hudson, *The Premature Reformation: Wycliffite Texts and Lollard History* (Oxford: Clarendon Press, 1988), esp. 'The Context of Vernacular Wycliffism', pp. 390–4.

[26] Recalled by Carter Revard, a Rhodes Scholar at Merton College 1952–4.

would suffer setbacks. Disagreements over length delayed *Gawain* somewhat, though Tolkien proved his acumen for the editing and glossary-compiling while E. V. Gordon took charge of the introduction and greater part of the notes. Since Tolkien had succeeded at this first outing, Sisam was confident that the two other editions would come speedily to fruition. He was wrong. In hindsight, E. V. Gordon exercised a degree of self-discipline when annotating *Gawain* impossible for Tolkien to match when annotating Chaucer. Their *Pearl* edition's long travails before and after Gordon's death in 1938 have become generally known (SH 3:974–80), but the saga of *Selections from Chaucer's Poetry and Prose* can only now be told.

In his fine essay on *The Lord of the Rings*, W. H. Auden observed that a quest typically leads to some unexpected outcome discovered only when the quester has come to the end.[27] This was true of Tolkien when starting what would become his career-long engagements with Chaucer, culminating with his lectures on the Pardoner's Tale in the mid-1950s. It is also true of my own search for the Clarendon Chaucer materials without knowing in advance what exactly would come to light in the archives. Both stories converge upon the OUP correspondences spanning more than two decades with letters mostly by Tolkien, Sisam, and George Gordon. Those letters provide the best starting-point for tracing this project as well as supplementing our knowledge of the author's career, since Tolkien's published *Letters* contain a notorious twelve-year gap between 1925 and 1937.[28]

Three is Company

In 1951, Tolkien's last letter about the Clarendon Chaucer provided an inventory of what a researcher might hope to find in the OUP archives (Fig. 1). After Sisam's retirement, the new Press Secretary Dan Davin encouraged Tolkien to finish the edition but finally sent a car to retrieve the materials when no progress seemed likely. Tolkien replied indignantly on 8 June:

Dear Davin,
   I sent back today all that might prove useful of *my* material (I know nothing of G. S. Gordon's, which indeed I never saw) for the 'Clarendon Chaucer.'
   The chief items were: (1) working copy made of galleys of the *text*, with 2 copies of the resultant *revises* in page-proof (not themselves, I think, again corrected throughout):

---

[27] W. H. Auden, 'The Quest Hero' (1961), *Prose: Volume IV, 1956–1962*, ed. Edward Mendelson (Princeton: Princeton University Press, 2010), 360–73 at p. 360; see SH 3:1043–7 'Quest'. Tolkien had been one of Auden's examiners who awarded him a Third.

[28] Carpenter, ed., *Letters*, 1: 'Between 1918 and 1937 few letters survive.' SH 2:681 remark that a lifetime total of some 1,500 letters are now known in libraries, archives, and private collections.

Jan ref.
279.20/D.M.D.

MERTON COLLEGE,
TELE. 2259. OXFORD.

[stamp: CLARENDON PRESS OXFORD 9 JUN 1951 SECRETARY'S OFFICE]

June 8, 1951

Dear Davin,

I sent back today all that might be useful of my material (I know nothing of G.S. Gordon's, which indeed I never saw) for the Clarendon Chaucer.

The chief items were: (1) working copy made of galleys of the text, with 2 copies of the resultant revises in page-proof (not themselves, I think, a great concern though — out).

(2) The correct proof of glossary.

(3) The draft of notes for all pieces but the last two (from Monk's Tale and Nun's Priest's Tale); the earlier items revised and reduced, the rest progressively in need of revision, and those for the Reeve's Tale possibly too illegible. [Part of the machination of the text of that Tale that I made was published in the Transactions of the Philological Society 1934 — not 1936, a my pencilled note. What seemed suitable of the results, as far as concerned the text of the Tale, was in-

corporated in the Revise of the text except for yeer L.158 of solochicon: a form which in my opinion should be removed from glossary and text in favour of yeer; the note, if any, should merely refer to Transactions.]

I deeply regret the whole affair. The material contains much that is fresh, and a prodigious amount of labour esp. in the emendation, reduction, and revision of the glossary. [But I was given no very steady end of the stick, and had say we more. I shall be interested to hear what, if anything, the Press decides to do about it. If this is abandoned, I should be grateful for the return of the unprinted material; and if this is used I should also be grateful for its eventual return if possible — there are a good many works which, though useless for the purpose (such as that on later by Legend of Cle... ha 59), I should find useful.

Yours sincerely,
JRRTolkien

000120

(2)
The correct proofs of *glossary*.
(3)
The draft of notes for *all* pieces but the last two (from *Monk's* Tale and *Nuns' Priest's Tale*): the earlier items revised and reduced, the rest progressively in need of revision, and those for the *Reeves Tale* possibly too illegible. [Part of the investigation of the text of that Tale that I made was published in the Transactions of the Philological Society 1934—not 1936, as my penciled note.[29] What seemed suitable of the results, as far as concerned the *text* of the Tale, was incorporated in the Revise of the text—except for *geen* l. 158 of selection: a form which in my opinion should be removed from glossary and text in favour of *gaan*: the note, if any, should merely refer to Transactions.]

I deeply regret the whole affair. The material contains much that is fresh, and a prodigious amount of labour, especially in the construction, reduction, and revision of the glossary. But I was given the very sticky end of the stick, and need say no more. I shall be interested to hear what, if anything, the Press decides to do about it. If it is abandoned, I should be grateful for the return of the *unprinted* material; and if this is used I should also be grateful for its eventual return if possible: there are a good many notes which, though useless for the purpose (such as that on *heterly* Legend of Cleopatra 59), I should find useful.

Yours sincerely
J R R Tolkien.[30]

This letter described precisely what awaited discovery: Tolkien's working copy of the Text proofs; his two copies of revised proofs; his corrected galleys of the Glossary; and his drafts of Notes except for the Monk's Tale and Nun's Priest's Tale. Tolkien repeated his longstanding claim that he never saw any of Gordon's contributions with the strong implication they had never materialized. He makes reference to his article 'Chaucer as a Philologist' as a continuation of his 'investigation of the text' of the Reeve's Tale. Though Tolkien did not say so outright, having the materials back would have been welcome because he still lectured on Chaucer and had already used (and held back for possible future use) his editorial notes on the *Parlement of Foules* for his teaching.

Now to turn back almost three decades to the project's beginnings in 1922, no formal contract for the textbook survives in the OUP archives and may never have existed, the two scholars proceeding with an informal gentlemen's agreement with Press officials. Gordon made decisions about the *Selections* with a list of contents date-stamped by the Secretary's Office on 15 AUG 1922. A copy was mailed to Tolkien at Leeds, and there is no indication that he raised any objections to

---

[29] Tolkien must have looked at these materials before surrendering them and noticed the wrong date pencilled in the margins of his notes on the Reeve's Tale; see Fig. 13.

[30] Partially quoted by SH 1:397 and Gilliver, 'Word as Leaf', 69–70; the brackets are Tolkien's.

Gordon's choices. This handwritten roster with a precise total of 4,291 lines was typed with a cover memo calculating 128 pages for the final book. Already a problem appeared on the horizon. The Chaucer texts extended considerably longer than the 2,530 lines of *Gawain*, but Tolkien was allowed considerably fewer pages for notes than E. V. Gordon had been given for that other Clarendon edition also begun in 1922.

Sisam approved organizing the selections in chronological order, beginning with extracts from Chaucer's translation of the thirteenth-century *Roman de la Rose*, and Tolkien later provided a table of contents in the headnote to his Glossary (see Appendix II):

I.   The Romaunt of the Rose (extracts).
II.   The Compleynte unto Pite.
III.   The Book of the Duchesse (extracts).
IV.   The Parlement of Foules.
V.   The Former Age.
VI.   Merciles Beaute.
VII.   To Rosemounde.
VIII. Truth.
IX.   Gentilesse.
X.   Lak of Stedfastnesse.
XI.   Compleint to his Empty Purse.
XII.   Boethius de Consolatione Philosophie.
Book II, Metre V.
Book II, Prose VII.
Book II, Metre VII.
Book IV, Metre VI.
XIII. The Prologue to the Legend of Good Women.
XIV.   The Legend of Cleopatra.
XV.   The Astrolabe (extract from introduction).
XVI.   The Prologue to the Canterbury Tales (extracts).
XVII. The Reeve's Tale (extract).
XVIII. The Monk's Tale (extract).
XIX.   The Nonne Preestes Tale.

Here another miscalculation emerges. No modern edition would tilt so heavily toward Chaucer's earlier poems. These lyrics did appear on the Oxford syllabus and Tolkien's notes from Michaelmas Term 1914 for 'Chaucer and his Contemporaries' contained many references to them,[31] but Chaucer's shorter pieces have not proved his most engaging, least of all with students.

---

[31] Bodleian MS Tolkien A 21/4, fols. 12–20. Tolkien mentioned 'Chaucer and his Contemporaries' in the version of his 'Valedictory Address' printed in Salu and Farrell, eds., *J. R. R. Tolkien, Scholar and Storyteller, Essays In Memoriam* (Ithaca: Cornell University Press, 1979), 16–32 at p. 26. Catherine

Yet Gordon and Sisam were not alone in their preferences for these courtly-love poems. C. S. Lewis's landmark article on *Troilus and Criseyde* argued that fourteenth-century readers valued Chaucer chiefly as the greatest English interpreter of *amour courtois*,[32] and his book *The Allegory of Love* intentionally neglected the *Canterbury Tales* to focus instead upon love poems such as *Rosemounde* and *Merciles Beaute*.[33] This preference matched somewhat George Gordon's enthusiasm for the lyric poems of Shelley in his 1922 Warton Lecture, yet Chaucer's conventional, formulaic verses were not what the marketplace wanted because they were not what readers enjoyed. Even Skeat's *Minor Poems* served mostly as preliminary work for his six-volume *Works of Geoffrey Chaucer*.[34]

As a further miscalculation, Gordon and Sisam followed Skeat's practice of arranging the works in what was presumed to be their order of composition, placing the less interesting pieces like *Romaunt of the Rose* first. Robinson's 1933 *Riverside Chaucer* would establish the precedent for placing these early works strategically at the end of the volume, almost as leftovers in the author's career with the *Romaunt* coming last, not first.

From a teaching viewpoint, Gordon and Sisam made another mistake by including nothing from *Troilus* and a minimum from the *Canterbury Tales*. Missing are the Miller's Tale, the Pardoner's Tale, and the Wife of Bath's Tale found in nearly every modern textbook such as *The Norton Anthology of English Literature*. Sisam's long-range strategy envisioned separate editions from the *Canterbury Tales*, publishing his own *Clerk's Tale* in 1923 and *Nun's Priest's Tale* in 1927,[35] but these plans would have further hampered the Clarendon Chaucer's prospects with its duller contents such as *Lak of Stedfastnesse*.

This fatal skewing of contents cannot be blamed solely upon Gordon. His own preliminary notes indicate grand ambitions for including the Knight's Tale, the Miller's Tale, the Shipman's Tale, the Pardoner's Tale, the Friar's Tale, the Summoner's Tale, the Clerk's Tale, the Canon's Yeoman's Tale, and even the Parson's Tale.[36] This scope was rendered impossible by Sisam's insistence upon 128 pages as the absolute maximum for pricing the volume.[37] Not until 1946 did

---

McIlwaine, *Tolkien: Maker of Middle-earth* (Oxford: Bodleian Library, 2018), 176, reproduces Tolkien's timetable for Michaelmas Term 1914 with 'Chaucer' scheduled on Tuesdays and Thursdays at 11:00.

[32] C. S. Lewis, 'What Chaucer Really Did to *Il Filostrato*', *Essays & Studies* 18.1 (1932), 56–75 at pp. 57 and 75.
[33] C. S. Lewis, *The Allegory of Love* (London: Oxford University Press, 1936), 'Chaucer', 157–97.
[34] Chaucer, *The Minor Poems*, ed. Walter W. Skeat (Oxford: Clarendon Press, 1888); see A. S. G. Edwards, 'Walter W. Skeat (1835–1912)', in Paul Ruggiers, ed., *Editing Chaucer: The Great Tradition* (Norman, OK: Pilgrim Books, 1984), 172–89 at p. 174.
[35] Chaucer, *The Nun's Priest's Tale*, ed. Kenneth Sisam (Oxford: Clarendon Press, 1927), p. v: 'In preparing this edition I have had in mind the needs of schools and colleges who keep up the good practice of studying a few short texts minutely.'
[36] Bodleian MS Tolkien A 39/3, fols. 282–3.
[37] Letter to Gordon, 5 January 1925, in Bodleian MS Tolkien A 39/3, fol. 284.

Sisam finally acknowledge to his OUP successor the blunder of too many early poems and too few *Canterbury Tales*. Again Robinson's *Riverside Chaucer* made the shrewder decision of positioning the *Tales* at the beginning since it was the work first approached by most readers.[38] Nearly all subsequent editors have followed this non-chronological order.

Only one title on Gordon's trimmed-down 1922 list was dropped—the Prioress's Tale—and this would prove a fateful decision. Tolkien liked this story of a boy-martyr, and in 1947 he recalled Chaucer's allusion to 'younge Hugh of Lincoln, slayn also | With cursed Jewes' when visiting the saint's tomb in Lincoln Cathedral.[39] But problems with the Prioress's anti-Semitism went back as far as Wordsworth's objection to her ferocious bigotry,[40] and Sisam expressed misgivings about a work potentially offensive to Jewish readers. Gordon acquiesced: 'We want sales.'

Though Tolkien imagined his Dwarves as alienated exiles like the Jews,[41] his own lack of prejudice was forcefully voiced in 1938 when the German publisher of *The Hobbit* wanted to ascertain the author's racial identity. 'If I understand that you are enquiring whether I am of *Jewish* origin,' Tolkien wrote back, 'I can only reply that I regret that I appear to have *no* ancestors of that gifted people' (*Letters*, 37). Years later he continued to reply when asked about his last name, 'It is not Jewish in origin, though I should consider it an honour if it were' (*Letters*, 410n.). Since the Clarendon Chaucer included so few selections from the *Tales*, it was easy enough to find a replacement for the Prioress's Tale.

By October 1923 Sisam decided to substitute the Reeve's Tale. Presumably he and Gordon thought that a student edition should include stories about students, if not the Prioress's pious little schoolboy, then the Reeve's rowdy Cambridge undergraduates. Tolkien may have been glad enough with this switch because the two undergraduates escaping the miller's wrath conformed with what his later lecture 'On Fairy-Stories' would describe as an audience's 'oldest and deepest desire, the Great Escape'.[42] The Nun's Priest's Tale, their only other Canterbury selection, also provided this happy ending when the rooster escapes from the hungry fox.

---

[38] F. N. Robinson, ed., *Poetical Works of Chaucer* (Boston: Houghton Mifflin, 1933), 1; see George F. Reinecke, 'F. N. Robinson (1872–1967),' in Ruggiers, ed., *Editing Chaucer*, 231–51.

[39] Ratcliff, *The Story of The Hobbit*, 79–80, cites the Prioress's Tale as a prime example of the medieval anti-Semitism which Chaucer resisted in his depiction of his Dwarves. He also cites, p. 758, an unpublished letter in which Tolkien further recounted his visit to the dubious reliquary of 'Little Saint Hugh (the supposed martyr)' as well as Chaucer's 'Prologue'.

[40] Florence H. Ridley, *The Prioress and the Critics* (Berkeley and Los Angeles: University of California Press, 1965), 2.

[41] Rebecca Brackmann, 'Dwarves are not Heroes: Antisemitism and the Dwarves in J. R. R. Tolkien's Writing', *Mythlore* 28 (2010), 85–106, is rebutted by Renée Vink, '"Jewish" Dwarves: Tolkien and Anti-Semitic Stereotyping', *Tolkien Studies* 10 (2013), 123–45.

[42] *Essays* 153; see also SH 2:359–61 'Escape'.

The Reeve's fabliau created the different challenge of maintaining decency. Sisam had already approved minor censorship, with the exclusion of two offensive passages in the Nun's Priest's Tale where a rooster 'feathered' a hen, but bowdlerizing the Reeve's Tale required omitting the text's entire second half where the two students sexually assault the miller's daughter and wife. Tolkien's editorial work, thus limited to the first half, still meant dealing with the Northern speech of the Cambridge clerks, and this in turn provided him with the impetus for further studying Chaucer's handling of dialect.

Gordon's original list of contents referenced Skeat's one-volume *Student's Chaucer*, its texts coming directly from the six-volume Oxford Chaucer, with the understanding that they would simply reprint from it. Although OUP already owned the rights, Sisam made a point of writing to Skeat's daughter for permission and offering five guineas, which she readily accepted, so that he could write triumphantly to Gordon, 'it is a very cheap way out.'

Tolkien had been gravely ill during the summer of 1923, but still Gordon wrote optimistically that his co-editor could knock things off before October. This letter confirmed that their edition would consist of twenty pages of Introduction and forty-eight pages of Essays (his assignments) followed by 128 pages of Text and twenty-eight pages of Notes and Glossary (Tolkien's jobs). Already the disproportion of Gordon's sixty-eight pages versus Tolkien's twenty-eight pages should have looked problematic.

As early as October 1923, Tolkien began raising questions about Skeat's texts. Besides new capitalization and word-divisions, he wanted to add diacritical marks as guides to pronunciation. Sisam resisted any changes that would increase the costs of production, but Tolkien went ahead anyway. The drawbacks with long-distance collaboration were showing.

The first two batches of the Text were typeset by early December 1923.[43] One copy was sent to Gordon for checking line-numbers and subheadings, and he entrusted Tolkien with reading carefully through the proofs themselves. Gordon would always remain aloof from such details. Tolkien received the next batch and replied in January 1924 with a long letter which survives in a typed in-house extract. There Tolkien noticed three misprints but argued for more extensive changes: 'There are a dreadful lot of semi-colons!' Though not extensively re-editing Skeat, Tolkien grew dogged about specific emendations such as restoring *buskes* for *busshes* in Chaucer's *Romaunt*. Sisam wrote back reminding him of the typesetting realities: 'these trifles will cost us 6d. each.' That would be about £1.37 in today's valuation.[44]

---

[43] For explanation of OUP's cumbersome process before computer printing, see Martin Maw's 'Printing Technology, Binding, Readers, and Social Life', in *History of Oxford University Press*, 3:277–307.

[44] Relative pound–sterling valuations have been calculated at www.measuringworth.com.

Tolkien's first surviving letter arrived on Sisam's desk in February 1924 when he returned another batch of proofs and almost boasted of restraints, despite insisting upon the minor change of *gniden* to *gnodded* in Chaucer's *Former Age*. A postscript explained a second layer of corrections in pencil: 'I lean in the direction (esp. in a normalised and to some extent modernised text like this) of boldly smoothing out the most apparently stumbling lines in metre.' Here Tolkien no doubt recalled how spelling variants had greatly complicated the glossary-making for their *Fourteenth Century Verse and Prose*, but he was already indicating his disrespect for the scribal spellings which would become central to his 1934 'Chaucer as a Philologist'.

By February 1924 Sisam was grumbling to Gordon about their slow progress. He worried that Tolkien was correcting lines which needed no corrections. He worried about the distractions from his *Gawain* edition. And for the first time he worried about Gordon's own introductory sections: 'Could you send us some copy?' Here is the first evidence Tolkien was not the only truant.

Sisam shifted blame back again in March when writing to David Nichol Smith, the Press's chief adviser on English Literature, that he did not think Tolkien should be allowed to hold up the Clarendon Chaucer as he was holding up all his other projects. 'If he would put the same time into working that he devotes to writing excuses, we might make some progress.' Tolkien's later editor Rayner Unwin would apologize for these excuses as 'a defence against his failure to achieve some rashly-promised goal'.[45] Even at this early date in the publication process, Sisam raised the possibility of finding a new co-editor.

Gordon's letter of May 1924 indicated that matters had come to a head with Tolkien: 'he has retired from the *Chaucer*.' Sisam replied philosophically: 'Tolkien is so overwhelmed with work and domestic troubles that I think he is wise to give up the *Chaucer*.' Then something happened not recorded in the correspondence. In July, Tolkien was in Oxford dining with Gordon at the Randolph Hotel, and they dined together again a day or two later at Gordon's home. When Tolkien appeared again in the correspondence in October, he was back at the Chaucer proofs and making headway on the glossary. Clearly he had changed his mind about abandoning the edition, and his visit in Oxford, albeit brief, seems to have persuaded Gordon that they could carry on together.

Besides setting the deadlines of December 1924 for the glossary and January 1925 for the notes, Sisam cracked the whip when insisting that the edition could not stand the cost of the extensive etymologies which were Tolkien's specialty: 'it will only bore the readers who are not supposed to be interested in philology.'[46]

---

[45] Rayner Unwin, *George Allen & Unwin: A Remembrancer* (London: Merlin Unwin Books, 1999), 114–15. See SH 3:1365–8 'Unwin, Rayner'.

[46] See SH 3:982–8 'Philology' for superb survey of this now-arcane subject. Tolkien repeated this excess when compiling the etymological index of names which caused delays in publishing *The Return of the King*, and it was finally abandoned because 'the size and cost were ruinous'; quoted by

He reminded Tolkien that he himself had kept his glossary to thirty-two pages for the complete *Canterbury Tales* in the World's Classics series. This prohibition for the Glossary would force Tolkien to shift these word-origins to his Notes and thereby augment what would become an impossibly long commentary. Gordon received a draft of the glossary by early December but asked Sisam not to pressure Tolkien for his annotations in January. He was exhausted from completing his *Gawain* edition as well as welcoming into the household a new baby—Christopher—born less than three weeks earlier.

When Gordon wrote again at the end of December 1924, he sent along Tolkien's corrected Text proofs—'Very good, it seems to me: he has taken trouble.' But he sounded an alarm that Tolkien had altered the *Boece* passages after comparing them to the original Latin. For verse, the printer needed simply to change a single line; for a prose piece like *Boece*, the change could require resetting a whole page.[47] At the end of 1924 Sisam issued grave warnings about the Glossary's length, then reckoned at thirty-eight pages, while pointing out that Tolkien should have been charged £70 for excess proof corrections in their *Verse and Prose*.

By the last day of December, Sisam wrote about limiting the Glossary and Notes to a total of forty-four pages. He added that Tolkien was wrong about *Boece* and his emendations had been cancelled. Gordon must have received a similar letter and replied on New Year's Day 1925, agreeing about Tolkien's excesses and advising they watch him carefully in the Notes. Little did they suspect how many surplus pages were to come.

There is a great deal of surviving correspondence during 1925, mostly between Sisam and Gordon (in Oxford) placing blame for missed deadlines on Tolkien (in Leeds). On 5 January, Sisam sent back the draft Glossary and instructed Tolkien to reduce it by ten pages. Tolkien's unhappiness with these restraints surfaced in his chapter for the *Year's Work in English* where he bemoaned 'the deadness of the treatment of long lists of words in isolation owing to the ever-pressing need for economy of space'.[48] When the January deadline for the revised Glossary passed without delivery—Tolkien was busy correcting *Gawain* proofs at the same time—Sisam sent a Latin note with a half-joking reference to the Doomsday: '*Dies irae adpropiat!*'

Christopher in Tolkien's *Unfinished Tales of Númenor and Middle-earth* (Boston and New York: Houghton Mifflin, 1980), 12.

---

[47] Tolkien was seldom shy about making drastic revisions in page proofs, as Rayner Unwin would recall in *A Remembrancer*, 75. Unwin, 'Publishing Tolkien', *Proceedings of the J. R. R. Tolkien Centenary Conference, 1992*, ed. Patricia Reynolds and Glen H. GoodKnight (Milton Keynes: Tolkien Society, and Altadena, CA: Mythopoeic Press, 1995), 26–9 at p. 26, recalled how Tolkien defended fitting revisions to the existing text: 'I have calculated the space line by line as carefully as possible.' See also *Letters*, 16.

[48] J. R. R. Tolkien, 'Philology: General Works', *Year's Work in English Studies* 4 (1924), 20–37 at p. 26.

By the beginning of March 1925, Gordon jubilantly forwarded the handwritten revision: 'Herewith Tolkien's copy for the *Glossary*: neat and workmanlike, and please God, of the right length.' By May, Tolkien received his galley sheets for the Glossary, and Gordon quickly returned his own copy with the apology that he had read it only 'here and there'. He was more assiduous as a letter-writer than an editor. Tolkien did not immediately return his corrected Glossary because he first wanted to finalize the Text and make headway on the Notes. As things turned out, he would not get around to returning these galleys to OUP until 1951.

July 1925 became something of a crossroads. First, Gordon approved Tolkien's revisions of the Text and forwarded them to the Press. Then, Sisam pushed for Gordon's contributions as well as Tolkien's commentary: 'if you could give us the Introduction and Essays, it might provoke emulation.' The long bonhomie between the two Oxford men gave way to the realization that Tolkien alone was not responsible for delays. Though impossible to know for certain, friction with Sisam may have played some role in Gordon's academic politics during these same busy weeks.

The third event of July 1925 was the election of Oxford's Rawlinson and Bosworth Professor of Anglo-Saxon. After R. W. Chambers of University College London declined the position and became instead an elector, the two finalists emerged as Sisam and Tolkien, and after Vice-Chancellor Joseph Wells was called upon to cast the tie-breaking vote, Tolkien was elected.[49] This outcome has always seemed deeply mysterious since Sisam had published a good deal more, including an important 1916 study of the *Beowulf* manuscript and a 1919 piece on the Old English *Epistola Alexandri*.[50] Tolkien had seen into print his *Middle English Vocabulary* for Sisam's anthology and had co-edited the *Gawain* edition, but he had published absolutely nothing on Anglo-Saxon and little criticism beyond his three highly learned surveys in *The Year's Work in English*.[51] Tolkien's formal letter of application explained that a heavy burden of teaching and administration had 'seriously interfered with my projects for publishable work' but promised, if elected to the professorship, 'I should endeavour to make productive use of the

---

[49] SH 2:218–19 'Chambers'. Douglas A. Anderson, 'R. W. Chambers and *The Hobbit*', *Tolkien Studies* 3 (2006), 137–47, traces the scholarly friendship between the two *Beowulf* scholars. Tolkien later described another elector, C. T. Onions, his OED supervisor, as his 'old protector, backer, and friend' (*Letters*, 353), so he too must have been a supporter.

[50] Kenneth Sisam, 'The *Beowulf* Manuscript', *Modern Language Review* 11 (1916), 335–7, and Henry Bradley and Kenneth Sisam, 'Textual Notes on the Old English *Epistola Alexandri*', *Modern Language Review* 14 (1919), 202–5; see Raymond Edwards, *Tolkien* (London: Robert Hale, 2014), 107–8.

[51] Wayne G. Hammond and Douglas A. Anderson, *J. R. R. Tolkien: A Descriptive Bibliography* (Winchester: St. Paul's Bibliographies, 1993), 'Contributions to Periodicals', 344–6, listed for the years 1910–31 only Tolkien's 'The Devil's Coach-Horses' (1925) on an odd word from *Hali Meiðhad* in Middle English, not Anglo-Saxon. Tolkien had listed as forthcoming an article on *Ancren Riwle* and the Katherine Group, though this seems to have been the piece not published until 1929 in *Essays and Studies* (SH 2:58–60).

opportunities which it offers for research' (*Letters*, 13). His promise must have sounded credible at the time.

Carpenter guessed the election's outcome was the doing of George Gordon, 'a master hand at intrigue' (*Biography* 115), and if the tie-breaker Joseph Wells harboured hard feelings toward Sisam over his stinginess in publishing his second edition of Herodotus without permitting updates in scholarship, who is to say Gordon did not fan the flames of his resentment?[52] Yet if Gordon had *opportunity* to work effectively behind the scenes, he did not appear to have a compelling *motive* beyond admiring the younger scholar's brilliance and showing himself persistent in patronage.

One incidental factor not previously taken into this account, though only one among many, was the advantage of bringing Tolkien to Oxford where the two editors could make swifter progress on their Clarendon Chaucer. All of his troubles with missed deadlines and overdone assignments occurred while Tolkien was labouring alone at Leeds. George Gordon could not have failed to notice that E. V. Gordon as an on-site collaborator kept Tolkien on task for completing their *Gawain* edition. If George Gordon were no longer in Leeds, where he had been Professor of English during 1913–22, he could finagle behind the scenes for his co-editor transferring to Oxford. Long before Tolkien became famous for *The Lord of the Rings*, Gordon merited the title 'Lord of the Strings' for all the strings he successfully pulled in academic affairs.

Tolkien's election as Professor of Anglo-Saxon, as it turned out, actually created even more distractions. The old and new appointments overlapped so that he taught at both Leeds and Oxford for two terms during 1925–6. Then there was the matter of moving his wife and children to 22 Northmoor Road. And then there was the matter of preparing seven Old English lectures and classes every week during Michaelmas Term of 1926. He had not been teaching exclusively Anglo-Saxon at Leeds, but now at Oxford his responsibilities included Gothic and Old Icelandic as well as Old English to the exclusion of his well-prepped lectures on Chaucer. Not that he would have felt any obligation to dazzle the undergraduates. He had reached the pinnacle of an academic career at the age of 33. He had arrived. As an Oxford professor, Tolkien no longer felt the keen spur for advancement which had fuelled his three editorial projects in the early 1920s. Oxford's 1925 *Statutes* did not in fact stipulate that a professor actually publish anything, only contribute to the advancement of knowledge, and it was not until the 1945 revisions that these duties included original work by the professor himself. To put matters crudely, there was no compelling need for Tolkien to rush his Clarendon Chaucer to completion.

Though Sisam's OUP correspondence betrays no obvious resentment over the election's outcome, his patience grew thin with both of his unpunctual editors

---

[52] Edwards, *Tolkien*, 129, suggests this motive for Wells voting against Sisam.

after his loss of the professorship. Later in the same week *The Times* announced Tolkien's triumph, Sisam wrote to Gordon threatening the penalty clause for overdue contributions. Gordon responded in August by sending some version of his Essays and Testimonials, probably still quite sketchy, but with no mention of his still-missing Introduction.

In October 1925 he sent another version of the Testimonials. If surviving materials are a fair indication, he had done little more than crib from Caroline Spurgeon's *Five Hundred Years of Chaucer Criticism and Allusion* then newly published in three hefty volumes.[53] Almost as a diversionary tactic, Gordon raised the new question of a frontispiece for their textbook and suggested the well-known Chaucer portrait from Hoccleve's *Regement of Princes*. Despite his later concerns with illustrating his own books, Tolkien appears to have voiced no opinion on a frontispiece. Only near the end of his letter to Sisam did Gordon promise the Introduction during the upcoming term. Rare, however, is the Oxford don who can accomplish much actual writing during the busy Michaelmas Term, and yet Gordon also offered a rosy outlook on behalf of Tolkien's efforts at abbreviating his Notes. Sisam was not easily appeased: 'I look forward to Introduction and Notes.'

The correspondence trailed off after Tolkien assumed his professorship at Oxford and could communicate in person. The next extant letter from Sisam to Gordon in July 1927 suggested expanding the range of essays beyond 1900 in order to include more modern scholars such as Carleton Brown and Robert K. Root. Gordon's reply does not survive but must have been negative, since Sisam next wrote proposing a separate volume of contemporary essays sometime in the future, with nothing for the time being which might interfere with progress on their Chaucer edition.

It had become clear that George Gordon, for all his academic eminence, was not following through. A look at his publication record during the 1920s confirms he was no powerhouse. His early reputation rested upon his essay collection *English Literature and the Classics* (1912) for which he contributed only 'Theophrastus and His Imitators'. Although he did produce a solid scholarly study on the historical concept of the 'Middle Ages',[54] he otherwise ushered into print only his popular Shakespeare lectures.[55] Like Tolkien, he promised a great deal more

---

[53] Caroline F. E. Spurgeon, *Five Hundred Years of Chaucer Criticism and Allusion, 1357–1900*, 3 vols. (Cambridge: Cambridge University Press, 1925). On the career of this remarkable scholar, see Renate Haas, 'Caroline F. E. Spurgeon (1869–1942): First Woman Professor of English in England', *Women Medievalists and the Academy*, ed. Jane Chance (Madison: University of Wisconsin Press, 2005), 99–109.

[54] George Gordon, '*Medium Aevum* and the Middle Ages' (Oxford: Clarendon Press, Society for Pure English, no. 19, 1925), 3–28.

[55] George Gordon, *Nine Plays of Shakespeare* (Oxford: Clarendon Press, 1928), and *Shakespeare's English* (Oxford: Clarendon Press, Society for Pure English, no. 29, 1928), 256–76.

than he delivered and was therefore not favourably remembered in the annals of Oxford University Press: 'he failed to perform.'[56]

By 1928 Tolkien had vastly exceeded the page-limits for the Notes and found it impossible to cut what he had drafted. Little could he have known that this impasse would become a permanent blockage impeding also his other long-promised editions of *Pearl, Exodus,* and *Ancrene Wisse.* At this point he passed the large bundle of annotations to Gordon and asked for help shortening what he had produced, but his timing was unlucky. This was the year in which his co-editor was elected President of Magdalen College and had even less time for scholarly projects. Always a social animal, Gordon became much in demand for committees and dining clubs, even becoming an early 'media don' broadcasting talks on BBC Radio. In a 1928 broadcast, for example, he praised the *OED* as a dictionary 'not merely of modern English but of *all* English—the English of Chaucer, of Spenser, of Shakespeare'.[57] Ironically this broadcast coincided with the start of his two-year period neglecting Chaucer's English in Tolkien's notes without providing any real help at reducing them. Years later his widow explained how he stored work-in-progress in the Founder's Tower at Magdalen for vacation breaks in the hope of productive labours. 'Before anything was quite ready for print,' she regretted, 'the academical term had again begun, and his work lay untouched until the next vacation.'[58]

Tolkien himself was hardly idle in 1928, preparing lectures on Old English works like the *Battle of Maldon,* directing B.Litt. research for distinguished future scholars such as Rosemond Tuve, and readying his important article on the literary language of the West Midlands,[59] all the while pursuing after-hours literary projects such as *Mr. Bliss* and *The Lay of Leithian.* The last years of the 1920s also saw *The Hobbit* taking shape as a bedtime story for the boys on Northmoor Road. When he did write to Sisam in November 1930, he took the offensive by shifting blame for the long-overdue Chaucer edition to the President of Magdalen College:

> I am not the sole or even chief culprit in this matter. And all the work so far done has been done by me. I have made one more effort to get back my draft of notes from my 'collaborator'! So far without success. His elevation is some excuse, but when one thinks of the labour of the glossary disturbed by alteration in selection, the notes, and the text, which have all fallen to my share, there is

---

[56] *History of Oxford University Press,* 3:342.
[57] *The History of the University of Oxford, Volume VIII: The Twentieth Century,* ed. Brian Harrison (Oxford: Clarendon Press, 1994), 459.
[58] Mary Campbell Gordon, *The Life of George S. Gordon, 1881–1942* (London: Oxford University Press, 1945), 160.
[59] J. R. R. Tolkien, '*Ancrene Wisse* and *Hali Meiðhad*', *Essays and Studies* 14 (1929), 104–26. Another B.Litt. student, Rosemary Woolf, went on to publish 'The Ideal of Men Dying with Their Lord in the *Germania* and in *The Battle of Maldon*', *Anglo-Saxon England* 5 (1976), 63–81.

some justification for my attitude—I will do no more unless I am given some help in the difficult task of selecting notes and reducing them to the somewhat narrow limits which are presumably contemplated.

I have returned again to the attack and demanded my stuff back—two years old now—with comments, from its prison in Magdalen.

This tirade got results. At the end of December 1930 Gordon returned the long-slumbering packet with a cover letter that claimed he had read through the annotations 'as far as they go'. The last phrase was a dig at Tolkien's failure to extend his commentary to the Monk's Tale and the Nun's Priest's Tale. Though encouraging, Gordon's few scribbles were hardly useful, extending to no more than four sketchy pages with vague comments like 'A jolly note!' But his one remark about the 'penciled [ ] for excision' does indicate that Tolkien had made efforts at identifying possible cuts with brackets even if he was unable actually to carry out these deletions. Years later he would write to his publisher about his similar inability to make cuts to *The Lord of the Rings*: 'it cannot be docked or abbreviated' (*Letters*, 113).

By January 1931 Tolkien acknowledged the return of the Notes but complained to Sisam about the lack of help for moving forward:

I did what I could with a shortened vacation to work at Chaucer, and at last re-extracted my notes from my collaborator (two years old). Nothing in this difficult task of reducing their bulk, for which they went to him, has been done; so I suppose that must fall to my lot. But I am rather appalled at the job, and also feel foggy as to ultimate bulk possible, and precise nature of audience addressed.

It is strange to hear him puzzling over the scope of his assignment at this late date: 'I must get quite clear as to number of pages allowable, before starting, and avoid any double-work.'[60] The page limits had long been spelled out as well as the prospective student audience, though Tolkien's performances as lecturer, publishing scholar, and fiction-writer indicate that he seldom kept his audience's needs clearly and steadily in mind.

Sisam did not write back until April 1931 when he patiently explained, one more time, that they wanted fewer notes, and he offered the assistance of David Nichol Smith who had overseen other Clarendon volumes. By December 1932 Tolkien acknowledged that Nichol Smith was helping to curtail the 'overwhelming mass of notes'. This meant adding more brackets but leaving final decisions on cuts to Tolkien. My own rough calculations suggest that these proposed deletions, if they had been made, would not have reduced the length of the Notes

---

[60] In the preface to his *Beowulf* translation, Christopher quotes his father's 1965 letter to Rayner Unwin again complaining he was 'not sure of my target' for his *Gawain* translation.

even by half, therefore still exceeding by four times the number of pages allowed by Sisam.[61]

In October 1931, R. W. Chapman entered the correspondence by informing Gordon ominously, 'I am investigating derelicts.' As Press Secretary for the years 1920–42, he took pride in running an efficient operation and reminded the President of Magdalen, 'I believe you are under an engagement to pay rent for the type!' This was not altogether a laughing matter, since plates for the Text and type-trays for the Glossary had already been stored for some six years. Chapman was willing to believe Tolkien the criminal but urged Gordon to 'knock your hands together and produce the book'. Though Chapman generally resisted commercializing OUP, he understood the need for running a business.[62] 'We want all the sellers we can get,' he ended his memo about the Clarendon Chaucer.

Only after another full year, in October 1932, did Tolkien write to Chapman asking whether a typist could be hired to assist with compressing his notes. His later manuscripts often survived in what Christopher has termed 'amanuensis typescripts', and Tolkien wrote to his London publisher in 1957 about plans 'to install a typist in my room in college'.[63] In his letter to Chapman, however, he admitted for the first time two other impediments: 'I am (a) a pettifogging scholar rejoicing in the minute and the intricate, and such games as textual criticism; or else (b) which does not concern you, a writer in modern English, a verse-writer and a metrist.' Here Tolkien confessed to diverting his time and energy to what universities now call Creative Writing, then an embarrassing sideline at Oxford, perhaps thinking specifically of *Mythopoeia* and *The Lay of Leithian* as well as the early version of *The Hobbit* which C. S. Lewis would read in January 1933.[64]

This letter also contains his histrionic exclamation—'if only I could free my mind and conscience of the Chaucerian incubus!'—to which Chapman responded with sympathy as well as practical support: '*Do* get Chaucer off your mind. I know myself that remorse of that kind prevents one from working at anything else.' His offer for typing assistance apparently called Tolkien's bluff, because he did not avail himself of the help, nor did he correspond again for two months.

When Tolkien next wrote to Sisam in December 1932, his letter adroitly camouflaged bad news by tucking it between happier tidings. He began by thanking his old tutor for kind words about his two-part article 'Sigelwara Land' and then announced putting the finishing touches on his paper about the Reeve's

---

[61] Tolkien would later create a similar impasse, not by excessive length, but by his insistence EETS print his *Ancrene Wisse* exactly as the text appeared line by line in the manuscript (SH 2:52–8).

[62] *History of Oxford University Press*, 3:20–1.

[63] SH 1:176–7; J. R. R. Tolkien, *Morgoth's Ring: The Later Silmarillion, Part I*, ed. Christopher Tolkien (Boston and New York: Houghton Mifflin, 1993), 141; and *Letters*, 262.

[64] *The Lay of Leithian* in *Lays of Beleriand*, 183–374; see also John D. Rateliff, '*The Hobbit*', in *Companion*, ed. Lee, 120, and SH 2:519–22 'The History of the Hobbit'.

Tale for *Transactions of the Philological Society*.[65] Only then did he admit no progress on the Clarendon Chaucer, but hoped somehow to trim his annotations in order to return to the good grace of the Press. The letter's very next sentence turned to prospects for publishing his *Beowulf* translation[66]—before complaining about overwork as an examiner at Manchester and Reading as well as Oxford— and concluding about the demands of his children.

Correspondence lapsed again until October 1936 when Tolkien was awarded his Leverhulme Research Fellowship and hopes were kindled that leave-time might result in finishing his Chaucer project. Chapman's letter to Gordon began with exasperation about the edition's type-trays which had gathered dust for more than ten years despite several warnings. The President of Magdalen coyly replied that he often wondered about their derelict work and understood Tolkien's reluctance to endure the tedium of abbreviating his notes. He ended by asking, 'May I have one more shot at Tolkien myself?' Gordon must have followed through on this offer, because a week later brought this note: 'Tolkien will have another try.'

George Gordon became Vice-Chancellor in 1938 for a three-year term and grew even busier, now charged with putting the University on a wartime footing and negotiating terms for government departments to occupy Oxford buildings. History records that he was highly successful in these efforts and even persuaded the War Office against barring military-age men from matriculating at Oxford.[67] Thus he ensured that the University would not shut down as it had during the First World War when it had been converted into a military camp. War also meant that OUP was called into service for printing official documents, instructional manuals, and codebooks.[68] *Selections from Chaucer's Poetry and Prose*, already stalled for more than a decade, became a casualty of these wartime priorities. The Printer's logbook noted that the glossary's trays were broken up and their type redistributed in October 1939. A memo to the Printer in November 1940 announced the fate of the text: 'Please melt the plates and let us have credit for the metal.' The Clarendon Chaucer's doom appeared sealed when George Gordon died of cancer in 1942.

The Second World War greatly altered academic life at Oxford—even as work on *The Lord of the Rings* preoccupied Tolkien's life—although there are indications that Sisam had not entirely abandoned hope for their Chaucer edition. His in-house memo of May 1946 suggested a fresh start with a new co-editor, perhaps

---

[65] See SH 2:223–5; the Reeve's Tale essay was reprinted with corrections from the author's own copy in *Tolkien Studies* 5 (2008), 109–71. Tolkien, 'Sigelwara Land' (1934), 99, acknowledged Sisam's help.

[66] Tolkien's *Beowulf* translation, first announced to Sisam in 1926 during correspondence about his *Pearl* edition, would not be published until 2014.

[67] See Lord Halifax's 'Introduction' to *The Life of George S. Gordon*; *History of the University of Oxford: Volume VIII*, ed. Harrison, 169, 173; and R. H. Darwall-Smith, 'Gordon, George Stuart', *ODNB* 22:909–10.

[68] *History of Oxford University Press*, 3:242–3.

J. A. W. Bennett, and with fewer minor poems and more selections from the *Canterbury Tales*. He signalled no great haste, despite the London office's keenness for international sales, apparently worried about upsetting the original editor. 'Tolkien is still a Professor, and it would only raise unhappy memories.'

Nor had Tolkien completely abandoned his ambitions. After becoming Merton Professor of Language and Literature in 1945, he assumed responsibilities for lecturing on Chaucer for the first time since leaving Leeds. Teaching for him always meant looking closely at individual words, and these investigations raised questions about the ways medieval texts were edited. At a gathering of the Inklings in November 1947, Warnie Lewis reported that Tolkien showed them a very beautiful facsimile of an early *Canterbury Tales* manuscript costing him £55, a considerable investment.[69] This would have been the 1911 facsimile of the Ellesmere Chaucer with its famous pilgrim portraits.[70] Skeat had relied heavily upon this manuscript as his base-copy for the *Canterbury Tales*, and now in the late 1940s Tolkien's Chaucer lectures began weighing its authority, for example announcing in his discussion of the Clerk's Tale, 'I myself am inclined to accept Ellesmere for the following reasons....'.[71]

After Sisam retired from OUP in 1948, Dan Davin was appointed Assistant Secretary with special responsibility for the Clarendon Press. He would later earn acclaim as one of the greatest editors of his time: 'no academic publisher before him initiated and saw to completion so many major projects.'[72] Davin's workload was legendary, dictating some eighty letters per day while managing on the side to publish seven novels as well as his memoir *Closing Times* featuring literary friends such as Louis MacNeice, Enid Starkie, and Dylan Thomas. With so much drive of his own, he showed little patience with donnish dithering, and one project that had been languishing far too long was the Clarendon Chaucer.

In June 1949, Davin contacted the surviving editor in person, jotting down a memorandum of the conversation: 'Tolkien says that it would be a great relief to him if he could hand over the materials of this and if we would see someone else to finish it off.' As early as 1924, it should be remembered, Sisam had raised the possibility of a replacement editor or even a third collaborator. Among the candidates mentioned over the years had been E. V. Gordon, Dorothy Everett, Angus MacIntosh, Phyllis Hodgson, Celia Sisam (Kenneth's daughter), Patricia Kean, and even Helen Gardner. Davin's 1949 memo echoed the optimism of his predecessor: 'Not much remains to be done, and most of this lies in finishing off the notes.'

---

[69] Warren Lewis, *Brothers and Friends*, 215.

[70] *The Ellesmere Chaucer Reproduced in Facsimile*, ed. Alex Egerton, 2 vols. (Manchester: Manchester University Press, 1911) was produced because the manuscript itself was leaving England after the Earl of Ellesmere sold it to Henry E. Huntington.

[71] Bodleian MS Tolkien A 13/2, fol. 34.

[72] Jon Stallworthy, 'Davin, Daniel Marcus', *ODNB* 15:424–6 at p. 425; see also *History of Oxford University Press*, 3:108.

Davin was overly confident about Tolkien's readiness to withdraw, however, writing to remind him some four months later: 'When you were last here, you were going to return to us the material for the Clarendon English Series Chaucer.' Currency devaluation had increased the price of Robinson's *Riverside Chaucer* so that their Clarendon edition had a better chance of competing in the British marketplace.[73]

In May 1951, Davin took the extreme measure of sending a car around to the college to collect the materials. Almost as if foreseeing this dire event back in 1945, Tolkien's *Leaf by Niggle* pictured the black-clad Driver who arrived to summon Niggle from unfinished work,[74] and therefore the arrival of Davin's car could not have been a jolly prospect for the truant editor. The transfer of Chaucer materials was made on 8 June and provoked the angry letter already quoted from Tolkien: 'I deeply regret the whole affair...'. Davin replied quite graciously, thanking Tolkien and adding that if at any time he would like to have back anything for consultation, 'we should of course be glad to send it to you.'

The year 1951 offered so many distractions, one wonders why Tolkien troubled himself about the long-slumbering textbook. In addition to updating his *Gawain* edition, he oversaw major revisions for a reprint of *The Hobbit*—particularly the chapter 'Riddles in the Dark' about Bilbo finding the Ring—and he was corresponding with Allen & Unwin about publishing *The Lord of the Rings*. Hoping that Collins might publish *The Silmarillion* as a companion piece, he composed the 10,000-word summary now printed as a preface to the published work. By the time he was correcting galleys and compiling an index for *The Lord of the Rings*, he had also undertaken the time-consuming duties as Sub-Warden of Merton College. Furthermore the year 1951 saw him rewriting and greatly expanding his undergraduate lectures on the Pardoner's Tale and preparing a formal lecture on the Chaucerian word *losenger* for the Congrès International de Philologie Moderne meeting in Liège.

OUP staffers kept Sisam regularly informed of developments during his retirement on the Isles of Scilly, now updating him that 'Tolkien has handed all his Clarendon Chaucer material over to us so that we are free to go ahead—if only we can find the right man.' Sisam was reluctant to inflict further insult and advised professional courtesy: 'You must leave the *Clarendon Chaucer* alone while Tolkien is professor—a sad story.'

Davin was impressed by the bundle, now tucked away in his strongroom, and he took a more positive view that a 'determined and commonsense editor' could whip the textbook into publishable form. He was still casting about for this fresh

---

[73] Tolkien had consulted the *Riverside Chaucer* because his lecture on the Clerk's Tale explained their text was 'Skeat (based as usual primarily on Ellesmere) with few notes F. N Robinson' (MS Tolkien A 13/2, fol. 91).

[74] J. R. R. Tolkien, *Poems and Stories* (Boston and New York: Houghton Mifflin, 1994), 203–4, and SH 2:658–63.

editor in October 1960 when a strong contender emerged, 'a young man named Burrow at Christ Church, according to Norman Davis'. Now considered one of the foremost medievalists of his generation, J. A. Burrow would have made a superlative candidate. His *Geoffrey Chaucer: A Critical Anthology* (1969) provided the reception history which Gordon had promised for his Testimonials, and Burrow went on to co-edit his own *Book of Middle English* (1992) with many of the same works such as *Gawain* and *Sir Orfeo* which Tolkien had glossed for Sisam's 1921 anthology. In addition to Chaucer's *Parliament of Fowls*, Burrow's textbook included the complete Reeve's Tale, unbowdlerized, as well as the Prioress's Tale which Sisam and Gordon had shied away from because of its perceived anti-Semitism.[75]

Davin took no action on any replacement editor, however, and no correspondence survives beyond 1960. Thereafter the Clarendon Chaucer file was closed and the project marked DROPPED.

The Shadow of the Past

As this outline of the Clarendon Chaucer's history emerged from reading Scull and Hammond's survey of the OUP correspondence, I began wondering what had become of the editorial materials returned by Tolkien in 1951 and deposited by Dan Davin in his strongroom. Thus my own unexpected journey began with emails to Oxford colleagues and led to the cellar of Oxford University Press. There, in autumn 2012, Tolkien's lost book was located by archivist Martin Maw and given an initial inspection by *OED* editor Peter Gilliver. The Clarendon Chaucer pages plus other related materials had been put into an unmarked grey box and shoved onto a bottom shelf in a remote part of the basement storage area. It is impossible to know when it arrived there and how often it had been accessed over the years, but some batches had been sorted into modern acid-free folders in the early 1990s by archivist Peter Foden and his assistant Jenny McMorris.

Here fact and fiction converge in a curious fashion. When Tolkien was drafting his time-travel novel *The Notion Club Papers* in the mid-1940s, he set the future action in 1987 with 'the greatest storm in the memory of any living man'—which Christopher described as his father's prevision of the Great Storm of 1987.[76] As a second uncanny glimpse into the future, the work's pseudo-scholarly foreword provided a fictional account of how these manuscript pages came to light at an even later date: 'They were found after the Summer Examinations of 2012 on the top of one of a number of sacks of waste paper in the basement of the Examination

---

[75] J. A. Burrow and Thorlac Turville-Petre, eds., *A Book of Middle English* (Oxford: Blackwell, 1992).
[76] J. R. R. Tolkien, *The Notion Club Papers* in *Sauron Defeated*, ed. Christopher Tolkien (London: HarperCollins, 1993), 157–8, 211, 250–2.

Schools at Oxford.'[77] As a remarkable coincidence of place and date, Tolkien's Clarendon Chaucer papers came to light also in an Oxford basement and also in the year 2012!

Martin Maw's ingenuity at locating the grey box was matched by his surprise at its survival. Dropped projects were usually discarded, much as Tolkien imagined for the drafts constituting *The Notion Club Papers*: 'They were found at the University Press waiting to be pulped, but no one knew how they had got there.'[78] In 1951, after all, Tolkien had not published *The Lord of the Rings* and was many years away from becoming a literary superstar. The prior OUP archivist Foden recalls destroying abandoned manuscripts in the 1960s with few exceptions. By that date Tolkien's name might have drawn some attention so that his materials would have been stored in the cellar instead of being pulped. Whatever the case, this chance survival of his Chaucer edition into the twenty-first century would likely have pleased Tolkien because medievalists like himself were always troubled by lost books. His friend R. W. Chambers's 'The Lost Literature of Medieval England' lamented, for example, the disappearance of Chaucer's *Origenes upon the Maudeleyne* and his *Wrecched Engendryng of Mankynd* along with the missing 'balades, roundels and virelays' mentioned in his *Legend* Prologue.[79] Here in an Oxford archive was a bundle of yellowing pages which had defied the odds much as Tolkien imagined for *The Notion Club Papers*—as well as Isildur's scroll about the Ring coming to light in the archives of Minas Tirith (*FR* II/2).[80]

Once opened, the grey box contained exactly what Tolkien described in the letter to Dan Davin—plus a good deal more—no doubt because of the penchant noted by John and Priscilla Tolkien: 'As a family we hoard relics from the past.'[81] Again Tolkien's *Notion Club Papers* eerily anticipated these muddled materials:

> On examination the bundle was found to contain 205 foolscap pages, all written by one hand, in a careful and usually legible script. The leaves were disarranged but mostly numbered...but they are defective and several leaves appear to have been lost; some of the longer entries are incomplete.[82]

OUP's grey box actually contained far more than two hundred pages comprising proof pages, revised proofs, hand-corrected galleys, typescripts, and handwritten drafts. Much of it resembled the jumble which Rayner Unwin recalled from an

---

[77] Ibid. 155.   [78] Ibid. 149.

[79] R. W. Chambers, 'The Lost Literature of Medieval England', *The Library*, 4th ser. 5 (1925), 293–321 at p. 319. A book Tolkien followed toward publication was R. M. Wilson's *The Lost Literature of Medieval England* (London: Methuen, 1952) which added to the list of Chaucer's lost works *The Book of the Leoun* named in his Retraction.

[80] We can add to this list of rediscovered manuscripts C. S. Lewis's *Lost 'Aeneid': Arms and the Exile*, ed. A. T. Reyes, foreword Walter Hooper, preface D. O. Ross (New Haven: Yale University Press, 2011)—which Tolkien heard Lewis read in 1944 (*Letters*, 93).

[81] *The Tolkien Family Album* (Boston: Houghton Mifflin, 1992), 7.

[82] Tolkien, *Sauron Defeated*, 156. Stuart D. Lee, 'Manuscripts', in *Companion*, ed. Lee, 59–62, notes how often lost, fragmented manuscripts figure in Tolkien's fiction.

even larger unfinished project: 'I was shown from time to time the serried ranks of box files that contained, as I was told, like beads without a string, the raw material of *The Silmarillion*.'[83]

Mysteriously, the grey box contained five rather than three copies of Text proofs and two copies of the Glossary's galley sheets rather than the single copy which Tolkien reported returning. There was also an eight-page 'Introduction on Language', part neatly typed and the rest handwritten in drafts, probably intended as preface to the Notes and anticipating several claims elaborated later in 'Chaucer as a Philologist'.[84] Next followed a thick 160-page batch of annotations showing exactly how far Tolkien had exceeded Sisam's limit, the first twenty pages in typescript and the rest handwritten, descending to illegibility before trailing off part way through his commentary on the Reeve's Tale.

In addition to the extra proofs, the grey box contained other surprises. Although Tolkien repeatedly claimed that he never saw Gordon's introductory materials, several large batches of them showed up herein. Again the OUP correspondence explains how this came about. In March 1956 Mary Gordon, the Vice-Chancellor's widow, had mailed these papers with a cover note: 'I am sending you this material which concerns a project in which my husband and Professor Tolkien were to have shared the work.' Davin then wrote to Sisam apprising him of this development: 'Mrs. Gordon lately sent us in a dump of the late lamented *C.E.S. Chaucer* which was found among G. S. Gordon's papers.' In addition to Gordon's copies of the Text proofs and Glossary galleys, her bundle contained drafts of his Introduction and Testimonials which were repeatedly mentioned in letters between Gordon and Sisam, but which Tolkien insisted he never saw, here revealed to have been very much as described by Davin—*a dump*.

Because students were required to know the critical tradition, Gordon's reception history started with Chaucer's earliest readers Thomas Hoccleve, John Lydgate, and William Caxton and extended to nineteenth-century admirers William Blake, William Morris, and Matthew Arnold. For these Testimonials, Gordon had simply copied long passages from Spurgeon's *Five Hundred Years of Chaucer Criticism and Allusion*, page after page, resembling nothing other than a graduate student struggling with an author outside his prior training. Nor did he tackle this note-taking as a single preparatory exercise, but in five separate attempts ranging from nine to eighteen pages each. Apparently stymied by Spurgeon's plenitude, Gordon never brought any of these efforts to a final stage—so far as the surviving documents indicate—and certainly he did not reduce them to a manageable number of pages. He seemed destined for the worst

---

[83] Rayner Unwin, 'Early Days of Elder Days', in *Tolkien's 'Legendarium': Essays on 'The History of Middle Earth'*, ed. Verlyn Flieger and Carl F. Hostetter (Westport, CN and London: Greenwood Press, 2000), 3–6 at p. 4.

[84] Bodleian MS Tolkien A 39/2/2/, fols. 138–42; see Appendix I.

possible outcome which C. S. Lewis imagined for such an undertaking: 'the author who transfers relentlessly to his article all the passages listed in his private notes can expect nothing but weariness from the reader.'[85]

Gordon's Introduction looks like the work of a novice shuffling research notes in no particular order. The jumble even includes a nameless undergraduate's essay on Chaucer's personality, probably from one of Gordon's weekly discussion groups, as well as a single page from another student's essay on *Troilus* observing, 'while Criseyde understands Pandarus perfectly, even she is a mystery to herself.'[86] For all his industry, Gordon got no further than a handwritten draft running to 127 pages without rising above the breeziness of the opening paragraph:

> When George III visited Norwich he remarked to the Mayor, 'You have a very ancient town, Mr. Mayor.' And the Mayor said, 'Yes, your Majesty, and formerly it was much more ancient.' The reply, like all Irish bulls, was good sense, and it may be applied to Chaucer. He is an ancient writer, and formerly he was much more ancient.

Gordon provided headings for subsequent sections of unequal lengths and unclear organization. Here is a sampling: Life of Chaucer—Chaucer's Political Opinions—Literature of the Court—Advance from Allegory to Portraiture of Real Life—Chaucer's Works—Chaucer as a Metrical Artist—Portraiture of Chaucer—The Limited Range of Chaucer—Chaucer's Scepticism—Chaucer the Comic Poet—Chaucer's Irony—Chaucer and Gower—and Chaucer's Choice of Themes for Humour. The last section on Chaucer's Language begins: 'Impossible to over-emphasise his mastery. Here at the beginning, as it is commonly reckoned, of Modern English Literature, is a treasury of perfect speech.'[87] And thus throughout.

In some fairness to Gordon, he had inherited a critical tradition already daunting in its abundance. The Chaucer Society had gathered a mass of life-records throughout the later nineteenth century, and Spurgeon presented this biographical evidence in the first fourteen pages of *Chaucer Criticism and Allusion* while her remaining 1,170 pages surveyed responses from Lydgate in 1400 to Skeat in 1900. We know that Gordon had her three volumes at his elbow as he struggled to condense the author's career and critical legacy, and yet the resulting hodgepodge is all the more startling because his letters to Sisam suggested that his assignment had reached a far more finished state. Gordon's cover-letter from August 1925 was explicit: 'Herewith Introductory Essays and Testimonia for the Clarendon Chaucer.'

Sisam's reply leaves doubt that Gordon really had completed his task: 'I look forward to Introduction and Notes.'[88] The missing Notes were Tolkien's, to be

---

[85] Lewis, 'What Chaucer Really Did to *Il Filostrato*', 74.
[86] Bodleian MS Tolkien A 39/3, fols. 140, 274.   [87] Bodleian MS Tolkien A 39/3, fol. 261.
[88] Bodleian MS Tolkien A 39/3, fol. 286.

sure, but the long-awaited Introduction would have been Gordon's. Because Davin reported in 1960 that the Chaucer materials did contain 'very full and numerous notes for the introduction, together with selected testimonials and notes upon them', the charitable view would be that Gordon did bring his work to a more advanced stage, but those pages never reached the grey box because misplaced after his death or discarded when the project was abandoned.

But if the bundle sent by Mary Gordon in 1956 was the best that her husband produced—and her *Life of George S. Gordon* apologizes repeatedly for scholarly projects begun but never finished—Tolkien had more reason for indignation than he himself knew. Gordon not only failed to make real progress but also outrageously exceeded the constraints imposed upon Tolkien, all the while heaping blame for delays on his junior colleague.

The grey box contained another surprise. In July 1939, Tolkien had accepted an invitation from John Masefield, then Poet Laureate, to dress up as Chaucer and recite the Reeve's Tale from memory for the Summer Diversions in Oxford. This feat seems less remarkable now that we know Tolkien had closely studied this fabliau while working on his article 'Chaucer as a Philologist: *The Reeve's Tale*' and, before that, while editing the text and glossing its vocabulary for his Clarendon Chaucer. When given an opportunity to prepare a programme for this performance, Tolkien did something remarkable. He completely re-edited the Reeve's Tale according to what he had learned about the poet's use of Northern dialect, and, as a more daring experiment, he sought to re-create what he believed to have been Chaucer's original language without allegiance to the standard copy-text, Ellesmere. Tolkien's goal matched what Christopher de Hamel has recently described: 'it is the dream of all scholars to reach back as nearly as possible to the primeval moment when the words left the pen of the author.'[89] Tolkien's souvenir copy of this programme, with a few marginal markings, somehow found its way into the grey box, too. Angry that OUP was forcing him to return his editorial materials, he probably dispatched the business so hastily that he failed to notice his Reeve's Tale programme had ended up with the rest of his Chaucer hoard.

There were some other odds and ends, such as bits of correspondence that never reached the official OUP file, but the obvious question that arises when surveying the helter-skelter of *Selections from Chaucer's Poetry and Prose* is what to do with this lost, forgotten textbook by a one of the most-read authors in literary history? This is the question which the remainder of my book tries to address.

---

[89] Christopher de Hamel, 'The Hengwrt Chaucer', in *Meetings with Remarkable Manuscripts: Twelve Journeys into the Medieval World* (New York: Penguin, 2017), 426–65 at p. 445.

3
Four Chaucerians
Walter W. Skeat, Kenneth Sisam, George S. Gordon, C. S. Lewis

Just as no artist works in total isolation, academic writers too have their predecessors, collaborators, publishers, and friends who to various degrees encourage, complicate, and in some cases sabotage their projects. This chapter focuses upon four scholars of medieval literature who played their various roles in Tolkien's Clarendon Chaucer. Their names have already figured throughout the Press correspondence in the previous chapter, but their careers and personalities deserve fuller notice for understanding the fate of *Selections from Chaucer's Poetry and Prose*.

Walter W. Skeat (1835–1912)

Walter W. Skeat was an eminent Victorian whose pioneering scholarship and voluminous publications are almost impossible to imagine in an age before photocopying and personal computers (Fig. 2). Because he requested his family to destroy his personal papers, we know little about his life except for the autobiographical introduction to his *Student's Pastime* supplemented by Kenneth Sisam's entry in the *Dictionary of National Biography*.[1] More than a century after his death, however, his influence remains profound especially in Chaucer and Langland studies. During the past generation, Harvard's Derek Pearsall routinely advised young medievalists just starting out, 'When in doubt, trust Skeat!'

As an undergraduate at Cambridge, Skeat studied theology and mathematics before taking holy orders and embarking upon a series of curacies. When a throat condition made preaching impossible, he returned to Cambridge as a lecturer in mathematics at Christ's College. In 1864 when Furnivall founded the Early English Text Society with the immediate goal of providing printed texts for citation in the *Oxford English Dictionary*, he learned of Skeat's philological interests and persuaded him to edit *Lancelot of the Laik*. At first baffled by the

---

[1] Walter W. Skeat, 'Introduction', *A Student's Pastime: Being a Selection of Articles Reprinted from 'Notes and Queries'* (Oxford: Clarendon Press, 1896), and Kenneth Sisam, 'Skeat, Walter William' in *DNB 1912–21*, 495–6, now revised by Charlotte Brewer, *ODNB* 50: 817–19.

Tolkien's Lost Chaucer. John M. Bowers, Oxford University Press (2019). © John M. Bowers.
DOI: 10.1093/oso/9780198842675.001.0001

Fig. 2. Walter W. Skeat. Portrait by Charles Edmund Brock.

fifteenth-century Scottish handwriting, Skeat advanced quickly under the tutelage of Henry Bradshaw, the University Librarian, and saw his edition rapidly into print in 1865. Thereafter he concentrated on Old and Middle English and became Professor of Anglo-Saxon at Cambridge in 1878.

It is truly mind-boggling to imagine that only a year after publishing *Lancelot*, Skeat tackled the most complicated text in the vernacular canon, Langland's *Piers Plowman*. He was the first to realize that the fourteenth-century poem survived in three different versions with a huge amount of variation among its more than fifty manuscripts.[2] Though he saw his *A-Text* into print after only one year, this colossal undertaking would occupy him for the next twenty years until completing his two-volume Oxford edition with parallel texts, introductions, notes, and glossary. Even then, editing Langland's poem was not a full-time undertaking, since during this same period he published a range of works from Ælfric's *Lives of the Saints* to Shakespeare's *Two Noble Kinsmen*. By the time he came to editing

---

[2] Charlotte Brewer, *Editing 'Piers Plowman': The Evolution of the Text* (Cambridge: Cambridge University Press, 1996), 'Skeat: Introduction', 91–112.

The Complete Works of Geoffrey Chaucer in the 1890s, his methods had become much more sophisticated than when first undertaking *Lancelot* in 1865.

Famous even during his lifetime for the prodigious number of publications, Skeat attributed this productivity to rigorous self-discipline: 'It is astonishing how much can be done by steady work at the same subject for many hours every day.'[3] The preface to his *Etymological Dictionary of the English Language* went farther in explaining how he adhered to strict constraints of time: 'my usual rule has been not to spend more than three hours over one word.'[4] He admitted that this discipline left him unhappy with many results, but at least he finished one project and moved along to the next without allowing himself to be hobbled by the fastidiousness that plagued other scholars like Tolkien. Sisam made a point of emphasizing Skeat's virtue in this regard, working always with a time-limit rather than aiming at perfection,[5] with the result that his *Student's Pastime* could list seventy-three books in print by 1896.

Though his wealthy father provided generously, Skeat had a large family to support and soon learned there was money to be made in scholarly publications. His *Etymological Dictionary* pushed his earnings to about £400 in the single year of 1883—roughly the equivalent of £36,000 today—and later books netted him annually about £100, sometimes substantially more.[6] Chaucer had been reckoned a lucrative author as far back as the 1775 edition of the *Canterbury Tales* by Thomas Tyrwhitt, a fellow of Merton College, whose deluxe second edition was lavishly produced in the manner of Greek and Latin authors.[7] Dr Johnson famously believed that nobody but a blockhead wrote except for money, and within a decade of Tyrwhitt's achievement, he himself envisioned a Chaucer edition and spelled out the standards for future practices: 'from manuscripts and old editions, with various readings, conjectures, remarks on his language, and the changes it had undergone from the earliest times to his age, and from his to the present: with notes explanatory of customs, &c., and references to Boccace, and other authours from whom he has borrowed, with an account of the liberties he has taken in telling the stories; his life, and an exact etymological glossary.'[8] As if the fulfilment of Dr Johnson's grand ambitions, Skeat's Oxford Chaucer would prove a great financial as well as scholarly success, generating during its first year of publication an income of £246 or roughly £25,000 in today's valuation.[9]

---

[3] *Student's Pastime*, pp. liii–liv.
[4] Walter W. Skeat, *An Etymological Dictionary of the English Language*, rev. edn (Oxford: Clarendon Press, 1910), p. xiv.
[5] *DNB*, 496.
[6] *History of Oxford University Press*, 2:348.
[7] Ibid. 2:583; see B. A. Windeatt, 'Thomas Tyrwhitt (1730–1786)', in Ruggiers, ed., *Editing Chaucer*, 117–43.
[8] *Boswell's Life of Johnson*, ed. R. W. Chapman (London: Oxford University Press, 1953), 1363–4.
[9] *History of Oxford University Press*, 2:591–2.

Although the Merton Professorship of Language and Literature was founded in 1885 and English had been offered as a pass degree since 1873, the subject did not enter the University's curriculum by statute until 1894 when its advent boosted sales in Clarendon books as teaching texts.[10] Selections from Chaucer had already begun in 1867 when Skeat entered the field with his *Tale of the Man of Lawe*, *Pardoneres Tale*, *Second Nonnes Tale*, and *Chanouns Yemannes Tale*. Clearly there was a market for individual *Tales* published after the model of individual plays by Greek dramatists like Sophocles. Later campaigns to stiffen the degree by requiring Old and Middle English texts would build upon Skeat's backlist of titles.[11]

OUP's governing Delegates encountered difficulties when commissioning an edition of Chaucer's complete works, however, first approaching John Earle in 1870 and Henry Bradshaw a year later, but the project languished until entrusted to Skeat.[12] He was the obvious choice, having already edited Chaucer's *Treatise on the Astrolabe* for the Early English Text Society in 1872 followed by *The Minor Poems* in 1888 and *The Legend of Good Women* in 1889, both for OUP. Not only had he acquired editorial skills unmatched by any of his contemporaries, but he was able to move quickly by transferring texts and commentaries from his previous editions with little revision.[13]

Even with these prior instalments at hand, Skeat still faced a daunting task. Earlier editions offered little practical help and much accumulated error. He adapted a variety of editorial methods though seldom explaining what exactly those methods were. Charlotte Brewer has remarked that it is hard to find any overt comment by him on editing, whether in theory or practice, so that readers can only infer his methods by looking at the results.[14] His Chaucer edition had begun with what sounds sensible and straightforward: 'In each case, the best copy has been selected as the basis of the text and has only been departed from where other copies afforded a better reading' (1:vii). But he did not explain how he chose a particular manuscript as the best copy and how he then went about identifying a better reading in some other manuscript.

EETS editors often adhered to the mechanical reproduction of a manuscript almost as a facsimile. Furnivall's *Six-Text Edition of Chaucer's Canterbury Tales* typified a practice criticized as 'non-editing' because not assessing manuscripts for purposes of reconstructing the author's original.[15] Often Skeat approximated this course by reproducing a copy-text like the Ellesmere *Canterbury Tales* and allowing the manuscript to determine substantive readings as well as spellings.

---

[10] D. J. Palmer, *The Rise of English Studies* (London and New York: Oxford University Press, 1965), 'The Founding of the Oxford English School', 104–117, and *History of Oxford University Press*, 2:582–3.
[11] Ibid. 2:584–6.   [12] Ibid. 2:589–92.
[13] Edwards, 'Walter Skeat', 174, 179–89.
[14] Charlotte Brewer, *Editing 'Piers Plowman'*, 83.
[15] Donald C. Baker, 'Frederick James Furnivall (1825–1910)' in Ruggiers, ed., *Editing Chaucer*, 157–69.

A. S. G. Edwards judges this practice as one of his few shortcomings: 'Skeat's gifts as an editor did not include the patient sifting of manuscript evidence' (p. 185).

Although Skeat sometimes used the genealogical method of German scholars such as Karl Lachmann for tracing texts backward through affiliated copies to reclaim the poet's original, generally he was much more conservative, deciding upon the best-surviving version and then substituting variants from other manuscripts only when his copy-text offered something unsatisfactory. Nor did he resort to conjectural emendations when plausible readings appeared elsewhere in scribal copies.[16] But even here he was not consistent. He rejected faulty manuscript testimony for poems like the *Parlement of Foules* and inserted his own guesses for what Chaucer really wrote, preferring his own spellings, too, when unhappy with what the fifteenth-century scribes had to offer.[17]

All in all, he comes off as a practical-minded editor using whatever method the textual situation called for. 'In Boethius, for example, a manuscript consists of sense more or less all the way through,' he wrote about Chaucer's *Boece* translation, 'but the manuscripts of the *Astrolabe* frequently scorn sense. You can only get at it by collation.'[18] However inconsistent his methods, he produced texts and supporting apparatus which established the foundations for all subsequent editorial work on Chaucer. He immediately adapted the six-volume *Complete Works* to the one-volume *Student's Chaucer* which had a tremendous reach into the twentieth century.[19] James Joyce picked up his copy when writing *Ulysses*, probably to re-read the Wife of Bath's Prologue as a medieval version of Molly Bloom's soliloquy, and John M. Manly and Edith Rickert selected it as the base text for their eight-volume Chicago edition of the *Canterbury Tales*.[20]

Skeat had followed Furnivall's practice of making available for future scholars a great quantity of materials, particularly textual data and commentaries,[21] but his Chaucer Glossary running to 310 double-columned pages remains among his greatest achievements. Even the most recent *Riverside Chaucer* continued weighing his editorial choices and drawing steadily upon his annotations. The fact that James Simpson and Christopher Cannon based their 'Oxford Scholarly Edition Online' upon Skeat's Chaucer attests to the durability of this landmark publication into the twenty-first century.

In the age before online access to manuscript resources, scholarship depended much upon institutional connections. Because Skeat's research took him regularly to Oxford, he found it desirable to seek college membership: 'my choice was

---

[16] Brewer, *Editing 'Piers Plowman'*, 79.   [17] Edwards, 'Skeat', 185.
[18] Letter to Furnivall quoted by Brewer, *Editing 'Piers Plowman'*, 90.
[19] *The Student's Chaucer: Being a Complete Edition of his Works*, ed. Walter W. Skeat (Oxford: Clarendon Press, 1895), contained texts and glossary but no notes.
[20] George Kane, 'John M. Manly (1865–1940) and Edith Rickert (1871–1938)', in Ruggiers, ed., *Editing Chaucer*, 208–9. James Joyce's copy of *Student's Chaucer* found its way to SUNY Buffalo.
[21] Sisam, *DNB*, 496.

Exeter, which proved a very happy one.'[22] William Morris had been an undergraduate at Exeter College and in 1896 turned to Skeat's text for his beautiful Kelmscott Chaucer. Exeter later became Tolkien's undergraduate college where the library register indicates that he checked out Skeat's Chaucer.[23] The last year of Skeat's life was also Tolkien's first year at Exeter, though there is no evidence that he ever actually saw the great man. In 1914 Tolkien won the college's Skeat Prize and used his £5 award to buy three romances by William Morris as well as *A Welsh Grammar*.[24] Years later he would joke to his lecture audience, 'The shade of Walter Skeat, I surmise, was shocked when the only prize I ever won (there was only one other competitor), the Skeat Prize for English at Exeter College, was spent on Welsh' (*Essays*, 192). By 1955 when he delivered this lecture 'English and Welsh', Tolkien had other reasons, as we shall see, to worry about offending his benefactor's ghost.

As a later editor of both Chaucer and Langland, E. Talbot Donaldson understood that 'all stages of the editorial process represent psychological achievements as much as they do scholarly ones'.[25] Yet Tolkien would surely have recoiled at this suggestion since he heaped scorn upon 'so-called psychologists'. He disdained psychological analyses of his works and wrote mockingly about identifying personally with his character Faramir: 'let the psychoanalysts note!'[26] The Freudian critic Leonard Jackson admits Tolkien would have dismissed any family-romance interpretation despite the fact that *The Lord of the Rings* introduces father-figures who are either killed off like Denethor and Théoden or dispatched into exile like Bilbo and Gandalf.[27] Nonetheless C. S. Lewis's 1942 essay 'Psycho-Analysis and Literary Criticism' forms something of a companion-piece with Tolkien's 'On Fairy-Stories' by connecting the artistic imagination with wish-fulfilling fantasy.[28] As much as he would have objected to Freudian interpretations of his fiction, Tolkien would surely have objected to the impertinence of having his editorial efforts

---

[22] *Student's Pastime*, p. lviii.

[23] John Garth, *Tolkien at Exeter College: How an Oxford Undergraduate Created Middle-earth* (Oxford: Exeter College, 2014), 21–2, 44.

[24] *Biography*, 77 and SH 1:58, 2:798. Tolkien's copy of Sir John Morris-Jones's *Welsh Grammar* (1913) went with other books donated to Oxford's English Faculty Library, now in the Bodleian's Tolkien Archive.

[25] E. Talbot Donaldson, 'The Psychology of Editors of Middle English Texts' (1966), *Speaking of Chaucer* (New York: W. W. Norton, 1970), 102–18 at p. 103.

[26] *Letters*, 232 and 288, and Henry Resnick, 'An Interview with Tolkien', *Niekas* 18 (1967), 37–47 at p. 38. The word *psycho-analysis* officially entered the language only with publication of the OED Supplement in 1933, when the word was singled out in the banquet speech celebrating the Supplement's publication by George S. Gordon; see Charlotte Brewer, *Treasure-House of the Language: The Living 'OED'* (New Haven and London: Yale University Press, 2007), 67.

[27] *Literature, Psychoanalysis, and the New Sciences of Mind* (Harlow and New York: Longman, 2000), 77–80, reads the trilogy via the castration complex; see Shippey, *Road to Middle-earth*, 322–3.

[28] C. S. Lewis had read Freud's *Introductory Lectures on Psychoanalysis* as background for 'Psycho-Analysis and Literary Criticism', in *Selected Literary Essays*, ed. Walter Hooper (Cambridge: Cambridge University Press, 1969), 286–300 at p. 286.

psychoanalysed in terms of some Oedipal contest with his scholarly father-figure Skeat—yet this is exactly what I venture to do in the paragraphs that follow.

Old-fashioned but not entirely outmoded, Harold Bloom's 1973 *Anxiety of Influence* described an agonistic struggle between the literary newcomer and his powerful precursor which can readily be translated into the generational rivalries between scholars. Tolkien's lectures routinely enacted this pattern of establishing his own authority by first dispatching his father-figures. '*Beowulf*: The Monsters and the Critics' began with a dismissive anecdote about Joseph Bosworth, for example, before mocking wrong-headed critics like Archibald Strong and even expressing dissatisfaction with those he admired like W. P. Ker.[29] Derek Brewer recalled the 1946 lectures on *Gawain* in which Tolkien confined himself to 'doing obscure (to me) battle with some mysterious entity, prophetically as it may now seem, called something like "Gollancz"'.[30] This was Sir Israel Gollancz (1863–1930) whose editorial work on the *Gawain* Poet provided Tolkien with many opportunities for finding fault with a distinguished predecessor.

Bloom provides six models useful for assessing Tolkien's struggles with Skeat's enormous scholarly presence, especially his 420 pages of annotations distributed over four volumes of his Oxford Chaucer, even if those struggles never assumed the drama of 'major figures with the persistence to wrestle with their strong precursors, even to the death'.[31] Tolkien's responses were never so confrontational and were typically expressed by his omissions. He never acknowledged the Oxford Chaucer as the almost exclusive source for his own commentary, for instance, constantly cribbing from Skeat without ever admitting that he was cribbing. Skeat's name never even appears in the index to Tolkien's *Letters* apart from the Skeat Prize. Thus his editorial commentary did not openly disdain his predecessor as Tyrwhitt had done with John Urry's 1721 *Works*: 'Mr. Urry's edition should never be opened by anyone for the purpose of reading Chaucer.'[32] Far from looking incompetent, Skeat's achievements felt intimidating to successive generations of scholars. Nor was he a figure of the remote past, it should be remembered, but still alive as an Honorary Fellow during Tolkien's first year as an undergraduate at Exeter College.

---

[29] Jane Chance Nitzsche, *Tolkien's Art: A 'Mythology for England'* (New York: St Martin's Press, 1979), 'The Critic as Monster: Tolkien's Lectures, Prefaces, and Foreword', 8–30 at p. 9: 'the critics *are* the monsters—and Tolkien by defending Beowulf *is* the hero.'

[30] Derek Brewer, 'Introduction', in *A Companion to the 'Gawain'-Poet*, ed. Derek Brewer and Jonathan Gibson (Cambridge: D. S. Brewer, 1997), 2. J. R. R. Tolkien and E. V. Gordon, eds., *Sir Gawain and the Green Knight* (Oxford: Clarendon Press, 1925), p. xxv, acknowledged Gollancz's editorial work.

[31] Harold Bloom, *Anxiety of Influence* (New York: Oxford University Press, 1973), 5. Josh Long, 'Clinamen, Tessera, and the Anxiety of Influence: Swerving from and Completing George MacDonald', *Tolkien Studies* 6 (2009), 127–50, has provided a Bloomian model for Tolkien suppressing his debt to McDonald's *Golden Key* to create something original in *Smith of Wootton Major*.

[32] Quoted by Windeatt, 'Thomas Tyrwhitt', 119.

Tolkien's response as a novice editor in the 1920s certainly resembles Bloom's *clinamen* or 'swerve', not in the sense of an evasive manoeuvre, but more in accord with the word's Old English root *sweorfan* meaning to 'file or grind away, polish, wipe, rub, scour'.[33] This nicely describes Tolkien's efforts at refining the mass of scholarly material inherited from the Oxford Chaucer. For his glossary, Tolkien sought to improve upon his predecessor, sometimes devising better definitions and sometimes compressing two or three entries into a single one. To contend with Skeat's daunting annotations, however, he constantly pushed beyond the modest limits of a student edition laid down by Sisam. As much as he deleted and condensed, the more literary allusions and etymological explanations he sought to include. His 1926 'Philology' survey rationalized these excesses: 'there is not much use in etymologies unless they are fairly full.'[34]

Tolkien had ample reason to feel himself a latecomer lagging behind the great scholarly age of Skeat, Furnivall, and other Victorian trailblazers. Skeat as Professor of Anglo-Saxon at Cambridge could boast shelves of publications to his credit whereas Tolkien as Professor of Anglo-Saxon at Oxford had almost none. Thus he also enacted Bloom's *kenosis* or 'emptying out' when the new writer tries ridding his enterprise of the precursor's over-abundance. Skeat was certainly guilty of packing his Chaucerian commentary with everything he learned about language, literature, and history, even drawing upon conversations on-the-fly with colleagues. His commentaries are peppered with sentences like 'Mr. Gollancz tells me...'. Skeat remembered everything that he read or heard, and he seems to have operated under a divine injunction to leave out nothing. Tolkien's *kenosis* started by leaving out a great deal of source material and ended by abandoning the commentary itself, not even reaching the Monk's Tale and the Nun's Priest's Tale, so that he achieved his ultimate undoing of Skeat's authority by negating the project of annotation-writing itself.

Since rejecting the precursor was not possible, *kenosis* in the secondary sense of 'repetition' found Tolkien steadily taking from Skeat's commentary without acknowledging the debt. This scholarly thievery looked forward to elevating theft as the primary merit for his hero Bilbo Baggins. The hobbit was recruited specifically as a burglar who stole from the three trolls, from the Wood-elves, from Gollum when he pocketed the Ring, and from Thorin Oakenshield when he made off with the Arkenstone. Tolkien as a fiction-writer continued these acts of thievery when, for example, the taking of the goblet from the dragon's hoard in *Beowulf* was lifted and recast as Bilbo's taking of the goblet from Smaug's hoard

---

[33] John R. Clark Hall, *A Concise Anglo-Saxon Dictionary*, 4th edn suppl. Herbert D. Merritt (Cambridge: Cambridge University Press, 1969), 331. Stephen Greenblatt took this as the title of his Pulitzer Prize-winning book *The Swerve: How the World Became Modern* (New York and London: Norton, 2011); as Bloom's student at Yale, Greenblatt has faced his own Oedipal struggles.

[34] J. R. R. Tolkien, 'Philology: General Works', *Year's Work in English Studies* 5 (1926), 26–65 at p. 49.

in *The Hobbit*.[35] His pilfering of Skeat's annotations formed a practice exercise, as it were, for a long career of taking and re-using earlier materials when needed.

As a third reaction, Bloom's *tessera* used a mosaic-making term for describing the process by which the newcomer strives to complete what the precursor had left undone. Tolkien clearly enjoyed ferreting out words missing from the Oxford Chaucer, often skipping what Skeat glossed in order to gloss what Skeat had skipped. Early in his commentary on the *Romaunt of the Rose*, for example, he spotted a reference to shiny stones (127) and quoted a whole stanza from his own translation of *Pearl* with a vaguely similar line—'There stones were dazzling in its deep'[36]—in order to provide a fourteenth-century parallel which Skeat had missed. Later Tolkien would give free rein to this impulse by taking Skeat's concise commentary on the Northern dialect in the Reeve's Tale (5.121–2) and expanding it into his seventy-page study 'Chaucer as a Philologist'.

Skeat's compulsive source-hunting reinforced the point, driven home in Tolkien's letter to John Masefield in 1938, that Chaucer was not the first English poet but 'stands rather in the middle than the beginning' (*Letters*, 39). Like Tolkien himself, Chaucer was a latecomer who operated largely as an heir, not a begetter. To make the point that even the famous opening of the *Canterbury Tales* lacked originality, Tolkien devoted three pages to the word *Aprille* by documenting the poet's indebtedness to Latin sources like the *Speculum Naturalis* as well as vernacular poems like the *Sowdone of Babylone*.[37] Just as Bloom's latecomer strives for completing as well as repeating, Tolkien enlarged upon what he found in the Oxford Chaucer to make his note on *Aprille* longer than Skeat's, not shorter.

To judge Skeat's annotations as somehow incomplete required Tolkien to engage in a steady misreading of them. Although his own Notes would remain incomplete, Tolkien's last jottings on the Reeve's Tale—'Chaucer at Hatfield' and 'The dialect is Yorkshire'—suggested ways for remedying his predecessor's shortcomings.[38] Skeat had connected the poet's biography with his literary work by remarking that Chaucer's presence in the Countess of Ulster's retinue in Yorkshire at Hatfield House (not to be confused with the more famous Hatfield House in Hertfordshire) allowed him personal knowledge of the Northern dialect which he later employed in the Reeve's Tale (Skeat 1:xvii). Here Tolkien would break his own rule against applying biographical information, since he typically insisted that 'excessive interest in the details of the lives of authors' could 'only distract

---

[35] When the 1938 *Observer* review caught this appropriation, Tolkien protested: '*Beowulf* is among my most valued sources; though it was not consciously present to the mind in the process of writing, in which the episode of the theft arose naturally (and almost inevitably) from the circumstances' (*Letters*, 31).
[36] This was an early version of *Pearl*'s stanza 10 from J. R. R. Tolkien, *Sir Gawain and the Green Knight, Pearl, and Sir Orfeo*, ed. Christopher Tolkien (1975; New York: Ballantine Books, 1980), 127.
[37] Bodleian Tolkien MS A 39/2/1, fols. 86–8.
[38] Bodleian Tolkien MS A 39/2/1, fol. 136v.

attention from the author's works' (*Letters*, 288). This brand of interpretation was presumptuous, too, because 'only one's guardian Angel, or indeed God Himself, could unravel the real relationship between personal facts and an author's works'.[39] Yet biography was one of those resources that Tolkien used when he found it useful. In this case, he wanted to know how Chaucer acquired the knowledge of Northern dialect which enabled him to write authentic-sounding dialogue for John and Alain. Only hinting at these possibilities when drafting his Clarendon annotations, Tolkien stopped at exactly the point where Skeat's comments on dialect became most extensive, hence most challenging to the newcomer. Tolkien would need six more years to publish his exhaustive investigation in 'Chaucer as a Philologist'.

To sum up, Tolkien suspended work on the Clarendon Chaucer in 1928 when his notes were transferred to Magdalen College for George Gordon to assist with trimming them. Two years passed before their return, largely untouched, but during this interval Tolkien had been busy studying the dialect issues raised on the final pages of his drafts. He was already thinking about such questions when writing a foreword for the 1928 *Glossary of the Dialect of the Huddersfield District* from the West Riding of Yorkshire.[40] Another non-London dialect became the subject of his 1929 article '*Ancrene Wisse* and *Hali Meiðhad*'. But here Bloom's fifth response of *askesis* or 'lone effort' was forced upon him when his Oxford appointment deprived him of his in-person partnership with E. V. Gordon. He also had reason to feel abandoned by George Gordon, and yet decided against calling upon C. S. Lewis, so that his 'lone effort' remained intact.

After joining the Council of the Philological Society in 1929, Tolkien had his first opportunity for sharing his insights on the Reeve's Tale in the lecture 'Chaucer's Use of Dialects' at the organization's meeting in Oxford in May 1931. The Chaucerian subject must have come as some surprise to listeners since he had been lecturing on Old English and Icelandic since his appointment as Professor of Anglo-Saxon in 1925. He had not even directed a thesis on Chaucer. But the subject had interested him from his undergraduate career when he wrote tutorial essays on 'The Language of Chaucer', 'Problem of Dialects', and 'Scandinavian Influence on the English'.[41] Something that Tolkien did not divulge in the published version of this talk was that he had been editing Chaucer since 1922.

---

[39] SH 2:159–68 'Biographies' at 159; Diana Pavlac Glyer and Josh B. Long, 'Biography as Source: Niggles and Notions', in *Tolkien and the Study of His Sources*, ed. Fisher, 193–214, demonstrate the utility of biographical criticism for shorter works like *Leaf by Niggle* and *The Notion Club Papers*.

[40] J. R. R. Tolkien, 'Foreword' to Walter E. Haigh, *A New Glossary of the Dialect of the Huddersfield District* (London: Oxford University Press, 1928), pp. xiii–xviii. See SH 3:847–8.

[41] Bodleian MS Tolkien A 21/1, fols. 43–63, 86–94, and 98–120; he had chosen Scandinavian Philology as his Special Subject when he transferred to the English School.

'Chaucer as a Philologist' ran to seventy pages in *Transactions of the Philological Society* after he added critical texts and editorial notes as well as appendices. Yet amid all this hefty scholarly apparatus, he begrudged acknowledging his debt to Skeat and mentioned his name only in the second page's footnote where he unfairly accused his predecessor of not proceeding very far in investigating the dialect issues. Here Tolkien's dismissive gesture denied the true extent of the prior editor's discoveries. He tended to name Skeat only when correcting him.

In fact Skeat was fully aware of these dialect elements in the Reeve's Tale. He had founded the English Dialect Society in 1873 and thus paved the way for the six-volume *English Dialect Dictionary* dedicated to him by its compiler Joseph Wright, the Yorkshireman who tutored Tolkien as a first-year undergraduate in Greek and Latin philology.[42] Nor was Skeat the first to notice these language features, since Tyrwhitt anticipated these findings in his 1775 edition of the *Canterbury Tales*: 'Chaucer, it may be observed, has given his clerks a northern dialect.'[43] With typical thoroughness, the Victorian editor devoted an entire closely-packed page to commenting upon dialect forms, remarking upon words such as *boes* which particularly fascinated Tolkien, and he reached conclusions about Chaucer's comic intentions still generally accepted today: 'the poet merely gives a Northern colouring to his diction to amuse us; he is not trying to teach us Northern grammar. The general effect is excellent, and that is all he was concerned with.'[44] In short, Skeat advanced much farther than Tolkien acknowledged when documenting Northern usages and establishing the author's humorous intentions.

Much more will be said about Tolkien's work on the Reeve's Tale in Chapter 6. For present purposes, 'Chaucer as a Philologist' reflects the newer scholar's ongoing struggles with his mighty predecessor. Not only did Tolkien attempt polishing, emptying out, and completing the Oxford Chaucer wherever he spotted opportunities, but he also enacted the response described by Bloom as 'recollecting forward' (*AI* 83). By 1934 Tolkien extended his sketchy commentary on Chaucer's fabliau in this new, highly ambitious direction by repeating without properly conceding Skeat's prior achievements.

There remains the sixth and final of Bloom's responses for a writer under the anxiety of influence. This was *apophrades* or 'return of the dead'. After Skeat's death in October 1912, the great scholar remained a memorial presence with books

---

[42] Wright never abandoned his Yorkshire speech during all his years in accent-conscious Oxford, unlike R. W. Chapman, another Yorkshireman, whose speech bore no trace of his northern upbringing. C. T. Onions and Henry Bradley can be added to the list of Tolkien's mentors who were Yorkshiremen. In J. R. R. Tolkien, *The Return of the Shadow: The History of the Lord of the Rings, Part I* (Boston and New York: Houghton Mifflin, 1988), 174, Christopher used Wright's *Dialect Dictionary* to gloss his father's obscure word *yowk*.

[43] Thomas Tyrwhitt, ed., *The Canterbury Tales of Chaucer*, 5 vols. (London: T. Payne, 1775–8), 1:113.

[44] Skeat 5:121–2; see Simon C. P. Horobin, 'J. R. R. Tolkien as a Philologist: A Reconsideration of the Northernisms in Chaucer's *Reeve's Tale*', *English Studies* 2 (2001), 97–105.

on the Exeter Library's shelves and the Skeat Prize awarded to an undergraduate examined on Chaucer. Years later when he summoned up 'the shade of Walter Skeat' during his lecture 'English and Welsh' (*Essays*, 192), his joking remark (where the truth is often expressed) invoked the ghostly image of his father-figure still very much a lively presence whenever he lectured on Chaucer during the 1940s and 1950s. When he weighed Skeat's emendations against Sisam's student edition of the Clerk's Tale, for example, Tolkien continued slighting the eminent Victorian when telling the undergraduates: 'Skeat comes marching in. Kenneth Sisam has stepped very softly. Sisam is right, I think.'[45] All these years later, he still found it necessary to make Skeat wrong.

Kenneth Sisam (1887–1971)

In 1910 Kenneth Sisam arrived at Merton College, Oxford, as a Rhodes Scholar and early member of what medievalists good-humouredly refer to as the New Zealand Mafia[46] (Fig. 3). The list of subsequent New Zealanders would be impressive. Norman Davis succeeded Tolkien as Merton Professor of Language and Literature, J. A. W. Bennett followed C. S. Lewis as Professor of Medieval and Renaissance English at Cambridge, R. W. Burchfield oversaw Tolkien's EETS edition of *Ancrene Wisse*, and Douglas Gray became the first J. R. R. Tolkien Professor of English at Oxford. Tolkien himself acknowledged the debt that the School of English owed to the Antipodes in his 'Valedictory Address' (*Essays*, 238). To this roster might be added Press Secretary Dan Davin who ended Tolkien's involvement with the Clarendon Chaucer in 1951. It is another happy coincidence that Peter Jackson chose to film *The Lord of the Rings* in New Zealand.

Carpenter's *Biography* largely neglects Tolkien's camaraderie with other colonials. He was born in the Orange Free State, his father died and was buried in Bloemfontein, and in autumn 1911 he joined the cavalry regiment whose membership was restricted to colonials. 'There is something about nativity,' he wrote to Christopher in South Africa in 1944; 'there is always a curious sense of reminiscence about any stories of Africa which always move me deeply' and 'only increases the longing I have always felt to see it again'.[47] He might indeed have returned to South Africa in 1921 as De Beers Chair at the University of Cape Town. Though he did not accept the job offer, his early childhood memories were 'still pictorially available for inspection' (*Letters*, 213), and these 'beautiful blends

---

[45] Bodleian MS Tolkien A 13/2, fol. 31v.
[46] Brewer, *Treasure-House*, 149, attributes the phrase to R. W. Burchfield, another New Zealander and editor of the *OED* Supplement 2; Burchfield pursued doctoral research on the *Ormulum* under Tolkien's supervision.
[47] *Letters*, 82, 90; see SH 3:1250–2 'South Africa'. He also asked Christopher to visit the house where he was born and his father's grave in Bloemfontein (*Letters*, 75).

Fig. 3. Kenneth Sisam standing on Middle Carn, the outcrop of rock from which his retirement house on the Scilly Isles took its name.

of African and English details' can be traced into the landscapes of Middle-earth, especially the wide-open barrenness of Rohan (*Letters*, 85, 90–1). His 'Valedictory Address' went out of its way to remind his audience that he had come to Oxford from 'lands under the Southern Cross' (*Essays*, 238).

Kenneth Sisam, who retired to the Scilly Isles because the landscape reminded him of his native New Zealand, therefore had reason to feel sympathy for Tolkien's colonial status otherwise downplayed in the official record. The two men had much else in common.[48] Sisam's father had emigrated from Warwickshire where Ronald courted Edith and, before that, had spent the idyllic boyhood later recalled when describing The Shire. Both men had played rugby football at school. Both were accomplished Latinists who turned to the study of English. Both overcame considerable obstacles to study at Oxford where they specialized in Old English. Both served apprenticeships as lexicographers at the *Oxford English Dictionary*. Both would become members of Merton College and eventually Honorary Fellows. Both had children who followed them into the profession.

---

[48] See Neil Ker, 'Kenneth Sisam, 1887–1971', *Proceedings of the British Academy* 58 (1972), 409–28; Peter J. Sisam, *Roots and Branches: The Story of the Sisam Family* (Marlow: Peter J. Sisam, 1993); SH 3:1205–7; and Brewer, *Treasure-House*, 16–18 *et passim*.

Like Tolkien's son Christopher who became a Fellow of New College, Sisam's daughter Celia was a medievalist at St Hilda's College and later worked collaboratively with her father on their *Salisbury Psalter* (1959) and *Oxford Book of Medieval English Verse* (1970).

This search for Sisam's sympathy with Tolkien is useful for explaining an abiding mystery in this scholarly story—namely, why he showed so much patience over so many years with the unpunctual, unproductive editor. Much as he badgered Tolkien about finishing the Clarendon Chaucer, he did not follow through on threats to dismiss him. When Tolkien himself proposed withdrawing in 1924, Sisam allowed him to continue trying. Even years after George Gordon's death when it was clear their *Selections* was going nowhere, Sisam sent letters from the Scilly Isles insisting that no replacement should be appointed while Tolkien continued as a professor. Why so much forbearance over decades?

Sisam had assisted Professor A. S. Napier and covered his classes on subjects such as Skeat's *Specimens of Early English* when his supervisor's health declined. Though only five years younger, Tolkien attended these lectures after switching from Classics and soon had Sisam as his tutor. Late in life, Tolkien would recall his good fortune for teaching 'spiced with a pungency, humour and practical wisdom which were his own. I owe him a great debt and have not forgotten it' (*Letters*, 406). Part of this debt included an introduction to the used-book catalogues which would help greatly in building his professional library. On Sisam's side, he had early experience with the undergraduate's brilliance but also his habitual excuse-making. In 1914 Tolkien was already writing to Edith: 'I went and saw Mr. Sisam and told him I could not finish my essay till Wednesday' (*Letters*, 7). It was the first of many postponements.

In 1920 Sisam drew Tolkien's attention to the advertisement for Reader in English Language at the University of Leeds, and he showed loyalty to a gifted pupil again when commissioning him to compile the glossary for his *Fourteenth Century Verse and Prose*. Though late in arriving, Tolkien's *Middle English Vocabulary* inspired confidence for future projects.[49] Work on this textbook further benefited Tolkien by focusing his attention on the Middle English works like *Pearl* which would engage his efforts for the remainder of his career. In 1921 before joining Oxford University Press, Sisam suggested the need for a new edition of *Sir Gawain and the Green Knight*. Tolkien had already glossed 360 lines for Sisam's anthology as a warm-up exercise, so to speak, and proceeded to what would become his most successful achievement with the Clarendon *Gawain* in 1925.[50]

---

[49] The anthology would enjoy long success as a textbook, selling more than 60,000 copies by 1972. Charlotte Brewer offers this statistic in the footnote to her website's entry on Sisam: http://oed.hertford.ox.ac.uk/main/content/view/349/340/.

[50] Shippey, 'Tolkien as Editor', 42, and SH 3:1193–9 '*Sir Gawain*'. Sisam's judgement was not entirely laudatory according to his daughter Celia: 'I gathered from my father that that edition was

Glossary-making for *Verse and Prose* set the agenda for much of Tolkien's later work starting with *Gawain* and gave him a close knowledge of the Breton lay *Sir Orfeo* which served as his chief source for medieval fairy lore.[51] Like the Wood-elves in *The Hobbit*, these fairies ventured into the forest but lived deep inside a mountain realm; like Bilbo reciting poetry for Lord Elrond's court, Sir Orfeo performed songs for the Fairy King's court. This indebtedness was typical of Tolkien's imaginative economy. He wasted little.[52] What he learned while glossing pieces for Sisam's anthology—even from the short song *The Maid of the Moor*—would find their ways into his fantasy novels.[53] The same would be true for his own editorial work on Chaucer.

Some Oxford history is useful for better understanding Sisam's recruitment of Tolkien as an editor. After the English School was founded in 1894, the question of the syllabus immediately arose.[54] Chaucer was already required for the Pass Degree in 1873 and remained on the syllabus for both Language and Literature. When Professor Walter Raleigh arrived in 1904 with the intention of rescuing poetry from the vassalage of philology, Chaucer was already firmly ensconced alongside Shakespeare as compulsory authors. Courses I, II, and III all included him. Tolkien's undergraduate notebook for Raleigh's lectures, 'Chaucer and His Contemporaries', attests to the thoroughness of this literary history.[55] Whatever reforms ensued, including Tolkien's own push for Language over Literature, Chaucer always figured in the final proposal.[56] OUP's Clarendon Series had been profitable from the 1860s but already looked old-fashioned by the late 1890s. While the London office sought general readers, Oxford redoubled its commitment to the English classics as Sisam set about transforming Clarendon textbooks for the twentieth century.[57]

As late as 1930 C. S. Lewis complained about the lack of a proper *Canterbury Tales*: 'there has not been a new edition since my undergraduate days, so that most

almost entirely the work of his co-editor E. V. Gordon, as Tolkien was so dilatory and didn't produce his share.' (Private email correspondence, by permission)

---

[51] Thomas Honegger, 'Fantasy, Escape, Recovery, and Consolation in *Sir Orfeo*: The Medieval Foundations of Tolkienian Fantasy', *Tolkien Studies* 7 (2010), 117–36; Kelley M. Wickham-Crowley, '"Mind to Mind": Tolkien's Faërian Drama and the Middle English *Sir Orfeo*', *Tolkien Studies* 12 (2015), 1–19; and SH 3:1203–5 '*Sir Orfeo*'.

[52] Around 1943 Tolkien prepared a mimeographed edition for cadets at Oxford and produced the verse translation which was published posthumously; see Carl F. Hostetter, '*Sir Orfeo*: A Middle English Version by J. R. R. Tolkien', *Tolkien Studies* 1 (2004), 85–123. Who knows but Tolkien's couplet describing Sir Orfeo's shagginess—'His *beard* is dangling to his knees! | He is gnarled and knotted like a *tree*!' (507–8)—gave subliminal suggestion for the name Treebeard?

[53] Bowers, 'Tolkien's Goldberry and *The Maid of the Moor*' (2011).

[54] SH 3:950–73 'Oxford English School' provide an excellent history.

[55] Bodleian MS Tolkien A 21/4, fols. 12–20v; see SH 3:1050 'Raleigh'.

[56] Palmer, *Rise of English Studies*, 104–17, 139.

[57] *History of Oxford University Press*, 3:79, 346, 540.

of my knowledge—it was never very exact—on Chaucer is out of date.'[58] Chaucer volumes like Skeat's *Minor Poems* had been designed for schools as well as ambitious amateurs, but they were not cheap, not aligned with the examination reading-list, and not competitive with offerings from Macmillan. 'We ought to be plugging away at cheap texts' became the refrain of Press Secretary R. W. Chapman.[59] When Sisam came on board, a debit of £148 was reported against the Clarendon Series. For secondary schools and colonial markets, he did not wince at the editions with the glossaries (such as Tolkien's) otherwise disdained by Press mandarins. These were still workaday volumes at the time; only in the 1930s did the Clarendon imprint achieve prestige status. Nor did Sisam shy away from rolling up his sleeves. Previous pressmen seldom read proofs, but Sisam reviewed galley pages with the scrutiny of a second editor.

Sisam's hands-on assistance with the Clarendon Chaucer must have caused him particular frustration since he busied himself with so many other projects that moved rapidly into print. Thirty new titles were added to the World's Classics series in 1925 alone. By 1927 Sisam's idea for the *Oxford Companion to English Literature* began what would become the highly profitable Oxford Companion volumes which continue to this day. In 1929 he conceived of the ambitious *Oxford Latin Dictionary* to replace the old Lewis and Short.[60] Other decisions remain noteworthy such as recruiting William Butler Yeats to edit *The Oxford Book of Modern Verse*.[61]

Around the same time Tolkien became bogged down on the Clarendon Chaucer, Sisam's attentions were diverted by another Press project of far greater importance. Already a proponent of the *Shorter Oxford English Dictionary*, Sisam moved forward with the *OED* Supplement almost before the ink was dry on the just-finished *Dictionary* itself. He reckoned ten years but saw its completion in half the time, an astonishing feat considering the long gestation of the parent publication. Archival memos indicate that Sisam was constantly concerned with staff management, the flow of supply between printers and lexicographers, and the rate of progress.[62] His readiness to answer letters from the general public helps explain why he wrote less frequently to Tolkien and Gordon during these years. These other successes may also account for his reluctance to broadcast problems with the Clarendon Chaucer—as partial explanation of why hardly anybody knew of its existence.

---

[58] *They Stand Together: The Letters of C. S. Lewis to Arthur Greeves (1914–1963)*, ed. Walter Hooper (New York: Macmillan, 1979), 330.
[59] Peter Sutcliffe, *The Oxford University Press: An Informal History* (Oxford: Clarendon Press, 1978), 131, 243, and *History of Oxford University* Press, 3:445.
[60] Brewer, *Treasure-House*, 86–94.
[61] Sutcliffe, *An Informal History*, 205–32, on the range of Sisam's achievements before the Great Depression.
[62] Brewer, *Treasure-House*, 44.

In addition to his Press duties, Sisam found time to publish first-rate student editions of his own. His Clarendon *Clerk's Tale*—chosen perhaps because narrated by an Oxford scholar—set a new standard when it appeared in 1923 at seventy-eight pages, hence modestly priced.[63] It provided everything that a reader could want. Its concise introduction was followed by an up-to-date bibliography, remarks on editing, and the text itself starting with the Clerk's portrait in the General Prologue. Sisam allowed himself the textual footnotes rejected for Tolkien's Clarendon Chaucer. While he restricted his glossary to seven pages, he allotted twenty pages of explanatory notes in addition to six pages on 'Chaucer's English' and 'Note on the Metre'. Though he cited cost as a factor when rejecting George Gordon's plans for a frontispiece, his own edition boasted twelve manuscript illustrations, two maps, two Ellesmere pilgrim-portraits, and the Chaucer portrait which he rejected for Tolkien's edition. In short, if he could complete his textbook single-handedly as a side project, he had good reason to feel annoyed that Gordon and Tolkien were not finishing their joint effort.

Sisam's student edition of *The Nun's Priest's Tale* followed four years later.[64] His introduction offered a succinct account of Chaucer's treatment of the beast-fable tradition and its setting within the *Canterbury Tales*. Again the text was conservatively edited as a welcome change from what has been described as Skeat's 'emendatorial impetuosity'.[65] In addition to maps and Ellesmere portraits, Sisam included two manuscript miniatures and four pictures of misericords showing barnyard chase scenes like the one in Chaucer's Aesopic fable.

Sisam's explanatory notes struck just the right balance between learned and introductory, eschewing the arcane philology for which he chided Tolkien, and yet the tidy volume contained a glossary of greater relative length than he allowed for the Clarendon Chaucer. At the time of its publication in 1927, Sisam's edition coincided with Tolkien's failure even to draft notes for his own Nun's Priest's Tale, and therefore one wonders whether his old tutor's edition might have created an inhibiting effect in addition to Skeat's. His *Nun's Priest's Tale* did indeed represent an ideal beginner's edition which stayed in print for thirty years until edged out of the market by the new textbook by Nevill Coghill and junior co-editor Christopher Tolkien.[66]

In all of these Chaucer editions, Sisam agreed with Tolkien and Gordon on one point: protecting students from indecency. After the 1857 Obscene Publications Act outlawed any book that might corrupt young minds, children became the

---

[63] Chaucer, *The Clerkes Tale of Oxenford*, ed. Kenneth Sisam (Oxford: Clarendon Press, 1923).
[64] Chaucer, *The Nun's Priest's Tale*, ed. Kenneth Sisam (Oxford: Clarendon Press, 1927).
[65] Edwards, 'Skeat', 184.
[66] Chaucer, *The Nun's Priest's Tale*, ed. Nevill Coghill and Christopher Tolkien (London: Harrap, 1959). See SH 2:246-7 'Coghill'.

focus of so much anxiety that Henry James bemoaned 'the tyranny of the young reader'.[67] Sisam's *Nun's Priest's Tale* bowdlerized the text to leave out Chanticleer's sexual relations with his hens,[68] although these missing passages sometimes merely sparked youthful curiosity. The distinguished medievalist A. C. Spearing remembers using Sisam's edition at school in the 1950s: 'Needless to say, it encouraged us (all boys) to find a complete text and look up the disappointingly harmless material omitted.'[69]

This prudery had not always prevailed. In 1801 Dorothy Wordsworth reported sitting comfortably by the fire after tea and reading aloud the Miller's Tale.[70] Victorian puritanism was nowhere evident with the genuine Victorian editor Skeat who did not shy away from including frank accounts such as Nicholas's sexual advances upon Alisoun: 'And privately he caughte hir by the queynte' (I, 3275). In addition to shielding students, Sisam felt that these excisions protected schoolmasters who could assume any book with the Clarendon imprint had undergone the moral review behind which they could take shelter.[71] Beyond Oxford, however, such guardedness jarred with the freer spirit after the Great War. When reading Chaucer in the 1920s, Virginia Woolf praised his freedom 'to speak without self-consciousness of the parts and functions of the body'.[72] And yet, as we will see in Chapter 6, Tolkien would follow Sisam's lead when sanitizing the Reeve's Tale in his 1939 pamphlet edition.

On the face of things, Sisam had an additional reason to feel annoyed with Tolkien after 1925 when he was passed over for the Professorship in Anglo-Saxon. It was rumoured that Chapman urged the committee to choose Tolkien so that Sisam could continue at the Press despite publications on *Beowulf*, *Exodus*, *Seafarer*, *West-Saxon Psalms*, and *Letter of Alexander* which far surpassed Tolkien's meagre output.[73] Years later Eugene Vinaver, editor of the Oxford *Morte Darthur*, was still giving vent to this sense of outrage: 'Everyone knows what a terrible mistake Oxford made when they by-passed him for the Chair of Anglo-Saxon.'[74] Sisam's personality may have factored in this loss, because he could strike people as a hard man, combative and stubborn, with a practicality bordering

---

[67] John Sutherland, *A Little History of Literature* (New Haven and London: Yale University Press, 2013), 162.

[68] Chaucer, *The Nun's Priest's Tale*, ed. Kenneth Sisam (Oxford: Clarendon Press, 1927), 5 (lines 4357–9, 4367–8).

[69] Private email with permission.

[70] Quoted by J. A. W. Bennett, *Chaucer at Oxford and at Cambridge* (Oxford: Clarendon Press, 1974), 9.

[71] Sutcliffe, *An Informal History*, 162.

[72] Virginia Woolf, 'The Pastons and Chaucer', *The Common Reader: First Series* (1925; rpt. New York: Harcourt, Brace and Co., 1953), 3–23 at p. 15: 'with the advent of decency, literature lost the use of one of its limbs. It lost its power to create the Wife of Bath.'

[73] Compare the two lists of publications in Ker, 'Kenneth Sisam', 427, and Carpenter, *Biography*, 'Appendix C: Published Writings of J. R. R. Tolkien', 266–7.

[74] Sutcliffe, *An Informal History*, 270.

upon parsimony. His fondness for winning arguments made him unpopular among dons who did not like losing.[75] He was overlooked by the *DNB*, for example, and was only recently included in the *ODNB*.[76]

Sisam's sense of aggrieved merit showed itself only after years of forbearance. His 'Compilation of the *Beowulf* Manuscript' (1953) undercut Tolkien's 'Monsters and the Critics' by observing that *all* of this manuscript's works shared an interest in monsters.[77] Then his compact volume *The Structure of 'Beowulf'* (1965) devoted more space to correcting Tolkien than any other prior scholar. Tolkien was wrong about contrasts between youth and age; he was wrong about the poem's two-part structure analogous to the two halves of an alliterative line; he was wrong about the narrative weakness of Beowulf's return; and he was especially wrong about the warrior's hopeless battle against evil. 'There is no word of his defeat in the poem.'[78] In the years immediately following his disappointment in 1925, however, Sisam maintained a stiff upper lip when dealing with Tolkien and Gordon as their Chaucer edition inched forward.

Even in his retirement Sisam was firing off stern memos: 'The Delegates are interested in performances, not excuses.'[79] If he had so many reasons for sacking Tolkien, then, why did he show such tolerance? Tolkien often cited family problems probably because they were effective as excuses. Sisam also had a family and understood the pressures of a father and breadwinner. Their annual salaries were both about the same at £1,000 by the late 1920s, although Tolkien had twice as many children whose schools as well as doctors cost him dearly. Sisam's grumblings about the Tolkien children's chickenpox and appendicitis probably cloaked a father's soft-hearted understanding. In December 1932 when Tolkien apologized for the demands of children, Sisam would probably have felt less sympathy if he knew the truant editor was squandering time on his *Father Christmas Letter* about goblins in caves beneath the North Pole.[80]

Tolkien's complaints about his own maladies also found a receptive audience since Oxford's climate had proven injurious to both men. From his earliest days Tolkien complained of the Thames Valley's *sleepies* later recalled as the drowsiness of the four hobbits along the Withywindle. Though robust and athletic in his native New Zealand, Sisam also fell victim to Oxford's weather. A botched surgery in 1912 left him unfit for military service, and thereafter he became a chronic

---

[75] Ibid. 270; *History of Oxford University Press*, 3:55, 106.
[76] Christopher Stray kindly sent me his Sisam entry forthcoming in *ODNB*.
[77] Kenneth Sisam, *Studies in the History of Old English Literature* (Oxford: Clarendon Press, 1953), 65–96 at p. 67; this collection reprinted with some new footnotes his 1916 'The *Beowulf* Manuscript', 61–4.
[78] Kenneth Sisam, *The Structure of 'Beowulf'* (Oxford: Clarendon Press, 1965), 25.
[79] Gilliver, *Making of the Oxford English Dictionary*, 455.
[80] J. R. R. Tolkien, *The Father Christmas Letters*, ed. Baillie Tolkien (Boston: Houghton Mifflin, 1976); see also SH 2:420–4.

invalid. Despite his stamina for desk work, he remained a valetudinarian always delicate of his diet.[81]

And then there was Tolkien and the Great War. Because Sisam had known him during his undergraduate days, he was in a position to gauge the psychological as well as physical trauma which his former student had suffered at the Battle of the Somme. Tolkien had been invalided home with trench fever and recovered only after repeated stays in hospitals, but this was only the physical recovery. Tolkien himself recalled the long-term psychological toll in his 1965 Foreword to *The Lord of the Rings*: 'One has indeed personally to come under the shadow of war to feel fully its oppression.' Though his name appears only twice in John Garth's *Tolkien and the Great War*, Sisam could appreciate how this shadow of combat had fallen over his star student's life. If some undercurrent of survivor's guilt ran through their later relationship, it surfaces in Sisam's perennial patience with Tolkien's missed deadlines.

After Chapman's retirement in 1942, Sisam assumed responsibly for guiding the Press through the challenges of the Second World War. His many anonymous kindnesses, especially to refugee scholars, go far toward redeeming his reputation. After his own retirement in 1948, he continued to exert influence from the Scilly Isles where, for example, he wrote his memorandum determining the course of the *OED*'s Second Supplement.[82] His advice was also decisive on the much smaller matter of doing nothing about the Clarendon Chaucer until after Tolkien's own retirement. By the time his successor Dan Davin was free to consider fresh candidates, however, the project initially tied to Skeat's nineteenth-century edition itself looked hopelessly antiquated. Sisam's respect for his former student, which launched the venture, had ultimately doomed it.

George S. Gordon (1881–1942)

George Gordon hardly qualifies for a chapter about Chaucerians because he never published on Chaucer (Fig. 4). He did not even lecture on Chaucer in his wide-ranging repertoire from ancient philosophers to contemporary poets, and he was best known during his scholarly career for discovering a cache of Shelley letters in Oxford's Bodleian Library.[83] But OUP wanted to adorn its Clarendon title-pages with names of famous academics who could provide breezy little prefaces,[84] and Gordon's name was certainly famous during his lifetime and might have endured if paired with Tolkien's on a title-page. Though their talents seemed complementary, the one a witty popularizer and the other a serious-minded philologist, they

---

[81] Sutcliffe, *An Informal History*, 178, 197–8.   [82] Brewer, *Treasure-House*, 136–51.
[83] R. H. Darwall-Smith, 'Gordon, George Stuart', *ODNB* 22:909–10, and SH 2:466–9.
[84] Sutcliffe, *An Informal History*, 132.

Fig. 4. George S. Gordon.

shared the fatal flaw of perfectionism which made completing projects rare throughout their separate careers. Sometimes, it is true, Gordon did work effectively as a collaborator, such as when he teamed with R. W. Chapman on a compilation of modern jargon,[85] but the Clarendon Chaucer was not so lucky.

Gordon remarked in his essay about the Athenian author of *Characters*: 'Theophrastus has had the fate of many great men and great workers to be best remembered by the slightest of his performances.'[86] It has been Gordon's fate to be remembered (if at all) for his inaugural address as Merton Professor *mis*quoted in Terry Eagleton's *Literary Theory: An Introduction* where his statement 'England is sick, and English literature must save it' seemed to resound of Victorian optimism.[87] Gordon was actually speaking ironically, mocking the 1923 report *Teaching of English in England* by asserting that Oxford dons had plenty to do without saving the nation. One mission was resisting the tedium of German scholarship by

---

[85] L. F. Powell and M. Clare Loughlin-Chow, 'Chapman, Robert William', *ODNB* 11:66.
[86] G. S. Gordon, 'Theophrastus and His Imitators', in *English Literature and the Classics*, ed. G. S. Gordon (Oxford: Clarendon Press, 1912), 49–86 at p. 49.
[87] Terry Eagleton, *Literary Theory: An Introduction* (Minneapolis and London: University of Minnesota Press, 1983), 23, went wrong by quoting second-hand from an Oxford D.Phil. thesis.

preferring the humane example of Furnivall who did 'the work of a half a dozen seminars without ever having seen one'.[88] As an early media don on the BBC in 1925, Gordon continued the mission of rescuing English literature from Teutonic pedantry.

Gordon had taken his undergraduate degree in Classics at Glasgow where he attracted the notice of Walter Raleigh who helped him to a scholarship at Oriel College, Oxford. There he won the Stanhope Prize on his way to earning a First Class degree in Classics.[89] After a year's study in Paris, he returned to Oxford in 1907 with a prize fellowship in English at Magdalen College until hired away as Professor of English at Leeds. After military service when he was wounded in France and caught fever at Gallipoli,[90] he returned to Leeds where he began the transition to administration, thereafter effective more as an organizer than a scholar. This is where his professional life intersected with Tolkien's.

In 1941 when everyone knew that Gordon was dying of cancer, Tolkien replied to a request for reminiscences meant for his obituary (*Letters*, 56–7). He owed a huge debt for Gordon's support at two turning-points in his career, first with his hire as a lecturer at Leeds and later with his election as a professor at Oxford. His memories reached back to Gordon's time at Magdalen before the War and the disappointment felt by undergraduates when he went northward, though Tolkien added somewhat uncharitably, 'as a stiff-necked young philologist I did not myself regard the event as important'. Here is an allusion to the English Faculty's Lang./ Lit. schism which would also complicate his first meeting with C. S. Lewis, perceived at the time as a mere enthusiast like Gordon.[91]

Tolkien's 1941 letter recalled interviewing for the job at Leeds where Gordon met him at the railway waiting-room and took him home. Once Tolkien accepted the position, Gordon's kindness continued beyond what might have been expected, assisting with lodgings and even sharing his office. Thus Tolkien would write that 'my first thoughts of him are always of personal gratitude, of a friend rather than of an academic figure' (*Letters*, 56). In return, Tolkien sent him a copy of *The Hobbit* when it was published and was glad to report: 'Professor Gordon has actually read the book (supposed to be a rare event) and assures me that he will recommend it generally and to the Book Society' (*Letters*, 20).

Although Gordon returned to Oxford as Merton Professor in 1922 and became President of Magdalen in 1928, Tolkien's recollections focused upon his 'doctrine of lightheartedness, dangerous, perhaps, in Oxford, necessary in Yorkshire',

[88] George Gordon, 'The Discipline of Letters: Inaugural Lecture as Merton Professor, 9 May 1923', in *The Discipline of Letters*, ed. Mary Gordon (Oxford: Clarendon Press, 1946), 1–8.
[89] George Stuart Gordon, *The Fronde: The Stanhope Essay, 1905* (Oxford: Blackwell, 1905).
[90] Though he planned a book on the Gallipoli Campaign, he managed only one wartime account: Capt. G. S. Gordon, *Mons and the Retreat*, preface by Field-Marshal Lord French (London: Constable and Company, 1918).
[91] Shippey, *Road to Middle-earth*, 'Lit. and Lang.', 1–27.

implying that Gordon really belonged at the less academically rigorous northern university. 'I associate Leeds with Gordon', said Tolkien despite overlapping for nearly two decades in the still-small English Faculty at Oxford.[92] Harsh comments run throughout the rest of Tolkien's letter—'he neglected some sides of his own work'—coloured no doubt by years of struggling with him as the collaborator on their Clarendon Chaucer. But this is inference. Tolkien never mentioned their failed edition in comments meant for the obituary.

Gordon had many real talents, and one of these was spotting talent in others. 'I may take Tolkien from you', he warned the *OED*'s Chapman when recruiting the young lexicographer in 1920, 'to give him the leisure to do texts' (*Letters*, 437n.). Already he foresaw a future for Tolkien editing works like *Gawain* which was in fact completed while at Leeds. Later in 1925 Gordon supported Tolkien's candidacy for the Rawlinson and Bosworth Professorship and wrote a glowing recommendation which now sounds part ironic, part portentous: 'There is no philological (or literary) scholar of his generation from whom I have learned so much, with whom I have worked more happily, or from whom, in my opinion, greater things may be expected' (SH 2:468).

He also spotted talent in C. S. Lewis and helped him to a fellowship without actually supplying a written recommendation—always the behind-the-scenes operator, as Lewis himself confided to his diary: 'Gordon said he wouldn't write anything as he was going to be consulted personally by the Magdalen people, but he would *back* me.'[93] Later in the 1930s Lewis referred to him jokingly as Smoothboots and Gentleman George, but his opinion had been higher in the 1920s after securing his position at Magdalen: 'he is an honest, wise, kind man, more like a man and less like a don than anyone I have known.'[94] He stopped short of praising Gordon as a scholar rumoured to have been elected Merton Professor merely on the strength of his *TLS* pieces. As might be expected for such an effective administrator, his time was consumed as a committeeman legendary for keeping meetings short and getting things accomplished. His time spent as an avid golfer probably caused serious scholars to look askance, as suggested by Gandalf's explanation for golf's discovery when the goblin king's head was knocked off and went down a rabbit hole (*Hobbit*, 48).

Unlike Tolkien, Lewis respected him as a teacher who continued Raleigh's practice of hosting weekly discussion groups where undergraduates read and debated their papers. He rated Gordon's lectures on Shakespeare 'capital' but 'too chatty'—'sensible rather than brilliant'—and always prone to 'raise a cheap laugh'. It is hard not to smile when Lewis chided Gordon for catering to large

---

[92] J. S. Ryan, 'Tolkien and George Gordon: Or, a Close Colleague and His Notion of "Myth-maker" and of Historiographic Jeux d'esprit', in *Shaping of Middle-earth's Maker: Influences on the Life and Literature of J. R. R. Tolkien* (Highland, MI: American Tolkien Society, 1992), 30–3.
[93] *Diary of C. S. Lewis*, 357.   [94] Ibid. 240–1.

audiences of 'semi-educated people',[95] since Oxford colleagues would later disparage Lewis for his popularity with the same general public.

That talent for reaching a wide audience made Gordon much sought after as a speaker, remembered in his *Times* obituary as Oxford's most delightful talker. He was elected Gresham Professor of Rhetoric in 1930 and Professor of Poetry in 1933. For the banquet celebrating publication of the *OED* Supplement, the organizers wanted Winston Churchill but were very happy to have George Gordon instead.[96] Nearly all his publications began under the spur of specific occasions such as his fifteen-minute radio talks 'Pepys's Diary' and 'Lamb's Letters' later included in the volume *Companionable Books*.[97] Although he wrote enough BBC talks to be collected in the second volume, *Lives of Authors*, he was unable over two decades to complete his potted biography of Chaucer. Like Tolkien with his invited lectures, he needed a fixed deadline.

Without these deadlines, Gordon had difficulty finishing anything. 'He always professed to envy the man who could write to a time-table,' his wife recalled; 'he drew up many of them and schemes of work: but he could never write automatically.'[98] He himself confessed this failing in a letter to David Nichol Smith: 'I am indeed full of schemes: I wish I were fuller of performance.'[99] He penned this letter in 1922 when his latest scheme was the Clarendon Chaucer. Pairing him with Tolkien meant OUP relying upon two procrastinators too easily distracted from their assignments. Though unhappy results seem inevitable with benefit of hindsight, Gordon and Tolkien looked like safe choices at the time.

Oxford University tried returning to normal after the Great War without quite realizing how much the world had changed. The age of the man of letters was passing away and the age of the academic specialist had begun, but Matthew Arnold's 'home of lost causes' had not yet awakened to these new realities.[100] Neither had George Gordon. It never occurred to him that he might have been ill-suited to a Chaucer edition. Certainly he had read the fourteenth-century poet and could make apt references. When discussing Desdemona's handkerchief in *Othello*, he alluded to the fact that Chaucer's Venus wore a 'subtle kerchief of Valence' in *Parlement of Foules*.[101] This dream-vision may have come more readily to mind because it was included in the Clarendon Chaucer. His radio talk 'Boswell's Life of Johnson' and his brief biography of Shakespeare serve as

---

[95] Ibid. 139, 185, 190, 220.   [96] Brewer, *Treasure-House*, 64.
[97] Mary Gordon's 'Preface' to *Discipline of Letters*, p. v; these included 'Shelley and the Oppressors of Mankind' as the Warton Lecture and 'Poetry and the Moderns' for his inaugural lecture as Professor of Poetry.
[98] Mary Gordon, *Life of George S. Gordon*, 151.
[99] *The Letters of George S. Gordon, 1902–1942*, ed. Mary Gordon (London: Oxford University Press, 1943), 150.
[100] Sutcliffe, *An Informal History*, 194. Arnold famously described Oxford as 'home of lost causes, and forsaken beliefs, and unpopular names, and impossible loyalties'.
[101] George Gordon, *Shakespearean Comedy and Other Studies* (Oxford: Oxford University Press, 1944), 106 for *Parlement of Foules* (line 272).

evidence that Gordon knew what was involved in writing an author's life,[102] so it remains a mystery why Chaucer defeated his best intentions.

The problem was not simply the remoteness of the fourteenth century. Gordon established his credentials as a medievalist by publishing a weighty investigation of the terms *medium aevum* and 'Middle Ages' in an article that rewards reading even today because he explained how the word *medieval* and the term 'Middle English' entered the scholarly lexicon.[103] The rigour of this study makes it even more puzzling that he struggled with a simple, straightforward preface to Chaucer. If Tolkien's trajectory from the Clarendon Chaucer to 'Chaucer as a Philologist' shows a deepening, more sophisticated understanding of what was involved in editing the fourteenth-century poet, Gordon's surviving materials suggest that he started largely befuddled and ended utterly hopeless. It is unfair to judge how he ended, of course, because he never completed his contribution during two decades when the edition was promised. But this was not a lone instance. He planned several books over his academic lifetime, he gathered research materials, and occasionally he wrote a few passages, but mostly his efforts remained a hodgepodge of jottings. In 1935 he wrote to a friend about the yellowing manuscripts in his drawer: 'I wish someone would diagnose the disease I suffer from of literary inhibition.'[104]

Still Gordon developed a special relationship with OUP during the era when publishers relied heavily upon professors as consultants contributing their time as well as their manuscripts. He had inherited from his predecessor Raleigh a vision for advancing the causes of the University by supporting the work of the Press, and he reckoned the Clarendon Series played a particular role for training future generations of English editors—which may partly explain his patience with Tolkien's apprenticeship. His own education in such matters, he admitted, took place in the Secretary's Room, where he spent a great deal of time.[105] In any event, Sisam and others at OUP risked applying no real arm-twisting with this academic eminence, especially after he became a Press Delegate.

Medieval historian and long-time Magdalen colleague Bruce McFarlane visited George Gordon shortly before his death and left this poignant recollection:

> He had no business to discuss. He merely lamented the cruel fate which prevented him from finishing his books. He said that he had been justly punished for neglecting them for administration, though he hoped that he had been moved in part by a sense of duty and only partly by ambition. He said he was really meant to be a scholar and a writer.[106]

---

[102] *Nine Plays of Shakespeare* (Oxford: Clarendon Press, 1928), pp. vii–x.
[103] Gordon, '*Medium Aevum* and the Middle Ages' (1925), is a substantial work, crowded with learned footnotes worthy of *Speculum*, with a useful appendix on the term 'Middle English' (pp. 26–8).
[104] *Letters*, ed. Mary Gordon, p. vii.   [105] Gordon, *Discipline of Letters*, 5, 15.
[106] Robin Darwall-Smith forwarded this passage from Magdalen College MC P27/C1/604; thanks to the President and Fellows of Magdalen College, Oxford, for permission to quote.

Oxford University was fortunate to have a Vice-Chancellor with his administrative skills and sense of duty as the Second World War approached, and in the grand scheme of things, these contributions to the academic institution as well as the nation surely outweighed whatever books he might have finished, including his little edition of Chaucer.

Immediately after his passing in 1942, the Press remained loyal and hoped that treasures might emerge from his dusty files. R. W. Chapman assisted with the publication of *Anglo-American Literary Relations* after Gordon had insisted for years that the 1931 lectures needed more work. What Chapman found was the rubble of any professor's unfinished project:

> The materials entrusted to me comprised: (1) a typescript of perhaps four-fifths of the whole, corrected both in ink and in pencil; (2) a duplicate typescript of most of (1), hardly corrected; (3) manuscript which had presumably not been typed (as well as most of that which had); (4) typed extracts. All these were filed, with substantial accuracy, in six folders, one for each lecture. There was also a considerable mass of raw material in notebooks and loose sheets.[107]

Thus Chapman had reason to recall ruefully in his *DNB* entry for Gordon, 'Of anything much more than a lecture, his friends learned to despair.' These lecture drafts were nonetheless further advanced than what survived of his Chaucer Introduction.

A total of five volumes by or about George Gordon were published through the good offices of his widow. Mary Gordon edited a selection of his letters, wrote a concise biography, and published draft materials with the help of colleagues like E. K. Chambers who supplied the preface for *Shakespearean Comedy and Other Studies*. Mrs Gordon took pains to discount her husband's shortcomings as the result of neither indolence nor total preoccupation with administration, though certainly these distractions abounded.[108] An introduction to the biography by Lord Halifax, University Chancellor 1933–59, emphasized his acquiring the Wytham Estate where the science departments would be built and especially readying Oxford for the Second World War. Vice-Chancellor Gordon had convinced the War Office that young officers needed coursework for gaining maturity, and his success on this score kept the University operating during England's darkest hours—and even had an impact on Tolkien's writing career, since teaching these cadets led to his translation of *Sir Orfeo*.

Mrs Gordon herself looked back at these institutional achievements in addition to her husband's heavy schedule of lectures throughout England, plus college duties such as cheering the boat races and even auditioning choirboys, as well as

---

[107] R. W. Chapman's introduction to George Stuart Gordon, *Anglo-American Literary Relations* (Oxford: Oxford University Press, 1942), 6.
[108] *Letters of George S. Gordon*, pp. vi–vii.

club activities such as attending Tolkien's saga-reading Kolbítar, a forerunner of the Inklings.[109] Her conclusion seemed obvious: 'the wonder is not why he did not publish more, but rather how he contrived to do so much.'[110] Yet these noteworthy accomplishments do not fully account for Gordon's lack of productivity. Although his fastidiousness partly explains why he shrank from proof-sheets, his insistence upon craftsmanship cloaked an almost pathological distaste for the finality of print.[111] His minimal work on the proof-sheets of the Clarendon Chaucer attests to this aversion.

Mary Gordon reached the bottom of the drawer by 1956 when she despaired of doing anything with her husband's Chaucer materials. She had already contacted Tolkien some years before, as she said in her cover-letter to OUP, but without a definite answer. Now after ushering so many unfinished writings into print, she had a good sense of what could be salvaged, what not. She herself was astonished at the messiness of his manuscripts with their illegible interpolations and crossings-out.[112] She therefore did not express much confidence for posthumous publication when posting the Chaucer bundle. 'I shirk the responsibility of destroying it,' she wrote to Dan Davin; 'Will be you kind enough to do so if you find it to be useless.'

Far from dismissing the material, Davin promised to consult the files and see if anything could be done to resurrect the Clarendon Chaucer. This was not mere politeness, because he almost immediately wrote to Sisam with new hopes that the edition might go forward: 'As I already have Tolkien's material, we should be in a position to go on if a suitable editor could be found.' So instead of destroying what had been described as a *dump*, Davin filed away Gordon's unfinished drafts along with the corrected page-proofs of texts and glossary—and Tolkien's own galleys and drafts of explanatory notes retrieved in 1951—in hopes that some younger medievalist might be found, even entertaining the possibility of Sisam's daughter: 'I suppose that it is not the kind of thing that would interest Celia...'. Apparently it was not.

C. S. Lewis (1898–1963)

In 1930 C. S. Lewis wrote his friend Arthur Greeves bemoaning the lack of an up-to-date Chaucer text,[113] and yet he did not add anything to the effect that his friend Tolkien would soon remedy the situation with his Clarendon Chaucer. (Fig. 5) This is because Lewis did not seem to know about this edition, which

---

[109] Andrew Lazo, 'Gathered round Northern Fires: The Imaginative Impact of the Kolbítar', in *Tolkien and the Invention of Myth: A Reader*, ed. Jane Chance (Lexington: United Press of Kentucky, 2004), 191–226, and SH 3:1234 'Kolbítar'.
[110] Mary Gordon, *Life*, 164.
[111] Ibid. 166, and George Gordon, *More Companionable Books*, ed. Mary Gordon (London: Chatto & Windus, 1947), p. vi.
[112] *Life*, 107.   [113] *They Stand Together*, 330.

Fig. 5. C. S. Lewis.

included the courtly-love lyrics featured in his own *Allegory of Love* as well as the Nun's Priest's Tale, his favourite from the *Canterbury Tales*.[114] Both men's lives are so abundantly documented that we know a great deal about the role Lewis played in encouraging Tolkien to complete other projects in danger of permanently stalling.[115] Tolkien admitted as much. Though trained as a Classicist and publishing on a wide array of literary works, notably *The Faerie Queene* and *Paradise Lost*, Lewis came to define his Oxford identity to match Tolkien's: 'Professionally I am chiefly a medievalist.'[116] Why, then, did Lewis not nudge his friend to complete *Selections from Chaucer's Poetry and Prose*?

If George Gordon does not qualify as a Chaucerian, C. S. Lewis certainly does. In 1916 he was already reading the poet closely and criticizing his *Canterbury Tales*: 'He has most of the faults of the Middle Ages—garrulity and coarseness—without

---

[114] Ibid. 371 about the Nun's Priest's Tale: 'it's *delicious*: homely & ridiculous in the best possible way.'

[115] This linkage has become commonplace: Carpenter, *Biography*, 'Jack', 147–55; Colin Duriez, *Tolkien and C. S. Lewis: The Gift of Friendship* (Mahwah, NJ: HiddenSpring, 2003); and Diana Pavlac Glyer, *The Company They Keep: C. S. Lewis and J. R. R. Tolkien as Writers in Community* (Kent, OH: Kent State University Press, 2007).

[116] *Collected Letters of C. S. Lewis*, Vol. 2: *Books, Broadcasts, and the War, 1931–1949*, ed. Walter Hooper (New York: HarperCollins, 2004), 161.

their romantic charm.'[117] Later he would clarify his objections: 'Chaucer was very like Dickens—a virtuous, bourgeois storyteller fond of highly moral vulgarity and indecency for its own sake, incapable (at the *Tales* period, not in his early life) of appreciating romance.'[118] When attending undergraduate lectures by C. T. Onions, he read the *Book of the Duchess* and the Prologue to the *Legend of Good Women* where he discovered the romance as well as beautiful language lacking in the ribald *Tales*.[119] Thus Lewis was poised to make major contributions to Chaucer criticism.

In 1932 he published an article on *Troilus and Criseyde* which remains influential in the critical tradition, and in 1936 he completed his book *The Allegory of Love* which included an important reassessment of Chaucer.[120] Though encouraged by Sisam, the book was not commissioned in advance (like Tolkien's edition) but was offered as a completed manuscript to Oxford University Press.[121] Helen Gardner judged it his greatest work.[122] Its 'Chaucer' chapter positioned the poet as a pivotal figure between the thirteenth-century *Roman de la Rose* and the sixteenth-century *Faerie Queene*. To make this case, Lewis shifted away from the standard syllabus: 'For many historians of literature, and for all general readers, the great mass of Chaucer's work is simply a background to the *Canterbury Tales*' (p. 161).

Lewis argued for a more historically accurate appreciation, not the bawdy Chaucer of the Miller's Tale but the courtly poet of the dream-visions, allegories, and amatory debates (p. 162). This meant concentrating upon love ballads like *Merciles Beaute* and dream poems like the *Parlement of Foules*. This preference was not strictly personal. Chaucer's shorter poems had featured prominently in the Oxford lectures of Sir Walter Raleigh, and even Ezra Pound esteemed them for extending the artistry of the troubadours.[123] When Lewis decided to exclude the *Tales* from his discussions, he ended up privileging the same titles which Tolkien had edited in his Clarendon Chaucer—though Lewis gave no sign of knowing about this concurrence.

Lewis dedicated *The Allegory of Love* to Owen Barfield,[124] and although his preface thanked Tolkien for reading the opening chapter 'Courtly Love', it is difficult to detect his influence except for one sentence describing how a lover

---

[117] *They Stand Together*, 109.   [118] Ibid. 250.
[119] *Diary of C. S. Lewis*, 117.
[120] Lewis, 'What Chaucer Really Did to *Il Filostrato*', and *The Allegory of Love* (London: Oxford University Press, 1936), 'Chaucer', 157–97.
[121] *History of Oxford University Press*, 3:405–8, includes *Allegory of Love* as one of its 'Eleven Case Studies'.
[122] Helen Gardner, 'Clive Staples Lewis: 1898–1963', *Proceedings of the British Academy* 51 (1965), 417–28 at p. 423; see SH 2:450 'Gardner'.
[123] Ezra Pound, *The ABC of Reading* (London: Routledge, 1934), 87, 92–100.
[124] Philip Zaleski and Carol Zaleski, *The Fellowship: The Literary Lives of the Inklings: J. R. R. Tolkien, C. S. Lewis, Owen Barfield, Charles Williams* (New York: Farrar, Straus and Giroux, 2015), place Barfield more squarely in his Oxford context.

speaks to his lady: 'He addresses her as *midons*, which etymologically represents not "my lady" but "my lord"' (p. 2). Tolkien always pounced on etymologies. Lewis had started this book in 1928 when Tolkien had been studying Chaucer for half a decade and would have been superbly qualified to comment on the 'Chaucer' chapter, but he seems not to have been asked. Why?

The book's first sentence suggests one answer: 'The allegorical love poetry of the Middle Ages is apt to repel the modern reader.' Lewis's goal was the historical reclamation of allegory as a mode of thinking, and as early as 1929, when his literary connection with Tolkien was growing stronger, Lewis read his friend's *Lay of Leithian* and praised a work which 'should have no taint of allegory to the maker and yet should suggest incipient allegories to the reader'.[125] Tolkien probably did not welcome this remark because he himself was one of those modern readers repelled by allegory.[126] His *Letters* are peppered with denials that *The Lord of the Rings* can be read allegorically, and his 1965 Foreword asserted bluntly: 'I cordially dislike allegory in all its manifestations, and always have done so since I grew old and wary enough to detect its presence.' One place where he would detect its presence with displeasure was in Lewis's *Chronicles of Narnia* (*Letters*, 352).

Shippey has nonetheless described Tolkien as a 'serial allegorist', citing as evidence the allegory of the tower in 'The Monsters and the Critics' and the autobiographical allegory of *Leaf by Niggle*.[127] But Tolkien's introduction to *Pearl* defined the term narrowly as a point-by-point set of equations—'a poem must *as a whole*, and with fair consistency, describe in other terms some event or process' (p. xii). In the allegory of the tower, for instance, the tower's builder would parallel the *Beowulf* Poet, but looking from the tower's top out upon the sea has no single meaning; the reader can apply any number of interpretations such as perceiving truth, beauty, the transcendent, and so on. Little wonder that Tolkien recoiled when Rayner Unwin felt that *The Lord of the Rings* veered in the direction of allegory (*Letters*, 120–21). Earlier on, as we shall see, Tolkien had occasion to disparage allegory in his commentary on Chaucer's translation of the *Roman de la Rose* and responded in his own fiction by literalizing the female figure of the Rose. When Sam Gamgee embarks upon his own romantic quest, his goal is not an allegorical flower, as in the French courtly classic, but rather a real woman—Rose Cotton.

As one of the oldest modes of literary interpretation, *allegoresis* searched for meanings beyond the literal words. Although Tolkien allowed that 'any attempt to explain the purport of myth or fairytale must use allegorical language' (*Letters*, 145), he preferred digging deeper into words themselves rather than launching

---

[125] *Lays of Beleriand*, 184; see 'C. S. Lewis's Commentary on the *Lay of Leithian*', 374–92.
[126] SH 2:44–9 'Allegory'.
[127] Shippey, 'Allegory versus Bounce: (Half of) an Exchange on *Smith of Wootton Major*', in *Roots and Branches*, 351–62 at p. 352.

into airy flights of speculation. 'I am a *pure* philologist,' he wrote to his son Christopher; 'I like history and am moved by it, but its finest moments for me are those in which it throws light on words and names' (*Letters*, 264). In short, Tolkien approached literary texts in radically different ways from the author of *The Allegory of Love*, and their divergent paths help to explain why Lewis was never apparently summoned to help with advancing the Clarendon Chaucer.

Otherwise the two men had a great deal in common. Lewis developed a schoolboy enthusiasm for Northernness after reading Longfellow's *Saga of King Olaf* and admiring Rackham's illustrations to Wagner's operas.[128] Later at Oxford he became a regular member of the Kolbítar group reading the sagas in the original Icelandic. Like Tolkien, he had a talent for languages and read rapidly in Greek, Latin, French, Italian, and German as well as Old Norse. His undergraduate training had followed much the same trajectory, only with greater distinction, since he took First Class honours in Classics in 1922 before earning another First in English in 1923. Years later when he wrote his essay 'Friendship', Lewis had Tolkien specifically in mind when he told how the two men were drawn together, standing side by side absorbed in some shared interest which set them apart from the common herd.[129] Yet there were interests that Lewis did not share with Tolkien, and this area of exclusion was evident from their first meeting.

In May 1926 as a newly elected Fellow of Magdalen, Lewis wrote about an English Faculty tea where Tolkien, himself now an Oxford professor, brought the discussion around to changes in the syllabus. Afterwards, the two scholars had their first sit-down conversation, just the two of them, and Lewis took his new friend's measure in his diary:

> He is a smooth, pale, fluent little chap—can't read Spenser because of the forms—thinks the language is the real thing in the school—thinks all literature is written for the amusement of *men* between thirty and forty—we ought to vote ourselves out of existence if we were honest—still the sound-changes and the gobbets are great fun for the dons. No harm in him: only needs a smack or so.[130]

Lewis must have brought up *The Faerie Queene*, the subject of his final chapter of *The Allegory of Love*, and Tolkien condemned Spencer's pseudo-Chaucerian language for not producing authentic forms of fourteenth-century English. This is precisely where the two dons parted company in the long-running debate over Language versus Literature. Because Lewis bristled at the notion of literature as the

---

[128] *Letters of C. S. Lewis*, ed. W. H. Lewis (New York: Harcourt Brace & World, 1966), 110–11, and C. S. Lewis, *Surprised by Joy: The Shape of My Early Life* (Orlando, FL: Harcourt, 1955), 17, 72–8. See also Tom Shippey, 'Tolkien and "That Noble Northern Spirit"', in McIlwaine, *Tolkien: Maker of Middle-earth*, 58–69.

[129] C. S. Lewis, *The Four Loves* (New York and London: Harcourt, 1960), 'Friendship', 57–90.

[130] *Diary of C. S. Lewis*, 393; see SH 1:145 and Duriez, 'Meeting of Minds and Imaginations (1926–1929)', 24–44.

amusement of middle-aged men, Tolkien would have seen him as belonging to the Lit. camp and thus his natural adversary (*Biography*, 147). Never in his later studies of *The Faerie Queene*, however, did Lewis really address Tolkien's objection to the poet's flawed re-creation of Middle English, only once acknowledging it as a problem: 'what he called "Chaucer" included many un-Chaucerian works and was so textually corrupt that Spenser could not have read it metrically even if he had understood Middle English metre (which he did not).'[131] In his report on their first conversation in 1926, it is noteworthy that Lewis made no mention of the Clarendon Chaucer as an effort at retrieving authentic Middle English forms because Tolkien apparently made no mention of his edition. This reticence seems to have persisted.

As a Classicist and philosopher who had migrated to English studies, Lewis sounded more amused than threatened by Tolkien's commitments to philology. The debate was hardly new. Already back in the 1890s Skeat defended the linguistic side against accusations that philologists like himself had no real love for literature.[132] In terms of institutional history, the philologists had won an advantage when Richard Rawlinson endowed a professorship for Anglo-Saxon in 1755; when the Merton Professorship of Language and Literature was established in 1885, its first occupant was the philologist A. S. Napier. The founding of Oxford's English School in 1894 was meant to strike a balance between dry-as-dust philology and 'mere chatter about Shelley',[133] but academic rivalries seldom subside so quickly.

Tolkien had been encouraged by George Gordon to develop the linguistic side at Leeds and was determined to do the same at Oxford, hence his talk about changing the syllabus at his first faculty meeting. When he placed a formal proposal before the English Faculty, however, Lewis was one of those who voted against him.[134] Not daunted, Tolkien proclaimed in his manifesto of 1930 that he favoured ending the survey of English literature after the first thousand years and thereby jettisoning the whole nineteenth century.[135] By this time, Lewis had been persuaded to support his plan for granting more coverage to Old and Middle English, and none at all to Victorian literature, with a syllabus stopping with the death of Lord Byron. Twenty years later when the question came up again, Lewis was actually more adamant than Tolkien on keeping this medieval-slanted syllabus.[136]

Lewis's amused response to Tolkien in 1926 is noteworthy. He could be ferocious in debate, hectoring, bullying, and on some occasions actually giving a smack. There is a story that he once grew so enraged at an Australian

---

[131] C. S. Lewis, 'Edmund Spenser, 1552–99', in *Studies in Medieval and Renaissance Literature*, ed. Walter Hooper (Cambridge: Cambridge University Press, 1966), 121–45 at p. 130.
[132] Skeat, *Student's Pastime*, p. xiii.
[133] Palmer, *Rise of English Studies*, pp. vii, 72–7.   [134] *Inklings*, 24.
[135] J. R. R. Tolkien, 'The Oxford English School', *The Oxford Magazine* 48 (1930), 778–80.
[136] *Inklings*, 55, 229–30.

undergraduate during a tutorial, he grabbed a broadsword and drew blood. Another student got off easier, chased from the room and yelled at down the staircase, 'If you think that way about Keats, you needn't come here again!'[137] Little wonder that most undergraduates were frightened, and many colleagues cowed, by these fierce assaults backed by a deep fund of literary knowledge. William Empson described Lewis as 'the best read man of his generation, one who read everything and remembered everything he read'.[138] Even in her otherwise warm reminiscences, Helen Gardner described a violent streak that flared up during some harmless intellectual discussion,[139] although Tolkien was usually spared this darker side.

This does not mean Tolkien had no reason to feel intimidated. Though six years younger, Lewis had academic proficiencies more far-ranging. His grounding in Classics qualified him for teaching philosophy to undergraduates in 1925. The next year, he started his career as an Oxford lecturer with courses such as 'Some English Thinkers of the Renaissance (Elyot, Ascham, Hooker, Bacon)' and 'Some Eighteenth-Century Precursors of the Romantic Movement' which aimed at the grand overviews which Tolkien never attempted. When Tolkien's 'Valedictory Address' admitted that his own sparsely attended classes lacked 'the wide view, the masterly survey' (*Essays*, 224), he was probably thinking back to Lewis's success at packing the University's largest lecture halls with four hundred attendees.[140]

Lewis did more than outshine Tolkien at lecturing. In terms of publishing, Lewis could chide his friend's dilatoriness because he himself was amazingly productive despite late-night carousing with chums. He impressed Tolkien as 'a man of immense power and industry' who published his sci-fi trilogy while also completing 'much other work,' notably his 702-page *English Literature in the Sixteenth Century*.[141] Tolkien himself *wrote* fast to the point of illegibility, but he then took endless pains over revision before committing himself to print—'I compose only with great difficulty and endless rewriting' (*Letters*, 113)—whereas Lewis *worked* fast and made few revisions before sending his stuff off. Thus he left very few unpublished works at the time of his death because he either mailed pieces to publishers or tossed them into the wastepaper basket.[142] The

---

[137] *Inklings*, 214.
[138] Paul Tankard, 'William Empson on C. S. Lewis's Reading and Memory', *Notes and Queries* 61 (2014), 614–16.
[139] Gardner, 'Clive Staples Lewis', 418.
[140] John Wain, 'C. S. Lewis as a Teacher', in *Masters: Portraits of Great Teachers*, ed. Joseph Epstein (New York: Basic Books, 1981), 236–52.
[141] *Letters*, 209. Derek Brewer told how Lewis would return to his Magdalen rooms after a late night of drinking, sit down, and write another twenty pages before going to bed; see 'The Tutor: A Portrait', in *C. S. Lewis at the Breakfast Table*, ed. James T. Como (New York: Macmillan, 1979, 41–67 at p. 43.
[142] *Inklings*, 47–8, and Walter Hooper in his introduction to C. S. Lewis, *Studies in Medieval and Renaissance Literature*, p. vii.

sheer volume was staggering with a bibliography running to over eighty pages.[143] Besides *The Allegory of Love* and many volumes of Christian apologetics, his major books included *A Preface to 'Paradise Lost'* (1942), *An Experiment in Criticism* (1961), and the posthumously published *Discarded Image: An Introduction to Medieval and Renaissance Literature* (1964). This output was made possible because he was not prone to the distractions that bedevilled Tolkien. Helen Gardner recalled his extraordinary powers of concentration in the Bodleian Library: 'To sit opposite him in Duke Humfrey when he was moving steadily through some huge double-columned folio in his reading for his Oxford history was to have an object lesson in what concentration meant. He seemed to create a wall of stillness around him.'[144]

Tolkien later recalled 'C.S.L. was my closest friend from about 1927 to 1940' (*Letters*, 349), and if Lewis did not give his friend any actual smacks during these years, he gave many nudges by way of encouragement.[145] He shared Tolkien's early ambitions for writing poetry, publishing *Spirits in Bondage* in 1919 and *Dymer* in 1926, and Tolkien loaned him drafts of his own poems besides the *Lay of Leithian*. Lewis was also an early reader of *The Hobbit* in 1933 and gave support for completing the novel by way of improving the ending.[146] Around 1936 when they agreed to write the sorts of novels that they themselves enjoyed reading, Lewis assigned himself the space-travel story *Out of the Silent Planet* as the first volume of what would grow into a trilogy. Tolkien was supposed to write the time-travel novel *The Lost Road* but never finished it. In a sense *The Hobbit* qualifies as time-travel, however, because Bilbo leaves his Edwardian home and steps backward through time into a mythic landscape of goblins, elves, and dragons. Lewis himself later described this effect: 'As the humour and homeliness of the early chapters, the sheer "Hobbitry", dies away we pass insensibly into the world of epic.'[147] But in terms of this friendly partnership in writing adventure stories, Tolkien came up short.

In 1954 after publishing *The Fellowship of the Ring*, Tolkien wrote to Rayner Unwin acknowledging Lewis's role in this vast undertaking: 'only by his support and friendship did I ever struggle to the end of the labour' (*Letters*, 184). After his friend's death in 1963, Tolkien clarified their fiction-writing relationship:

> The unpayable debt that I owe to him was not 'influence' as it is ordinarily understood, but sheer encouragement. He was for long my only audience. Only

---

[143] Walter Hooper, *C. S. Lewis: A Companion and Guide* (London and New York: HarperCollins, 1996), 'A Bibliography of the Writings of C. S. Lewis', 799–883.
[144] Gardner, 'Clive Staples Lewis', 419.
[145] Andrew Lazo, 'A Kind of Mid-Wife: J. R. R. Tolkien and C. S. Lewis—Sharing Influence', in *Tolkien the Medievalist*, ed. Chance, 36–49.
[146] *Biography*, 181, and *Letters*, 14.
[147] C. S. Lewis, 'On Stories', in *Essays Presented to Charles Williams*, ed. C. S. Lewis (London: Oxford University Press, 1947), 90–105 at p. 104. See SH 2:744–53 '*The Lost Road*'.

from him did I ever get the idea that my 'stuff' could be more than a private hobby. But for his interest and unceasing eagerness for more I should never have brought *The Lord of the Rings* to a conclusion.... (*Letters*, 362)

By March 1944, for example, Tolkien ended a lengthy dry spell only when Lewis began 'putting the screw' to him (*Letters*, 68). Lewis admitted not really influencing the contents of his friend's writing, but 'my continual encouragement, carried to the point of nagging, influenced him very much to write at all'.[148]

Tolkien did not always accept Lewis's suggestions, but he did take the trouble to rewrite almost every passage that his friend found lacking. Lewis himself observed that Tolkien responded to encouragement but had only two reactions to direct criticism: 'Either he begins the whole work over again from the beginning or else takes no notice at all' (*Biography*, 149). When Lewis heard the chapter 'The Voice of Saruman' read aloud and reacted with an outburst—'You can do better than that. Better, Tolkien, please!'—Tolkien revised the section, over and over, until the confrontation between the two wizards became for a time what he considered the best chapter in *The Lord of the Rings* (*Letters*, 376).

Lewis even pressed his friend to complete *The Silmarillion* and yet—this is the key point—the same encouragement was not apparently invited for Tolkien's academic writings. Lewis knew Old English poetry, he taught *The Battle of Maldon* to undergraduates, and he hosted his famous 'beer and Beowulf' evenings in his rooms at Magdalen. We know that he commented on Tolkien's *Beowulf* translation because his handwriting survives in the typescripts where he suggested improvements.[149] And yet Tolkien did not apparently seek his advice before delivering 'The Monsters and the Critics' where he had so many nasty things to say about literary critics—such as Lewis was. Nor does Lewis's handwriting crop up in the two unfinished drafts of *'Beowulf' and the Critics*, the book-length version of the lecture.[150] If they ever discussed Tolkien's Old English projects over beer, no evidence of this scholarly conversation has come down to us.

For one thing, the two men's willingness to share work-in-progress came only after the fateful 1931 walk around Magdalen grounds when Tolkien proved persuasive on the question of religious faith. His success at hastening Lewis's conversion to Christianity marked a major turning point. If their friendly support for each other's writing is viewed as an evolving bond, this trust developed only subsequent to the period 1926–30 when the Clarendon Chaucer could have used a forceful boost.

---

[148] *Collected Letters of C. S. Lewis*, Vol. 3: *Narnia, Cambridge, and Joy, 1950–1963*, ed. Walter Hooper (New York: HarperCollins, 2007), 1458.
[149] Christopher identified the hand of C. S. Lewis in his father's *Beowulf* translation (pp. 108–12).
[150] Tolkien did quote Lewis's poem 'The Northern Dragon' in *'Beowulf' and the Critics*, ed. Drout, 57–8.

What would have been his response to Tolkien's textbook? Lewis certainly felt the need for better editions from his earliest encounters with Chaucer. Though he appreciated affordability, he found the Everyman version mutilated by abridgement and he grumbled about the scrubbiness of the Oxford World's Classics edition.[151] Not that he felt inclined to remedy the situation himself. Even though he taught textual criticism, Lewis admitted to his student Derek Brewer, 'I can't *edit* any more than I can audit. I'm not accurate.'[152] This does not mean he did not understand how editors went about their business. In 1929 when Tolkien sent his *Lay of Leithian* for comments, Lewis jokingly treated it as if it were a medieval text surviving in multiple manuscripts already analysed by previous scholars—'added by a later hand to supply a gap in the archtype', says Peabody—and then inserted his own editorial judgements such as 'This passage, as it stands, is seriously corrupt', just as Tolkien had done in the margins of his Chaucer proofs.[153]

Lewis also lacked the temperament for compiling editorial notes. In 1930 while working on *The Allegory of Love*, he lampooned the scholarly annotations found in Chaucer editions:

> One minute you are puzzling out a quotation from a French medieval romance: the next, you are being carried back to Plato: then a scrap of medieval law: then something about geomancy: and manuscripts, and signs of the Zodiac, and a modern proverb 'reported by Mr. Snooks to be common in Derbyshire,' and the precession of the equinoxes, and an Arabian optician (born at Balk in 1030), five smoking-room stories, the origins of the doctrine of immaculate conception, and why St Cecilia is the patroness of organists. So one is swept from East to West, and from century to century, equally immersed in each oddity as it comes up.[154]

To read Tolkien's draft annotations for Chaucer is to realize that Lewis, though surely recalling Skeat in this caricature, understood the quirks and excesses that plagued such projects. Although he later admitted that Tolkien had cured his old prejudice against trusting a philologist,[155] here Lewis heaped derision on exactly the philological waywardness which caused his friend's edition to founder.

By the 1930s when Christian faith and common cause in reforming the English syllabus drew the two men closer together, Tolkien's Chaucer edition had been stalled for several years while Lewis's reputation rose with publication of *The Allegory of Love*. Tolkien may have entrusted him with reading his first full draft of *The Hobbit*, but, academics being academics, some degree of competitiveness

---

[151] *Surprised by Joy*, 147, and *They Stand Together*, 140, 148.
[152] Brewer, 'The Tutor', 63.
[153] *Lays of Beleriand*, 374–92 at pp. 375, 386. McIlwaine, *Maker of Middle-earth*, 222, reproduces the first page of *Leithian* which Tolkien had written and rubricated to resemble a medieval manuscript.
[154] *They Stand Together*, 330.   [155] *Surprised by Joy*, 216.

persisted. No man likes admitting failure to another; showing weakness did not figure among Lewis's definitions of 'Friendship' in *The Four Loves*. So it is understandable that Tolkien would have been unwilling to admit that he had stumbled—and his philological enterprise had come to ruin as well—for what should have been the elementary assignment of publishing a student reader of Chaucer.

4
Tolkien as Editor: Text and Glossary

Tolkien apparently played no role in selecting texts for the Clarendon Chaucer and was not expected to do much actual editing. He was asked simply to tidy up extracts from Walter W. Skeat's *Student's Chaucer* reprinted from his monumental 1894 *Works of Geoffrey Chaucer*. Consequently he made almost no substantive emendations, although he insisted upon better punctuation as well as diacritical marks to help newcomers with pronouncing Middle English. When he did make some minor change in spelling or word-order, however, he grew stubborn about it. Later in his fiction–writing when printers changed 'dwarves' to 'dwarfs' and 'elven' to 'elfin' in the first edition of *The Lord of the Rings*, he demanded that the original forms be restored throughout (*Letters*, 169). This is the sort of obstinacy already on display when editing Chaucer.

Once Tolkien had established the text largely through negotiations with Kenneth Sisam, with little real assistance from George Gordon, the project had reached only the midpoint of the process described by OUP's Martin Maw: 'a first read; corrections in the compositors' room to produce a second read; a submission to the author for any emendations, which were inserted by Press compositors; a further check on the amended text by the Readers; and a final copy check by a Reader outside the Press.'[1] The Clarendon Chaucer had therefore reached a fairly advanced stage, its main text emended and reset while awaiting further work by the co-editors on supporting sections, specifically Gordon's Introduction and Tolkien's Notes. As his second assignment, Tolkien's Glossary was straightforward, workmanlike, and impressive in its economy after Sisam's insistence upon reducing its length. If Text and Glossary had been Tolkien's only responsibilities, as had been the case when editing *Gawain* with E. V. Gordon, his Chaucer edition might have been published soon after this other Clarendon textbook in 1925.

As a study of editorial practices and lexicography, this chapter might be brain-numbingly dull for general readers, even for today's Chaucer specialists no longer routinely trained in textual criticism and historical linguistics, if not for the fact that it allows us to watch Tolkien in his role as a scholar and catch glimpses of the future author of *The Lord of the Rings*. Carpenter has established the

---

[1] 'Printing Technology, Binding, Readers, and Social Life', in *History of Oxford University Press*, 3:277–307 at p. 292; see for example Gilliver, *Making of the Oxford English Dictionary*, 'Proofs and Revises', 270–4.

Tolkien's Lost Chaucer. John M. Bowers, Oxford University Press (2019). © John M. Bowers.
DOI: 10.1093/oso/9780198842675.001.0001

commonplace view that the philologist and the novelist were always the same man, the two sides of his literary life overlapping so completely that readers cannot fully appreciate the one without the other.[2] Tolkien himself maintained that language always came first in his writings, and his work on *Selections from Chaucer's Poetry and Prose* invited the minute care for words that would run throughout his fiction.

Text

A mystery surrounds the Text's proofs discovered in the grey box in OUP's basement. Tolkien's 1951 letter to Dan Davin (Fig. 1) indicated he was returning the 'working copy made of galleys of the *text*, with 2 copies of the resultant *revises* in page–proof', but there were five sets of proofs in the box, two working copies and three copies of the revises. The problem is deciding which copies belonged to Tolkien and which found their ways into the box by other routes.

Date-stamped 4 DEC 1923 when sent out to the editors, Proof 1, Copy 1 was clearly Tolkien's working copy and holds most interest for showing more than six hundred changes that he wanted in 119 pages.[3] Stamped with the same date, Proof 1, Copy 2 became Tolkien's second working copy sent back to OUP by way of George Gordon.[4] Tolkien was still at Leeds while both Gordon and Sisam were in Oxford, so this second working copy becomes the key record of their long-distance collaboration. Tolkien transferred most (but not all) of his changes from his original working copy and used pencil notes in the margins explaining why his changes should stand.

An in-house typescript headed Extract from letter from J. R. R. Tolkien Jan 5th 1924 reflects what we find in Copy 2:

> I have only discovered 3 actual misprints... The remainder of my marks are alterations of Skeat, such as *God, th'effect* already agreed upon; *pité, attempré* (to which I imagine you will readily assent); restorations of MS e.g. *buskes* (p. 4, l.102) where Skeat substitutes *busshes* with a note that *busk* is not Chaucerian... In any case the complete renovation of Skeat's somewhat lavish punctuation is doubtless out of the question. There are a dreadful lot of semi-colons!... they give me pain.... I have also abolished the occasional hyphens that crop up.

Tolkien had accomplished much over his Christmas vacation. Sisam wrote back in January 1924 approving most of Tolkien's edits, but not all, cautioning about the expense of changing those dreadful semicolons.

---

[2] *Biography*, 136; see Thomas Honegger, 'Tolkien's "Academic Writings"', in *Companion*, ed. Lee, 27–40.
[3] Bodleian MS Tolkien A 39/1, fols. 1–120.
[4] Bodleian MS Tolkien A 39/1, fols. 121–240.

This second copy had gone from Tolkien directly to Gordon, who remained mostly a bystander contributing the occasional question-mark or *Yes* initialled GSG wherever Tolkien inserted a comment justifying a change. The handwritten instruction to return his copy of the page-proofs did not prevent Gordon from keeping it almost a year, date-stamped 22 DEC 1924 when finally received back at the Press.[5] The Text then went forward after Sisam marked it up, approving or disallowing changes, with the printer's receipt stamped 19 MAY 1925.

Stamped REVISE 23 JUN 1925 when sent back to the editors, Proof 2, Copy 1 represents the printer's resetting to accommodate these changes. The 119 pages had now been printed on both sides, front and back, as they would have appeared in the published book. The names of the two editors were still missing from the title-page, however, and there remained no table of contents. These pages contain some further alterations by Tolkien, always the niggler, as indication that this copy remained in his possession as he worked on the Glossary and Notes. Stamped with the same date, Proof 2, Copy 2 contains more changes by Tolkien still insisting upon emendations already rejected by Sisam. So this was the second copy of the *revise* mentioned in his letter to Davin.[6]

The mystery of the grey box begins to unfold. Tolkien used Proof 1, Copy 1 as his working copy and kept it for future reference. He transferred his edits to Copy 2 before sending it to Gordon and thence to Sisam. Proof 2, Copies 1 and 2 were sent to Tolkien who used both of them for recording minor changes. Proof 2, Copy 3 shows no tinkering by Tolkien and seems never to have been in his possession—which tallies with his letter to Davin.

For the Glossary's galleys, Copy 1 was corrected by Tolkien and kept aside as he awaited the completion of his Notes to add cross-references. What, then, about the other materials in the grey box not specified in Tolkien's 1951 letter? The Glossary galley Copy 2 with some slight corrections by Gordon was sent back in two instalments to Sisam as indicated by two cover-letters. Copy 3 is largely untouched except for the General Prologue's new subheadings not in Tolkien's hand. Since Gordon originally took charge of subheadings, it is reasonable to suppose this was a copy that he also kept for tinkering. So here is my best guess for what survives of the Glossary galleys. Dan Davin's Clarendon Chaucer file contained Copy 2 inherited from Sisam in 1948, Copy 1 returned by Tolkien in 1951, and Copy 3 sent by Mrs Gordon in 1956, all shelved together after the project was dropped in 1960.

---

[5] The grey box contained a mailing envelope addressed 'To the Secretary / Clarendon Press / Proofs of Text / from GS Gordon;' see Bodleian MS Tolkien A 39/3, fol. 291.

[6] Bodleian MS Tolkien A 39/1, fols. 241–300. Like any prudent writer in those pre-photocopying, pre-computer days, Tolkien sent one copy back to the printer and kept a duplicate for himself; see Rateliff, *Story of the Hobbit*, p. xxxix. The two other copies of the *revises*, not being Tolkien's, have not been catalogued among the Tolkien Papers at the time of this writing.

The following sections focus only upon those proof pages of Text and Glossary corrected in Tolkien's hand.

The first proof of the Text was printed on unbound pages, front only, with holes punched in the upper left-hand corners with brass fasteners binding each of the original gatherings.[7] Always frugal with paper, Tolkien used the title-page for compiling his own table of contents in black ink, starting just below the title *Selections from Chaucer's Poetry and Prose* and, when he ran out of space, continuing at the top of the same page; red-pencil lines indicate the five gatherings (Fig. 6).

As a draft for the table of contents later printed at the head of his Glossary (see Appendix II), the Arabic numbers indicated the order of the selections while keeping Skeat's Roman numerals as references to Chaucer's shorter poems.

Tolkien jotted 'working copy' on page 2 where extracts from the *Romaunt of the Rose* began. First he searched for printer errors. Though his January 1924 letter mentioned only three in the first batch, he now corrected a total of nine misprints throughout.[8] His change of *theerly* to *heterly* in the *Legend of Cleopatra* may seem a dry-as-dust detail, but these were the dry-as-dust details about which Tolkien cared passionately, in his own writings no less than Chaucer's. He was still thinking about *heterly* when drafting his Notes, writing his article 'Chaucer as a Philologist' (p. 47), and finally dashing off his letter to Davin in 1951: 'there are a good many notes which, though useless for the purpose (such as that on *heterly* Legend of Cleopatra 59), I should find useful.'

Next came his editorial changes. Textual critics speak of two classes of emendations. The first involves 'accidentals' such as spelling, capitalization, and punctuation. There was no standard spelling in Middle English, even in London, but since spelling was a phonetic representation of a writer's personal language, Tolkien saw editing as the opportunity to return the poetry closer to Chaucer's own pronunciation. This was no trivial concern for him, and it felt like an imperative the longer he spent with his author. These alterations, averaging about five per page, represented what he believed was the poet's authentic pronunciation. He would make some 130 spelling changes such as *pite* to *pité*, *prively* to *privély,* and *attempre* to *attempré* indicating loan-words new to English but retaining their French pronunciations.

Concern for precise pronunciation led Tolkien to pepper his texts with diacritical marks of this sort, especially where accents clarified metre. He was notably fussy when changing *unreprovable* to *unréprováble* for proper scansion in *Legend of Cleopatra* (112). Whenever he encountered the word *dayesye*, he changed it to

---

[7] Archivist Peter Foden reports removing rusty fasteners to prevent damage to the documents in the 1990s.

[8] *That* for *Than* (p. 3), *ekk* for *eek* (p. 6), *made* for *make* (p. 12), *O* for *I* (p. 36), *even* for *ever* (p. 42), *OE* for *OF* (p. 51), *got* for *god* (p. 71), *theerly* for *heterly* (p. 75), and *soon* for *noon* (p. 95).

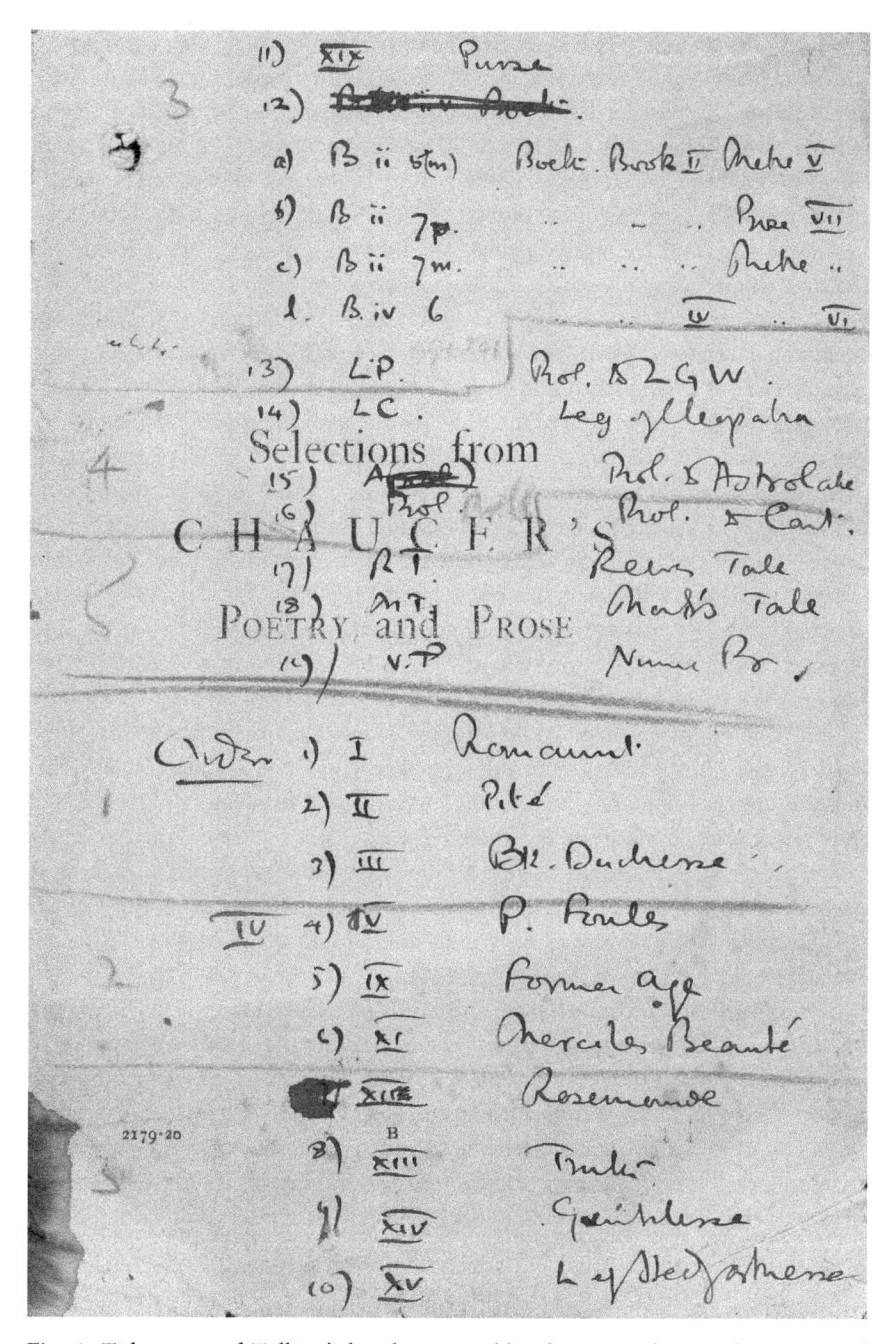

Fig. 6. Title-page and Tolkien's handwritten table of contents for Proof 1, Copy 1 of *Selections from Chaucer's Poetry and Prose* (Oxford, Bodleian Library, MS Tolkien A 39/1, fol. 1).

dayësye in his first copy and then *dayèsye* in his second copy. This addiction to diacritical marks would carry over to his fiction, as every reader knows all too well, where he was scrupulous about names such as Sméagol and Ghân-buri-Ghân.[9] Schooled by phoneticians like Henry Sweet—a model for G. B. Shaw's Henry Higgins—Tolkien had studied Sweet's *History of English Sounds* as an undergraduate and delivered a college talk on 'Visible Speech' in which he argued that writing should indicate exactly how to articulate sounds.[10] This became his objective wherever possible while editing Chaucer.

Besides being a stickler for pronunciation, Tolkien wanted some 477 changes in punctuation, bothered less by Skeat's semicolons than by his hyphens. He steadily corrected *her-of* to *herof* and *al-though* to *although* so that his letter of January 1924 greatly understated the extent to which he abolished hyphens. Despite his initial warnings over costs, Sisam raised no fuss about these trivial changes.

Besides accidentals, textual critics designate 'substantives' as their more important category of emendations. Tolkien marked some thirty-two words which he wanted changed, although nearly all were what might be termed 'indifferent variants' somewhere between substantive and accidental. For example, Tolkien objected to Skeat's *busshes* instead of *buskes* in the *Romaunt* (102) because 'not Chaucer's form'. Skeat's Oxford Chaucer actually lent support by recording that *buskes* appeared in two witnesses, the Glasgow manuscript and Thynne's early edition. Tolkien further justified the change by drawing attention to a line where Skeat accepted *busk* previously in the same work, and he was so confident of his emendation that he entered *busk* in his Glossary. Some years later when reflecting on editorial goals in 'Chaucer as a Philologist' (p. 11), he admitted that problems with Chaucer's texts seldom involved different words (substantives) but most often 'dialectal forms and spellings' (indifferent variants). Nearly all his changes fall under this second rubric as early indication of how much Tolkien distrusted fifteenth-century scribes to transmit precisely what Chaucer had written.[11]

It is difficult identifying a single substantive variant among Tolkien's many emendations. In *Compleinte unto Pité* where he found the line 'For, sothly for to seyne, I bere the sore' (96), he rewrote it at the bottom of page as 'for sothe they desdeyn I bere so sore'—a true substantive change—and yet he failed to transfer the line to Copy 2 for Sisam's approval. Other cosmetic changes typify Tolkien's eagle-eyed search for Chaucer's originals after consulting the full range of manuscript evidence. When he declared in his 1934 study of the Reeve's Tale that it was

---

[9] Perhaps encouraged by spellings like Väinämöinen in *Kalevala*, he grew more scrupulous with names like Ilúvatar, Manwë, and Fëanor in his *Silmarillion*; see Tom Shippey, 'Tolkien and the Appeal of the Pagan: *Edda* and *Kalevala*', in *Roots and Branches*, 19–38.

[10] Garth, *Tolkien at Exeter*, 39.

[11] Donaldson, 'The Psychology of Editors', 110, adjusted the editorial bias against scribes ('all they ever do is make mistakes') by noting how often medieval copyists spotted errors in their exemplars and corrected them.

'the duty of an editor to weigh such gossamer—in cases where mere spelling is important' (p. 16), no reader knew exactly how much time he had already spent weighing such gossamer in his Clarendon Chaucer.

If Tolkien took pains with small details like deciding between *buskes* or *busshes*, this is because Chaucer had already taken pains that his texts not suffer the same corruption evident in other Middle English works such as *Piers Plowman*. In the famous Tearing of the Pardon scene, for example, Piers in Skeat's 1886 edition proclaims his intention 'Ne about my *bely-ioye* so bisi be namore!' (B.VII.118), but Kane–Donaldson's 1975 edition renders this line 'Ne about my *bilyue* so bisy be na moore.' Extreme variations such as 'belly-joy' or 'belief' seldom occur in Chaucer's texts because he supervised their copying by professional scribes such as the one who produced early copies of his *Boece* and *Troilus*. Even then the poet found reason to complain about his copyist's carelessness in his witty lyric *Chaucers Wordes Unto Adam, His Owne Scriveyn*. Though it was not included in the Clarendon Chaucer, Tolkien alluded to this one-stanza poem in his 1926 'Philology' survey and cited it again in his Clarendon notes when pondering the problem of scribal corruption:[12]

> We have the words of wrath written by Chaucer to Adam his own scribe. It is only too likely that the texts we now use would enrage him still more; poets are peculiarly impatient of bungled detail.[13]

What were these bungled details? Chaucer accused his scribe of inaccuracy through 'negligence and rape'. Adam made some errors through carelessness but others through *rape*, a much-discussed word which could mean violating the body of the text but also, through the Latin *raptus*, implied abducting his words and robbing the author.[14] Tolkien came to believe that the scribes were guilty of kidnapping Chaucer's authentic spellings and a modern editor had a duty to rescue these lost pronunciations.

Another instance of an orthographic variant comes in *Compleinte unto Pité* where Tolkien emended *virtues* to *vertues* (50) with a pencil sidenote explaining that all manuscripts agreed. That is, when Tolkien consulted the textual apparatus in Skeat's Oxford Chaucer, he found *vertues* was the unanimous reading of all seven manuscripts where the poem survived. Shippey has observed that Tolkien worked more effectively as editor with a work like *Gawain* extant in a single

---

[12] Tolkien, 'Philology' (1926), 64. Adam was identified as Adam Pinkhurst by Linne Mooney, 'Chaucer's Scribe', *Speculum* 81 (2006), 97–138, and Linne R. Mooney and Estelle Stubbs, 'Adam Pinkhurst, Scrivener and Clerk of the Guildhall, c.1378–1410', in *Scribes and the City: London Guildhall Clerks and the Dissemination of Middle English Literature, 1375–1425* (York: York Medieval Press, 2013), 66–85. Lawrence Warner, 'Scribes, Misattributed: Hoccleve and Pinkhurst', *SAC* 37 (2015), 55–100, has joined others challenging this identification.
[13] Bodleian MS Tolkien A 39/2/1, fol. 12, about line 95 of *Compleinte unto Pité*.
[14] Carolyn Dinshaw, *Chaucer's Sexual Poetics* (Madison: University of Wisconsin Press, 1989), 3–10.

manuscript.[15] With the *Canterbury Tales* surviving in more than eighty manuscripts, the wide range of variants opened the possibility that the author's original words might survive somewhere other than the editor's copy-text Ellesmere. These variants further suggested that the author's authentic spellings may have been lost in the welter of scribal variations and could be recovered only by an intelligent editor bold enough to reach beyond all the manuscripts and engage in 'conjectural emendations'. Even after the Clarendon Chaucer stalled, Tolkien continued his quest for authentic readings as late as the 1940s when his Oxford duties included lecturing on the *Parlement of Foules*, the Clerk's Tale, and the Pardoner's Tale.

The fullness of the Oxford Chaucer's textual apparatus enabled Tolkien to spot and challenge Skeat's conjectural emendations where he had judged all manuscripts corrupt and attempted repairs. In *Compleinte unto Pité*, for example, the prior editor inserted *ne* in the line 'Me [ne] lakketh but my deth, and than my bere' (105), but Tolkien rejected this change with the sidenote 'not in manuscript, not used by XIV-century syntax'. Skeat had been forthright about enclosing [*ne*] in brackets, and his endnote explained that the great German scholar Bernhard ten Brink recommended the change (1:461). But Tolkien was not convinced. He preferred his own sense of fourteenth-century usage supported in this case by the manuscripts.

Like Skeat, Tolkien argued for Chaucer's authentic language by citing testimony from the poet's other works. For the *Book of the Duchess*, he changed *ageyn* to *ayen* with a sidenote referencing two instances of this spelling in the *Parlement of Foules*.[16] His meticulous attention to Chaucer's word-choices meant that he acquired a deep knowledge of the poetry which he carried forward into his later career. So, too, it reflected the meticulous craftsmanship which Tolkien brought to his own writings, claiming about *The Lord of the Rings*: 'Hardly a word in its 600,000 or more has been unconsidered.'[17]

Just as Tolkien the lexicographer possessed an intimate understanding of Chaucer's vocabulary, Tolkien the poet felt that he understood Chaucer's prosody well enough to make corrections based on metre. His first letter of Sisam in 1924 already spoke of 'boldly smoothing out the most apparently stumbling lines'. In the *Parlement of Foules* where he objected to the scansion 'Than som man doth that hath served ful yore' (476), he transposed the word-order for smoother iambic pentameter—'Than som man doth that served hath ful yore'—without the support of a single manuscript.

---

[15] Shippey, 'Tolkien as Editor', 45.
[16] Tolkien's Glossary included the word as a variant of the one he rejected: '**aye(i)n, ayens**, *adv.* back, again; *prep.* exposed to; at the approach of. See Agein.'
[17] *Letters*, 160; see John D. Rateliff, '"A Kind of Elvish Craft": Tolkien as Literary Craftsman', *Tolkien Studies* 6 (2009), 1–21.

Skeat's transparency enabled such disagreements. For example, his text of *The Former Age* contained a cross † signalling his departure from the manuscripts for the word *gniden*—'The which they †gniden, and eete nat half y-nough' (11)—and even his slimmed-down *Student's Chaucer* provided an endnote explaining why.[18] Tolkien reverted to *gnodded* on the authority of a Cambridge manuscript, although he allowed Chaucer might have written the smoother *gnīden*. He picked this fight because *Ancrene Wisse* gave him confidence of this word's authenticity, deferring his fuller defence for his Notes.[19]

Besides these skirmishes, Tolkien questioned larger matters such as whether the Cambridge Gg manuscript preserved the earlier version of the Prologue to *The Legend of Good Women*—Skeat's Text A. Already by 1892 Bernhard ten Brink had reversed this order, giving priority to the version preserved in the Fairfax manuscript—Skeat's Text B.[20] Tolkien took issue with Skeat and crossed out *Earlier Version* as the subtitle in his working copy of the proofs, recommending in his Notes to consider more interesting questions:

> Even if we could reach certainty as to the order in which A and B were made, the chief importance of this would be in the chance offered of observing Chaucer in his workshop, not in the interpretation of the allegory and contemporary allusion—which is hotly debated, and of little ultimate importance, except in so far as it may help to fix the order of A and B.[21]

Though the *Legend* Prologue contained the sort of allegory that Tolkien disliked, he did enjoy catching Chaucer in the act of rewriting extensively. Already as an undergraduate he jotted down from Raleigh's lecture: 'Chaucer continually revised his work.'[22] Thus he found in the medieval author a role-model unafraid to set aside the first version of a text and completely rewrite it. Michael Drout's edition of *'Beowulf' and the Critics* reveals a text somewhat like Chaucer's *Legend* surviving in two distinct versions, and Christopher has done a masterful job of tracing the multilayered composition of *The Lord of the Rings*. Tolkien never stopped revising materials for his *legendarium* from 1917 almost till his death.

---

[18] *Student's Chaucer*, 726: 'I gnodden; Hh. knoddyd; *correctly* gnīden, *pt. pl. of* gnīden.'
[19] MS Tolkien A 39/2/1, fol. 24v: 'The manuscripts have *gnodded*, which in earlier and better spelling would be *gnoddede*, *gnuddede* (with elision of the final *e*). This is a genuine word, used for precisely this action of roughly crushing and rubbing corn in the hands, already before Chaucer. We should therefore retain it, since the bisyllabic word foot is not impossible, even if we suspect that Chaucer really wrote the smoother *gnīde(n)*, past. pl. of *gnīden* (OE. *gnīdan*), which had the same sense. Compare the same variation in the *Ancren Riwle* (Camden Soc. p. 260): *and þer ase he eode bi þe weie mid his deciples, summe cherre heo breken þe eares bi þe weie and gniden þe cornes ut bitweanen hore honden* (another Ms. *gnuddeden þe curnles ut*).'
[20] John S. P. Tatlock, *The Development and Chronology of Chaucer's Works* (London: Chaucer Society, 2nd ser., no. 37, 1907), 86–102, agreed with ten Brink against Skeat.
[21] Bodleian MS Tolkien A 39/2/1, fol. 42r.
[22] Bodleian MS Tolkien A 21/4, fol. 14v.

Corruption of the *Legend* Prologue in the Cambridge manuscript encouraged other editors to conjecture what Chaucer originally wrote, and Tolkien was always ready to pursue a lost original.[23] The following couplet scanned poorly and failed to make sense:

> Somme songyn on the braunchis clere
> Of love & that joye it was to here (A, 127-8)

Skeat used brackets to signal his reconstruction (3:75):

> Somme songen [layes] on the braunches clere
> Of love and [May], that Ioye hit was to here.

Tolkien ventured his own conjecture, more conservative for not introducing the word *May* and more sonorous for introducing the alliterative doublets *somme songen* and *love and layes*:

> And somme songen on the braunches clere
> Of love, and layes that joy hit was to here.[24]

In terms of his own writings, Tolkien's close study of Chaucer's decasyllabic couplets gave insights for revising his poem 'Over Old Hills and Far Away' in 1927 and then composing *Mythopoeia* in the same verse-form early in the 1930s: 'Blessed are the legend-makers with their rhyme | Of things not found within recorded time....'[25]

The Clarendon Chaucer was limited in its selections from the *Canterbury Tales*. Of the General Prologue's pilgrim portraits, Gordon and Sisam chose only the Knight, Squire, Prioress, Monk, Clerk, Shipman, Wife of Bath, Parson, Miller, and Reeve. Next came the Reeve's Tale in a truncated version breaking off after only 228 lines before the raucous bedroom scene. The snoring and farting of Simkin's family were gone; the wife going outside to piss was gone; and the sexual assaults upon the miller's daughter and wife were gone. Though he engaged in less censorship in his 1939 edition of the Reeve's Tale, any bowdlerizing caused Tolkien some uneasiness because he regretted whenever poetry was lost. His lecture 'On Fairy-Stories' would complain about the old tales 'bowdlerized instead of being reserved' (*Essays*, 136).

Even partial inclusion of the Reeve's Tale had the unintended consequence of focusing Tolkien's attention on the dialect issues which would occupy him

---

[23] For the latest reconstruction, see Geoffrey Chaucer, *The Legend of Good Women*, ed. Janet Cowen and George Kane (East Lansing: Colleagues Press, 1995).

[24] His Notes continued defending this emendation (Bodleian MS Tolkien A 39/2/1, fol. 50).

[25] 'Over Old Hills and Far Away', in *Book of Lost Tales, Part I*, 116-17, and *Mythopoeia* in J. R. R. Tolkien, *Tree and Leaf*, intro. Christopher Tolkien (Boston: Houghton Mifflin, 1989), 97-101 at p. 99; see SH 2:822-3 and Carl Phelpstead, 'Myth-Making and Sub-Creation', in *Companion*, ed. Lee, 82-6 ('Mythopoeia').

throughout the 1930s. Specifically the proof-pages required the editor to consider the proverb uttered by the northern cleric John: 'Him boës serve himselve that has na swayn.' (The rustic lad falls back upon proverbial wisdom much as will Sam Gamgee.[26]) At first Tolkien emended *boës* to *bos* on Skeat's authority: 'In northern poems, the word is invariably a monosyllable, spelt *bos*' (5:122). Then Tolkien had second thoughts, crossed out his own emendation, and reverted to Ellesmere's *boës*. Vacillation persisted into the Glossary where he entered *boes* as Northern.

As he explored dialect issues at greater length in 'Chaucer as a Philologist', Tolkien grew increasingly distrustful of the ability of London's scribes to preserve Chaucer's Northern forms even as he gained confidence in his own aptitude for restoring the poet's original spellings. He retained Ellesmere's *boes* in his 1934 study but emended to *bos* in his 1939 edition of the Reeve's Tale. This emendation may seem a trivial change, but Chaucer's dialect usages carried further implications. How expertly had the poet reproduced regional language? To what extent was he mocking the clerks for speaking in a country-bumpkin idiom? How did he develop an ear for a dialect so remote from his native London? And if early scribers miscopied these Northern words, how much more pervasively did they miswrite the rest of Chaucer's texts? These questions are addressed in Chapter 6.

Tolkien as editor had no difficulty with the Monk's Tale and the Nun's Priest's Tale. Unlike the lyrics and dream-visions, *The Canterbury Tales* survived in the reliable-looking Ellesmere manuscript (not yet challenged by Tolkien) so that he did little more than cross out Skeat's commas and capitalize the *G* in God.

Proof 1, Copy 2

Tolkien's real editorial debates took place in Copy 2 date-stamped 4 DEC 1923 but not forwarded to OUP by Gordon until December 1924 with a cover letter: 'Here is Tolkien's text. Very good, it seems to me: he has taken trouble.' Gordon had simply glanced over these pages with the occasional *Yes GSG*. Sisam then moved quickly to accept or cancel Tolkien's changes, and by 31 December he sent the page proofs to David Nichol Smith for confirmation of his decisions: 'I think Tolkien is wrong in all his emendations in Boethius, and have cancelled them.'

Professor Nichol Smith was not the only outsider to review these proofs. An unknown hand wrote on the first page 'insert [ ] and + as in book', the book being *Student's Chaucer*, and then proceeded throughout the entire text to mark Skeat's emendations—a huge undertaking—only to have these insertions crossed out by Sisam with an emphatic red-pencil *NO*.[27] The prospect of so many pedantic

---

[26] Tom Shippey, '"A Fund of Wise Sayings": Proverbiality in Tolkien', in *Roots and Branches*, 303–19, points to the importance of this 'survivor-genre' in *TLOR*.

[27] Comparison with writing samples from George Gordon, David Nichol Smith, and E. V. Gordon eliminates most who might have had access to the proof pages.

changes at 6d. each must have struck him as unthinkable as well as unattractive. He allowed brackets only in special cases as in *The Former Age* where Skeat invented a line to replace one missing in the manuscript and Tolkien wanted it duly noted: 'This line (very bad in point of content) is wholly Skeat and must be in [ ].'

The final stamp 19 MAY 1925 indicates when the printer received Copy 2 for making his typesetting changes. Tolkien's presence at a faculty meeting at Leeds on this same date serves as a reminder that these editorial negotiations had not proceeded face-to-face. Editing *Gawain* during the same period, Tolkien and E. V. Gordon were both at Leeds and could sit down together for hashing out differences. Since Tolkien did not begin lecturing in Oxford until October 1926, his editorial communications with co-editor George Gordon and OUP's Sisam had proceeded long-distance mostly in the margins of Copy 2. While the 170 miles of separation surely hampered progress, this proof's inserts, crossings-out, and notations in the margins tell an interesting story of how these negotiations moved forward.

Tolkien continued to spot mistakes, noting that the first two lines of the Prioress's portrait had been left out. Skeat's oversight of a single word in the General Prologue drew a sidenote: 'Omission of this in Oxford Chaucer is apparently an accident. It's clearly required, and appears (without textual comment) in other editions, Skeat or not.' He also defended his views on punctuation, inserting new changes even while bringing forward his original emendations from Copy 1. Not even tiny matters were overlooked: 'this *comma* wrong.' Despite prior warnings, Sisam was surprisingly indulgent with these minor corrections.

Tolkien inserted pencil balloons in the margins to defend the rescue of the poet's lost wordings. Accordingly he wrote about a line in the *Book of the Duchess*: 'If any emendation is to be done, this is what we would naturally suppose Chaucer to have really written.' Thus he also defended switching word-order in the *Parlement of Foules*: 'not so manuscripts but it is much better.' Skeat sometimes served as his ally as when justifying a change in the *Legend of Good Women*: 'Skeat takes this liberty elsewhere.' Tolkien's confidence about knowing what Chaucer had really written would grow over the next dozen years.

There is something comical about the three scholars struggling with lines dropped for decency's sake from the Nun's Priest's Tale (Fig. 7). Sisam had inserted dots to indicate the omissions where Chanticleer 'feathered' his hens, but Tolkien objected: 'Rhyme and numbering are sufficient signposts.' After Gordon took the trouble to agree with Tolkien, Sisam approved crossing out the ellipses.

Tolkien caused the most trouble with Chaucer's prose translation of Boethius. Selections from *Boece* reflected interest at the time in the evolution of English prose evidenced by R. W. Chambers's *On the Continuity of English Prose from Alfred to More and His School* (1932) as well as James Joyce's 'Oxen of the Sun'

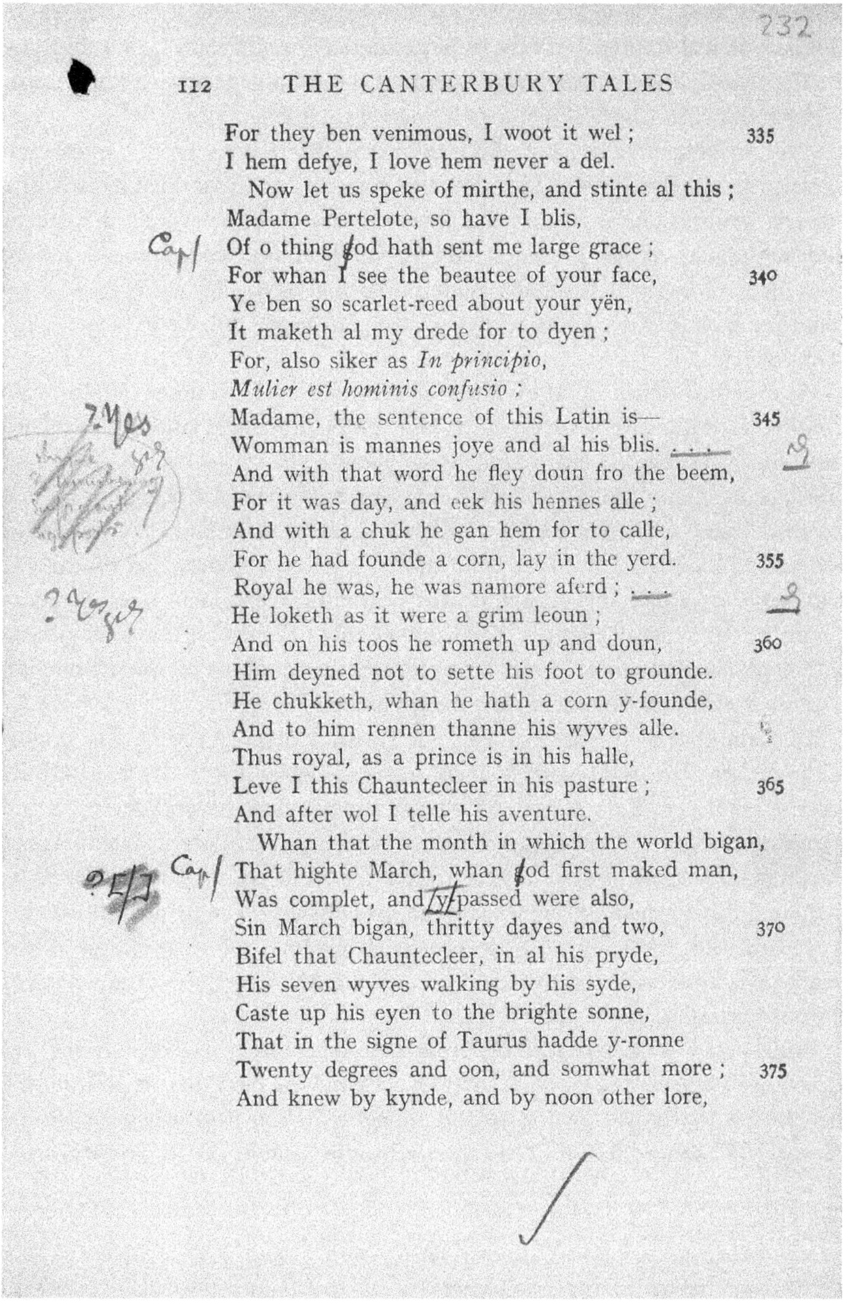

112   THE CANTERBURY TALES

  For they ben venimous, I woot it wel; 335
  I hem defye, I love hem never a del.
   Now let us speke of mirthe, and stinte al this;
  Madame Pertelote, so have I blis,
  Of o thing god hath sent me large grace;
  For whan I see the beautee of your face, 340
  Ye ben so scarlet-reed about your yën,
  It maketh al my drede for to dyen;
  For, also siker as *In principio*,
  Mulier est hominis confusio;
  Madame, the sentence of this Latin is— 345
  Womman is mannes joye and al his blis.
  And with that word he fley doun fro the beem,
  For it was day, and eek his hennes alle;
  And with a chuk he gan hem for to calle,
  For he had founde a corn, lay in the yerd. 355
  Royal he was, he was namore aferd;
  He loketh as it were a grim leoun;
  And on his toos he rometh up and doun, 360
  Him deyned not to sette his foot to grounde.
  He chukketh, whan he hath a corn y-founde,
  And to him rennen thanne his wyves alle.
  Thus royal, as a prince is in his halle,
  Leve I this Chauntecleer in his pasture; 365
  And after wol I telle his aventure.
   Whan that the month in which the world bigan,
  That highte March, whan god first maked man,
  Was complet, and *y*-passed were also,
  Sin March bigan, thritty dayes and two, 370
  Bifel that Chauntecleer, in al his pryde,
  His seven wyves walking by his syde,
  Caste up his eyen to the brighte sonne,
  That in the signe of Taurus hadde y-ronne
  Twenty degrees and oon, and somwhat more; 375
  And knew by kynde, and by noon other lore,

Fig. 7. Tolkien's 'working copy' of the first page-proofs of the *Canterbury Tales* (Oxford, Bodleian Library, MS Tolkien A 39/1, fol. 232).

episode in *Ulysses*.[28] Tolkien knew one way to salvage Chaucer's translation was to compare scribal readings with the original Latin. He had already been consulting *De Consolatione Philosophiae* while drafting the commentary where he recommended the Loeb Classical Library's facing-page edition.[29]

After looking at the Latin, Tolkien concluded that Chaucer's translation was not accurately represented in Skeat's copy-text MS Cambridge Ii.iii.21. The current *Riverside Chaucer* agrees that this manuscript's bad readings are frequent and substantial. When the latest editors Ralph Hanna and Traugott Lawler consulted the original Latin for establishing their text, they were unwittingly following Tolkien's lead for justifying changes. 'Sense and Latin demand it', said Tolkien.

Here his insistence upon accuracy collided with OUP's desire for low-cost production. Although Sisam would favour conjectural emendation in Old English texts,[30] he rejected changes in *Boece* because they would require resetting whole pages. Never mind that Tolkien had correctly spotted problems: 'This line does not make sense nor does it translate *quid enim furor hosticus ulla / Vellet prior arma movere*.' And never mind that he guessed correctly that the copyist had picked up a marginal gloss and written it into his text. Sisam's response was simply to cross out all changes. Tolkien won only one victory: 'No good putting in *Skeat's* line numbers.' Sisam accepted the clarification of line-numbering because it would not interfere with the printed text.

This editorial tug-of-war resulted from Tolkien's obsession with a lost originality which he believed philology could rescue. Shippey has nicely described the *asterisk-reality* of words, songs, and legends reconstructed beyond the support of surviving evidence[31]—in this case Chaucer's authentic text—and Tolkien was not happy that his spadework had been rejected for the *Boece*. He later retaliated by including this warning in the headnote to his Glossary: 'The frequent references to the extracts from *Boethius* are usually cautionary, for in these pieces the language is unnatural, and the uses of words often due to clumsy translation or misunderstanding of the Latin original.'[32]

And where was George Gordon during these skirmishes over *Boece*? As early as December 1923, he was devising subtitles such as 'The First Age' and 'Death the Leveller'. Now he was having second thoughts in the page-proofs. 'Love the Mover' was changed first to 'The Order of Nature' and finally to 'The Universal

---

[28] On the two authors' shared philological interests, see Shippey, *Author of the Century*, 'Tolkien and Joyce', 310–12.
[29] Bodleian MS Tolkien A 39/2/1, fol. 37v.
[30] Kenneth Sisam, 'Notes on Old English Poetry', *RES* 22 (1946), 257–68 at p. 268.
[31] Shippey, *Road to Middle-earth*, 19–23; his 'Views of Evil: Boethian and Manichaean', 140–6, suggests why Tolkien took such interest in Chaucer's *Boece*.
[32] Bodleian MS Tolkien A 39/3, fol. 1; see Appendix II.

Love'. With his usual deference, Sisam accepted Gordon's humdrum changes while rejecting Tolkien's smart emendations.

Proof 2, Copy 1

The next set of proofs was stamped 23 JUN 1925 when leaving the Press. Here the printer had made the changes which Tolkien marked and Sisam approved, often grudgingly. Tolkien's handwriting indicates this was one of the two *revises* returned in 1951.

Tolkien carefully reviewed the new pages and never quit pushing for greater accuracy. Besides noticing a previously overlooked misprint in the Reeve's Tale, he suddenly focused upon a line spoken by the northern clerk Alain: 'What? whilk way is he geen?' He substituted *gaan* for *geen* and added a note in the margin: 'See Tolkien / Philo Soc / "Chau as a Philologist".' This indicates his interest in the edition continued after publishing his article on the Reeve's Tale in 1934. There he defended *gan(e)* as a northernism witnessed by three other manuscripts instead of Skeat's *geen* supported by Ellesmere (p. 22). Tolkien remained resolute about this change, still arguing in his 1951 letter to Davin against printing *geen*: 'a form which in my opinion should be removed from glossary and text in favour of *gaan*.'

Proof 2, Copy 2

This proof, also stamped 23 JUN 1925 with '2nd copy of revise' written on the title-page, was Tolkien's second copy as indicated by a few niggling changes in his hand. He again noted the misprint in the Reeve's Tale and again wanted *geen* emended to the Northern variant *gaan*.

Proof 2, Copy 3

Since there are no changes written in these pages, Tolkien must never have had this copy in his possession. A letter from Gordon to OUP stamped 27 JUL 1925 says briefly, 'Herewith Revise corrected for press.' This must have been Gordon's copy, then, and found its way to the grey box by a different route.

Thus some of the grey box's mysteries have been solved. When Tolkien wrote in 1951 that he was returning 'working copy made of galleys of the *text*, with 2 copies of the resultant *revises* in page-proof', he referred to (1) Proof 1, Copy 1 with his changes prior to negotiations with Sisam; (2) Proof 2, Copy 1 with one change based on his 1934 study of Northern dialect in the Reeve's Tale; and (3) Proof 2, Copy 2 where he continued insisting upon these late changes.

The other two proofs in the box probably came from Sisam's 'Clarendon Chaucer' file inherited after his retirement in 1948 by Davin. Or possibly Sisam may have sent these two batches of proof-pages back to Gordon, whose widow in turn returned them to OUP along with his other materials in 1956. Whatever the circumstances of its survival, Proof 1, Copy 2 remains the most useful for recording the give-and-take between Tolkien as the scrupulous editor and Sisam as the promoter of an inexpensive textbook.

Glossary

When his military service ended in 1918, Tolkien returned to Oxford as an assistant lexicographer at the *Oxford English Dictionary* then housed in the Old Ashmolean on Broad Street. He always recalled learning more about languages during the next two years than in any equal period of his life. With the *OED* then nearing the end of the alphabet, his supervisor Henry Bradley assigned him Germanic *W* words such as *wander, warlock, water, wild,* and *winter,* and he later praised the young scholar's mastery of Anglo-Saxon and comparative linguistics.[33] Tolkien remained immensely proud of his contributions and remarked whenever etymologies were challenged, 'The *OED* is me!'[34] Thus he was ready, by talent and training, for the linguistic projects that came his way thereafter.

The return of undergraduates after the Great War pressed the need for new textbooks, and Tolkien produced his glossary to Sisam's *Fourteenth Century Verse and Prose* while working simultaneously at the *OED*. Skeat had provided expert guidelines:

> The best way is to make a note of every word that requires explanation on a *separate slip* of paper, with a reference to the place where it occurs. I keep the slips *in the order in which the words occur in the book*, and afterwards go over each one again separately, adding the part of speech and the sense (unless this has already been done), at the same time *verifying the references* and making sure that the sense is correct. Then, and *not till then*, the slips are all sorted into alphabetical order... The rejected slips can be thrown away; the rest go to press without rewriting.[35]

Sisam reported how Skeat enjoyed fireside conversations, 'all the while sorting glossary slips as tranquilly as a woman does her knitting'[36] Skeat wrote with some pride that his Chaucer slips considerably exceeded 30,000 and 'the whole *depth* of them was quite two inches over *nine feet*'.[37] If this sounds like a brain-numbing

---

[33] Carpenter, *Biography*, 108, and Gilliver, Marshall, and Weiner, *Ring of Words*, 'Tolkien as Lexicographer', 42.
[34] *Tolkien Family Album*, 42.   [35] Skeat, 'Introduction', *Student's Pastime*, p. liv.
[36] Sisam, 'Skeat', *DNB*, 496.   [37] *Student's Pastime*, pp. liv–lv.

enterprise, Tolkien found himself agreeing in 1928 after assembling three of them for student editions: 'Compiling a glossary, even the most humble word-list, is a long and wearisome labour.'[38]

Sisam's anthology had required only a humble glossary with definitions, but the more Tolkien grappled with the 43,000 words in the texts, the more elaborate the project grew and the longer he took to complete it. Because it was not finished when *Verse and Prose* was published in 1921, the Press printed it separately in 1922 as *A Middle English Vocabulary* to become the young academic's first book. The results were impressive, offering some 4,740 entries with nearly 6,800 definitions and almost 15,000 references to words in the texts. There were some 1,900 cross-references as well as an index of 236 proper names.[39] Though the pages were unnumbered when printed at the end of Sisam's volume, Tolkien's glossary ran to 167 pages.

Although Tolkien was able to draw expertly upon the *OED* still in progress, his work had independent value because no standard Middle English dictionary existed at the time. He could therefore claim quite justly in his introductory note: 'I have given exceptionally full treatment to what may rightly be called the backbone of the language.' Though he would later complain about the ordeal, he also admitted that 'Middle English is an exciting field—almost uncharted I begin to think, because as soon as one turns detailed personal attention on to any little corner of it, the received notions and ideas seem to crumple up and fall to pieces' (*Letters*, 11). These reflections came in 1923 just when turning his attention to the glossary for the Clarendon Chaucer.

In July 1923 George Gordon reported on Tolkien's progress with their *Selections*: 'He is equal, or will be soon, to making the Chaucer Glossary; and would like to knock this off before October.' He was far too optimistic. Only in December 1924 had Sisam seen enough of the word-list to urge shortening it, and Gordon replied confidently that he was looking over Tolkien's draft manuscript. This reference to a *manuscript* indicates that Tolkien, rather than following Skeat's method of sending slips directly to the printer, had taken the extra time and trouble of writing out a complete draft, hence another reason for missing his deadline.

At the end of December 1924, Sisam wrote to David Nichol Smith about Tolkien's failure to divide his contributions between twenty-four pages for notes and twenty pages for his glossary, instead producing thirty-eight pages for the glossary alone. Sisam then reminded Tolkien of these realities in January 1925: 'We cannot possibly allow more than 28 pages for the Glossary.' A letter to

---

[38] 'Foreword' to Haigh's *A New Glossary of the Dialect of the Huddersfield District*, p. xiii. By this date Tolkien had compiled word-lists for his *Gawain* and Chaucer editions as well as Sisam's *Verse and Prose*.

[39] SH 2:783–6 and Gilliver, Marshall, and Weiner, *The Ring of Words*, 35–7.

Gordon on the same day spelled out the restrictions sure to displease Tolkien: 'omission of practically all references, shortening of the preliminary note, and shortening of some of the longer articles.'[40]

Tolkien did his best, and in March 1925 Gordon could write to Sisam with the good news that the Glossary had been reduced. Since the prior version does not survive, we cannot know what exactly Tolkien cut out. There are no etymologies as there had been in *Gawain* and *Verse and Prose*, so probably these were dropped only to reappear in his draft Notes. His manuscript version was typeset, and the grey box contained eleven long-sheet galleys which would have translated to twenty-seven printed pages, one fewer than Sisam's maximum. Tolkien then proofread these pages, correcting a variety of errors introduced mostly because the printer worked from his handwritten draft. But the marked-up galleys were never sent back for resetting because he was waiting to include references to the Notes still in progress at the time—and never finished.

Even shortened, the Chaucer glossary included some 1,760 entries with nearly 3,400 definitions and almost 700 references to words in the texts. Though pressed for space, he nonetheless recorded thirty-four dialect variants. There were some ninety-seven cross-references but no separate index of proper names. Instead, Tolkien shifted names like Agathon, Cybele, and Nimrod to his annotations. His glossary for the *Gawain* edition makes a clear contrast, extending to seventy-eight pages with a separate two-page index of names at the end. Here is how he and E. V. Gordon justified its length: 'There are approximately as many distinct individual words as there are lines in the poem: a new word for every line.' Justly proud of their achievement, they could not resist tossing out a challenge to future Chaucer editors: 'the vocabulary and idiom of *Sir Gawain* deserve as much as even Chaucer's best work (which has not received it) a full and careful analysis.'[41] Tolkien brought forward to his Clarendon Chaucer this challenge for more careful analysis of vocabulary. His many discoveries did not contribute to the legacy of lexicographers, unfortunately, and even his student Norman Davis knew nothing about this possible resource when compiling his own *Chaucer Glossary* in the 1970s. 'Norman was close to him in those last years,' the volume's co-editor Douglas Gray recalls, 'and if he knew about the book, he would certainly have mentioned it.'[42]

The grey box contained two copies of these galleys.[43] Galley 1, Copy 1 was Tolkien's working copy where he wrote at the top of the first page: '*Corrected* but

---

[40] Bodleian MS Tolkien A 39/3, fol. 284.
[41] Tolkien and Gordon, 'Preface' to *Sir Gawain and the Green Knight*, p. vi; Tolkien wrote with pride of the etymologies included in his Glossary (p. 133).
[42] Private email communication, 2 December 2016, with permission; see *A Chaucer Glossary*, compiled by Norman Davis with Douglas Gray, Patricia Ingham, and Anne Wallace-Hadrill (Oxford: Clarendon Press, 1979).
[43] Bodleian MS Tolkien A 39/A, fols. 1–11 and 12–22. The first gathering is stamped 2 MAY 1925 for columns 1 to 5 (the first three sheets) and 8 MAY 1925 for the second batch, columns 6–11 (the

shall need check with "revise" texts.' Clearly he kept this copy for further tinkering because no date-stamp indicates its return to the Secretary's Office. Galley 1, Copy 2 was accompanied by two handwritten notes from George Gordon saying that he looked these over before sending them back to OUP.[44] His two batches were stamped upon their receipt 7 MAY 1925 and 14 MAY 1925, each of them just one week after being sent out. Gordon obviously wanted them off his desk.

Galley 1, Copy 1

Tolkien's Glossary began with a three-paragraph introduction wholly different from Skeat's two-page overview for his 1894 Glossorial Index (6:1–2). Tolkien's first paragraph explained spelling variations for newcomers to Middle English. (See Appendix II.) These matters had engaged his interests since his 1913 undergraduate essay 'The Language of Chaucer'.[45] The second paragraph gave instructions on finding variant spellings especially for verbs. Since his early plea to Sisam for normalized spellings had gone unheeded, he now needed to account for these variants. The third paragraph explained difficulties with the *Boece* where the language was unnatural; his reference to passages 'otherwise interpreted by other editors' points to his unspoken rivalry with Skeat. This headnote was followed by ORDER OF PIECES ASSUMED IN NUMBERING THE GLOSSARY which expanded the table of contents originally handwritten on the book's title-page.

Sisam's complaints about length had forced Tolkien to compress. His definitions were therefore more concise than Skeat's, he combined noun/verb forms into single entries, and he minimized references to the Text. Yet besides correcting misprints, he could not resist inserting into his galleys a large number of improvements and additions (Fig. 8).

Below, my analysis of words beginning with *a*– shows Tolkien catching misprints—for example, correcting **aguiter** to **aguiler** for 'needle-case' and amending the definition for **allye** from 'many (into)' to 'marry (into).' Otherwise he responded to the challenge of Skeat's massive glossary by finding words previously left out and sometimes giving fuller accounts of words. The glossary-making gave further scope to his 'anxiety of influence' by aiming at definitions as different as possible from Skeat's.

fourth to sixth sheets), the third batch, columns 12–17 (seventh to ninth sheets), and the final gathering for columns 18–21 (tenth and eleventh sheets).

[44] Bodleian MS Tolkien A 39/A, fols. 23–4.
[45] Bodleian MS Tolkien A 21/1, fols. 43–63.

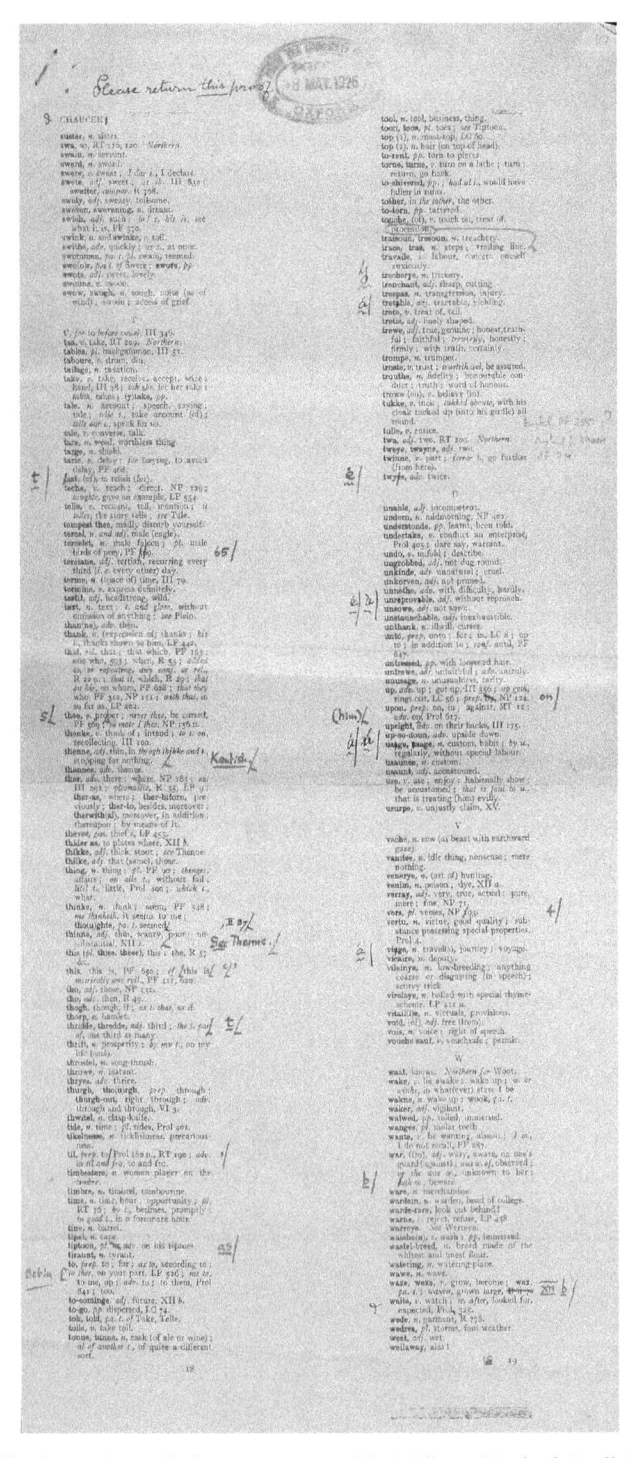

Fig. 8. Galley long-sheet of Glossary corrected by Tolkien (Oxford, Bodleian Library, MS Tolkien A 39/3, fol. 10).

Tolkien was scrupulous about including words which Skeat had missed like 'abidinge, *n.* duration, XII *b.*' and '**acloye**, *v.* embarrass.' Sometimes he changed the spelling along with the definition. Skeat's '**Asyde**, *adv.* aside, 3.558, 862; A 896, E 303' becomes Tolkien's '**aside**, *adv.* sidelong, III 862.' Or he condensed Skeat's entries such as the three for **Accord** (s.), **Acord** (s.), and **Acorde** (v.) into the single entry '**acorde**, *n.* concord, harmony; consent, wish, will; *in a., of oon a.*, in tune; *v.* come to an agreement.'

Reading through a glossary can be almost as tedious as writing one, but some words deserve attention because they figure thematically in Tolkien's later fiction. Notice for example how Skeat's *aventure* stressed the negative with 'peril' and 'mishap' in his *Student's Chaucer* entry:

> **Aventure**, *s.* chance, 4.21; peril, B 1151; misfortune, L. 657; fortune, 18.22; luck, T. ii. 288, 291; circumstance, L. 1907; *of a.*, by chance, HF 2090; *on a.*, in case of mishap, T. v. 298; *in a.*, in the hands of fortune, T. i.784; *per a.*, perchance, A. ii.12. 6; *in a. and grace*, on luck and favour, 4.60; *good a.*, good fortune, 5.131, 7.324; *pl.* adventures, A 795; accidents C 934.

Tolkien's succinct entry—'**aventure**, *n.* chance; misfortune; *pl.* adventures; *good a.*, good luck; *his a.* what befell him'—reflects the positive value upon adventure in *The Hobbit* and even looks forward to the debate on the last page whether Bilbo's 'adventures' had been 'mere luck' or something more like divine intervention.[46] Tolkien's lecture 'On Fairy-Stories' recalled this special sense in Middle English: 'Most good "fairy-stories" are about the *aventures* of men in the Perilous Realms or upon its shadowy marches.'[47] Chaucer was more ambivalent about this force in men's lives. His Canterbury pilgrims met at the Tabard Inn 'by aventure' as a purely random happenstance, but then the Knight benefited from the luck of the draw—'Were it by aventure, or sort, or cas' (844)—as if destined by his social status to tell the first tale. Tolkien himself would maintain a similar uncertainty over whether key events, like Bilbo's finding of the Ring and Gollum's falling into Mount Doom, resulted from mere chance or some higher destiny overseen by the Valar.[48]

Tolkien's abbreviation *n* signalled a word intended for further discussion in his Notes. The entry for **overthwert** was very brief, for example, because he drafted a whole paragraph on the word in his commentary on the *Book of the Duchess*, as we shall see in Chapter 5. Other words sometimes continued to fascinate him years later. His entry for *losengeour* grew into the 1951 lecture which he coyly described as 'no more than a footnote': 'It was in Chaucer that I first made the acquaintance

---

[46] His undergraduate Chaucer notebook already inclined toward the positive: 'The motto of Comedy is *Here is Luck!*' (Bodleian MS Tolkien A 21/4, fol. 15v).

[47] *Essays*, 113; Solopova, 'Middle English', in *Companion*, ed. Lee, 235, provides a fine paragraph on *aventure*.

[48] See Shippey, *Road to Middle-earth*, 'Luck and Chance', 150–4, and *Author of the Century*, 'Luck', 143–7.

of that dubious character the *losengeour*.'[49] He did not tell his conference audience that this acquaintance improved during the 1920s when glossing the line 'For in your court is many a losengeour' in the *Legend of Good Women* (A, 328).

Because Tolkien largely strove to condense entries, instances in which he added extra information deserve notice, particularly in matters of dialect. When he began teaching the course 'Language of Chaucer' during his first year at Leeds, he produced mimeographed pages on the Kentish dialect as an aid to his students (SH 1:122). This alertness to South-East variations carried forward in seven entries:

abegge, *v.* pay for it. *Kentish.*
dreye, *adj.* dry; as *n.* PF 380. *Kentish.*
hed, y-hed, *pp.* of Hide. *Kentish*
melle, *n.* mill, V 6, RT 3. *Kentish.*
shette, *v.* shut, enclose. *Kentish.*
stente, *Kentish form of* Stinte.
thenne, thin, in *throgh thikke and t.,* stopping for nothing. *Kentish.*

Skeat could be faulted for noting only the first and fifth of these words as Kentish.

Why Tolkien's interest in Kentish? Skeat's 'Life of Chaucer' reminded readers that the poet represented Kent as MP in the parliament of 1386, and he speculated that the poet's residence in Greenwich had been the source of his dialect forms.[50] Tolkien's commentary for *Complaint unto his Purse* wondered if Chaucer had actually been exiled from the court to Greenwich, which formed part of Kent until 1889.[51] This biographical fact seemed to explain how local elements infiltrated his language. If the family of Chaucer's mother Agnes originally came from Kent, however, the dialect may have been literally Chaucer's mother-tongue.[52] Since the Kentish word *melle* at the beginning of the Reeve's Tale makes no sense for a Norfolk narrator, this dialect variant for 'mill' must have belonged to Chaucer, not the Reeve.[53]

By noting these Kentish words, Tolkien assembled further evidence that Chaucer's personal language was a hybrid of dialects converging upon the capital.

---

[49] Tolkien, 'Middle English "Losenger"', 63–4.

[50] Skeat 6:xxiii–xxv and *Student's Chaucer*, p. xi; see Tolkien's undergraduate notebook for lectures 'Chaucer and his Contemporaries': '1386 member of Parliament for the County of Kent' (Bodleian MS Tolkien A 21/4, fol. 14). Tolkien wrote on the next page: 'Chaucer living at Greenwich at time of Prologue.'

[51] 'In his *Envoy to Scogan*, written probably in 1393, he complains that while Scogan is living near to the source of favour (*at the stremes heed of grace*) he was living forgotten in a solitary wilderness at the end of the stream. A MS. note explains the head of the stream, Thames, as *Windesore* and the end as *Grenewich*.'

[52] John Matthew Manly, *Some New Light on Chaucer* (New York: Henry Holt, 1926), 26; see also 'Chaucer and Kent', 46–9.

[53] Tolkien provided a note on this word's occurrence in Chaucer's *Former Age* (p. 6): 'a striking example of the specially Kentish (South-Eastern) forms that are frequent in Chaucer.' Simon C. P. Horobin, 'Chaucer's Norfolk Reeve', *Neophilologus* 86 (2002), 609–12. In a private email Dr Horobin points out that Tolkien's Kentish forms could occur also in East Anglian.

His 1913 undergraduate essay had already made this argument about London English.[54] Although his glossary singled out only one instance of West Midland dialect—'**mury**, *Western form of* Mery'[55]—Tolkien was assiduous at recording Northern words. These were not regional variants assimilated into his own language, like Kentish, but rather outlandish words used for comical effect in the Reeve's Tale:

alswa, *adv.* also. *Northern.*
anes, once. *Northern for* Ones.
banes, *pl.* bones, RT 153 *Northern.*
bath, *Northern for* both. RT 167.
boes, it behoves. RT 107. *Northern.*
capul, *n.* horse. *Northern word.*
fra; *till and fra,* to and fro. *Northern.*
ga, *v.* go, RT 182. *Northern.*
gas, *3 sg.* goes, RT 117. *Northern.*
ham, *adv.* home. *Northern.*
hethen, *adv.* hence. *Northern.*
hething, *n.* contempt. *Northern.*
is, *v.* is; is it, there is, that is. *Northern uses* am, RT 111; art, 169.
lathe, *n.* barn. *Northern word.*
na, *adj.* no, RT 106, 214. *Northern.*
pit, *pp.* put, RT 168. *Northern.*
raa, *n.* roe-buck. *Northern. See* Roo.
sal, *Northern form of* shall, RT 123.
slik, *adj.* such, RT 210. *Northern.*
swa, so, RT 110, 120. *Northern.*
taa, *v.* take, RT 209. *Northern.*
twa, *adj.* two, RT 209. *Northern.*
waat, knows. *Northern for* Woot.
werkes, *v.* aches, RT 110. *Northern.*
whilk, *adj.* which. *Northern.*
y, *for* **i**, *Northern form of* in, RT 102.

Skeat noted most of these Northern forms but missed *capul, fra, ga, hething, twa,* and *werkes*, and therefore Tolkien, bettering his elder, made space to include them as separate entries and signal their dialect in italics. Not even the latest *Riverside Chaucer* records *slik*.

---

[54] MS Tolkien A 21/1, 'The Language of Chaucer', fols. 43–63: see Simon Horobin, *The Language of the Chaucer Tradition* (Cambridge: D. S. Brewer, 2003), 'Chaucer's Language and the London Dialect', 16–35.

[55] Tolkien's undergraduate essay on Chaucer's language had noted this Western form: 'Examples of dialectal variants / mery . merie . mury' (MS Tolkien A 21/1, fol. 43v).

Though Tolkien was already an accomplished typist by the 1920s, the OUP printer was clearly working from a handwritten draft. 'The compositors always make mistakes in setting from my handwriting!' Tolkien would later recall (*Letters*, 222). Thus *rob* had become *206* in the entry for '**reve**, *v.* 206', and Tolkien twice corrected *ironic* for the printer's *Doric*—as if Chaucer had introduced words from the Greek dialect spoken at Sparta![56] Irony is not something usually noted in glossaries, but Tolkien as an undergraduate had come to appreciate Chaucer as 'the most gently ironic poet of our tongue'.[57]

The printer never incorporated these corrections because Tolkien withheld the marked-up galleys, first wanting to insert references to his Notes and then to check entries against final revises of the Text. Such matters remained in flux as indicated by deletion of **prime** as a word appearing in the Nun's Priest's Tale. Why? Because Gordon and Sisam had dropped lines which might have shocked younger readers: 'He fethered Pertelote twenty tyme | And trad as ofte, er that it was *pryme*' (4367–8). This suggests Tolkien got a head start on his glossary-making before these offending lines had been deleted. His 1930 complaint to Sisam that his efforts had been 'disturbed by alteration in selection' suggests that he might even have begun when the Prioress's Tale was still included. He was often impetuous at starting projects even if delinquent about finishing them.

Galley 1, Copy 2

George Gordon quickly looked over this other copy date-stamped 2 MAY 1925 and jotted down a few changes. He queried the spelling of *farandaway* as a definition for **away** and suggested expanding the definition of **daun**. He sent back the first batch only five days after it had been mailed out and wasted little time glancing over the second batch before returning it to the Secretary's Office. Besides inserting a few commas, he suggested the entry for **gauded** needed clarifying and questioned whether **smoterlich** meant *smirched*. This copy was stamped 14 MAY 1925 upon its receipt at the Press with a handwritten note to Sisam: 'Hold till Tolkien returns his.' This, as it turned out, would never happen.

To sum up about the sections actually typeset for *Selections from Chaucer's Poetry and Prose*. The Text had been selected by George Gordon from Skeat's Oxford Chaucer and approved by Kenneth Sisam with some adjustments, notably replacement of the Prioress's Tale with a truncated version of the Reeve's Tale. These extracts were then typeset in page-proofs by December 1923, lightly

---

[56] '**gent**, *adj.* refined (*Doric*), PF 558' and '**halle**, *n.* hall; general place for household to eat and assemble; (*Doric*) NP 12.' Doric was also the popular name for Mid-Northern Scots, hence not such an absurd slip by the printer.
[57] Bodleian MS Tolkien A 21/4, fol. 15.

emended by Tolkien, and reset with the approval of Gordon and Sisam by June 1925. Tolkien compiled the Glossary in a handwritten manuscript, it was judged too long, he shortened it for Gordon and Sisam, and he received back the printed galleys in May 1925. He then began correcting mistakes and adjusting entries in light of work undertaken for the Notes. His galley sheets were never returned and never reset, however, as he wrestled with reducing the length of his annotations. Gordon skimmed through his own copy of the Glossary galleys and returned them to Sisam with a few superficial changes.

Thereafter in 1928 Tolkien sent his draft Notes to his co-editor for help with trimming them, but Gordon let the bundle gather dust for two years while Tolkien focused his attention on dialect issues in the Reeve's Tale. Meanwhile the print trays languished. Press Secretary R. W. Chapman had practical experience editing Jane Austen's novels as well as *Boswell's Notebooks*,[58] and he therefore showed little patience when writing to Gordon in 1931 about what should have been their straightforward student edition of Chaucer. Almost our last view of the printing process comes when Chapman writes again in 1936: 'The type has been standing for more than ten years.' The type-trays continued standing till melted down during the Second World War. Gordon's galley pages were inherited by Dan Davin in 1948, they were reunited with Tolkien's proofs and drafts in 1951, and the whole batch was joined by Gordon's leftover materials in 1956 when sent by his widow—all eventually stashed in the grey box in the cellar of Oxford University Press.

---

[58] L. F. Powell and M. Clare Loughlin-Chow, 'Chapman, Robert William (1881–1960)', *ODNB* 11:64–6.

5
The Chaucerian Incubus: The Notes

In October 1932, four years after halting work on his Clarendon edition, Tolkien wrote to Press Secretary R. W. Chapman about his hopes for future publishing projects—'if only I could free my mind and conscience of the Chaucerian incubus.' He meant the 160-page commentary that he was unable to shorten.[1] These excessive Notes now have considerable value for revealing the range of his linguistic, historical, and aesthetic engagements with Chaucer as a founding author of the English tradition when he himself still stood at the threshold of his own epoch-making literary career.

The word *incubus* has a distinctly Chaucerian resonance. The *OED* cites the Wife of Bath's Tale as one of the earliest attestations and offered as its first definition an evil spirit that descended upon sleepers especially seeking carnal intercourse with women—a sense altogether appropriate for Chaucer's lusty Alisoun.[2] The *OED*'s third definition comes closer to Tolkien's sense of something weighing him down and oppressing him like a nightmare. Tolkien probably knew that *incubus* was also the most widely used scholastic term for 'fairy'.[3] C. S. Lewis's *Discarded Image* included the Incubus in his list of supernatural figures from Reginald Scot's *Discouerie of Witchcraft* (1584), and he had already included Incubuses in his mob of monsters tormenting Aslan in *The Lion, The Witch, and the Wardrobe*.[4] When editors of the *OED*'s Second Supplement asked Tolkien about the origins of the word *hobbit*, he reported finding himself 'in a very tangled wood—the clue to which is, however, the belief in *incubi* and changelings' (*Letters*, 406n.). The word was also associated with sinister fairies waylaying their victims much as the Wood-elves did with Thorin Oakenshield and his companions. Mostly completed by the time Tolkien wrote to Chapman in 1932, *The Hobbit*'s Mirkwood episode could almost be read as an allegory for his own editorial impasse. Abandoned by the fatherly guide Gandalf (George Gordon), the stalwart Thorin (Tolkien)

---

[1] For the main body of Notes recovered from OUP archives, see Bodleian MS Tolkien A 39/2/1, fols. 6–71 (*Romaunt* to *Legend of Cleopatra*), and A 39/2/2, fols. 72–143 (*Legend of Cleopatra* to Reeve's Tale).

[2] Tolkien and Gordon, eds., *Sir Gawain and the Green Knight*, 115, mention how Geoffrey of Monmouth represented 'Merlin to be the son of a nun and an incubus'.

[3] Green, *Elf Queens*, 3, 16; see also his chapter 3, 'Incubi Fairies', 76–109.

[4] C. S. Lewis, *The Discarded Image: An Introduction to Medieval and Renaissance Literature* (Cambridge: Cambridge University Press, 1970), 125, and *The Lion, the Witch, and the Wardrobe* (1950; New York: HarperCollins, 1978), 151.

Tolkien's Lost Chaucer. John M. Bowers, Oxford University Press (2019). © John M. Bowers.
DOI: 10.1093/oso/9780198842675.001.0001

was held hostage by the king of the Wood-elves (the Chaucerian incubus of his annotations).

Because Walter W. Skeat included no explanatory notes in his *Student's Chaucer*, Kenneth Sisam always reckoned the commentary would be a strong selling point for *Selections from Chaucer's Poetry and Prose*. Tolkien was already teaching classes on the Prologue to the *Canterbury Tales* at Leeds and therefore had some notion of what undergraduates needed to have explained. Though the dates for Tolkien's drafts are not indicated, he was already considering the project by 1925 when compiling his Glossary and inserting *n*'s to direct readers to fuller explanations in the Notes. What Sisam had failed to consider was Tolkien's lack of proven talents for this particular assignment, since E. V. Gordon had annotated their *Gawain* edition and he himself had provided the commentary for *Fourteenth Century Verse and Prose*.

Tolkien's composition of the Notes seems to have followed what Carpenter described for the writing of *The Lord of the Rings*: 'Each chapter would begin with a scribbled and often illegible draft; then would come a rewriting in a fairer hand; and finally a typescript done on the Hammond machine.'[5] The Tolkien children retained a vivid memory of this contraption as 'a splendid-looking machine with twin castle-like turrets that operated the upper-case keys, and a wooden frame and lid which made it enormously heavy.'[6] The opening pages of his Chaucer commentary represent the third and final phase of this process, all neatly typed even with italics. Tolkien implied as much when writing to Dan Davin in 1951: 'the earlier items revised and reduced, the rest progressively in need of revision.' (See Fig. 1.) This transition began four pages into the *Parlement of Foules* where the typescript switched to fairly neat handwriting, some pages neater than others. And finally the commentary on the *Canterbury Tales* became sketchier until stopping halfway through the Reeve's Tale. What Christopher said of later writings applies also to his father's Chaucer commentary: 'The texts are never obviously concluded, and often end in chaotic and illegible or unintelligible notes and jottings.'[7]

The Notes offer all six challenges faced by anyone dealing with Tolkien's manuscripts.[8] Legibility: Tolkien's handwriting varies from very neat to unreadable. Reworking: he was a compulsive rewriter who sometimes composed two or three versions on the same page. Rolling revision: he made some changes while drafting and other changes at later dates. (My transcriptions reproduce ink revisions made during the initial writing, only occasionally the pencil changes

---

[5] *Biography*, 193; Carpenter reported seeing two typewriters in his garage office when he visited Tolkien at home in 1967; see also SH 2:261–7 'Composition'. Tolkien wrote in 1964 that 'I like typewriters' and hoped for an electric one that could produce Fëanorian script.

[6] *Tolkien Family Album*, 72. The machine had interchangeable typefaces on a revolving disc to produce Old English þ and æ as well as italics.

[7] J. R. R. Tolkien, *The Peoples of Middle-Earth*, ed. Christopher Tolkien (Boston and New York: Houghton Mifflin, 1996), 'Late Writings', 294.

[8] Lee, 'Manuscripts', in *Companion*, ed. Lee, 62–5.

inserted later.) Lost material: Tolkien, though something of a packrat, did discard prior drafts no longer useful. Dating: the timeline becomes a matter of guesswork in the absence of external evidence like OUP date-stamps. Foliation: this problem has been remedied with the transfer of the materials to the Bodleian Library where archivist Catherine McIlwaine has sorted the drafts into booklets and assigned page numbers. Collections: pages had been shuffled and some sections separated, notably his commentary on the *Parlement of Foules* which he removed for teaching purposes in late 1940s and never returned.[9] Christopher reported a more extensive muddle with *TLOR* manuscripts, some of them accidentally remaining in England while most were shipped to Wisconsin after their purchase by Marquette University.[10]

We know these draft annotations reached a stopping point by 1928 when they disappeared for a two-year limbo with co-editor George Gordon. Once returned, his five pages of comments sound much like Chaucer's Franklin condescending to the younger Squire: 'I have gone on and finished my reading of your notes, as far as they go.'[11] Gordon's reference to brackets inserted to signal possible excisions does answer one question about dating. Whoever added these brackets, whether Tolkien or David Nichol Smith or both, had done the work before 1928 when Gordon took delivery.

Sisam was not losing hope, only patience: 'you will have to decide on less notes than an ordinary school edition.' By the time Gordon returned the draft annotations at the end of 1930, however, Tolkien had other distractions. In addition to faculty and college duties, he was writing his *Father Christmas Letter* while drafting the earliest versions of *Annals of Valinor* and *Annals of Beleriand*. He had joined the Council of the Philological Society and invested considerable work on a lecture delivered to its members at Oxford in May 1931—'Chaucer's Use of Dialects'—which would be published three years later as 'Chaucer as a Philologist'. Tolkien probably considered this hefty article on the Reeve's Tale as an extension of work on his Chaucer edition, not yet an admission of defeat.

Anne Middleton has written smartly about the mundane-looking labour of annotating a medieval text, an undertaking which, like editing itself, functions as an act of literary restoration. In keeping with the philologist's grand mission of rescuing what has been lost, an editorial commentary bridges historical gaps and explains what modern readers would not otherwise know. With her hands-on experience of annotating *Piers Plowman*, Middleton found much more in an operation which otherwise seems so workaday that its critical intentions might pass largely unnoticed:

> In each of its minute iterations, annotation theorizes the entire text to which it is nominally in service, while in no single place is it forced out from underground to

---

[9] These notes on Chaucer's *Parlement* survive separately in Bodleian MS Tolkien A 38/2, fols. 96–126, the first two pages added when Tolkien began lecturing on the work in January 1948 (SH 1:348).

[10] Tolkien, *Return of the Shadow*, 1.   [11] Bodleian MS Tolkien A 39/2/1, fols. 1–5.

acknowledge this dimension of its enterprise, which it presents on each occasion as merely an ordinary practical activity, a modest attestation that a working public utility is indeed working as it should for the general benefit.[12]

Looking back over his career in 1959, Tolkien reckoned that he was singularly equipped for the job: 'I would always rather try to wring the juice out of a single sentence, or explore the implications of one word, than try to sum up a period in a lecture, or pot a poet in a paragraph' (*Essays*, 224). He had anticipated this claim allegorically in *Leaf by Niggle* when describing his hero: 'He used to spend a long time on a single leaf, trying to catch its shape, its sheen, and the glistening of dewdrops on its edges.'[13] With Middleton's caveats in mind, we readily spot two considerations that Tolkien excluded from his Clarendon annotations: (1) Chaucer's fourteenth-century England as literary context and (2) Chaucer the man. Skeat's 1894 *Works* provided a gigantic amount of historical and biographical information which Tolkien largely ignored while wringing the juice out of single words.

The challenge of his Chaucer annotations came in limiting the amount of juice. After compiling concise notes for his own *Verse and Prose*, Sisam appreciated how prudently Skeat had resisted the counsels of perfection: 'If he had waited until everything was cleared up to his satisfaction, we should have been without a major Chaucer.'[14] Tolkien found it difficult to resist these temptations, however, still proposing new emendations long after his Chaucer text had been corrected and re-typeset.[15] The counsels of perfection would steadily dog all future plans for publication.

Tolkien's section 'Introduction on Language' was probably drafted as a preamble to his Notes (see Appendix I) where he stated that his comments on words 'have been necessarily limited to specially hard cases'. He loved minutiae, and his annotations compensated for cuts in the Glossary by discussing hard cases such as *overthwert* in the *Book of the Duchess*—'Therto hir look nas not asyde | Ne *overthwert*, but beset so wel' (862–3):

> This is usually translated 'askance' here, but this sense is given by *asyde*. The lady's chief merit is her *mesure* (881), she steered the golden middle course between all extremes. *overthwert* is then the exact opposite of *asyde*, and refers to a bold and challenging stare straight in the eye. The original sense of the word and its other form *thwertover* is 'at right angles' the opposite of *endelong* (cf. the Knight's Tale 1133), and it is especially used of the arms of a cross; it thus got the sense of going clean contrary to any one, right across one's path, and is used

---

[12] Anne Middleton, 'Life in the Margins, or What's an Annotator to Do?', *New Directions in Textual Studies*, ed. Dave Oliphant and Robin Bradford (Austin: University of Texas Press, 1990), 167–83 at p. 169.
[13] Tolkien, *Leaf by Niggle*, in *Poems and Stories*, 195.
[14] Letter to R. W. Chambers quoted by Brewer, *Editing 'Piers Plowman'*, 105.
[15] He added this note in the finished text of *The Book of the Duchess* (836) at some later date: 'This is a feeble line metrically. Possibly *espied hadde* is nearer to what Chaucer wrote.'

figuratively of flat contradiction or the 'lie direct' (*þweartouer leasinge* in the Ancren Riwle). In the Romance of the Rose 292 f. *for she (Envy) ne loked but awry, or overthwart, al baggingly* there is certainly no question of Envy looking anything but askance, but this is due to bad translation of *ele ne regardast noient fors de travers en borgnoisant*. Two translations, as it were, are offered of *de travers* of which only *awry* is in this case right, though in some cases *overthwert* would be good enough.   (Bodleian MS Tolkien A 39/2/1, fol. 22)

An extended note of this sort could become a miniature essay, and once Tolkien invested time and energy in one of these philological forays, he had real difficulty considering it for excision.

Shippey has rightly observed that Tolkien's notes in his completed editions have been overlooked as a critical resource:

> These data of course come very often in the form of glosses, comments on single words, and are not formed into connected arguments; but as I have said again and again, that is the way Tolkien's mind worked. Nor is the activity of the glossator (which is what Tolkien started as) to be despised.[16]

My following sections focus only upon those notes which offer special insights into his enterprises as poet, translator, and especially fiction-writer. I have done no justice to the bulk of his commentary on individual words. A specialist on Chaucer's language would write a completely different book. Although Tolkien insisted that delving into an author's life revealed little of the workings of his mind (*Biography*, 127), his Chaucer commentaries do provide steady insights into his own creative imagination. If Goethe described his literary output as 'fragments of a great confession' and Nietzsche thought a philosophy was an 'unconscious memoir', Christopher believes that his father's ceaseless construction of an imaginary world made *The History of Middle-earth* into 'a record of his life, a form of biography'.[17] So why cannot the Oxford professor's scholarly writings provide another version of autobiography? Tolkien's adaptations from Skeat's 420 pages of commentary, taken together with his own excursions into particular words, contribute richly to the mosaic of this literary life.

I. *The Romaunt of the Rose*

Tolkien began his commentary with three typewritten pages on lines 21–134 from Fragment A of Chaucer's *Romaunt* (Fig. 9).[18] Since he was a two-finger typist who did

---

[16] Shippey, 'Introduction', in *Roots and Branches*, p. iv.
[17] Tolkien, *Peoples of Middle-Earth*, p. x. *Letters*, 52–3, provided a rare instance of 'autobiography' when Tolkien described to his son Michael his courtship and marriage to Edith.
[18] Bodleian MS Tolkien A 39/2/1, fols. 6–8.

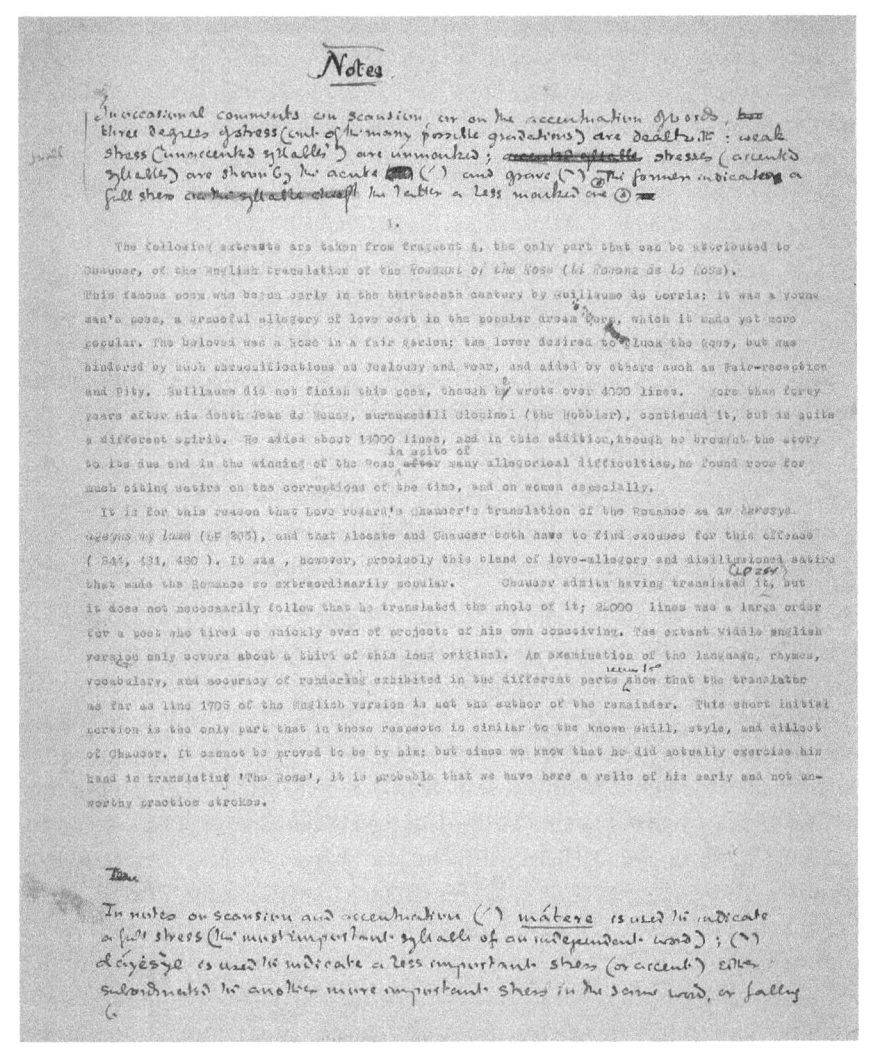

Fig. 9. Tolkien's typed commentary on Chaucer's *Romaunt* (Oxford, Bodleian Library, MS Tolkien A 39/2/1, fol. 6).

not normally compose at the keyboard, he probably started with handwritten drafts, now lost.[19] Rayner Unwin recalled that the manuscript of *The Hobbit* arrived in their publishing offices as a single-spaced typescript much like these pages.[20] Impressively,

---

[19] Composing *Farmer Giles* and *Smith of Wootton Major* at the typewriter departed from Tolkien's normal practice; see *Biography*, 244, and SH 3:1215–16. Christopher reported that other late writings were drafted at the keyboard; see *Peoples of Middle-Earth*, 294.

[20] Unwin, 'Publishing Tolkien', 73.

his machine produced italics when citing titles like the *Romaunt of the Rose* (*li Romanz de la Rose*).

At some point after completing these typed pages, he realized that newcomers to Middle English needed guidance on pronunciation, and so he wrote out longhand at the bottom of the page a short section which began 'In notes on scansion and accentuation...'. Not satisfied, he inserted at the top of the page a new section which began 'In occasional comments on scansion, or on accentuation of words...'. Still not satisfied, he turned over the page and filled most of the reverse side with a much longer handwritten description of Chaucer's language: 'In notes on accentuation and scansion (´) indicates a stressed syllable...'. Here we see in miniature Tolkien's habit of revising his work by setting aside a prior version and starting anew.[21]

On the question of the French poem's dual authorship, he transmits Skeat's information that the continuator of the *Rose* was Jean de Meung, 'surnamed li Clompinel (the Hobbler)'. For those looking for subconscious inspirations for the word *hobbit* in the later 1920s, here is another entry for the list of possibilities.[22] It is noteworthy that hobbits were by nature continuators like the Hobbler. Frodo continued Bilbo's *There and Back Again*, Sam Gamgee continued Frodo's *History of the War of the Ring*, Peregrin produced a version containing material otherwise missing or lost, and Meriadoc supplemented these accounts with treatises such as *Old Words and Names in the Shire* (FR Pro). Tolkien's Epilogue, later cancelled, pictured Sam 'struggling to finish off the Red Book, begun by Bilbo and nearly completed by Frodo.'[23] Like the thirteenth-century Hobbler whose 18,000-line completion dwarfed the original 4,000-line fragment by Guillaume de Lorris, these hobbits produced continuations that eventually overshadowed Bilbo's original story in *The Hobbit*.

Recognition of the historical importance of the *Roman de la Rose* increased after C. S. Lewis's lectures in 1928, prepared no doubt as background for his chapter on this French dream-vision in *The Allegory of Love*, but Tolkien already knew Chaucer's *Romaunt* well enough to cite it in his *Gawain* edition.[24] Here he summarized the love-allegory succinctly: 'The beloved was a Rose in a fair garden; the lover desired to pluck the Rose, but was hindered by such personifications as Jealousy and Fear.' How deeply did this story lodge in the editor's memory? On the slopes of Mount Doom where the jealous Gollum and the fearsome Nazgûls have hindered him, Sam Gamgee conceives a love-quest homeward to his own Rose. Unlike the film adaptation which showed Sam mooning over the barmaid in

---

[21] *Biography*, 143, quotes C. S. Lewis on Tolkien's habits of revision.
[22] Marjorie Burns, 'Tracking the Elusive Hobbit (in Pre-Shire Den)', *Tolkien Studies* 4 (2007), 200–11.
[23] Tolkien, *Sauron Defeated*, 132.
[24] Tolkien and Gordon, eds., *Sir Gawain and the Green Knight*, 81, also alludes to Chaucer's Prologue to the *Legend of Good Women*.

the opening scenes, Tolkien's story did not introduce the name of Rose Cotton until this late point in *The Return of the King*. Only after their quest to destroy the Ring did Sam pursue his own 'romance of the Rose' back to the Shire.[25]

Tolkien's commentary served as a reminder that Chaucer started his career as an English translator. As if to align himself with this precedent, Tolkien provided a lengthy gloss on a line not noticed by Skeat—'With gravel, ful of stones shene' (127)—by quoting a whole stanza from his own *Pearl* translation:

> *The adornment of that wondrous deep*
> *Was blissful banks of beryl bright;*
> *In swirling music the waters sweep*
> *Ever faring on in murmurous flight.*
> *There stones were dazzling in its deep*
> *Like glint through glass a-gleaming light,*
> *Like the streaming stars when strong men sleep*
> *That stare in the welkin in winter night;*
> *For emerald, sapphire, and chrysolite*
> *Was every pebble in pool there pent,*
> *So that all was lit with liquid light,*
> *Such wealth was in its wonderment.*[26]

Even George Gordon roused himself to remark: 'A jolly note, but can *The Pearl* here be justified against the limits of space?'[27] The image of pebbles at the bottom of a clear stream nevertheless exercised a strong appeal, one that even Lewis could not resist in his own dream-vision *The Great Divorce*.[28]

Chaucerian translation remained one of Tolkien's key concerns. He disapproved the use of French as a literary language in England after 1066 and indeed deplored the imposition of any imported language: 'Literature shrivels in a universal language, and an uprooted language rots before it dies.'[29] Nonetheless his notes drew steady attention to Chaucer's renderings from Latin and Italian as well as his ongoing debt to the French *Rose*. 'A translation may be a useful form of commentary', Christopher quoted his father in his 1975 *Sir Gawain and the Green Knight, Pearl, and Sir Orfeo*; 'a translator must first try to discover as precisely as he can what his original means, and may be led by ever closer attention to understand it better for its own sake' (p. viii). Thus Chaucer stood as a

---

[25] Tolkien valued this plotline: 'I think the simple "rustic" love of Sam and his Rosie (nowhere elaborated) *is absolutely essential* to the study of his (the chief hero's) character' (*Letters*, 161).

[26] This early version differs in nearly every line from the later one published in *Sir Gawain and the Green Knight, Pearl, and Sir Orfeo* (1975), 127; see SH 3:976–8 on the long history of the *Pearl* translation.

[27] Bodleian MS Tolkien A 39/2/1, fol. 2.

[28] Robert Boenig, *C. S. Lewis and the Middle Ages* (Kent, OH: Kent State University Press, 2012), 102–3.

[29] Tolkien, 'Philology' (1927), 59.

role-model for Tolkien's verse translation of *Pearl* as novice work for honing his own poetical craft. 'English is an instrument of very great capacity and resources', he learned in some measure by closely studying Chaucer; 'it has long experience not yet forgotten, and deep roots in the past not yet all pulled up' (SH 3:999). Tolkien in his commentary on *Truth* would cite the French poet Deschamps's commendation to the *grant translateur, noble Geffrey Chaucier*, and it is therefore apt that his longtime collaborator Simonne d'Ardenne would honour him with the same phrase *grant translateur* in the 1979 memorial volume.[30] Because Tolkien understood that poetic craft required an apprenticeship, he praised Chaucer's *Romaunt* as 'a relic of his early and not unworthy practice strokes'.

When Skeat failed to mention the *Romaunt*'s references to the herbs mint and fennel, Tolkien again recalled the anonymous English dream-vision. 'At the beginning of *The Pearl* there is a mound "*with gilly-flower (cloves), ginger, and gromwell crowned, and peonies powdered all between*"...'.[31] Thereafter his commentary seldom missed an opportunity to expound upon plants such as *hertes reste* in the *Legend* Prologue:

> 'heart's ease' (Chaucer also uses *hertes eese*). This, it is interesting to note, became a flower-name, recorded from the 16th century as a name of the wallflower and pansy. It is quite possible that it was a flower-name in the 14th century. Why the name was given is unknown. It is probably due to the same sort of gentle sentiment that we have here (genuine doubtless, even if others had praised the daisy first). (Bodleian MS Tolkien A 39/2/1, fol. 68)

Tolkien's mother taught him some botany as a boy, it was a required subject at King Edward's School, and years later Lewis marvelled at his friend's almost idolatrous love of flowers as well as trees.[32] When asked late in life what book influenced him as a teenager, he replied that his most treasured volume had been *Flowers of the Field* by C. A. Johns.[33] He was a frequent visitor to Oxford's Botanic Garden, and his 1927 entry for *The Year's Work in English Studies* used this analogy for a philologist's responsibilities: 'a man who tells us the names of plants as we walk with him does not rid himself of all responsibility for misinforming us by saying he is no botanist.'[34] Nor was he alone in the family; his aunt Jane Neave went 'botanizing' in Switzerland before the age of 90 (*Letters*, 308). It is therefore noteworthy that Bilbo's fondness for flowers marked him out early as an

---

[30] S. T. R. O. d'Ardenne, 'The Man and the Scholar', in Salu and Farrell, eds., *Tolkien: Scholar and Storyteller*, 33–7 at p. 36. She made a point of remembering her mentor specifically as a Chaucerian (p. 35). See SH 2:290–2.

[31] Stefan Ekman, 'Echoes of *Pearl* in Arda's Landscape', *Tolkien Studies* 6 (2009), 59–70, shows how Tolkien never forgot the poem's natural beauties.

[32] *The Times* obituary was reprinted in Salu and Farrell, eds., *Tolkien, Scholar and Storyteller*, 11–15 at p. 12; see also *Biography*, 163.

[33] McIlwaine, *Tolkien: Maker of Middle-earth*, 198.

[34] Tolkien, 'Philology' (1927), 59.

exceptional hobbit. A whole book could be written about plants in Tolkien's fiction—and indeed Dinah Hazell has done so.[35]

As one of the great landscape writers in our tradition, Tolkien had learned much from the *Gawain* Poet about woodlands, but it was from Chaucer that he drew inspiration for flowers. Later in the *Legend* Prologue, he explained about Queen Alceste transformed into a daisy: 'Classical mythology, especially as known from the *Metamorphoses* of Ovid, provided plenty of suggestive parallels.' Then he included a note about how Cybele originally created the daisy: '*Cybele*, the Phrygian Mother Goddess, of the earth and of fertility. Producing flowers is thus properly attributed to her; her functions were similar to those of the Latin *Ceres*.' Lore of these mother-figures probably lurks somewhere behind legends of the vanished Entwives: 'The Elves made many songs concerning the Search of the Ents, and some of the songs passed into the tongues of Men' (*TT* III/4).[36]

The *Roman de la Rose* was the most influential dream-vision of the late medieval period, and Tolkien already knew the genre intimately from teaching the Old English *Dream of the Rood* and editing as well as translating *Pearl*. Chaucer would follow the French vogue for dream poetry in his *Book of the Duchess*, while the Nun's Priest's Tale, the final selection of the Clarendon Chaucer, included an extended debate over the validity of dreams as predictors of future events.[37] Tolkien remarked how the *Parlement of Foules* provided 'a summary neither very interesting nor very well done' of Macrobius' commentary on Cicero's *Somnium Scipionis*—the chief authority for all medieval dream-lore—but he did not reject these longstanding categories of dream interpretation.[38] Even before Freud's *Interpretation of Dreams*, Andrew Lang had published his psychical research in *The Book of Dreams and Ghosts* (1897), and Tolkien acknowledged the allure of this tradition in his Lang Lecture: 'In dreams strange powers of the mind may be unlocked' (*Essays*, 116).

Nor was this tradition neglected in his own works. In *The Hobbit*, for example, Bilbo's dream of the cave floor cracking open became a vivid warning of the goblin attack. By one count, there are forty-six references to dreams in *The Lord of the Rings*, and this number rises to nearly a hundred when including visions of other sorts.[39] The chapter 'In the House of Tom Bombadil' tells how the four hobbits experience a variety of dreams recognizable from the centuries-old categories of

---

[35] *The Plants of Middle-earth: Botany and Sub-creation* (Kent, OH: Kent State University Press, 2006).

[36] Corey Olsen, 'The Myth of the Ent and the Entwife', *Tolkien Studies* 5 (2008), 39–53.

[37] Rateliff, *Story of The Hobbit*, 'Bilbo's Dreams', 147, attributes these features to Tolkien's work on the Nun's Priest's Tale.

[38] Tolkien had no fondness for the Roman orator. 'My love for the classics', he once said, 'took ten years to recover from lectures on Cicero' (Salu and Farrell, eds., *Tolkien: Scholar and Storyteller*, 12).

[39] Sean Lindsay, 'The Dream System in *The Lord of the Rings*', *Mythlore*, 13, no. 3 (1987), 7–14 at pp. 10–14, and Amy M. Amendt-Raduege, 'Dream Vision in J. R. R. Tolkien's *The Lord of the Rings*', *Tolkien Studies* 3 (2006), 45–55 at p. 47.

Macrobius (*FR* I/7).[40] Nightmares inspired by recent events (*insomnium*) befall Pippin and Merry, the one dreaming of Old Man Willow again attacking them and the other, with the noise of rain outside, fearing that he will drown in the Withywindle. Tolkien remarked on the *Parlement*: 'This is the class of dreams called ἐνύπνιον in Macrobius' commentary, dreaming about things that occupy the waking mind.' For his part, Frodo has a revelatory dream (*oraculum*) in which he sees Gandalf trapped on the top of a high tower until he is rescued by the Eagles. Tolkien's Introduction to *Pearl* recalled 'a period when men, aware of the vagaries of dreams, still thought that amid their japes came visions of truth'[41]—in Frodo's case, the truth of Gandalf's imprisonment on the top of Orthanc.

The chapter 'Fog on the Barrow-downs' begins with their final night under Tom Bombadil's roof when Frodo experiences what Macrobius termed a prophetic vision (*visio*) in which he sees pale light behind a curtain of grey rain until turning to glass and silver (*FR* I/8). This dream will be confirmed as true prophecy when he does finally approach the Undying Land (*RK* VI/9). Merry's dream might also have been a *visio* looking forward to his encounter with the Black Rider outside the *Prancing Pony* where he loses consciousness and thinks he had fallen into deep water. Tolkien's efforts at annotating Chaucer's visionary poems, in short, reinforced his appreciation for the dream's role in the literary tradition, including the work by another Oxford don—'Lewis Carroll's *Alice* stories with their dream-frame and dream-transitions' (*Essays*, 117). What Tolkien neglected in his own fiction was Macrobius' *somnium* or truth veiled in allegorical form, probably because of his oft-repeated dislike of allegory.

The French *Rose* had also secularized and eroticized the image of the *hortus conclusus* from the Song of Songs (4:12) which for centuries had been interpreted as an image of the Virgin Mary. Even when real walled-in gardens became luxury retreats for the wealthy, as Chaucer described in the Merchant's Tale, they routinely had at their centre a fountain like the Well of Narcissus at the end of Fragment A of Chaucer's *Romaunt* (1462–1659). There the Dreamer looks into the silvery 'mirour perilous' and sees the rosebud for which he conceives an ardent desire. These long-established ingredients would find their way into the Lothlórien episode where Galadriel, in some ways a Marian figure of compassion and mercy, leads Frodo and Sam into her own 'enclosed garden' where there was a 'fountain on the hill' providing water for the silver mirror. In it, the two hobbits glimpse visions fuelling their desire to go forward on their quest (*FR* II/7). Of course Tolkien knew these ingredients from many medieval texts, but his close

---

[40] Lewis, *The Discarded Image*, 60–9, provided a section on Macrobius.
[41] *Pearl*, ed. E. V. Gordon (Oxford: Clarendon Press, 1953), p. xv; this anonymous introduction is reprinted in his *Pearl* translation volume, pp. 10–19. Lewis, *Discarded Image*, 54, notes that Chalcidius added *revelatio* to the better known classifications of Macrobius and Chaucer recalled it in his *House of Fame*.

work with Chaucer's *Rose* provided him with a literary precedent firmly established within the English tradition from the fourteenth century onward.

II. *Compleinte unto Pité*

Already pushing against Sisam's limits, Tolkien's commentary on the 119-line *Compleinte unto Pité* covers four and a quarter typed pages and begins with a rejection of any true biographical contents: 'we may feel certain that the love was literary, not real.'[42] Later he remarks about the unreality of the lady herself: 'Pity is addressed in the conventional manner of a lover petitioning his mistress. Most of the last two stanzas are only applicable to the lady in whose heart pity is lying dead and not to Pity at all.' His unhappiness with Chaucer's trite handling of Pité looks forward to the centrality of the virtue in *The Lord of the Rings*. When Frodo says it was a pity that Bilbo did not kill Gollum, Gandalf quickly replies, 'Pity? It was Pity that stayed his hand.' (Notice how Tolkien himself capitalizes and personifies Pity.) As the wizard further reflects upon the mercy shown to the creature, he muses that 'the pity of Bilbo may rule the fate of many—yours not least' (*FR* I/2), and in the long trajectory of the plot, the Ring is destroyed only because Gollum bites it from Frodo's finger. If not for Bilbo's pity, in short, Frodo's quest would have failed. Tolkien reflected after publication that 'the "salvation" of the world and Frodo's own "salvation" is achieved by his previous *pity* and forgiveness of injury.'[43] Already in the 1920s he sensed that the virtue *pité* deserved better than Chaucer's clumsy, artificial treatment.

Tolkien proceeded to an explanation and an apology. First he explained how this lyric introduced into the English poetic tradition the seven-line stanza known as rhyme royal because King James I of Scotland used it in his *Kingis Quair*. 'Rhyme Trojan would be a better name', he wryly suggested, because 'the most remarkable example of its use is Chaucer's *Troilus and Criseyde*.' It is not an easy verse-form to master, as C. S. Lewis discovered when using it for his poem *Dymer* (1926). Then came Tolkien's apology that their Clarendon edition included no extracts from *Troilus* because its 'length and excellence forbade its being laid under piecemeal contribution to the present selection'. He greatly admired Chaucer's tragic love-story set against the backdrop of the Trojan War, and, as we shall see in Chapter 7, the lovers Troilus and Criseyde provided inspiration for the happy-ending romance of Faramir and Éowyn set against the backdrop of the War of the Ring. *Troilus* would assert influences small as well as large. In *The Hobbit* when Bilbo looks down from his flight with the Eagles and sees the 'little

---

[42] Bodleian MS Tolkien A 39/2/1, fols. 9–13. See Douglas Gray, 'Chaucer and *Pite*', in Salu and Farrell, eds., *Tolkien: Scholar and Storyteller*, 173–203.

[43] *Letters*, 234. See SH 3:989–94 'Pity and Mercy'.

spot of earth', Tolkien was recalling how Troilus looked down from the eighth sphere and saw the 'litel spot of erthe' (5.1815).[44]

Next Tolkien voiced one of his pet peeves: 'The allegory of this poem does not bear close examination. Chaucer has not worked it out well—it was hardly worth it.' Lewis would agree in *The Allegory of Love* that this lyric illustrates 'the use of personification at its lowest level—the most faint and frigid result of the popularity of allegory' (p. 167). Tolkien's *Pearl* Introduction would apply strict standards for allegorical writing: 'its entire narrative and all its significant details should cohere and work together to this end' (p. xii). Later he was furious when the Swedish translator interpreted *The Lord of the Rings* as an allegory of contemporary politics (*Biography*, 228), and C. S. Lewis joined this rejection by classifying it as the sort of myth discussed in his friend's lecture 'On Fairy-Stories': 'Into an allegory a man can put only what he already knows; in a myth he puts what he does not yet know and could not come by in any other way.'[45]

Tolkien's 1965 Foreword favoured the term *applicability* instead of allegory. Readers were free to exercise their own critical faculties, that is, rather than accepting the author's single predetermined meaning. If this appeal to the reader's freedom sounds somewhat like what Jean-Paul Sartre proposed in *What Is Literature?*, we have only to recall that Lewis read Sartre and Tolkien showed himself no stranger to these contemporary writers when citing Simone de Beauvoir in his 1968 BBC interview.[46] As early champions of allegory, Augustine and Dante permitted multiple meanings to arise out of a story's literal sense, and therefore Tolkien was simply following a long-established tradition when allowing for a range of applications. Because Chaucer's *Pité* enforced an obvious this-means-that equation, Tolkien readily dismissed its 'tottering allegory' and 'flimsy fabric of the allegory'.

For Tolkien personally, another problem with allegory was its longstanding linkage with Catholicism. C. S. Lewis put the matter bluntly in *The Allegory of Love*: 'all allegories whatever are likely to seem Catholic to the general reader' (p. 322). Evelyn Waugh's *Brideshead Revisited* attested to bigotry against Catholics at the university and in English society at large in the 1920s, and Tolkien, mindful how much his mother suffered for her faith, was always cautious about not being so identified.[47] His Exeter College report card branded him as 'R.C.' for Roman Catholic,[48] and his physician R. E. Havard, when he converted as a student, was

---

[44] His 1915 tutorial essay 'Chaucer: Troilus & Cressida' (MS Tolkien A 21/7, fols. 1–7) showed he was even aware of the manuscripts used by Skeat when editing his Oxford Chaucer.

[45] *Letters of C. S. Lewis*, ed. W. H. Lewis, 271.

[46] Renée Vink, 'Immortality and the Death of Love: J. R. R Tolkien and Simone de Beauvoir', in *The Ring Goes Ever On: Proceedings of the Tolkien 2005 Conference*, ed. Sarah Wells, 2 vols. (Coventry: Tolkien Society, 2008), 2:117–27. See *Letters of C. S. Lewis*, ed. W. H. Lewis, 297–8, on his own reading of Sartre as 'a great rhetorician'.

[47] See Edwards, *Tolkien*, 'Appendix—Tolkien the Catholic', 291–9.

[48] McIlwaine, *Tolkien: Maker of Middle-earth*, 144–5; the sub-rector added 'v. lazy' immediately after 'R.C.'.

forced to switch to Queen's College because Keble barred Catholics. Twentieth-century Christians often felt threatened, as Tolkien hinted parenthetically in his *Beowulf* lecture—'A Christian was (and is) still like his forefathers a mortal hemmed in a hostile world' (*Essays*, 22)—and Tolkien sometimes endured rude remarks like the one about the election of a Rector for Lincoln College: 'Thank heaven they did not elect a Roman Catholic' (*Letters*, 84). Even his fellow Christians among the Inklings harboured prejudice. Hugo Dyson was not alone in objecting to the Catholic underpinnings of *The Lord of the Rings* and even objected to J. A. W. Bennett joining them because he was Catholic.[49] C. S. Lewis felt no compunction about referring to Irish Catholics as 'bog rats',[50] and later, when admitting that Tolkien had broken down old prejudices, he kept using the pejorative term *Papist* into the 1950s.[51] Tolkien remarked to his son Michael as late as 1968, 'Has it ever been mentioned that Roman Catholics still suffer from disabilities not even applicable to Jews?' (*Letters*, 395).

From Leeds onward, therefore, Tolkien avoided dealing with religious texts such as *Piers Plowman* despite his fondness for its Worcester dialect—'Any corner of that county (however fair or squalid) is in an indefinable way "home" to me' (*Biography*, 27)—because these discussions would have required dealing with Langland's theological allegories. Though *Gawain* mentioned sacramental rituals in passing, Tolkien let his Catholicism show only late in his career when suggesting the story's whole meaning hinged upon Gawain's confession prior to rendezvousing with the Green Knight.[52] Early when staking out his scholarly projects, the Arthurian myths underlying *Gawain* proved problematic for him because they contained explicitly Christian elements (*Letters*, 144). This avoidance of religious discussions may partly explain why he balked at completing his edition of *Pearl* with its doctrinal debates; he even asked that his name not appear on its title-page when the edition was finally published in 1953. His work on texts like *Hali Meiðhad* focused exclusively upon language, not religious contents, and he faced years of difficulties finishing his EETS edition of *Ancrene Wisse*, a thirteenth-century manual for anchoresses. He provided no critical introduction when it finally appeared in 1962, only a three-page prefatory note on his transcription of the manuscript.[53]

Tolkien's career focused instead upon more secular-looking works like *Beowulf*, and he remarked about his own *Smith of Wootton Major*, 'As usual there is

---

[49] Dyson was often a disruptive presence at these gatherings. SH 2:321–2 includes the famous report, perhaps apocryphal, of how he reacted to Tolkien's reading by snorting, 'Oh, fuck, not another elf!'
[50] Carpenter, *Inklings*, 51–2, recounts Tolkien's reaction to the anti-Catholic bias.
[51] *Surprised by Joy*, 216.   [52] *Essays*, 87, and SH 3:1199–200 'Ker Lecture'.
[53] See Chance, *Tolkien, Self and Other*, 185–9, on this edition's troubled history. Donaldson, 'The Psychology of Editors', 116, notes how an editor's basic instinct for invisibility verges upon the wish for non-existence—'the state where the editor does not even claim to edit; he just transcribes'—which nicely describes Tolkien's desire for invisibility as editor of *Ancrene Wisse*.

no "religion" in the story.'[54] But he was not completely candid and elsewhere confided to Fr. Robert Murray, grandson of the *OED*'s founding editor: '*The Lord of the Rings* is of course a fundamentally religious and Catholic work; unconsciously so at first, but consciously in the revision.' He went on to explain: 'That is why I have not put in, or have cut out, practically all references to anything like "religion", to cults or practices, in the imaginary world.'[55] Not all readers were placated, and some reviewers reacted hostilely even if the anti-Catholic grounds for this hostility were not overtly expressed.[56]

The Clarendon Chaucer triggered none of these inhibitions because it included love lyrics, courtly dream-visions, philosophy, and even a scientific manual, but none of the poet's religious works like the Second Nun's Tale of St Cecilia. One of Tolkien's undergraduate jottings made this important distinction: 'Chaucer is insensitive of religion rather than irreligious.'[57] Even his elegy *Book of the Duchess* lacked any hint of Christian consolation, while the pagan settings of *Troilus* and the Knight's Tale automatically excluded Christian elements. The boisterous Canterbury pilgrims at the Tabard Inn almost immediately forget their destination at the shrine of St Thomas Becket (not named) once they are distracted by the tale-telling competition. Tolkien's note on the Prioress's rosary beads provided the rare departure with its catechism-sounding instructions: 'The complete devotion consists of reciting the fifty-five prayers twice, meditating successively upon the Five Joyful Mysteries (one to each decade, e.g. the Annunciation, Visitation, Nativity etc); the Five Sorrowful Mysteries (e.g. the Agony in the Garden); the Five Glorious Mysteries (e.g. the Resurrection).' In 1944 he wrote to Christopher recommending the 'praises' in Latin as a source of personal comfort (*Letters*, 66), but this openness about Catholic devotion was little evidenced outside the family circle.

His habitual dodge in *Compleinte unto Pité* was to focus instead upon language. Corruption of the proper name *Herenus* for the Furies prompted reflection on such aberrations:

> The strange forms taken by Classical names in Middle English are sometimes confusing, sometimes charming. They are the product of actual alteration in pronunciation (French), increased by the transference to English, and at the mercy throughout their traditions of mere letter confusion in the copying, not to speak of deliberate variation to make them look more natural or more pleasant or more convenient to the poet.

This vulnerability would encourage Tolkien as an author to provide diacritical marks to safeguard the pronunciation of names such as Éowyn and Lothlórien.

---

[54] *Biography*, 245; see SH 3:1075–84 'Religion in Tolkien's Writings'.
[55] *Letters*, 172; see Pat Pinsent, 'Religion: An Implicit Catholicism', in *Companion*, ed. Lee, 446–60.
[56] Shippey, *Author of the Century*, 309.   [57] Bodleian MS Tolkien A 21/4, fol. 10v.

Since he pronounced his own last name with the accent on the second syllable, but often heard others stress the first syllable, he was perhaps unusually sensitive to the correct pronunciation of proper names overall.[58]

III. *The Book of the Duchess*

Gordon had selected 363 of the 1,334 lines from the *Book of the Duchess* and divided them into three sections entitled 'Proem' (44–216), 'Dream of the Hunt' (291–386), and 'Lover's Portrait of his Lady' (817–913). Tolkien's headnote then explained how the elegiac dream-poem was composed in the octosyllabic couplets popularized in French works like the *Roman de la Rose*. Editing a poem in a particular metre seems to have impacted his own versifying. In the wake of editing the alliterative *Gawain*, Tolkien had written *The Children of Húrin* in alliterative verses running to over 2,000 lines, but sometime in the summer of 1925, after editing the octosyllabic *Book of the Duchess*, he began writing his *Gest of Beren and Lúthien* in the same Chaucerian verse-form:

> A king there was in days of old:
> ere Men yet walked upon the mould
> his power was reared in cavern's shade,
> his hand was over glen and glade.[59]

He composed his *Lay of Aotrou and Itroun* in the same verse-form after interrupting composition of *The Lay of Leithian*, also in eight-syllable couplets, and years later he remarked about the challenge: 'octosyllabic couplets are defeating for a translator; there is no room to move' (SH 3:1000).

His commentary on *The Book of the Duchess* extended over nine typed pages explaining which manuscripts preserved the work and what was known about its occasion: 'The poem was written to lament the death of Duchess Blanche of Lancaster, wife of John of Gaunt, on September 12th, 1369.'[60] He later recalled these same particulars to his aunt Jane Neave in 1962 when comparing the poem to *Pearl* which he explained was 'contemporary with Chaucer' (*Letters*, 317). He even knew the elegy well enough when editing the *Pearl* to quote lines 948–51 though this passage had not been included in his Clarendon Chaucer. His own

---

[58] As a Rhodes Scholar at Merton College in the 1950s with digs on Sandfield Road near the Tolkiens, Reynolds Price recalled in his memoir *Ardent Spirits: Leaving Home, Coming Back* (New York: Scribner, 2009), 258: 'he pronounced his name *Toll*-KEAN, not TOLL-*kin* as most Americans miscall him.' Price's Rhodes classmate and Tolkien's supervisee V. A. Kolve has confirmed to me this pronunciation.

[59] *Lays of Beleriand*, 150–363 at p. 189 (lines 1–4). Christopher in J. R. R. Tolkien's *Narn I Chîn Húrin: The Tale of the Children of Húrin* (Boston and New York: Houghton Mifflin, 2007), 269, 272, notes this switch in verse-forms from alliterative long-lines to octosyllabic couplets.

[60] Bodleian MS Tolkien A 39/2/1, fols. 14–22.

bereavement after the early death of his mother might partly explain his interest in elegies on the deaths of young women like Fair White in *The Book of the Duchess*,[61] and Tolkien found much to praise in Chaucer's authenticity of feeling:

> In many respects it is the most charming of his minor poems, not only because it is complete, but also because through the conventions which he uses there runs a real sincerity of feeling—though it may be only art, and the sign of the awakening of his power to give new life to the matter he borrowed from books and learning, and to join the pieces with cunning into a new whole.

The touchstones for his own literary aesthetics were emerging: completeness, authenticity of feeling, borrowings from earlier books, and craftsmanship aimed at a sense of unity.

Chaucer's pre-dream section contains Ovid's story of Ceyx and Alcyone included also in the *Confessio Amantis* (IV, 2927-3123). Tolkien knew Gower's version after glossing it for Sisam's *Verse and Prose* and could remark with confidence, 'the comparison with Gower is by no means entirely in Chaucer's favour.' This was largely due to what was missing at the end: 'the omission in Chaucer of any reference to the changing of the dead husband and wife into seabirds, in which shape they renewed their tender love.' That Ovid's loving couple partly inspired his own creation of Elwing—who also turns into a bird and flies over the water seeking her beloved Eärendil—gains greater credence now that we know Tolkien invested time editing and annotating Chaucer's version of this love-story from the *Metamorphoses*.[62]

His prefatory remarks speculated on the genesis of this Ovidian adaptation: 'it is probable that a version of the legend of Ceyx and Alcyone was once made by Chaucer for its own sake separately. It was his way to adapt and rearrange his own work.' The Man of Law's report that Chaucer wrote 'Ceys and Alcion' in youth (*CT* II, 57) had served as evidence that the author took this early material and inserted it into the later, longer work. This recycling of earlier pieces would offer a notable precedent for Tolkien's own practices.

In the same letter to Chapman bemoaning the Chaucerian incubus, Tolkien confessed that he was distracted from OUP projects because he was a verse-writer. His first published work was the poem *Goblin Feet* in 1915, and *The Lord of the Rings* would be studded with some seventy-five poems, many of them written and even published previously in his career.[63] Tom Bombadil's songs, for example,

---

[61] Zaleski and Zaleski make much of the impact of his mother's death in *The Fellowship: The Literary Lives of the Inklings*, 13-21.

[62] *Silmarillion*, 296-300; see Kristine Larsen, 'Sea Birds and Morning Stars: Ceyx, Alcyone, and the Many Metamorphoses of Eärendil and Elwing', in Fisher, ed., *Tolkien and the Study of His Sources*, 69-83.

[63] Verlyn Flieger, 'Poems by Tolkien: *The Lord of the Rings*', in *Tolkien Encyclopedia*, 522-32; Christopher, 'Tolkien's Lyric Poetry', in Julian Eilmann and Allan Turner, eds, *Tolkien's Poetry* (Zurich and Jena: Walking Tree Publishers, 2013); Corey Olsen, 'Poetry', in *Companion*, ed. Lee, 173-88: and

were extracted from the longer version appearing in the *Oxford Magazine* in 1934. The rhyme which Frodo rattles off at the *Prancing Pony* was originally published as 'The Cat and the Fiddle' in *Yorkshire Poetry* in 1923. When Strider recites his tale of Beren and Lúthien, the stanzas have several precursors in Tolkien's verse-writing going back to 'Light as Leaf on Lindentree' published in *The Gryphon* in 1925. And so on.

Germanic philology's *Liedertheorie* maintained that the earliest epics were really medleys of shorter, pre-existent songs cobbled together by poets like Homer.[64] Anglo-Saxon scholars, many of them German or trained in Germany, speculated that *Beowulf* was constructed in this manner from heroic lays gathered and fitted together. Tolkien's allegory of the tower ridiculed such scholars interested more in the old building-stones than in the magnificence of *Beowulf* itself.[65] With *The Book of the Duchess*, however, Tolkien believed that he had actually caught a great poet in the act of re-appropriation by taking one of his own early poems and fitting it into place as part of a new organic whole.

Most Chaucerians no longer accept 'Ceyx and Alcyone' as a pre-existent piece, but Tolkien did not waste his own earlier poems any more than he wasted paper, and so he was quick to believe that he had found in Chaucer an eminent predecessor for adapting prior work. The challenge was making sure each act of repurposing functioned in its new context: 'the verses in *The Lord of the Rings* are all dramatic: they do not express the poor old professor's soul-searching, but are fitted in style and contents to the *characters* in the story that sing or recite them' (*Letters*, 396). Though he appreciated the *Beowulf* Poet's handling of the Sigemund episode as a dragon story within the larger dragon story,[66] the use of an inset story as an entryway into the personality of the storyteller became one of Chaucer's most brilliant innovations in his *Canterbury Tales*. The Knight's Tale may have been written years earlier as 'The Love of Palamon and Arcite', for example, but it was perfectly adapted to this pilgrim narrator. As a prime example of Tolkien's own adaptations, Aragorn's *Tale of Tinúviel* (FR I/11) fits perfectly into the hero's psychological profile because it functions as an analogue of his human love for the Elf maiden Arwen.[67]

In the dream section of *The Book of the Duchess*, the Chaucerian narrator awakens inside a magnificent room with stained-glass windows showing the

---

SH 3:995–1002 'Poetry'. *Goblin's Feet* can be read in J. R. R. Tolkien, *The Annotated Hobbit*, rev. edn Douglas A. Anderson (Boston and New York: Houghton Mifflin, 2002), 113. Wayne G. Hammond and Christina Scull, *The Lord of the Rings: A Reader's Companion* (London: HarperCollins, 2005), document the publication histories of all the inset poems.

[64] F. A. Wolf, *Prolegomena to Homer (1795)*, trans. and intro. Anthony Grafton, Glenn W. Most, and James E. G. Zetzel (Princeton: Princeton University Press, 1985).
[65] *Essays*, 7–8; see Shippey, *Author of the Century*, 'Allegory and Applicability', 161–8.
[66] Tolkien, *Beowulf: A Translation and Commentary*, 284–6.
[67] C. S. Lewis judged these inset verses as 'on the whole poor, regrettable, and out of place' (*Letters*, 169), but then Lewis was also out of sympathy with what Chaucer had accomplished in his *Canterbury Tales*.

famous Trojan War figures Hector, Priam, Achilles, Paris, Helen, and so forth. Tolkien explained: 'Poets have at all times been fond of lists of fair names, which are often none the less effective though the audience's knowledge of the legends attached to them was small or vague.' Later Tolkien felt that 'the magic of mere names' functioned successfully for Chaucer's inset ballade in the *Legend* Prologue. He invoked Spenser and Milton as later English authors also fond of listing names and would insert himself in this distinguished line-up when indulging his own impulse, for example memorializing Rohan's warriors who fell at Minis Tirith— Harding, Guthláf, Dúnhere, Déorwine, Grimbold, Herefara, Herubrand, Fastred, Hirluin, Forlong, Derufin, and Duilin (*RK* V/6)—even if his audience's knowledge of them was not even small or vague, but wholly non-existent.

Gordon had chosen the excerpt 'Dream of the Hunt' for their edition, and Tolkien's fascination with deer-hunting went back to his youthful experience of poaching and butchering a deer, a fact he sometimes mentioned in his lectures on *Gawain* (SH 1:82). A dash of Chaucerian humour carried over to *The Hobbit* when a deer's sudden arrival disrupted the company's travel to the far shore of the enchanted stream. Thorin was quick-witted enough to shoot the fleeing beast as it landed on the farther bank, but Bombur's fall into the water distracted the dwarves and lost them the boat that would have enabled them to claim the fallen deer for a venison dinner. They are next distracted by the Wood-elves on a great hunt which proves just as elusive for them as the deer hunt for the Chaucerian dreamer.

The deer hunt in *The Book of the Duchess* begins with the blowing of a horn. Chaucer's *gret horne* thus became one more source, along with many others such the oliphant-horn in the *Chanson de Roland*, for Boromir's great Horn of Gondor sounded during the attack of the Orcs (*TT* III/1). Tolkien's younger brother Hilary was proud of his service as a bugler in the Royal Warwickshire Regiment— 'I became (though I say it as shouldn't) a very good bugler'[68]—and a photograph of him in uniform with his bugle in *The Tolkien Family Album* (p. 39) suggests it was part of family lore. 'One of the things I remember moving me most', Tolkien reported late in life about *The Lord of the Rings*, 'was the horns of the Rohirrim at cockcrow.'[69]

The blowing of the hunting horn three times also brought to Tolkien's mind his own training as a signalling officer in the Great War:

> The fourteenth-century horn had only one note, but various calls were made by combining notes of different lengths, a sort of Morse-code...Three long G's is still used on the military bugle as a similar sort of signal.[70]

---

[68] *Black and White Ogre Country: The Lost Tales of Hilary Tolkien,* ed. Angela Gardner (Moreton-in-Marsh: ADC Publications, 2009), 50.
[69] *Letters*, 376, and Resnick, 'Interview with Tolkien', 39. See Shippey, *Author of the Century*, 215–21, on Tolkien's various war horns.
[70] Tolkien and Gordon, eds., *Sir Gawain and the Green Knight*, 100, had included a note on the fourteenth-century horn but without comparing its notes to Morse code.

Tolkien had learned how to send messages by Morse code with a buzzer by day and a lamp by night, though even buzzers were later prohibited because the enemy could detect dots-and-dashes through the hard ground.[71] A new portable Morse telegraph lessened this threat without otherwise eliminating battlefield confusion. Later, as wish-fulfilling alternatives, *The Lord of the Rings* included other wartime communications such as the beacons of Gondor and especially the *palantíri* for instant communication, although the seeing-stones, like Morse buzzers, were susceptible to eavesdropping.[72]

One specific moment from *The Book of the Duchess* may have stuck in Tolkien's memory for his own storytelling. When the dreamer realizes that everyone has gone into the forest for an adventure, he jumps out of bed and rushes after them without any mention of getting dressed. In *The Hobbit*, Bilbo also jumps out of bed when he discovers that he had been left behind by the Dwarves and rushes after them so quickly that he forgets not his clothes but at least his handkerchief.

IV. *The Parlement of Foules*

When I first examined the Clarendon Chaucer materials in summer 2013, I discovered that annotations for the *Parlement of Foules* were missing. By a happy coincidence on the same day, an email arrived from Bodleian archivist Catherine McIlwaine with a list of Chaucer holdings among the Tolkien Papers— and there was an entry for the *Parlement* with commentary and notes.[73] Tolkien's handwritten coversheet, added in January 1948, clarified the situation: 'The *Parlement of Foules* is now set "for examination" as from the first of the month instead of the *Clerkes Tale*.'[74] No longer Professor of Anglo-Saxon, Tolkien was required to teach Chaucer's 699-line dream poem and had simply snatched the nearly thirty pages of notes from his long-stalled *Selections* to adapt to the needs of undergraduates: 'It is my practice to begin with a line-by-line commentary.'[75] Derek Brewer, later an eminent medievalist in his own right, recalled in the 1940s how Tolkien confined himself entirely to single words in single lines, though often forgetting to tell his students which lines he was discussing.[76] Tolkien's editorial

---

[71] John Garth, *Tolkien and the Great War: The Threshold of Middle-earth* (New York and Boston: Houghton Mifflin, 2003), 114–15; see also *Biography*, 85–6, 91.

[72] Tolkien, *Unfinished Tales*, 'Beacons of Gondor', 300–1, and 'The Palantíri', 403–15.

[73] Bodleian MS Tolkien A 38/2, fols. 98–126: 'introduction and commentary on Chaucer's *Parlement of Fowles*, 1948.' Tolkien knew this poem well enough to quote it in both versions of *'Beowulf' and the Critics*, ed. Drout, pp. 42, 96, 164, and 264–5.

[74] Bodleian MS Tolkien A 38/2, fols. 96–7. His older teaching notes for the Clerk's Tale survive in MS Tolkien A 13/2, fols. 5–38: 'I am going to deal this term with two of the *Canterbury Tales*—The *Clerk's Tale* and the *Pardoner's Tale*.' I discuss his two series of lectures on the Pardoner's Tale in Chapter 7.

[75] In a reversal of sorts, Christopher took his father's lecture notes for *Beowulf* and adapted them as endnotes for his 2014 edition of the translation.

[76] Brewer, 'Introduction', in *A Companion to the 'Gawain'-Poet*, 2.

notes on single words therefore readily adapted to these lectures that hopped from crux to crux.

When drafted in the 1920s, Tolkien's *Parlement* commentary switched after three pages from typescript to black-ink handwriting, still clear and easy to read for the time being, though over the years of classroom use, the margins acquired extra blue-ink jottings more difficult to decipher. Tolkien started by praising the dream-vision as 'a remarkable and on the whole successful poem', with a backward look at the *The Book of the Duchess* which already 'showed that he could match the masters of grace and charm, and already reveals himself as unrivalled in tender sensibility; his dream is really dreamlike and filled with a soft and gentle air'. His praise for the *Parlement* continued by acknowledging the poet's skill at what would become his own practice of adapting sources:

> Now we first get hints of his real originality and begin to savour his own peculiar temper. Still blending and adapting various sources, French (*Romance of the Rose*), Latin classical and medieval (Cicero and Alanus de Insulis), and Italian (Boccaccio), he constructs a poem that is not only a complete new thing, but is in places very individual and Chaucerian in tone. At last we get the clear touches of Chaucerian humour...

Tolkien was most impressed by early instances of Chaucer's self-deprecating humour. Though his original headnote reported the common interpretation of the poem as 'an allegory of the marriage of Richard II with Anne of Bohemia', he later let his dislike of this mode show when telling students in the lecture version about interpreting the various birds: 'whenever one touches "allegory," one is in difficulties.'

'Greek *galaxia*, translated in Latin *orbis lacteus* of which our *Milky Way* is in turn a rendering, though influenced by more native notions of the Milky Way as a road... behind which lurk legends now almost entirely lost.' This note on Chaucer's *galaxye* (56) deserves notice because he had already discussed the Milky Way in his 1924 'Philology',[77] and he would allude to the word, again in italics, in the opening sentence of 'Chaucer as a Philologist' where he imagined his author 'surveying from the *Galaxye* our literary and philological antics'. His Clarendon commentary explained Cicero's *Somnium Scipionis* as the poet's source and took time to sketch the career of the Roman general Scipio Africanus: 'As a matter of history, Scipio did not approve of the unjust and horrible third Punic War, nor after its conclusion of the burning, levelling, and ploughing up of the city which he was obliged to see carried out.' Here Tolkien perhaps recalled the wartime horrors which he witnessed first-hand at the Battle of the Somme—as well as the scorched-earth tactics used during the Boer War in his native South Africa—and he would later imagine how Sauron pursued his own scorched-earth

---

[77] Tolkien, 'Philology' (1924), 21–2.

policy to destroy the gardens of the Entwives during the War of the Last Alliance (*Letters*, 179). His commentary on *galaxye* concluded with an explanation of the medieval planetary system and music of the spheres: 'The idea of the harmony of the concentric spheres of the "planets" revolving all in a similar direction was thus bound up with the notion of the excellence of the number seven. Each of these seven planetary spheres emitted one of the notes of the gamut.' Heavenly music, of course, formed a major part of Tolkien's own creation myth in his *Silmarillion*.[78]

He felt a close kinship with Chaucer when dealing with the natural world, and nothing so much engaged Tolkien's interests as the *Parlement*'s catalogue of trees (176–82):

> The bilder ook, and eek the hardy asshe;
> The piler elm, the cofre unto careyne;
> The boxtree piper; holm to whippes lasshe;
> The sayling firr; the cipres, deth to pleyne;
> The sheter ew, the asp for shaftes pleyne;
> The olyve of pees, and eek the drunken vyne,
> The victor palm, the laurer to devyne.

Tolkien was himself fond of what he called the 'Homeric catalogue', such as naming the various reinforcements arriving at Minis Tirith,[79] and his fascination with these trees was fuelled by Skeat's remark that the poet had added six species to those derived from the *Roman de la Rose*. Tolkien even makes the valid point that the General Prologue's portraits qualify as a catalogue:

> Chaucer's list of trees is of literary origin; its items show that it comes largely from the Mediterranean. The list has been traced back as far as Ovid (*Metamorphoses* x.90), whence, with variation, it appears in Seneca's *Œdipus*, Lucan, Statius, and (from Statius) in Boccaccio and the *Romance of the Rose*. Actually Chaucer is here combining the list in Boccaccio's *Teseide*, xi.22–24, with one in *Romance of the Rose* 1338–1368. Chaucer was fond of a descriptive catalogue; the Prologue in the *Canterbury Tales* is an elaborate product of the same partiality. Here the brief characterisation, however, is mainly derivative. Compare the twenty-one trees in the Knight's Tale (A.2921). The present passage was closely imitated by Spenser (*Faerie Queene* i, I, 8 and 9).

The section here mentioned from the Knight's Tale must have given Tolkien a pang when recalling the large grove of trees cut down by Theseus to clear ground for his jousting stadium. From early childhood Tolkien hated seeing trees cut down for no good reason, like the willow felled beside the mill-pond outside

---

[78] This began with *The Music of the Ainur* in *Book of Lost Tales: Part I*, 40–62; see Bradford Lee Eden, 'The "Music of the Spheres": Relationships between Tolkien's *The Silmarillion* and Medieval Cosmological and Religious Theory', in *Tolkien the Medievalist*, ed. Chance, 183–93.

[79] *The War of the Ring*, 229, 287, 293, on origins of the Homeric catalogue in *RK* V/1.

Sarehole, and Chaucer's scene of deforestation at Athens may have lingered in Tolkien's memory when describing how Saruman, also presiding over a vast walled circuit at Isengard, ordered the cutting down of trees in Fangorn Forest. Somewhat like the list of trees in the *Parlement*, Tolkien described how the Ents represented a variety of species such as birch, beech, oak, fir, chestnut, ash, rowan, and linden (*TT* III/4).

Tolkien would become one of the twentieth century's great nature writers and the godfather of environmental literature,[80] and here he took evident pleasure when including notes on individual trees such as the yew for making bows:

> The yew for bows and the aspen (black poplar) for arrow-shafts are items added from English usage. They are not in Ovid. They both appear in the Chaucerian translation of the list in *Romaunt*, although the original does not mention yew.

Tolkien would recall this particular lore in his fiction. The archer Beleg Cúthalion was buried with his great bow of yew-wood, the Lord of Eagles refused flying near Men because of their yew bows, and Aragorn noticed the Uruk-hai warriors fought with superior yew bows.

Tolkien's note on 'holm to whippes lasshe' contained more tree-lore which resurfaced in his own writings:

> Skeat defines this as 'holly', but it is probably the *ilex* or 'holm-oak', an evergreen with dark pointed leaves, somewhat like holly, and slender shapely acorns... *holm* is etymologically the same word as *holly*, O.E. *holegn*, M.E. *holy* and *holin* (surviving dialectally as *hollin*). From *holin* partly by purely scribal confusion *holm* was produced; *holin* is the reading of some MSS here.

Here we find the origin of Hollin as the region where Frodo and his friends encounter holly trees near the West Gate of Moria. Tolkien later explained this place-name in his *Nomenclature*: 'The CS name (short for *Hollin-land*) of the country called in Elvish *Eregion* "holly–region". *Hollin* is an old form, still used locally, of *holly*.'[81] Clearly this explanation recalled his note written years earlier for Chaucer's *Parlement*.

The Mediterranean homeland of these trees impressed Tolkien the most and looked forward to the same southern species of olive, tamarisk, cypress, and junipers encountered by Frodo and Sam when arriving in Ithilien (*TT* IV/4). Commenting later about the geography of Middle-earth, Tolkien reckoned Gondor lay on the equivalent of the north coasts of the Mediterranean and Minas Tirith itself about the latitude of Florence (*Letters*, 376). Chaucer had actually visited Italy as Tolkien noted about the poem's dating: '*Parlement of*

---

[80] Liam Campbell, 'Nature', in *Companion*, ed. Lee, 431–45, and SH 2:345–52 'Environment'.
[81] Hammond and Scull, *Reader's Companion*, 772, and Cynthia M. Cohen, 'The Unique Representation of Trees in *The Lord of the Rings*', *Tolkien Studies* 6 (2009), 91–125.

Foules is usually assigned to the year 1382—that is, after Chaucer's two visits to Italy in 1378 and 1379.' Tolkien himself was famously averse to foreign travel and visited Italy only after completing *The Lord of the Rings* (SH 2:580–2), and therefore his trees are actually more book-based than the medieval poet's. The flora of his Ithilien grottoes, for instance, recalled Mediterranean flowers like asphodels from Book IX of Milton's *Paradise Lost*, aptly enough, because Ithilien was the 'garden of Gondor' fallen into neglect and 'now desolate'.

Skeat made another remark which perhaps encouraged Tolkien's thinking about these trees: 'The reader will observe the life and spirit which the personification of the several trees gives to this catalogue' (1:512). Chaucer had indeed endowed them with many human traits: the oak is a builder, the boxwood is a piper, and the cypress is a lamenter of death. Tolkien had his own impulse to personify trees and endow them with life and spirit, first Old Man Willow and later, to a degree which surprised the author himself, Treebeard and his fellow Ents.

Chaucer also provided a catalogue of birds firmly rooted in the medieval bestiary tradition. When *The Hobbit* introduced the Lord of the Eagles who 'had eyes that could look at the sun unblinking' (p. 150), Tolkien was partaking in the longstanding tradition which he explained about Chaucer's royal bird: 'The idea that the eagle could gaze unblinking at the sun is an old one and is supported by the most undaunted of all etymologists, Saint Isidore of Seville.' The thrush was credited with wisdom, the raven lived to an old age, and the crow was ill-omened because of its black feathers. 'The starling can be taught to talk, but the reference is clearly "mythological" to some story in which a malicious talking starling gave away a secret', Tolkien wrote; 'Chaucer's Manciple tells just such a story, though it is of a talking crow.' He himself would recall this lore of thrushes, starlings, crows, and ravens in *The Hobbit* where talking birds announce the death of Smaug and warn of the army of Elves and Lake-men approaching the Lonely Mountain. Tolkien's late essay about mythology probably recalled Chaucer's talking birds: 'These have been rather lightly adopted from less "serious" mythologies, but play a part which cannot now be excised.'[82]

Because *Ent* derives from Old English for 'giant', it is not entirely surprising that his note on 'crane the geaunt with his trompes soune' (*PF* 344) focused mostly on the word *geaunt*: 'derived from the adjective *giganteus* used in Alanus' description (referring to its long legs).' When Gandalf and his companions first spot Ents below Helm's Deep, they are described as 'walking like wading herons in their gait' (herons belong to the same family as cranes) and 'their legs in their long paces beat quicker than the heron's wings'.[83] Ents also have ringing voices 'clear as notes of a horn', and this was another trait mentioned in Tolkien's *Parlement* note: 'Where

---

[82] Tolkien, 'Myths Transformed', in *Morgoth's Ring*, 409.
[83] *TT* III/8; *The War of the Ring*, 30, indicates that Tolkien's earliest description of an Ent was 'walking stilted like a wading heron'.

the bird is still familiar, "clarys" or "trumpets" are still used of its cry.' It has not been previously noted, so far as I know, but the battle at Isengard between the giant Ents and much smaller Orcs recalls the mythological war between Cranes and Pygmies first reported in Homer's *Iliad* and repeated by Pliny the Elder, later picked up in the English tradition by Mandeville's *Travels* and Milton's *Paradise Lost*.

V. *The Former Age*

Tolkien provided four handwritten pages for Chaucer's 64-line Boethian lyric.[84] The poem's nostalgia for an earlier, simpler time in mankind's prehistory naturally spoke to Tolkien's own interests, sharing as he did a longing for the deep-rooted past.[85] The poet had recalled the Golden Age from Ovid's *Metamorphoses* when adapting these lines from his own translation of Boethius, and for their Clarendon edition, Gordon selected this passage from *Boece* (II, m. 5) because it was the lyric's immediate source.

Looking back into mankind's far-distant past, Chaucer envisaged a culture much more primitive than we find in Hobbiton, which Tolkien imagined as a Warwickshire village around the time of Queen Victoria's Diamond Jubilee in 1897 (*Letters*, 230). These men were even more primitive than his Drúedains who made flint tools, carved figures in stone, practised the arts of magic, and possessed botanical skills rivaling the Elves (*UT* 377–87). Chaucer's prehistoric people knew no fire, no ploughing, no metallurgy, no coinage, no jewellery, no sailing ships, no warfare, and no cities with walls and towers. This range of privations must have struck Tolkien as too primitive. When the Númenóreans took pity on the peoples of Middle-earth during the Dark Years, they bestowed upon them the basics which Chaucer withheld: 'Corn and wine they brought, and they instructed Men in the sowing of seed and the grinding of grain' (*Sil* 314).

Grinding grain was crucial to the advance of civilization, and Tolkien's annotations, though sparse, focused on the word *quern* as an instance when 'the poor philologist will have to call on some archaeological expert' (*Letters*, 270). Where Skeat provided the single remark 'Quern, a hand-mill for grinding corn' (1:539), Tolkien wrote an entire paragraph as if an archaeologist lecturing about an artefact (Fig. 10):

> *quern*: O.E. *cweorn* 'handmill', the most primitive apparatus for grinding. In essentials it consisted of two large round slabs of hard stone, pierced and joined

---

[84] Bodleian MS Tolkien A 39/2/1, fols. 23–6.
[85] Shippey, *Road to Middle-earth*, 308–17; Chaucer's classical sources took him back to ancient Troy and even more ancient Athens. Even his comic *Thopas* was an echo-chamber of formulas from deep-rooted English romances.

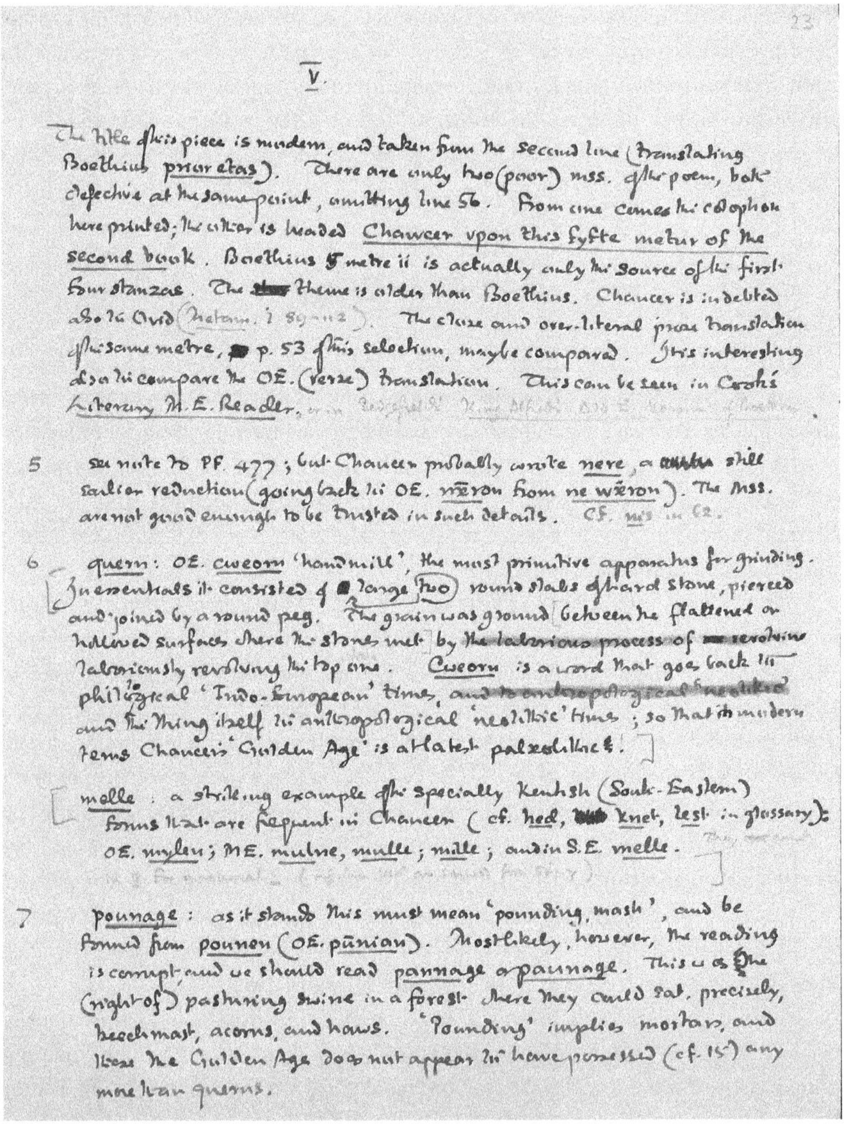

V.

The title of this piece is modern, and taken from the second line (translating Boethius prior aetas). There are only two (poor) mss. of the poem, both defective at the same point, omitting line 56. From one comes the colophon here printed; the other is headed Chaucer vpon this fyfte metur of the second book. Boethius metre ii is actually only the source of the first four stanzas. The theme is older than Boethius. Chaucer is indebted also to Ovid (Metam. I 89–112). The close and over-literal prose translation of the same metre, p. 53 of this selection, may be compared. It is interesting also to compare the OE. (verse) translation. This can be seen in Cook's Literary M.E. Reader.

5 see note to PF. 477; but Chaucer probably wrote nere, a still earlier reduction (going back to OE. nǣron from ne wǣron). The MSS. are not good enough to be trusted in such details. Cf. ...

6 quern: OE. cweorn 'handmill', the most primitive apparatus for grinding. In essentials it consisted of two large round slabs of hard stone, pierced and joined by a round peg. The grain was ground between the flattened or hollowed surfaces where the stones met by the laborious process of revolving laboriously revolving the top one. Cweorn is a word that goes back to philological 'Indo-European' times, and the thing itself to anthropological 'neolithic' times; so that in modern terms Chaucer's 'Golden Age' is at latest palaeolithic!

melle: a striking example of the specially Kentish (South-Eastern) forms that are frequent in Chaucer (cf. hed, knet, lest in glossary): OE. mylen; ME. mulne, mulle; mille; and in S.E. melle.

7 pounage: as it stands this must mean 'pounding, mash', and be formed from pounen (OE. pūnian). Most likely, however, the reading is corrupt, and we should read pannage or paunage. This was the (right of) pasturing swine in a forest where they could eat, precisely, beechmast, acorns, and haws. 'Pounding' implies mortars, and these the Golden Age does not appear to have possessed (cf. 15) any more than querns.

Fig. 10. Handwritten notes on Chaucer's *The Former Age* (Oxford, Bodleian Library, MS Tolkien A 39/2/1, fol. 23).

by a round peg. The grain was ground between the flattened or hollowed surfaces where the stones met by laboriously revolving this top stone. *Cweorn* is a word that goes back to philological 'Indo-European' times, and the thing itself to anthropological 'neolithic' times; so that in modern terms Chaucer's 'Golden Age' is at latest palæolithic!

Tolkien's interest was probably encouraged by the *Prose Edda*'s legendary ruler Fróthi whose magical quern established peace throughout his realm. 'Monsters and the Critics' mentioned his Anglo-Saxon counterpart Froda who had connections with the Norse Golden Age—and whose name partly inspired Frodo's.[86] *The Lost Road* would include an account of another golden age ruled over by King Sheaf whose mill produced 'gold grain, and there was no want in the land'.[87] Elias Lönnrot had interpreted the *Kalevala*'s Sampo as a quern that magically produced flour, salt, and gold. This was an important point for Tolkien, not simply because he admired Lönnrot's compilation as a model for his own project of resuscitating national mythology, but also because his Silmarils represented an effort at explaining the mystery of the Sampo.[88]

Nor is it surprising to find Tolkien using the terms Neolithic and Palaeolithic so expertly. He had a boyhood interest in British archaeology shared with his schoolmate Christopher Wiseman, who made a point of visiting prehistoric barrows when stationed on the Orkney Islands.[89] Tolkien preferred delving linguistically to digging in the dirt, however, and later when studying Chaucer's dialect humour, he talked about the 'exhuming of ancient jokes buried under years' and retrieving comedy by 'digging it up and examining it'.[90] George Steiner, who had been a Rhodes Scholar when Tolkien was still teaching, saw in the don's linguistic archeology more than merely unearthing dead languages:

> To study the grammar of a language, particularly an ancient or partly-lost language, is to engage in mental archaeology. The philologist and the grammarian bring out to the light of day the conventions of dreams, the fundamental concepts of art, the historic memories of a buried world.[91]

Archaeology operated as the philology of prehistory, and Tolkien had opportunity for aligning the two disciplines when recalling prehistoric sites around Oxford to picture his own Barrow-downs where buried treasures testified to the disappearance of the men of Cardolan.

In 1928, about the time he suspended work on his Chaucer notes, archaeologists at Lydney Park in Gloucestershire recruited Tolkien to explain the name

---

[86] *Essays*, 16; *Letters*, 224; and *Beowulf: A Translation and Commentary*, 331, on the two Fródas of the Heathobards, 'one the historical father of their last king Ingeld, and one the remoter (perhaps mythical) ancestor: the Fróda of the Great Peace'. See also Shippey, *Author of the Century*, 'The Myth of Frodo', 182–7.

[87] J. R. R. Tolkien, *The Lost Road and Other Writings*, ed. Christopher Tolkien (New York: Del Rey, 1996), 95–107, where Christopher connects King Sheaf with Snorri's account of Fróthi.

[88] Shippey, *Road to Middle-earth*, 206, 242–3; *Author of the Century*, 244; and SH 2:588–98 'Kalevala'.

[89] John Garth, 'Wiseman, Christopher (1893–1987)', *TE* 708–9; Garth, *Tolkien and the Great War*, 141; and SH 2:491–2 'Prehistory'.

[90] Tolkien, 'Chaucer as a Philologist', 2.

[91] George Steiner's 1973 *Le Monde* reminiscence 'Tolkien, Oxford's Eccentric Don' has been reprinted in *Tolkien Studies* 5 (2008), 186–8 at p. 187.

Nodens inscribed on bronze plates from the Roman level.[92] Other discoveries included quern-stones like those mentioned by Chaucer.[93] Because the place was known locally as Dwarf's Hill and honeycombed with abandoned mines, it naturally suggested itself as background for the Lonely Mountain and the Mines of Moria.[94] In 1926 Tolkien had written that 'an archaeologist never visits in vain any site associated in local nomenclature with giants, old wives, fairies, King Arthur, Puck, Robin Hood, or Michael Scott'.[95] As a strategic hillfort, Dwarf's Hill joined with nearby examples such as Uffington Castle as further inspiration for the hill-top watchtower of Amon Sûl.

For the name Nodens, Tolkien reconstructed its Indo-European origin and assembled Irish myths, his passion for proper names compelling him backward in time much as he traced the name Eärendil to its lost roots.[96] He decided Nodens went back to the Irish royal figure Núadu of the Silver Hand who had lost his hand in battle with the giant Firbolg and replaced it with a silver one.[97] Interestingly the Elf smith Celebrimbor's name means 'hand of silver' in Sindarin. Lost hands would become a recurrent theme in Tolkien's own writings. Maedhros lost his hand when escaping Morgoth's fortress, Barahir's hand was cut off by Orcs as a trophy for Sauron, and Beren had his hand bitten off by the wolf Carcharoth. Frodo got off light by having only his finger bitten off by Gollum so that he became known thereafter as Frodo of the Nine Fingers.[98]

Tolkien then turned to Germanic etymologies for Núadu: 'ON. *nat-r* means any piece of valuable personal property, a sword, a ring' (p. 136). By this date he was already telling his boys the bedtime story about a valuable ring, and Firbolg's name would find an echo in the name of the goblin captain Bolg. Tolkien's comparison of the giant to the Titan in Greek mythology recalls how his own Balrog drew inspiration from the Titan in Hesiod's *Theogony*.[99] Nor is it too farfetched to imagine the hand of King Nodens, as part of a healing cult lasting into Roman

---

[92] J. R. R. Tolkien, 'The Name "Nodens"', Appendix I in R. E. M. Wheeler and T. V. Wheeler, *Report on the Excavation of the Prehistoric, Roman, and Post-Roman Site in Lydney Park, Gloucestershire* (London: Society of Antiquaries, 1932), 132–7, reprinted *Tolkien Studies* 4 (2007), 177–83; see Carl Phelpstead, *Tolkien and Wales: Language, Literature and Identity* (Cardiff: University of Wales Press, 2011), 'Nodens and the Comparative Method', 53–7, and Chance, *Tolkien, Self and Other*, 140–1.

[93] Bee Wilson, 'Querns and Curtains', *TLS* 5842 (14 November 2014), 3–4, confirms them as defining features of the prehistoric British household.

[94] Helen Armstrong, 'And Have an Eye to That Dwarf', *Amon Hen: The Bulletin of the Tolkien Society* 145 (May 1997), 13–14.

[95] Tolkien, 'Philology' (1926), 65.

[96] Tom Shippey, 'History in Words: Tolkien's Ruling Passion', in *Roots and Branches*, 157–73.

[97] Shippey, *Road to Middle-earth*, 35–6; see also J. S. Lyman-Thomas, 'Celtic: "Celtic Things" and "Things Celtic"—Identity, Language, and Mythology', in *Companion*, ed. Lee, 281.

[98] Tolkien, *Peoples of Middle-Earth*, 242; Leonard Jackson, 'The Castration Complex: Nine-Fingered Frodo', in *Literature, Psychoanalysis, and the New Sciences of Mind*, 77–8, does not survey all the other lost appendages in Tolkien's fiction.

[99] Hammond and Scull, *Reader's Companion*, 393.

times, suggested one of Aragorn's kingly powers according to the old nurse Ioreth: 'The hands of the king are the hands of a healer' (*RK* V/8).

This field report was published in 1932 when Tolkien's mind turned again to prehistoric remains. His *Father Christmas Letter* for that year regaled the children with an account of the caves beneath the North Pole: 'Many of the pictures were done by these Cave-men—the best ones, especially the big ones (almost life-size) of animals, some of which have since disappeared: there are *dragons* and quite a lot of mammoths.'[100] Tolkien's drawings took their inspiration from the prehistoric paintings in northern Spain,[101] but caves always held a powerful allure for him. He had taken his bride Edith to visit the Cheddar Caves on their honeymoon in 1916 and visited them again in 1940 when hard at work on *The Lord of the Rings*.[102] Here in 1903 the Cheddar Man's remains had been discovered, dating back some nine thousand years, still Britain's oldest complete human skeleton.

By 1932 when Tolkien was drawing his caves beneath the North Pole, *The Hobbit* envisioned the Lake-town of Esgaroth as resembling the Neolithic sites pictured in Ferdinand Keller's *The Lake Dwellings of Switzerland*. Neolithic Britain (4000–2500 BC) also witnessed the construction of large megalithic tombs across the landscape. Fifteen miles from where Tolkien sat writing, the Nine Barrow Down rose above the Oxfordshire plain, where Stone Age peoples had buried their royalty. Another barrow at Avebury provided a close model for his 'standing stones, pointing upwards like jagged teeth out of green gums' (*FR* I/8). In the 1930s, when he had a car, Tolkien drove his family to the ancient long-barrow known as Wayland's Smithy, and during this same decade he lectured on 'The Legend of Wayland the Smith'. Constructed about 3500 BC, its entrance inspired the Barrow-wight's lair with its two standing stones like pillars of a headless door (*FR* I/8). Dunharrow's standing stones carved in the likeness of men (*RK* V/3) were modelled after the Rollright Stones at Long Compton twenty-four miles north-east of Oxford; these also inspired the Standing Stones where the dog Garm first encountered the dragon in *Farmer Giles of Ham* (*Letters*, 130–1). Tolkien probably recalled one of the stone formations nicknamed the 'Whispering Knights' when describing how his ghostly shadow-knights gathered at the Hill of Erech, 'thronging round the Stone and whispering' (*RK* V/2). But he calculated Chaucer's prehistoric utopia much further backward in time to the Palaeolithic, lasting in Britain until some 10,000 years ago.

Chaucer's final stanza claimed that during this innocent age no ambitious kings built *toures hye*, and Tolkien's last note reads: 'In medieval accounts, Nimrod

---

[100] McIlwaine, *Tolkien: Maker of Middle-earth*, 258–9, reproduces two pages of these cave drawings.
[101] Christopher recalled that his father relied upon M. C. Burkitt's *Prehistory: A Study of Early Cultures in Europe and the Mediterranean Basin* (1925); see Christina Scull, 'The Influence of Archaeology and History on Tolkien's World', in *Scholarship and Fantasy: Proceedings of the Tolkien Phenomenon*, ed. K. J. Battarbee (Turku, Finland: Anglicana Turkuensia, no. 12, 1993), 33–51 at pp. 34–5.
[102] The Cheddar Caves inspired the glittering caves of Aglarond behind Helm's Deep (*Letters*, 407).

was made the originator of the disastrous project of building Babel.' Though he admired monumental structures such as the Argonath as remnants of Gondor's past grandeur, Tolkien inherited this biblical prejudice against towers like Nimrod's as structures inherently evil because God 'does not look kindly on Babel-builders' (*Letters*, 116). He passed this prejudice along to his hobbits who also 'did not go in for towers' (*FR* Prol). Sauron asserted a corruptive influence upon the Númenóreans by encouraging them to build high towers,[103] and a late interview with Tolkien extended this condemnation to the whole modern world: 'It's like the tower of Babel, isn't it? All noise and confusion.'[104] A list of Tolkien's own high towers makes the point about their intrinsic wickedness—Dol Guldur, Orthanc, Minas Morgul, Minas Ungol, Towers of Teeth, Towers of the Black Gate, and the Dark Tower of Barad-dûr—and their destiny over time to fall into ruins.[105]

VI. *Merciles Beaute*

Described as 'perhaps the most Chaucerian of all his short minor poems,' this 39-line lyric encouraged Tolkien to exercise lexicographical skills honed at the *OED*.[106] Although the line 'For Daunger halt your mercy in his cheyne' did not prompt much comment from Skeat, Tolkien found a great deal to add about the word *halt*:

> halt: 'holds', 3rd. sg. of *hōlden*—this is from O.E. *hăldan*, later *hāldan*, but in the 3rd sg. *halt* (from *haldeþ*) the vowel remained short in O.E. and was still retained unchanged in the 14th century, although this made it now differ considerably from the changed long vowel of other parts of the present. See II 101 note, and Legend Prologue 252 note.

These pedantic forays freed the annotator from discussing contents, since the poem's courtly-love posturing, which C. S. Lewis found exquisite, did not rouse much appreciation from Tolkien. As further avoidance, his note on line 28— 'I never then to ben in his prison lene'—noticed a problem with scansion and suggested omitting the preposition *in*:

> *prison* (etymologically 'captivity') in Middle English also meant 'prisoner', but this sense became obsolete. To restore it here gives a smoother line (and a roundel is the place for smoothness and regularity) and a more natural position for the adjective *lene*.

---

[103] Tolkien, *The Lost Road*, 74–5.   [104] Resnick, 'Interview with Tolkien', 42.
[105] Michael D. C. Drout, 'The Tower and the Ruin: The Past in J. R. R. Tolkien's Works', in Helen Conrad-O'Briain and Gerald Hynes, eds., *Tolkien: The Forest and the City* (Dublin: Four Courts Press, 2013), 175–90.
[106] Bodleian MS Tolkien A 39/2/1, fols. 27–8.

Tolkien must have boasted about this minor emendation because, years later, his friend Nevill Coghill acknowledged the improvement when quoting the line in his book *The Poet Chaucer*.[107]

VII. *To Rosemounde*

Tolkien's commentary for this 24-line ballade said nothing about its contents or rhyme-scheme but devoted most of its one and a half pages to bickering with Skeat over the mysterious word *tregentyll*.[108] The word was not even Chaucer's but the scribe's, written in his colophon to *Troilus* previous in the manuscript, and yet Tolkien could not help indulging the pedantry that Sisam warned would only bore students:

> This little jest of Chaucer's was discovered by Skeat in 1891 on the flyleaf of a MS at Oxford in which it follows a copy of *Troilus and Criseyde*. To the latter is added the colophon: *Tregentyll/here endeth the book of Troylus and of Crisseyde/Chaucer*. On the next leaf is the ballade, without title, but with the colophon: *Tregentil Chaucer*. Skeat thought *Tregentil* might be the scribe's name (which one would then have expected after *here endeth* etc.) and rejected indignantly the notion that it was an enthusiastic comment of the copyist—chiefly because of the wide space between the words in the colophon to the ballade, and because we ought to have *tres gentil*. But the objections have not much weight. In Old French *tres* was frequently compounded with the following adjective, instead of being used separately, and in this case the loss of the *s* could be natural in Anglo-French; indeed the imagined scribe's name could hardly have any other origin. Certainly the comment 'Very polished. Chaucer' is just to *Troilus*, and it adds much to the joke of the little piece. Only with regret could we lose it—it reads almost like Chaucer's own signature.

When annotating the text itself, Tolkien commented upon the scribal insertion of *that* in the phrase *whan that* instead of explaining the more interesting term *mappemounde* as a map of the world (Skeat did), and he provided a translation of the line 'I am pickled in love like a pike in spicy sauce' without remarking on the silliness of this conceit in a love-poem (Skeat did).

VIII. *Truth*

Tolkien's headnote to this 28-line ballade rehearsed information about its manuscripts, titles, sources, and textual variants over the course of three

---

[107] Nevill Coghill, *The Poet Chaucer*, 2nd. edn rev. (London: Oxford University Press, 1967), 81n. The current *Riverside Chaucer* failed to make this improvement.
[108] Bodleian MS Tolkien A 39/2/1, fols. 29–30.

handwritten pages,[109] but its many commonplaces did not impress him: 'The piece has been highly praised, but scarcely deserves it.' The closing envoy survives in only one manuscript and its first line—'Therefore, thou vache, leve thyn old wrecchedness'—prompted Skeat to remark that the sense of *vache* (cow) was obscure. Two decades later, Edith Rickert's biographical research led her to propose that Chaucer was addressing his friend Philip de la Vache.[110] Tolkien did not wholeheartedly embrace this new suggestion—one of his few notices of any other scholar—probably because the stanza revealed a nastiness that readers do not like discovering in their genial Chaucer:

> Miss Rickert has argued that the *envoy* directs the poem to (rather at?) Sir Philip (de) la Vache, who married Elizabeth, daughter of Sir Lewis Clifford—a friend of Chaucer's—since it was by his hand that the French poet Deschamps sent a *balade* addressed to the *grant translateur, noble Geffrey Chaucier*. The details of the poem she also urges are applicable to the incidents of Sir Philip's life. Nonetheless the strongest argument in favour of the proper name is the absence of any other evidence for the use of the ordinary French *vache* in an English context. The author could not have been innocent or the recipient unobservant of the play on the name implied (which is pointed by the *thou*). The latter can hardly have relished it. If Sir Philip is really meant, the *balade* can hardly be counted a tactful sermon, and it is not altogether surprising that the envoy is found in one manuscript only. Doubts have been expressed as to its genuineness, for its continuation of the rhyme-scheme proves little. But it may have been written later than the rest, to point lines once written without special aim, perhaps to settle some small score of which we now know nothing.
> (Bodleian MS Tolkien A 39/2/1, fols. 32–3)

Rickert's argument has prevailed for identifying Sir Philip as the recipient before 1390, even though Paul Strohm, one-time Tolkien Professor of English at Oxford, was still wrestling with the envoy's full implications six decades after Tolkien himself.[111]

IX. *Gentilesse*

In his single-page commentary on this 21-line poem, Tolkien repeated the fifteenth-century scribe John Shirley's account of how Henry Scogan 'inserted it bodily into a "moral balade" he wrote for his pupils, the sons of Henry IV'.[112]

---

[109] Bodleian MS Tolkien A 39/2/1, fols. 30–3. See Ralph Hanna III, 'Authorial Versions, Rolling Revision, Scribal Error? Or, the Truth about Truth', in *Pursuing History: Middle English Manuscripts and Their Texts* (Stanford: Stanford University Press, 1996), 159–73.

[110] Edith Rickert, 'Thou Vache', *Modern Philology* 11 (1913–14), 209–26.

[111] Paul Strohm, *Social Chaucer* (Cambridge, MA: Harvard University Press, 1989), 74; see also *Riverside Chaucer*, 1084–5.

[112] Bodleian MS Tolkien A 39/2/1, fol. 34r–v; Tolkien begins using both sides to save paper. See Bowers, *Chaucer and Langland*, 87–92.

These Lancastrian scions included the illustrious Henry V, later a model for Aragorn leading his outnumbered troops through enemy territory to the Black Gate much as Henry had led his outnumbered forces to Agincourt. Nearly all of Tolkien's remarks focused on the phrase *firste stok* in the opening line as the occasion for discussing *gentilesse* as inborn virtue: 'nobility, both actual worldly eminence and true nobility of character, is by the grace of God.' He went on:

> Chaucer also wrote a 'poetical essay' on this subject in *The Tale of his Wife of Bath*, 253 ff. Indeed, though it has been said that the conviction that real nobility lies in virtue was more rare in Chaucer's day than our own, this is not likely to be true. It was a common theme, and doubtless the practice and the preaching accorded as closely then as now.

Though the bawdy Wife of Bath had been rejected for the Clarendon Chaucer, Tolkien often cites her because her Arthurian romance provided an authentically medieval vision of the Elf Queen's dancing company. But the 'poetic essay' to which he refers was the wedding-night lecture by the Loathly Lady (really the Elf Queen shapeshifted from her true form) who cited Boethius and Dante to argue the natural nobility of *gentilesse*, pointing out that many well-born men with old money behaved worse than poor men of humble birth: 'he is gentil that dooth gentil dedis' (314). Like nearly all English novelists, Tolkien confronted issues of class. The Tooks may have been socially elevated in the Shire because rich, but the two Bagginses showed virtue as well as heroism, as did Samwise Gamgee when the challenge arose, beyond the expectations of their somewhat lower status. The well-spoken Bilbo and Frodo embodied this *gentilesse* by granting mercy and acting magnanimously when opportunities came their way.[113]

Tolkien's commentary then added a theological dimension missing in Chaucer:

> Eminence and good qualities are the free gifts of God and not only to be got by breeding; God can endow a man of humble stock with noble qualities and lift him to high rank.... All good qualities, as also their recognition in the world, are granted by God.

His old teacher Joseph Wright, the Yorkshire mill-worker who rose to become Professor of Comparative Philology, considered Oxford a meritocracy: 'A man could make his way there if he had the will: it did not depend upon birth or social status, but upon work.'[114] The poor orphan Tolkien had his own experience of upward mobility as if some divine grace lifting him to higher rank. He brought to his best-known fiction this same confidence that loyal, well-intentioned men rose while corrupt, self-serving men fell and even died as a result.

---

[113] Shippey, 'Noblesse Oblige: Images of Class in Tolkien', in *Roots and Branches*, 285–301.
[114] Quoted by Douglas Gray in his inaugural lecture as J. R. R. Tolkien Professor of English Literature and Language, *A Marriage of Mercury and Philology* (Oxford: Clarendon Press, 1982), 19n.

X. *Lak of Stedfastnesse*

Tolkien drafted less than a page on this 28-line poem and began with the question of attribution.[115] The fifteenth-century bookman John Shirley reported that Chaucer sent this poem to the king at Windsor, thus allowing researchers to date it between 1393 and 1399 when, Tolkien noted, 'Richard II was rapidly degenerating.' Skeat had referred only to the last years of Richard II's reign without any disparaging remark. Tolkien's Shakespearean view of the headstrong monarch, very much the creation of his Lancastrian successors, supported this notion of a decadent courtliness which Tolkien's fictional alter-ego Faramir invoked when describing the decline of Gondor's past greatness (*TT* IV/5).

Offering reflections on 'martial glory and true glory' from his inception as a character (*Letters*, 79), Faramir's condemnations found steady parallels at Richard II's court. The Men of Númenor grew enamoured of the black arts; Richard II was accused of occult practices and kept a book of geomancy in his personal library. Gondor's kings made tombs more splendid than the houses of the living; Richard II invested lavishly in royal tombs in Westminster Abbey. Gondor's kings counted the old names of their ancestors more dearly than their sons; Richard II installed a genealogical series of statues from Edward the Confessor to himself in Westminster Hall. Childless men sat musing on heraldry; the childless Richard II had an obsession with heraldry, affixing his insignia of the White Hart wherever possible, most famously on the back of the Wilton Diptych. Old Númenorean scholars asked questions of the stars; Richard II's mania for astrology prompted Chaucer to write his *Treatise on the Astrolabe* commending 'the king that is lord of this langage'. The last king of Anárion's line left no heir; Richard II had no children with Queen Anne and therefore left no heir when deposed by his cousin Henry Bolingbroke.

The list of books dealing with Richard II's reign has grown steadily since the landmark volume *The Court of Richard II* by Gervase Mathew, longtime member of the Inklings.[116] Mathew's foreword thanked Tolkien, who must have heard a good deal about this project over their years at the *Eagle and Child* just down from Blackfriars where the scholarly priest lived. But what Fr. Mathew admired as opulent and cosmopolitan at the Ricardian court, Tolkien found degenerate at Minas Tirith. Though Tolkien was notorious for making dismissive remarks about Shakespeare, his own historical transition from the Third Age to the Fourth Age parallels the narrative trajectory from *Richard II* to *Henry V*; his final

---

[115] Bodleian MS Tolkien A 39/2/1, fol. 34v.
[116] SH 2:779–80. Gervase Mathew, *The Court of Richard II* (New York: W. W. Norton, 1968), has been followed by Nigel Saul, *Richard II* (New Haven and London: Yale University Press, 1997); Anthony Goodman and James Gillespie, eds., *Richard II: The Art of Kingship* (Oxford: Clarendon, 1999); and John M. Bowers, *The Politics of 'Pearl': Court Poetry in the Age of Richard II* (Cambridge: D. S. Brewer, 2001).

examinations in 1915 covered the two central plays of this tetralogy, *Henry IV, Part 1* and *Henry IV, Part 2* (SH 3:1146–8). The victory of Henry V over numerically superior French forces, followed by a royal wedding promising a new era of peace and prosperity, offered a ready-made template for Aragorn's ascent to Gondor's throne and his coronation with Arwen as his queen.

Otherwise Tolkien commented upon only four words in *Lak of Stedfastnesse*, his longest note devoted to the sixth line 'Is al this world for *mede* and wilfulnesse':

> for *mede*: because of (his love of) gain and pecuniary rewards—especially as shown in taking bribes; cf. *Parlement of Foules* 228. In *Piers Plowman* Mede is bribery and corruption personified. See C Passus iv 127 ff. There Richard is told that Mede and her allies '*haue maked almost...that no lond loueth the, and yut leest thyn owene.*'

Tolkien's references are noteworthy because Skeat's commentary did not cite *Piers Plowman*, even though he himself had published the work in his monumental two-volume edition of 1886. This means that Tolkien took the trouble to pull down Skeat's edition, knew where to consult the long passage on Lady Mede, and quoted the C-text's lines 209–10 six pages beyond the start of the satire against bribery at line 127. Though Langland did not name the corrupt King, Tolkien automatically identified him as Richard II.

If Tolkien has been little recognized as a Chaucerian, he is even less known as a Langlandian beyond the poem *Doworst* written as a lampoon of Oxford undergraduates: 'In a summer season when sultry was the sun | with lourdains & lubbers I lounged in a hall' (SH 2:304–5). His avoidance of *Piers Plowman* in both research and teaching seems mysterious because the poem was written in the Worcester dialect which he cherished as his mother-tongue.[117] Part of the answer probably lies in the words omitted from the middle of the quotation cited in his note—*bote Marie the helpe*—because veneration of the Virgin Mary was Catholic-sounding and Tolkien always avoided being identified as a Catholic medievalist. Yet here in his Chaucer commentary, he showed himself expert at referencing *Piers Plowman* even if he never wrote about it elsewhere.

XI. *Compleint to his Empty Purse*

Tolkien wrote in his introduction to this 26-line poem: 'This is probably the last thing ever written by Chaucer. This must almost certainly be true of the not altogether pleasing envoy.'[118] Then he crossed out the two sentences and wrote

---

[117] David Bratman, 'Tolkien and the Counties of England', *Mallorn* 37 (1999), 5–13 at p. 7. The idyllic hamlet of Sarehole was still officially in Worcestershire when he lived there as a boy.

[118] Bodleian MS Tolkien A 39/2/1, fols. 35–6.

above them: 'The unpleasing *envoy* to this poem, if not the whole, is probably the last thing Chaucer ever wrote.' Thus Tolkien's two messy pages show him entering the later phase when his drafts are crowded with strike-outs, inserts, and rewrites leading finally to the extreme sketchiness of his notes for the Reeve's Tale.

Commenting on Chaucer's five-line envoy to Henry Bolingbroke after seizing the throne, Tolkien the monarchist (who as a cadet had attended the coronation of George V) could not approve the illegal usurpation any more than he could approve Denethor's efforts at keeping Aragorn from the throne of Gondor. His *LOTR* Appendix A tells how, much earlier, the decline of the Númenor began when King Tar-Palantir's nephew usurped the sceptre and consequently became the last king of the Númenóreans. Even so, Tolkien found the poet's toadying supplication to King Richard in the main three stanzas objectionable and provided more than the usual biographical background about the poet's 'occasion of poverty':

> This does nothing to increase our respect for the language in which Henry IV the conqueror of his former patron Richard II is addressed by Chaucer. Nor can Chaucer have wasted much time in changing sides. The answer (presumably) to the complaint, a grant of an additional forty marks a year, came only a few days after Henry's 'election' on September 30th, 1399. About a year later, traditionally Oct. 25th, 1400, Chaucer died. The contrast between the first stanzas and the last is not a happy one to end on—between the elvish Chaucer who could still turn a begging occasion to a witty mockery of his own need, and Chaucer, now probably ailing as well as in need, forced to go begging once more, and scraping lower than ever.

The phrase *elvish Chaucer* formed part of the Host's characterization of the pilgrim-narrator so withdrawn from his travelling companions that he seemed in some other world.[119] The tradition of the elf-enchanted songster had its roots in poems like *Thomas the Rhymer* quoted by Tolkien in 'On Fairy-Stories' (*Essays*, 110). Bilbo Baggins becomes prolific as a poet after retreating into the elvish realm of Rivendell, it should be noted, and Smith's creativity also comes alive when he leaves Wootton Major and journeys into the realm of Faery.

Chaucer later used the terms 'elvysshe craft' and 'elvysshe lore' in his Canon's Yeoman's Tale to describe the mysterious art of alchemy and, by implication, his own literary art for transforming the slippery stuff of human experience into the solid, orderly substance of literature. Tolkien's 'On Fairy-Stories' recalled this phrase when describing a Secondary World summoned into existence by 'elvish craft' (*Essays*, 140). Why specifically *elvish*? For one thing, the alchemist's work with super-heated metals recalled the metalwork of elvish smiths starting with Eöl,

---

[119] *CT* VII, 1893–4; see J. A. Burrow, 'Elvish Chaucer', in *The Endless Knot: Essays on Old and Middle English in Honor of Marie Borroff*, ed. M. Teresa Tavormina and R. F. Yeager (Cambridge: D. S. Brewer, 1995), 105–11.

the Dark Elf of the First Age. In 1936 Tolkien's lecture 'The Legend of Wayland the Smith' discussed how the *Poetic Edda*'s Völundr was called 'prince of elves' when forging magical golden rings. Only a short leap of imagination leads to Celebrimbor forging the three rings for the Elves and eventually all of the Rings of Power.

Tolkien's picture of an ailing, begging Chaucer violated his usual ban on using an author's life to explain his work, even a work as ostensibly personal as this *Compleint*. Skeat's own difficulties reconciling Chaucer's poverty with the wealth of the son Thomas (1:xlix) resulted from the 'autobiographical fallacy' whereby critics take the poet's statements about himself literally, not ironically.[120] Not financially distressed, Chaucer was more likely politically distressed by the Lancastrian usurpation and drew upon the begging-poem tradition to place himself in a supplicating position.[121] It is also tempting to see Tolkien's phrase *ailing as well as in need* as projecting his personal concerns upon his author, since ill-health and financial worries were recurrent themes throughout his letters and conversations. A note on the *Parlement* (117) indicated his willingness to believe Chaucer about himself: 'It is actually quite in accordance with the ways of literary composition that accidental exterior things such as the battered book in need of binding, and the glimpse of a star though his window, should be genuine and personal and embedded in references to feigned personal feelings and experiences.'

Chaucer's phrase *out of this toune* prompted more biographical speculation on Tolkien's part:

> Hardly 'help me to retire from London to some cheaper place'. A heavy purse would deliver him from economy. At any rate, as a result of the increase in its weight, we find him leasing a tenement in Westminster on Dec. 24, 1399. This has been conjectured that he wished to come back to London from Greenwich. In his *Envoy to Scogan*, written probably in 1393, he complains that while Scogan is living near to the source of favour (*at the shremes heed of grace*), he was living forgotten in a solitary wilderness at the end of the stream. A manuscript note explains the head of the stream, Thames, as *Windsore*, and the end as *Grenewich*.

Chaucer's residence in Greenwich had already served to explain Kentish elements in his personal dialect.

Then came the closing envoy which caused Tolkien the most unhappiness:

> O conquerour of Brutes Albioun!
> Which that by lyne and free eleccioun
> Ben verray king, this song to you I sende;
> And ye, that mowen al our harm amende,
> Have minde up-on my supplicacioun!

---

[120] George Kane, 'The Autobiographical Fallacy in Chaucer and Langland Studies' (1965), in *Chaucer and Langland: Historical and Textual Studies* (Berkeley and Los Angeles: University of California Press, 1989), 1–14.

[121] Robert F. Yeager, 'Chaucer's "To His Purse": Begging or Begging Off?', *Viator* 36 (2005), 373–414.

His long note on 'Brutes Albioun' displayed a knowledge of Welsh lore not shared by his predecessor, thus partly accounting for his joke, years later, about spending his Skeat Prize money on *A Welsh Grammar*.[122]

> *Brutus* or *Brut* was in mediæval tradition a descendant of Æneas of Troy and founded the kingdom of *Britain* in this island. Name and tradition probably go back to early Welsh tales ascribing the name of the island to an eponymous founder whose name was assimilated to Latin *Brutus* when he was connected later with Æneas and Vergil. Since mediæval chronicle histories usually began with *Brut*, this name acquired also the sense of 'chronicle', now obsolete in English, but surviving today in Welsh *brut*. *Albion* was a traditional name in such chronicles for Britain before the Roman occupation. It is probably an old name, derived from the white southern cliffs; according to plausible conjecture, this may also be the etymological sense of Welsh *Prydain* (Britain).

Skeat had drawn upon Geoffrey of Monmouth's account of Brutus, but Tolkien preferred imagining more ancient Welsh sources, as he did in his *Notion Club Papers* when Ramer (Tolkien's stand-in) dreams of discovering 'a unique fragment of a MS. in very early Welsh, before Geoffrey, about the death of Arthur'.[123] The Geoffrey here is of course Monmouth. Their *Gawain* edition's note on the opening Brutus stanza had also gone back to the Welsh *Prydain* with further reference to Morris-Jones's *Welsh Grammar*.[124] His avoidance of naming the twelfth-century Latin authority is curious because the pseudo-scholarly introduction to *Farmer Giles of Ham* offers what amounted to a precis of Monmouth: 'Since Brutus came to Britain, many kings and realms have come and gone' (p. 227). Because Tolkien described himself as historically minded—'Middle-earth is not an imaginary world' (*Letters*, 239)—he would have been naturally attracted to Monmouth's *History of the Kings of Britain* as exactly the sort of fictional history-writing—or historical fiction-writing—that stood as a precedent for his own invocation of Britain's lost past.

'I much prefer history, true or feigned', he wrote in his 1965 Foreword to *The Lord of the Rings*, and Monmouth stood as Britain's earliest master of the sort of feigned history described by Francis Bacon in 'The Advancement of Learning': 'The use of this feigned history is to give some shadow of satisfaction to the mind of man in those points wherein the nature of things denies it.' Recuperating a nation's lost past in a well-made narrative that combined the factual and the imaginative can be traced back to Virgil's *Aeneid*[125]—Monmouth's own

---

[122] Tolkien, 'English and Welsh', in *Essays*, 192; see also Dimitra Fimi, 'Tolkien's "Celtic Type of Legends": Merging Traditions', *Tolkien Studies* 4 (2007), 51–71.
[123] Tolkien, *Sauron Defeated*, 192. 'Such a manuscript leaf', Christopher remarked in a footnote, p. 216, 'would be of superlative importance in the study of the Arthurian legend.'
[124] Tolkien and Gordon, eds., *Sir Gawain and the Green Knight*, 80–1.
[125] Sandra Ballif Straubhaar, 'Roman History', in *Tolkien Encyclopedia*, 576; see also Judy Ann Ford, 'The White City: *The Lord of the Rings* as an Early Medieval Myth of the Restoration of the Roman Empire', *Tolkien Studies* 2 (2005), 53–73.

model—and Chaucer produced his versions of feigned history in many works, notably his Man of Law's Tale where Custance was said to rekindle Christianity in England a generation before the official version in Bede's *Ecclesiastical History*. Custance's voyage westward to Britain can also be compared with St Brendan's *imram* to the Isles of the Blessed, both of them bolstering the core-story behind Eärendel's mission of salvation into the Uttermost West.[126]

XII. *Boethius De Consolatione Philosophiae*

Up to this point in his Notes, Tolkien provided information only about manuscripts and titles, but here he showed a keen interest in the historical Boethius and mined Skeat's commentary to fill six pages assiduously revised even as he drafted them[127] (Fig. 11). His interest was not exceptional. C. S. Lewis boldly declared about *The Consolation of Philosophy*: 'Until about two hundred years ago it would, I think, have been hard to find an educated man in any European country who did not love it.'[128] Skeat had emphasized *Boece*'s importance as the main philosophical source for *Troilus*, and Tolkien liked citing *Adam Scriveyn* where Chaucer chastised his scribe for carelessly copying both works.[129] For his own purposes, Tolkien would prize Boethius as the model of a Christian writer whose masterpiece eschewed any explicit Christian contents even as he grappled with evil's sway in human affairs.[130]

His own late work *Athrabeth Finrod ah Andreth* ('Debate of Finrod and Andreth') offers an intriguing example of a Boethian dialogue covering questions of mortality, death's origins, its divine rationale, and the immortality of human as well as elvish souls. There is gender reversal, however, with the male Elf Finrod taking the role of Lady Philosophy and the mortal woman Andreth speaking from a personal sorrow whose cause is revealed only at the end—her loss in youth of her lover Aegnor, brother of Finrod.[131] Previous critics guessed that Tolkien gained familiarity with the *Consolation* by studying King Alfred's Old English translation,[132] but clearly his most careful attention to the original Latin came

---

[126] Tolkien's *Notion Club Papers* included 'The Death of St. Brendan' as well as another version entitled 'Imram'; see *Sauron Defeated*, 261–4, 296–9, and SH 2:566–7.
[127] Bodleian MS Tolkien A 39/2/1, fols. 37–41. Their *Selections* included Book II, Metre v; Book II, Prose vii; Book II, Metre vii; and Book IV, Metre vi.
[128] Lewis, *Discarded Image*, 'Boethius', 75–91 at p. 75.
[129] Mooney and Stubbs, *Scribes and the City*, 68, have identified Adam's copy of *Boece* in Aberystwyth, National Library of Wales, MS Peniarth 393D.
[130] John Wm. Houghton and Neal K. Keesee, 'Tolkien, King Alfred, and Boethius: Platonist Views of Evil in *The Lord of the Rings*', *Tolkien Studies* 2 (2005), 131–59.
[131] Tolkien, *Morgoth's Ring*, 303–60, and SH 2:73–80 '*Athrabeth Finrod ah Andreth*'.
[132] Shippey, *Road to Middle-earth*, 140–6, and Kathleen E. Dubs, 'Providence, Fate, and Chance: Boethian Philosophy in *The Lord of the Rings*', in *Tolkien and the Invention of Myth*, ed. Chance, 133–42.

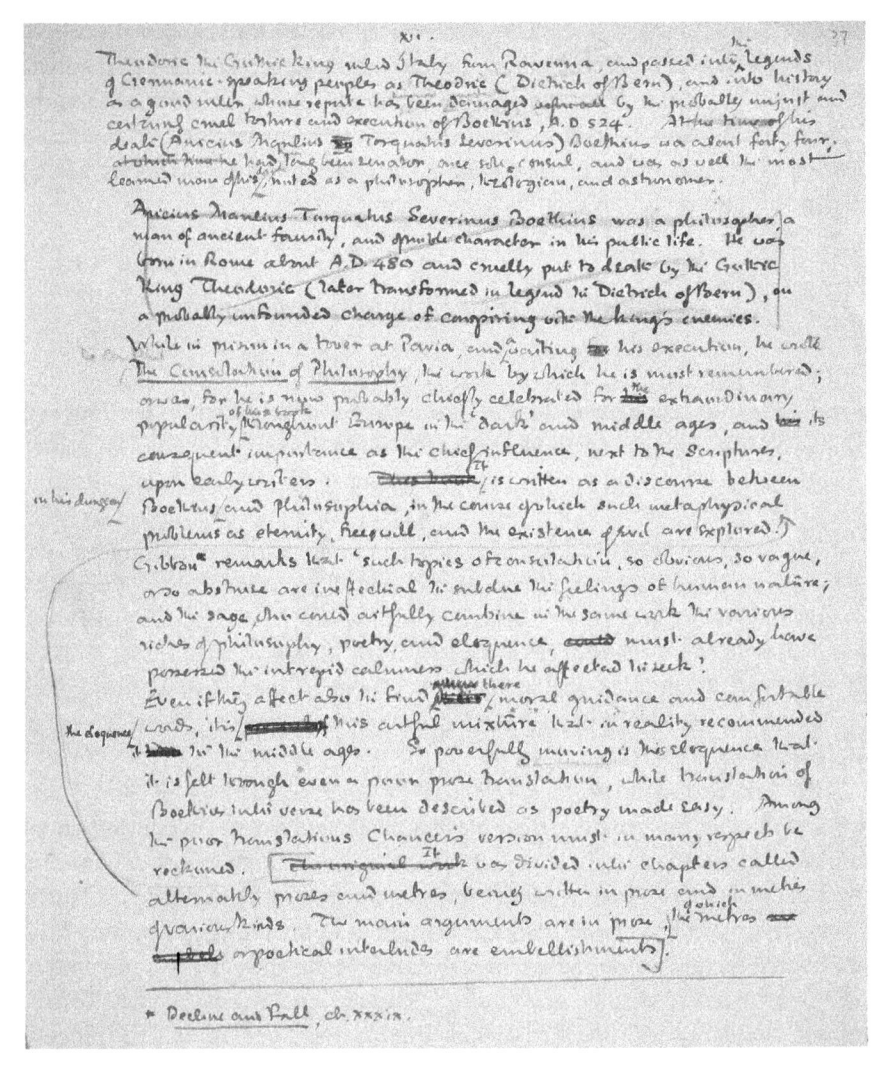

Fig. 11. Rewritten commentary on Chaucer's *Boece* (Oxford, Bodleian Library, MS Tolkien A 39/2/1, fol. 37).

while editing and annotating Chaucer's *Boece*, particularly the selection which Gordon entitled 'Death the Leveller', and he was still pondering these profound issues in his own Boethian dialogue of 1959.

Tolkien's headnote typifies his practice of writing a complete draft, cancelling it to write a new version, and then putting both of them aside to write yet another version. His first effort rehearsed the basic facts—leaving us to suspect the philosopher's five-part name later inspired the king's five-part name Augustus Bonifacius Ambrosius Aurelianus Antonius in *Farmer Giles of Ham*:

Anicius Manlius Torquatus Severinus Boethius was a philosopher, a man of ancient family, and of noble character in his public life. He was born in Rome about A.D. 480 and cruelly put to death by the Gothic King Theodoric (later transformed in legend to Dietrich of Bern) on a probably unfounded charge of conspiring with the king's enemies.

He crossed out this paragraph and tried again at the top of the page, now shifting emphasis away from the philosopher to the ruler who executed him:

Theodoric the Gothic king ruled Italy from Ravenna and passed into the legends of Germanic-speaking peoples as Theodric (Dietrich of Bern), and into history as a good ruler whose repute has however been much damaged by his probably unjust and certainly cruel torture and execution of Boethius, A.D. 524. At the time of his death Anicius Manlius Torquatus Severinus Boethius was almost forty-four, had then long been senator, once sole consul, and was as well the most learned man of his day, noted as a philosopher, theologian, and astronomer.

This focus on Theodoric the Great (454–526) gave priority to *legends* over *history*, perhaps recalling how Alfred the Great also prefaced his Boethius translation with an account of Theodoric. Tolkien had studied late Roman history even after transferring to Oxford's English School, and so he knew that the Gothic king, far from a brutish barbarian, had lived for many years at the court of Constantinople where he learned the basics of Roman government and the military tactics that served him well when he became ruler of a largely Latinized populace. Seeking to restore the glory of ancient Rome, Theodoric reigned over Italy during its most peaceful, prosperous period since the fourth century.[133] Nor was Boethius his only scholar-administrator, succeeded by Cassiodorus whose history of the Goths, written for Theodoric, was condensed by Jordanes in *De Origine Actibusque Getarum*. Tolkien's fascination with the Goths meant that he also read this work closely; his description of the Battle of Pelennor Fields followed Jordanes' account of the Battle of the Catalaunian Plains and the Roman defeat of Attila's Huns.[134]

Tolkien had admired *OED* editor Henry Bradley's *The Goths* with its encomium to Theodoric as 'among the noblest men who ever wore a crown',[135] and he lectured on 'Legends of the Goths' at Oxford in 1929 not long after drafting these comments about *Boece*. His later 'English and Welsh' told how the Gothic language moved him deeply—'I have since mourned the loss of Gothic literature'—and his study of Wright's *Primer of Gothic Language* inspired him to try inventing lost Gothic words (*Essays*, 191–2). Christopher notes that the

---

[133] John Moorhead, *Theoderic in Italy* (Oxford: Clarendon Press, 1992).
[134] Shippey, *Road to Middle-earth*, 16; Miryam Librán-Moreno, '"Byzantium, New Rome!" Goths, Langobards, and Byzantium in *The Lord of the Rings*', in *Tolkien and the Study of His Sources*, ed. Fisher, pp. 84–115, goes into great detail on the author's treatment of Goths (good) and Byzantines (bad).
[135] Henry Bradley, *The Goths from the Earliest Times to the End of the Gothic Dominion in Spain*, 5th edn (London: T. Fisher Unwin, 1898), 190; on Theodoric's treatment of Boethius, see pp. 183–4.

forefathers of the Kings of Rohan have names constructed from Gothic, not Old English (*UT* 311), and the only complete poem in the Gothic language is Tolkien's own *Bagme Bloma*.[136] He regretted that the Goths' embrace of the Arian heresy created a rift with Latin Christianity so that Roman civilization was not backed by Gothic power—except during the short-lived rule of Theodoric.[137]

Theodoric had indeed 'passed into the legends'—always a powerful phrase for Tolkien—to become the Germanic folk-hero Dietrich of Bern (Verona) whose name crops up in the Old English poems *Waldere*, *Deor*, and *Widsith* as well as the Middle High German *Nibelungenlied*. These legends told of his battles with dragons, dwarves, and giants. His grandson-in-law became the Wadga grafted to the family tree of Wayland the Smith.[138] The Old Norse *Þiðreks saga af Bern* contained the Nibelung story with its disaster-producing gold ring and served as one of Richard Wagner's sources for his *Ring des Nibelungen*.[139]

Tolkien's third draft of his *Boece* headnote returned focus to Boethius, starting with his execution instead of his birth and singling out the detail of the philosopher's imprisonment in a tower. Visitors to Pavia are still shown a tower said to have been the one where Boethius met his end. Chaucer may have seen it when he travelled there to negotiate with the Lombard tyrant Barnabo Visconti, whose downfall he inserted into his Monk's Tale,[140] and Tolkien himself seldom missed a chance to mention towers. If he had gotten around to annotating their edition's extract from the Monk's Tale, Tolkien would have no doubt drawn attention to Hugelino's imprisonment in a tower: 'But litel out of Pyse stand a tour | In whiche tour in prisoun put was he' (3599–600). Was he recalling this detail of Boethius' imprisonment when picturing Gandalf's captivity atop the tower of Orthanc? Was he still recalling it in 1971 when he said sadly that personal letters were 'like bread to a prisoner starving in a tower' (*Letters*, 415)?

Here is the headnote's final version:

> Anicius Manlius Torquatus Severinus Boethius was in A.D. 524 cruelly executed (on a probably unfounded charge) by Theodoric the Gothic King, who at that time ruled Italy from Ravenna, on the whole very well. At his death Boethius was, at an age of about forty-four, in spite of a long tenure of high office, renowned also as a philosopher, theologian and astronomer, probably the most learned man of his day. In a tower at Pavia, where for a year he awaited death, he wrote

---

[136] Printed and translated by Shippey, *Road to Middle-earth*, 354.

[137] Tom Shippey, 'Goths and Romans in Tolkien's Imagination', in Conrad-O'Briain and Hynes, eds., *Tolkien: The Forest and the City*, 19–32 at p. 27; he concludes that Aragorn is the obvious parallel to Theodoric the Great (p. 28).

[138] Shippey, *Road to Middle-earth*, 22–3, 29, untangles these references; see also Sandra Ballif Straubhaar, 'Myth, Late Roman History, and Multiculturalism in Tolkien's Middle-earth', in *Tolkien and the Invention of Myth*, ed. Chance, 101–17.

[139] Shippey, 'The Problem of the Rings: Tolkien and Wagner', in *Roots and Branches*, 97–114.

[140] As a trick of fate, the poet's great-great-grandson and last male descendant Richard de la Pole was slain at the Battle of Pavia in 1525.

his last and most famous book, *The Consolation of Philosophy*, in the form of discourse between himself and Philosophia, who appeared to comfort him in his dungeon.

For a fuller account of Boethius, Tolkien directed readers to the same chapter of Gibbon's *Decline and Fall of the Roman Empire* which Skeat had quoted at length. Scholars often take these shortcuts, though Tolkien knew Gibbon from his own reading and shared the historian's sense of decline when writing about the 'long defeat' in Middle-earth (*FR* II/7).[141] William Morris had borrowed liberally from Gibbon's portrayals of the Gothic tribes in *The House of the Wolfings* and *The Roots of the Mountains,* two of Tolkien's favourites from undergraduate days.[142] Citing the importance of Boethius' book 'as the chief influence, next to the Scriptures, upon early writers', Tolkien traced the lineage of the *Consolation*'s admirers even as he disparaged its translators:

> Boethius was the teacher of Dante before Chaucer. Jean de Meun, second author of the *Romance of the Rose*, used him freely, so that Chaucer is often indebted to the philosopher through the *Romance* as well as direct.... Translations of Boethius were to be found both before the *Romance* and after Chaucer. In English, however, there appears to have been only one, the famous rendering in which the original is freely handled by King Alfred in the 9th century; there exists also a translation of the metres into (very poor) Old English verse, which is also ascribed to King Alfred.

After translating *Beowulf* into prose in 1926, Tolkien was quick to defend Chaucer's failure to render Boethius' poems into English verse: 'So powerfully moving is this eloquence that it is felt through even a poor prose translation.' And how did he rate *Boece* overall? 'Among the poor translations, Chaucer's version must in many respects be reckoned.' Here he took the fourteenth-century writer to task, almost as if criticizing a student's essay, by focusing upon Chaucer's confusion of two Latin words:

> His translation is often faulty through sheer mistakes in Latinity (e.g. in one place he takes *clauus* as *clauis*)—errors which many would nowadays make as often, but for the dictionaries which did not then exist.... Most often his translation is defective through slavish following of the idiom, or word-order, of the original, or use of words of Latin origin that were no longer good renderings of their ancestors—a fault to be seen at all periods of English. It has taken many centuries for English to shake off the trembling awe of the slave in the presence of Lord Latin.

---

[141] *Letters*, 255: 'I do not expect "history" to be anything but a "long defeat"...'. Shippey, *Road to Middle-earth*, 350, remarked how Gibbon 'certainly stayed in Tolkien's mind'.

[142] He purchased a copy of *House of the Wolfings* with money from the Skeat Prize in 1914; see also Rachel Falconer, 'Earlier Fantasy Fiction: Morris, Dunsany, and Lindsay', in *Companion*, ed. Lee, 307–9.

Tolkien perhaps recalled the advice of his schoolmaster George Brewerton to prefer plain English words; Tolkien never calls Mount Doom a *volcano* or its molten outpourings *lava* because both words came from Latin. Perhaps chastened by his critique of Chaucer's prose, Tolkien rewrote his own remarks in a clearer, smoother, and more concise style, even making room for a bit of praise: 'he often reveals his talent in finely chosen words and phrases.' Next Tolkien drafted two pages of notes gleaned from Skeat's forty-page commentary, still chafing at the corrupt passages which Sisam prevented him from correcting. 'This is not sense as it stands', he wrote. 'It can be rectified by...'.

XIII. Prologue to *The Legend of Good Women*

Despite Sisam's warnings not to exceed a total of twenty pages, Tolkien showed no sign of imposing economy even as he drew nearer the end and could see how much he had written. Here he drafted twenty-eight pages on the Prologue to the *Legend of Good Women*, two pages of general introduction followed by twenty-six pages of notes, some particularly long.[143] He spent two full pages glossing names in Chaucer's inset 'Balade' and another two pages on the misogynist author *Valerie*. Blue pencil was used to cross out sentences and whole entries during the drafting process, and later pencil brackets indicated how excessive notes might be trimmed, but never were.

Tolkien's headnote started with the standard question of how many of Cupid's martyrs were meant for inclusion: 'The number Chaucer intended to write (if he ever made up his mind) is unknown.' The author whose own *legendarium* never reached any finished state seems unperturbed, almost comforted, that the founder of the English tradition left unresolved the length and final form of his own unfinished story-collections, here the *Legend* and later the *Canterbury Tales*.

His next question addressed the Prologue's two versions. Like Tolkien with his two versions of 'Riddles in the Dark' for *The Hobbit*—'the revised version is in itself better in motive and narrative' (*Letters*, 141)—Chaucer was a revising author who produced two versions of his *Troilus*, an earlier text of the Knight's Tale entitled 'the Love of Palamon and Arcite', and the first-draft version of the Wife of Bath's Tale later assigned to the Shipman. Skeat believed that the Cambridge Gg manuscript of the *Legend* Prologue preserved the earlier A Version later rewritten as the B Version found in Fairfax and six other manuscripts. Though Tolkien was open-minded to the idea that 'B is the better of the two—favoured by the author', he was obliged to annotate the A text chosen by Gordon for their *Selections*. In his working copy of the Text's proof, however, Tolkien made bold to strike out the

---

[143] Bodleian MS Tolkien A 39/2/1, fols. 42–70.

subtitle *Earlier Version* and now explained why: 'there is a tendency at present to put B before A.'[144]

Tolkien found value in these two versions because they allowed us to observe Chaucer in his workshop, but he objected to the Prologue's topical allegory: 'That the God of Love and his queen were intended for Richard II and his queen, Anne of Bohemia (see *Parlement of Foules*) is often argued, but not proved.' This identification of Queen Alceste with Queen Anne was established by Fairfax's compliment—'And whan this book is maad, yive hit the quene | On my behalf at Eltham or at Shene' (496–7)—which was dropped in Cambridge Gg presumably because the English queen had died. Tolkien used this evidence to establish an end-date for the Fairfax version: 'Anne died in 1394 and the king, whose grief was extravagant, forsook his palace of Shene for good; it had been their favourite house. The lines must have been written therefore before 1394.' Because these references now carry significance beyond routine commendations to the poet's royal patrons, the critical tradition has caught up with Tolkien's challenge to any simple equation of the two royal couples, the historical and the fictional.[145]

Chaucer's beautiful and merciful Queen Alceste in her garden, freed from any fourteenth-century courtly context, provided several important ingredients for Tolkien's own creative imagination. The first was her sacrifice on behalf of her husband:

> Alcestis was wife of Admetus of Pherae in Thessaly (not Thrace, as here). Apollo obtained of the Fates a promise that he should be delivered at the hour of death if father, mother, or wife would die for him. Alcestis died for her husband, and so is taken as a type of pure love and of devotion. Gower tells her story in *Confessio Amantis*.

Already by the late 1920s, Tolkien imagined his Lúthien making a similar sacrifice, first by dying and going to the Halls of Mandos where she sang so sorrowfully that the Lord of the Dead summoned Beren back to life—what he called 'a kind of Orpheus-legend in reverse' (*Letters*, 193)—and then again by choosing to abandon her Elvish immortality to face a human death.[146] It was the same price that Lúthien's descendant Arwen was willing to pay for her marriage to Aragorn. Years later after his wife Edith's death, Tolkien would lament the reversal of roles in his own personal mythology: 'But the story has gone crooked, & I am left, and *I* cannot plead before the inexorable Mandos' (*Letters*, 420).

---

[144] *Riverside Chaucer*, 1059–60, has established the orthodoxy of Fairfax first, then Cambridge Gg second.

[145] See Paul Strohm, 'Queens as Intercessors', *Huchon's Arrow: The Social Imagination of Fourteenth-Century Texts* (Princeton: Princeton University Press, 1992), 95–119, and David Wallace, '"If That Thou Live": Legends and Lives of Good Women', in *Chaucerian Polity: Absolutist Lineages and Associational Forms in England and Italy* (Stanford: Stanford University Press, 1992), 337–78.

[146] J. R. R. Tolkien, *Beren and Lúthien*, ed. Christopher Tolkien (Boston and New York: Houghton Mifflin Harcourt, 2017), assembles and dates the many versions of this episode.

Once the Chaucerian legacy is established, Alceste joins Galadriel's literary genealogy beginning with Lady Philosophy in *The Consolation of Philosophy* and continuing with Beatrice in the *Divine Comedy* and the Pearl Queen in *Pearl*. C. S. Lewis had thanked Tolkien for reading his 'Courtly Love' chapter in *The Allegory of Love*, and Galadriel enacts the lady's role from medieval *amour courtois* when becoming the object of Gimli's adoration despite the fact that she already had a consort. The Dwarf looks into her eyes and falls in love, she gently asks him to name his desire, and when he asked for a single strand of her hair, she bestows three golden hairs as he stammers his thanks.[147] Queen Alceste's story, however, added an ingredient missing from the courtly-love model as well as the Boethian traditions. All prior female instructors were virginal or virago-like, Beatrice like an admiral and the Pearl Queen like a duke or earl. None of them belonged to a loving husband–wife couple. Only Alceste enacts the role of a queen loyal to her consort, much as Galadriel did when deciding to remain in Middle-earth because Celeborn refused to leave.

Tolkien came to imagine Celeborn ruling over Lórien much as Chaucer's God of Love held dominion over his garden realm.[148] Here he was joined by Galadriel who resembled Alceste in her wise, compassionate treatment of the Chaucerian dreamer: 'she had a marvellous gift of insight into the minds of others, but judged them with mercy and understanding' (*UT* 230). Like Chaucer the poet, Celebrimbor the artisan played the role of an attendant preoccupied with his craft. Also like Chaucer forced to repent works like the *Romaunt* and *Troilus* defaming ladies, Celebrimbor came to repent using his artistry to forge of the Rings of Power (*UT* 235–7).

The *Legend* Prologue describes the poet rising early in the morning to venerate the daisy, and Tolkien's annotation on the Old English *dæges ēage* as 'eye of day' allowed him to indulge his own love of the flower: 'as the sun shines in the heavenly fields, so does the daisy, with its golden centre and surrounding rays, shine from the grass below.' One of his late letters would recall at length a daisy in his lawn: 'it had put out from its flower, on delicate stalks rising in a ring out of the rim of the disc, six pink-tipped little elvish daisies like an airy crown' (*Letters*, 403). His Clarendon text always took care with the word's pronunciation by adding accent-marks—some as elaborate as *dáyèsẏe*—and his notes placed the word's formation squarely in the riddle tradition: 'The name is probably connected with ancient riddles and "kennings" (conventional poetic descriptive compounds) and enshrines a double comparison, the riddle once removed.'[149]

---

[147] FR II/8. Gimli continues as the courtly lover when almost coming to blows with Éomer for speaking disrespectfully of the Lady of the Golden Woods, and this love-narrative continues in the Appendix A where Gimli sails from Middle-earth out of his desire to see her beauty again and Galadriel obtains grace for him to be received by the Lords of the West.

[148] 'The History of Galadriel and Celeborn', *UT*, 228–67 at pp. 230, 235, and 237, varies considerably from the oft-revised history in Appendix B of *The Return of the King*, 363.

[149] Tolkien discussed Old English kennings in 'On Translating *Beowulf*', *Essays*, 59–60. McIlwaine, *Tolkien: Maker of Middle-earth*, 304, remarks that Tolkien's hyphenated words like *stone-slide* and *wolf-ring* resemble Anglo-Saxon kennings.

Tolkien lectured on Old English Riddles in 1931, but *The Hobbit*'s key chapter 'Riddles in the Dark' was already in the earliest drafts from around 1930.[150] It is therefore noteworthy that one of Bilbo's riddles matched what Tolkien explained about Chaucer's daisy:

> *An eye in a blue face*
> *Saw an eye in a green face.*
> *'That eye is like to this eye'*
> *Said the first eye,*
> *'But in a low place*
> *Not in high place.'*

To solve the riddle, Gollum needed to cast his memory back to when he still lived by the river before retreating underground: 'Sun on the daisies it means, it does.'[151] Writing to his publisher in 1947, Tolkien denied any particular source because it was simply 'the etymology of the word "daisy" expressed in riddle-form' (*Letters*, 123). He himself had gone back to this etymology about 1925 in his *Lay of the Children of Húrin* when writing 'the eye of day was opened wide' about the same time he finished editing Chaucer's texts and proofing the galleys.[152]

Tolkien continued sparring with Skeat in his *Legend* notes. For the line 'Ther-as ther is non assay by preve', his predecessor commented upon *ther* while Tolkien remarked instead upon the phrase *assay by preve*. When Skeat said nothing about *halyday*, Tolkien took a quarter-page to explain: 'The sense is that he always put aside his week-day studies on Sunday (and other "holidays"); in May he did this even on week-days.' When Skeat came up short on *coroun*, Tolkien supplied half a page on the word's earliest appearances into Old English, Old French, and Middle English, the scansion of its various forms, and its appearance in the Second Nun's Tale. And when Skeat decided that Chaucer's fondness for Maytime poetry was a mere commonplace, Tolkien replied: 'These lines may be taken as one of the genuine references to Chaucer's personal tastes.'

Tolkien steadily documented the poet's debt to precursors Guillaume de Machaut and Jean Froissart and interpreted lines 62–5 to mean 'French poets, first in the field, have reaped all the harvest and left only the gleanings.' But his distaste for everything French brought him to the defence of Chaucer as a fellow English writer: 'Though derivative in many ways from their work, especially in conventional details, his imitation is clever enough to bear comparison with its models, and individual enough to stand on its own merits.'

---

[150] Rateliff, *History of The Hobbit*, p. x; see p. xx for his conclusion 'the story was indeed begun in the summer of 1930 and completed in January 1933'.
[151] *Annotated Hobbit*, 122; see also Adam Roberts, *The Riddles of the Hobbit* (London: Palgrave Macmillan, 2013), 62–3.
[152] *Lays of Beleriand*, 38 (line 718); Christopher makes this connection 'Cf. Bilbo's second riddle to Gollum' (p. 56).

When Chaucer set the initial action 'in a litel erber that I have', Tolkien again violated his rule against using the author's life by explaining that the lines 'refer to Chaucer's house at the time of the first writing of the prologue'. Would Tolkien have been distressed by connecting this note with the fact that 22 Northmoor Road's back garden also had an newly-built arbour, not yet covered with greenery, where he was photographed napping somewhat like the dreamer in the *Legend* Prologue?[153] His Chaucer note certainly expanded upon the luxury of having such an arbour:

> Chaucer gave up the lease (received in 1374) of his house above the city gate of Aldgate in October 1386. It is thought that an *erber*, which was a green space with shady walls of trained trees and climbing plants, would hardly be connected with such a house, and that we should look in Kent for his dwelling when he wrote this. He was appointed Justice of the Peace for Kent in October 1385, and so perhaps left his Aldgate house even before the date when he relinquished the lease. But then as now, town-dwellers could doubtless (if they could afford it) have an *erber* detached from their house. The *erber*, and the servants strewing flowers, need not be much closer to reality than the ensuing dream. The sense of freedom which runs through the prologue is, however, unmistakeable, and it may be connected with the privilege granted to Chaucer in February 1385 of performing his duties as Controller of the Customs and Subsidies through a deputy. He thus had unwonted leisure, without loss of income, until by a sudden twist of 'hir that turned as a bal' he lost his appointment in December 1386.[154]

His aborted *TLOR* sequel *The New Shadow* got as far as imaging the leisure of its two main characters 'sitting in an arbour near the steep eastern shore of Anduin' more than a hundred years after the fall of the Dark Tower.[155]

Tolkien's closing allusion to Chaucer's *Truth*—'In trust of hir that turneth as a bal' (9)—looks like donnish wit meant to impress the reader whether or not the reader caught the reference. One wonders how many of Chaucer's own first readers actually caught his bookish references and showy name-dropping. Often the humour depended upon recognizing how he twisted his sources, as when the God of Love cited Valerius and St Jerome as authorities on virtuous wives. Tolkien needed to explain the joke: 'But *Valerie* and *Ageyns Jovinian* were notorious, and well-known by name, to many more than ever read them, as types of the condemnation of women. Love's appeal to them therefore was probably intended to sound comic (to some ears).' Bookishness was, after all, another trait shared by the two authors. The *Legend* Prologue reported that Chaucer owned a library of 'sixty bokes olde and newe', a large personal collection at the time, and Tolkien too

---

[153] Two photographs in *Tolkien Family Album*, 50–1, show wooden trellises for the arbours where Tolkien was sleeping with young Christopher. See also McIlwaine, *Tolkien: Maker of Middle-earth*, 277.

[154] Paul Strohm, *Chaucer's Tale: 1386 and the Road to Canterbury* (New York: Viking, 2014), greatly expands upon this biographical background.

[155] Tolkien, *Peoples of Middle-Earth*, 411.

became an avid book-collector, often photographed in front of bookshelves at home and in college rooms, his walls lined with hefty volumes from floor to ceiling, unlike the rooms of C. S. Lewis whose visitors were struck by the meagreness of his personal library.[156]

Alceste's plea for her royal husband's restraint summoned the negative example of the 'tiraunts of Lumbardye' (354) who, in Tolkien's note, 'frequently obtained supreme power in the "free cities" of Lombardy and often made their names odious for their cruelty and tyranny'. He said more about the Visconti family's iron-fisted rule in northern Italy because, as an author who would create the good rulers Théoden and Aragorn, he thought long and hard about what good kingship meant according to 'the sentence of the philosophre' (365):

> This probably refers to Aristotle, who was supposed to have educated Alexander the Great, and taught him all his philosophy (under three heads: *Theoric*, *Rhetoric*, and *Practic*). *Practic* deals with the ordering of a king's life, of his person, household, and realm. Gower sets out all this 'education of Alexander' in the seventh book of the *Confessio Amantis*. There Aristotle says that a king must govern all classes in the realm, clerk, knight, merchant, and common people alike; *o lawe must governe hem alle*. The third 'point of Policy', after Truth, and Liberality with Discretion, is Justice.

He then paraphrases Chaucer's lines 368–9: 'This is no new obligation; a king has been solemnly pledged by his oaths to administer the law justly since very ancient times.' Eventually in his own Middle-earth, these *very ancient times* would reach back to the Third Age when Bard of Dale extended his royal rule to Lake-town, which previously had become a commercial republic like Venice with the Master as its Doge. Like a proper Tolkien hero hostile to change and innovation, Bard reverted to the older model by assuming the role of a traditional Germanic king.

Commenting upon England's royal succession in Chaucer's *Compleint to his Empty Purse*, Tolkien questioned the legitimacy of the Lancastrian succession: 'Henry IV proclaimed himself king by conquest, inherited right, and election. One ground was sufficient in theory. The first was the most real.'[157] Aragorn becomes the clearest embodiment of this kingly ideal when accepting his crown with consent of the governed: 'and all the people cried *yea* with one voice' (*RK* VI/5). If Henry Bolingbroke had a dubious claim because he came to the English throne by force of arms, not popular consent, Aragorn became King of Gondor legitimately by election as well as inheritance. Though victorious in battle after lifting the siege of Minis Tirith, he refused to enter the city by right of conquest, only going

---

[156] *Tolkien Family Album*, 56. Lewis's prodigious memory did not require him to keep books handy for reference; see W. H. Lewis, 'Memoir of C. S. Lewis', in *Letters of C. S. Lewis*, 16.

[157] Bodleian MS Tolkien A 39/2/1, fol. 36. W. H. Lewis, 'Memoir of C. S. Lewis', 14, reported an Inkling session that discussed the contractual theory of medieval kingship; see also Christopher Scarf, *The Ideal of Kingship in the Writings of Charles Williams, C. S. Lewis and J. R. R. Tolkien: Divine Kingship Is Reflected in Middle-earth* (Cambridge: James Clarke, 2013).

disguised to the Houses of Healing to assist with the wounded. As King Elessar, he brought order to his realm exactly as Aristotle prescribed.[158] He tempered liberality with discretion when pardoning the Easterlings, he gave Mordor's freed slaves their own lands around Lake Núrnen, and he enforced justice when condemning Beregond for spilling blood in the Hallows but punished him with nothing harsher than exile to Ithilien in the service of Faramir (*RK* VI/5). His royal rule bore no resemblance to the tyrants of Lombardy.

Queen Alceste's catalogue of Chaucer's works seemed calculated to improve the chances for the poet's literary corpus surviving intact. Some did not make it. Tolkien speculated about the 'balades, roundels, virelayes' and lamented, 'It seems certain that a great many "minor poems" of this sort written by Chaucer are now lost altogether.' About the work called 'Wreched Engendring of Mankinde' he offered a flicker of hope: 'It has perished entirely, unless, as is often held, it was originally written in seven-line stanzas and fragments of it appear worked into the prologue to the Man of Law's Tale.' But for the third lost work 'Origenes upon the Maudeleyne', Tolkien sounded a despairing note: 'No trace of it is left, not even worked into later poems.' Already in a sombre mood, he ended with mention of a linguistic casualty: 'This form of Magdalen was once universal, though now only preserved in the pronunciation (*maudlin*) of Magdalen College, Oxford, and in *maudlin tears*.'

XIV. *The Legend of Cleopatra*

Of the ten love-martyrs from *The Legend of Good Women*, Gordon picked Cleopatra probably because Shakespeare's *Antony and Cleopatra* made her a more attractive choice for undergraduate readers than Hypsipyle or Hypermnestra. Tolkien's twelve-page commentary on this 126-line text gave him opportunities for revisiting Roman history, focusing on curious etymologies, citing Germanic as well as Classical traditions, and making the case for his London poet's knowledge of the provincial-sounding Alliterative tradition.[159]

Tolkien understood that Chaucer's background readings had cast a wide net: 'The sources of this legend are probably various, and Chaucer has certainly not presented the "naked text" of any one authority.' He followed Skeat on crediting the ancient authors Orosius and Annæus Florus as well as Boccaccio's *De Claris Mulieribus*, even citing the version of Cleopatra's suicide in *Confessio Amantis* because Gower 'shows signs of having read Chaucer's *Legend*'. Much as critics like

---

[158] Judy Ann Ford and Robin Anne Reid, 'Councils and Kings: Aragorn's Journey towards Kingship in J. R. R. Tolkien's *The Lord of the Rings* and Peter Jackson's *The Lord of the Rings*', *Tolkien Studies* 6 (2009), 71–90.
[159] Bodleian MS Tolkien A 39/2/2, fols. 71–80.

to imagine great authors working in solitude, Chaucer and Gower clearly enjoyed a special rapport as friends, fellow readers, and poetry-writing rivals. So close was their literary camaraderie that it is not always clear in which direction the influence flowed, whether Gower had read Chaucer's *Legend* first or Chaucer worked from Gower's *Confessio*. John Fisher imagined a relationship like the one between Coleridge and Wordsworth or later Eliot and Pound.[160] Now of course we can add Tolkien and Lewis to that list of close literary friendships.

Tolkien remained a stickler about scansion, remarking grumpily about line 17: 'If Chaucer really passed this line as it stands, we can only say that he was not doing his best.' When the poet said the Egyptian queen was 'fair as is the rose in May' (34), Tolkien objected to a simile not befitting her exotic beauty: 'But Chaucer was repainting the picture for a northern audience in the colours he knew and they expected.' Although Chaucer slighted the wedding feast, Tolkien took time to provide a sample medieval menu which included barnacle-geese in butter, rabbits in coloured sauce, and pheasants in gleaming silver—'not to mention a long wine-list'—closer to the fancy French cooking that he deplored than the simple rustic meals that he included in his stories.

As with the ancient names listed in *The Book of the Duchess*, he reflected upon the spelling *Tholomee* for Cleopatra's brother Ptolemy to illustrate what changes occurred over time:

> Their pronunciation and spelling were thus far removed from their originals, but they had become familiar and survived the acquaintance often with their forms in Latin texts. Some still do. We cling to Homer, Aristotle, Virgil in spite of our knowledge that these people were really named *Homēros, Aristotélēs, Vergilius*. There were corruptions, of course, especially of less familiar names, some deliberate because pedantic exactitude was not in fashion, some accidental because copyists will always stumble when faced with unfamiliar words.

That scribes misspelled unfamiliar words as well as names would become central to Tolkien's argument about lost dialect forms in the Reeve's Tale. His own exactitude was hardly exemplary, as Christopher remarked in the introduction to his *Beowulf* translation: 'In the matter of proper names my father was inconsistent and sometimes found it difficult to decide between several possibilities' (p. 11).

Strange words were the stock and trade of a philologist, and Tolkien took a keen interest in *heterly* (59):

> This word only occurs here in Chaucer, and elsewhere it belongs only to the Alliterative tradition, whether the alliterative prose of the life of *St Katharine* and

---

[160] John H. Fisher, *John Gower: Moral Philosopher and Friend of Chaucer* (London: Methuen, 1965); see also John M. Bowers, 'Rival Poets: Gower's *Confessio* and Chaucer's *Legend of Good Women*', in *John Gower, Trilingual Poet: Language, Translation, and Tradition*, ed. Elisabeth Dutton with John Hines and R. F. Yeager (Cambridge: D.S. Brewer, 2010), 276–87.

related works, or to such poems as *Sir Gawain and the Green Knight, Wars of Alexander, William of Palerne*. It is foreign to the South East of England, and belongs to the North and West, a blend probably of Old Norse *hatrliga* and Old English *hetelīce*. Almost certainly *heterly they hurtlen* is a reminiscence of some of Chaucer's miscellaneous reading in contemporary English, more lively than the foreign learning he is more proud to parade. In addition to hints of this sort, the style and rhythm of Chaucer, when attempting to describe scenes of action, sometimes becomes very similar to that of the Alliterative poets. This passage should be compared with the tourney in the Knight's Tale, 1747–1762. There the vague resemblance becomes almost identity. Alliteration is frequent, and sometimes used exactly as in a professedly Alliterative poem (e.g. 1747, 1750, 1753, 1754, 1758), while metrically these lines (and others) would seem natural in such poems, and some (e.g. 1758) are the same as the normal lines of Old English verse.

This last sentence reminds us that Tolkien always intended to publish a study of Old English prosody and even recorded a talk entitled 'Anglo-Saxon Verse' for BBC Radio in January 1938.[161] His ongoing commitments to Alliterative poetry made him especially alert to Chaucer's debt to the native English tradition, and he later repeated this claim about *heterly* when writing 'Chaucer as a Philologist' (p. 47):

And significantly we here come upon *heterly*. This word occurs only here in Chaucer; indeed it probably occurs here alone in Middle English outside actual alliterative writings... Chaucer's *heterly they hurtlen* has been taken from some now lost piece he once conned and did not forget. *heterly* is dialect, but it is more. There was, after all, a literature of merit, especially in the West, before Chaucer's day, and before anything literary was written that can be ascribed to London. Chaucer is not independent either of the past or of the contemporary, and neither was his audience.

Because Chaucer's alliterative lines were first officially noticed by F. N. Robinson in 1933 and given further attention by Dorothy Everett in 1947, Tolkien's preliminary discussion in his Clarendon Chaucer, though never published, represented truly groundbreaking discoveries.[162]

But Tolkien had more to say on the subject. Among the draft pages of his *Cleopatra* commentary, he inserted two separate leaves on which he wrote, front and back, a self-contained essay somewhat like one of his appendices for 'Chaucer as a Philologist' and later at the end of *The Return of the King*. A few excerpts highlight his conviction that Chaucer knew native Alliterative poetry and did not

---

[161] J. R. R. Tolkien, *The Fall of Arthur*, ed. Christopher Tolkien (Boston and New York: Houghton Mifflin Harcourt, 2013), includes extracts from a later version of the talk as 'Appendix: Old English Verse', 223–33. Here Tolkien took his habitual swipe at standard literary history: 'If you have ever heard that Chaucer was the "father of English poetry", forget it' (p. 225).

[162] Robinson, ed., *Poetical Works of Chaucer*, 783, and Dorothy Everett, 'Chaucer's "Good Ear"', *RES* 23 (1947), 201–8. Everett arrived as a tutor at Oxford in 1921 and later had Priscilla Tolkien as a student; Tolkien in 1951 suggested her as someone who might complete his Clarendon Chaucer (SH 2:366).

disparage it: 'The frequent alliterative phrases to be found in his work are mainly due to the language itself, not the poet. They are there partly as an indication of the liking for alliteration in everyday speech, partly as traces of the drill which the language had received from countless Alliterative poets...'. At this point he compiled a full page of Chaucer's alliterative phrases beginning with *'fresshe floures* PF 259, 854, Prol 90, NP 382; *forweped and forwaked*, III 126; *wake or winke*, PF 7, 482; *for lust or lore*, PF 15...'—and continuing with forty-nine more examples until ending with *'blood and bones*, NP 607'. These citations span the full range of the *Selections* which he knew thoroughly as glossary-maker, and he probably compiled a running list as he encountered them while editing, not blessed with the almost photographic memory of his friend Lewis.[163]

Years later Tolkien would write to Auden about the impact of children's literature on *The Hobbit*: 'it has some of the silliness of manner caught unthinkingly from the kind of stuff I had had served to me, as Chaucer may catch a minstrel tag' (*Letters*, 215). Tolkien detected these minstrel tags surfacing as alliterative formulas in *Cleopatra*:

> Apart, however, from those phrases embedded in the language, or echoes through minstrel's verse of ancient, nearly forgotten traditions, it is noticeable that where Chaucer is describing scenes, such as battles, that require a forcible and graphic method, his style and rhythm approach close to that of the alliterative poets. The passage here (*Legend of Cleopatra* 56–74) should be compared especially with the tourney in the Knight's Tale (A, 2602–2620).

The almost magical phrase *ancient, nearly forgotten traditions* reflects Tolkien's view that Old English versification entered a long period of oral performances by minstrels, persisting over the generations after 1066 to re-emerge during the fourteenth century more as an Alliterative Survival than as an Alliterative Revival.[164] Nor was alliterative poetry an entirely alien presence in the poet's London. Tolkien believed Chaucer knew *Gawain* and probably its author also.[165]

Thus alliteration surfaced in action-packed passages like the one he cited from the Knight's Tale despite its immediate narrative source in Boccaccio's *Teseida*:

> There the resemblance passes beyond a mere hint or echo, and becomes so great that it is impossible to deny that English reading has played a significant part in his adaptation of an Italian original. Not only is the alliteration frequent, but it is used in some lines exactly as in an Alliterative poem; and metrically, while it is still perfectly possible for us (and Chaucer) to carve up the lines into the approved five feet, they fall naturally into the Alliterative line, having two main accented syllables in each half, with the caesura in between.

---

[163] When asked whether her father had a photographic memory, Priscilla Tolkien replied, 'No, he had to work at it like everyone else.' (Private communication from Verlyn Flieger.)

[164] See Ralph Hanna, 'Alliterative Poetry', in *The Cambridge History of Medieval English Literature*, ed. David Wallace (Cambridge: Cambridge University Press, 1999), 488–512.

[165] Tolkien, '*Sir Gawain and the Green Knight*' (1953), *Essays*, 73.

Tolkien then scanned four representative lines. It is indeed awkward for teachers explaining Chaucer's versification when immediately confronted with the first line of the General Prologue—'Whan that Aprille with his shoures sote'—which scans more naturally as a four-stress alliterative line, with caesura in the middle, than a five-foot iambic line like the one that comes next: 'The droghte of Marche hath perced to the rote'. Tolkien himself would explore this hybrid verse-form of alliterating four-stress lines with rhyming couplets in his poem *The Hoard* first published in 1923 when he had begun work on his Clarendon Chaucer.[166]

Tolkien's training prepared him to spot lines in the Knight's Tale 'correctly arranged even according to the strictest Old English poem', and he guessed at their use because 'Chaucer was writing at a time when Alliterative verse, preserved unrecorded in popular verse, doubtless often wide enough, was being written once more (for gentle audiences) in large quantities and sometimes of great merit—to judge even by what chance has saved of it.' He probably had in mind specifically the courtly poems of the Cotton Nero manuscript preserving the sole surviving copy of *Sir Gawain and the Green Knight*.

The fact that poems like *Gawain* were written in a non-London dialect was not a negative for Tolkien. He felt strong loyalty to family roots in Worcestershire, and he specialized in West Midland texts such as *Le Morte Arthur* which could be traced back linguistically to Mercian. His Riders of the Mark were meant as Mercians, and his Shire occupied the same square miles as the ancient kingdom of Mercia.[167] Even though the old diocese of Worcester was believed to be the heartland of early Alliterative texts, Tolkien took pains to narrow the cultural if not the geographical gap with Chaucer:

> He never wrote any verse himself that was alliterative except by way of adornment or reminiscence. That he despised the work of Alliterative poets as provincial is improbable. They were as dependent on French models and sentiment as he was. But the practice of Alliterative verse was associated with a region (the North and West Midlands) removed from the places he normally lived in, and especially with an unfamiliar vocabulary.

Tolkien took particular interest in the young Chaucer's visit to Yorkshire, where he heard the 'unfamiliar vocabulary' which he later put into the mouths of his northern clerks in the Reeve's Tale. Tolkien's inset essay continued about Alliterative verse-making as a distinct poetic craft:

> Also it needed its own early training, and Chaucer's had been in rhyme. In any case it was not (though it might by a master have been made) an instrument for the lighter kinds of music; and no master could make it as easy to write as rhyme.

---

[166] SH 2:508–9; Shippey, 'The Versions of "The Hoard"', in *Roots and Branches*, 341–9 at p. 348, remarks on his hybrid form.

[167] Bratman, 'Tolkien and the Counties of England', 10.

Chaucer makes his Parson say:—

> But trusteth wel, I am a Southren man,
> I kan nat geeste 'rum ram ruf' by lettre,
> Ne, God woot, rym holde I but litel bettre.

But this (as is sometimes forgotten) is spoken in character, and the Parson by these very words (and his later tale!) shows himself no poet or judge of poetry. His words have not the weight of Milton censuring rhyme after first showing his mastery of it.[168] What Chaucer himself thought of *rum ram raf* is better to be gauged, delicate matter though it be, from his own work set against the background of Middle English. The just conclusion probably is that he read it, liked it when it was good, but knew that his own taste and talent were different.

Tolkien would further remark upon the Parson's phrase 'by lettre' when he discussed alliterative verse in *Beowulf*.[169] Later he reflected in 1955 that 'I write alliterative verse with pleasure' (*Letters*, 219), and when W. H. Auden sent his *Song of the Sibyl*, Tolkien planned on sending back his own attempt at 'the art of writing alliterative poetry', probably the work later published as part of *Legend of Sigurd and Gudrún*.[170] He wrote not only with pleasure but with real success in poems as fine as any other modern practitioner, including Auden. Back in the early 1920s he composed more than 2,200 lines in the alliterative *Lay of the Children of Húrin* (as mentioned earlier) but abandoned it early in 1925 (when working on Chaucer) to recast his accounts of Beren and Lúthien in octosyllabic couplets for the *Lay of Leithian*.[171] After suspending work on the Clarendon Chaucer, however, he returned to experimenting with alliteration in his verse-drama *The Homecoming of Beorhtnoth Beorhthelm's Son* as early as 1931 (SH 2:545–50). Next he undertook the alliterative *Fall of Arthur*, mentioned in a 1934 letter by R. W. Chambers, though not appearing in print until nearly seventy years later.[172] C. S. Lewis referenced this poem in the opening paragraph of his 1935 essay 'The Alliterative Metre' where he included his famous six-line specimen starting 'We were talking of dragons, Tolkien and I...'.[173] The example that most readers know is the alliterative elegy for Rohan's dead warriors buried in the Mounds of Mundburg—'We heard of the horns in the hills ringing...' (*RK* V/6).

---

[168] Milton's note on 'Verse' in the 1668 second edition of *Paradise Lost* defended his use of blank verse instead of rhyming couplets. [My note]

[169] Tolkien, *Beowulf: A Translation and Commentary*, 280–4.

[170] *Letters*, 379; see Tolkien, *The Legend of Sigurd and Gudrún*, 364–7, for his own 'Prophecy of the Sibyl'.

[171] SH 2:652–6 '*The Lay of the Children of Húrin*' and SH 2:648–52 '*Lay of Leithian*'.

[172] Tolkien, *The Fall of Arthur* (2013); see also T. S. Sudell, 'The Alliterative Verses of *The Fall of Arthur*', *Tolkien Studies* 13 (2016), 71–100; Chance, *Tolkien, Self and Other*, '"Queer Endings" After *Beowulf*: *The Fall of Arthur* (1931-1934)', 111–31; and SH 2:381–7. For Chambers as a mentor, see Edwards, *Tolkien*, 125–6.

[173] Lewis, *Selected Literary Essays*, 15–26. Tolkien later remarked these were not 'entirely accurate examples of Old English metrical devices' (*Letters*, 389).

In Aragorn's lament for the kings of Rohan, his adaptation of the famous *ubi sunt* lines from *The Wanderer* combined alliteration with rhyme somewhat as Chaucer had done in the Knight's Tale: 'Where now the horse and the rider? Where is the horn that was blowing? | Where is the helm and the hauberk, and the bright hair flowing?' (*TT* III/6).[174]

When Tolkien completed his excursus on Alliterative verse and returned to annotating *Cleopatra*, he confronted the grotesque scene of the Egyptian queen's suicide. Chaucer's heroine did not simply apply a single asp to her breast; she jumped naked into a snake-pit teeming with 'all the serpents that she myghte have'. Skeat's commentary shuttled between North's Petrarch and Shakespeare's *Antony and Cleopatra* to avoid the utter strangeness of Chaucer's account. Tolkien turned to Germanic sources to explain what Skeat had neglected:

> But the crowd of serpents and the pit (99, 118) are probably due to Northern ideas of burial, and to the legendary use of serpents in a pit as a cruel and horrible death. Of this the death of Gunnar, King of the Burgundians, in the snake-pen of the Hun king is the most famous example. King Ella of Northumbria in legend gave the same death to Ragnar Lodbrók.[175]

King Alla's example fitted handily in this context because the Northumbrian king figured as a main character in the Man of Law's Tale. One of Tolkien's last supervisees, V. A. Kolve, later wrote about this same suicide scene in *Cleopatra*, drawing upon medieval visual traditions of grave-worms and *transi* tombs.[176] Tolkien certainly knew these religious images and could have seen the splendid double-decker tomb of the poet's granddaughter Alice Chaucer at nearby Ewelme, but he preferred the older Northern legends such as the version of Gunnar in the snake-pit included in his own *Lay of Gudrún*.[177] Tolkien would draw upon the same Germanic lore when describing the terrors that Beren and Lúthien faced at Morgoth's stronghold: 'Black chasms opened beside the road, whence forms as of writhing serpents issued' (*Sil* 211). In *The Hobbit* when the Great Goblin becomes enraged by the sight of the sword Orcrist, he orders the dwarves to be taken away to 'dark holes full of snakes'. In this bedtime story told to his sons in the late 1920s, the deadly reptile lurking in a dark underground chamber would take final form as the dragon Smaug.

---

[174] Tolkien quoted these same lines from *The Wanderer* in his 'Valedictory Address' (*Essays*, 239); see SH 3:1393–5 '*The Wanderer*'.

[175] On King Ælla's execution of Ragnar, see Katherine Holman, *Historical Dictionary of the Vikings* (Lanham, MD: Scarecrow Press, 2003), 220. Ragnar's last words in the snake-pit provide the title for Tom Shippey's *Laughing Shall I Die: Lives and Deaths of the Great Vikings* (London: Reaktion Books, 2018).

[176] V. A. Kolve, 'From Cleopatra to Alceste: An Iconographic Study of *The Legend of Good Women*' (1981), in *Telling Images: Chaucer and the Image of Narrative II* (Stanford: Stanford University Press, 2009), 28–65, notes 267–77. His B.Litt. project with Professor Tolkien on the 'Religious Grotesque' evolved into his landmark study of Middle English religious drama, *The Play Called Corpus Christi* (Stanford: Stanford University Press, 1966).

[177] Tolkien, *Legend of Sigurd and Gudrun*, 9–10, 297–9, 330.

XV. *The Astrolabe*

Skeat's Oxford Chaucer had incorporated a huge amount of technical information from his 1872 *Treatise on the Astrolabe*, and Tolkien's two-page commentary on their 73-line extract referred curious readers to this edition with its plates illustrating the device's operation.[178] No great fan of technology himself, Tolkien understood that literature students needed coaxing to read even the Prologue to one of the earliest scientific texts in English: 'The chief interest of the treatise now, for those not specially concerned with the history of mathematics, astronomy, and scientific instruments, lies in the example it offers of Chaucer in a prose not so directly under the direction of a Latin original.' Unlike *Boece*, that is, his *Astrolabe* was freely adapted from various texts such as Messahala's *Compositio et Operatio Astrolabi* so that the editor could not check the English against a single Latin source. For once Tolkien does not burden his readers with information about manuscripts. Nor, strangely, does he remark on Chaucer's reference to 'the king that is lord of this langage' now taken as an early claim for the King's English as the official language of the realm.[179] Perhaps Tolkien harboured loyalties to the West Midland language of the *Gawain* Poet as an equal contender for this status during the fourteenth century.

As a student edition, the Clarendon Chaucer steadily appealed to students by including selections *about* students, as in the Reeve's Tale, and so the *Astrolabe* guaranteed its inclusion because its 'affectionate and familiar prologue' addressed a boy named Lewis. When the fifteenth-century poet John Lydgate saw this address to 'litel Lowis my sone', he decided the treatise's recipient was Chaucer's own younger son, otherwise a shadowy figure in the documentary records.[180] Tolkien endorsed this view of a son 'beginning to show tastes of a mathematical kind like his father'—in a sense anticipating his own son Christopher's tastes for things such as medieval literature like his father. Christopher as a lad also enjoyed looking at stars through his telescope, and Priscilla recalled how she too felt encouraged when given the book *The Starry Heavens*: 'My father also talked to us about eclipses of the sun and the moon and about the planets and their satellites' (SH 3:1130). Tolkien later reported that as a teenager he was interested more in astronomy than in literature (SH 2:84).

The treatise made another appeal to local undergraduates because 'the calculations are directed to be made after the latitude of Oxford'. Fourteenth-century mathematicians at Merton College were pre-eminent in the field, and Chaucer's connections with this college are evidenced by his commendation of *Troilus* to

---

[178] Bodleian MS Tolkien A 39/2/2, fols. 81–2; see Geoffrey Chaucer, *A Treatise on the Astrolabe Dedicated to his Son Lowys (A.D. 1391)*, ed. Walter W. Skeat, EETS e.s. 16, 1872.

[179] Andrew Cole, 'Chaucer's English Lesson', *Speculum* 77 (2002), 1128–67.

[180] *Chaucer Life-Records*, ed. Martin M. Crow and Clair C. Olson (Oxford: Clarendon Press, 1966), 544–5.

one-time Merton fellow Ralph Strode.[181] But little Lewis at the age of 10 would have been too young for matriculation and too ill-prepared for university because 'his Latin was not precocious'. Here Tolkien hints at his own dissatisfaction with the poorly prepared undergraduates mocked in *The Clerkes Compleinte* modelled after Chaucer's General Prologue: 'Whanne that Octobre mid his schoures derke | The erthe hath dreint, and wete windes cherke' (SH 2:245).

After noting that Chaucer's summary 'gives more in the nature of a forecast of hopes than an account of what actually appears', Tolkien pondered the unfinished status of Chaucer's treatise around 1391: 'He seems aware of his own tendency to alter plans or abandon them.'[182] This statement sounds prophetic in terms of Tolkien's many literary plans altered and abandoned over his career, including the edition at hand. To account specifically for the unfinished *Astrolabe*, he ventured the guess that Part V was never written due to astrology's ill repute as a dark science: 'Chaucer may have had some qualms in spite of his own half-sceptical interest in the science.' The Miller's Tale poked fun at the Oxford clerk Nicholas for using his astrolabe to predict rain (no great feat in England), but a good Christian had graver qualms because of the residual pagan belief that the stars rather than God steered men's destinies: 'where matters astrological are alluded to, he says such things are "rytes of payens in which my spirit ne hath no feith".' Chaucer's conclusion to *Troilus* had also condemned 'payens corsed olde rytes' as wholly inadequate to provide consolation to the Trojans.

Tolkien himself was drawn to the glamour of ancient star-lore and readily included astrological myths throughout his *legendarium*.[183] His curiosity as an undergraduate had been aroused by the line *Eala Earendel, engla beorhtast* from the Old English poem *Christ I*—'Hail Earendel, brightest of angels'—and his research into Jacob Grimm's *Teutonic Mythology* led him to conclude that it was the lost name of a planet or star. This became the flashpoint in his imagination so that Eärendil took shape in his private mythology as the sky-borne ancestor of both Elrond and Aragorn.[184] The star-voyager oversaw the welfare of Middle-earth and provided light for Galadriel's Nenya, the Ring of Adamant, as well as her phial that saved the two hobbits in Shelob's cave.[185] But Tolkien was not much interested in the text of Chaucer's *Astrolabe* and provided less than a

---

[181] Bennett, *Chaucer at Oxford and at Cambridge*, 'Men of Merton', 58–85 at pp. 63–5, 75.

[182] Tolkien crossed out this later comparison: 'The Prologue to the *Canterbury Tales* is a prospectus to a work that was never finished. In this respect it is like the table of contents for the treatise on the *Astrolabe*.'

[183] Jim Manning, 'Elvish Star Lore', *Planetarian* (December 2003), 14–22, and Kristine Larsen, 'Myth, Milky Way, and the Mysteries of Tolkien's *Morwinyon, Telumendil,* and *Anarríma*', *Tolkien Studies* 7 (2010), 197–210.

[184] Shippey, *Road to Middle-earth*, 'Eärendil: A Lyric Core', 244–7.

[185] Tolkien had occasion to gloss this word 'adamauntes' in Chaucer's *Parlement* (148): 'the word is derived from Greek *adamas* (*adamant-*), our "diamond". Partly through a fanciful etymology from Latin *adamans* ("falling in love"), this name became applied to the lode-stone or natural magnet. The product of this verbal confusion was an entirely legendary stone that combined the properties of both.'

page of hit-and-miss annotations such as the one for *seyn*—'the proper form of the past participle of *see* (O.E. *segen*)'.

XVI. *Prologue to the Canterbury Tales*

'It is easier to plan a big book than to write it.' Tolkien's headnote to his commentary on the *Canterbury Tales* sounds prophetic in terms of his own ambitious projects (Fig. 12). The difference lay in his intentions. He did not originally plan *The Lord of the Rings* as a big book but rather a sequel on the same scale as *The Hobbit*, and he

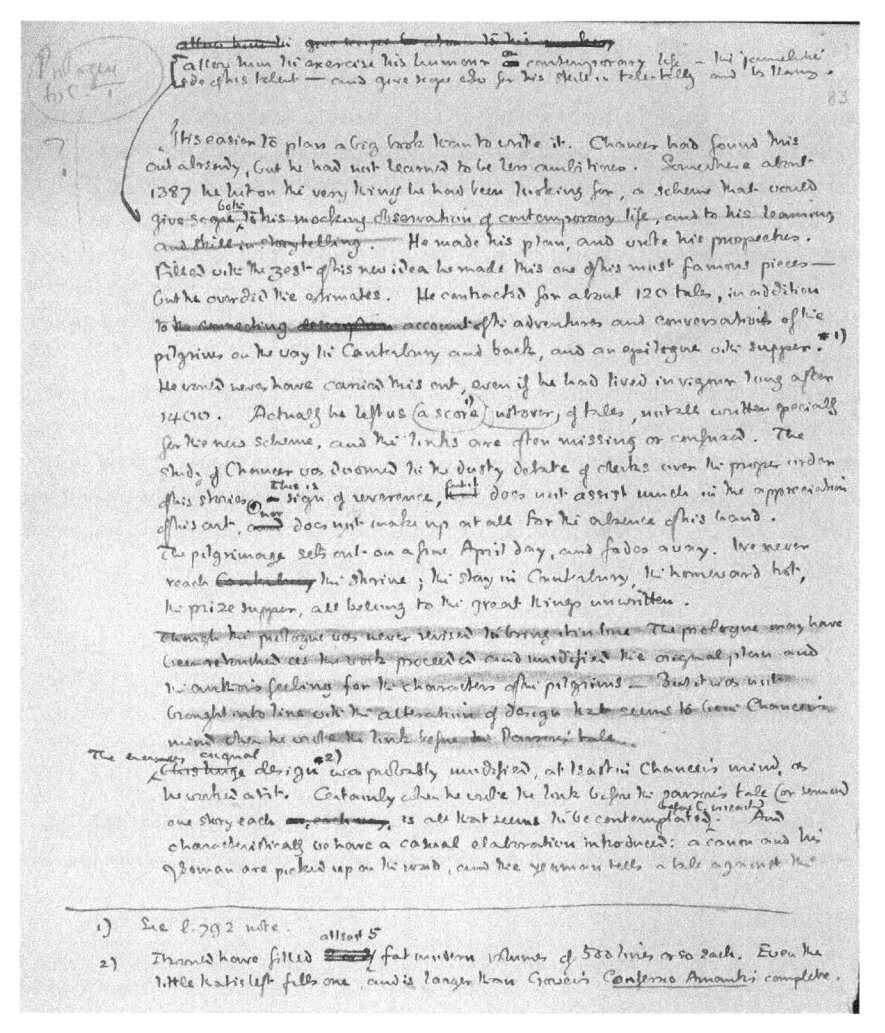

Fig. 12. Handwritten introduction to *Canterbury Tales* (Oxford, Bodleian Library, MS Tolkien A 39/2/2, fol. 83).

never exactly planned *The Silmarillion* as a book as such (novel, epic, or saga) but rather as an ever-expanding compilation of myths no more consistent than the body of Greek mythology. Gordon had extracted 511 lines out of the General Prologue's 858 and supplied subheadings for these selections: the Beginning, the Knight, the Squire, the Prioress, the Monk, the Clerk, the Shipman, the Wife of Bath, the Parson, the Miller, the Reeve, and the Plan of the Tales.[186] Tolkien then drafted sixty-one pages of annotations, three times the total which Sisam had allowed for the Notes altogether, as his own enactment of the gap between plan and performance.

'Chaucer had found this out already, but he had not learned to be less ambitious.' Here Tolkien recalled Chaucer's two previous unfinished works *Astrolabe* and *Legend of Good Women* as grand projects that fell short. Thus his *Canterbury Tales* became another instance in which Chaucer 'made his plan and wrote his prospectus. Filled with the zest of his new idea, he made this one of his most famous pieces—but he overdid the estimates.' Tolkien had already made a similar remark about the *Romaunt*, the poet's first incomplete project: '22,000 lines was a large order for a poet who tired so quickly even of projects of his own conceiving.' For his last over-ambitious project, Chaucer's mortality also loomed: 'He would never have carried this out, even if he had lived in vigour long after 1400.' Tolkien remarked elsewhere that 'it is the untold stories that are most moving' (*Letters*, 110), and so the *Canterbury Tales* offered a poignant example with some ninety-seven of the proposed 120 stories left untold.

While Tolkien announced famously that *The Lord of the Rings* grew in the telling, Chaucer's *Canterbury Tales* actually shrank in scope from what was announced, perhaps reduced in plan from four tales to one tale per pilgrim, but certainly lacking its promised conclusion back at the Tabard Inn. What survives contains incomplete tales, missing and confused links, and a frame-narrative broken into ten fragments whose sequence had sparked much scholarly disagreement:[187]

> The study of Chaucer was doomed by the dusty debate of clerks over the proper order of his stories. This is a sign of reverence, but it does not assist much in the appreciation of his art, nor does it make up at all for the absence of his hand. The pilgrimage sets out on a fine April day and fades away. We never reach the shrine; the stay in Canterbury, the homeward trot, the prize supper, all belong to the great things unwritten.

Tolkien then added: 'This huge design was probably modified, at least in Chaucer's mind, as he worked at it.'[188] Here the editor was beginning to identify

---

[186] Bodleian MS Tolkien A 39/2/2, fols. 83–131.

[187] Christopher admitted a similar challenge with his father's manuscript fragments when editing *Lost Tales, Part I*, p. xix; see also 'Note on the Order of the Tales', 228–30. Even when Tolkien provided links between tales, he was not always certain which tales he was linking, something like Chaucer's uncertainty in his Man of Law's Endlink; see *Lost Tales, Part II*, 147.

[188] Chaucer's vagueness about the Canterbury journey may have encouraged Tolkien to devise precise chronologies for his plots and draw detailed maps for the travels of his characters. See

personally with his author, years before knowing how deeply would run his resemblance to this great starter of literary projects, later writing to his publisher about his sequel to *The Hobbit*: 'I find it only too easy to write opening chapters.'[189]

While neglecting to provide tales for his Yeoman, Plowman, and Five Guildsmen, Chaucer allowed new characters to show up unannounced: 'characteristically we have a casual elaboration introduced: a Canon and his Yeoman are picked up on the road.' Tolkien later confessed to W. H. Auden his own tendency to let new characters show up in *The Lord of the Rings*: 'Strider sitting in the corner at the inn was a shock, and I had no more idea who he was than had Frodo' (*Letters*, 216). Other unplanned, unexpected characters would include Treebeard and Faramir.[190]

Despite some lively episodes such as the spat between the Host and the Pardoner, Chaucer's frame-narrative achieved no organic unity. Instead of a dramatic plotline, individual pilgrims are allowed to speak at great length, in their own voices with their own rhythms and registers, marking an achievement which Tolkien brilliantly matched in 'The Council of Elrond' where some twenty distinctive voices are heard. Falling short of novelistic expectations, Chaucer's story collection better qualifies as a medieval compilation, a term actually used in a colophon of the Ellesmere manuscript—'the tales of Caunterbury, *compiled* by Geffrey Chaucer'. Because Tolkien's own *legendarium* grew in scope without ever coalescing into a definitive structure, Christopher reached the same conclusion about which literary label to apply: 'my father came to conceive *The Silmarillion* as a compilation' (*Sil* x).

Tolkien admired his medieval precursor's audacity as an innovator: 'There is nothing in English before Chaucer quite like the plan of the *Canterbury Tales*.' Just as *The Lord of the Rings* extended the fantasy genre beyond predecessors such as William Morris and Lord Dunsany, Chaucer worked from the antecedents of 'collected sermons, legends of saints, moral tales, or recipes'. The influence of Boccaccio's *Decameron* was hardly necessary: 'He would have had to exercise as much originality in reshaping the suggestion they afforded and adapting it to England.' Besides Gower's *Confessio Amantis,* his own *Legend of Good Women* stood as a sufficient English-language forerunner with its stories unified by a common theme. 'Chaucer could have bridged the gap between such things as these and his *Canterbury Tales* by his own invention unaided.' Tolkien's own creativity operated in much the same way, aided or unaided by prior texts, but it is probably no coincidence that his frame-narrative *Book of Lost Tales* with Vëannë

McIlwaine, *Tolkien: Maker of Middle-earth*, 352–3, 'Timeline for the Breaking of the Fellowship', and 377–403, 'Mapping *The Lord of the Rings*'.

[189] *Letters*, 29: 'I am sure I could write unlimited "first chapters". I have indeed written many.'
[190] *Letters*, 79 to Christopher in 1944: 'A new character has come on the scene (I am sure I did not invent him, I did not even want him, though I like him, but there he came walking into the woods of Ithilien): Faramir, the brother of Boromir.'

offering 'The Tale of Tinúviel' as a tale-within-a-tale (for example) dates from the same decade when he was teaching, editing, and drafting commentary on Chaucer's story collection.

What common theme connected the tales told along the road to Canterbury? 'Chaucer would indeed have been hard put to it to write a single tale (let alone twenty or 120) of interest to men and women of his day that do not deal with Love'—more specifically 'conjugal relations'. Tolkien saw more clearly than Kittredge that *all* of the tales were about marriage, not just those starting with the Wife of Bath's Tale.[191] Here he also challenged Lewis's insistence upon placing Chaucer narrowly in the courtly-love tradition in his *Allegory of Love* then in progress.[192]

'That the germ of the Prologue was an actual pilgrimage is perfectly possible,' Tolkien continued about the frame-narrative: 'Chaucer may in fact have been at the Tabard. It is the way that books are begun.' His suggestion anticipated current speculation that Chaucer actually resided in Southwark during the last decade of his life and would have known the real-life Host much as Tolkien supposed: 'Chaucer's sketches do not suggest, usually, that they are portraits of individuals—except, perhaps, Harry Bailey.' Not that Tolkien faulted the poet on this score: 'I tried a diary with portraits (some scathing some comic some commendatory) of persons and events seen; but I found it was not my line' (*Letters*, 85). As an accomplished artist, he imagined Chaucer at the Tabard making 'sketches' stored in his memory for 'excellent little pictures if a little external and superficial'. Later his commentary would renew the painting metaphor when suggesting the poet's description of the Prioress's grey eyes as 'one of those happy touches on the canvas, taken direct from life, which give individuality to Chaucer's portraits'. In any case, the notion that Chaucer and his chums gathered at the Tabard Inn for drinking, talking, and even reading aloud from their works provided a fine precedent for the Inklings later gathering at the *Eagle and Child*.[193] We know that Gower resided in Southwark and was completing his *Confessio Amantis* during the same years when Chaucer was making headway on his *Canterbury Tales*.[194]

Gordon and Sisam had agreed upon reducing selections from the General Prologue by including only nine of these portraits between the famous April opening (1–100) and the 'Plan for the Tales' at the end (715–858).[195] Even with

---

[191] George Lyman Kittredge's *Chaucer and His Poetry* (Cambridge, MA: Harvard University Press, 1915), 185–210, proposed the Wife of Bath's 'marriage debate' as unifying the sequence of tales only to the Franklin's Tale.

[192] Lewis, *Allegory of Love*, 162–3.

[193] See two chapters in Stephen H. Rigby and Alastair J. Minnis, eds., *Historians on Chaucer: The General Prologue to the 'Canterbury Tales'* (Oxford: Oxford University Press, 2014): Martha Carlin, 'The Host', 460–80 at pp. 475–80; and Caroline M. Barron, 'Chaucer the Poet and Chaucer the Pilgrim', 24–41.

[194] Robert Epstein, 'London, Southwark, Westminster: Gower's Urban Context'. *A Companion to Gower*, ed. Siân Echard (Cambridge: D. S. Brewer, 2004), 43–60 at pp. 51–7.

[195] When Tolkien began his *Book of Lost Tales* with the traveller's desire for 'strange lands', he seemed to be recalling Chaucer's pilgrims desiring what he glossed here as 'distant (*ferne*) shrines in foreign (*straunge*) countries'.

this pared-down roster of pilgrims, Tolkien correctly estimated the challenge for readers recapturing the historical sense of the poet's satires: 'Time has seen to it that the Prologue is now one of the hardest things in Chaucer to really understand.' He appreciated what all classroom teachers quickly learn. The General Prologue, though widely anthologized in textbooks, offers the usual challenges for redeeming medieval meanings dimmed by the passage of centuries: 'we can only partly understand the significance of his descriptions now, and that only after a research which the author never intended us to endure.'

Tolkien had not fully profited from this lesson when writing his own 'Prologue' to *The Lord of the Rings*. Many first-time readers find these pages just as challenging as Chaucer's Prologue because 'Concerning Pipe-weed' and 'Of the Ordering of the Shire' delay the storytelling while burdening readers with an excessive amount of Middle-earth history and hobbit ethnography—their manner of living in holes, their fondness for smoking pipes, the records preserved in the Red Book of Westmarch—mostly relayed by a coy narrator with his ironic Chaucer-like smile. For better storytelling in the 1990 audiobooks, *The Fellowship of the Ring* began with 'A Long-Expected Party' and the 'Prologue' was repositioned at the end of *The Return of the King*.

Now that we know about his close attention to Chaucer's Prologue with its jovial pilgrims at the Tabard Inn, Tolkien's 'Prologue' with its hobbits given to merry conviviality begins to look familiar: 'And laugh they did, and eat, and drink often and heartily, being fond of simple jests at all times.' His first-person narrator of *The Hobbit* would intrude almost as a separate character, much like the Chaucerian narrator warning readers of the Miller's Prologue to 'turne over the leef and chese another tale' (I, 3177). Later Tolkien would take a different strategy when casting the narrator of *The Lord of the Rings* as a translator sorting through different versions of the War of the Ring, more like the narrator of *Troilus* claiming to rely upon the made-up historian Lollius for his account of the Trojan War.

In his landmark study *Anatomy of Criticism*, Northrop Frye provided a five-part taxonomy of literary modes, all of which were cunningly deployed in the *Canterbury Tales*. Chaucer's multiplicity of genres span the range from myth and romance (Apollo and Custance), to high and low representations (Emelye and the Wife of Bath), and down the scale to the ironic satires in his fabliaux (Reeve's Tale).[196] As a seasoned Chaucerian, Tolkien went about the business of combining much the same range from myth and romance (Sauron and Aragorn) down the scale to the satirical (Samwise) thereby achieving much the same successful hybrid of literary modes for his *Lord of the Rings*.[197] Certainly the seeds had been planted

---

[196] Shippey, *Author of the Century*, 'Style and Genre', 221–5, makes this point based on Frye's literary modes.
[197] *Anatomy of Criticism* (1957) did not take into consideration Tolkien's trilogy, but Victoria University Library at the University of Toronto does preserve a first edition of *The Lord of the Rings*

for this successful amalgamation during the 1920s when he drafted his commentary for Chaucer's masterpiece.

Despite the patchiness of his annotations in later pages, Tolkien continued focusing on particular details, for example taking three whole pages to discuss *Aprille* from Chaucer's famous first line. 'The description is not inapplicable to a favourable specimen of April weather in England, but it is nonetheless mainly of learned and literary origins.' He then traced those origins to vernacular texts like *Kyng Alisaunder* and Latin works like Guido delle Colonne's *Historia Destructionis Troiae*, another of his sources for *Troilus*. Following Chaucer's move away from liturgical time to the secular calendar, Tolkien's own fiction-writing would follow the action according to the months of the year.[198] Frodo begins his journey after Gandalf's departure in June and the removal of his furniture in September, and he travels from Bree to Rivendell in October. Because *The Hobbit* starts in the same month as Chaucer's *Tales*—'it was April' (p. 44)—perhaps it is not altogether surprising that Tolkien filled three pages on *Aprille*.

For 'holy blisful martir' Tolkien surpassed Skeat with a much longer note on St Thomas Becket, his hagiographical information including the miraculous water in which a tiny drop of the saint's blood was dissolved as medicine: 'This water was carried away in little lead ampules (*ampullae*), which became the special sign of a completed pilgrimage to Canterbury.' For anyone wanting a picture, Tolkien offered one of his rare references to secondary scholarship, E. L. Cutts's *Scenes and Characters of the Middle Ages* (1872), also one of Skeat's favourites. His page-long note on *palmers* as 'persons going on long pilgrimages to distant (*ferne*) shrines in foreign (*straunge*) countries' looks forward to one of Tolkien's few Continental trips when he and his daughter Priscilla travelled to Italy as pilgrims to the shrine of St Francis at Assisi (SH 1:493–8). If Chaucer's pilgrims headed to Canterbury to give thanks for recoveries from illness, it might not be fanciful to imagine Tolkien visiting Assisi to give thanks for completing his final volume of *The Lord of the Rings* then in press in August 1955.

He included other details which caught his interest: 'the shrine and its treasures of gold and silver and jewels were of great value and magnificence.' Tolkien had been born in South Africa with the Kimberley diamond mines to the west and the Witwatersrand gold mines to the north. Visions of mineral riches were in his blood, so to speak, and he found the glamour of gold and jewels irresistible throughout his fiction. His Chaucer commentary included two and a half pages on the Prioress's swearing by St Loy, the patron saint of goldsmiths, and therefore

---

personally annotated by Frye. See SH 3:966 for Frye's recollections of attending Tolkien's *Beowulf* lectures.

[198] Appendix D 'The Calendar' shows Tolkien's concern with precise dating systems; see also Hammond and Scull, *Reader's Companion*, 'Chronologies, Calendars, and Moons', pp. xliv–l.

the object of special devotion by Madam Eglentyne with her fondness for jewellery.

Maybe because of his own Army experience, Tolkien's commentary on THE KNIGHT—the first pilgrim portrait—devoted a half-page note to *armee* as 'a technical word for an armed expedition or the assembly of troops and material for war'. This seems to have been the first recorded instance in English: 'There cannot be much doubt that Chaucer wrote *armee* using a technical French military word which, however successful since, had apparently not been used much in English before.' This resulted in much confusion among scribes: 'That the bungling produced something which might possibly make sense is probably simply an unfortunate accident.' Tolkien would have harsher things to say about how scribes bungled Chaucer's dialect variants in the Reeve's Tale.

Fascinated with place-names, he glossed the Knight's travels to *Pruce* (Prussia) and *Lettow* (Lithuania) and devoted several pages to individual campaigns in lands of *hethenesse* as distant as Russia: 'He had together with other English knights taken service with the Teutonic Knights on the eastern marches where constant warfare went on against the still heathen peoples of N.E. Europe.' Tolkien went on to explain that Edward III's son the Duke of Gloucester along with the Earl of Derby joined these campaigns against the Lithuanians, whose capital fell in 1390. His interest in 'heathen peoples' would find fuller expression in 'The Monsters and the Critics', and, in a strict sense, all the brave warriors of Rohan and Gondor were heathens, too, though the best of them rose above their pagan limitations. He took the time to write a note to *The Parlement of Foules* (46–9) on Chaucer's summary of Macrobius: 'whatever virtuous man loves his country's good shall go to Heaven.' *The Lord of the Rings* uses the word *heathen* only twice, when describing Denethor's mad obsession with burning himself and his son Faramir on a funeral pyre (*RK* V/7). Naturally Tolkien preferred the Christian chivalry embodied in Chaucer's Knight, who was always victorious *in listes*: 'he had fought as Christian champion against three pagan challengers.'

The Knight's campaigns in Turkey served as a reminder of the Moslem threat lurking just to the east of Christian Europe. Family lore held that Tolkien's forefather fought at the Turkish siege of Vienna in 1529 and was sufficiently foolhardy (*tollkühn*) to lead a raid that captured the Sultan's standard (*Biography*, 26). The Gallipoli Campaign with 43,000 British casualties lingered as a painful memory, particularly for Tolkien as a veteran of the Lancashire Fusiliers who suffered massive losses there. Collective memories reached back much deeper into Europe's medieval past. Saracen armies in Spain had become the subject of the *Chanson de Roland*, its hero's blast upon his great horn transformed into Boromir's horn-call when overrun by Orcs. The siege of Minas Tirith recalled many prior episodes of siege warfare. 'Algeciras (*Algezir*) on the South coast of Spain was taken from the Moorish prince of Granada in 1344.' The Knight's campaigns extended to the other side of the Mediterranean—'*Belmarye* and *Tramyssene* refer to the Moorish kingdoms of North Africa'—and North Africa's Barbary pirates in turn provided Tolkien with inspiration for his Corsairs of Umbar. On the other hand, he could write with some relief about *Palatye*: 'Palathia in Anatolia was a small Christian lordship still held after the Turkish conquest.' Similarly Minas Tirith shrank to a small lordship held against Sauron's territorial expansions won by his scimitar-wielding warriors.

Tolkien's many references to the Knight's Tale throughout his notes indicate his familiarity with it even though no excerpts had been included in the Clarendon Chaucer. The King of Thrace and the King of India arriving to joust at Athens allowed Chaucer to indulge in Orientalist fantasies of the exotic and monstrous, much like Tolkien's depiction of the Dark Númenórean known only as the Mouth of Sauron. Chaucer's 'eastern marches' would become the approximate location of Mordor on his map of Middle-earth, and Tolkien's Easterlings fought with scimitars like Moslem warriors. Both writers, however, were able to look beyond stereotypes. When one of these swarthy Haradrim warriors falls dead, Sam gazes down at the man and recognizes his humanity, wondering if he had rather have stayed home in peace (*TT* IV/4).[199]

Chaucer uses his far-travelling Knight as narrator entering into his own sympathetic engagement with pre-Christian fighters when tracing the fortunes of his pagan princelings Palamon and Arcite. There is even an unnoticed parallel in Tolkien's other writings. In the Knight's Tale, the exiled Arcite won the favour of Theseus and rose at the Athenian court under the assumed name Philostrate. Likewise in the *Silmarillion*, the outlaw Túrin won the favour of Orodreth and rose to prominence in Nargothrond under the assumed name Agarwaen. Chaucerian texts not included in his *Selections*, that is, inspired plotlines throughout Tolkien's creative processes.

In 1980 Terry Jones would publish an entire book on the Knight as a mercenary like the renowned English freebooter John Hawkwood,[200] yet half a century earlier, Tolkien accepted without the least irony the oft-quoted line describing this pilgrim as *a verray parfit gentil knight*. For clarifying the pilgrim's *curteisye*, Tolkien showed a donnish interest in whether the Knight was seated at high table: 'The table was not necessarily the chief or high table set on a raised platform (*deis, des*) at the upper end of the hall, but might be one of the tables ranged down the length of the hall.' His *Gawain* edition had provided a note on the high table at Camelot 'like the dining hall of an Oxford or Cambridge college',[201] and such seating arrangements mattered as much in Middle-earth as they did at Oxford. The Master of Lake-town made a display of honouring Thorin and the Dwarves

---

[199] Margaret Sinex, '"Monsterized Saracens": Tolkien's Haradrim and Other "Fantasy Products"', *Tolkien Studies* 7 (2010), 175–96.

[200] Terry Jones, *Chaucer's Knight: The Portrait of a Medieval Mercenary* (London: Eyre Methuen, 1980).

[201] Tolkien and Gordon, eds., *Sir Gawain and the Green Knight*, 85.

by seating them at high table, and Gandalf and Glorfindel are seated on either side of Elrond upon the dais at Rivendell (*FR* II/1). Tolkien singled out a telling detail when he was elected Merton Professor in 1945: 'I dined for the first time at Merton high table on Thursday and found it very agreeable' (*Letters*, 116).

Tolkien himself had served as a cavalry cadet galloping across the Kentish plains during the summer of 1912,[202] and he would always value *chivalry* like the Knight's in the root sense of horsemanship. He even took time to note that the word *hors* was plural, remarking about this humbly attired pilgrim's three horses: 'The Knight put his money into good mounts and not fine clothes.' Since Chaucer's affluent pilgrims ride on horseback rather than walk to the shrine of St Thomas, Tolkien took a steady interest in all their horses, not just the Knight's. Later his own fiction gave prominent roles to horses like Gandalf's Shadowfax, Théoden's Snowmane, and even Tom Bombadil's Fatty Lumpkin. His Riders of Rohan corrected the view that ancient Englishmen avoided fighting on horseback, and he reintroduced the lost word *éored for these mounted troops.[203]

Skeat's information on the Knight's attire prompted Tolkien to draft two paragraphs on the *habergeoun* which had stained his jacket:

> The hauberk was a long coat or shirt of chain mail and the principal body armour of the knight through all but the later part of the Middle Ages, though modern artists have created the impression that he went about encased in beautifully fitted shining plates (of enormous weight and costliness) from King Arthur's day until knights were no longer bold. Such plates were at end of the fourteenth century only beginning to come in and only for such as could afford them. However, the use of plate armour specially as a protection for the thighs was already making the long full-shirted hauberk old-fashioned and increasing the use of the *habergeoun*, a shorter and originally less effective form.

Because Tolkien generally followed his own advice from 'On Translating *Beowulf*' and avoided the archaic vocabulary favoured by William Morris (*Essays*, 56), he did not clothe his warriors in Chaucer's *fustians* and *gipons* and used *habergeon* only once when describing Eärendil's attire (*FR* II/1). He could not resist the old-fashioned hauberks which he imagined Beowulf wearing when arriving in Denmark,[204] and thus the storerooms of Edoras provided hauberks for Aragorn and Legolas, the long-dead Baldor was found wearing a gilded hauberk under the Dwimorberg, and the Lord of the Nazgûl was wearing a hauberk when slain by Éowyn. Aragorn used the term when translating the ancient dirge of the Rohirrim, itself adapted from *The Wanderer*: 'Where is the helm and the hauberk

---

[202] *Biography*, 66; SH 3:1230 'King Edward's Horse'; and Janet Brennan Croft, 'The Hen that Laid the Eggs: Tolkien and the Officers Training Corps', *Tolkien Studies* 8 (2011), 97–106.
[203] Thomas Honegger, 'The Rohirrim: "Anglo-Saxons on Horseback"? An Inquiry into Tolkien's Use of Sources', in *Tolkien and the Study of His Sources*, ed. Fisher, 116–32.
[204] Tolkien, *Beowulf: A Translation and Commentary*, 195.

and the bright hair flowing?' Tolkien's 'Valedictory Address' also used the term when rendering the Old English *byrnwiga*—'Alas, the knight and his hauberk!' (*Essays*, 239).

Annotations proceeded from one pilgrim to the next without subheadings, moving next to the Knight's son. Tolkien's admiration of the fashion-conscious SQUIRE recalled his own youthful dressiness which continued into later life with impeccably tailored suits—'I like, and even dare to wear in these dull days, ornamental waistcoats' (*Letters*, 289)—and his comments on the portrait recalled, too, his undergraduate efforts in poetry and drawing in addition to sports. 'He was an accomplished and well-educated young man after the pleasant fashion of his day,' Tolkien remarked, 'in which "athletics" left room for poetry, dancing, drawing and music, accomplishments not demanded of the ruder heroes of older romance or the duller ones of later days.' He seemed unimpressed in the 1920s by the 'duller' undergraduates at Leeds and even Oxford. Poetry and music were accomplishments shared by Bilbo, Aragorn, and Treebeard. Villains like Saruman and Denethor never burst into song.

Tolkien took special interest in the Squire's sleeplessness *by nightertale* and drafted nearly a whole page exploring the 'interesting and possibly significant word' in dialects remote from London: 'The expression is of Scandinavian origin and would be expected in consequence to belong to the N.W. and N.E. of England.' Always on the look-out for Norse loan-words, Tolkien had written an undergraduate essay on 'Scandinavian Influence on the English' and continued pondering these dialect features in his 1934 study of the Reeve's Tale. In the north-eastern reaches of Middle-earth, he imagined the language of Dale and Lake-town 'more or less Scandinavian in character' (*Letters*, 175). Though the Squire's Tale was not included in their *Selections*, he knew the work well enough to cite its allusion to Gawayn 'comen ageyn out of fairye' in his edition of *Gawain*.[205] He may later have recalled it in *The Hobbit*, too, since the Squire's Oriental romance featured a magical sword like Sting and a ring like the one that permitted Bilbo to understand the spiders in Mirkwood. The Squire's Tale also included an enchanted mirror like Galadriel's allowing glimpses into the future and a marvellous horse like Shadowfax with gait so smooth for a rider like Pippin to sleep on its back.[206]

Next among the pilgrims came THE PRIORESS. Her swearing by the French bishop St Loy emphasized what set the lady apart from the anglicizing poet Chaucer: 'the lady spoke French.' Even her name smacked of affectation: 'Eglentyne,

---

[205] Tolkien and Gordon, eds., *Sir Gawain and the Green Knight*, 97.

[206] Tolkien probably knew W. A. Clouston's *On the Magical Elements in Chaucer's Squire's Tale, with Other Analogues* (London: Chaucer Society, 2nd ser., no. 26, 1890) since his lectures on the Pardoner's Tale drew steadily upon Clouston's 'The Three Robbers and the Treasure-Trove: Buddhist Original and Asiatic and European Versions of *The Pardoner's Tale*' (1872).

the French for Sweet Briar, is very unconventual.'[207] (Sam will notice eglantine growing where Orcs made a dreadful feast in Ithilien.) Unlike other upper-class pilgrims such as the Man of Law, the Prioress must actually have spoken some French even if it was recorded nowhere in the *Tales*:

> And Frensh she spak ful faire and fetisly,
> After the scole of Stratford atte Bowe
> For Frensh of Paris was to hir unknowe.
>
> (*CT* I, 124–6)

Tolkien himself began learning French from his mother, he improved his proficiency at school, and he used it when escorting some Mexican schoolboys to France in summer 1913. If searching out reasons for his later aversion, we need only recall that his next chance to use French found him approaching the trenches at the Somme. Though he knew the language well enough to read scholarly books in French for his 'Philology' surveys during the 1920s, he later took pains to disparage it: 'French has given to me less of this pleasure than any other language with which I have sufficient acquaintance for this judgement' (*Essays*, 191). He was blunter with one correspondent: 'I dislike French' (*Letters*, 288). Nobody knowing his strong feelings about all things French, including the cuisine, should be surprised that he was prompted to write a mini-essay on the Prioress as a French-speaker:

> There was a Benedictine nunnery at Stratford-at-Bow, an ancient foundation dating back probably as far as about 1100. Presumably it was where the Prioress had been educated, or had been a novice and young nun. Doubtless the French spoken by the ladies there was good enough, but it is useless to deny that Chaucer is mocking or to assert that he is merely jotting down facts without comment or malicious motive. This would leave precious little point in the next line. The rather old-fashioned, and indeed at the end of the 14th century very provincial and decadent French of the gentry of England, probably still satisfied many of them who felt its use to mark them off plainly from the common folk (more plainly than the command of *h* does now). But people of larger wealth or wider travel and reading were only too well aware of the inferior position which their transplanted and anglicized dialect occupied with regard to the literary language of Paris. Gower (who wrote French probably a deal better than the Prioress could) is full of apologies for his idiom. The fact that at this time books were made to teach people to speak French, who by descent should have needed no teacher but the conversation of their homes, shows that all was not well with domestic French in England. Many in fact were abandoning it in daily life, even if they made efforts to have their children taught Continental French as an

---

[207] Tolkien's hobbits also chose the names of flowers for girls such as Rose Cotton and Elanor Gamgee, *elanor* being a flower that her father recalled from Lothlórien (*RK* VI/9).

accomplishment. No special sneer is probably intended at the Stratford nunnery, or at any rate not at its French, which may have been of the highest kind obtainable in England. It is mentioned very likely to fix in the minds of an audience, naturally more alive to topical allusions than we are, precisely the culture and degree to which the Prioress belonged: a conservative, old-fashioned type, proud of its gentility and traditions, but unconscious of its own narrowness and provinciality and the changing times. Very likely such was the reputation of the house in Chaucer's time. It is not so much the use of French, or even its badness, of course that Chaucer smiles at, as the secure feeling of belonging to a higher order that its use gave to its possessors, unaware (as he knew perfectly well) that a Parisian would esteem their dialect little higher if at all than the patois of country bumpkins.   (Bodleian MS Tolkien A 39/2/2, fols. 102–3)

Tolkien had taken to heart the urgings of his teacher George Brewerton, who encouraged his boys to avoid French loan-words in favour of their English equivalents: 'Manure? Call it muck!' (*Biography*, 35–6). In 1910 at his school's debating society, Tolkien had spoken in favour of the motion 'This house deplores the occurrence of the Norman Conquest', and he always regretted the influence of French on the purity of the Saxon language (SH 2:617–18). Nonetheless he followed Skeat in softening the poet's censure of the ladylike nun's French as yet another ingredient in Chaucer's 'vision of an anxious gentility'. Spouting a few French phrases could be taken as a sign of pretentiousness, as it does with the hobnobbing friar's *je vous dy sanz doute* in the Summoner's Tale, but Tolkien dismissed one critic's 'older satirical view' of Madame Eglentyne in his 'Philology' survey in 1927 when drafting these annotations, and he embraced a more generous view of her French as a natural part of elevated rank.[208] Since speaking a foreign language has always been a mark of distinction, it is noteworthy that Bilbo and Frodo are both conversant in Elvish, Gildor dubbing the younger hobbit 'a scholar in the Ancient Tongue' because he could address them in high-elven speech (*FR* I/3).

Chaucer's religious ladies never indulged in the lechery of nuns in Boccaccio's *Decameron* possibly because there was a fourteenth-century nun named Elizabeth Chaucer, maybe the poet's sister or daughter,[209] and Tolkien's criticism of the Prioress was no doubt tempered by his own friendships with nuns. He was visited by the Sisters of Mercy when recuperating from trench fever in Hull, thereafter corresponding with their mother superior Mary Michael for the rest of her life. An early version of his poem *The Last Ship* was published in the *Chronicle of the Convents of the Sacred Heart*, and Priscilla recalled that he was a famous entertainer at holiday parties hosted by the convent on Norham Gardens (SH 3:1071–2). His support for the other Oxford convent at Cherwell Edge and

---

[208] Tolkien, 'Philology' (1927), 47.   [209] *Chaucer Life-Records*, 545–6.

specifically his friendship with its superior Mother St Teresa Gale—who read the manuscript of *The Hobbit* while recovering from flu—put him in touch with the lodger Elaine Griffiths who, in turn, did us the huge favour of bringing his novel to the attention of Allen & Unwin (*Letters*, 215, 346, 374). Because nursing duties had fallen to nuns for centuries, a nurse is still sometimes called 'sister' in England. C. S. Lewis always remembered fondly the 'exquisite Sister' who nursed him as a young soldier wounded by artillery fire.[210] Ioreth, the oldest nurse at the Houses of Healing, has something of the talkative, warm-hearted nun about her and refers to her fellow healers as 'sisters' when chattering to Aragorn about kingsfoil (*RK* V/8).

Tolkien's 1923 review of Furnivall's *Hali Meidenhad* launched his career-long engagement with works on female spirituality from the Katherine Group—already at this early date connected in his mind with Chaucer's Clerk's Tale—and he mentored Catholic research students such as Simonne d'Ardenne and Mary Salu.[211] He published on the Katherine Group in 1929 after suspending work on the Clarendon Chaucer and long planned an edition of *Seinte Katerine* with d'Ardenne.[212] His 1930 proposal to Kenneth Sisam for his next project after the ill-fated Clarendon Chaucer—'I would like to cooperate in an edition of the *Ancrene Riwle*'—indicated an unspoken regard for the religious women addressed in this guide for holy living. Naturally his reverence for nuns would have prevented him from mentioning (if he knew it) that the convent of Stratford-at-Bow, where the Prioress learned her French, was landlord for the Unicorn brothel in Southwark not far from the Tabard Inn.[213]

Next there was the matter of the Prioress's dogs. While embodying feline cruelty in Tevildo Prince of Cats, Tolkien had an Englishman's fondness for dogs like the great wolfhound Huan that saved Beren and Lúthien and even Farmer Maggot's watchdogs that barked ferociously at Frodo and his travelling companions. *The Story of Kullervo* retained the magical dog Musti from the *Kalevala*, his *Lay of Leithian* made a point of mentioning 'Hounds there were in Valinor' (2,238), and *Farmer Giles of Ham* featured the talking dog Garm borrowed from the *Prose Edda*. Having already discussed hunting dogs in *Gawain*,[214]

---

[210] *Surprised by Joy*, 197. Tolkien was amazed to find that Lewis 'admires nuns!' (*Letters*, 96).

[211] J. S. Ryan, 'J. R. R. Tolkien and the *Ancrene Riwle*, or Two Fine and Courteous Mentors to Women's Spirits', in *In the Nameless Wood: Explorations in the Philological Hinterland of Tolkien's Literary Creations* (Zurich and Jena: Walking Tree Publishers, 2013), 261–300.

[212] Tolkien, '*Ancrene Wisse* and *Hali Meiþhad*' (1929); see SH 2:58–60 and 2:598–9 'Katherine Group'. D'Ardenne's *Seinte Katerine*, co-edited with E. J. Dobson, finally appeared as EETS s.s. 7, 1981; she had previously published the related text *þe Liflade ant te Passiun of Seinte Iuliene*, EETS o.s. 248, 1961, dedicated to Tolkien and thanking him for help on the glossary and grammar. Norman Davis remarked that the edition 'presents more of Tolkien's views on early Middle English than anything he himself published' (SH 2:291).

[213] Richard Rex, 'Madame Eglentyne and the Bankside Brothels', in *'The Sins of Madame Eglantyne' and Other Essays on Chaucer* (Newark: University of Delaware Press; London: Associated University Presses, 1995), 78–94.

[214] Tolkien and Gordon, eds., *Sir Gawain and the Green Knight*, 100–1, 105–6.

Tolkien drafted a long note about the hunting hounds in *The Book of the Duchess* and the lone dog that led the dreamer to the Black Knight:

> *forloyn*: a call blown when the beast had outdistanced or outwitted hounds and left them behind 'weary and sore', whether it was still being pursued by another pack or not. Presumably it was a signal for the lagging and tired dogs to come back to the huntsman, and it marked the end of the hunt, so far as that particular pack was concerned. Hereupon a whelp comes and fawns upon the poet and then makes off. (Bodleian MS Tolkien A 39/2/1, fol. 21)

Despite his liking of hunting dogs, Tolkien joined others chiding the Prioress for pampering her little pups: 'The dogs were fed on the best food, much better than many people could obtain—a folly of sentimental pet-keepers (with tender hearts) that did not perish with the fourteenth century.' Mrs Tolkien kept chickens for their eggs during the Second World War, but the closest the family came to a dog was Michael's toy lost on the beach during a vacation on the Yorkshire coast and later memorialized in the story *Roverandom* told from the dog's viewpoint.[215] It is probably no coincidence that Tolkien wrote this story in 1927 about the same time that he was commenting on the Prioress's dogs.

Tolkien drafted two full pages about the Prioress's eye-colour 'greye as glas'. Only excerpts are quoted below, particularly those statements looking forward to the Reeve's Tale where the miller's daughter also has 'ÿen greye as glas':

> The Prioress is described now in terms as conventional, if less obviously burlesqued, as Sir Thopas. She is the romance fair lady, slightly spoiled, in a gently malicious manner fitting to the author speaking in his own elvish person. In the Reeve's Tale we see the same conventional portrait rudely and coarsely parodied, as is more fitting to Chaucer pretending to be a Reeve... There, even his duller readers must have perceived the inversion of the familiar picture of the lady 'gent and small', with only her grey eyes left undamaged, a nasty comment on the pretended gentility of the maiden's mother. In the description of the Prioress, the joke is milder and dawns on us more slowly. The original of the picture (if there was any single one) may indeed have had 'grey eyes', not uncommon, and those who wish may see in this line one of those happy touches on the canvas, taken direct from life, which give individuality to Chaucer's portraits. It is far more probable (and more amusing) to believe that English literary tradition and convenient rhyme (and a jesting purpose) dictated the colour of her eyes and found the alliterative phrase. The latter is one of those familiar things, embedded in everyday language, which are very difficult to track, and which escape glossaries of hard words and learned commentaries alike. Actually Chaucer, here and

---

[215] SH 3:1110–14 '*Roverandom*'. John Garth told me, 'If the Tolkien family had had dogs, I would know about it.' McIlwaine, *Tolkien: Maker of Middle-earth*, 281, includes a photograph of the Tolkien chickens.

in the Reeve's Tale 54, provides the only two examples of *grey as glas* we can find in Middle English.... Not only great ladies such as Guinevere, all fair ladies' standard (if we do not begin with Olympian Athene *glaukōpis* of the Greeks!), had grey eyes—or blue, for such was the range of the sense, the colour of the sea in most of its northern moods—but almost all fair ladies and maidens beside...[216]
(Bodleian MS Tolkien A 39/2/2, fols. 107–8)

Another fair lady was Arwen, first appearing at the banquet in Rivendell when 'the light of stars was in her bright eyes, grey as a cloudless night' (*FR* II/1). Tolkien also created the grey-eyed Éowyn who embodied something of Madame Eglentyne's doubleness. Much as the Prioress had the twofold aspects of the courtly lady and the mother superior, Éowyn starts as a courtly lady in Théoden's hall but then transforms into the warrior Dernhelm riding to the siege of Minas Tirith. The first clue to her true identity comes when Merry spots her 'clear grey eyes' (*RK* V/3). As a shield-maiden, Éowyn resembles the warrior-maiden Athena denoted by the epithet 'grey-eyed' (γλαυκῶπις). Tolkien would recall that *grey* included the colour of the sea when describing Éowyn at the moment she confronts the Lord of the Nazgûl: 'Her eyes grey as the sea were hard and fell' (*RK* V/6). Tolkien may well have been partial to this colour because he himself had grey eyes—as did Aragorn, Elrond, and his fictional counterpart Faramir.[217]

Perhaps Madame Eglentyne's courtly affectations even planted a seed for the upper-class pretentions of Lobelia Sackville-Baggins. Her hyphenated name, as Tolkien pointed out, had more aristocratic connotations than mere Baggins.[218] If the Prioress showed extravagant manners at the dinner table, Lobelia coveted Bilbo's silver spoons for her own table and first entered *The Lord of the Rings* when attending her cousin's birthday dinner because 'his table had a high reputation' (*FR* I/1). When Chaucer finally added that the dainty nun was in fact quite large—'The lady "gent and small" is middle-aged and *en bon point*'—Tolkien at last admitted 'we are perhaps right in feeling the first hint of malice' in what he interpreted as a 'mild version of the cruelty of the Reeve's Tale.' He himself would indulge this degree of malice toward Lobelia, though what he said satirically about the Prioress could apply to hobbits in general: 'a conservative, old-fashioned type, proud of its gentility and traditions, but unconscious of its own narrowness and provinciality and the changing times.'

Truly cutting satire of religious corruption was reserved for THE MONK, whose duties as an *outridere* overseeing monastic properties had become occasions for worldly pleasures: 'The opportunities offered were no doubt seized on and abused by such as preferred horses to books and prayer.' Even his horse was

---

[216] See Richard Rex, '"Grey" Eyes and the Medieval Ideal of Feminine Beauty', in *Sins of Madame Eglentyne*, 54–60.
[217] SH 2:63–5 'Appearance'.
[218] Tolkien, 'Nomenclature of *The Lord of the Rings*', in Hammond and Scull, *Reader's Companion*, 762.

fashionably decorated to impress: 'the Monk is singled out by his bells, which are meant to point to his copying of the gear and ways of the secular people of rank.' Glorfindel rode a horse with harness ringing with bells because he was an Elf Lord of rank, but when Tolkien came to describe the more austere Dúnedain warriors, he made a point of mentioning their horses were not decorated.

The Monk specifically flaunted St Benedict's rules against outdoor enjoyments: 'Hunting, hawking and dicing were forbidden to priests by canon law, and were in any case contrary to monastic rule and spirit, and only possible, certainly as habitual pursuits, at a time of laxity.'[219] As a devout Catholic, Tolkien responded to the portrait's worst anti-monasticism by rejecting a particularly unflattering passage as spurious: 'we can scarcely accept 180–4, as they stand in our text, as Chaucer unadulterated.' Editors sometimes rationalize censoring their texts by claiming anything they dislike could not have been by their author. Skeat raised no doubt about the authenticity of the lines that Tolkien questioned, nor does the current *Riverside Chaucer*.

During the Reformation, Chaucer acquired the reputation of an early advocate for dissolving monasteries because of his rule-breaking Monk, although the poet's satire during the fourteenth century was surely intended for correction, not destruction.[220] Tolkien recalled such censure when concluding about the Monk, 'neither ecclesiastic nor lay observers seem ever to have considered such conduct as anything but worldly and improper, and it was reprobated in laws, homilies, and literature throughout the Middle Ages.' In 1421 Henry V took an interest in the laxity of Benedictine foundations and ordered the General Chapter to convene at Westminster, and his thirteen articles of complaints, not coincidentally perhaps, closely followed Chaucer's own profile of monastic abuses.[221] Years later when writing to his son Michael about those (like Chaucer) scandalized by Church corruption, he balanced this criticism with praise for the work of monastic scribes: 'I think we should remember the enormous debt we owe to the Benedictines, and also remember that (like the Church) they have always been in a state of succumbing to mammon and the world' (*Letters*, 337n.).

Tolkien displayed his impulse for explaining the obvious when next he wrote about THE CLERK OF OXENFORD. In a poem published in 1913, he had described Oxford as 'the city by the fording' when it was not yet mere nostalgia; undergraduates in his day still encountered cattle travelling to market along Broad Street outside Exeter College:[222]

---

[219] Tolkien did not turn a blind eye to clerical failings: 'I have met snuffy, stupid, undutiful, conceited, ignorant, hypocritical, lazy, tipsy, hardhearted, cynical, mean, grasping, vulgar, snobbish, and even (at a guess) immoral priests' (*Letters*, 354).

[220] Linda Georgianna, 'The Protestant Chaucer', in *Chaucer's Religious Tales*, ed. C. David Benson and Elizabeth Robertson (Cambridge: D. S. Brewer, 1990), 55–69.

[221] Bowers, *Chaucer and Langland*, 'The Monk: Prologue to the *Siege of Thebes*', 206–15.

[222] Garth, *Tolkien at Exeter College*, 5, 7.

Oxenford : O.E. *Oxnaford*—one of the few place-names that appears to have really meant what it seems to say: 'ford for oxen'. The name probably originally arose from a ford for cattle coming into the market from the west over one of the shallow branches of the then unconserved and more meandering Thames. The ford was probably to the west of the town, near the Osney where the carpenter of Chaucer's Miller's Tale lived.[223]

Tolkien belaboured the point perhaps because he had invested time in his *Book of Lost Tales* associating Hengst's brother with *Oxenaford* as the Old English equivalent of the Qenya *Taruktarna*; Tolkien once suggested to Tom Shippey that Hincksey outside Oxford preserved the name Hengst itself.[224] He continued his liking for the older version of the city's name and used it sarcastically in 'On Fairy-Stories': 'I heard a clerk of Oxenford declare...' (*Essays*, 149). Again, in *Farmer Giles of Ham*, he gave credit for an obscure definition to the 'Four Wise Clerks of Oxenford', alluding jokingly to the *OED* editors Murray, Bradley, Craigie, and Onions. Though the Clarendon Chaucer did not include the Miller's Tale set in Oxford, Tolkien seems to have recalled the fabliau's wooden tubs when describing the Dwarves in their barrels in his most fabliau-like episode of *The Hobbit*.

English professors always show a fondness for Chaucer's Clerk as much for his precarious livelihood as for his love of books, and Tolkien, perhaps recalling his own early pursuit of academic employment, focused upon the line 'Ne was so worldly for to have offyce':

> A result of the opportunities offered by the church was that there were too many qualified persons in orders (minor or major) for the benefices, and many of these were persons who entered on such a life from more or less worldly motives. Their services, as educated men, were more and more employed in secular offices, by the king as by lords. To this we owe ultimately our modern use of 'clerk'. This Clerk, however, was not worldly; he desired a cure of souls, not a secular post. The service of clerks in the king's exchequer, or as stewards to lords and landowners, is censured in *Piers Plowman* (B...)

Tolkien's uncertainty about line-numbers from *Piers Plowman* indicates that he was scribbling hastily and merely glanced at the scholarly source at his elbow, because Skeat had specified passus and line numbers. Nevill Coghill, later a fellow Inkling and Merton colleague, would confirm Chaucer's debt to Langland when matching his zeal for social satire in the General Prologue's pilgrim portraits.[225]

---

[223] Tolkien knew the Miller's Tale well enough to quote it offhand: 'This would be to investigate "Goddes privitee", as the Medievals said' (*Letters*, 234).
[224] Tolkien, *Lost Tales, Part II*, 297 and 355–6; Shippey, *Author of the Century*, 57.
[225] Nevill Coghill, 'Two Notes on *Piers Plowman*: I. The Abbot of Abingdon and the Date of the C-Text; II. Chaucer's Debt to Langland', *Medium Ævum* 4 (1935), 83–94.

Tolkien glossed the joke about the Clerk's lack of money—'But al be that he was a philosophre | Yet hadde he but litel gold in cofre'—so that the wordplay would not be lost upon undergraduates:

philosophre: this word meant both philosopher (in modern sense) and scientist (cf. Natural Philosophy, Experimental Philosophy)—and scientist was at the time equated with alchemist. The clerk was not a philosopher of the latter sort whose pursuit was the 'philosopher's stone' that could transmute base metal into gold, so (whatever might be true of alchemists) he had little gold.

Since students of previous generations first encountered the term *philosopher's stone* in this passage from the General Prologue, it may have been where J. K. Rowling got an early hint for her title *Harry Potter and the Philosopher's Stone*. Obvious as her many debts to Tolkien, Rowling readily admits her indebtedness to Chaucer, too, specifically the Pardoner's Tale in the core-story's version of 'Tale of the Three Brothers' about greed leading to death in *Harry Potter and the Deathly Hallows*. We shall see in the final chapter that Tolkien shared this fascination with the Pardoner's Tale.

Not from a well-to-do family like so many undergraduates in those days, Tolkien recalled something of his own privations when explaining the poverty of the Clerk of Oxford: 'He appears also to have come of a poor family that had made sacrifices to send him to Oxford—as many do still, if not as much as they did in days before pious benefactors had somewhat eased the way.' Tolkien's nod to *pious benefactors* recalled his guardian Father Morgan's generosity as well as Exeter College's Exhibition of £60 which maintained him as a poor scholar at Oxford.[226] As his better-off friend Rob Gilson remarked, 'He has always been desperately poor.'[227] Since his last sketchy note for the Reeve's Tale took much the same notice of John and Alain—'They are called *povre* clerks'—it is hardly surprising that Tolkien did not join Chaucer's mockery of these two underprivileged students nor the threadbare Clerk of Oxford. It is perhaps noteworthy that Bilbo charged nothing for teaching his poor student Sam Gamgee to read and write.

Tolkien's annotations grew sketchier and more idiosyncratic as he neared the end of the General Prologue. For THE SHIPMAN, he continued his practice of commenting on horses by glossing the pilgrim's *rouncy*—'a rough heavy horse chiefly used for cartage or general agricultural work, not for riding'. The word as well as the image of the Shipman as an ungainly rider had already figured in his article 'The Devil's Coach-Horses' from 1925: 'The devil appears to have ridden his coach-horses like a postilion, but he was in worse case than Chaucer's Shipman who "rood upon a rouncy as he couthe"; his steeds seem indeed to have been

---

[226] Garth, *Tolkien at Exeter*, 15; see *Biography*, 60.
[227] Garth, *Tolkien and the Great War*, 44; see also SH 2:453–4 'Gilson'.

heavy old dobbins that needed all his spurring' (p. 336). He would never have occasion to use the word in *The Lord of the Rings* where all the horses possess a degree of equine nobility, even Bill the Pony. Though he took time to explain the joke of Don Quixote having a horse named Rocinante—from the cognate Spanish *Rocín* for work-horse—it is not perhaps too much of a stretch that *roch* became the Sindarin word for 'horse', King Fingolfin rode a mighty steed named Rochallor, and the name *Rohan* derived from *Rochand* meaning 'land of horses'.

Tolkien's Shipman notes focused mostly upon seafaring terms, aptly enough, remarking at length on *tydes* (skipped by Skeat) and crossing through the half-page draft for *tydes* only to write a full-page replacement. Here are his introductory sentences:

> This description is meant to have a nautical air and a smack of genuine sailors' language. It contains some words used in what are now their chief or sole senses, though these are still rare in Middle English, which suggests that they represent contemporary nautical talk, and that our uses have been influenced by the language of the ports, especially London. *tydes* still normally 'times'. Since the times specially observed by a coastal navigator were those of ebb and flood, this use is probably older among sailors than in ordinary language. It is not recorded in O.E. and is uncommon in M.E.

One older speaker who uses the word in this dual sense is Gandalf when encountered in Fangorn Forest: 'We meet again. At the turn of the tide. The great storm is coming, but the tide has turned' (*TT* III/5). Tolkien's love of the sea is well-attested, treating his family to beach holidays whenever possible, and later he transferred this deep yearning for the sea to his Elves (SH 3:1132–5). When his Appendix B traced the lives of all the Fellowship's members to their ends, Legolas sailed down Anduin and thence over the sea with his companion Gimli, and even Samwise went to the Grey Havens and passed over the sea. He had greater recourse to nautical lore in *Akallabêth* when describing the seafaring Númenóreans when their voyages increased during the reign of Tar-Aldarion.

When his commentary focused on the phrase *Ypres and Gaunt* after a note on the Shipman's *barge*—both Elves and Orcs employed barges upon the Anduin—Tolkien had moved along to THE WIFE OF BATH without signalling the changeover. He provided no name or summary of her background to identify this pilgrim, one of only three women among the thirty pilgrims, the only one not a nun. Chaucer's neglect of female characters in his frame-narrative to the *Tales* would be shared by Tolkien, who created 'gender imbalance' in his fiction by including very few women in *The Lord of the Rings*—where Éowyn spends much time disguised as the male warrior Dernhelm—and featuring no named women in *The Hobbit* except briefly Lobelia Sackville-Baggins plus a passing reference to Belladonna Took. Always an enthusiast for manly adventure stories like *King Solomon's Mines*, he was no fan of women's literature and had a loathing for

Dorothy Sayers (*Letters*, 82); Lewis doubted the two Oxford writers ever met despite the fact that Tolkien otherwise encouraged younger women scholars and Sayers contributed to Lewis's volume of memorial essays for Inkling member Charles Williams.[228] The chatty nurse Ioreth (meaning 'old woman' in Elvish) comes closer to the Wife of Bath as a purveyor of old wives' tales without posing the sexual threat of Chaucer's Alisoun.

Kittredge had identified the Wife of Bath as a key figure who initiated the debate about marriage as the unifying theme throughout the middle section of the *Tales*, but Tolkien avoided this colourful but morally disturbing character by simply singling out words in her portrait such as *offring*, *coverchiefs*, *chirchedore*, and *carpe*—the latter 'a word belonging exclusively to the North and West, especially to alliterative writings'. He noted her pilgrimages to Jerusalem, Rome, Boulogne, Galicia, and Cologne but without remarking how extraordinary that she had travelled to Jerusalem thrice, offering instead the pedantic comment that 'the modern accentuation of the word would require *thryes* as a monosyllable'. One detail that did merit his attention was her first marriage at the age of 12— hence 'she is not yet old' as a useful corrective—and he repeated Skeat on the folklore about someone who was *gat-toothed*. Little else of her boisterous personality entered his commentary.

Tolkien felt some relief in next describing THE PARSON in an altogether positive manner: 'Chaucer has made the cleric more particular and vivid, though in fact he is describing only one who lived up to the precepts for the proper behaviour of a parish priest.' He drafted a note on the line *Ful looth were him to cursen for his tythes* only to cross it out and write almost a full page explaining tithes as the Parson's main income: 'failure or refusal to pay them, or any fraud in their payment was a serious sin—usually enumerated under the fruits of avarice in treatises on the sins such as *Ancren Riwle*.' Tolkien always intended to write more about this thirteenth-century rule for female hermits after his preliminary 1929 article '*Ancrene Wisse* and *Hali Meiðhad*', and in any case he included references to it throughout his Chaucer commentary even when Skeat did not. Here he also outdid his predecessor by citing John Mirk's *Instructions for Parish Priests* on excommunication as the punishment for parishioners not paying their tithes.

Hereafter Tolkien's drafts become increasingly difficult to decipher as he moved from the Parson directly to his first note on THE MILLER as a *carl*. He described this as 'a Scandinavian word', and he recalled it late in life in his unfinished *Tal-Elmar* when describing the unsavoury town-master as a

---

[228] *Letters of C. S. Lewis*, ed. W. H. Lewis, 287, and Zaleski and Zaleski, *The Fellowship*, 352, on Dorothy Sayers. See John D. Rateliff, 'The Missing Women: J. R. R. Tolkien's Lifelong Support for Women's Higher Education', in *Perilous and Fair: Women in the Works and Life of J. R. R. Tolkien*, ed. Janet Brennan Croft and Leslie A. Donovan (Altadena, CA: Mythopoeic Press, 2015), 41–69; Chance, *Tolkien, Self and Other*, 'Tolkien's Women: Students, Saints, and Holy Women', 184–9; and SH 3:1426–9 'Women and Oxford'.

'blear–eyed carl'.[229] His other notes concerned the rare words *knarre*, *harre*, and *harlotryes* which he would have included in the Glossary if allowed more space there. He ended by silently appropriating Skeat's reference to William Thorpe's 1407 complaint about Canterbury pilgrims like the Miller making an uproar with their bagpipes.

Tolkien began his commentary on THE REEVE eight lines into the pilgrim's portrait with the unexceptional word *winne*, otherwise crossing out false starts while allowing some sketchy entries to stand. One topic never failed to produce a long note—horses—and here he took an interest in the Reeve's *stot*, which Skeat defined simply as 'a low-bred undersized stallion'. Tolkien produced a half-page note beginning: 'The sense of this word is disputed. It is first found in late Old English in documents from Bury St. Edmunds where *stoltās* is glossed "equi viles".' His messy remark on the horse's name *Scot* is decipherable only because he took it verbatim from Skeat (5:51): 'to this day there is scarcely a farm in Norfolk or Suffolk, in which one of the horses is not called Scot.' His hobbits also had homely names for horses like Bill and Bumpkin. Tolkien's cavalry experience gave him more first-hand knowledge about horses than most Chaucerians, and more interest as well, so that among his last notes for the General Prologue was this explanation for *St. Thomas a Waterings*—'a place for watering horses'.

For the final section entitled 'Plan of the Tales' in the Clarendon Chaucer, Tolkien produced six pages that look more like note-taking than note-drafting. For the meaning of the phrase *sitting by this post*, he admitted rather refreshingly, 'I don't know.' If we are expecting a description of the innkeeper Harry Bailey as inspiration for Barliman Butterbur, we are disappointed, finding instead random notes like this one on *thoughte*: 'the O.E. verb *þencan* (*þōhte*) "think actively", "cogitate", "intend" and *þyncan* (*þūhte*) "appear" "seem" became similar or identical in many of their forms in M.E.' Certainly Tolkien had scrutinized Chaucer's lines on the Host when editing the text and compiling his glossary so that he had enough knowledge about him for later bringing Barliman more colourfully to life.

Here, too, he struggled with the perennial problem of how many tales Chaucer intended, whether the original plan for two tales toward Canterbury and two tales on the way back, as specified in the General Prologue, or a revised design of one tale for each pilgrim as suggested in the Parson's Prologue.[230] Tolkien cited witnesses from the next generation in the early fifteenth century to clarify the audience's expectations: 'The Chaucerian continuators who tried their hand at carrying on the unfinished tales took no notice of this line or the next, but went by the apparent later intention of Chaucer "one tale each" (Lydgate and the unknown

---

[229] Tolkien, *Peoples of Middle-Earth*, 428.
[230] Christopher noted similar revision after the fact in his father's own story collection *Book of Lost Tales*: 'when he abandoned them he had also abandoned his original ideas for their conclusion' (*Part I*, p. 13).

author of the *Tale of Beryn*, who told what happened at Canterbury).' John Lydgate's *Siege of Thebes* imagined himself as a pilgrim who joined Chaucer's original company in Canterbury and was invited by the Host to tell a story on the way back to London, obliging them with a prequel to the Knight's Tale so long-winded that it extended along the entire route homeward. The anonymous *Tale of Beryn* provided a much fuller, more colourful account of the pilgrims' stay in the cathedral town, including the Pardoner's fabliau-like misadventure with their inn's barmaid, after which the Merchant tells the initial tale on the homeward journey, his second. Tolkien's offhand comment therefore pre-empted later Chaucerians who insisted that the pilgrimage had been allegorized as a one-way spiritual ascent to the Celestial Jerusalem and no return trip to London was conceivable.[231] Tolkien knew better. He knew that medieval readers naturally expected a pilgrimage, like a quest, to follow the familiar pattern of 'there and back again'.

Calculating the number of intended tales was tangled up with deciding the number of taletellers, and Tolkien used asterisks to indicate which pilgrims actually told their tales in Chaucer's completed sections:

> In addition to the *ten* pilgrims represented in this selection, the Prologue also describes a Yeoman, Friar*, Merchant*, Lawyer*, Franklin*, Haberdasher, Carpenter, Weaver, Dyer, Tapicer, Cook*, Physician*, Ploughman (the Parson's brother), Manciple*, Summoner*, Pardoner*; and mentions a Nun* (the Prioress' *chaplain*) with her three Priests, one* of whom tells a story (Nun's Priest's Tale). This makes 30—or 31 with Chaucer*—the Host as umpire is not to be included in the storytellers. *Wel nyne and twenty* (l. 24) was probably intended as exact when written. (*One and thirty* would have fitted the line as well.) It is possible that the *three* priests, only one of whom is ever heard of again, is an unrevised error, or a later confusion. The original plan is thus for 31 (or 29) × 4 = 124 (or 116) tales.

All modern editions reckon twenty-nine pilgrims plus the Chaucerian narrator, not counting the Host or the late-arriving Canon's Yeoman, for a company of thirty and therefore a projected collection of 120 tales. But English professors, like poets, are better at number symbolism than numerical calculations.[232] Barely able to count change, C. S. Lewis repeatedly failed the mathematics section of his Oxford entrance exams and was later admitted only because ex-servicemen were exempted.[233] The comic confusion of having so many travellers arriving singly and in pairs, however, prepared Tolkien to write his own opening chapter of

---

[231] See my article 'The Tale of Beryn and The Siege of Thebes: Alternative Ideas of the *Canterbury Tales*', SAC 7 (1985), 23–50.

[232] Christopher Kreuzer, 'Numbers in Tolkien', in *The Ring Goes Ever On*, ed. Wells, 2:325–38.

[233] *Surprised by Joy*, 186–7, and Zaleski and Zaleski, *The Fellowship*, 75.

The Hobbit where thirteen dwarves—rather than thirty-one pilgrims—arrive at Bilbo's front door. Dwalin and Balin arrive one after another, but Kili and Fili come as a pair somewhat like the Franklin and Man of Law arriving together in Southwark. Just as Chaucer had the Five Guildsmen as his largest party of arrivals, Tolkien had as his largest group the five dwarves Dori, Nori, Ori, Oin, and Gloin (*Hobbit*, 39–40).

Set against this Chaucerian source-text, 'An Unexpected Party' has Gandalf assuming the role of the Host, organizing this rambunctious group and laying out plans for their journey, with Bilbo assuming the role of Chaucer who will later write an account of their adventures. Personal gain is the motive in both stories. The Canterbury pilgrim who tells the best tale will win a free dinner back at the Tabard Inn, while Bilbo and the Dwarves hope each to receive a share of the dragon's treasure. In both narratives, too, the organizer himself has an ulterior motive. Besides booking the company's return stay and prize dinner, Harry Bailey wants to escape for a few days from his mean, violent wife while Gandalf's true motive—which readers discover only in Appendix A. III 'Durin's Folk'—is the elimination of Smaug as a potential ally of Sauron.

Tolkien thought 'a journey is a marvellous device' (*Letters*, 239) and ended his commentary on the General Prologue by explaining how much Chaucer fell short in his itinerary:

> Actually a single story is extant (each probably belonging to the outward journey) for the *ten* characters of the selection, and for those marked * above. Chaucer recites the parody of contemporary verse *Sir Thopas*, and when this is cut short by the Host, gives a long sermon (*Tale of Melibeus*). The Cook's tale and the Squire's were never finished. Thus we have, with the Canon's Yeoman's tale (see introductory note), 20 tales, 2 fragments, and a little parody, out of the projected total of 124 or 116 tales—later modified perhaps to 58.

If his *Selections* included meagre offerings from these *Tales*, at least Tolkien's commentary gave some idea of how many more had been written, or partly written, as well as how many the poet had promised. John M. Manly's edition of the *Canterbury Tales* brought greater clarity for sorting out these fragments and groups, but it was published in 1928, too late to provide any help for the Clarendon Chaucer.

When Tolkien continued on the following page—'The Reeve's name was Oswald...'—he ventured upon the truncated version of the Reeve's Tale with a commentary which itself trailed off halfway through. He never came anywhere near annotating the Monk's Tale or the Nun's Priest's Tale. If he found the burden of the 'Chaucerian incubus' too crushing, the problem was largely of his own making, again and again digressing to trace etymologies and write two-page entries on single words when told repeatedly that he had only a total of twenty pages for his Notes. Yet he plodded onward in evident fatigue in these final pages with what Harold Bloom might have diagnosed as 'the exhaustion of being a latecomer' (*AI* 12)—or what we might recognize as the bone-tired determination of Frodo and Sam staggering through Mordor toward Mount Doom. The following chapter explores how his faltering engagements with the Reeve's Tale nonetheless elicited important responses from Tolkien as scholar and storyteller over the next two decades.

6

Tolkien as a Chaucerian: *The Reeve's Tale*

In 1922 George Gordon planned on including the Prioress's Tale in their *Selections from Chaucer's Poetry and Prose* until Kenneth Sisam persuaded him that its anti-Semitic contents would cause problems. Their solution was to substitute the first half of the Reeve's Tale while omitting the second half to avoid 'certain offensive passages'. For Tolkien, this meant undertaking only 228 lines for the straightforward job of editing and sorting words into his Glossary before commenting upon obscure and interesting points in his Notes.[1] Like Bilbo carelessly picking up a ring in a cave, his encounter with the Reeve's Tale would occasion far greater consequences than anyone could have imagined, including Tolkien himself.

In terms of his ongoing responses to Skeat who had provided a single-page note on the Northern language of the two Cambridge students, Tolkien in 1934 would publish the seventy-page article 'Chaucer as a Philologist: *The Reeve's Tale*'. Five years later when asked to dress up as Chaucer and perform for a summer entertainment in Oxford, Tolkien chose to recite the Reeve's Tale and did extra duty by preparing the text for a printed programme. Though his brief introduction claimed 'Only in the words of the clerks is there any material departure from the text as printed by Skeat', Tolkien's candour fell short (Fig. 14). He had actually done something quite daring and completely re-edited the work, abandoning the Ellesmere manuscript which Skeat had used as his a copy-text and rewriting every line and almost every word to conform to what he believed were Chaucer's authentic spellings.[2] Tolkien had lamented in his 1927 *Year's Work in English* that editors could go only so far in reconstructing a past poet's original achievement:

> It is of the nature of things that the skeleton lasts longest. Palæontology rescues rather bones than flesh, it give us little information concerning the cry of the tyrannosaurus; the history of language recovers for us many word-forms whose

---

[1] Bodleian MS Tolkien A 39/2/2, fols. 132r–136v; the commentary, itself incomplete, covered only lines 3921–4148 from Skeat.
[2] Shippey, 'A Look at *Exodus* and *Finn and Hengst*', in *Roots and Branches*, 175–86, shows Tolkien exercising his zeal for emendation elsewhere, but nothing like his thoroughgoing reconstruction of the Reeve's Tale's text.

Tolkien's Lost Chaucer. John M. Bowers, Oxford University Press (2019). © John M. Bowers.
DOI: 10.1093/oso/9780198842675.001.0001

full richness of tones and of meanings escapes us—it can hardly hope to drag back much of the syntax and idiom of the lost past.[3]

Unable as a philologist to give full voice to the lost past in deeds as well as words, Tolkien would seek this recovery in his fantasy writings.

Some other medievalists before him wrote fiction, Montague Rhodes James famous for supernatural thrillers such as *Ghost Stories of an Antiquary*,[4] but because Skeat never published novels, Tolkien could stake a claim in an area which his Victorian predecessor chose never to enter. About the time he was teaching the Reeve's Tale to military cadets in the 1940s, the story of John, Alain, and the Cambridge miller worked a peculiar alchemy in his imagination, and he appropriated Chaucer's fabliau to imagine two young hobbits battling Isengard's evil mill-master in what would become *The Two Towers*.

Already Chaucer's story attracted him because he and his younger brother had an adventure as boys with the fearsome miller outside their village of Sarehole.[5] Because this real-life miller was covered in white dust when he chased them away, young Ronald dubbed him the White Ogre and begrudgingly acknowledged this background at the end of his 1965 Foreword. Memories were still vivid when looking back in 1968:

> As for knowing Sarehole Mill, it dominated my childhood. I lived in a small cottage almost immediately beside it, and the old miller of my day and his son were characters of wonder and terror to a small child. (*Letters*, 390)

In Tolkien's wish-fulfilling version of this story, Merry and Pippin are not frightened away as were the Tolkien boys, nor are they beaten, bloodied, and run off like the two Cambridge students, but instead they join forces with the Ents to attack Saruman and destroy his dark Orc-infested mills. Tolkien's imaginative process routinely fixed upon a medieval text for mediating between his personal experiences and his literary creations. Even alliteration bolsters the genealogy from the Sarehole miller and Simkin the miller of the Reeve's Tale, and then to Tolkien's Sandyman the miller of Hobbiton and Saruman of Isengard.

---

[3] Tolkien, 'Philology' (1927), 56. Tolkien remembered this image of dinosaur bones when describing Smaug's skeleton as if the fossils of a tyrannosaurus at the bottom of the Long Lake (*Hobbit*, 313); a year after publishing *The Hobbit*, he lectured on dragons at Oxford's natural history museum and compared them to dinosaurs (SH 1:225).

[4] See Patrick J. Murphy, *Medieval Studies and the Ghost Stories of M. R. James* (University Park: Pennsylvania State University Press, 2017).

[5] Shippey, *Road to Middle-earth*, 171; SH 3:1126–8 'Sarehole', and McIlwaine, *Tolkien: Maker of Middle-earth*, 130–1, with photograph of the miller Mr Andrew with his son. The *Oxford Dictionary of English Place-Names* takes the first element of Sarehole as *Searu* meaning 'sere' or 'withered', which Tolkien automatically corrected to the Mercian *Saru* for the name of his wizard Saruman, also dry and withered.

The Reeve's Tale in the Clarendon Chaucer

Tolkien suspended work on his Clarendon Chaucer after sketching nine pages of notes on the Reeve's Tale. To be more accurate, he spottily annotated 94 of the 228 lines representing the first half of the fabliau excerpted by Sisam and Gordon. Even the quality of Tolkien's penmanship worsened by the time he stopped one-third down the almost unreadable last page, although his commentary remained scholarly even as his script grew sloppy. This deterioration was typical, as Christopher remarked about just one manuscript of *The Lord of the Rings*: 'Here the draft stops, the ending being very ragged.'[6] Tolkien himself acknowledged this muddle when later scribbling in the margin: 'These in so far as legible need revising...' (Fig. 13).

After identifying the Reeve as the pilgrim named Oswald, Tolkien cribbed information from Skeat (5:113) to remark upon his regional language: 'we have learned already that he came from Baldeswelle in Norfolk; in his own words in the prologue to his tale, there are dialectal traces as *so thee'k, ik am*.' This Norfolk spelling of the first-person pronoun would become what his student Norman Davis called 'the *ik* which everybody notices'.[7] Tolkien went on about regionalisms: 'Having decided on this localization of the Reeve, Chaucer proceeds to make him localize the tale he tells also in the Eastern districts, in Cambridge.' This place-setting in the university town formed part of the Reeve's retaliation against the Miller whose tale was set in the other university town, Oxford. His fabliau begins when a local miller's thefts upset the *wardeyn* of a Cambridge hall, and Tolkien's gloss on the word would gain meaning for him personally in future years: 'a title for a head of a hall or a college still preserved in several Oxford colleges, notably the oldest Merton'. Although he knew Chaucer's connections with Merton College, what Tolkien could not have known in 1928 was that he would become Merton Professor of Language and Literature in 1945 and write gleefully of his good fortune: 'It is incredible belonging to a real college' (*Letters*, 116).

But in 1928 Tolkien's main question about the Reeve's Tale was how the poet gained his precise knowledge of dialects: 'It is unlikely that Chaucer would carefully localize the tale in places he did not know personally. The dialects are accurate enough to allow us to believe that he did know Cambridge and its neighbourhood.' Although the Reeve came from Norfolk and set his tale at Trumpington outside Cambridge, which were places southerly enough for Chaucer to have contact with

---

[6] J. R. R. Tolkien, *The History of the Lord of the Rings*, ed. Christopher Tolkien, 4 vols. (Boston and New York: Houghton Mifflin, 1988), *The War of the Ring*, 3:65; see *Biography*, 183–4.

[7] Norman Davis, *RES*, n.s. 27 (1976), 336–7 at p. 336, was reviewing Bennett's *Chaucer at Oxford and at Cambridge*. Tolkien's 'Chaucer as a Philologist', 7, had mentioned these unusual touches; see Alan J. Fletcher, 'Chaucer's Norfolk Reeve', *Medium Ævum* 52 (1983), 100–3. Philip Knox, 'The "Dialect" of Chaucer's Reeve', *Chaucer Review* 49 (2014), 102–24, has revisited the question of Norfolk dialect and finds this evidence less compelling.

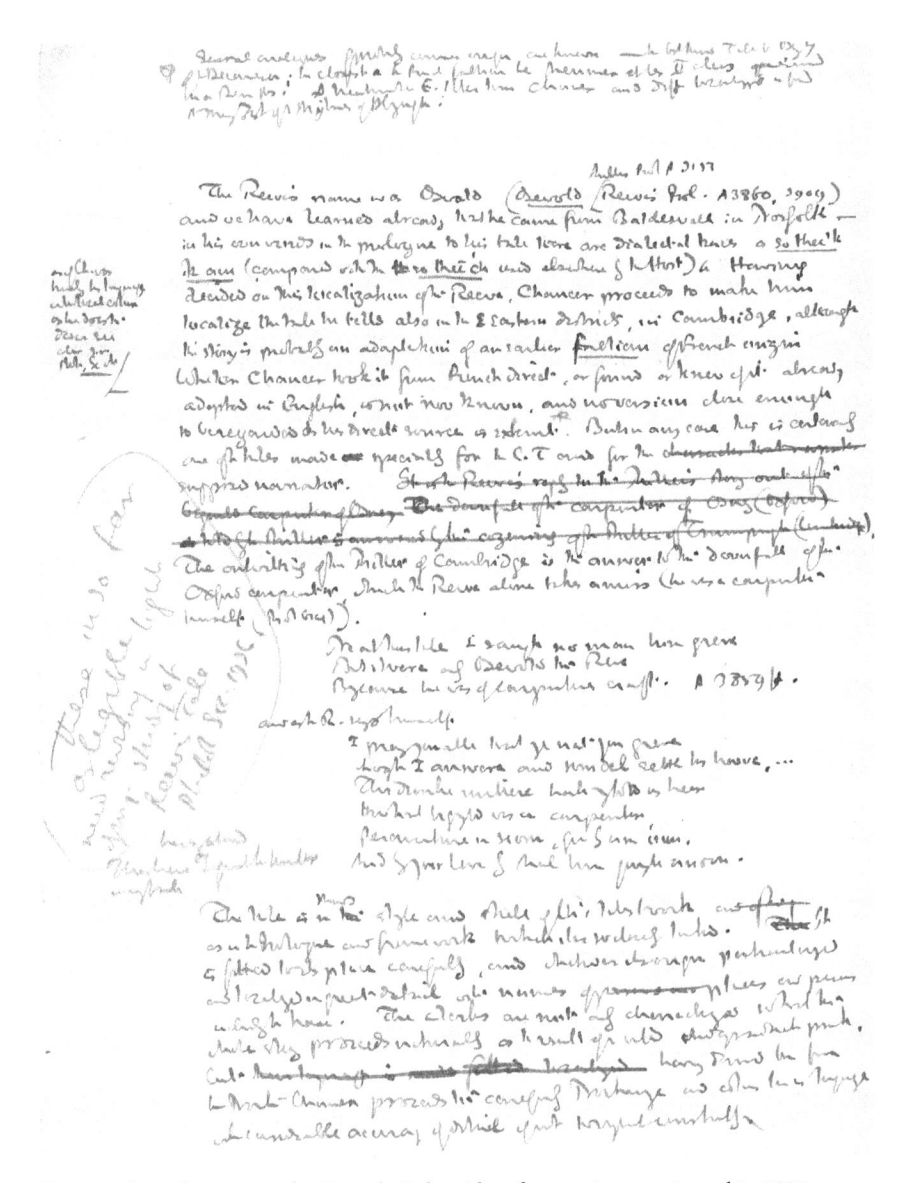

Fig. 13. Introduction to the *Reeve's Tale* with reference in margin to his 1934 "Chaucer as a Philologist." (Oxford, Bodleian Library, MS Tolkien A 39/2/2, fol. 132).

them and their residents, what really interested Tolkien were the two students from Strother and the Northern dialect that Chaucer had them speaking.[8]

---

[8] The elusive place-name is identified with Castle Strother in Northumberland, geographically and linguistically *terra incognita* beyond Chaucer's first-hand experience, and so the poet simply used the more familiar dialect of Yorkshire.

English dialectology was still a relatively new field in the wake of Richard Morris's *Specimens of Early English* (1867), and yet Skeat could remark that almost every beginner in the study of Middle English had grown familiar with the Northern, Midland, and Southern dialects unknown before Morris.[9] Skeat himself had founded the English Dialect Society in 1873 and prepared the way for the six-volume *English Dialect Dictionary* dedicated to him by Joseph Wright, Tolkien's tutor during his first year at Oxford. Skeat was therefore equipped to identify the Northern speech of the clerks in the Reeve's Tale and filled a whole page explaining how Chaucer used regional forms such as the long *ā* instead of his usual long *ō*, giving as examples *na* instead of *no*, *ham* instead of *hoom*, *gas* instead of *gooth*, *banes* instead of *bones*, *bathe* instead of *bothe*, and *twa* instead of *two* (5:121–2). He also pointed out Northern words such as *boes* for 'behoves', *lathe* for 'barn', *fonne* for 'fool', and *taa* for 'take' which occur nowhere else in Chaucer's works. These were the same examples which Tolkien would use in the introduction to his 1939 edition (Fig. 14).

One can only suspect that Skeat's tour-de-force had some inhibiting effect, since Tolkien stopped drafting his explanatory notes at exactly the point where he

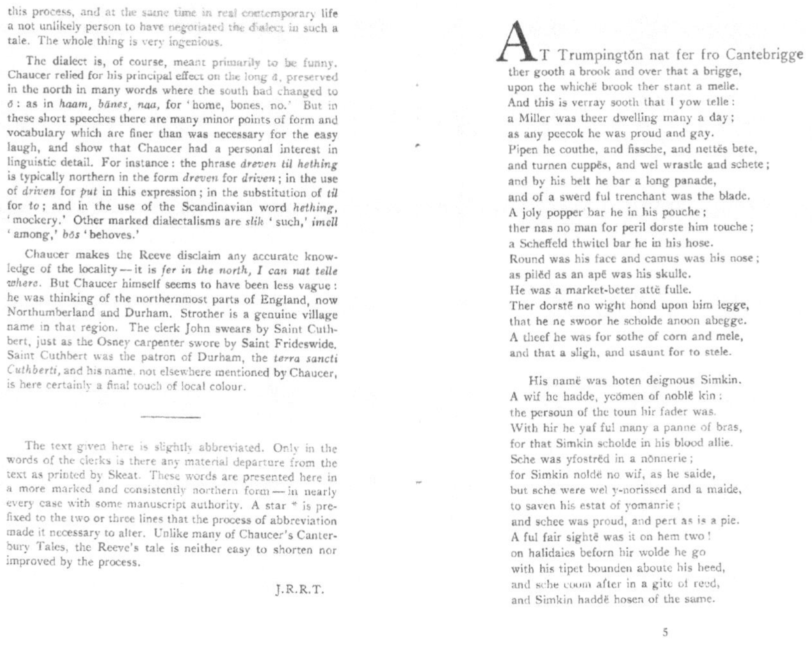

this process, and at the same time in real contemporary life a not unlikely person to have negotiated the dialect in such a tale. The whole thing is very ingenious.

The dialect is, of course, meant primarily to be funny. Chaucer relied for his principal effect on the long ā, preserved in the north in many words where the south had changed to ō: as in *haam*, *bānes*, *naa*, for 'home, bones, no.' But in these short speeches there are many minor points of form and vocabulary which are finer than was necessary for the easy laugh, and show that Chaucer had a personal interest in linguistic detail. For instance: the phrase *dreven til hething* is typically northern in the form *dreven* for *driven*; in the use of *driven* for *put* in this expression; in the substitution of *til* for *to*; and in the use of the Scandinavian word *hething*, 'mockery.' Other marked dialectalisms are *slik* 'such,' *imell* 'among,' *bōs* 'behoves.'

Chaucer makes the Reeve disclaim any accurate knowledge of the locality—it is *fer in the north, I can nat telle where*. But Chaucer himself seems to have been less vague: he was thinking of the northernmost parts of England, now Northumberland and Durham. Strother is a genuine village name in that region. The clerk John swears by Saint Cuthbert, just as the Osney carpenter swore by Saint Frideswide. Saint Cuthbert was the patron of Durham, the *terra sancti Cuthberti*, and his name, not elsewhere mentioned by Chaucer, is here certainly a final touch of local colour.

The text given here is slightly abbreviated. Only in the words of the clerks is there any material departure from the text as printed by Skeat. These words are presented here in a more marked and consistently northern form—in nearly every case with some manuscript authority. A star * is prefixed to the two or three lines that the process of abbreviation made it necessary to alter. Unlike many of Chaucer's Canterbury Tales, the Reeve's tale is neither easy to shorten nor improved by the process.

J.R.R.T.

AT Trumpingtŏn nat fer fro Cantebrigge
ther gooth a brook and over that a brigge,
upon the whichë brook ther stant a melle.
And this is verray sooth that I yow telle:
a Miller was theer dwelling many a day;
as any peecok he was proud and gay.
Pipen he couthe, and fissche, and nettës bete,
and turnen cuppēs, and wel wrastle and schete;
and by his belt he bar a long panade,
and of a swerd ful trenchant was the blade.
A joly popper bar he in his pouche;
ther nas no man for peril dorste him touche;
a Scheffeld thwitel bar he in his hose.
Round was his face and camus was his nose;
as pilĕd as an apē was his skulle.
He was a market-beter attë fulle.
Ther dorstē no wight hond upon him legge,
that he ne swoor he scholde anoon abegge.
A theef he was for sothe of corn and mele,
and that a sligh, and usaunt for to stele.

His namë was hoten deignous Simkin.
A wif he hadde, ycŏmen of noblë kin:
the persoun of the toun hir fader was.
With hir he yaf ful many a panne of bras,
for that Simkin scholde in his blood allie.
Sche was yfostrēd in a nŏnnerie;
for Simkin noldë no wif, as he saide,
but sche were wel y-norissed and a maide,
to saven his estat of yomanrie;
and schee was proud, and pert as is a pie.
A ful fair sightē was it on hem two!
on halidaies beforn hir wolde he go
with his tipet bounden aboute his heed,
and sche coom after in a gite of reed,
and Simkin haddë hosen of the same.

5

Fig. 14. Tolkien's 1939 programme edition of *The Reeve's Tale*—last page of introduction and first page of text (Oxford, Bodleian Library, MS Tolkien A 39/3, fols. 28v–29r).

[9] Skeat, *Student's Pastime*, p. xxiii.

began considering Strother as the two clerks' hometown—'Fer in the north, I can nat telle where' (4015)—though he still found occasion to make Skeat wrong:

> The next line is of course a jest—a Southern shrug of the shoulders at the unknown geography of the barbarous North (which Chaucer had nonetheless visited) ... But it also implies that the village was thought of in the extreme north of England. Skeat says how no such town was, but there are two villages in Northumberland of the name ... It appears to have meant 'marsh' and to have been related to O.E. *strōd* ...   (Bodleian MS Tolkien A 39/2/2, fol. 136r)

Tolkien would explore this word *strōd* in his edition of *Pearl* where he had found the word *stroþe-men*. There he connected it with the place-name Strother and glossed *stroþe* as 'marshy land'. He then translated *stroþe-men* as 'men of this world' suggesting 'the dark, low earth onto which the high stars look down'.[10] This image fits the two lads from Strother and (as we shall see later) their earthy hobbit counterparts Merry and Pippin found lazing about and smoking pipe-weed among the ruins of Isengard. This etymology's comic implications might have been extended further, since John and Alain chase their runaway horse into a marshy fen, which they would have called a *strod* in their native dialect. All wet when they returned to Simkin's house after nightfall, the students would indeed have qualified as *stroþe-men*.

The Chaucerian narrator's 'Southern shrug of the shoulders at the unknown geography of the barbarous North' raises the question whether England's northern dialects had become markers of social status by the late fourteenth century. Robert Epstein suggests that the answer is complicated: 'Chaucer invites social prejudices based on linguistic differences only to challenge and undermine them.'[11] Probably because Tolkien championed the non-London texts of the Katherine Group and the *Gawain* Poet, his 1934 study would focus more on Chaucer as a skilled philologist and less on the northern speakers as lower-class rustics. Tolkien never engages in the condescension of John Trevisa's famous 1387 translation of Hidgen's *Polychronicon*: 'Al þe longage of þe Norþhumbres, and specialych at 3ork, ys so scharp, slyttyng, and frotyng, and vnschape, þat we Souþeron men may þat longage vnneþe vndurstonde.' Certainly he knew this passage because he had glossed it in Sisam's *Verse and Prose*—quoted here[12]—but he did not bring forward Trevisa's linguistic bias and did not endorse the pilgrim-narrator's shrug at the barbarous North.

---

[10] *Pearl*, ed., 51–2 on line 115. Shippey, 'Tolkien and the *Gawain*-Poet', in *Roots and Branches*, 76–7, suggests this note was contributed anonymously by Tolkien, who included in it a reference to his own 'Chaucer as a Philologist'.

[11] '"Fer in the north; I kan nat telle where": Dialect, Regionalism, and Philologism', *SAC* 30 (2008), 95–124 at p. 102.

[12] Sisam, *Fourteenth Century Verse and Prose*, 150. Tolkien glossed *scharp*, *slyttyng*, *frotyng*, and *vnschape* as 'harsh', 'piercing', 'grating', and 'formless'.

Tolkien's last scratchy annotations for his Clarendon Chaucer took issue with Skeat's speculations that these *povre clerks* might have belonged to a prominent local family, and he ended with two pencil notes indicating topics for further attention:

Chaucer at Hatfield
the dialect is Yorkshire

Both jottings suggest that his commentary, had it continued, would have discussed Chaucer's first-hand knowledge of Yorkshire and his handling of the local dialect.

Chaucer at Hatfield indicates an intention to use biographical facts to elucidate literary matters. Nineteenth-century researchers had scoured the archives for information about Chaucer's life, and Skeat reported (1:xvii) that the earliest record placed him in Yorkshire in December 1357 when he belonged to the household of the Countess of Ulster and her husband Prince Lionel, son of King Edward III. Also present at Hatfield was the young John of Gaunt, and Chaucer's connection with the future Duke of Lancaster may have started during this holiday visit. His *Book of the Duchess*, occasioned by the death of Gaunt's first wife, reinforces the link with the line 'By seynt Johan, on a riche hil' (1319) alluding cryptically to John's Richmond Castle in Yorkshire. Hatfield House stood in a deer park which can be connected with the poem's setting; the Clarendon Chaucer's excerpt 'Dream of the Hunt' no doubt resonated with Tolkien because he too, as a young man in Yorkshire, had hunted and killed a deer.

In 1357 the teenage Chaucer—so the speculation runs—heard enough of the local Yorkshire dialect to realize how different it sounded from his native London speech. Years later his *Troilus* ended ruefully about the lack of a standard literary language: 'ther is so greet diversitee | In English and in wryting of our tonge' (5.1793–4). The future poet would have realized at this early age, too, how comically outlandish this Northern patois sounded to courtiers in the royal entourage. Chaucerian connections with Yorkshire did not end there, however, and in the last year of the poet's life, his son Thomas was appointed constable of Knaresborough Castle and forester for the North Yorkshire lordship.[13] Nor did Chaucer's linguistic interests end with the Reeve's Tale. He set his Summoner's Tale in Holderness in Yorkshire where the local householder speaks an old-fashioned version of English with hardly any loan-words from French.[14] Thus Chaucer made the further joke that Northern speech was not only outlandish in pronunciation but also backward in its vocabulary.

---

[13] J. S. Roskell, 'Thomas Chaucer of Ewelme', in *Parliament and Politics in Late Medieval England* (London: Hambledon, 1983), 151–91 at p. 153. John of Gaunt had acquired Knaresborough Castle in 1372 and added it to the vast holdings of the Duchy of Lancaster.

[14] Tom Shippey, 'Bilingualism and Betrayal in Chaucer's Summoner's Tale', in *Speaking in the Medieval World*, ed. Jean Godsall-Myers (Leiden and Boston: Brill, 2003), 125–44.

Tolkien's second jotting *dialect is Yorkshire* represented no sudden discovery. His 1914 undergraduate notebook included the jotting 'Reeve's Tale: northern students' so that Professor Raleigh must have included this fact as part of his survey of Chaucer's life and works.[15] Even if these linguistic features were generally known, however, Tolkien did not accept Skeat's view that dialect functioned simply as a casual jest. 'The poet merely gives a Northern colouring to his diction to amuse us,' wrote the earlier scholar; 'he is not trying to teach us Northern grammar' (5:121–2). When returning to these passages as a seasoned philologist around 1928, Tolkien decided that Chaucer did indeed handle Northern dialect with real expertise and his achievement deserved serious investigation.

Before trailing off, Tolkien's notes on the Reeve's Tale showed a specific interest in mills and millers: 'The outwitting of the miller of Cambridge is the answer to the downfall of the Oxford carpenter which the Reeve alone takes amiss.' He then copied out nine lines from the Reeve's Prologue not included in their edition (3859–61, 3910–11, and 3913–16) to explain how the Reeve's fabliau served as retaliation against millers generally as a profession. His first note then dealt with the setting at Trumpington: 'the old mill (whose pool remains) is almost a quarter of a mile above the old bridge.' When Tolkien came to envision his own village of Hobbiton, he automatically included the same features of the mill and bridge over the river. He then returned to Simkin: 'Chaucer makes the Reeve's description approach fairly closely his description of the pilgrims' Miller.' The General Prologue had portrayed his Miller as a violent, dishonest brute who later told the famously bawdy story about an old carpenter, his young wife, and two amorous Oxford clerks. Tolkien emphasized the violence of the Reeve's miller with notes on his *panade* as a 'knife with two edges', his *popper* as a 'small dagger', and his *thwitel* as a 'small knife for whittling'. Simkin's weapons were not merely for self-defence. 'The miller frequented markets,' Tolkien remarked about the term *market-beter*, 'to swagger up and down in search of quarrels.'

Why this preoccupation with millers? We know that Tolkien, aged about 5, experienced a primal scene of fright when chased away from Sarehole Mill by the angry miller dubbed the White Ogre. His lecture 'On Fairy-Stories' translated the scene into mythic form: 'In Faërie one can indeed conceive of an ogre who possesses a castle hideous as a nightmare.'[16] His brother Hilary also remembered the dark cavern of the mill's interior where two men worked great leather belts, pulleys, and shafts. These memories became more troubling in 1933 when Tolkien discovered that a willow overhanging the mill-pool had been cut down for no

---

[15] Bodleian MS Tolkien A 21/4, fol. 15.
[16] *Essays*, 151; see also p. 133: 'A child may well believe a report that there are ogres in the next county.'

apparent reason.[17] Later he would write to his American publisher about his love of trees—'I find human maltreatment of them as hard to bear as some find ill-treatment of animals' (*Letters*, 220)—and a late letter to the *Daily Telegraph* was still defending his loyalties: 'In all my works I take the part of trees as against all their enemies' (*Letters*, 419). *The Two Towers* gave him the opportunity of allowing the trees to avenge themselves when the Ents march on Isengard.

Although his 1965 Foreword denied any connection between the two millers of Sarehole (George Andrew and his son) and the two Hobbiton millers (Sandyman and his son Ted), his own older miller starts off at the *Ivy Bush* as an unsavoury character who spreads the rumour that Frodo's parents had drowned each other on the river. Later when Sam looks into the Mirror of Galadriel, he is outraged by the vision of the miller's son felling trees, and in the end Ted is found collaborating with Saruman's ruffians in 'The Scouring of the Shire'. As literary embodiments of the author's boyhood memories, Chaucer's treacherous millers lurk somewhere in the background of Hobbiton's traitorous miller.

'Chaucer as a Philologist: *The Reeve's Tale*'

If the young Chaucer first encountered dialect differences when visiting Yorkshire, the young Tolkien had a similar realization when his mother settled them in Sarehole in 1896 and his middle-class accent stood out against the Worcestershire speech of the local boys.[18] Later Tolkien made a pleasant acquaintance with Yorkshire speech when studying with Joseph Wright, Oxford's Professor of Comparative Philology. Wright had begun as a poor mill-worker in Yorkshire and used his savings to study in London, Heidelberg, and Leipzig, earning his doctorate before arriving in Oxford as a lecturer in 1888. Wright kept his Yorkshire accent throughout his Oxford career and even published a study of his home dialect.[19] Tolkien as a schoolboy had discovered Wright's *Primer of the Gothic Language* and began attending his lectures on Gothic Grammar in 1911. He went for tutorials at the professor's home the following year. Long afterwards, in his 'Valedictory Address', Tolkien warmly recalled these sessions at his teacher's dining table when he sat at one end learning about Greek philology from the professor with his glinting glasses in the farther gloom (*Essays*, 238). He enjoyed the huge Yorkshire teas.

---

[17] See SH 3:1126–8 for the mill-related recollections of both brothers. His return visit in 1933 presented the 'violent and peculiarly hideous change' brought about by urban encroachment from Birmingham.

[18] *Biography*, 29; now part of Warwickshire, Sarehole still belonged to Worcestershire until 1911.

[19] SH 3:1444–5; see Joseph Wright, *A Grammar of the Dialect of Windhill in the West Riding of Yorkshire* (London: K. Paul, Trench, Trübner & Co., 1892).

Tolkien had steady encounters with Yorkshire speakers beginning in 1910 when he sketched the ruins of Whitby Abbey, again in 1916 when he took a signalling course at Otley, and yet again in 1917 when he convalesced from trench fever in Holderness, the setting for the Summoner's Tale. Over a mile away near the village of Roos was the woodland glade where Edith danced for him among the hemlocks, an experience which would inspire him to imagine Beren watching his dancing elf-maiden Lúthien (*Letters*, 345, 420). Later in 1917 Tolkien worked on *The Tale of Tinúviel* while recuperating at a hospital in Hull, with subsequent postings in Easington, Kilnsea, and Harrogate before he was transferred out of Yorkshire in autumn 1918.

He returned in autumn 1920 when starting his academic career at the University of Leeds. Here he would complete his *Middle English Vocabulary* and his edition of *Sir Gawain and the Green Knight*, although he did not look back with much fondness upon the dour undergraduates. 'Probably England's most (at least apparently) dullest and stodgiest students', he later wrote about the young men and women who arrived from 'home backgrounds bookless and cultureless' (*Letters*, 403). He vented his playful calumny in the Chaucerian pastiche *The Clerke's Compleinte* published anonymously in 1922:

> & specially from euery schires ende
> In al þe north to Leedis clerkes wende
> & in þe derkest toune in Yorkeschire
> Seken of lore welles depe & schire.[20]

He made one allowance: 'A surprisingly large proportion prove "educable": for which a primary qualification is the willingness to *do some work*.'[21] Their work included the study of Middle English, and Tolkien began immediately offering lectures on the Language of Chaucer and another series on the General Prologue to the *Canterbury Tales*.

Tolkien bought a house and started settling his family, since Leeds might well have remained his home for the rest of his academic career. In January 1922 he delivered a talk on the *OED* to the Yorkshire Dialect Society, founded a quarter-century earlier by his mentor Joseph Wright, and in summer of that year he treated his wife and young son John to a holiday on the Yorkshire coast at Filey. This seaside visit would inspire his poem *Progress in Bimble Town* and a subsequent holiday there led to writing *Roverandom*. The 1922 issue of *Yorkshire Poetry* published his *The Cat and the Fiddle*—a later version of which was performed by Frodo at the *Prancing Pony* (*FR* I/9)—and his student Hugh Smith brought out his

---

[20] Anders Stenström, 'The Clerkes Compleinte Revisited', *Arda* 6 (1990 for 1986), 1–13.
[21] *Biography*, 111. Gilliver, *Making of Oxford English Dictionary*, 391, 397, notes that four of Tolkien's Leeds students were trained expertly enough to join the staff of the *OED*.

Yorkshire-dialect poems in the 1923 collection *The Merry Shire*.[22] In short, if Chaucer had a brief holiday contact with Yorkshire speakers, Tolkien gained much more extensive familiarity.

This 'friendly foreigner to the district', as Tolkien described himself, took an interest in the South Yorkshire dialect project of Walter E. Haigh, and when his *New Glossary of the Dialect of the Huddersfield District* was published by OUP in 1928—just when Tolkien was focusing upon the Yorkshire dialect in the Reeve's Tale—he provided a preface declaring that Haigh's efforts had value 'not only to local patriotism, but to English philology generally.'[23] As a one-time lexicographer, he was probably aware that Yorkshire words collected by Furnivall and other sub-editors had never been included in the *OED*.[24]

In addition to the many Scandinavian words unearthed, Tolkien took particular interest in the local dialect's relation to the language of *Gawain* and *Pearl*, remarking, 'their connexion with the modern dialects, of which that of Huddersfield is an interesting example, is immediately apparent to any one glancing at this glossary' (p. xvi). He carried over these lessons into his own scholarly and imaginative writings. Haigh's dialect words *il*, *til*, and *wight* would find their ways into 'Chaucer as a Philologist', and Douglas Anderson traces *The Hobbit*'s phrase 'shrieking and skriking' back to Haigh's entry for *skrīk*. Janet Croft has increased the range of indebtedness:

> A number of the words in the *Glossary* can be found in the Common Speech of Middle-earth as spoken by the hobbits. Some appear as elements in place-names like Bree (*breę*, *bru*, the brow of a hill), Staddle (*stæddl*, *staddle*, a timber stand or base for a stack), or the element Brock- (*brok*, a badger) in Brockenborings. Others are used in family names like Baggins (*bæggin*, a meal, particularly a brown-bag lunch). However, several are used in exactly the same way as in the Huddersfield dialect: gaffer (*gæffer*), a corruption of grandfather, for an old man; vittles (*vittlz*) for food, nowt (*nout*) for nothing, nosey (*nuęzi*), of one who pries into things, or nuncle (*nunkl*) for uncle.[25]

When Bilbo's household goods are up for auction upon his return to Bag End, the word *auction* itself goes back to this study of Yorkshire dialect.[26] Even the name of the innkeeper Butterbur can be traced back to what he learned from Haigh.[27]

---

[22] Mark Atherton, 'Old English', in *Companion*, ed. Lee, 222.

[23] Tolkien, 'Foreword' to Haigh's *New Glossary of the Dialect of the Huddersfield District*, pp. xiii–xviii at p. xiii. Tolkien's copy of Haigh was included with the books donated in 1959 to Oxford's English Faculty Library along with others such as Wright's *Dialect of Windhill* (1892), Mackinzie's *The Early London Dialect* (1928), and Orton's *Phonology of South Durham Dialect* (1933).

[24] Gilliver, *Making of the Oxford English Dictionary*, 69; only in 1993 did the OED make a commitment to include varieties other than Standard British English.

[25] Janet Brennan Croft, 'Walter E. Haigh, Author of *A Glossary of the Huddersfield Dialect*', *Tolkien Studies* 4 (2007), 184–8 at pp. 186–7.

[26] Anderson, *Annotated Hobbit*, 111, and Shippey, *Road to Middle-earth*, 93n.

[27] Shippey, 'Why Source Criticism?', 11.

What Tolkien noted about the 'humour' and 'raciness' of Haigh's examples was already evidenced in the Yorkshire-speakers John and Alain in the Reeve's Tale.[28]

All this background explains why Tolkien was supremely qualified to detect Northern elements during the Clarendon Chaucer project begun while he was actually living in Yorkshire. Yet he soon suspected Skeat had not fully appreciated Chaucer's linguistic competence, and by 1928 when his annotations sputtered to a halt, he felt the need for fuller answers. That opportunity came when presenting a paper to the Philological Society in Oxford in May 1931. Because Joseph Wright had died in February 1930, Tolkien may have felt some duty for taking up the torch. His dialect study also coincided with his manifesto 'The Oxford English School', published in *The Oxford Magazine*, where he argued that historical linguistics should be taught with the same range and rigour as literary history: 'Chaucer should be recovered for such students as a mediæval author, and part of his works become once more the subject of detailed and scholarly study' (p. 782). Even after returning to Oxford as Professor of Anglo-Saxon, he never lost sight of Chaucer as the central figure in English literature. Thus his ongoing concern with the poet's uses of dialect, prompted by his Clarendon edition, explains the genesis of what always seemed an oddity in his scholarly career—his 1934 article 'Chaucer as a Philologist: *The Reeve's Tale*'.

Skeat had already done a thorough job of identifying these dialect words, observing also some of the poet's mistakes in reproducing Yorkshire speech, but he concluded that Chaucer aimed only at casual humour. Tolkien set out to challenge his predecessor by demonstrating that Chaucer had actually done an expert job at reproducing Northern speech, but his achievement had been blurred by fifteenth-century scribes. Rather ungenerously, he consigned Skeat's name only to an easy-to-miss footnote on the second page where he belittled the discovery: 'As plainly perceived by Skeat, though his enquiry amid the mass of his general labour in the service of Chaucer did not proceed very far.' The Bodleian Library preserves several batches of draft materials as evidence that Tolkien invested heavily in the general labour for his own study.[29] Most of these notes would find their way into the body of the lecture, while his ruminations on *geen* and *neen* required their own five-page appendix. Tolkien's quest for Chaucer's authentic words was, typically with him, the recovery of something lost.

As if to establish his credentials as a Chaucerian, Tolkien's first paragraph wittily inserted three quotations from the *Parlement of Foules* (1, 56-7, 65) starting with the italicized word *Galaxye* previously annotated in his Clarendon

---

[28] Chance, *Tolkien, Self and Other*, 141–2.
[29] MS Tolkien A 14/1, MS Tolkien A 17/2, fol. 122, MS Tolkien A 30/2, MS Tolkien A 32/2, and MS Tolkien E 16/45.

Chaucer, now proposed as the poet's heavenly vantage-point for passing judgement on faulty scholarship. This leads to a swipe at source-hunters with a line from the General Prologue about the derelict Monk—'Lat Austin have his swink to him reserved' (188)—a line included and annotated in his Clarendon Chaucer.[30] Chaucer's lament in *Troilus* over the 'greet diversitee in English' served Tolkien as ammunition in his ongoing dispute over Language versus Literature, and Chaucer, as the article's title makes clear, would have sided with the philologists because he was one of them. Some recent Chaucerians have questioned the pervasiveness of Northern dialect and the degree to which scribes bungled copying these elements,[31] but Tolkien's article remains the *locus classicus* for Chaucerian language study while in the process, unfortunately, distancing linguistic analysis farther from literary interpretation.[32]

The problem with Chaucer's dialect variants arose, as Tolkien saw it, when fifteenth-century scribes did not get the joke and miscopied these forms, substituting what they and their London readers found more familiar. This observation led to the far-reaching and indeed unsettling conclusion that these scribes as a group could not be trusted for transmitting the poet's other authentic spellings. He believed that Chaucer heard a welter of dialects in his native London and that works like *Gawain* and *Piers Plowman* reached the metropolis where the poet read them in their regional dialects.[33] Recalling how Chaucer's little poem *Adam Scriveyn* condemned his personal copyist to scratching his scalp as much as the poet scraped his vellum to correct mistakes, Tolkien had his own witty riposte: 'if the curse he pronounced on scribe Adam produced any effect, many a fifteenth-century penman must early have gone bald' (p. 2).[34]

Tolkien accused the copyists but found them hard to convict: 'it is difficult to catch Adam and his descendants at their tricks' (p. 5). He would therefore have been intrigued by identification of the Ellesmere scribe's handwriting in a Scriveners Company document, signed Adam Pinkhurst, because he would have felt vindicated that this same Adam, scolded by the poet for miscopying his *Troilus* and *Boece*, later miscopied the Reeve's Tale in the Ellesmere manuscript after

---

[30] '*Austin*: the great St. Augustine of Hippo is meant, after whom the Augustinian canons were named. He did not found their order, of course, but their rule was compiled from his writings.'

[31] Simon Horobin, 'J. R. R. Tolkien as a Philologist: A Reconsideration of the Northernisms in Chaucer's *Reeve's Tale*'; see also N. F. Blake, 'The Northernisms in "The Reeve's Tale"', *Lore and Language* 3.1 (1979), 1–8, and Shippey, 'Tolkien as Editor', 50. See SH 2:223–5.

[32] Wendy Scase, 'Tolkien, Philology, and *The Reeve's Tale*: Towards the Cultural Move in Middle English Studies', *SAC* 24 (2002), 325–34 at pp. 330–1.

[33] Chaucer 'knew *Sir Gawain*, and probably the author also' (*Essays*, 73). See Simon Horobin, '"In London and Opelond": Dialect and Circulation of the C Version of *Piers Plowman*', *Medium Ævum* 74 (2005), 248–69, shows how Langland's London scribes preserved his Worcestershire dialect.

[34] Though this one-stanza lyric was not included in the Clarendon Chaucer, Tolkien took the trouble to copy it on a scrap of exam paper (Bodleian Tolkien 14/2, fol. 100).

Chaucer had died and could not correct his errors.[35] Tolkien knew that Ellesmere and Hengwrt were probably copied by the same scribe, but the two manuscripts differed 'in notable points' when representing the northernisms of the two Cambridge clerks (p. 11). The same professional copyist worked on both commissions, that is, and yet he reacted differently to the dialect elements. If he was working from the same exemplar, at least one of his scribal copies must have been unfaithful to Chaucer's originals.

Like so much else in his 1934 study, Tolkien's views on scribal behaviour had been anticipated during work on the Clarendon Chaucer. The typescript of his 'Introduction on Language', probably meant to precede his glossary as in his *Gawain* edition, began with his bold assertion that Chaucer's genuine texts were lost behind the alterations of his fifteenth-century copyists:

> The language of these selections from Chaucer is substantially that of the latter part of the fourteenth century. It must not, however, be overlooked that our extant copies, in varying degrees according to their age and carefulness, have at haphazard altered Chaucer's language not only in spellings but also in accidence, syntax and even occasionally in vocabulary, in conformity with the uses of a later century. In the process they have often doubtless disregarded the finer points of style and versification; sometimes they have obviously neglected metre altogether. If we had Chaucer's own autographs, or copies certainly seen and passed by him, we should of course find a language more uniform (and somewhat more uniformly archaic) than that presented by these selections drawn from various manuscripts of various dates.[36]

These ruminations from the 1920s anticipate the thoughts and even the wording of his 1934 article—'His holographs, or the copies impatiently rubbed and scraped by him, would doubtless be something of a shock to us' (p. 2)—and serve as evidence that Tolkien had already begun pondering these matters during his prior editorial labours.[37]

Tolkien's impulse for emendation, previously constrained by Sisam, had freer rein when producing critical texts for the ninety-eight lines in which the two clerks speak in their native dialect (pp. 17–20). He identified some 127 points of grammar, inflection, and vocabulary without a single instance of 'false dialect' in what he imagined as Chaucer's original. Side-by-side comparison with Skeat shows the thoroughness of his restored spellings:

---

[35] Linne R. Mooney, 'Chaucer's Scribe', *Speculum* 81 (2006), 97–138; Warner, 'Scribes, Misattributed: Hoccleve and Pinkhurst', has raised doubts about this naming of the Ellesmere scribe.

[36] 'Introduction on Language', Bodleian Tolkien MS A 39/2/2, fols. 138–140r (typescript) and fols. 140v–143 (handwritten); see Appendix I.

[37] Having the author's own handwritten copies does not guarantee the perfect text that editors idealize; see Bowers, 'Hoccleve's Two Copies of *Lerne to Dye*: Implications for Textual Critics'.

Skeat, (1894), A, 4036–45	Tolkien (1934), p. 17
'By god, right by the hoper wil I stande,' Quod Iohn, 'and se how that the corn gas in; Yet saugh I never, by my fader kin, How that the hoper wagges til and fra.' Aleyn answerede, 'Iohn, and wiltow swa, Than wil I be bynethe, by my croun, And se how that the mele falles doun In-to the trough; that sal be my disport. For Iohn, in faith, I may been of your sort; I is as ille a miller as are ye.'	'Bi god, right bi þe hoper wil I stand,' quod Iohn, "and se hougat þe corn gas in. ʒit sagh I neuer, bi mi fader kin, hou þat þe hoper waggës til and fra.' Alain answeredë: 'Iohn, and wiltou swa þen wil I be binëþën, bi mi croun, And se hougat þe melë fallës doun In til þe trogh. þat sal be mi desport; For, Iohn, i faiþ, I es al of ʒour sort: I es as il a miller as er ʒe.'[38]

Tolkien has not only restored the northernisms *il* and *I es* but also reverted to the archaic thorns (þ) and yoghs (ʒ) which Chaucer probably used but modern editors consistently modernize. The editor's diacritical marks signal pronouncing of final *-e* as in *melë* later discussed in detail (pp. 48–50).[39] Insertion of *hougat* as a contraction of 'how that' was justified because it was purely Northern and occurred in manuscripts other than Ellesmere: 'Skeat's failure to record its presence in the MSS. used for his edition is curious' (p. 33). And where did Chaucer obtain this acquaintance with Northern forms? The author's 'knowledge was not acquired casually in London, and was founded on the study of books (and people)', although for the moment Tolkien does not specify where the poet encountered these Yorkshire-speakers (p. 46).

Tolkien's newly edited lines were then followed by exhaustive annotations revealing the full extent of his philological ambitions always resisted by Sisam. There was little overlap with his Clarendon Notes because he had quit drafting his commentary before Alain and John began talking at any length—and the entire second half of the fabliau, where their bedroom conversations take place, had been omitted for the sake of decency—but we do find some words such as *boës/bos* and *gaan/geen* previously queried when he emended Skeat's text. Now finally he could lavish attention on words marked as Northern in his Clarendon Glossary: *alswa, banes, bath, capul, gas, ham, hething, lathe, pit, raa, sal, swa, taa, twa, waat, werkes,* and *whilk*. His particular interest in *slik*—'a word of more limited currency than any of the others here used as dialect by Chaucer' (p. 34)—earned two long notes and its own appendix (pp. 23–4, 64–5). Because he was producing a critical edition of these lines, he recorded all variants from the seven landmark manuscripts printed in Furnivall's *Six-Text Edition of the Canterbury Tales* as well as Harley 7334. While almost every line came under close scrutiny, Tolkien gave absolutely

---

[38] If John's plan seems childish, we should recall that Cambridge undergraduates began their studies as young as 14.
[39] 'Final *e* is never mute', he would say also about Sindarin in *TLOR*'s Appendix E; 'To mark this final *e* it is often (but not consistently) written ë.'

no sense of the story's sexual mischief which he dismissed merely as 'the knock-about business'. His philological business meant wringing the juice out of words, not analysing plots or characters.

If Chaucer operated as a philologist whose dialect jokes were missed by later scribes, Tolkien's argument looks more clearly like an extension of his editorial project. 'I believe that a close examination of all the manuscripts of the *Canterbury Tales* with respect to the northernisms in this tale would have a special textual value,' he wrote in 1934; 'in fact, purely accidentally, the *Reeve's Tale* is of great importance to the textual criticism of the *Canterbury Tales* as a whole' (p. 5). Tolkien's passing phrase *purely accidentally* described in retrospect, perhaps as a private joke to himself, the original impetus for this study from the 1920s. If not for the accident of Sisam persuading Gordon to substitute the Reeve's Tale for the Prioress's Tale, he would never have undertaken a study which he expanded in the lengthy version published 'with the addition of a "critical text", and accompanying textual notes, as well as of various footnotes, appendices and comments naturally omitted from the reading' (p. 1). Clearly this paper grew in the writing.

Tolkien had mined his own Clarendon commentary for facts such as the Reeve's East Anglian dialect inserted as a footnote where the regional phrases *ik am* and *thee'k* invited further digressing: 'one is tempted, in the middle of an enquiry into mere dialect, to turn aside and emphasize the occasional concomitant *literary* suggestions of some of the words already dealt with' (p. 47). Once again he cited Chaucer's use of alliterative verses for describing the naval battle in *Cleopatra* and the tourney in the Knight's Tale—the dialect word *heterly* prominent in this tradition—and he could not help reminding readers of the literary achievements of the West prior to any comparable achievements in London: 'Chaucer was not independent either of the past or of the contemporary, and neither was his audience' (p. 47). If Tolkien did not actually consult his four-page excursus on Chaucer's alliterative practices in his edition's explanatory notes, he recalled that prior discussion well enough to reproduce its main points in almost identical wording.

Tolkien's critical edition restored some 130 dialect forms to demonstrate what some future editor needed to accomplish for rescuing Chaucer's authentic forms throughout all his works (p. 48). Particularly he came to realize how unfounded the slavish reliance on Ellesmere as a copy-text had been. Years earlier when editing *Piers Plowman*, Skeat had developed a tendency to trust beautiful books, fixing upon the Vernon manuscript for his A-Text largely because it was physically attractive, then granting it an authority beyond its reliability as a copy-text.[40]

---

[40] He invested even greater trust in the Laud manuscript of the B-Text because its attractiveness convinced him it might have been Langland's autograph; see Brewer, *Editing 'Piers Plowman'*, 126, 140–1.

When Skeat later came to edit the *Canterbury Tales*, he exercised a similar bias in favour of the gorgeous Ellesmere, as Tolkien realized:

> A proper text of the Canterbury Tales (or other major works of his), not to mention the recapturing to some extent of Chaucerian spelling and grammar, is not to be obtained from devout attachment to any one MS., certainly not Ellesmere, however attractive it may look.[41]

This unsettling conclusion was to be ignored for practical reasons by future editors, and indeed the 1957 and 1987 *Riverside Chaucer* continued privileging Ellesmere for their *Canterbury Tales*. Tolkien's radical view nonetheless placed him in the forefront of textual critics at a time when a complete collation of all manuscripts formed the basis of the eight-volume *Tales* edition of John M. Manly and Edith Rickert under way in the 1930s. Their analysis challenged the authority of Ellesmere, too, concluding that Hengwrt came closer to preserving the poet's authentic text.[42] E. Talbot Donaldson later agreed that an editor 'should certainly not be permitted to use the authority of a MS instead of his own head', and he also preferred Hengwrt as the base text for his edition of the *Tales*, making bold to include other improvements as well: 'in a number of lines, which the scholar will recognize, I have adopted a reading I consider superior to the one generally accepted.'[43] This was the editorial freedom to which Tolkien clearly aspired.

His jotting *the dialect is Yorkshire* at the end of his Clarendon commentary became the subject of the first fifty-four pages of his 1934 study before considering his second jotting: *Chaucer at Hatfield*. Certainly Yorkshiremen travelled to London, and the poet had access to books such as *Prick of Conscience* and *Speculum Vitæ* written in Yorkshire dialect and circulating as far south as London during his lifetime.[44] 'But Chaucer did not stay in the study', Tolkien wrote about the poet's contacts with the language:

> Once at least he is believed to have been in Yorkshire; and though a residence at Hatfield as a very young man would not provide even an inquisitive person, less biased than usual by southern prejudices against dialectal harring, garring, and grisbitting, with much opportunity for observation on the local vernacular, we may probably take this fleeting glimpse of Chaucer in Yorkshire as a reminder

---

[41] 'Chaucer as a Philologist', 48. He later repeated the point: 'after textual examination, no MS., and certainly not Ellesmere, can escape the charge of casual alterations, careless of the detail of Chaucer's work and its intent' (p. 54).

[42] John M. Manly and Edith Rickert, eds., *The Text of the Canterbury Tales Studied on the Basis of All Known Manuscripts*, 8 vols. (Chicago and London: University of Chicago Press, 1940), 1:266–83. Bodleian MS Tolkien 14/2, fol. 99, indicates Tolkien was aware of their project: 'Manly & Rickert have studied 84 MSS.'

[43] Donaldson, 'The Psychology of Editors', 116, and *Chaucer's Poetry: An Anthology for the Modern Reader* (New York: Ronald Press Co., 1958), p. v.

[44] *Richard Morris's 'Prick of Conscience': A Corrected and Amplified Reading Text*, prepared by Ralph Hanna and Sarah Wood, EETS o.s. 342, 2013, pp. xiv, xxxiv–xlvii, 'Authorship and the Poet's Dialect'.

that people moved about, especially those of his class and station. On such occasions Chaucer would not shut his ears. (p. 55)

Though Tolkien later opposed investigating an author's life—particularly when the author was himself—here he bent this rule by resorting to 'established facts of Chaucerian biography' (p. 56) to explain how the young would-be poet heard the Yorkshire language where it was actually spoken in Doncaster as well as at Hatfield House while travelling in the entourage of the Countess of Ulster.[45] But Tolkien did not pry into more personal matters, nor did he ponder why Chaucer used non-London dialect in this tale but not in any other. The Man of Law's Tale was set in Northumbria where the constable and his wife would have spoken an ancestor of the same Northern dialect, but Tolkien did not speculate why his author included no dialect features there. 'To guess is not, in any case, the province of the philologist' (p. 55).

But he had not finished applying biographical information. Next he considered the reference to Strother as the hometown of John and Alain. Strother actually placed the two clerks in Northumberland, as Tolkien knew when writing his introduction to the 1939 programme (see Fig. 14):

> Chaucer makes the Reeve disclaim any accurate knowledge of the locality—it is *fer in the north, I can nat telle where*. But Chaucer himself seems to have been less vague: he was thinking of the northernmost parts of England, now Northumberland and Durham. Strother was a genuine village name in that region. The clerk John swears by Saint Cuthbert, just as the Osney carpenter swore by Saint Frideswide. Saint Cuthbert was the patron of Durham, the *terra sancti Cuthberti*, and his name, not elsewhere mentioned by Chaucer, is here certainly a final touch of local colour.

But Chaucer's stay at Hatfield House and Tolkien's own times in Leeds, Roos, Filey, and Holderness predisposed both writers toward the Yorkshire dialect instead. After correcting Skeat's statement that no such town existed, Tolkien produced two likely candidates for Strother. Such names were an abiding interest reflected by his membership in the English Place Name Society,[46] and he pursued etymological forays into Old English and Old Norse to arrive at the root *strōd* for 'marsh' carried over from his Clarendon Notes. Without reliable maps in the fourteenth century, Chaucer could only have known about the town's existence by visiting the region or having contact with its natives (p. 57). Tolkien refuted Skeat's suggestion that the young clerks might have been related to the local grandees Aleyn de Strother and his son John—information already sketched

---

[45] *Chaucer Life-Records*, 18, provides a fuller account of the documentary evidence than Skeat's.
[46] Tolkien, 'Philology' (1924), 20, ranked the study of place-names next to lexicography. Shippey, *Road to Middle-earth*, 100, reckoned some six hundred place-names in *The Lord of the Rings*. See SH 3:1239 'English Place-Name Society'.

in his Clarendon commentary—because unlike the well-to-do constables of Roxburgh Castle, John and Alain were 'clerks and poor' (p. 58).[47] His last Clarendon note made the same point that these clerks were *povre*. Tolkien's fiction would later show considerable respect for poorer characters like Sam Gamgee,[48] and in his personal conduct, too, Tolkien was remarkable for crossing class boundaries and befriending college servants such as his scout Charlie Carr. Tolkien had also been a poor student, it must be remembered, and like Chaucer's rowdy Cambridge students, he was far from a cloistered bookworm, engaging in undergraduate shenanigans like driving a hijacked bus down a major Oxford thoroughfare. There might also have been some identification with Chaucer's character John based on his name. When asked about his own name in 1969, Tolkien wrote back: 'It is *John*: a name much used and loved by Christians, and since I was born on the Octave of St. John the Evangelist, I take him as my patron' (*Letters*, 397). He had named his oldest son John, too.

Before proceeding to eleven pages of appendices on the words *tulle*, *slik*, and *geen/neen*—these last two particularly worrying because they did not belong to any spoken dialect during Chaucer's lifetime (p. 66)[49]—Tolkien made his final effort at recruiting Chaucer to the cause of Language in his disciplinary warfare with Literature. The poet would have appreciated all of this scholarly attention to his linguistic joke, Tolkien was certain, and he would 'have more sympathy with such pother, and with such of his later students who attach importance to the minutiæ of language, and of his language, even to such dry things as rhymes and vowels, than with those who profess themselves disgusted with such inhumanity' (p. 59).

The fruits of these philological labours were not lost upon the fiction-writer whose enjoyment of dialect humour did not disdain Uncle Remus; even Frodo and Sam's fall into the briars in Mordor (*RK* VI/2) quite possibly came from his recollection of Brer Rabbit in the briar patch. When writing to the BBC producer of *The Homecoming of Beorhtnoth* in 1954, however, Tolkien suggested using no rural accents in the spoken dialogue because they were dealing with a period when dialect connoted 'no social implications' (*Letters*, 187). But Anderson's *Annotated Hobbit* (p. 70) connects the comic dialogue of the Three Trolls with Chaucer's linguistic joke from the Reeve's Tale, and this humour was based very much upon class—'not drawing-room fashion at all', Bilbo thought.[50] Their words like *blimey* and *blighter* as well as expressions like "'Ere, 'oo are you?' suggest specifically the

---

[47] See Bennett, *Chaucer at Oxford and at Cambridge*, 'Appendix A: Poor Scholars', 117–19.
[48] Chance, *Tolkien, Self and Other*, 'Chaucer's Rustics and Other "Dubious Characters"', 147–51, believes Tolkien found models for characters like Sam among Chaucer's fabliau characters.
[49] Jeremy J. Smith, 'Chaucer and the Invention of English', *SAC* 24 (2002), 335–46 at 344, agrees with Tolkien about these forms.
[50] Tolkien later derived class-based humour from Sam's references to words like *taters*. 'Chaucer as a Philologist' decided the colloquialisms of the two clerks were 'quite intelligible and yet all the more odd and laughable in alien shape because of their very familiarity' (p. 9).

cockney dialect already exploited for comic effect in George Bernard Shaw's *Pygmalion*.[51] As early as 1928 when Tolkien stopped work on his Chaucer edition and began thinking more closely about the Reeve's Tale, his *Mr. Bliss* made fun of characters dropping their aitches and mangling their syntax. His note on the Prioress had said her French set her apart from common folk more plainly than the command of *h* did.

The *OED* says the Reeve's Tale introduced the word *cockney* into the language when John fretted that classmates would mock him for not getting his share of sex: 'I sal be haldën daf, a cokenai' (288). With attention to every dialect detail, 'Chaucer as a Philologist' confronted the awkward fact that *cokenai* was an Eastern word, not Northern, and Tolkien decided that John probably picked it up from the student slang which comingled regional languages at Cambridge (p. 53).

John is anxious about being mocked as a sissy when his misadventures are later talked about. He imagines himself a character in a story, that is, but not one who will be considered clever or sexually enterprising by an audience back in Cambridge. Later Tolkien's own characters will develop this same self-conscious sense of their roles within unfolding narratives. Sam, as simple-minded in his way as the Yorkshire clerk, is given a magnificent monologue in which he realizes how he and Frodo have entered upon an adventure which is really an extension of the exploits of Beren and Eärendil: 'Why, to think of it, we're in the same tale still!' (*TT* IV/8). He wonders whether he and Frodo, too, will figure in tales told years later by the fireside. Of course they will. Sam himself will be reading them to his children seventeen years later.[52]

Eventually Tolkien decided that dialect differences mattered in Middle-earth as well as Middle English. The Sindarin language became so 'divergent and dialectal' that the Elves coined the word *lambe* as the equivalent of the English term 'dialect', and the speech of the Silvan Elves had evolved so far from the language of Beleriand that even Frodo noticed the difference.[53] *TLOR*'s Appendix F on the Common Speech explained how 'Hobbits indeed spoke for the most part a rustic dialect, whereas in Gondor and Rohan a more antique language was used'. Even Orcs had 'as many barbarous dialects as there were groups or settlements of their race'. When the four hobbits arrive at Bree, the gatekeeper can tell by their speech that they are from the Shire (*FR* I/9), and shortly afterwards when Frodo announces his interest in writing a book about history and geography, his listeners at the *Prancing Pony* are baffled because 'neither of these words were much used

---

[51] Tolkien, 'Philology' (1924), 29, had already remarked upon the 'cockney accent'. *TLOR*'s Appendix F said Trolls 'spoke a debased form of the Common Speech'.

[52] Tolkien described this scene in the 'Epilogue' later cancelled; see *The History of the Lord of the Rings, Part Four*, 114–35.

[53] Tolkien, *Unfinished Tales*, 216 and 257, and J. R. R. Tolkien, *The War of the Jewels*, ed. Christopher Tolkien (Boston and New York: Houghton Mifflin, 1994), 394.

in the Bree-dialect' (*FR* I/9). The implication is that Bree, far in the east, was just as non-intellectual as Strother far in the north.

Oxford Summer Diversions 1939

Even before Tolkien arrived at Oxford as an undergraduate, Eleanor Prescott Hammond had already identified the challenge for Chaucer's future editors to improve upon Skeat's efforts: 'an edition of the *Canterbury Tales*, based upon the seven MSS (out of more than fifty) which the Chaucer Society had issued when Skeat prepared his text, cannot be considered as final.'[54] After Tolkien confirmed her observations in his 1934 study of the Reeve's Tale, he gave no indication of taking this challenge back to his Clarendon Chaucer. Most of the dialect passages had been cut along with the bedroom sex-farce, and besides, the text had already been corrected and re-typeset after Sisam squelched Tolkien's efforts at amending just two lines in *Boece*. Moreover the prospect of considering all manuscripts of the *Canterbury Tales* must have seemed overwhelming, then as now.

'Chaucer as a Philologist' rejected the consensus of the seven landmark manuscripts because Tolkien was certain, for example, 'Chaucer did not write *at þe fulle*' (p. 63). Two decades later, Donaldson took up this challenge on behalf of a single line in the Wife of Bath's Prologue and found the authentic reading in three 'bad' manuscripts, not Ellesmere.[55] In 1934, however, Tolkien left the task of rejecting faulty readings like *geen* and *neen* to future editors because such thoroughness was the work of a lifetime, as Manly and Rickert were discovering. Then, as luck would have it, he found himself in 1939 with an opportunity for applying these lessons to a free-standing edition of the Reeve's Tale.

For all his admitted shortcomings as a lecturer—and Kingsley Amis joined the chorus of undergraduates recalling him as 'incoherent and often inaudible'[56]— Tolkien did have a flair for theatrics. Douglas Gray admitted that Tolkien was 'one of the world's worst lecturers' but nonetheless recalled the spellbinding moment from his 1959 retirement address 'when he began to recite the *Ubi Sunt* lines from the Old English *Wanderer* and there was a stillness in the room as if the Green Knight himself had come in'.[57] W. H. Auden also recalled him reciting lines of

---

[54] Eleanor Prescott Hammond, *Chaucer: A Bibliographical Manual* (London: Macmillan, 1908), 145; she refers to the Chaucer Society's *Six-Text Edition of Chaucer's Canterbury Tales* edited by Furnivall.

[55] Donaldson, '*Canterbury Tales*, D117: A Critical Edition' (1965), in *Speaking of Chaucer*, 119–30. Ralph Hanna revisits this crux in 'The Application of Thought to Textual Criticism in All Modes—with Apologies to A. E. Housman', *Studies in Bibliography* 53 (2000), 163–72.

[56] Kingsley Amis, *Memoirs* (New York and London: Simon and Schuster, 1991), 53 and 102, described Tolkien as 'the worst technically in delivery'; he also recalled Philip Larkin doing a hilarious imitation of Tolkien (p. 52). For a more balanced assessment of Tolkien as a lecturer, see SH 3:962–6.

[57] Gray, *Marriage of Mercury and Philology*, 20–1.

Beowulf as if hearing the voice of Gandalf in a mead hall (*Biography*, 138). In his student days, this dramatic aptitude showed itself when tackling the role of Hermes in a school production of Aristophanes' *The Peace* (in the original Greek) and he again distinguished himself in the cross-dressing role of Mrs Malaprop in Sheridan's *The Rivals*.[58] About hamming up his interviews in the 1968 documentary *Tolkien at Oxford*, he confessed, 'my histrionic temperament (I used to like "acting") betrayed me' (*Letters*, 390).

Tolkien first appeared in Oxford's Summer Diversions in 1938 when Nevill Coghill and John Masefield invited him to perform something from Chaucer. For that occasion he decided upon the Nun's Priest's Tale, the poet's comic masterpiece. Officially Professor of Anglo-Saxon in the 1930s, he maintained a clear remembrance of the tale which he had edited and glossed during the 1920s, and his *Beowulf* lectures cited it as an example of an earlier, simpler story enlarged with many intrusive passages. Tolkien even felt chummy enough to jest with his author for the amusement of the undergraduates:

> *The Nun's Priest's Tale* is obviously based on old material, and obviously much elaborated by Chaucer. You can here and there lift whole chunks and say 'Ha! Master Geoffrey, you stuck that in. You think it an improvement, do you? Well, perhaps it is. Perhaps.'[59]

On the merrymaking occasion in summer 1938, Tolkien strode upon the stage costumed as Chaucer in a green robe, a turban, and fake whiskers parted in the middle like the forked beard shown in early portraits like Ellesmere's. Such an impersonation was itself a distinctly Chaucerian gesture, since this is exactly what the *Canterbury Tales* accomplished when invoking a character like the Nun's Priest and having him tell a story, each of the pilgrim narratives ingeniously suited to the personality and even the deeper psychology of the individual taleteller.

Tolkien recited from memory the mock-epic of Chanticleer and Pertelote with the aid of a microphone at the Oxford Playhouse. His Clarendon commentary on the *Book of the Duchess* anticipated the challenge which the fourteenth-century poet himself must have faced when reciting in the manner of minstrels 'who had to keep a wary eye on their patrons and check any incipient yawns':

> They also had to prevent if possible the chatter of the people in the back rows from spoiling the best bits, and so we get prayers for silence not only at the beginnings of poems but in the middle when a new part of the tale or an important scene was entered upon. Chaucer himself was not above giving us the hint that his store of knowledge and his skill was greater than the patience of our inattentive minds.   (Bodleian MS Tolkien A 39/2/1, fol. 15)

---

[58] SH 2:315–17 'Tolkien as Performer'.
[59] Tolkien, *Beowulf: A Translation and Commentary*, 163.

The *Oxford Mail* ran an enthusiastic review praising Professor Tolkien's bravery for reciting without a script a tale 'fraught with endless perils and difficulties for the speaker' (SH 1:233–4). The Nun's Priest's Tale is indeed notorious for its obscure names such as *Kenulphus* as well as technical vocabulary on medicine and dream-lore, but what the newspaper did not know—because hardly anyone knew—was that Tolkien had already worked over the text, word by word, as part of his Clarendon project more than ten years before.

Masefield had composed a prologue to be read before the performance, but when shown it, Tolkien took exception to his far-reaching claims about Chaucer. 'These lines seem to me to allude to the erroneous imagination that Chaucer was the first English poet, and that before and except for him all was dumb and barbaric.' Just two years earlier Tolkien had published his British Academy *Beowulf* lecture arguing for the literary excellence of this Old English masterpiece centuries before the *Canterbury Tales*. 'I do not personally connect the North with either night or darkness, especially in England, in whose long 1200 years of literary tradition Chaucer stands rather in the middle than the beginning.' Then he added for good measure: 'I also do not feel him springlike but autumnal.'[60] Some dozen years earlier, his Clarendon Chaucer's 'Introduction on Language' had ended with a similar caveat that 'it is better to dismiss the falsehoods enshrined in "first warbler" and "father of English poesy" than to forget that (accomplished) English verse had been written, and had developed many tricks and devices and formulas, long before Chaucer was born.' (See Appendix I.)

Though Masefield had come to poetry by way of Chaucer and could himself recite the Monk's Tale by memory, he readily acknowledged the true expert: 'Professor Tolkien knows more about Chaucer than any living man and sometimes tells the Tales superbly, inimitably, just as though he were Chaucer returned.'[61] Tolkien's thorough knowledge derived not simply from studying Chaucer as an undergraduate and lecturing on him at Leeds, of course, but had come to fruition during the half-dozen years labouring upon his edition with Skeat at his elbow.

Invited for an encore performance the next year, Tolkien chose to recite the Reeve's Tale. Perhaps because the *Oxford Mail* previously remarked that Chaucer's Middle English had frightened the audience, he prepared a pamphlet with a printed text to help listeners follow along. The fourteen-page programme entitled simply *The Reeve's Tale* began with all the preliminaries that might have gone into his Clarendon edition: 'Among Chaucer's pilgrims was a reeve,

---

[60] *Letters*, 39. Though dismissive of Masefield's later elegy for T. S. Eliot (*Letters*, 353), Tolkien did know his poetry. Mark Atherton, *There and Back Again: J. R. R. Tolkien and the Origins of 'The Hobbit'* (London and New York: I. B. Tauris, 2012), 119–20, notes similarities between the verses recited by Legolas—'To the Sea, to the Sea! The gulls are crying!'—and Masefield's most famous work, 'Sea-Fever'.

[61] John Masefield, *Letters to Reyna*, ed. William Buchan (London: Buchan & Enright, 1983), 72. See SH 2:777–8 'Masefield'.

Oswold of Baldeswell in Norfolk.' Although not truncated like the version in his Clarendon edition, the text was nonetheless bowdlerized to remove the grosser moments, even when the miller's wife suckles her baby. (Ten-year-old Priscilla Tolkien was in the audience.) This sanitizing of the Reeve's Tale looks forward to the prudishness of Tolkien's fiction in the tradition of boyhood classics like *Treasure Island* and *King Solomon's Mines*. Though hobbits eat a great deal, they do not seem to have grosser bodily functions, except perhaps in the rare moment on Weathertop when Sam and Merry walk away from the campfire apparently to urinate (*FR* I/11). Does anyone actually have sex in Middle-earth?

The *Oxford Mail* regretted the text's abbreviation for a local audience 'broad-minded enough to accept the distinctly broad humour of Chaucer in a story of his which can least afford to be cut because of the amazingly ingenious way in which the plot is worked out' (SH 1:244). As if anticipating this rebuke, Tolkien had admitted in his introduction's last sentence: 'Unlike many of Chaucer's Canterbury Tales, the Reeve's tale is neither easy to shorten nor improved by the process.'[62] Yet he tried anyway.

Certainly Tolkien knew full well the editorial challenges after glossing and annotating his Clarendon Chaucer, and he repeated in the preface his central claims from 'Chaucer as a Philologist':

> Even in the usual printed text of Chaucer the northern dialectal character of the speeches of Alain and John is plain. But a comparison of various manuscripts seems to show that actually Chaucer himself went further: the clerks' talk, as he wrote it, was probably very nearly correct and pure northern dialect, derived (as usual with Chaucer) from books as well as from observation. A remarkable feat at the time. But Chaucer was evidently interested in such things, and had given considerable thought to the linguistic situation in his day. It may be observed that he presents us with an *East-Anglian* reeve, who is amusing *southern,* largely London, folk with imitations of *northern* speech brought southward by the attraction of the *universities*. This is a picture in little of the origins of literary and London English.

Next he explained the dialect feature of long –*ā* in words like *bānes* for 'bones' as well as specific Northern vocabulary such as *slik* and *bōs*. A separate note explained how the text had been altered as well as abbreviated: 'Only in the words of the clerks is there any material departure from the text as printed by Skeat. These words are presented here in a more marked and consistently northern form—in nearly every case with some manuscript authority.' Here Tolkien was modest about investigating the manuscripts yet not altogether frank about merely

---

[62] Tolkien's handwritten sidenote in his souvenir copy approved one cut as 'effective and wholly intelligible' (p. 13). The programme has been reprinted as J. R. R. Tolkien, 'The Reeve's Tale: Version Prepared for Recitation at the "Summer Diversions" Oxford: 1939', *Tolkien Studies* 5 (2008), 173–83.

reprinting Skeat. In addition to omitting some forty-six lines for the sake of decency, he resisted the tyranny of Ellesmere as a copy-text for determining accidentals such as final *-e* and indeed he took far greater liberties.

When this pamphlet was reprinted in *Tolkien Studies* in 2008, a brief headnote explained the occasion for which it was written but said nothing about the text which Tolkien actually produced. He had complained to Masefield that if authentic fourteenth-century poetry was not sufficiently intelligible for a listening audience, it could be delivered in a 'modified modern pronunciation' (*Letters*, 40). But this is not what he did in 1939. What he attempted instead was recovering fully what he believed to have been Chaucer's authentic language and even some spellings, specifically those that preserved fourteenth-century practices like u/v in the word like *serue* and *neuer*. He even changed words such as *what* to *quat* although previously admitting the evidence for Chaucer actually using these spellings was slender (1934, p. 16).

For an English editor in the first half of the twentieth century, he naturally aligned himself with A. E Housman's application of common sense for identifying mistakes and judging the merits of emendations. Housman came from a Worcestershire family, had preceded Tolkien at King Edward's School by more than three decades, and taught at London's University College where one of his former students, Tolkien's friend R. W. Chambers, concluded his book *Man's Unconquerable Mind* with a chapter on Housman. There he quoted his old teacher as saying, 'for the last hundred years individual German scholars have been the superiors in genius as well as learning of all scholars outside Germany',[63] and yet Housman dismissed the German method of editing as 'thoughtlessness in the sphere of recension'.[64] The ferocity of Housman's editorial prefaces had once been the topic of conversation among the Inklings (SH 1:347), but Tolkien went further than liberating himself from stemmatics when deciding to extend conjectural emendation to grammar and spellings as well as substantive readings.[65] Manly and Rickert, working at the same time, had not set as their goal retrieving the author's perfectly proof-read autograph—which may never have existed with an unfinished work like the *Canterbury Tales*—but rather the archetype of all surviving manuscripts. For his bold adventure at re-creating Chaucer's lost originality, Tolkien extended into new territory the common-sense English tradition

---

[63] R. W. Chambers, *Man's Unconquerable Mind: Studies of English Writers from Bede to A. E. Housman and W. P. Ker* (London: Jonathan Cape, 1939), 'A. E. Housman', 365–86 at p. 383. Chambers admired Tolkien's *Beowulf* lecture enough to insert two mentions of it, pp. 68–9 and 91.

[64] A. E. Housman, 'The Application of Thought to Textual Criticism', *Proceedings of the Classical Association* 18 (1922), 67–84 at p. 77.

[65] See Jerome J. McGann, *A Critique of Modern Textual Criticism* (Chicago: University of Chicago Press, 1983), 'Modern Textual Criticism: The Central Problems', 23–36. For editing medieval texts, Lee Patterson's 'The Logic of Textual Criticism and the Way of Genius: The Kane–Donaldson *Piers Plowman* in Historical Perspective', in *Negotiating the Past: The Historical Understanding of Medieval Literature* (Madison: University of Wisconsin Press, 1987), 77–113 at pp. 80–3, provides a concise critique of stemmatics and best-text editing.

memorably described in Housman's conclusion to his landmark 1921 lecture: 'Knowledge is good, method is good, but one thing beyond all others is necessary; and that is to have a head, not a pumpkin, on your shoulders and brains, not pudding, in your head.'

Years of careful study had informed Tolkien's notions of Chaucer's language, and now finally, with his head solidly on his shoulders, he had freedom for a speculative re-construction of what he believed the poet's lost language sounded like. Side-by-side comparison demonstrates the rewriting's thoroughness beyond what was attempted in his 1934 reconstruction:

Skeat, *Tales*, A, 4036-45	Tolkien (1939), pp. 7-8
'By god, right by the hoper wil I stande,' Quod Iohn, 'and se how that the corn gas in; Yet saugh I never, by my fader kin, How that the hoper wagges til and fra.' Aleyn answerede, 'Iohn, and wiltow swa, Than wil I be bynethe, by my croun, And se how that the mele falles doun In-to the trough; that sal be my disport. For Iohn, in faith, I may been of your sort; I is as ille a miller as are ye.'	'By god, right by the hoper wil I stand,' quoth Jon, 'and see hougat the corn gaas in! Yit sagh I neuer, by my fader kin, hougat the hoper waggis til and fra.' Alain answeredë: 'Jon! and wiltu swa then wil I be binethen, by my croune, And see hougat the melë fallis doune in til the trogh. That sal be me desport; For Jon, i faith, I es al of your sort: I es as il a miller as er ye.'

Even the quickest look reveals how far changes went beyond his claim of simplifying for non-specialists. Certainly 'Yit sagh I neuer' was not clearer than Skeat's 'Yet saugh I never'. This passage not only added the northernisms *es, il, gaas*, and *hougat* from his 1934 study—this last variant from the Corpus manuscript now accepted in the *Riverside Chaucer*, but only for its first appearance—finally he could follow through on emending *boes* to *bos* after concluding in 1934 that 'Chaucer probably wrote *bos* as genuine N. texts' (p. 20).

He was not methodical about checking his 1934 study, however, his programme announcing his preference for the rhyme *wille/tille* instead of *wulle/tulle* despite an entire appendix to the contrary in his article (pp. 59–63). In some places he grew even bolder. His 1934 text had read 'þou *hast* as a coward ben agast' even though he believed 'we may assume Chaucer wrote northern *has* here' (p. 26). So his 1939 version reads 'thow *has* as a coward been agast!'

Donaldson offered an amusing allegory likening an editor's dilemma when choosing between two readings to a young man's choice between two women to marry. Equally unhappy with both of his wedding candidates—that is, with the two readings offered by the manuscripts—the editor was 'uniquely privileged to be able to bring his dream-girl into existence'.[66] This creation of an ideal text,

---

[66] Donaldson, 'The Psychology of Editors', 104.

superior to any offered by the scribes, was exactly what Tolkien believed that he was bringing into existence by educated instinct, glancing back and forth between Skeat's text and his own editorial re-creation, sometimes remembering his earlier emendations from 'Chaucer as a Philologist', sometimes not, and always in quest of spellings closer to Chaucer's own. With over 700 alterations from Skeat, sometimes six per line not counting punctuation, he proceeded with confidence that Chaucer 'would chiefly esteem the efforts to recover the detail of what he wrote, even (indeed particularly) down to forms and spellings, to recapture an idea of what it sounded like' (1934, p. 1). As a performer of the Reeve's Tale in 1939, he was chiefly concerned with the sounds of words but also relished the opportunity to recover details of the poet's grammar and spelling practices.

Far from taking reckless liberties, he saw himself as a trained philologist dutifully removing the corruptive influence of fifteenth-century scribes. This was precisely what he believed Chaucer would have wanted: 'the acquiring of as good a knowledge as is available of the language of his day would certainly have seemed to him a preliminary necessity, not a needless luxury' (1934, p. 2). Such precision was no new concern on his part. When the two Oxford dons first met in 1926, C. S. Lewis wrote in his diary that Tolkien could not read Spenser because of the forms.[67] Lewis must have mentioned *The Faerie Queene* because he planned a chapter on it for his *Allegory of Love*, and Tolkien immediately pounced upon Spencer's failure to reproduce authentic forms of Middle English.[68] Ben Jonson had already launched this complaint when quipping, 'Spencer in affecting the Ancients writ no language', but Lewis himself would dodge the question, making no mention of the poet's linguistic archaisms in his 'Spenser' chapter in *The Allegory of Love* (1936) or 'Sidney and Spenser' in *English Literature in the Sixteenth Century* (1954). Venturing in 1939 to succeed where Spenser had failed, Tolkien intended rescuing Chaucer's Middle English from the overbearing authority of Skeat's edition based upon the untrustworthy Ellesmere manuscript. His spelling of the saint's name *Cudbert*, for example, departed from all the witnesses *Cutberd*, *Cutbert*, and *Cuthberd* previously recorded from the manuscripts (1934, p. 23) since he was confident of knowing better than any scribe what Chaucer actually wrote. Ironically, his rewriting of the Reeve's Tale harkened back to Skeat's own impulse when editing *Boece* in the absence of reliable manuscripts: 'I found that the only satisfactory way of producing a really good text was to rewrite the whole of it' (2:xlviii).

---

[67] *Diary of C. S. Lewis*, 392–3. In *English Literature in the Sixteenth Century*, Lewis enacted his own linguistic re-creation: 'When I have quoted from neo-Latin authors, I have tried to translate them into sixteenth-century English' (p. v).

[68] In his lecture to cadets during the Second World War, Tolkien used a phrase from *Troilus* to illustrate Spenser's linguistic incompetence: 'a misreading of *dorring do(n)* as *derring do*, and a misunderstanding of the passage, is derived through Spenser the bogus mediaeval word *derring-do* "chivalry, knight-errantry"' (Bodleian MS Tolkien 14/2, fol. 92).

Near the beginning of 'Chaucer as a Philologist', Tolkien had speculated about what we would find if the poet's own handwritten copies ever surfaced. Therefore in 1951, a dozen years after dismissing Ellesmere in his edition of the Reeve's Tale, he would have felt vindicated by the discovery of a work entitled *Equatorie of the Planetis* which was quite possibly a long-lost Chaucer holograph offering a language somewhat different from Ellesmere. The manuscript at Cambridge's Peterhouse College contains the date 1392—contemporary with Chaucer's long-accepted *Treatise on the Astrolabe*—and its tables were computed for London where the poet was living at that time. Most compelling was the 'Radix Chaucer' inscription comparable to his signature in a document from his time at the customhouse.[69] The editor Derek Price's preface made a point of thanking Professor Tolkien for his assistance, and twenty-five photostat pages from the Peterhouse manuscript, which Tolkien donated to the English Faculty Library at the time of his retirement, must have formed the basis for his expert judgements. Although he was engrossed during this period with seeing *The Lord of the Rings* into print, it is hardly surprising, given his hopes for the survival of a Chaucer holograph, that he took the time to clip and save two *Times* pieces and two *TLS* articles on the discovery of the *Equatorie*.[70]

Ever since the *Equatorie*'s publication in 1955, opinion has been divided over its status as Chaucer's working-copy written in his own hand. Strongest opposition came from those such as Larry Benson, general editor of the *Riverside Chaucer*, invested in the language of Ellesmere.[71] Paleographers A. S. G. Edwards and Linne R. Mooney have also raised doubts, whereas other manuscript experts, Pamela Robinson and John H. Fisher, found compelling evidence in support.[72] Fisher even made bold to include the work in his *Complete Poetry and Prose of Geoffrey Chaucer*. As a specialist on medieval astronomy, J. D. North readily connected its contents with the poet's celestial references as part of a circumstantial case in favour.[73] It is noteworthy, for instance, that the *Equatorie* frames its calculations

---

[69] *The 'Equatorie of the Planetis' Edited from Peterhouse MS. 75.I*, ed. Derek J. Price with linguistic analysis by R. M. Wilson (Cambridge: Cambridge University Press, 1955), 'Ascription to Chaucer', 149–66. This manuscript was the first chosen by Peterhouse College to digitalize: https://cudl.lib.cam.ac.uk/view/MS-PETERHOUSE-00075-00001/5.

[70] These newspaper clippings were also part of his 1959 donation to the English Faculty Library, now transferred to the Bodleian's Tolkien Archive.

[71] Larry D. Benson, 'Chaucer's Spelling Reconsidered' (1992), in *Contradictions: From 'Beowulf' to Chaucer*, ed. Theodore M. Andersson and Stephen A. Barney (Aldershot: Scolar; Brookfield, VT: Ashgate, 1995), 70–99. See also Stephen Partridge, 'The Vocabulary of The Equatorie of the Planetis', *English Manuscript Studies, 1100–1700* 3 (1992), 29–37.

[72] A. S. G. Edwards and Linne R. Mooney, 'Is the *Equatorie of the Planets* a Chaucer Holograph?', *Chaucer Review* 26 (1991), 31–42; Pamela Robinson, 'Geoffrey Chaucer and the *Equatorie of the Planetis*', *Chaucer Review* 26 (1991), 17–30; and John H. Fisher, 'Historical and Methodological Considerations for Adopting "Best Text" or "Usus Scribendi" for Textual Criticism of Chaucer's Poems', *Text: Transactions of the Society for Textual Scholarship* 6 (1994), 165–80.

[73] J. D. North, *Chaucer's Universe* (Oxford: Clarendon Press, 1988), 'Authorship of The Equatorie', 169–81.

from the beginning of Aries to the latter end of Libra—that is, following the same astrological sequence as the frame-narrative of the *Canterbury Tales* from Aries in the General Prologue to Libra in the Parson's Prologue.

Linguistic analysis has identified words in the *Equatorie* recorded nowhere else in Middle English except in the works of Chaucer, especially technical vocabulary shared with his *Astrolabe*. The *Equatorie* actually refers to 'the tretis of the astrelabie' as a companion piece.[74] Peterhouse's mingling of dialects matches Tolkien's sense of Northern intrusions, and linguistic analysis by R. M. Wilson echoed his own long-held views on Chaucer's language: 'If he lived in an area of mixed dialect, such as that of London, he might well be familiar with a variety of forms, any of which he could use when necessary for the sake of rhyme' (p. 146). The *Equatorie*'s inclusion of *overthwart* would certainly have caught Tolkien's attention as the distinctive Chaucerian word for which he had supplied an especially long note on its appearance in *The Book of the Duchess*.

In a volume honouring Tolkien's student Norman Davis, the historical linguist M. L. Samuels made the case that Ellesmere's spellings really belonged to its scribe, not Chaucer.[75] The poet's personal spelling, he concluded, must be found instead in the *Equatorie*—'an authentic and autograph work of Chaucer' (p. 35)—with distinctive forms such as *moche*, *shollen*, *yif*, *agayn*, and *thorw*. Tolkien's reconstruction of Chaucerian language did not precisely match what Samuels proposes since he did not write *thorw* in his 1939 rendering of the Reeve's Tale (4066-7). Even professional scribes of the period were inconsistent, however, and the Chaucerian poet and Privy Seal clerk Thomas Hoccleve varied his spellings when making two copies of one of his own poems.[76] Yet it is surprising that Tolkien did not employ the Northern *agayn* throughout his edition of the Reeve's Tale since Samuels based the poet's first-hand knowledge of this dialect variant on the same biographical evidence of Chaucer's service at Hatfield in the later 1350s (p. 29). All in all, Samuels points in the direction already taken by Tolkien for freeing future editions of the *Canterbury Tales* from overdependence upon Ellesmere.[77]

To return to the Reeve's Tale, what will really interest readers today is the connection between Chaucer's fabliau and Tolkien's early drafts of what would become *The Lord of the Rings*. Evidence of this linkage survives in a single draft page of *The Return of the Shadow*, dated July 1939, on which he wrote 'Summer Diversions' and then squeezed into the left margin two lines from the Reeve's

---

[74] *Equatorie of the Planetis*, ed. Price, 'Linguistic Analysis', 137–48; see p. 22 for the *Astrolabe* reference.
[75] M. L. Samuels, 'Chaucer's Spelling', in *Middle English Studies Presented to Norman Davis in Honour of his Seventieth Birthday*, ed. Douglas Gray and E. G. Stanley (Oxford: Clarendon Press, 1983), 17–37 at p. 21. Simon Horobin, *Language of the Chaucer Tradition*, 36–59, makes a case against the *Equatorie* preserving Chaucer's spelling.
[76] See Bowers, 'Hoccleve's Two Copies of *Lerne to Dye*'.
[77] N. F. Blake took up this challenge with his *Canterbury Tales, Edited from the Hengwrt Manuscript* (London: Arnold, 1980).

Tale describing Simkin the miller—'as ani pecok he was proude & gai | pipen he couþe & fissche & nettes bete' (*CT* I, 3926–7). This is neither Skeat's text nor his own, so it must have come off the top of his head. This page has been produced in facsimile by Christopher as an important moment in the evolution of the narrative when Treebeard was introduced as a giant who seemed hospitable but was really in league with the Enemy.[78] Clearly from Treebeard's inception, there was some connection in Tolkien's mind between Simkin the miller and Sauron's agent later replaced in the story by Saruman. The subliminal influence of the Reeve's Tale will become clearer in the final version where the hobbits Merry and Pippin (like John and Alain) join the attack upon Saruman at Isengard (like Simkin at Trumpington).

'Flotsam and Jetsam'

Tolkien was not finished with the Reeve's Tale in 1939. As one of his civilian services during the Second World War, he oversaw the teaching of Navy and Air Force cadets taking six-month short courses at Oxford before heading into combat. His duties included working out a plan of English classes, arranging for tutors and lecturers, and teaching his own courses aimed at a non-specialist audience. This was an offshoot of Vice-Chancellor George Gordon's arrangements before his death to keep the University operating. Even from the grave, Gordon devised ambitious schemes and left Tolkien to handle the 'sticky end of the stick'.

To serve the linguistic needs of these future officers, Tolkien prepared a single-spaced mimeograph *Chaucerian Grammar (with special reference to the 'Reeve's Tale')* running to eleven pages and providing a guide to Middle English's nouns, adjectives, adverbs, pronouns, and verbs.[79] To squeeze maximum text onto a minimum number of pages because of paper rationing, Tolkien employed his Hammond typewriter with the same 'midget type' used for airletters to Christopher in South Africa.[80] But if this guide was keyed to the Reeve's Tale, the question arises what text was assigned for the cadets to read? The safest guess is that Tolkien distributed leftover copies of the programme from the 1939 Summer Diversions. That booklet would have superbly served his teaching needs even if its

---

[78] Tolkien, *Return of the Shadow*, 382–4; see also McIlwaine, *Tolkien: Maker of Middle-earth*, 354–5, for an enlarged colour facsimile of the page.

[79] Bodleian MS Tolkien 14/2, fols. 82–92. Fols. 93–5 continued with handwritten notes on verbs also drawn from the Reeve's Tale and fol. 117 with 'Vocabulary of the Reeve's Tale'. In the early 1940s Tolkien produced a similar linguistic guide to his made-up Adunaic language which Christopher printed in *Sauron Defeated*, 430–9.

[80] Christopher in *The War of the Ring*, 233–4, dates his father's drafts to 1944 on the basis of the midget type. McIlwaine, *Tolkien: Maker of Middle-earth*, 266–7, reproduces a page of Tolkien's *Beowulf* translation in midget type.

prudish omissions would have disappointed the future officers. Chaucer's story would also have appealed to these cadets with the self-congratulatory sense of being Oxford students less likely than their counterparts at Cambridge to speak with country-bumpkin accents.

The Reeve's Tale, in short, remained central to Tolkien's attention as he struggled forward drafting and revising chapters of *The Lord of the Rings*, writing to Stanley Unwin in December 1942 that he had reached the chapter that would become 'Flotsam and Jetsam'.[81] Teaching cadets destined to lead their troops upon the battlefields of Europe, Tolkien set about transforming Chaucer's story of two students fist-fighting in a bedroom to the far more heroic vision of the two hobbits joining with the Entish army in an assault upon Isengard.

Toward the end of his life when *The Lord of the Rings* was subjected to biographical interpretations, Tolkien left no doubt about his feelings on this score: 'One of my strongest opinions is that investigation of an author's biography (or such other glimpses of his "personality" as can be gleaned by the curious) is an entirely vain and false approach to his works—and especially to a *work of narrative art*' (*Letters*, 414). While he did allow that an author could not remain wholly unaffected by personal experiences, his 1965 Foreword insisted 'the ways in which a story-germ uses the soil of experience are extremely complex, and attempts to define the process are at best guesses from evidence that is inadequate and ambiguous.' Yet three decades earlier when 'Chaucer as a Philologist' speculated about the medieval poet's imaginative processes, he made larger allowance for using what we know about a writer's biography: 'The chance events of the actual lives of authors get caught up into their books, but usually they are strangely changed and intricately woven anew one with another, or with other contents of the mind' (pp. 55–6). Thus the young Chaucer's winter holiday in Yorkshire explained how he first heard the Northern dialect later put into the mouths of his two clerks. Just as his medieval poet worked from books as well as overheard conversations, Tolkien's own imagination wove together the literary and the real-life.

If Chaucer had his youthful experience at Hatfield, Tolkien's boyhood adventures occurred outside the village of Sarehole where he had a first-hand encounter with mills and millers:

> Over the road a meadow led to the River Cole, little more than a broad stream, and upon this stood Sarehole Mill, an old brick building with a tall chimney. Corn had been ground here for three centuries... [Ronald and Hilary] would stare through the fence at the water-wheel turning in its dark cavern... Sometimes they would venture through the gate and gaze into an open doorway, where

---

[81] *Letters*, 58. *The War of the Ring*, 12, 26, 40–2, confirms that Tolkien was working on the Isengard episode in 1942–3 when teaching the Reeve's Tale to cadets.

they could see the great leather belts and pulleys and shafts, and the men at work. There were two millers, father and son. The old man had a black beard, but it was the son who frightened the boys with his white dusty clothes and sharp-eyed face. Ronald named him 'the White Ogre'. When he yelled at them to clear off they would scamper away from the yard... At the foot of the pool the dark waters suddenly plunged over the sluice to the great wheel below: a dangerous and exciting place.[82]

Loud as medieval watermills were with their large turning wheels, Sarehole Mill, originally built in the 1760s, had become scarier after a coal-burning steam engine grinding bones for fertilizer was installed in the 1850s. Its tall redbrick chimney would have belched black smoke, exactly as Sam envisioned when he looked into the Mirror of Galadriel. The encroachments of the modern world had worsened by the time Tolkien revisited it in 1933. 'The old mill still stands,' he wrote, 'but the crossing beyond the now fenced-in pool, where the bluebell lane ran down into the mill lane, is now a dangerous crossing alive with motors and red lights.' The White Ogre's house, so frightening to him as a youngster, had become a petrol station. Tolkien was especially saddened by the disappearance of the elm trees. 'How I envy those whose precious early scenery has not been exposed to such violent and peculiarly hideous change' (*Biography*, 129–30).

These personal memories then got caught up in his imaginative process with his reading, editing, and teaching of Chaucer. Although Sisam and Gordon selected the Reeve's Tale for their edition apparently without Tolkien's involvement, its story of two young men going into the countryside and having a dangerous encounter with a miller would have resonated with his own youthful recollections. Sarehole was not nearly so far north as Strother, to be sure, but Tolkien was officially a poor scholar like John and Alain at Cambridge when he later found his way southward to the other ancient university at Oxford.

Finally came the imaginative alchemy that transformed both brands of experience, the personal and the literary, into a thrilling story. Undergraduates noticed that Tolkien seldom mentioned anything about storytelling, just single words in single lines, as Diana Wynne Jones recalled from attending his lectures in the 1950s: 'he never talked about narrative at all.'[83] Even his seventy-page study of the Reeve's Tale utterly neglected the story which clearly meant something special to him personally. Enough early readers learned about this boyhood escapade that Tolkien's 1965 Foreword strongly discouraged pursuing this connection: 'Recently

---

[82] *Biography*, 28. *Black and White Ogre Country: The Lost Tales of Hilary Tolkien* preserves the childhood remembrances by Ronald's younger brother. McIlwaine, *Tolkien: Maker of Middle-earth*, 296–7, shows Tolkien's 1937 watercolour of Hobbiton's mill with a tower as if a memory of the chimney of Sarehole mill.

[83] 'The Shape of the Narrative in *The Lord of the Rings*' (1983), *Reflections on the Magic of Writing*, 5–6; her official online biography reports that C. S. Lewis and J. R. R. Tolkien were both lecturing then, 'Lewis booming to crowded halls and Tolkien mumbling to me and three others'.

I saw in a paper a picture of the last decrepitude of the once thriving corn-mill beside its pool that long ago seemed to me so important. I never liked the looks of the Young miller, but his father, the Old miller, had a black beard, and he was not named Sandyman.' His overreaction failed to conceal, indeed it strongly suggested, the full reach of his childhood experience into his fiction.

To begin with just an isolated example from *The Two Towers*. Aragorn and his companions under the eaves of Fangorn Forest have their horses stampeded away—'wild with some sudden gladness' (*TT* III/5)—in an episode that recalls John and Alain having their horse released to run off with 'wilde mares' in the marshes. In Chaucer's version, it was Simkin who played this trick while Saruman is the prime suspect in Tolkien's version.[84] The muddle over the culprit's identity, as well as the carryover of the adjective *wild* for the horses, suggests something surfacing from subterranean memories. It was as if Tolkien recalled Simkin's deceit with the horse from the Reeve's Tale, he transferred it to his early draft of *The Treason of Isengard*, and only later did he puzzle out the trickster's true identity. But Chaucerian inspirations ran deeper.

It is now a critical commonplace that Tolkien's literary imagination took inspiration from his medievalist training.[85] For more than twenty years Tolkien had worked on the Reeve's Tale as editor, glosser, and annotator without ever discussing its core narrative. Even the introduction to his 1939 programme avoided even the briefest summary. His commitment to Chaucer's storytelling surfaced only when drafting the chapters 'Treebeard' and 'Flotsam and Jetsam'. Here it is tempting to connect his 1939 impersonation of Chaucer with his lecture 'On Fairy-Stories', delivered just four months earlier at the University of St Andrews, as prelude to the transformation of Chaucer's town-and-gown comedy into an epic battle with a fairy-story's joy of the happy ending in *The Two Towers*.

This transformation begins when the younger hobbits Merry and Pippin stray into Fangorn Forest (as Ronald and Hilary had wandered into the forest along the River Cole) and they learn about the trees cut down by Orcs for no reason (as Tolkien grieved over the elms felled near the old mill). 'Some of the trees they just cut down and leave to rot', Treebeard reported angrily (*TT* III/4). Tolkien had long wished to rewrite the scene in Shakespeare's *Macbeth* in which Birnam Wood came to Dunsinane Hill so that 'the trees might really march to war' (*Letters*, 212n). Now he had his chance when the Ents decide to fight back against Saruman.

The two hobbits join the attack against the mill-master who had turned Isengard into an industrial wasteland. Instead of being frightened off—and here

---

[84] In *Treason of Isengard*, 385, 389, and 403, even Christopher is forced to guess whether the old man who released the horses was Gandalf or Saruman.

[85] See for example Thomas Honegger, '*The Homecoming of Beorhtnoth*: Philology and the Literary Muse', *Tolkien Studies* 4 (2007), 189–99 at p. 195.

is where the storyteller's imagination rewrites personal memory—the heroic hobbits join the Ents to take revenge for the felled trees, defeat the wicked wizard, and destroy his machines. Merry and Pippin do better than escape injury and death. They achieve what Tolkien described with his newly coined word *eucatastrophe* or 'the sudden happy turn in a story which pierces you with a joy that brings tears'.[86] Each story also has its surprise reward. John and Alain in victory make their escape by snatching something round, valuable, and hidden by Simkin—the loaf of bread baked from their stolen grain. And Pippin in their victory also snatches up something round, valuable, and hidden by Saruman—the palantír. Tolkien confessed that he knew nothing about the Orthanc-stone until it fell from the wizard's window (*Letters*, 217). Just possibly a hint lay deeply buried in his memory of the Reeve's Tale.

Was Tolkien thinking specifically of John and Alain when writing about his two hobbits? Notice that when Merry later introduces himself to King Théoden, he explains about his people: 'Far in the North is our home.'[87] This is not strictly true about the Shire's position on the map. Esgaroth and Erebor are farther north, Arnor and Angmar much farther, and Forodwaith so far north to become the home of the Snowmen. But his statement does recall, consciously or unconsciously, the exact phrase *fer in the north* (4015) about the home of the two young clerks from Strother. It was a phrase that Tolkien took the trouble to quote in the introduction to his 1939 edition (Fig. 14).

In 'The Scouring of the Shire', the Sarehole miller again emerges from Tolkien's recollections to be reimagined as Ted Sandyman. Under Sharkey's orders, the Hobbiton mill had been rebuilt as a steam-driven factory with its tall brick chimney belching black smoke just as in Tolkien's boyhood memories: 'They're always a-hammering and a-letting out a smoke and a stench, and there isn't no peace even at night in Hobbiton' (*RK* VI/8). On a more menacing scale, the Sarehole miller, mingled with memories of Chaucer's Simkin, once again metamorphoses into Saruman in the guise of Sharkey. In this more frightening version of a fairy-tale, the enemy has pursued the heroes and penetrated into their homeland, much like the old hag following the knight back to the king's court in the Wife of Bath's Tale. Tolkien had already learned the terror of this home invasion from *Beowulf*: 'Grendel is an enemy who has attacked the centre of the realm and brought into the royal hall the outer darkness' (*Letters*, 242). In this instance, Saruman has invaded the Shire and subjugated the hobbits with his gang of ruffians until another *eucatastrophe* unfolds. Tolkien's earliest sketches had a warrior-like Frodo heading the resistance, but the former Ring-bearer was later

---

[86] *Essays*, 153; *Letters*, 100; and SH 2:364–5 'Eucatastrophe'.
[87] *TT* III/8; *The War of the Ring*, 26, indicates that Merry's exact wording was already present in the earliest draft.

reimagined as a pacifist so that Captain Meriadoc and Captain Peregrin take the lead fighting to liberate their homeland.

For Tolkien, his real-life experiences and his scholarly pursuits converged in his fiction, the two never sealed off in airtight compartments. As an example of what C. S. Lewis called the 'wishful thinking' of the new psychology,[88] the White Ogre who had terrorized the Tolkien boys outside their village underwent this creative alchemy—with Chaucer's story serving as catalyst—to be transformed into the White Wizard defeated by the two hobbits, first at Isengard and finally at the very door of Bag End.

The chance events of the author's actual life *had* got caught up into his book—as Tolkien claimed about the poet's creative process in the Reeve's Tale—but strangely changed and intricately woven anew with the Chaucerian contents of his own mind.

[88] *Surprised by Joy*, 203.

7
Chaucer in Middle-earth

Umberto Eco has examined our ongoing fascination with the Middle Ages and listed ten different versions including the 'shaggy medievalism' of works like *Beowulf*.[1] Much of Tolkien's success as a fiction-writer derives from assimilating several of these fantasies of the past including the decadent Middle Ages described by Faramir at Minas Tirith. Strangely missing from Eco's literary types was the jolly, earthy, boisterous Middle Ages of the *Decameron* in his Italian tradition and the *Canterbury Tales* in ours. This Chaucerian legacy, so clearly embodied in Tolkien's hobbits, is easy enough to miss because it has been so thoroughly normalized in English literature that it no longer seems 'medieval' at all, especially in Oxford where Chaucer had been a steady literary presence for more than five centuries.

Some listeners inside Merton Hall in 1959 might nonetheless have been surprised that Tolkien, best known for his work on Old English poetry, devoted a section of his 'Valedictory Address' to recruiting Chaucer to the cause of Language against Literature in a debate still very much alive in the retiring professor's mind:

> His merits as a major poet are too obvious to be obscured; though it was in fact Language, or Philology, that demonstrated, as only Language could, two things of first-rate literary importance: that he was not a fumbling beginner, but a master of metrical technique; and that he was an inheritor, a middle point, and not a 'father'. Not to mention the labours of Language in rescuing much of his vocabulary and idiom from ignorance or misunderstanding.[2]

Repeating views about Chaucer from his letter to John Masefield in 1938, this encomium would have sounded surprising only because nobody knew about Tolkien's efforts at rescuing fourteenth-century vocabulary and idiom during his own long labours on *Selections from Chaucer's Poetry and Prose*.

Like almost all medievalists in the twentieth century, Tolkien as a youngster had come to the field by way of Chaucer and took some delight in noting that his son John, at the age of 2, had already added 'Chaucer' to his vocabulary.[3] His

---

[1] Umberto Eco, 'Dreaming of the Middle Ages', *Travels in Hyper Reality: Essays*, trans. William Weaver (San Diego, New York, and London: Harcourt Brace Jovanovich, 1986), 61–72.
[2] *Essays*, 233–4; see SH 3:1373–4 and Jill Fitzgerald, 'A "Clerkes Compleinte": Tolkien and the Division of Lit. and Lang', *Tolkien Studies* 6 (2009), 41–57.
[3] McIlwaine, *Tolkien: Maker of Middle-earth*, 118: 'name of bell the handle of which was figure of Chaucer on a horse—stood always on table at meals.' The poet on a horse was probably based on the famous Ellesmere portrait.

Tolkien's Lost Chaucer. John M. Bowers, Oxford University Press (2019). © John M. Bowers.
DOI: 10.1093/oso/9780198842675.001.0001

teacher George Brewerton, himself a medievalist, sparked Tolkien's earliest interest by reciting the *Canterbury Tales* to their class at King Edward's School. Unlike other medievalists like C. S. Lewis, however, Tolkien insisted that English literature ended rather than began with Chaucer (*Biography*, 77). With the fourteenth-century poet seldom far from his thoughts as the culmination of all that came before, even his famous *Beowulf* lecture opened with a witty allusion to the General Prologue (574–5): 'it may seem presumption that I should try with *swich a lewed mannes wit to pace the wisdom of an heep of lerned men*' (*Essays*, 5–6). His 1947 purchase of the Ellesmere facsimile testified to his ongoing concern with Chaucer, and in 1951 when invited by his former student S. R. T. O. d'Ardenne to deliver a paper at a conference in Liège, he decided to investigate the word *losenger* which had engaged his attention when glossing the *Legend of Good Women* almost three decades earlier for his Clarendon Chaucer.[4]

It is worth digressing to ponder why, from among all the words in Old and Middle English, Tolkien chose this word *losenger* as the subject for what would become one of the last scholarly studies published during his lifetime. He had provided no entry for the word in his Chaucer Notes and may have felt that the omission represented unfinished business. But with so many other loose ends in this edition, there must have been something else weighing on his mind. Here he defined the word in its original Chaucerian context as 'slanderer', 'liar', and 'backbiter' related to the word *losel* for 'idle wastrel'. Perhaps it would not be far-fetched to suggest that at this point in his career, after more than a quarter-century as an Oxford professor, Tolkien looked back guiltily upon all the unkept promises to publishers and all the accusations of idleness from colleagues, and he produced this paper as a sort of *mea culpa*. His research student V. A. Kolve recalled him reflecting upon these shortcomings: 'He confessed to me once that some were disappointed by how little he had done in the academic way, but that he had chosen instead to explore his own vision of things.'[5]

Already by 1932 he admitted to Chapman the weight of the Chaucerian incubus upon his conscience. His *Gawain* edition, 'Chaucer as a Philologist', and 'The Monsters and the Critics' had all appeared before the Second World War. Set against this relatively slender résumé were undelivered assignments such as his *Pearl* edition, the book-length *'Beowulf' and the Critics*, and his EETS edition of *Ancrene Wisse*. If his own harsh remarks about George Gordon holding up their Chaucer edition did not quite qualify him as a 'slanderer', these complaints did deflect blame from his role as an 'idler' who failed to reduce his annotations to a

---

[4] In 'Middle English 'Losenger'', 64, Tolkien said that he first puzzled over the word forty-five years earlier, that is, in 1906 when still at King Edward's School.

[5] Private email communication, 15 September 2008, with permission.

publishable length. He would confess during a newspaper interview in 1968, 'I have always been incapable of doing the job at hand.'[6]

For so many years, in short, he had been loafing in his scholarly career as a *losel* who squandered time on children's stories when he should have been whipping his *Beowulf* book into shape. He confided to his publisher in 1937 that Oxford would merely add *The Hobbit* to his 'long list of never-never procrastinations' (*Letters*, 18). Fiction-writing simply did not count in terms of academic production, especially after Tolkien had idled away his two-year Leverhulme Research Fellowship.[7] 'The authorities of the university', he would lament when *The Lord of the Rings* was in press, 'might well consider it an aberration of an elderly professor of philology to write and publish fairy stories and romances' (*Letters*, 219). He explained to his American publisher this widespread view of his failings: 'Most of my philological colleagues are shocked (cert. behind my back, sometimes to my face) at the fall of a philological into "Trivial literature"; and anyway the cry is: "now we know how you have been wasting your time for 20 years"' (*Letters*, 238). His enormous effort during the late 1940s in the cramped row-house without even a desk—'I typed out *The Hobbit*—and the whole of *The Lord of the Rings* twice (and several sections many times) on my bed in an attic of Manor Road' (*Letters*, 344)—was little known because it simply did not count. Then in May 1951 when struggling to deliver *The Lord of the Rings* to his publisher, OUP's Dan Davin forced him to surrender all his Clarendon Chaucer materials. So it does not seem entirely accidental that in July of this same year, when he was asked to deliver a paper at Liège in the autumn, his thoughts turned automatically to Chaucer—and he decided upon tracing the etymology of *losenger* as 'liar' with a degree of unspoken self-reproach as a scholar who promised so much and delivered so little.

To return to his remarks on Chaucer in his 'Valedictory Address', Tolkien was correct when reminding his audience that the fourteenth-century poet was as much an inheritor as an inventor. Thus he was also the first English writer to feel his own 'anxiety of influence' generated by all the Classical and Continental predecessors ceaselessly named throughout his works, as well as the native English writers such as Langland and the *Gawain* Poet never even acknowledged. These would have included the Alliterative poets to whom Chaucer was indebted in his *Cleopatra* and Knight's Tale, as Tolkien had documented in his draft commentary.

Nietzsche had described the flashpoint for a certain kind of creativity:

Great men, like periods of greatness, are explosives storing up immense energy; historically and physiologically speaking, their precondition is always that they

---

[6] Charlotte Plimmer and Denis Plimmer, 'The Man Who Understands Hobbits', *London Daily Telegraph Magazine* (March 1968), 32.
[7] *Letters*, 18–19 (1937): 'I am under research-contract since last October, and not supposed to be indulging in exams or in "frivolities".'

be collected, accumulated, saved, and preserved for over a long period—that there be a long period without explosions. Once the tension in the mass becomes too great, then the most accidental stimulus is enough to bring 'genius', 'action', a great destiny into the world.[8]

This nicely describes Chaucer's long apprenticeship and late start as a poet, his first major poem, *The Book of the Duchess*, written when he was around 30. It also describes Tolkien's lengthy period of reading, researching, and drafting unpublished writings before the spark for an ignition came when Stanley Unwin requested a second hobbit book—and his great destiny as a writer of genius took shape. Already loaded with Old English, Old Norse, and Middle English texts as well as great authors such as Spenser, Shakespeare, and Milton, the jam-packedness of Tolkien's literary imagination included Chaucer abundantly in his storehouse of explosives. Isn't it altogether fitting, then, that *The Lord of the Rings* should begin with Gandalf's fireworks?

The Clarendon Chaucer may have found him in 1922, not the other way around, but once he accepted the commission, he came to recognize a writer with unexpected resemblances to himself in storytelling and craftsmanship, even in his biographical profile. As a Saxonist, he acknowledged the similarity between the scene of Bilbo stealing a gold goblet from Smaug's hoard and the episode of the nameless burglar stealing a goblet from the dragon's hoard in *Beowulf* (*Letters*, 31), but as with so many writers in the English tradition, his narrative artistry was steadily and inescapably Chaucerian. Sometimes Tolkien himself discovered these resemblances only after the fact, as when lecturing on the Pardoner's Tale in the 1950s, while other parallels emerge only now that we know about his career-long engagements with Chaucer. If readers have not previously detected *Troilus* and the *Canterbury Tales* in Tolkien's Middle-earth, it is because nobody was alert for noticing these ingredients.

Chaucer and Tolkien: Affinities

Perhaps the first thing to appreciate about Chaucer and Tolkien is that both men worked within institutions which kept records and preserved 'paper trails', Chaucer's life-records considerably more numerous than Shakespeare's documented life two centuries later, so that biographies can be written and careers outlined with some confidence. Chaucer's poetry also preserved a sense of his personality so that Tolkien's commentary on the *Parlement of Foules*, originally drafted for his Chaucer edition and later adapted for undergraduate lectures in 1948, provided

---

[8] Friedrich Nietzsche, *Twilight of the Idols or How to Philosophize with a Hammer*, trans. and intro. Duncan Large (Oxford: Oxford University Press, 1998), 69 (ix.44).

him with evidence for portraying the wily fourteenth-century author who denied knowledge of love except by way of his reading (line 8):

> This disclaimer is very Chaucerian. The comic contradiction (at first sight) of the preceding stanza is neatly turned into his favourite description of himself as a book-lover, and so serves to introduce a variation on the machinery of the *Book of the Duchess*, a book and the dreams begotten by it. Humorous self-consciousness, with a touch of vanity—he was well aware of it, Chaucer could mock his own foibles and retain them—prompted many jokes against himself, and disparagement of his own wit and appearance. This is all of a piece with his literary character: if ever the wings of his poetry bid fair to exalt him for a moment in strong flight, they were promptly withered by the flame of his own mockery, and he fell down into (intentional) bathos, a jesting Icarus. This is usually to the delight but sometimes despair of the reader.
> (Bodleian MS Tolkien A 38/2, fols. 98–9)

The passage hints at parallels between the lecturer and the subject of his lecture. First of all, Tolkien was a great disclaimer. Many of his statements about his own work took the form of denying some interpretation or influence. He insisted not to remember being bitten by a tarantula when a toddler in South Africa, denied that 'The Scouring of the Shire' reflected the sorry state of England in the late 1940s, and rejected any debt to Wagner's *Der Ring des Nibelungen*: 'Both rings are round, and there the resemblance ceases.'[9]

Particularly Tolkien was struck by Chaucer's personal library of sixty books— 'a big library for the time, if the number is to be taken as approximately true to reality'[10]—because he also was a book-lover often photographed in front of shelves lined with the scholarly volumes which provided resources for his fiction as well as research projects. Both authors drew upon prior literary traditions to make their own books into seamless continuations of those traditions.

Both writers also maintained the playful pretense that their books were simply translations of previous books. Just as Chaucer sustained the fraud that *Troilus* was translated from his made-up historian Lollius, Tolkien's Prologue to *The Lord of the Rings* claimed it as a redaction from the Red Book of Westmarch already subjected to scholarly editing with a great deal of annotation and many corrections, especially for the names and quotations. His Appendix F's final section 'On Translation' took this pretence to a comically pedantic extreme. Tolkien's other pseudo-scholarly introductions, notably his late 1920s Foreword to *Farmer Giles of Ham* and his 1962 Preface to *The Adventures of Tom Bombadil*, mocked academics (like himself) by mimicking them with the tongue-in-cheek humour long established as the hallmark of English satire since Chaucer. Tolkien's famous

---

[9] *Letters*, 306; see SH 3:1382–91 'Wagner'.
[10] Bodleian MS Tolkien A/39/2/1 on the *Legend* Prologue's 'sixty bokes olde and newe' (273).

declaration 'I am in fact a Hobbit' (*Letters*, 288–9) neatly aligns with Chaucer's talent for mocking his own foibles while proudly retaining them.

The main characters of their works were bookish, too. The narrator of the *Book of the Duchess* decided to read a romance when he could not fall asleep, and the dreamer of the *Parlement* ended his story as it began—with books: 'and thus to rede I nil not spare'. Bilbo leaves Bag End and heads to Rivendell in order to finish writing his book, and when Frodo wants to be ignored at the *Prancing Pony*, he announces that he is thinking about writing a book about history (*FR* I/9). This ruse turns out to be prophetic, foretelling how he would eventually write his own history of the War of the Ring.

Tolkien's 'Introduction on Language' in his Clarendon edition had identified a literary characteristic which would carry over from Chaucer into his own writings—sometimes cunningly derivative and sometimes self-consciously poking fun at using derivative material:

> In some ways Chaucer offers special difficulty in this respect. Rumours of his 'debt' to this or that foreign author for material or thought need make no one afraid to recognize him principally as an original author, not only using older literary material for his own purposes, but writing the contemporary English skilfully, wittily and with point, giving a felicity or a twist to common phrases as well as striking out ones of his own. And he was a man of whimsical humour, not always content to say and mean only one thing at a time. Yet he was not always able to show this, nor by any means always careful to try. He could use hackneyed tags or devices to fill a line or help his rhyme like any minstrel or popular story-teller. It is not always easy to be sure when he is the individual and when he is handing on the common stuff of the poetry of his day. Sometimes he does the latter, but is aware of it and smiling. (See Appendix I.)

Tolkien had his own debts to prior literary works but nonetheless considered himself, like Chaucer, an innovator using these earlier texts for fresh purposes. He wrote his fiction in contemporary English, having recognized the disadvantages of William Morris's archaic usages and reserved such vocabulary for figures such as Isildur and even to some extent Faramir. He elevated popular storytellers like Jules Verne and H. Rider Haggard to a respectable status alongside Homer and Shakespeare and must have smiled when passing along 'common stuff' from *Peter Pan* and *Wind in the Willows*. His friend Simonne d'Ardenne nicely described him in Chaucerian terms as 'a humorist caught at his own trick'.[11]

Though 'lively language' and 'comic conception' were evident in his earliest fiction,[12] Tolkien concentrated Chaucerian humour mostly in the hobbitry of

---

[11] D'Ardenne, 'The Man and the Scholar', 37.
[12] Christopher's 'Foreword' to his father's *Book of Lost Tales, Part I*, p. xviii, contrasts its humour with the later gravity of *The Silmarillion*.

Bilbo and his fellow citizens of the Shire. 'I love the vulgar and simple as dearly as the noble', he later reflected, and he admitted that the *Silmarillion* suffered from the absence of these elements because there was 'little fun or earthiness but mostly grief and disaster' (*Letters*, 232, 303). He acknowledged his odd traits such as ornamental waistcoats and a simple sense of the comical (*Letters*, 288–9), and he cultivated Chaucerian eccentricity with other donnish quirks such as the Gallophobia that prompted him to launch tirades against French cooking. All of these self-confessed oddities recall the medieval poet who 'prompted many jokes against himself'. Laughter when all hope was lost may have belonged to the heroic North, but the good humour steadily displayed by hobbits took its inspiration from the Chaucerian legacy.

Tolkien's description of *The Book of the Duchess* as 'a book and the dreams begotten by it' points to Chaucer's insomnia and the late-night reading which inspired his writings. The poet was an extremely busy public man whose career included service in royal households, diplomatic missions abroad, a twelve-year tenure as Controller of the Wool Customs, and a briefer period as Keeper of the King's Works. These daytime duties left him with only his evenings for literary work. He was perhaps one of those men who need only a few hours of sleep, and this late-night diligence must have seemed so strange to onlookers that he made the point of complaining of 'defaute of slepe' as if a clichéd symptom of love-sickness in *The Book of the Duchess*. Tolkien took note: 'Chaucer begins by bewailing that he cannot sleep. This leads naturally to the bedside book, convenient machinery for introducing stories.'[13] Chaucer's reputation for nighttime reading must have been fairly well known because Geffrey, the self-named dreamer in *The House of Fame*, was chided for leaving his office register only to go home and pore over another book (653–8).

D'Ardenne connected this specific passage from Chaucer's dream-vision with what she had witnessed about Tolkien at 20 Northmoor Road: 'Although I stayed at his house frequently, I never knew when he got any sleep at night.'[14] With his own sense of hours stolen guiltily from professional duties, Tolkien's habits of late-night writing are better documented than Chaucer's. 'I go to bed late and get up late', he wrote of himself, explaining how he completed work only 'by sitting up all hours' (*Letters*, 83). His daughter Priscilla offered one reason why: 'In order to take part in family life as he did and be so available to our needs and interests he often had to work far into the night when the household was quiet' (SH 2:229). C. S. Lewis went so far as to attribute these late nights to his friend's Johnsonian horror of going to bed.[15] Whatever the case, Carpenter pictured what must have

---

[13] Bodleian MS Tolkien A 39/2/1, fol. 14.   [14] D'Ardenne, 'The Man and the Scholar', 36.
[15] Lewis's anonymous *Times* obituary was reprinted in Salu and Farrell, eds., *Tolkien, Scholar and Storyteller*, 15. Some doubt has been raised recently about Lewis's authorship, but he used the same phraseology about Johnson's horror of annihilation in *Surprised by Joy*, 117.

been a familiar scene with Tolkien 'at his desk until half past one, or two o'clock, or perhaps even later, with only the scratching of his pen to disturb the silence'.[16] If *The Hobbit* began as a bedtime story for his boys, all his narrative writings were in a sense bedtime stories for himself.

Early in his career, Tolkien said that he could not bear a 'compartmented life' which would keep his friends and wife apart,[17] but this partition did eventually divide family life from university life throughout his Oxford years. Some five centuries earlier, Chaucer seems to have accepted starker divisions. We suspect his marriage to Philippa Roet was a love-match because she was not a rich heiress. Her service to Edward III's queen brought advantages, to be sure, but separate courtly careers meant that husband and wife lived apart for much of their married life, Geoffrey mostly in London and Philippa wherever the royal household went, at the end of her life in Lincolnshire. They had at least one son Thomas who made a brilliant career, perhaps another son Lewis to whom the *Astrolabe* was addressed, and maybe even a daughter Elizabeth who became a nun. Termination of Philippa's annuity payments in 1387 indicates that she had died after some twenty-one years of marriage. Her husband seems never to have remarried.[18]

Operating apart from his wife during most of their married life, Chaucer became a man of cronies as Tolkien himself was memorably described.[19] His poetry contains some of their names, confirmed by documents assembled in *Chaucer Life-Records*, as indication of the extent to which these courtiers and men in royal service valued poetry.[20] Sir Lewis Clifford brought Chaucer's translation of the *Roman de la Rose* to the attention of the French poet Eustache Deschamps. Sir John Clanvowe quoted the Knight's Tale in his Chaucerian imitation *The Boke of Cupide, God of Loue*.[21] Occasional poems were addressed to Sir Peter Bukton and Sir Philip de la Vache. Famed as the venue for the General Prologue, the Tabard Inn may actually have served as a precursor to Tolkien's *Eagle and Child* where this literary circle assembled to drink, talk, and share work-in-progress such as the *Canterbury Tales*. Derek Pearsall has imagined this clubbable, men-only gathering where Chaucer could try out his latest stuff with

---

[16] *Biography*, 126. Rateliff, *Story of The Hobbit*, p. xxi, adjusts this view with backing from Christopher: 'almost all his creative writing was done not in term-time but during his too-brief vacations between academic semesters.'

[17] Garth, *Tolkien and the Great War*, 100, quotes Tolkien's words to his schoolfriend Christopher Wiseman.

[18] *Chaucer Life-Records*, 'Philippa Chaucer, Wife of Geoffrey Chaucer', 67–93, and 'Chaucer's Children', 541–6.

[19] C. S. Lewis in Salu and Farrell, eds., *Tolkien, Scholar and Storyteller*, 15.

[20] Derek Pearsall, *Life of Geoffrey Chaucer: A Critical Biography* (Oxford: Blackwell, 1992), 'The "Chaucer Circle"', 181–5.

[21] John M. Bowers, 'Three Readings of The Knight's Tale: Sir John Clanvowe, Geoffrey Chaucer, and James I of Scotland', *Journal of Medieval and Early Modern Studies* 34 (2004), 279–307.

a live audience.[22] The gathering is easy enough to picture as a kind of fourteenth-century Inklings.

Chaucer found a particular friend in John Gower much as Tolkien did in C. S. Lewis. The relationships between their literary works can be explained only if the two poets were in constant contact, passing their manuscripts back and forth, and commenting on what they found good, what not.[23] Gower held Chaucer's power of attorney when he travelled abroad and later received commendation as 'moral Gower' at the end of *Troilus*. Tolkien's diary made explicit a bond with Jack Lewis that can only be guessed for their fourteenth-century forerunners: 'Friendship with Lewis compensates for much, and besides giving constant pleasure and comfort has done me much good from the contact with a man at once honest, brave, intellectual—a scholar, a poet, and a philosopher' (*Biography*, 152). Later this friendship cooled, as the relationship also appears to have chilled between the two medieval poets, Gower dropping his reference to Chaucer from the second version of his *Confessio Amantis* and Chaucer mocking Gower in his Prologue to the Man of Law's Tale. Nonetheless Tolkien gave Treebeard the booming voice of Lewis in *The Two Towers* (*Biography*, 198), and Lewis modelled the philologist Elwin Ransom after Tolkien in his Space Trilogy and envisaged him as the ideal companion in his chapter 'Friendship' in *The Four Loves*.

Each author was identified with the city where he spent most of his life, Chaucer in London and Tolkien in Oxford. Though Chaucer travelled to France, Spain, and Italy, he went always on diplomatic missions, never apparently for any personal reason, not even as the sort of pilgrim whose role he enacted in the *Canterbury Tales*. He inherited his father's house on Thames Street in London's Vintry Ward and later was given rent-free chambers in Aldgate during his tenure as Controller of the Wool Custom. When he removed to Kent, he probably went no farther than Greenwich. This was a quiet retirement from the tumult of London and the royal court, something like Tolkien's escape to Bournemouth during his retirement years. Chaucer's last address was a garden house in the precincts of Westminster Abbey, near where he had spent so much of his professional career, in a way presaging Tolkien's return after his wife's death to college life at 21 Merton Street.

For his part, Tolkien admitted, 'I do not travel much' (*Biography*, 180) and showed little of the itch for visiting distant places that infects so many academics. Even Chaucer's threadbare Clerk of Oxford had journeyed to Padua. If Tolkien travelled to Scotland or Ireland, he typically went to lecture or serve as an outside examiner. Oxford was home. He spent his undergraduate years there, he returned

---

[22] Derek Pearsall, 'The *Canterbury Tales* and London Club Culture', in *Chaucer and the City*, ed. Ardis Butterfield (Cambridge: D. S. Brewer, 2006), 95–108.
[23] Fisher, *John Gower*, 32–3.

there for employment at the *Oxford English Dictionary*, and he returned again for the remainder of his university career, first for a professorship attached to Pembroke College and then for another at Merton. After a few years of retirement on the southern coast, mostly for his wife's sake, he returned to Oxford with his last settled address in a Merton College flat. We do not know if Chaucer enjoyed the abbey garden, but Tolkien wrote beautifully about his: 'The great bank in the Fellows' Garden looks like the foreground of a pre-Raphaelite picture.'[24]

Each author visited the other's city. Chaucer the Londoner had a detailed knowledge of Oxford and knew several prominent Oxonians, though it is unlikely he ever studied there. Royal business took him north of Oxford to Woodstock– where the grey-stone 'Chaucer's House' is said to have belonged to his son—and indeed Thomas Chaucer established himself fifteen miles to the south-east of Oxford at his country manor in Ewelme. (Tolkien took time in a lecture to trace Ewelme's name back to the Old English *ǽ-welm* or 'out-gush' from the name of a local spring.[25]) His Miller's Tale was set in the up-scale suburb of Osney made prosperous by the nearby Augustinian abbey; Chaucer knew that the carpenter's house was close enough for Nicholas to hear the friars singing in their chancel. Osney was also where Richard II confirmed Chaucer's election to parliament in 1386.

Elsewhere Chaucer showed real familiarity with the university town and specifically Merton College's scholars. He commended *Troilus* to 'philosophical Strode', almost certainly the Ralph Strode who was a Fellow of Merton before becoming Common Sergeant of the City of London; Strode lived over Aldersgate during the same period when Chaucer had his room at Aldgate. Bishop Thomas Bradwardine, another Mertonian, was cited as an authority on predestination in the Nun's Priest's Tale. Chaucer's *Treatise on the Astrolabe* provided calculations after the latitude of Oxford, and these calculations match an instrument still on display upstairs in Merton's old library. His authorship of the *Equatorie of Planetis* is argued partly by its connection with a Latin treatise by Simon Bredon of Merton College. The range of the poet's learned references matches closely the roster of Merton Library's books which Tolkien's student J. A. W. Bennett detailed in *Chaucer at Oxford and at Cambridge*.[26] Not that Chaucer had the privilege of reading in Merton's library, fascinated though he was with history, philosophy, and science, but conversations with Strode and other Oxford friends afforded him enough second-hand knowledge to make him sound conversant with these scholarly works. Oxford men also knew something of Chaucer. Report of the poet's

---

[24] *Letters*, 417. John Gardner, *The Life and Times of Chaucer* (New York: Knopf, 1977), 309–14, concocted a picture of the elderly poet spying on young lovers in the abbey garden.
[25] Tolkien: *Beowulf: A Translation and Commentary*, 187.
[26] Bennett, 'Men of Merton', 58–85, with the book-list, 67–8. See SH 2:119–20 'Bennett'.

deathbed repentance came from Dr Thomas Gascoigne, Chancellor of the University in the fifteenth century.

While the poet's knowledge of Oxford was extensive, his sense of Cambridge was much vaguer. The *Life-Records* never place him there; for example, Chaucer was no longer a knight of the shire when parliament convened there in 1388. Specialists have trouble identifying his reference to Soler Hall in the Reeve's Tale— maybe King's Hall, though the poet himself seemed foggy—and terms like *warden* and *manciple* were not recorded at Cambridge but more likely transposed from Oxford. He set his fabliau outside the university town and yet invoked little of the local colour of Trumpington, perhaps knowing about its mill only by report. Sir Roger de Trumpington had served with him in the royal household. Since Merton College owned five properties in Cambridge, including Grantchester near Trumpington, Chaucer may have known about these places from friends at Oxford, not Cambridge.[27]

Tolkien sometimes went to London, though not as often as George Gordon, C. S. Lewis, and other Oxford colleagues, and always for very specific purposes (SH 2:704–5). In younger days, he travelled there as a school cadet for the coronation of George V, and he went again for a last reunion with his three closest schoolmates in 1914. In later years, he delivered his *Beowulf* lecture at Burlington House, he saw his publisher Sir Stanley Unwin on special occasions, he attended a luncheon when getting the International Fantasy Award in 1957, and he received his CBE at Buckingham Palace in 1972. Though London was an easy commute by rail—and Tolkien did travel to Cambridge for professional reasons such as studying his manuscript of the *Ancrene Wisse*—he did not spend nearly as much research time at London's British Museum as one would expect, relying instead upon facsimiles of manuscripts such as the one containing *Pearl* and *Gawain*.[28]

Imagining escapes from the filth and stench of London, Chaucer anticipated Tolkien's longing for a countryside free of urban pollution. 'Quantities of dung and other ordure, both from the droppings and entrails of beasts slaughtered, and other filth, are thrown and cast into ditches, rivers, and other waters,' Henry Knighton's fourteenth-century *Chronicle* reported, 'so that the air thereof is greatly polluted and infected, and many lethal maladies and other diseases come from one day to another both upon the inhabitants.'[29] Obviously Virginia Woolf's description of an idyllic realm during Chaucer's lifetime held true only beyond the city walls: 'His eyes rested on a virgin land, all unbroken grass and wood except for the small towns and an occasional castle in the building. No villa roofs peered

---

[27] Bennett, *Chaucer at Oxford and at Cambridge*, 'Appendix C: Merton and Cambridge', 124–5.

[28] *Pearl, Cleanness, Patience, and Sir Gawain: Reproduced in Facsimile from the Unique MS. Cotton Nero A.x in the British Museum*, intro. I. Gollancz, EETS o.s. 162, 1923.

[29] *Knighton's Chronicle, 1337–1396*, ed. and trans. G. H. Martin (Oxford: Clarendon Press, 1995), 522–5.

through Kentish tree-tops; no factory chimney smoked on the hillside.'[30] It is little wonder, then, that the poet neglected London as a setting for his stories except for the unfinished Cook's Tale and the Canon's Yeoman's Tale, the latter dwelling upon the smoke and stink from burning chemicals.[31] His poems pictured instead the idealized outdoors like the deer park in *The Book of the Duchess*, the garden in *The Parlement of Foules*, and the daisy-strewn countryside in the Prologue to *The Legend of Good Women*.

Their love for England's green and pleasant land was allied with a mutual dislike for the French. Tolkien forever judged the Norman Conquest as a catastrophe for imposing French rule and French language on the English peoples. Éomer's defiant statement about the Riddermark's freedom from foreign dominion expressed a linguistic as well as political stance (*TT* III/2). In 1913 Tolkien was disgusted by vulgar Parisian behavior like spitting in the street, and his French experience worsened when accompanying two Mexican students to Brittany where their aunt was killed by a car. Things turned far more harrowing with trench warfare during his three months at the Battle of the Somme. John Garth's *Tolkien and the Great War* makes clear how combat in France permanently coloured his emotional life and worked its way into his fiction with grim images like the Dead Marshes.

Chaucer as a young man saw the ugly side of warfare, too, when he joined the ill-fated Normandy Campaign of 1359–60. He was taken prisoner, probably while doing something as unheroic as collecting fodder for horses, and he was held hostage for some weeks until ransomed. It is hard to gauge the traumatic aftermath of this experience, though we know the winter weather was terrible, sickness and starvation were commonplace, and prisoners were routinely mistreated while under constant threat of execution if ransom money was not forthcoming. Chaucer wrote about warfare in the Knight's Tale and *Troilus*, but he never described actual battles or romanticized chivalric violence, unlike contemporary poets such as the author of the *Alliterative Morte Arthure*.[32]

Tolkien, with his traumatic memories of the Somme, also slighted battle sequences more than readers tend to remember. Bilbo was knocked unconscious and missed much of the Battle of the Five Armies; Frodo was stabbed by the Morgol blade and lost consciousness during the fight on Weathertop; and Pippin missed the heat of battle at the Black Gate as he too blacked out, hearing only, 'The Eagles are coming!' The opening page of *The Two Towers* does not show Boromir's fight with the Orcs, only the aftermath with the warrior pierced by arrows. Faramir's rearguard action in retreat from the Rammas is seen mostly

---

[30] Woolf, 'The Pastons and Chaucer', 12.
[31] Wallace, *Chaucerian Polity*, 'Absent City', 156–81.
[32] J. A. Burrow, *Ricardian Poetry: Chaucer, Gower, Langland and the 'Gawain' Poet* (London: Routledge & Kegan Paul, 1971), 93–102, and Pearsall, *Life of Geoffrey Chaucer*, 40–6.

from a distance by spectators atop the walls of Minis Tirith. Not until he is brought back wounded into the city is he described close up, much as Troilus is seen only returning from battle with helmet shattered, shield bristling with arrows, and horse bleeding. On the Pelennor Fields, the charge of the Rohirrim focused mostly on running horses and singing warriors rather than the clash of fighting men. Peter Jackson's films needed to expand these battle scenes to show Orcs firing arrows at the horsemen and Théoden's cavalry trampling Sauron's infantry. Meanwhile Frodo's quest took him on a separate path so that he missed the siege of Helm's Deep, the assault on Isengard, the attack on Minas Tirith, and the muster of troops before the Black Gate.

The best evidence of Chaucer's lifelong hostility to the French was his decision to write exclusively in English.[33] He certainly spoke French at the court and the customhouse, probably even in the bedroom with his Hainault wife, but he charted a different career from his friend John Gower who wrote his *Mirour de l'Omme* and *Cinkante Ballades* in the language.[34] Even the *Gawain* Poet, it would seem, read more widely among French romances.[35] If Tolkien avoided French-derived vocabulary, Chaucer took a different tactic. He aggressively assimilated French words into his lexicon while translating French sources and appropriating French models, all in the process of domesticating these foreign elements to create a distinctively English literature.

When Tolkien admitted to his publisher in 1938 that he found it only too easy to write introductory chapters (*Letters*, 29), he disclosed another trait shared with his fourteenth-century predecessor. Chaucer may have penned one of the most famous openings in English literature—'Whan that Aprille with his shoures sote'—but he was notorious for not finishing his works. This tendency began early with only the first 1,750 lines translated for his *Romaunt of the Rose*, and it persisted until the end of his career with his incomplete *Canterbury Tales* surviving in ten disordered fragments. This ambitious work itself contained the unfinished instalments of the Cook's Tale, Sir Thopas, the Monk's Tale, and the Squire's Tale.[36] Even the highly accomplished General Prologue shows loose ends with its missing portraits of the Second Nun and the Nun's Priest. Chaucer's death cannot be blamed because he had also left unfinished earlier works such as *The House of Fame*, *Anelida and Arcite*, *A Treatise on the Astrolabe*, and *The Legend of Good*

---

[33] John M. Bowers, 'Chaucer after Retters: The Wartime Origins of English Literature', in *Inscribing the Hundred Years' War in French and English Cultures*, ed. Denise Baker (Albany: State University of New York Press, 2000), 91–125.

[34] R. F. Yeager, 'John Gower's French', in *Companion to Gower*, 137–51.

[35] Ad Putter, *'Sir Gawain and the Green Knight' and French Arthurian Romance* (Oxford: Clarendon, 1995).

[36] The Squire's sprawling romance breaks off just as he intends to tell about the brother–sister incest of Cambalo and Canacee; Tolkien was not so shy about brother–sister incest in his accounts of Kullervo and Túrin; see Shippey, *Road to Middle-earth*, 261–3.

Women. Even his *Boece* might be considered unfinished if Chaucer perhaps meant to return and versify the metrical passages which he had rendered as prose.

For Tolkien, this tendency to leave works unfinished started with his early *Story of Kullervo*,[37] and it continued over the decades with a multitude of fragments, revisions, second and third drafts, and new beginnings. His *legendarium*, always changing and ramifying, was only posthumously assembled in *The Silmarillion* and *The History of Middle-earth*.[38] Even the works which were eventually published had reached precarious stopping-points. Lewis suggested *The Hobbit* was unfinished or only messily finished when he read it in January 1933.[39] Christopher recalled this disappointing state of affairs: 'The ending chapters were rather roughly done and not typed out at all.'

Part typescript and part handwritten draft, the manuscript of *The Hobbit* did not often leave Tolkien's study where it might have remained, unrevised and unpublished, if not for the insistence of friends that he persevere to its completion.[40] 'Usually I compose only with great difficulty and endless rewriting,' he wrote to Stanley Unwin in 1945 about troubles with his hobbit sequel: 'I made an effort last year to finish it and failed' (*Letters*, 113). Looking back in 1957, he was astonished at bringing *The Lord of the Rings* to conclusion at all: 'A notorious beginner of enterprises and non-finisher, partly through lack of time, partly through lack of single-minded concentration, I still wonder how and why I managed to peg away at this thing year after year, often under real difficulties, and bring it to a conclusion' (*Letters*, 257).

On those happy occasions when Chaucer did finish a literary undertaking, he sometimes had difficulty at achieving real closure for it. *Troilus* ends with fifteen stanzas in which seven or eight separate conclusions can be identified, amounting to what Donaldson famously described as 'a kind of nervous breakdown in poetry'.[41] The ending of the Clerk's Tale also meanders from one stanza to the next before adding six more under the rubric 'L'Envoy de Chaucer'. In the Parson's Prologue, the final instalment for the Canterbury journey left a vague image of the narrator as a *shadwe* cast by the setting sun. (Tolkien abhorred shadows as an absence of real life: the Ringwraiths have become shadows of men

---

[37] J. R. R. Tolkien, *The Story of Kullervo*, ed. Verlyn Flieger (Boston and New York: Houghton Mifflin Harcourt, 2016).

[38] See three chapters in *Tolkien's 'Legendarium'*, ed. Flieger and Hostetter: Wayne G. Hammond, '"A Continuing and Evolving Creation": Distractions in the Later History of Middle-earth', 19–29; Charles E. Noad, 'On the Construction of "The Silmarillion"', 31–68; and David Bratman, 'The Literary Value of *The History of Middle-earth*', 69–91.

[39] *They Stand Together*, 449: 'Whether it is really *good* (I think it is until the end) is of course another question.' Rateliff, *Story of The Hobbit*, p. xvi, believes that Lewis read a completed draft; SH 2:511–19 'Dates of Origin and Completion' traces the novel's complicated history.

[40] Rateliff, *Story of the Hobbit*, pp. ix–xx, largely corrects Carpenter, *Biography*, 183–4, based on his study of Marquette University manuscripts.

[41] Donaldson, *Speaking of Chaucer*, 91.

and Mordor is where the shadows are.⁴²) In a sense his *Canterbury Tales* also fades into shadow as the Host voices one of the most poignant lines in English literature—'But hasteth yow; the sonne wole adoun.' Thereafter the Parson dismisses storytelling and rejects poetry itself as the physical world darkens. It is not even clear whether the *Tales* were meant to end here—or with the Parson's Tale which is really a treatise on penance—or with Chaucer's Retraction—or with no ending at all, since the pilgrims never return to the Tabard Inn for the Host's judgement of the prize-winning tale.

Tolkien also had difficulty providing closure for *The Lord of the Rings*. The story could have ended with the destruction of the Ring in Mount Doom and the fall of Sauron's Dark Tower—or with the marriage of Aragorn and Arwen and restoration of monarchy in Gondor—or with the arrival of the four hobbits back home in the Shire. Even when Sam returns from the Grey Havens after seeing Frodo off, Tolkien still could not let loose of his story. He wrote two versions of an 'Epilogue' set years later when Samwise reads their adventures one more time to his children.⁴³ Though this coda was cancelled, Tolkien's Appendices could not resist including 'Later Events Concerning the Members of the Fellowship of the Ring' which continued the saga until all the main characters were either dead or departed over the sea to the Undying Lands. Elijah Wood (Frodo in the films) recalls how Jack Nicholson made an early exit from the Hollywood premiere of *The Return of the King* and later at a party explained why: 'Too many endings, kid—too many endings!'

These excesses suggest Tolkien's tendency to disregard his audience's needs and limitations, as many Oxford undergraduates testified after sitting confusedly through his lectures, unable to hear or follow his text references. Surely *The Hobbit* makes demands beyond the capabilities of 'children between the ages of 5 and 9', as young Rayner Unwin reckoned in his reader's report. Later in *The Lord of the Rings*, his 'Prologue: Concerning Hobbits' challenged the audience's patience as the author himself acknowledged after the fact—'I have perhaps overweighted Part I too much with attempts to depict the setting and historical background' (*Letters*, 185)—and these demands upon the reader's commitment would continue over the next 1,100-some pages until reaching the final 'Note on three names: *Hobbit, Gamgee*, and *Brandywine*'. To take one famous example of neglecting his reader's basic needs, Gandalf exclaims when battling the Balrog that he is 'wielder of the flame of Anor' and that 'the flame of Udûn' cannot pass (II/5). What is Anor? What is Udûn? Tolkien did not explain. Therefore he may not have pretended when admitting to Sisam as late as 1931 that he felt 'foggy' about the

---

⁴² Shippey, *Road to Middle-earth*, 146–8.
⁴³ J. R. R. Tolkien, *The History of the Lord of the Rings, Part Four: The End of the Third Age*, ed. Christopher Tolkien (Boston and New York: Houghton Mifflin, 1992), 114–35; see *Letters*, 179 on Tolkien's decision to drop the 'universally condemned' epilogue: 'One must stop somewhere.'

audience of their Clarendon Chaucer. This edition had already occupied him for almost a decade, but the length and technical details of his annotations gave little indication that he ever fully understood the needs of student readers.

Chaucer specialists do not often admit it, but their author also made unrealistic demands upon his audience by including proper names and obscure allusions which scholars are still trying to explicate after six centuries. C. S. Lewis noted that Chaucer took the straightforward love-story from Boccaccio's *Filostrato* and loaded it up with historical and mythological allusions.[44] Even Chaucer's sophisticated London audience would have found these references challenging if not altogether baffling. To take only one example, Boccaccio started by addressing his lady-love, but Chaucer instead invoked *Thesiphone*. This was the Fury whose proper name was probably gleaned from Statius, much to the confusion of early copyists who variously miswrote it as *Simphone*, *Ciphon*, and *Cyphome*.[45] Tolkien believed that the General Prologue had been rendered obscure by the passage of time, but many of Chaucer's learned references were surely obscure at the moment of their creation. One has only to review the list of the Physician's medical authorities: Esculapius, Deyscorides, Rufus, Ypocras, Haly, Galyen, Serapion, Razis, Avycen, Averrois, Damascien, Constantyn, Bernard, Gatesden, and Gilbertyn (I, 429–34). Did anyone besides Ralph Strode know that Gadesden had been a Merton College fellow who authored the *Rosa Anglica*? Even modern commentators cannot make positive identification of names like Serapion. Tolkien had complained that 'copyists will always stumble when faced with unfamiliar words', and thus the Physician's simpler reference to Rufus appeared in manuscripts variously as *Ruphus*, *Rusus*, *Risus*, *Rufijs*, and *Platearius*. If professional scribes stumbled over these strange-looking names, how much more confounded were the poet's courtly readers? Nor were the copyists always at fault, as Tolkien's 'Introduction on Language' remarked about foreign and Classical names distorted for convenience: 'It is in fact just where we should not expect it, in these bookish elements, that freedom and quaintness can be found, and not in the native English.' (See Appendix I, note 2.)

Always with an eye to posterity, Chaucer made demands which would absolutely require the emergence of better informed, more inquisitive readers over later centuries. By doing so, he set an example for Tolkien to gamble that future readers would rise to his own challenges. Few if any of his early readers could have known that *Aiya Eärendil Elenion Ancalima* was a plea in an Elvish language for help from the sky-mariner Eärendil; now everyone knows from the scholarly enterprises of Carpenter and Shippey (and others) that it comes from the line

---

[44] Lewis, 'What Chaucer Really Did to *Il Filostrato*', 59–65, assumed that the poet would not have made these references if his readers were unable to understand and appreciate them.

[45] B. A. Windeatt's exemplary edition of Geoffrey Chaucer, *Troilus and Criseyde* (London and New York: Longman, 1984), 84–5, records the perplexities of the scribes.

Éala Éarendel engla beorhtast which first caught the young Tolkien's attention when studying the Old English poem *Christ I*.[46] As annotator of Chaucer's works during the 1920s, Tolkien had already internalized these high expectations for an audience committed to plumbing the depths of an author's writings, including eventually his own.

Tolkien oversaw the publication and revisions of The Hobbit and The Lord of the Rings, but he was not so scrupulous about his lesser works, some scattered in out-of-the-way journals and others never published at all, just crammed into drawers and files. His fourteenth-century predecessor had a similar attitude toward publication (as it was understood in a manuscript culture) by taking care primarily for his major works but letting others fend for themselves. His lyric *Adam Scriveyn* indicates commissioning a professional copy of *Troilus and Criseyde* during his lifetime, thus providing at least one first-rate exemplar for luxury editions like the Corpus Christi manuscript produced during the decade after his death. His dream-visions and minor poems, on the other hand, especially unfinished ones such as *The House of Fame* and *Anelida and Arcite*, followed more haphazard paths, finding their ways into less attractive, less carefully supervised collections like the Fairfax manuscript, often in the company of works by Chaucerian imitators like John Lydgate, with some confusion over who had authored what.

Other comparisons between the two writers can be multiplied. Tolkien was not particularly musical despite the fact that the family once manufactured pianos, and he admitted his youthful failure at learning the fiddle: 'I love music, but have no aptitude for it.'[47] The music of the Ainur may have created Arda for the children of Ilúvatar, but his friend Christopher Wiseman believed that Tolkien himself was tone-deaf. He enjoyed listening to his wife perform at the piano and was delighted when Donald Swann composed *The Road Goes Ever On: A Song Cycle*, but he himself was no tunesmith and could not set to music any of the poems embedded in his stories. 'Words took the place of music for him', Carpenter wrote by way of apology (*Biography*, 30), recalling Tolkien's own remark that his musical impulse had been 'transformed into linguistic terms' (*Letters*, 350). Chaucer, too, showed no talent for music, even though singing and flute-playing figured among his Squire's courtly accomplishments. Unlike his great French predecessor Guillaume de Machaut, who was a major composer as well as a poet, Chaucer did not produce lyrics meant for singing to instrumental accompaniment. When he did insert a roundel at the end of *The Parlement of Foules*, he claimed credit for the words only, not the melody—'The note, I trowe, imaked was

---

[46] *Biography*, 72, 79; Shippey, *Road to Middle-earth*, 244–7. Only years later did Tolkien explain to a curious reader that *Aiya Eärendil Elenion Ancalima* was the Quenya translation of the Old English (*Letters*, 385).

[47] *Letters*, 173; see SH 2:815–21 'Music'.

in Fraunce'—and even Tolkien spotted Chaucer's confusion over fitting these lines to music.[48] One likely reason Chaucer fashioned himself chiefly as a narrative poet was because he lacked the musical abilities required of a lyric poet.

One final resemblance. Both writers convey an autumnal sense of belatedness as heirs of a long procession of forerunners. When Chaucer tells his *Troilus* to kiss the footsteps of Virgil, Ovid, Homer, Lucan and Statius, the humble gesture grew out of an awareness that his English-language epic lacked the literary prestige and linguistic staying-power of Latin. Tolkien's elegiac conclusion to his *Beowulf* lecture, written after finishing *The Hobbit*, expressed his sense of the belatedness of the heroic poem, not primitive but 'a late one, using the materials (then still plentiful) preserved from a day already changing and passing' (*Essays*, 33). This remark applies equally to his own position both historically and personally. *The Lord of the Rings*, written largely during his fifties, bespeaks the late style of other great artists who looked back at their own early works, but only dimly forward to future developments, in Tolkien's case the explosive growth of the fantasy genre.[49] With this sense of living in some historical aftermath, he also embodied the pessimism of the philologist who surveyed ancient achievements and saw only the long defeat. *Leaf by Niggle* expressed this gloom in its ending where only a single leaf from the artist's masterpiece was framed and hung in the Town Museum: 'But eventually the Museum was burnt down, and the leaf, and Niggle, were entirely forgotten in his old country.'[50] Tolkien's late poems such as *The Last Ship* convey something like the sombre finality of Chaucer's *Retraction*. Even as an academic, Tolkien would have felt this belatedness as the heir of the nineteenth century's pioneering scholarship so powerfully represented by Skeat.

But literature also offered its consolations, as both writers knew from reading Boethius, and much of this joy arose from beautiful language as well as the glories of nature which language captured and preserved. Adapted from his long-idle Clarendon edition, Tolkien's 1948 lecture on *The Parlement of Foules* looked down into the deep well of the past and saw Chaucer's image as an Oxford philologist looking back:

> Chaucer, indeed, would (I think) have liked our English School and have been an enthusiastic member of it on all its ends (linguistic and literary). He had a humour that could keep learning in its place (and keep the scholar there too!); and yet he liked learning, and especially learning about literature and its technique

---

[48] Bodleian MS Tolkien A 13/2, fol. 124 on the roundel's French title *Qui bien aime a tard oublie*: 'the tune cannot have got its name from a French poem beginning with this line, for the French line is octosyllabic, the roundel decasyllabic.'

[49] Margaret Hiley, '*Lord of the Rings* and "Late Style": Tolkien, Adorno, and Said', in *Tolkien and Modernity*, ed. Thomas Honegger and Frank Weinreich (Zurich and Jena: Walking Tree Publishers, 2006), 53–73.

[50] Tolkien, *Poems and Stories*, 219.

and indeed about *language*. He was in fact, within his limits, a thoroughly *literary* man. Both an original poet with the impulse to make things and a living man with an eye for the life of his time—not only the people, but also the trees and flowers; he took sustenance from books and from accumulated literary experience.

(Bodleian MS Tolkien A 38/2, fol. 96)

Tolkien had a tendency to identify with early authors, even with nameless ones like the *Beowulf* Poet, because their anonymity became blank screens upon which he could project his own literary personality.[51] This sense of fellow-feeling then induced confidence that he knew what these poets were thinking and what they meant to say. His identification with the better-documented Chaucer was already heralded by his title 'Chaucer as a Philologist'. Since Tolkien understood himself as 'primarily a scientific philologist' (*Letters*, 345), he could hardly help picturing Chaucer as one, too. Aptly enough the *OED* attributes to Chaucer the earliest attestation of the word *philology* in his Merchant's Tale.

The Chaucerian humour which keeps erudition in its place is perhaps best represented in Tolkien's *Farmer Giles of Ham*, his late 1920s mock-medieval parody set in the same world as the *Canterbury Tales* with its burlesque of characters and literary conventions. The serious is made silly in the manner of Chaucer's own *Sir Thopas*, and the fabliau-like ridicule of knighthood recalls the Miller's takedown of the Knight. Like the decadence of Gondor bemoaned by Faramir, the knights of King Augustus have lost the true spirit of chivalry in their obsession with outward trappings. On the other hand, Tolkien's parson looks like a composite of Chaucer's hardworking Parson and his book-loving Clerk of Oxford. He also includes a blacksmith out of the Miller's Tale and a miller out of the Reeve's Tale. The story's bourgeois realism looks through a medieval lens at the Edwardian practicality of his hobbits. Though Tolkien set aside *The New Shadow* as a dark, depressing sequel to *The Lord of the Rings*,[52] his *Farmer Giles* represents life-or-death seriousness giving way to Chaucerian humour. Yet for all the work's spoofing, Tolkien felt the weight of 'accumulated literary experience' in the cyclical pattern of one king falling upon Fortune's Wheel while another rose up.[53] The Knight's Tale had been Chaucer's examination of this twofold operation of worldly renown with Arcite falling while Palamon rose, and his Monk's Tale transmitted from Boethius and Boccaccio this *de casibus* pattern to later English writers such as Shakespeare. Tolkien knew this pattern specifically from editing the Monk's tragedy of Count Ugolino which Chaucer himself had lifted from Dante's *Inferno*.

---

[51] Shippey, 'Tolkien and the *Beowulf*-Poet' and 'Tolkien and the *Gawain*-Poet', in *Roots and Branches*, 1–18 and 61–77.
[52] Tolkien, *Peoples of Middle-earth*, 409–21; see SH 3:848–9.
[53] Chance Nitzsche, '*Farmer Giles of Ham*: the Late Medieval English King', in *Tolkien's Art*, 85–90; see SH 2:398–405.

Chaucer in the Soup

Tolkien's 'On Fairy-Stories' offers the memorable comparison of a literary work to a soup simmered with various bones: 'By "the soup" I mean the story as it is served up by its author or teller, and by "the bones" its sources or material—even when (by rare luck) those can be with certainty discovered.'[54] Tolkien's own stories require this source-hunting because he steadily assimilated elements from ancient works which he had read, taught, translated, and written about, fitting and repurposing them with the same skill that he admired in the *Gawain* Poet as 'a man capable of weaving elements taken from diverse sources into a texture of his own' (*Gawain*, trans., 4). Discovery of the Clarendon Chaucer alerts us to a whole new collection of ingredients previously unrecognized in Tolkien's great Cauldron of Story.

Sometimes these are quite trivial. For example his commentary remarked about Chaucer's General Prologue—'The pilgrimage sets out on a fine April day and fades away'—and thereafter Bilbo and his companions set out in April, too, and fade away from the Shire into the world of myth. Chaucer's timid Sir Thopas offered a forerunner for the reluctant adventurer in *The Hobbit*. Even the dates of Bilbo's residence back in the Shire after returning from the Lonely Mountain in S.R. 1341 until departing again for Rivendell in S.R. 1401 look like a private scholarly jest, since these same years (plus one) conform to Skeat's dating of Chaucer's birth about 1340 and his death in 1400. After the gap in the *Canterbury Tales* between the trailing off of the Cook's Tale and a new start in Fragment II, the Host very precisely calculates the time as 'ten of the clokke'; after the gap when Frodo blacks out from his Nazgûl wound and awakens in Rivendell for a new start in Book II, Gandalf also calculates the time precisely as 'ten o'clock in the morning'. When starting his Book II of *TLOR*, that is, Tolkien repeated consciously or unconsciously the time-telling precision of Chaucer when starting Fragment II of his *Tales*.

Chaucerian remembrances flavour *The Lord of the Rings* throughout. Magically transported like the narrator in *The Book of the Duchess*, Frodo awakens in a Rivendell bedroom filled with otherworldly beauty, this one of elvish enchantment instead of literary dreams. Legolas the Wood-elf carries the same weaponry of bow, quiver, and sharp knife as the Knight's green-clad Yeoman, also a woodsman. Chaucer's reference to Sir Olifaunt in his *Sir Thopas* joined with other medieval bestiary lore to inspire Sam's recitation of his *Oliphaunt* poem; Tolkien would use the same jingle-jangle metrics of *Sir Thopas* for his Sindarin tail-rhyme stanzas.[55] Dame Nature in her garden in *The Parlement of Foules* joined with

---

[54] *Essays*, 120; see Shippey, *Road to Middle-earth*, 'The Bones of the Ox', 289–95.
[55] Patrick Wynne and Carl F. Hostetter, 'Three Elvish Verse Modes', in *Tolkien's 'Legendarium'*, ed. Flieger and Hostetter, 113–39 at p. 117.

Queen Alceste in *The Legend of Good Women* to provide important models for Galadriel in the Golden Wood. C. S. Lewis had noted that Chaucer inserted a stanza in his *Parlement* describing a far more paradise-like garden than in Boccaccio—'No man may ther wexe seek ne old'[56]—making it an additional source for Lothlórien where sickness and deformity held no sway (*FR* II/6). In the chapter 'Shelob's Lair', Gollum's attack on Sam failed because 'he had made the mistake of speaking and gloating' (*TT* IV/9)—which was exactly the mistake made by the fox when losing his prey in the Nun's Priest's Tale. This Chaucerian detail was not recalled from far-off schooldays, of course, since Tolkien had edited the Nun's Priest's Tale in the 1920s and memorized it in 1938 to recite for a summer entertainment. The year 1938 was the same in which he drafted the earliest chapters of what would become *The Lord of the Rings* and introduced his own talking fox who pauses in the woods to remark: 'I have seldom heard of a hobbit sleeping out of doors under a tree. Three of them! There's something mighty queer behind this.'[57] This odd-looking passage is now recognizable as an intrusion from Chaucer's Aesopic world of talking animals.

Tolkien's Eagles came to the rescue when the Dwarves were treed by Goblins and Wargs in *The Hobbit*, again when Gandalf was imprisoned atop Orthanc, and yet again when Frodo and Sam were stranded on Mount Doom. Although many sources provided these 'machines', as Tolkien called them after Horace's *deus ex machina*, Anderson quotes as the most likely source *The House of Fame* where the Eagle snatches up the Chaucerian dreamer.[58] Since literary fame would later vex Tolkien with demands upon his time and intrusions upon his privacy, it is unfortunate the Clarendon Chaucer did not include this dream-vision in which the fourteenth-century poet, too, expressed his desire to evade the heavy burdens of celebrity.[59]

And sometimes Tolkien recalled larger sequences of action. The General Prologue describes Chaucer's company assembling by accident at the Tabard Inn as a sociable place well supplied with drink. The innkeeper Harry Bailey enters the story as a colourful, talkative character; the pilgrims agree to tell tales along their journey; and Chaucer, incognito, decides to transcribe their tale-telling in a book. In his chapter 'At the Sign of the Prancing Pony' (*FR* I/9), Tolkien's four hobbits arrive at the inn also bustling with merry voices. The innkeeper Barliman Butterbur enters as a lively, talkative character; the hobbits accidentally fall into the company of a Ranger—'he can tell a rare tale', says Butterbur; and Frodo,

---

[56] Lewis, *Allegory of Love*, 175–6.
[57] *FR* I/3; Tolkien retained almost verbatim the talking fox (actually internal monologue) from his earliest drafts in *Return of the Shadow*, 51. Hammond and Scull, *Reader's Companion*, 96, remark upon the curiousness of the passage.
[58] *Annotated Hobbit*, 156–7, quotes two sections from Skeat's *Student's Chaucer* (lines 529–53, 896–909). Ratelliff, *Story of The Hobbit*, 220, cites the royal eagles in Chaucer's *Parlement of Foules*.
[59] Bowers, *Chaucer and Langland*, 80–102, considers Chaucer's strategy for achieving posthumous fame yet safeguarding his privacy while alive.

incognito as Mr Underhill, announces his plan for writing a book. Recalling stories like Strider's *Tale of Tinúviel* became an important structural device for which the *Canterbury Tales* provided a venerable model.[60]

When forced to provide a diversion at the Bree inn, Frodo begins a silly-sounding song based on the nursery rhyme *Hey Diddle Diddle* much as Chaucer the Pilgrim recites his jingle-jangle *Sir Thopas* when forced by the Host to contribute a tale. When Frodo inadvertently slips the Ring on his finger and disappears, the people imagine he is a travelling magician like the *tregetours* who make things disappear in the Franklin's Tale. Unlike Frodo at the *Prancing Pony*, the Chaucerian narrator did not exactly disappear at the Tabard Inn, but he was so successful at concealing his identity that later the Host needed to ask 'What man artou?' Tolkien may have recalled the Chaucerian pilgrim's knack for finding out everything about others, while surrendering nothing about himself, when Treebeard describes the similar information-gathering tactics of Saruman (*TT* III/4). If Chaucer's General Prologue denied responsibility for the racier tales by claiming only to repeat what each pilgrim said, Tolkien's 'Prologue' devises a similar ploy by claiming merely to have drawn his stories from the Red Book of Westmarch.

Frodo's journey with his companions to Rivendell was rooted in medieval antecedents like the *Canterbury Tales* where internal storytelling was set within a larger frame-narrative. Already by 1917 Tolkien was experimenting with these stories-within-stories in his *Cottage of Lost Play*.[61] Of course *Beowulf* contained inset stories like 'The Finnsburg Episode',[62] but Tolkien's interior tale-telling assumed a specifically Chaucerian quality in *The Fellowship of the Ring*. Its stories are told along the road rather than at court, the storyteller is a fellow traveller instead of a professional minstrel, and the inset story is not predictive of some future episode, like 'Sigemund and the Dragon' in *Beowulf*, but rather offers insights into the mind and heart of the storyteller himself. Strider comforts the four frightened hobbits on Weathertop by recounting the legends of Elves and Men, but his song of Beren and Lúthien also reflects his own romantic history and future hopes with Arwen. Nor is he the only storyteller. On the road to Amon Sûl, Sam had already recited *The Fall of Gil-galad* which he learned from Bilbo.

Chaucer's ingenious experiment of adapting each tale to the inner life of the tale-teller continues throughout *The Lord of the Rings*. These inset stories are 'all dramatic', as Tolkien later commented, 'fitted in style and contents to the *characters* in the story that sing or recite them' (*Letters*, 396). Though Aragorn starts in

---

[60] Verlyn Flieger, 'Frame Narrative', *TE* 216–18, and Solopova, 'Middle English', in *Companion*, ed. Lee, 239–41.

[61] *The Lost Road* was projected as another frame-narrative containing a series of stories; see SH 2:750.

[62] J. R. R. Tolkien, *Finn and Hengest: The Fragment and the Episode*, ed. Alan J. Bliss (Boston: Houghton Mifflin, 1983); see SH 2:433–7.

response to Sam's request for stories about Elves, his tale of Tinúviel (*FR* I/11) reflects his own anxieties over the love of a Man for an Elf Maiden—himself and Arwen—as a continuation of events stretching back to Tuor's love for Idril in *The Fall of Gondolin*. Tolkien reviewed these unfortunate unions of Elves and Men in his Appendix A where 'The Tale of Aragorn and Arwen' tells how Aragorn's mother reacted with foreboding when he announced his love for Elrond's daughter: 'it is not fit that mortal should wed with the Elf-kin.' In Chaucer's Man of Law's Tale, this taboo of human–elvish marriage had already become such a familiar motif that the wicked Donegild invoked it as a ready-made falsehood to discredit King Alla's newborn son: 'The moder was an elf, by aventure | Y-come, by charmes or by sorcerye' (*CT* II, 754–6).[63] Like tales from Chaucer's other pilgrims such as the Pardoner and the Wife of Bath, Aragorn's stories open a window into his private desires and fears—his desire for Arwen and his fear that they will end tragically like Beren and Lúthien.

A whole book could be written on *Troilus and Criseyde* as a masterwork midway in the English tradition between *Beowulf* and *The Lord of the Rings*. All three literary works explore from a Christian viewpoint the best-meaning efforts of pagans with no guarantee of reward in the afterlife. Though Chaucer's tragedy of the Trojan lovers thwarted what Tolkien valued as the joy of happy ending, his Clarendon commentary nonetheless praised the poem as 'his greatest achievement and his greatest exhibition of technical metrical skill'.[64] The image of Troilus in the Temple of Venus in *The Parlement of Foules* further occasioned Tolkien's high praise: 'The story was later the subject of Chaucer's masterpiece, and only work of first rank that he finished.'[65] Years later he again expressed his admiration when assessing *Gawain* among the narrative masterworks of the fourteenth century: 'It has a rival, a claimant to equality not superiority, in Chaucer's masterpiece *Troilus and Criseyde*. That is larger, longer, more intricate, and perhaps more subtle' (*Essays*, 105). Beyond these broad appreciative statements, he knew the text thoroughly enough to quote its Book V to his cadet students about courage: '*in no degree secounde in dorring don that longeth to a knight*—meaning that Troilus was second to none in daring to perform all deeds proper to a knight'.[66]

The Trojan romance was based on the *Filostrato* where Boccaccio's hero Troiolo was forsaken by his beloved Criseida for his more determined rival Diomede. In Chaucer's free adaptation, many readers lose patience with the diffident Troilus, as indeed did Tolkien in his early lecture on the *Kalevala* when mocking the courtly lover in contrast to the bold Finnish suitor: 'There is

---

[63] Stuart D. Lee and Elizabeth Solopova, *The Keys of Middle-earth: Discovering Medieval Literature through the Fiction of J. R. R. Tolkien* (New York: Palgrave Macmillan, 2005), 128–9.
[64] Bodleian MS Tolkien A 39/2/1, fol. 9.
[65] Bodleian MS Tolkien A 13/2, fol. 111, on the allusion to Troilus in *Parlement*.
[66] Bodleian MS Tolkien 14/2, fol. 92.

no Troilus to need a Pandarus to do his shy wooing for him.'[67] Thus he would have applauded instead Chaucer's aggressive Diomede, and indeed his chapter 'The Steward and the King' fused the two Chaucerian suitors in the person of Faramir. He woos Éowyn while both are confined together in the Houses of Healing, his courtship combining the sincere love of Troilus with the self-assurance of Diomede. Once Chaucer's Trojan love-tragedy is added to the list of Tolkien's sources, other parallels become clear. Troilus was the younger son of the king whose older son Hector, the better warrior, was killed by the Greeks; Faramir was the younger son of the steward whose older son Boromir, the better warrior, was killed by the Orcs. Like Diomede rather than Troilus, though, Faramir wastes no time pressing his love-suit upon Éowyn in an episode that grew in the telling. His courtship of the warrior-maiden had been largely absent in the earliest drafts and emerged only in later revisions.[68]

Just as Criseyde was initially distraught over her separation from Troilus, Éowyn grieves her impossible love for Aragorn, by now leading his army through Ithilien toward almost certain death at the Black Gate. This is what Tolkien later described as 'the theme of mistaken love seen in Éowyn and her first love for Aragorn' (*Letters*, 161). Though she is the niece of King Théoden and embodies a range of Germanic virtues, Latin poetry's amatory elements infiltrated her character by way of Boccaccio's classicizing romance adapted in the English *Troilus*.[69] Éowyn also owes something to Chaucer's Emelye in the Knight's Tale. Both are warrior-maidens, one an Amazon and the other a Shield-maiden of Rohan. Tolkien's earliest sketches encourage this resemblance by saying 'Éowyn goes as Amazon' and 'Make Éowyn the twin-sister of Éomund a stern Amazon woman'.[70] And both women have been forced from their homelands by war and find themselves in far-off cities courted by foreign noblemen. But the directness of Faramir has no basis in the standoffish knights Palamon or Arcite, who seem more interested in each other as friends and rivals. Interestingly, Tolkien's earliest conception of love in the Houses of Healing had aligned more with this homosocial dynamic: 'Faramir opens his eyes and looks on Aragorn and love springs between them.'[71] Unacceptable even in wartime England, this same-sex masculine bond between the two warriors was replaced by Faramir's love for Éowyn so that his nearer Chaucerian model becomes the audacious, successful Diomede.

---

[67] The two versions of his *Kalevala* lecture are printed in Tolkien's *Story of Kullervo*, ed. Flieger, 70; see also Chance, *Tolkien, Self and Other*, 'An Early Literary Model: Antihero Kullervo in the Finnish *Kalevala* (1914–1919)', 28–37.

[68] See *Sauron Defeated*, 52–9.

[69] Miryan Librán-Moreno, 'Greek and Latin Amatory Motifs in Éowyn's Portrayal', *Tolkien Studies* 4 (2007), 73–97, identifies these Classical elements without tracing their transmission through Boccaccio and Chaucer.

[70] Tolkien, *Treason of Isengard*, 437, 448.

[71] Tolkien, *The War of the Ring*, 385. He would have known from the Prologue to the *Legend of Good Women* (F 420–1) that the Knight's Tale was written prior to the *Canterbury Tales* and given the title 'The Love of Palamon and Arcite'. See Bowers, 'Three Readings of The Knight's Tale', 279–87.

After a hostage exchange in the midst of war, Criseyde finds herself alone in the Greek camp with little hope of seeing Troilus again. Also stranded among alien peoples against the backdrop of war, Éowyn is left behind in Gondor when Aragorn rides off to the Black Gate. Her brother and last surviving kinsman Éomer also rides into Ithilien, unlikely to return. The besieged city of Minas Tirith, it has been noted, incorporates a number of elements from Troy's legends.[72] The way C. S. Lewis described Criseyde applies equally to Éowyn: 'What cruelty it is, to subject such a woman to the test of absence—and of absence with no assured future of reunion, absence compelled by the terrible outer-world of law and politics and force (which she cannot face), absence amid alien scenes and voices.'[73] Tolkien, later commenting at length upon the courtship of Faramir and Éowyn, was aware that its rapid progress had been criticized: 'In my experience feelings and decisions ripen very quickly (as measured by mere "clock–time", which is actually not justly applicable) in periods of great stress, and especially under the expectation of imminent death' (*Letters*, 324).

Faramir gazed upon the wounded warrior-maiden and felt compassion, 'being a man whom pity deeply stirred'. The passage recalls Chaucer's favourite line *For pitee renneth sone in gentil herte* from the Knight's Tale, Merchant's Tale, Squire's Tale, and *Legend of Good Women*. But Faramir is not handicapped by the religious qualms about which Tolkien warned his son Michael when entering the military in 1941: '*Allas! that ever love was sinne!* as Chaucer says' (*Letters*, 48). Nor is Faramir enmeshed in the courtly tradition that required self-denial and worshipful service, as Tolkien explained to one reader:

> I do *not* think that persons of high estate and breeding need all the petty fencing and approaches in matters of 'love'. This tale does not deal with a period of 'Courtly Love' and its pretences; but with a culture more primitive (sc. less corrupt) and nobler.[74]

Gimli enacts the more traditional pattern of worshipful love for Galadriel, for example, even prepared to challenge Éomer to combat for insulting the Lady of the Wood.

Faramir is no starry-eyed lover lost in his romantic obsession. When Éowyn asks how she can relieve his cares, he gives her a straightforward answer without the flowery rhetoric of a courtier. He tells her that she is beautiful and his heart

---

[72] Leslie A. Donovan, 'Middle-earth Mythology', in *Companion*, ed. Lee, 92–106 at p. 95.
[73] Lewis, *Allegory of Love*, 187.
[74] *Letters*, 324; Tolkien had read and commented upon the 'Courtly Love' chapter in Lewis's *Allegory of Love*. Tolkien wrote further to his son Michael about courtly love: 'Its weakness is, of course, that it began as an artificial courtly game, a way of enjoying love for its own sake without reference to (and indeed contrary to) matrimony. Its centre was not God, but imaginary Deities, Love and the Lady. It still tends to make the Lady a kind of guiding star or divinity—of the old-fashioned "his divinity" = the woman he loves—the object or reason of noble conduct. This is, of course, false and at best make-believe' (*Letters*, 49).

would be eased to see her often. In order to learn more about the lady, he proceeds to find in Merry a friend somewhat like Pandarus as the intermediary for Troilus. Thereafter she joins him for daily walks without attempting to conceal their relationship. This is markedly different from the secrecy which Criseyde enforced upon Troilus. When Éowyn confides her anxieties about the Black Gate, he understands her concern for Aragorn as his rival. Faramir invokes Mordor's inescapable darkness while Éowyn, holding his hand, draws closer for comfort and assurance. After pledging his protection, he leans down and kisses her brow while standing on the city walls in full view of onlookers.

When Éowyn does not celebrate the news of Sauron's defeat, Faramir corners her with the direct question: 'do you love me, or will you not?' She replies with equal bluntness that she had wished to be loved by another man. Faramir explains that she loved Aragorn for his status and strength, much as a young soldier loves his captain. His own love is based on her renown and beauty, not mere pity, and he asks her frankly if she cannot love him in return. 'Then the heart of Éowyn changed, or else at last she understood it.' Though Faramir cannot make her a queen, he invites her to join him in Ithilien for transforming the wasteland back into a garden. When she jokes that men will mock him for marrying a shield-maiden, he takes her in his arms and kisses her under the sunlit walls. This public acknowledgement might have prevented the tragedy of Troilus and Criseyde.

Tolkien may have discouraged critics from using his biography to illuminate his writings, but a crucial episode in his own life helps to account for this love story's lengthy inclusion—some readers would say *too* lengthy. Like Troilus, he himself had pursued a romance with Edith Bratt in secret because his guardian Father Morgan disapproved. By the time he turned 21 and was free to proceed, she had become engaged to a man named George Field. On a fateful day in January 1913, Tolkien travelled by train to Cheltenham and took her walking into the country-side where they had a private talk. Tolkien could be persuasive when necessary. He convinced C. S. Lewis to convert to Christianity; he convinced George Gordon to let him continue on the Clarendon Chaucer; and later he convinced Rayner Unwin to make almost endless concessions when publishing *The Lord of the Rings*. Though Tolkien had begun his romance in secret like Troilus, he changed into an unrelenting Diomede who persuaded Edith to break with George Field and marry him instead.[75]

As with the Reeve's Tale, *Troilus* served as a Chaucerian lens through which a biographical episode was refracted to become the wish-fulfilling fantasy with a happy ending. Faramir not only embodied Tolkien's background as a soldier and a scholar with skills in archival research—sharing, too, his recurrent nightmare of a tidal wave—but he was also the resourceful suitor who persuaded his lady

---

[75] *Biography*, 69; Tolkien omitted mention of a rival in his account to his son Michael: 'I went back to her, and became engaged, and informed an astonished family' (*Letters*, 53).

to abandon her other lover and attach herself to him instead. Tolkien himself, in a rare instance of candour, admitted the resemblance: 'As far as any character is "like me" it is Faramir' (*Letters*, 232).

The Wife of Bath's Tale

Gordon and Sisam decided against including tales by the two pilgrims most familiar to today's readers of the *Norton Anthology* and singled out by Harold Bloom as the two most interesting in the *Canterbury Tales*,[76] and yet Tolkien knew the Wife of Bath and the Pardoner very well. But only gradually and in some sense grudgingly did he come to appreciate how these Chaucerian tale-tellers influenced the creation of his own characters and storylines.

To take an almost subliminal instance of indebtedness, the Wife of Bath's Prologue begins with *experience* and *authoritee* as the two means for establishing knowledge—that is, either by first-hand experience or by second-hand authority of books. Very much reflecting these medieval distinctions, Tolkien's chapter 'The Council of Elrond' dramatizes the same two methods when tracing the history of the Ring. First, Elrond speaks from eye-witness *experience* when he recalls the battle where he beheld Elendil fall on the slopes of Mount Doom and Isildur cut the Ring from Sauron's hand. Next, Gandalf related what he had learned from *authority* in the archives at Minas Tirith. A scroll written by Isildur recounted his brief possession of the Ring, telling how its elven-script was refreshed by fire and became 'precious to me'. Gandalf learned exactly what he needed to know from an old manuscript.

The Wife of Bath's Tale began with a striking medieval account of fairies and their disappearance. Tolkien thoroughly disliked post-medieval versions such as Michael Drayton's *Nymphidia* with its 'flower-fairies and fluttering sprites with antennae' (*Essays*, 111). He understood that authentic elves were far more powerful and dangerous than these Tinkerbell-like pixies.[77] For an authentic account preserving lore much more ancient, he looked to texts like *Sir Orfeo*, the Breton lay which Chaucer himself maybe knew from the Auchinleck manuscript.[78] In this same native tradition, the Wife of Bath offers a medieval romance with the same deep-rootedness which Tolkien valued in *Gawain*: 'Behind our poem stalk the

---

[76] Harold Bloom, *The Western Canon: The Books and Schools of the Ages* (New York: Riverhead Books, 1994), 'Chaucer: The Wife of Bath, the Pardoner, and Shakespearean Character', 99–118. Bloom's introduction to *J. R. R. Tolkien: Modern Critical Views* (Philadelphia: Chelsea House Publishers, 2000), 2, suggests his judgements were not always sound: 'I suspect that *The Lord of the Rings* is fated to become only an intricate Period Piece.'

[77] Tolkien also knew that Chaucer's late-medieval elves were quite different from their Anglo-Saxon antecedents: 'In all Old English poetry "elves" (*ylfe*) occurs once only, in *Beowulf*, associated with trolls, giants, and the Undead, as the accursed offspring of Cain' (*Letters*, 314).

[78] Laura H. Loomis, 'Chaucer and the Breton Lays of the Auchinleck MS.', *SP* 38 (1941), 14–33.

figures of elder myth, and through the lines are heard the echoes of ancient cults, beliefs and symbols remote from the consciousness of an educated moralist (but also a poet) of the late fourteenth century' (*Essays*, 73). Elsewhere Chaucer recollected figures of elder myth like the sea-giant Wade in an old wives' tale—'And eek thise olde wydwes, God it woot | They konne so muchel craft on Wades boot' (*CT* IV, 1423–4).[79] The Wife of Bath was an old wife, after all, and five times a widow, and therefore the perfect narrator for a tale drawing upon ancient folklore.

Skeat (5:315) had explained the theological concept which fitted fairies into a Christian framework, explaining how some cast-out angels did not fall all the way down into Hell but remained in the middle region of air where they took various shapes to tempt men into sin.[80] Chaucer had inherited this lore about exiled angels from religious works like the *South English Legendary*:

> And ofte in fourme of wommane, in many derne weye,
> Grete compaygnie men i-seoth of heom, boþe hoppie and pleiȝe,
> Þat Elvene beoth i–cleopede...[81]
>
> And often in the shapes of women, in many secret byways,
> Men see a great company of them, hopping and playing,
> Who are called Elves...

Dancing woodland elves had entered folklore by the time the Wife of Bath's Tale recalled bygone days when the land was filled with enchantment.[82] Despite the opening reference to King Arthur, her story's real protagonist is the Elf Queen with her dancing ladies:

> In th'olde dayes of the king Arthour,
> Of which that Britons speken greet honour,
> Al was this land fulfild of fayerye.
> The Elf-queen with hir joly companye
> Daunced ful ofte in many a grene mede.
>
> (*CT* D, 857–61)

This scene of elves dancing in the forest was magical for Tolkien, appearing many times in his early poems and thereafter, all of them enhanced for him personally

---

[79] Karl P. Wenterdorf, 'Chaucer and the Lost Tale of Wade', *Journal of English and Germanic Philology* 65 (1966), 274–86.

[80] W. P. Ker, respectfully taken to task in Tolkien's *Beowulf* lecture, had written on this subject in 'The Craven Angels', *Modern Language Review* 6 (1911), 85–7; see also Shippey, *Road to Middle-earth*, 238–9.

[81] *The Early South-English Legendary or Lives of Saints*, ed. Carl Horstmann, EETS o.s. 87, 1887, p. 307 (lines 253–5); see Shippey, *Road to Middle-earth*, 238–9. Tolkien owned a copy now part of the Bodleian's Tolkien Archive.

[82] Verlyn Flieger, *Green Suns and Faërie: Essays on Tolkien* (Kent, OH: Kent State University Press, 2012), 'When Is a Fairy Story a *Faërie* Story?', 65–73 at p. 67.

by the memory of Edith dancing in a field in Yorkshire (*Biography*, 56, 105). Nessa danced before the Valar upon the green grass of Almaren (*Sil* 28), and Beren first came upon Lúthien dancing in the unfading grass (*Sil* 193). The early version *Light as Leaf on Lindentree* had envisioned Tinúviel dancing in a hemlock glade and was later adapted by Strider on Weathertop (*FR* I/11). Appendix A's 'Tale of Aragorn and Arwen' recounted how Aragorn thought his song had brought Lúthien back to life as the Elf maiden he saw walking in the woods. The scene returned for the last time in *Smith of Wootton Major* when the hero comes upon fairy women dancing on a lawn beside a river.[83] Smith meets a young maiden who is really the Elf Queen in disguise, much as Chaucer's knight had met the Elf- Queen shapeshifted into an old hag after her dancing ladies have disappeared. Tolkien's 'On Fairy-Stories' remarked upon such illusions: 'The trouble with the real folk of Faërie is that they do not always look like what they are' (*Essays*, 113). The Wife of Bath's knight fails to recognize the Elf Queen even when she magically transforms herself into a beautiful young woman at the tale's conclusion.

'On Fairy-Stories' quoted *The Ballad of Thomas Rhymer* when describing how a mortal goes off with the elvish woman, never to return (*Essays*, 110, 113). In Chaucer's parody, the childlike Sir Thopas falls in love with the Elf Queen in a dream and goes searching for her into Fairyland, only to abandon his quest and rush home as soon as confronted by the giant Sir Olifaunt. In the Wife of Bath's reversal of the Breton lay *Lanval*, where an outcast knight escapes the Arthurian court with the fairy queen,[84] the Elf Queen arrives magically at Arthur's court and claims her right to marry the knight because she had provided him with the secret for saving his life. Only after a long lecture about natural inborn virtue—Tolkien's commentary on *Gentilesse* remarked, 'Chaucer also wrote a "poetical essay" on this subject in the Tale of his Wife of Bath'—does she transform back into her true form. The lusty knight is so spell-struck, however, that he fails to register what Tolkien called 'the fear of the beautiful fay that ran through the elder ages' (*Essays*, 151).

But unlike common variants of the Elf Queen story, the Wife of Bath's enchanted bride does not disappear, she does not transform into a monster like Melusine, and she does not transport her human lover off to fairyland. Instead, the couple live happily ever after 'un-to hir lyves ende'. This last phrase, so casually included that it is easy to miss, suggests that the Elf-queen sacrificed her immortality for the love of a mortal man, much as Arwen does when she leaves her

---

[83] J. R. R. Tolkien, *Smith of Wootton Major*, in *Poems and Stories*, illustrated by Pauline Baynes (Boston and New York: Houghton Mifflin, 1994), 303–42 at p. 322; see also SH 3:1214–22 'Smith of Wootton Major'.

[84] Tolkien's heavily annotated copy of Marie de France's *Breton Lais* was donated to Oxford's English Faculty Library, now housed in Bodleian's Tolkien Archive. Chaucer knew the genre of the Breton lay well enough to write his own version in the Franklin's Tale; see Shippey, *Road to Middle-earth*, 280.

kindred to live as Aragorn's wife in Gondor. Such domestication became an important Chaucerian legacy. It was the sort of thing Tolkien had in mind when he told John Masefield that the poet struck him as middle-class rather than regal (*Letters*, 40). Tolkien had offered just such a conventional moral to his *Lay of Aotrou and Itroun* where the husband remains faithful to his wife unto death by rejecting claims upon his love by the evil Corrigan, a Breton word for 'fairy'.[85] Marriage eclipses magic. Tolkien even hinted at a human/elven marriage in *The Hobbit* where Bilbo's adventuresome streak was explained by one of his Took ancestors having a fairy wife.

Tolkien had found fault with fairy elements in the native Arthurian tradition: 'For one thing its "faerie" is too lavish, and fantastical, incoherent and repetitive. For another and more important thing: it is involved in, and explicitly contains the Christian religion' (*Letters*, 144). The Wife of Bath's Tale provided a corrective. Her fairies are fleeting and mysterious, and the old hag's true identity as the Elf-queen is never explicitly stated. Also the role of the friars at expelling fairies from Britain is placed at the beginning and never again mentioned, so there is no further Christian element after this satirical swipe at the mendicants, no doubt in retaliation against Friar Hubert who had criticized the Wife's Prologue as too long.

The Wife of Bath's Tale is followed by the Friar's Tale. This quest into the forest tells how a vicious summoner meets a mysterious green-clad man with eyes concealed beneath his hat's black fringe. This sinister stranger turns out to be a devil after giving the obvious clue that his home is far in the north country. Tolkien knew the lore even if the summoner did not: 'The North was the seat of the fortresses of the Devil' (*Letters*, 376). But the summoner, instead of fleeing, forms a pact of brotherhood with this demonic travelling companion. The eerie story stuck in Tolkien's memory and returned in *Smith of Wootton Major* where a lone traveller in the forest meets a mysterious man who, like Chaucer's devil, was 'dressed all in dark green and wore a hood that partly overshadowed his face' (pp. 328–9). The stranger turns out to be instead Alf the Prentice—Alf of course meaning Elf—as Tolkien reverts to the older expectation that a green-clad figure should be a fairy, not a demon.[86] But nobody dies in *Smith*. Nobody faces eternal damnation as in the Friar's Tale. Again we are granted the consolation of a happy ending. Despite its simple language and appeal to children, Tolkien felt it represented an 'old man's book already weighted with the presage of "bereavement"' (*Letters*, 389). In some sense these last Chaucerian

---

[85] J. R. R. Tolkien, 'The Lay of Aotrou and Itroun', *The Welsh Review* 4/4 (1945), 254–66; see SH 2:645–7. A critical edition is now available: J. R. R. Tolkien, *The Lay of Aotrou and Itroun together with the Corrigan Poems*, ed. Verlyn Flieger with note on text by Christopher Tolkien (Boston and New York: Houghton Mifflin Harcourt, 2017).

[86] His *Gawain* edition, 86, had remarked, 'green was a fairy colour'. For Chaucer's substitution of a demon for a fairy in the Friar's Tale, see Green's *Elf Queens*, 52.

remembrances from 1967 deserve comparison with Shakespeare's *Tempest* as a summation and a leave-taking.

To clear space for her fairy-story's happy ending, the Wife of Bath positioned an *un*happy episode at the beginning. There she sounded an elegiac note which must have struck deeply the author of *The Lord of the Rings* when explaining how her tale took place many centuries in the past when 'Al was this land fulfild of fayeres' (859)—that is, before fairies were banished by intrusion of the friars:

> I speke of manye hundred yeres ago;
> But now can no man see none elves mo.
> For now the grete charitee and prayeres
> Of limitours and othere holy freres
>
> . . . .
>
> This maketh that ther been no fayeryes.
> For ther as wont to walken was an elf,
> Ther walketh now the limitour himself.
>
> (*CT* III, 863–74)

Tolkien recalled throughout his career similar scenes of vanishing fairies. His first published poem *Goblin Feet* lamented this disappearance of elvish enchantment— 'O! the magic! O! the sorrow when it dies!' The disappearance of the fairy dancers had already figured in the version of 'Light as Leaf on Linden' inserted into his alliterative *Lay of the Children of Húrin*.[87] In all his many versions of Lúthien dancing, she invariably eluded Beren when he first spotted her in the forest: 'Then sudden she vanished like a dream.'[88]

His early *Book of Lost Tales* proposed different accounts for the complete disappearance of fairies from Middle-earth. In one, they retired to Tol Eressëa and hid themselves in the woods; in another, they grew smaller and more transparent until men could no longer see them. Like Chaucer's rustic fairies displaced by friars, Tolkien imagined a zero-sum game whereby Elves grew smaller as Men grew stronger.[89] The repeated vanishing of the Wood-elves in Mirkwood Forest represented only their temporary escape from intruders, but Galadriel has foreseen a final departure with only a few stragglers left behind to 'dwindle to a rustic folk of dell and cave, slowly to forget and to be forgotten' (*FR* II/7).

This Chaucerian sense of disenchantment, centuries before Max Weber popularized the term, encouraged Tolkien's efforts at reclaiming enchantment in his

---

[87] *Lays of Beleriand*, 129 (lines 423–5); see Christopher's 'Note on the poem "Light as Leaf on Lindentree"', 142–7.
[88] *Lays of Beleriand*, 214 (line 617).
[89] Tolkien, *Lost Tales, Part II*, 288–95 and 332–3.

modern fairy-stories.[90] As a devout Catholic, however, he would not have blamed their disappearance on the arrival of Christianity in Britain. Specifically he would not have cast Franciscans as the villains. When he had money enough to travel, he took his daughter Priscilla on pilgrimage to the shrine of St Francis at Assisi. Instead of Christianity, he blamed the advent of machines; and instead of outcasts, he imagined his elves as voluntary exiles awaiting their return westward. As Tolkien explained at the time of *TLOR*'s publication, 'The High Elves met in this book are Exiles returned back over Sea to Middle-earth' (*Letters*, 176). Galadriel and Celeborn had refused the pardon of the Valar so that their eventual departure from the Grey Havens marked their return, a homecoming rather than a banishment (*Letters*, 386n). Tolkien's version came close to the notion of God eventually pardoning the elves in the *South English Legendary*—'And manie of heom a-domesday ʒeot schullen to reste come'—and thus amended Chaucer's utter eradication of fairies in the Wife of Bath's Tale.

The Pardoner's Tale

George Lyman Kittredge's influential 1915 *Chaucer and His Poetry* branded the Pardoner as the most abandoned figure among the Canterbury pilgrims (p. 211), and his disapproval became widespread. George Gordon excluded the unsavoury character's portrait from the General Prologue, and the Pardoner's Tale was never considered for the Clarendon Chaucer even though it had appeared on Tolkien's undergraduate syllabus at Oxford. But just as he was obliged to teach *Beowulf* after becoming Professor of Anglo-Saxon in 1925,[91] Tolkien found himself lecturing on the Pardoner's Tale after he became Merton Professor in 1945. 'For insensible Providence has guided the compilers of our syllabus and the prescribers of our lists to name these two texts', he informed his students grumpily about the Pardoner's Tale in addition to the Clerk's Tale.[92]

How fully conscious was he that Chaucer's narrative had already entered his imagination and was working an imaginative alchemy? Tolkien was surely disingenuous when caught lifting from *Beowulf* the scene of Bilbo stealing the goblet from the dragon's hoard: '*Beowulf* is among my most valued sources, though it

---

[90] Patrick Curry, 'Iron Crown, Iron Cage: Tolkien and Weber on Modernity and Enchantment', in *The Ring Goes Ever On*, ed. Wells, 1:128–32.

[91] In his preface to his father's *Beowulf* translation, Christopher described how Tolkien had the assignment 'not of his own conceiving, but [was] concerned with a specific work, of great celebrity and with a massive history of criticism extending over two centuries' (p. ix). *The Pardoner's Tale* had a longer critical tradition stretching back to the early fifteenth century.

[92] Bodleian MS Tolkien A 13/2, fol. 5. He was, of course, already familiar with the Pardoner's Tale; Rateliff, *Story of The Hobbit*, 108–9, connects Tom the Troll swearing by 'Oddsteeth' ('God's teeth') with the Three Rioters swearing in Chaucer's narrative.

was not consciously present to the mind in the process of writing' (*Letters*, 31). Even in the late 1940s he might have sworn that the Pardoner's Tale was not consciously present in his mind when completing *The Lord of the Rings*—and honestly meant it—though its core-story cannily anticipated the entire arc of his narrative from Sméagol's murder of Déagol to its climactic episode of Gollum fighting with Sam and Frodo inside Mount Doom.

Once we learn of Tolkien's teaching commitments with the Pardoner's Tale, it is easy enough to spot its bones turning up everywhere in his rich, complex soup. The Pardoner preached on a biblical text *radix malorum est cupiditas*—'greed is the root of all evils' (1 Tim. 6.10)—and then offered a sermon dramatizing how three young men went searching for gold and found only their own deaths. Tolkien would follow the Pardoner's homiletic lead by supplying scriptural verses illustrating Frodo's failure to resist the Ring's allure inside Mount Doom: 'Forgive us our trespasses...Lead us not into temptation...' (*Letters*, 233, 252). Avarice is a major evil in nearly all of Tolkien's writings going back to the Kings of Númenor whose decline began when they grew greedy for wealth. *The Hobbit* offered the same lesson when Thorin Oakenshield's lust for gold led to three deaths, his own along with his nephews Kili and Fili. Shippey has identified greed as a recurring theme elsewhere with characters such as the Master of Lake-town fleeing with his gold only to die of starvation in the wilderness.[93] As forerunner to these stories, the poem *The Hoard*, which Tolkien published in 1923 but kept revising until 1970, told how the elves, a dwarf, a dragon, and finally an old king were obsessed with gold until all were dead and only the gold itself was left, buried and ownerless.[94]

The Pardoner's Flemish tavern has all the noise and bustle of the *Prancing Pony*, and Butterbur's description of the mysterious Strider as 'one of the wandering folk' (*FR* I/9) sounds somewhat like the tavern-keeper telling about Death stalking the countryside. The Pardoner's Old Man met by the three questers in the forest can be glimpsed when Tolkien's old man appears to the three searchers outside Fangorn Forest (*TT* III/2) and again when Gandalf reappears as a white-haired old man inside the woods to Aragorn, Gimli, and Legolas. This figure's unnatural agedness comes back again at the doorway of the Path of the Dead: 'On the threshold sat an old man, aged beyond guess of years' (*RK* V/3). Like the Old Man's curse of deathlessness, Gollum's unnatural longevity was similarly

---

[93] *The Road to Middle-earth*, 87; he suggests *The Hobbit* as a whole can be read as an allegory of greed for gold (p. 91). The core-story is potent throughout our tradition; Martin Amis remarked in 2012 when presenting Elmore Leonard with a lifetime achievement award for his fiction: 'Mr. Leonard has only one plot. All his thrillers are reworkings of Chaucer's *The Pardoners Tale*, in which death roams the land, usually Miami or Detroit, disguised as money.'
[94] Shippey, 'The Versions of "The Hoard"', 342. Tolkien offered a contrary example in 'Fog on the Barrow-Downs' when Tom Bombadil spread out the treasure on the grass 'free to all finders' without any greed on his part.

conceived as 'a poor sort of long life' and 'frightfully wearisome' and 'finally tormenting'.[95] The image of the *vetus homo* descended in a theological tradition from St Paul's Epistle to the Romans (6.6), and these old-man figures in Tolkien's fiction, taken individually, would be unremarkable if not for the fact that he was lecturing on the Pardoner's Tale during the same period when completing *The Lord of the Rings*.

Two totally different versions of this lecture survive among the Tolkien Papers as evidence of an engagement that went beyond his basic teaching duties. The earlier version dates from Michaelmas Term 1947 when he found much to praise: 'We have come to one of Chaucer's best told tales, and one that is most clearly chosen, written, and designed for its place in the unfinished *Tales* and for the pilgrim who tells it, the Pardoner.'[96] It is not entirely clear when he began substituting the second lecture series, much enlarged and mostly negative, but completing *The Lord of the Rings* in 1948 and then proofreading the galley pages probably made him see resemblances between his core narrative and Chaucer's—and he completely changed his opinion about it. He returned to teaching the Pardoner's Tale in the autumn and winter terms 1951–2, repeating this sequence in Hilary and Michaelmas Terms 1953 and again in Hilary and Trinity Terms 1954—that is, immediately before publishing *The Fellowship of the Ring* in July 1954 and *The Two Towers* in November 1954. During the academic year 1955–6, his lectures on the Pardoner's Tale extended over all three terms following publication of *The Return of the King* in October 1955. The timing suggests much.

In the audience for these revised lectures was Diana Wynne Jones, the fantasy novelist whose *Fire and Hemlock* would feature a young woman longing to become an adventure writer like Tolkien.[97] In a superb appreciation of Tolkien as a narrative artist, Jones later recalled hearing him discuss the Pardoner's Tale for an ever-diminishing number of undergraduates:

> He started with the simplest possible story: a man (prince or woodcutter) going on a journey. He then gave the journey an aim, and we found that the simple picaresque plot had developed into a quest-story. I am not quite sure what happened then, but I know that by the end he was discussing the peculiar adaptation of the quest-story which Chaucer made in his Pardoner's Tale.
>
> As you see, Tolkien did not give away half of what he knew, even about plots, and I suspect he never talked about narrative at all, but it is clear from *The Lord of the Rings* that he knew all about narrative as well. The plot of *The Lord of the Rings* is, on the face of it, exactly the same simple one that he appeared to describe in his lectures: a journey that acquires an aim and develops into a kind of quest.[98]

---

[95] Tolkien, *Return of the Shadow*, 79.   [96] MS Tolkien A 13/2, fols. 86–98 at 86r.
[97] Shippey, *Author of the Century*, 319, 326.
[98] 'The Shape of the Narrative in *The Lord of the Rings*' (1983), *Reflections on the Magic of Writing*, 5–6. Tolkien's 1953 Ker Lecture on *Gawain* indulged another late-career interest in narrative.

Though Christopher reported that his father regularly used plot-outlines for his fiction,[99] narrative analysis was indeed a rarity for Tolkien as a scholar. His seventy pages on the Reeve's Tale gave hardly a hint of the story in which dialect features were embedded. Even his celebrated *Beowulf* lecture said less about the actual story than we tend to recall, instead mocking the contradictory views of prior critics—'it is feeble and incompetent as a narrative; the rules of narrative are cleverly observed in the manner of the learned epic'—and concluding that *Beowulf* was not actually a narrative poem at all (*Essays*, 8, 28). Because his original 1947 lecture focused as usual on linguistic issues in the Pardoner's Tale,[100] his technical analysis of story-elements in the 1950s indicates that something had sparked some special interest.

Tolkien conducted a great deal of research for his new series *The Pardoner's Tale: The Story and its Form*, putting aside his earlier lectures and starting again from scratch, as C. S. Lewis reported that he so often did during any revision process[101] (Fig. 15). His final version extends over some forty-four closely written pages, with a few more pages currently missing at the end. Although its legibility deteriorated somewhat, the text did not peter out as did his *Beowulf* lectures and was carefully drafted throughout without excessive abbreviations or sketchy sentences.[102] Although the 'Monsters and the Critics' had dismissed the research methods of folklorists—'The comparison of skeleton "plots" is simply not a critical literary process at all' (*Essays*, 14)—a comparison of skeleton plots is exactly what he pursued for the Pardoner's Tale. This approach probably resulted after he realized the Chaucerian narrative had operated as an important analogue for his own fiction, maybe even a subliminal source, more specifically than even Diana Wynne Jones concluded about the plot of *The Lord of the Rings* being exactly the same as he described in his lectures.

Tolkien began by admitting the necessity of source-hunting for this 'appearance in Chaucer of a *special* form, *specially* handled, of a wide-spread tale known from China to Portugal'. His 1940s lecture had already wondered where the poet got his story: 'it is very plain that many things that Chaucer had himself *read or heard* have disappeared. It is perfectly possible for Chaucer to have had a *direct source.*' In the early 1950s, Tolkien's habit of digging down to the deepest bedrock meant consulting the Chaucer Society's 'Buddhist Original and Asiatic and European

---

[99] *Unfinished Tales*, 8. McIlwaine, *Tolkien: Maker of Middle-earth*, 311, reproduces a page of 'plot notes' for chapters 7–9 of *The Hobbit*.

[100] MS Tolkien A 13/2, fol. 91r: 'I shall still esteem it my function (or duty) to examine this piece chiefly as a *cloth-merchant* rather than a *tailor* or *dress-maker*...I mean I shall pay considerable attention to all linguistic points that arise.' Another early draft of his lectures on the Pardoner's Tale also approached the text as a specimen of fourteenth-century language (MS Tolkien A 13/2, fol. 61).

[101] Bodleian MS Tolkien A 13/2, fols. 39–60. *Biography*, 143, quotes Lewis on Tolkien's habits of revision.

[102] Christopher's edition of the *Beowulf* translation (p. 132) reported that the lectures which he mined for his 'Commentary' had petered out toward the end, and Bliss, *Finn and Hengst*, p. viii, described these lectures as hastily written and cluttered with abbreviations throughout.

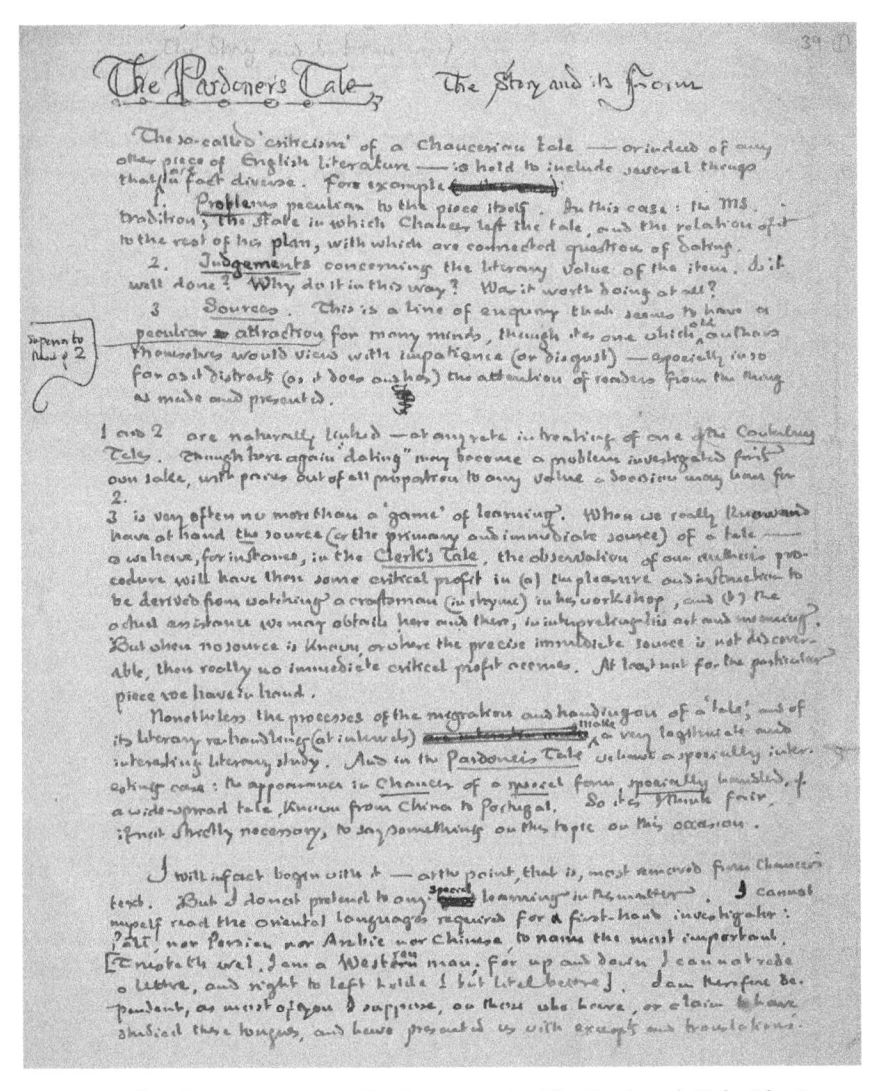

Fig. 15. Tolkien's opening page of his lecture series *The Pardoner's Tale: The Story and its Form* (Oxford, Bodleian Library, MS Tolkien A 13/2, fol. 39).

Versions of *The Pardoner's Tale*' (1872) in which William Alexander Clouston surveyed the earliest Indian, Persian, Arabian, and Tibetan versions.[103] These background texts were hardly unknown; Skeat reprinted the most ancient version

---

[103] W. A. Clouston, 'The Three Robbers and the Treasure-Trove: Buddhist Original and Asiatic and European Versions of *The Pardoner's Tale*', in *Originals and Analogues of Some of Chaucer's Canterbury Tales*, ed. F. J. Furnivall, Edmund Brock, and W. A. Clouston, Chaucer Society, 2nd series, no. 20 (London, 1872), 415–36 with the *Jātaka*'s version 420–1. Tolkien's lecture referred students to this volume as well as Skeat's reprint.

from the Buddhist *Jātaka* in his Oxford Chaucer (3:443–4). After Tolkien delved back as far as possible with apologies to his listeners—'I cannot myself read the Oriental languages required for a first-hand investigator: Pali, nor Persian nor Arabic nor Chinese, to name the most important'—he finally arrived at the basic ingredients of Chaucer's story:

> Here is the core... Two men find an unguarded or ownerless treasure. The effect on them is disastrous for it creates greed in their hearts, and they kill one another—and so neither of them enjoys any of it at all.... (fol. 41r)

Though he did not tell the undergraduates, Tolkien had no doubt spotted this core-story in his own version where Déagol found the lost Ring and was murdered by his friend Sméagol.[104] Over the long span of five centuries, Sméagol is also destroyed by his possessiveness, clutching the Ring one last time as he falls to his death in the fires of Mount Doom.[105] Tolkien had even embedded a miniature, truncated version in 'A Long-Expected Party' when Frodo and Merry apprehend three greedy treasure-seekers at Bag End:

> Then they went round the hole, and evicted three young hobbits (two Boffins and a Bolger) who were knocking holes in the walls of one of the cellars... The legend of Bilbo's gold excited both curiosity and hope; for legendary gold (mysteriously obtained, if not positively ill-gotten), is, as everyone knows, any one's for the finding—unless the search is interrupted.[106]

The basic Chaucerian ingredients are present here but without the fatal consequences. In some sense Tolkien would have considered his versions as the original 'asterisk-source' (to borrow Shippey's useful term) underlying the most ancient surviving versions from India. Because the same Indo-European tale-tellers had reached Britain before the invention of writing, their versions were lost until Tolkien recovered them in *The Lord of the Rings*.

Chaucer had made a good initial decision, Tolkien thought, by not casting this story as a beast fable like his Nun's Priest's Tale:

> The incident was turned into a tale about people. Several different things will—more or less inevitably—happen to it, not, of course, necessarily in this order....
> A setting must be devised to *account for the treasure* and *the way in which it was found*. Since the story could be many thousands of years old, and yet to be still in a time where things held *beautiful* (such as gold or silver or jewels) were hoarded and coveted... from that esteem, and the desire of possession which they aroused, the 'treasure' will take the shape of precious metals or gems.   (fol. 41r)

---

[104] Tolkien, *Treason of Isengard*, 23–4 and 27–8, shows that this core-story was already drafted in 1939.
[105] SH 3:1007–9 'Possessiveness' make a useful distinction from mere greed.
[106] FR I/1; this odd episode about the three young hobbits already appeared in earliest drafts of *Return of the Shadow*, 241, 276.

First, the story needed to establish the nature of the treasure and introduce the two friends (like Déagol and Sméagol) who found it before becoming deadly rivals:

> So the story begins to take shape, growing outwards from within like a seed. But it cannot develop abstractly unaffected by soil and climate. The account of the *treasure* and of its *origin*, or at least the explanation of how it was open to the finders to claim, will be done in terms of time and place of the story-teller—and these features will consequently be specially liable to variation and alteration. So also (if less so) will be the characterization of the finders and their evil dispositions which lay them open to cupidity. But we can follow them a little further. They must, of course, be at least *two*. They will be represented as friends, companions or confederates. Why? Well, partly for simple mechanical reasons: it is the simplest and most obvious way of explaining this joint discovery. Partly, as further growth from the *moralitas*: in this way, their fall under the influence of cupidity is enhanced, is made more shocking. Thus, if they are represented as professional thieves (one of the most obvious devices for the purpose even in a very remote and 'primitive' time) they will be likely under some bond to one another... (fol. 41v)

Next, the story needed a wise, well-informed character (like Gandalf) to explain its history and warn of its dangers:

> There now enters another element. A 'wise man.' In a sense he represents the teller of the moral story. But his place in the machinery is to *warn* the finders. Therefore he must already *know about the treasure*. At least he must know what it is, and where it is at the moment lying—but he *may* know more than that: he may know about its nature and origin. And a reason must be given for two things: (a) why he tells the finders about it, (b) why he himself eschews it.
> (fol. 41v)

Tolkien is vague about assigning this role of 'wise man' either to Chaucer's tavern-keeper who tells the three young men about Death in a nearby village, or to the Old Man who directs them to the eight bushels of gold, because he thought Chaucer had done a poor job of designating this role. At the same time he may have recognized, with unspoken self-congratulations, that his own Gandalf far more effectively fulfilled this function by discovering the Ring's sinister origins and tracing its history from Isildur to Gollum. So Tolkien's lecture was quick to identify the wise man as a wizard:

> The *wise man* is apt to be also a wizard. In such an atmosphere he is quite likely to become even closer connected with the *treasure*, as its discoverer or even producer, and will take on a mythological or saintly stature while the treasure itself will become 'magical' or demonic. (fol. 42r)

Gandalf does indeed have this 'saintly stature' as one of the incarnate angels or Istari, a Quenya word which Tolkien elsewhere translated as *wise*, the adjective here assigned to the wizard in the core-story. His fullest account of the Istari as wanderers who did not die, only looked older, dated from 1954 when also developing his thoughts on the deathless, wandering Old Man of the Pardoner's Tale.[107]

When he came to providing a schematic outline, Tolkien positioned the wizard-figure early in the narrative's archetypal design:

> The story thus had grown to what we may perhaps call its 'typical shape':
>
> (1) There is A, a Wizard or Sage. By his powers he discovers a great treasure—probably sinister in origin, made or guarded by evil spirits. He will have nothing to do with it. He instructs his disciple-companion B to beware of it. Here, probably at a very early stage, a form of words was used that later had considerable effect on the story: for example, A to B. 'That which you see is as perilous as a venomous snake' or 'There death lies hid.'
>
> (2) There are some wicked men C and D whose previous lives (e.g. as thieves) predisposes them to disastrous cupidity; but they are close friends, and bound to one another by vows of fellowship....
>
> (3) As soon as C and D find the treasure, the evil spell of Avarice begins to work; but at first they plan amicably how best to deal with good fortune...
>
> (4) As soon as they are separated, Avarice begins its deadly work. D thinks of the treasure left in C's hands...
>
> (5) The story then proceeds to the prepared catastrophe. D returns and is at once murdered by C (and E). C (and E) feast and drink, and in the moment of triumph succumb and die beside the treasure...
>
> (6) To wind up: A comes back to the scene of the catastrophe and draws the moral. It was at this point, I suggested, that the disciple B comes in: since dialogue is used effectively 'A to B' representing *inside the story*, the teller and his audience outside it. Thence B was transferred also to the beginning... (fols. 42v–43r)

First in the backstory, Sméagol and Déagol discuss good-naturedly how the Ring should be considered a birthday present; this jostling over ownership will be repeated between Gollum and Bilbo in *The Hobbit*. Later in *The Lord of the Rings*, Bilbo becomes the first 'disciple-companion B' instructed by the wizard to leave the gold Ring behind when he departs for Rivendell; eventually Bilbo is transferred back to the beginning as author of *The Hobbit* with its account of the Ring's discovery (FR I/1). In the chapter 'The Shadow of the Past', Gandalf provides the Ring's lengthy backstory which Tolkien's lecture described as part of the core: 'And just as he himself represents the story-teller inside the tale, so there will now come in an "inside audience" to whom he can speak' (fol. 42r). Here the second disciple-companion Frodo serves as this inside audience.

---

[107] 'The Istari', *UT*, 388–402. Tolkien in *Return of the Shadow*, 76 and 224, had quickly reassigned the role of warner from Gildor to Gandalf and made emphatic the wizard's cautions against using the Ring.

When Bilbo first offers the Ring to Gandalf for safekeeping (*FR* I/1), he reacts exactly as Tolkien predicted and will have nothing to do with it. The wizard recoils even more violently when offered the Ring a second time by Frodo: 'I dare not take it, not even to keep it safe, unused. The wish to wield it would be too great for my strength' (*FR* I/2). He then instructs his disciple-companion Frodo about its evil powers and the need to destroy it.

The Pardoner's three young men questing to kill Death matched Tolkien's recurrent theme of wrongly seeking immortality, as when the Númenóreans tried sailing westward to the Undying Lands. The Ring's promise of longevity as a sort of counterfeit immorality also became Sauron's chief bait for the Ringwraiths.[108] The 'wicked men' were originally thieves driven by greed, but they were also 'close friends and bound to one another by vows of fellowship'. Also in the 1950s, Tolkien revised his story of Morgoth stealing the Silmarils with the assistance of Ungoliant but then refusing to share the gems with her—'Thus there befell the first thieves' quarrel.' He then expanded this version 'Of the Thieves' Quarrel' in which the giant spider dies as a result of Morgoth's betrayal, thus bringing the primal myth of greediness closer to the core-story of the Pardoner's Tale.[109]

In all versions of the story, the main characters required their opponents. In Gollum's previous life as Sméagol, he turned into Déagol's enemy and killed him for the Ring. Because Tolkien had his two good characters Gandalf and Frodo, he needed two bad characters as foils. Now a sad old hobbit, Gollum becomes Frodo's corrupt counterpart who loses his one chance at redemption after Sam interferes (*Letters*, 330). As Gandalf's adversary, Saruman belongs to the same wizard order but betrays their friendship for the Ring.

Though the core-story involved only two men, the Pardoner's Tale offered an expanded variation in which three men plot each other's deaths. 'I have suggested that the number was enlarged to *three* for narrative reasons', said Tolkien in his lecture, perhaps thinking of his own enlargement of the story's cast of three hobbits fighting over the gold in the Cracks of Doom. His *The Lord of the Rings* had performed what Harold Bloom termed 'an act of creative correction' by giving these three characters different motives, and then his lecture on the Pardoner's Tale engaged in Bloomian 'self-saving caricature' and 'perverse, willful revisionism' (*AI* 30) when criticizing Chaucer. After launching the original two-man version of Sméagol and Déagol, Tolkien had followed Chaucer by expanding the

---

[108] *Letters*, 246, about *TLOR*: 'The real theme for me is about something much more permanent and difficult: Death and Immorality.' See also *Letters*, 286, and SH 2:803–14 'Mortality and Immortality'.
[109] Tolkien, *Morgoth's Ring*, 109, 295–9; Christopher noted that the standard account has Ungoliant retreat into the south (p. 299). An earlier version of 'the first thieves' quarrel' had already appeared in *The Lost Road*, 255.

number to three—Frodo, Sam, and Gollum—but he arrived at a quite different ending in which the two good hobbits survive.

Here *The Lord of the Rings* engaged in creative correction just where Chaucer's story 'proceeds to the prepared catastrophe'. Tolkien's use of the word *catastrophe* is significant because he had reshaped his events to conclude instead with a *eucatastrophe* or 'joy of the happy ending'. The two hobbits of the Shire survive because not driven by greed, whereas Gollum's murderous obsession with the Ring leads to his own death. Both retellings of the age-old story end with a fight over the gold. In Chaucer's version, the youngest is killed when wrestling with his two older fellows who then die by drinking poisoned wine; in Tolkien's version, the oldest dies after wrestling with the two younger hobbits who then survive by escaping the eruption of Orodruin. For all of his meanderings and revisions over many years, Tolkien had already decided upon this conclusion in his outline of 1939:

> When Bingo [> Frodo] at last reaches Crack and Fiery Mountain *he cannot make himself throw the Ring away*...At that moment Gollum—who had seemed to reform and had guided them by secret ways through Mordor—comes up and treacherously tries to take the Ring. They wrestle and Gollum *takes Ring* and falls into the Crack.[110]

Tolkien toyed with the idea of having Sam wrestle with Gollum and push him into the gulf, but a wrestling match and its outcomes remained constants.

Tolkien typically used sources only to improve upon them.[111] His improvement upon the Pardoner's Tale allowed for three different responses to the gold's temptation and three different outcomes for his characters. Gollum was fatally obsessed with the Ring and died clutching it; Sam felt a stronger loyalty to his master and survived largely unscathed; and Frodo's willpower weakened so that only Gollum's attack allowed him to complete his quest with the loss of a finger.[112] The Pardoner's sermon on the biblical verse 'greed is the root of all evil' was transformed into Tolkien's positive *exemplum* of two characters motivated by devotion to each other and duty to their fellows. If Merry and Pippin's victory along with the Ents at Isengard improved upon *Macbeth*—and improved, too, upon the misadventure of John and Alain in the Reeve's Tale—the success of Frodo and Sam at Mount Doom was transformed into a happy-ending version of the Pardoner's Tale.[113]

---

[110] Tolkien, *Return of the Shadow*, 380, and *Sauron Defeated*, 3–5.

[111] Jason Fisher, 'Tolkien and Source Criticism: Remarking and Remaking', in *Tolkien and the Study of His Sources*, ed. Fisher, 29–44.

[112] Eight years after his Pardoner's Tale lectures, Tolkien produced a lengthy narrative analysis of Frodo's inability to surrender the Ring; see *Letters*, 325–33.

[113] Tolkien in *Letters*, 233–5, reflected on the quest's final events which 'seemed to me mechanically, morally, and psychologically credible'.

After its lengthy narrative analysis, *The Pardoner's Tale: The Story and its Form* returned to Tolkien's critique of source-studies and specifically Clouston's confidence that the story originated in Asia and was then imported to Europe:[114]

> The fact therefore that the oldest known version (and one already fully elaborated, indeed already altered for a special purpose) is *Indian* and *Buddhist* is no proof that this tale arose in India and spread thence westward... Sanscrit language and its descendant, the primary vehicle of Buddhist literature, are not indigenous to India, but entered from the north-west, leaving behind people of very close connexion in language (and in religion and myth) in the wide lands right up to the borders of what is now named Europe. Buddhism, and therefore the roots of its literature, go back to a time that seems to us ancient; but the world of men was already very old in the days of Gautama... (fol. 44r)

Just as Indo-European languages had migrated from west to east, so too the earliest myths of the Aryan peoples passed along these same routes across Mesopotamia and Persia. The fact that the earliest texts were written in Sanskrit does not mean the same stories were unknown among other peoples in far-off lands. 'What indeed,' asked Tolkien, 'do we know of the tales of men in all the lost centuries in the lands we now call Europe?'

Here he echoes his own early exclamation, 'how complex are the linguistic and cultural events of Europe before the dawn of history!'[115] Though Chaucer's Old Man spoke of walking as far as India and Chaucer knew accounts of India from Mandeville's *Travels* (as did Tolkien from glossing the excerpt in Sisam's anthology), the fourteenth-century English writer had no way of deriving his Pardoner's Tale directly from the *Jātaka*. The core-story must have been rooted in native soil, and those roots reached deep into the unrecorded past, deeper no doubt than Chaucer himself understood. Anglo-Saxon monks no longer knew what a *Sigelhearwa* was, for example, but Tolkien believed the reasons they used the word to translate 'Ethiopian' were worth investigating: 'we seek to recapture what they had forgotten and examine each of the original elements in turn.'[116] Retrieving mythic figures of Europe's lost centuries and recovering the sources of its legends—here the three men struggling with each other to the death over a gold treasure—had become Tolkien's mission throughout *The Lord of the Rings*, completed and published by the time he was lecturing anew on the Pardoner's Tale in the 1950s.

Had Tolkien realized the resemblance to Chaucer's core-story when first writing about Frodo, Gollum, and Gandalf? Probably not. His original lectures

---

[114] Nevill Coghill and Christopher Tolkien, eds., *Pardoner's Tale* (London: George G. Harrap, 1958), repeated this view: 'The story itself had come half way round the world to find a man who could tell it properly' (p. 37). One student later recalled of Tolkien's lectures: 'it was from him that most of us heard the name *Mahabharata* in connection with *The Pardoner's Tale*' (SH 3:965).

[115] Tolkien, 'Philology' (1926), 44; see Simon J. Cook, 'The Cauldron at the Outer Edge: Tolkien on the Oldest Fairy Tales', *Tolkien Studies* 13 (2016), 9–29.

[116] Tolkien, 'Sigelwara Land' (1934), 95.

on the Pardoner's Tale in the late 1940s gave no hint of defensiveness. There he had told his students that it was one of Chaucer's best-told tales.[117] The potential for rivalry was always lurking, however, because Chaucer differed from the *Beowulf* Poet as a named author with a biography, a substantial canon of titles, a lineage of predecessors as prestigious as Dante and Boccaccio, and a genealogy of successors as illustrious as Spenser and Shakespeare. Only when reading proofs of *The Lord of the Rings* did Tolkien apparently recognize parallels between the two skeleton plots, and his attitude toward Chaucer's performance turned sharply negative as if enacting Harold Bloom's anxiety-ridden role: 'The poet confronting his Great Original must find fault that is not there' (*AI* 31). After years of considering Chaucer as a brother philologist, Tolkien suddenly confronted him as a father-figure and struggled for superiority against this formidable precursor. Therefore in the 1950s he found reasons to fault Chaucer as a narrative artist as he had not in the 1940s.

In a telling moment in 'Three Is Company' when Frodo recited *The Road Goes Ever On and On*, Sam asked if it was Bilbo's poetry or an imitation of it—and Frodo had to admit, 'It came to me then, as if I was making it up; but I may have heard it long ago' (*FR* I/3). With what amounts to an admission of unconsciously using prior material, Tolkien came to value source-studies at the end of his life: 'the particular use in a particular situation of any motive, whether invented, deliberately borrowed, or unconsciously remembered, is the most interesting thing to consider.'[118] Once he realized that he himself had unconsciously remembered Chaucer's core-story, he judged much more harshly its particular variation in the hands of the fourteenth-century poet. 'I do not approve of the *Pardoner's Tale*,' he declared to his undergraduates: 'it has a specious surface finish and attraction, but does not support examination or long familiarity.'[119]

Specifically Chaucer had neglected essential elements of the archetype. The origin of the gold is never explained. The Old Man does not clearly grasp the treasure's threat when directing the three young men to it. And the storyline is top-heavy and misshapen: 'It ends abruptly (as Chaucer's tales are apt to do), as if he had expended so much energy (or too much) on the beginning that he had barely breath to stay the course.' If T. S. Eliot famously remarked that bad writers defaced their sources while good writers made them better or at least different, Tolkien concluded that Chaucer had defaced whatever sources he drew upon and that he himself, to his own unspoken satisfaction, had taken the same inherited story and made it into something both different and better.

---

[117] Bodleian MS Tolkien A 13/2, fol. 86.

[118] *Letters*, 418. Tolkien admitted to Auden that *The Marvellous Land of Snergs* was 'probably an unconscious source-book' for *The Hobbit* (*Letters*, 215n.).

[119] Tolkien's harshness could apply even to his own work, as when Christopher quoted him from a 1937 letter: 'I don't much approve of *The Hobbit* myself' (*Return of the Shadow*, 7).

And what about the pilgrim tale-teller? Even more than Kittredge before him, Tolkien found the Pardoner an 'odious and noxious creature of bizarre shape and colouring and strange if disgusting habits'. It is not clearly stated whether *disgusting habits* alluded to the Pardoner's deviant sexuality as grounds for damning him as well as his tale. Not until the 1980s did Chaucerians write explicitly about this pilgrim as a homosexual, but the unspoken suspicion was always present to smirk at.[120] Living quietly as a homosexual during the bigoted 1950s, Nevill Coghill in his textbook used euphemisms such as 'effeminacy' and 'lack of manhood' but left little doubt what he meant.[121]

Although Gandalf chose Bilbo for the quest specifically because he was 'a bit queer' (*UT* 323), Tolkien may have become defensive because some early reviews of *The Lord of the Rings* had caught a whiff of homoeroticism between Frodo and Sam. Edwin Muir's notorious 1955 review of *The Return of the King* said about all the male characters, 'hardly one of them knows anything about women, except by hearsay.' Attacking hobbits as 'boys masquerading as adult heroes' meant in effect attacking their masculinity. They were not real men; they were not even the height of real men.[122] Tolkien bristled at the review—'Blast Edwin Muir and his delayed adolescence!' (*Letters*, 230)—and yet the nastiness of his own characterization of the Pardoner seems to have mobilized the homophobia of the 1950s as a sort of self-defence after depicting intimate male relationships throughout his trilogy.[123] The year 1955 when Tolkien launched his three-term lecture series on the Pardoner's Tale, it should be noted, was the year after persecution as a homosexual had hounded Alan Turing into committing suicide.

After taking issue with the odious Pardoner, Tolkien transferred his censure to the author himself: 'I do not think that Chaucer did all things well. In this case I think he did much that was ill.' To condemn Chaucer's narrative artistry meant tacitly to compliment himself on doing better. He had revived the most ancient and therefore most authentic two-man version in his account of Sméagol and Déagol. His gold treasure exerted more power than simple greed over its possessors. His wizard functioned better at knowing the true nature of the gold's threat

---

[120] This discussion began in a high-visibility journal with Monica E. McAlpine, 'The Pardoner's Homosexuality and How It Matters', *PMLA* 95 (1980), 8–22. Carolyn Dinshaw, *Getting Medieval: Sexualities and Communities, Pre- and Postmodern* (Durham, NC: Duke University Press, 1999), 122–6, focuses on Kittredge's fascination with the Pardoner's forbidden sexuality rendered as homophobia.

[121] *The Pardoner's Tale*, ed. Nevill Coghill and Christopher Tolkien, 17–18. Reynolds Price, *Ardent Spirits*, 128, recalls about the senior editor: 'Nevill himself was born in 1899, served in the First War, married, fathered a daughter, then separated from his wife and lived a quietly homosexual life thereafter.'

[122] Edwin Muir, 'A Boy's World', *The Observer* (27 November 1955), 11; see Patrick Curry, 'The Critical Response to Tolkien's Fiction', in *Companion*, ed. Lee, 370–1. Muir's complaint was not without merit; see Chance, *Tolkien, Self and Other*, 'The Failure of Masculinity', 215–39.

[123] David LaFontaine, 'Sex and Subtext in Tolkien's World', *The Gay & Lesbian Review* 22/6 (2015), 14–17; see also LaFontaine, 'The Tolkien in Bilbo Baggins', *The Gay & Lesbian Review* 23/6 (2016), 24–8.

and advising its owner about it. Finally Tolkien took up Chaucer's three-man version and transformed it into a positive *exemplum* by having Frodo and Sam resist temptation and rid themselves of the gold treasure, albeit with unintended help from Gollum. In one early version Frodo wrestled with Gollum over the Ring, in another Sam did the brawling, but the life-or-death struggle remained a consistent feature.[124] It would be exaggerating to suggest that Tolkien himself wrestled with Chaucer as a strong precursor—certainly not to the death, as Bloom put it—but he did see fit to stage a wrestling match between Gollum and the two hobbits as prelude to the *eucatastrophe* inside Mount Doom.

Tolkien's marathon lectures of 1955–6 became an act of leave-taking. *The Return of the King* was published in October 1955, three weeks into Michaelmas Term, and students curious about their professor's fiction-writing were then in a position to connect his trilogy with his remarks on the Pardoner's Tale. Diana Wynne Jones, later a great fan of the novels, does not mention knowing them or even knowing *about* them when she attended his Chaucer lectures, but she correctly guessed, 'Tolkien did not give away half of what he knew even about plots.' And one thing that he did not give away was his own narrative's resemblances to the Pardoner's Tale. The more time passed after publication of *The Lord of the Rings*, the more likely his undergraduates were to spot those resemblances. His final classes in Trinity Term 1959 covered *Sawles Warde*, and he emerged from retirement in 1962–3 to lecture on *Beowulf* for his colleague C. L. Wrenn,[125] but for the remainder of his teaching career at Oxford after 1956, he never again lectured on the Pardoner's Tale.

---

[124] Tolkien, *Treason of Isengard*, 209.
[125] Tolkien had co-authored with S. R. T. O. d'Ardenne '"Iþþlen" in *Sawles Warde*', *English Studies* 28 (1947), 168–70, as part of their ongoing study of the Katherine Group. Anne Hudson shared with me about attending these final classes on *Sawles Warde*: 'Christopher was the better lecturer.'

8
Coda: Fathers and Sons

Chaucer and Tolkien were both exceptionally lucky in the sons who served as literary executors sorting through their literary remains and overseeing posthumous publications. Without them, we would not have the Chaucer or the Tolkien that we read today. These parallels are purely coincidental, hardly the stuff of serious scholarship, to be sure, but they provide a fitting coda to a story founded on the twin coincidences of the Clarendon Chaucer's survival and its rescue from the basement of Oxford University Press. How might Tolkien have felt about these parallels? His own *The Lost Road* imagined a series of father–son incarnations recurring over the course of history, Elendil and Herendil in Númenor, Ælfwine and Eadwine in Anglo-Saxon times, and Alboin and Audoin in the twentieth century.[1] So he might have been intrigued, albeit begrudgingly, by this account of father–son affinities between the Chaucers and the Tolkiens.

Thomas Chaucer's responsibility as custodian of his father's literary papers remains a matter of speculation, but Christopher's ancillary role was already well established even during his father's lifetime. By the age of 5, he was catching inconsistency in the bedtime version of *The Hobbit*, such as whether the colour of Bilbo's door was green or blue, and later, at 13, he was paid twopence each for ferreting out misprints in the published novel.[2] When Tolkien was struggling with his sequel in 1945, he wrote to Stanley Unwin explaining his youngest son's role which continued via the mails while he was training as a RAF Spitfire pilot in South Africa:

> My Christopher was my real primary audience, who has read, vetted, and typed all of the new Hobbit, or The Ring, that has been completed. He was dragged off in the middle of making maps. I have squandered almost the only time I have had to spare for writing in continuing our interrupted conversations by epistle: he occupied the multiple position of audience, critic, son, student in my department, and my tutorial pupil. But he has received copies of all chapters I wrote in a spurt last year. (*Letters*, 112–13)

---

[1] Tolkien, *The Lost Road*, 85–7, and *Letters*, 347. Christopher remarked, 'Alboin's biography sketched in these chapters is in many respects closely modelled on my father's own life' (*Lost Road*, 58).
[2] SH 3:1301–2 and *Letters*, 28.

Tolkien's Lost Chaucer. John M. Bowers, Oxford University Press (2019). © John M. Bowers.
DOI: 10.1093/oso/9780198842675.001.0001

After the war when Christopher returned to Oxford to complete his degree, he became a member of the Inklings and undertook reading aloud the draft chapters of *The Lord of the Rings*. Everyone agreed that he read more effectively than his father. When Tolkien grew dissatisfied with his own efforts at cartography, Christopher undertook the job of drawing the Middle-earth maps for publication.

The Hobbit sold well and won prizes, and Tolkien lived long enough to witness *The Lord of the Rings* become a literary phenomenon, but there is little evidence that Chaucer, circumspect in the extreme, released the majority of his works during his lifetime. His writing desk at the time of his death would have been piled with uncirculated manuscripts of *The Book of the Duchess* and *The Parlement of Foules* as well as unfinished drafts of *The House of Fame* and *The Legend of Good Women*. His scribe Adam's fair copies of *Troilus* and *Boece* were probably produced for the author only, not for release beyond a small circle of friends like John Gower. These texts then became exemplars for posthumous copying. Anyone looking at the earliest manuscripts of the *Canterbury Tales* would conclude Chaucer belonged chronologically to the fifteenth century because that is when all the copies were produced. Some well-placed individual clearly took charge of the author's literary remains during the decade after his death in 1400 to preserve these works in grand fashion. Someone needed to provide exemplars, pay professional scribes, and finance production of lavish volumes like Ellesmere. Even Hengwrt without any pilgrim portraits was, as Christopher de Hamel so nicely says, 'not a cheap book'.[3] That individual was almost certainly the poet's son and heir.[4]

Thomas Chaucer was born in the late 1360s but does not enter the documentary record until retained by John of Gaunt in 1389.[5] He would have grown up with his mother mostly in the Lancastrian household, an exact contemporary of Gaunt's oldest son, the future Henry IV, and he would have been the playfellow of Gaunt's children by his longtime mistress and third wife, Katherine Swynford— the sister of Thomas's mother. Like his father, he travelled on diplomatic missions to the Continent but rose to a higher level of responsibility as Chief Butler providing wine for the royal household. Unlike his father, he married a wealthy heiress and established himself at a country seat in Oxfordshire where he served as sheriff, escheator, and member of several commissions. At his Ewelme manor, he

---

[3] De Hamel, 'Hengwrt Chaucer', 435–6: 'It uses gold. It is of some size, especially in comparison with many Middle English manuscripts of its time, such as *Piers Plowman* or the Wycliffite scriptures, which are often small and unimposing. It is written on parchment, not paper... and the skin here is of good quality, soft to the touch.'

[4] John H. Fisher, *The Importance of Chaucer* (Carbondale and Edwardsville: Southern Illinois University Press, 1992), 'Chaucer Since 1400', 141–69 at pp. 145–6, credits Thomas with these posthumous publications. About the Ellesmere project, Manly and Rickert, eds., *Text of the Canterbury Tales* (1:159), concluded Thomas Chaucer was 'logically the person to have had made what was clearly intended as an authoritative text'.

[5] Martin R. Ruud, *Thomas Chaucer* (Minneapolis: University of Minnesota Studies in Language and Literature, no. 9, 1926), assembled the biographical documents then known.

came to resemble Chaucer's Franklin as a mainstay of shire administration, enjoying a prosperous life without risking too much ambition. Oxfordshire became the centre of his property holdings that included Wootton Hundred—recalled by Tolkien's title *Smith of Wootton Major*.

When Richard II was deposed in 1399, Thomas was entrusted with custody of the young Queen Isabelle. Thereafter he became a reliable supporter of the Lancastrians during fourteen parliamentary sessions, five times as Speaker of the Commons—a record unmatched until the reign of George II. Here he showed himself a canny operator like his father, able to serve as intermediary between Henry V and Bishop Beaufort without losing the confidence of either.[6] He raised troops for Henry V's invasion of France, but perhaps mindful of his father's hardships during the Normandy expedition, he claimed illness before embarking and therefore did not fight at Agincourt. His tomb-brass in Ewelme church showing him in armour with a sword was a pious fiction probably conceived by his daughter, since he seems to have taken trouble to avoid the expenses and dangers of knighthood. Thomas, like Geoffrey, had been a survivor. His only child Alice Chaucer outlived three husbands, the last of them the Duke of Suffolk, so she had motivation for embellishing her father's image.

No book-list survives as evidence of literary interests, although Thomas did have connections with cultural activists like Humphrey, Duke of Gloucester. John Lydgate's ballade *On the Departing of Thomas Chaucer* establishes his relationship with the most prolific poet of the fifteenth century.[7] His son-in-law William de la Pole had custody of the aristocratic poet Charles d'Orléans and possibly penned some verses himself.[8] Yet the upwardly mobile Thomas seemed reluctant about acknowledging kinship with the author of the *Canterbury Tales* so that Geoffrey's arms were not even included on his tomb.[9] Though official documents give no hint that the poet was indeed his father, Thomas in all likelihood played the decisive role as the man behind the curtain, so to speak, for bolstering literary greatness on behalf of Geoffrey Chaucer.

Tolkien's friend the medieval historian Bruce McFarlane had occasion to investigate Thomas Chaucer's career and found an individual of exceptional talents: 'a self-made man of great wealth, acquisitive yet circumspect, politic and *affairé*, well-versed in all branches of administration and diplomacy, a practiced

---

[6] Roskell, 'Thomas Chaucer of Ewelme', 170.
[7] *The Oxford Book of Late Medieval Verse and Prose*, ed. Douglas Gray with Norman Davis (Oxford: Clarendon Press, 1985), 60-2. Derek Pearsall, *John Lydgate* (Charlottesville: University Press of Virginia, 1970), 161-2, speculates that Lydgate came to know Thomas Chaucer because Ewelme was just south-east of Oxford where the poet studied in 1408.
[8] Derek Pearsall, 'The Literary Milieu of Charles of Orléans and the Duke of Suffolk, and the Authorship of the Fairfax Sequence', in *Charles d'Orléans in England (1415-1440)*, ed. Mary-Jo Arn (Woodbridge and Rochester: Boydell & Brewer, 2000), 145-56.
[9] A. E. Greening Lamborn, 'The Arms on the Chaucer Tomb at Ewelme', *Oxoniensia* 5 (1940), 78-93.

chairman and envoy, influential and respected'.[10] The Lancastrian usurpation improved his prospects with an annual income of £1,000 from properties alone. The addition of annuities and stipends made him a very rich man, rich enough for investments on behalf of his father's posthumous literary standing. Certainly Thomas had motive and opportunity for commissioning the earliest, most reliable, and most expensive copies of *Troilus* and the *Canterbury Tales* as part of the nascent process of 'canon-formation' on behalf of the English literary tradition, but more specifically on behalf of his family's status.

Christopher de Hamel speaks of 'Chaucer's executors' without venturing to name names,[11] but most likely Thomas himself took charge of his father's literary papers by formal or informal arrangement with the author before his death. The younger Chaucer was never heavy-handed as a marketer and remained conspicuous by his absence from any record of promoting these works. At a time of ever-shifting political alliances and social upheavals—his first parliamentary session in 1401 passed the law *De heretico comburendo* that authorized the burning of Lollards—the earliest deluxe manuscripts do not contain his name, or the names of any aristocratic owners for that matter, except for the shield of Henry V as Prince of Wales in the Pierpont Morgan manuscript of *Troilus*.[12]

At some early point Thomas needed the help of professional bookmen in order to produce handsome, complete-looking copies of the *Canterbury* fragments which his father left in some disarray. In addition to his duties as Chief Butler, he had wide-ranging responsibilities for estates management, shire commissions, parliamentary business, and legal transactions as forester, castle constable, and justice of the peace. All of this paperwork required a staff of clerks associated with London's writing professionals, and Thomas thus had connections with scribes possessing the talent, training, and spare time for literary projects on the side. This much is clear: some entrepreneurial scribe did not simply come upon Chaucer's drafts wafting around London and start copying the Hengwrt and Ellesmere manuscripts.[13] A legitimate custodian needed to provide access to exemplars, and a wealthy patron needed to pay scribes as well as limners, illuminators, and binders to produce these sumptuous volumes.[14] There was only one man qualified in all these areas for overseeing these authorized editions. If Geoffrey Chaucer

---

[10] K. B. McFarlane, 'Henry V, Bishop Beaufort and the Red Hat, 1417–1421' (1945), in *England in the Fifteenth Century: Collected Essays*, intro. G. L. Harriss (London: Hambledon Press, 1981), 79–113 at p. 102; McFarlane had been a member of Tolkien's Kolbítar reading group.

[11] De Hamel, 'Hengwrt Chaucer', 445, 464.

[12] Terry Jones, *Who Murdered Chaucer? A Medieval Mystery* (New York: St. Martin's Press, 2003), 264–6 and 291–5, takes a somewhat sinister view of Thomas Chaucer's manoeuvres on the political landscape.

[13] Mooney and Stubbs, *Scribes and the City*, have identified Adam Pinkhurst as the copyist of Hengwrt and Ellesmere (pp. 66–85), though Warner's 'Scribes, Misattributed: Hoccleve and Pinkhurst' and De Hamel's 'Hengwrt Chaucer' cast doubts on these ascriptions.

[14] Martin Stevens and Daniel Woodward, eds., *Ellesmere Chaucer: Essays in Interpretation* (San Marino CA: Huntington Library, 1995), examines many aspects of this production.

became famous as father of English poetry, Thomas Chaucer deserves credit as father of English literary executors.

In 1900 Skeat was excited to discover that Thomas continued renting Geoffrey's house in the garden of Westminster Abbey until his own death in 1434.[15] For more than a century, however, scholars neglected to ask *why* Thomas continued leasing this residence when he had a larger, more luxurious London townhouse in Golding Lane. Parliament did not always convene in Westminster, but Thomas's first session did meet there in January 1401 not long after his father's death. The garden residence would have provided convenient lodging within walking distance of any parliamentary business, while in his spare hours Thomas faced the daunting task of sorting through the literary papers left there for safekeeping. Because 1401 is usually reckoned as the approximate date for the Hengwrt manuscript, it is tempting to picture Thomas recruiting one of his father's own experienced copyists to assist with piecing together the fragments of the *Canterbury Tales*, if not working on site, then receiving batches sent from Westminster. This first effort in Hengwrt achieved mixed results, preserving a text judged closest to the poet's original but failing to assemble the fragments in an order acceptable to modern readers. The copyist had access to authoritative exemplars, that is, but he had no well-informed directions on how the fragments fitted together.[16] The Hengwrt scribe did not even know to include the Canon's Yeoman's Tale, perhaps Chaucer's last and most sophisticated poetic work.

Secure within the precincts of the Benedictine monastery, the poet's last known residence most likely served as a repository for the author's fair copies and working papers, as well as his personal library, becoming in effect the first Centre for Chaucer Studies.[17] It was probably at the Westminster Abbey tenement that another early scribe was provided with exemplars for making the two other deluxe manuscripts Harley 7334 and Corpus Christi 198.[18] Here, too, the Hengwrt scribe returned between 1400 and 1410 for producing Ellesmere with its preferred tale-order and famous pilgrim pictures, all of which required the further outlay of funds for artists and limners. It is probably no coincidence that when William Caxton began printing in 1476, he set up his press in the precincts of Westminster Abbey and his first book was the *Canterbury Tales*.

It was probably here, too, that John Lydgate enjoyed almost unlimited access to Chaucer's works, composing his *Complaint of the Black Knight* and *Temple of*

---

[15] Walter W. Skeat, 'Thomas, Son of Geoffrey Chaucer', *Athenæum*, no. 3770 (27 January 1900), 116.

[16] Manly and Rickert, eds., *Text of the Canterbury Tales*, 1:266–83; see also Ralph Hanna, 'The Hengwrt Manuscript and the Canon of *The Canterbury Tales*', in *Pursuing History*, 141–55; Simon Horobin, 'Adam Pinkhurst, Geoffrey Chaucer, and the Hengwrt Manuscript of the *Canterbury Tales*', *Chaucer Review* 44 (2010), 351–67; and De Hamel, 'Hengwrt Chaucer', 438–49.

[17] Bowers, 'The House of Chaucer & Son: The Business of Lancastrian Canon-Formation', in *Chaucer and Langland*, 183–90, and Pearsall, *Life of Geoffrey Chaucer*, 280–2.

[18] Mooney and Stubbs, *Scribes and the City*, 'John Marchaunt', 38–65, identify the scribe who copied Harley and Corpus Christi between the two other productions of Hengwrt and Ellesmere.

Glass even before their models *The Book of the Duchess* and *The House of Fame* appeared in the earliest manuscripts. Lydgate was so well-informed about Chaucer's career that he was able to include the poet's literary biography in his *Fall of Princes*, itself a vastly expanded version of the Monk's Tale. In particular Lydgate had access to the unfinished *Canterbury Tales* and wrote a continuation of the pilgrimage and tale-telling in his *Siege of Thebes*. At a time when Chaucer was being installed as father of the English literary tradition, Lydgate was energetically positioning himself as the poet's literary heir even as Thomas acted behind the scenes as his legal heir.[19]

Documentary evidence of the sort lacking for Chaucer's son is abundant for Christopher Tolkien as overseer for his father's unfinished writing projects.[20] He immediately tackled the staggering task of editing 'Silmarillion' materials in publishable form. Much as Thomas Chaucer allowed his earliest scribes freedom to sift through the self-contradictory materials of the *Canterbury* fragments to produce different arrangements, even inserting *Gamelyn*, found among his father's papers perhaps as a source for an unwritten Yeoman's Tale, Christopher tackled the challenge of *The Silmarillion* (1977) by compiling materials 'so complex, so pervasive, and so many-layered that a final and definitive version seemed unattainable'.[21] Whereas Thomas Chaucer needed the help of the Hengwrt–Ellesmere scribe, Christopher was assisted by the Canadian writer Guy Kay in his 'difficult and doubtful task' (p. xi).

Tolkien's earlier versions of these legends were then assembled in the two-volume *Book of Lost Tales* and thereby became the first instalments of Christopher's twelve-volume *History of Middle-earth*. In particular his four-volume *History of the Lord of the Rings* stands as a monument to meticulous editing. It is sobering to imagine what a slapdash affair these posthumous publications might have become—if indeed they ever saw the light of day—had it not been for the dedication of a literary executor who was himself an exacting scholar long familiar with his father's writings. Rayner Unwin remarked about Tolkien's debt to his son: 'one man's imaginative genius has had the benefit of two lifetimes' work.'[22] One can only wonder whether Thomas Chaucer, looking over the shoulder of his scribes during the decade after his father's death, also took a personal hand in the Ellesmere version which has been widely accepted as definitive.

---

[19] Bowers, 'John Lydgate: The Outsider Let In', in *Chaucer and Langland*, 202–6.
[20] Douglas A. Anderson, 'Christopher Tolkien: A Bibliography', in *Tolkien's 'Legendarium': Essay on 'The History of Middle-earth*, ed. Verlyn Flieger and Carl F. Hostetter (Westport and London: Greenwood Press, 2000), 247–52, traces this extraordinary output up to 1996.
[21] *Sil*, p. ix; see Noad, 'On the Construction of "The Silmarillion"', in *Tolkien's 'Legendarium'*, ed. Flieger and Hostetter, 31–68.
[22] Unwin, 'Early Days of the Elder Days', ibid. 6.

Here I want to conclude with an early instance in which Christopher completed one unfinished project even during his father's lifetime, almost as a harbinger of things to come. When Tolkien returned his Chaucer materials to OUP in 1951, his letter to Dan Davin described what was missing: 'The draft of notes for *all* pieces but the last two (from *Monk's Tale* and *Nuns' Priest's Tale*).' For the Monk's Tale, George Gordon had excerpted the 55-line story of Ugolino based on Dante's *Inferno*, but the capstone of their *Selections* was the perennial favorite praised even by C. S. Lewis—the Nun's Priest's Tale. Tolkien had worked over the text and included its vocabulary in his Glossary, but he never proceeded to draft any commentary whatsoever on the tale which he knew well enough to recite from memory for Oxford's Summer Diversions in 1938.

A year after publishing a student edition of *The Pardoner's Tale*, Christopher ushered into print his own *Nun's Priest's Tale* in 1959.[23] Though he no longer had access to his father's editorial materials locked in Dan Davin's strongroom, the whole project gives a startling sense of *déjà-vu* beginning with the division of editorial labours. In the 1920s J. R. R. Tolkien served as junior co-editor with Merton Professor George Gordon; in the 1950s Christopher Tolkien served as junior co-editor with Merton Professor Nevill Coghill. The difference was that Christopher actually completed and published his student editions. He knew his Chaucer well. Later, when editing *The Lays of Beleriand*, he could trace references to Wade back to *Troilus* and the Merchant's Tale, even citing Speght's 1598 Chaucer annotations about the boat Gringelot as the source for Eärendel's sky-ship Wingelot.[24]

This handy little edition of *The Nun's Priest's Tale* does not state who did what, but it probably followed the earlier model with Professor Coghill contributing a chatty introduction of the sort expected from George Gordon. Coghill's apology for his deficiencies could easily have been written by Gordon: 'when we hunt for truffles, we use a pig to show us where they are and dig them out for us' (p. 9). Coghill had rehearsed this colloquial style in his Penguin translation of the *Canterbury Tales* where, for example, he explained why Edward III contributed to Chaucer's ransom from French captivity: 'Well-trained and intelligent pages did not grow on every bush.'[25]

Christopher then rolled up his sleeves for the heavy work of 'Chaucer's Language and Metre' before proceeding to edit the text, write the notes, and compile the glossary—just as his father had been assigned to do more than three decades

---

[23] Chaucer, *The Nun's Priest's Tale*, ed. Nevill Coghill and Christopher Tolkien (London: George G. Harrap, 1959). Coghill and Christopher Tolkien also published student editions of *The Pardoner's Tale* (1958) and *The Man of Law's Tale* (1969).
[24] *Lays of Beleriand*, 174–5; see Wenterdorf, 'Chaucer and the Lost Tale of Wade'. Tolkien's *Gawain* edition, 90–1, had already made this reference to Speght's 1598 Chaucer edition about Wade's boat.
[25] Geoffrey Chaucer, *The Canterbury Tales*, trans. Nevill Coghill (Baltimore: Penguin Books, 1952), 7. This paperback remains in print as a Penguin Classic, though Tolkien was not a fan of his verse-making: 'Mr Nevill Judson Coghill | Wrote a deal of dangerous doggerill' (*Letters*, 359).

before. He announced his intention to include dots and accent marks for clarifying pronunciation, especially for final *-e* and for words newly borrowed from French, exactly as Tolkien had done much to the irritation of Sisam. Christopher also carried forward his father's interest in the migration of Old Norse vocabulary from north to south: 'the Scandinavian nominative *they*, ousting the native English *hi*, was already completely established in London by this time' (p. 37). Old Norse had become his academic specialty, and the next year he published his edition of *The Saga of King Heidrek the Wise*.[26] When establishing his text of the Nun's Priest's Tale, Christopher shared his father's scepticism about Ellesmere for preserving Chaucer's spellings and even his original words: 'The Ellesmere scribe made, indeed, a fair number of quite obvious errors' (p. 44). He would record emendations of these errors at the bottom of pages while following the facsimile edition of Ellesmere as his copy-text. This may have well been the same facsimile that Warnie Lewis reported Tolkien showing off to the Inklings in 1947.[27]

His Nun's Priest's Tale was conscientiously edited without much showiness about its underlying erudition. It is also a complete text, the two passages describing how Chanticleer 'feathered' his wife Pertelote not deleted for decency's sake. Footnotes record sixty emendations of Ellesmere's readings. Comparison with prior editions show that fifty-two improvements were suggested by Skeat, six more gleaned from Sisam's 1927 student edition, and two more imported from Robinson's *Riverside Chaucer*. Thus Christopher produced a text in some ways superior to the current *Riverside Chaucer*. Though its editor Ralph Hanna did not record all departures from Ellesmere, his *Canterbury Tales* kept closer to the copy-text, not always with happy results. For example, Christopher's emendation 'But to that o man fil a greet mervaille' is metrically superior to Hanna's 'But herkneth! To that o man fil a greet mervaille' (3076) because he smartly omitted Ellesmere's *herkneth*.

Forty-five pages of notes gave Christopher the scope which his father aspired to. Reading them now gives the happy sense of an Oxford reunion where we encounter so many long-familiar names and revisit favourite topics of conversation. Coghill's Penguin translation had already explained courtly love by reference to C. S. Lewis's *The Allegory of Love*, and now Christopher made easy acknowledgement of the 1894 Oxford Chaucer: 'When Professor Skeat edited the Canterbury Tales...' (p. 99). He also deferred to the reigning student edition when acknowledging 'Dr. Sisam has suggested...' (p. 99) and 'Dr. Sisam has pointed out...' (p. 131).

Christopher pursued etymologies and commented upon single words like *aventure* familiar from his father's philological forays. He also made a point of

---

[26] *The Saga of King Heidrek the Wise*, ed. Christopher Tolkien (London: Thomas Nelson and Sons, 1960); see review of the 2010 reprint by Tom Shippey, *Tolkien Studies* 8 (2011), 136–42.

[27] Warren Lewis, *Brothers and Friends*, 215.

identifying the Kentish words *kyn* and *leste*. He paid silent homage to his father's interest in Chaucer's dialect words like *ill*: 'for him it was a word characteristic of the North and East of England (it was of Scandinavian origin), and he only used it to give an impression of dialect in the talk of John and Alain, the two Cambridge students from the North of England in the Reeve's Tale' (pp. 94–5). Even when annotating the Nun's Priest's Tale, Christopher could not resist alluding to his father's discoveries in the Reeve's Tale.

His more substantial notes almost always correspond with his father's key interests. When Pertelote expounded on laxatives, Christopher included information about plants and flowers which seemed a family obsession. His two-page discussion of the Mercian boy-saint Kenelm reflects ancestral ties to a region already brought back to life with the Riders of the Mark. His note on Scipio deferred to the *Parlement of Foules* which his father had taught in 1948 with notes salvaged from his Clarendon Chaucer. His comments on Boethius contain the same essential information which his father drafted. Finally, Christopher's glossary comprised some thousand words extending over twenty-eight pages, exactly the same number of pages allotted to his father's word-list in his *Selections*.

What Christopher produced in his *Nun's Priest's Tale* edition—though he could not have fully grasped its significance at the time—was early success at completing a project which his father had left unfinished. Far more important in practical terms, it represented apprentice work for the long series of editorial projects that lay ahead. Here we find the template of introduction, text, notes, and glossary carried over to *The Silmarillion* in 1977. If Coghill had joined him in reconstructing this *legendarium*, as was speculated at the time,[28] their teamwork would have been a large-scale repetition of their three Chaucer editions. Preparing these student textbooks during the first decade of his own academic career had become for Christopher, as the Clarendon Chaucer had been for his father thirty years earlier, a warm-up exercise for future endeavours. It further readied him to bring into print J. R. R. Tolkien's letters, lectures, essays, translations, narrative poetry, working drafts, and mythologies of Middle-earth which continue to enrich our understandings of *The Hobbit* and *The Lord of the Rings*.

---

[28] George Steiner reported in a 1973 piece reprinted in *Tolkien Studies* 5 (2008), 188: 'Professor Nevill Coghill, a poet and Chaucerian, was an intimate friend and will probably be responsible for editing a posthumous book called *The Silmarillion*.'

APPENDIX I

[Tolkien's 'Introduction on Language' was most likely intended as preface to his Notes, since it was typed on the same machine with the same paper stock as his commentary on the *Romaunt of the Rose*. These three pages have now been catalogued as Bodleian MS Tolkien A 39/2/2/, fols. 138–40, and there are another three pages, fols. 141r–143r, handwritten front and back in various degrees of legibility, much crossed through and rewritten. This handwritten section covers pronunciation, dialect, and spelling, sometime repeating matter from the typewritten pages, so that it is conceivable these pages represent an early draft later put aside when Tolkien completely rewrote this 'Introduction' in typescript. This was his practice elsewhere. If so, this would be the only instance among the Clarendon Chaucer materials in which the first-draft pages survive along with the later typed version. Whatever the case, only the clean, readable typewritten paragraphs are transcribed below. His footnotes are included exactly as he left them.]

An Introduction on Language

The language of these selections from Chaucer is substantially that of the latter part of the fourteenth century. It must not, however, be overlooked that our extant copies, in varying degrees according to their age and carefulness, have at haphazard altered Chaucer's language not only in spellings but also in accidence, syntax and even occasionally in vocabulary, in conformity with the uses of a later century. In the process they have often doubtless disregarded the finer points of style and versification; sometimes they have obviously neglected metre altogether. If we had Chaucer's own autographs, or copies certainly seen and passed by him, we should of course find a language more uniform (and somewhat more uniformly archaic) than that presented by these selections drawn from various Mss. of various dates. But we should not get rid of all variation. English of London, spoken and spelt, doubtless changed a good deal in Chaucer's lifetime, and with it to a lesser degree Chaucer's own uses. Also at any given moment the English of London in his day varied more from person to person (irrespective of class) than our present polite language does, written or spoken.

For instance, even when inaccuracy, present in all poets for different reasons, has been allowed for,[1] we see that many rhymes undoubtedly used by Chaucer depend on an amount of variation, both in the stems of certain groups of words, and in grammatical forms, to which we have today no parallel. We have our variations, such as *again* which we may rhyme with *rain* (cf. Chaucer's *agein, ayein*) or with *men* (cf. his *ayen*), but we have nothing quite like his *mirie, merie, murie* (or the many other words with variation *i—e—*occasionally *u*). We are today not certain about the conjugation of *wake,* but we cannot compete with the variation in the Chaucerian accidence of verbs, of which *see* may be taken as an example among many, or the forms of the third person of the present indicative as an important point (see below).

This does not of course prove that Chaucer himself hesitated in his own personal use, say in talking to his friends, but it certainly seems to show that such variations were heard about

---

[1] e.g. rhymes such as *hoom,* home, and *doom*—see note to . . .

him, or were already familiar in writings of various dialectal tinge, and were known by him to be familiar in one way or another to his audience. That they were not 'quaintnesses', nor signs of the happy freedom from grammar of a primitive using an unschooled tongue in which anything might happen or be allowed, is of course sufficiently shown by the fact that they were not arbitrary.[2] They may have been convenient for rhyme or metre, but they were not invented for these purposes. Thus if Chaucer uses both *knit* and *knet* it is because in different dialects (forming the ingredients of the mixed speech of the growing capital) *knit* and *knet* were the everyday developments of older *cnytt*, in which *y* was originally pronounced similarly to modern French *u* (a pronunciation preserved and still intended by the altered spelling with *u* in such forms as *murie*). The forms had a real existence quite independent of poets.

In spite of these variations which cannot be got rid of, the language of these texts could be regularized and approximated to modern usage[3] without much violence and made to look superficially even more like the English of to-day than it does. But this would not be an advantage. Chaucer should be read according to the Mss., or else translated, but not 'modernized'. His language is much further removed (in more than five centuries) from ours than appears at first sight, and the chief danger to those beginning the study of his works lies in underestimating not in exaggerating the degree of difference. It is better to set out with the suspicion that almost any word or phrase in the fourteenth century *may* prove to mean something different in some degree from its first suggestion to the modern reader than to be content to look up only those words that are no longer current or even literary (such as *fele* many, *wreen* cover).

This is sufficient warning without lengthy illustration. A glance at the glossary will show that the quite obsolete words are a very small proportion of the entries. A good many words have been included, perhaps unnecessarily, which only differ in spelling from modern written forms (as *deef* deaf); but most of the space has been taken up by words still recognizable or well-known whose uses or senses are different from those of the present day. This difference extends to meanings now quite lost (as *pay* please) to the colouring and associations of such words as *gentil* or *rody* (ruddy); important too are the idiomatic uses of common words, pronouns and prepositions, like *after*, *there*, *that*. The finer the distinction the more likely it is to be missed in dealing with 'one's own language', but the more desirable it is, for accuracy or full appreciation, not to miss it.

An attempt has been made in glossary and notes to provide sufficient material for the worthy exercise of following Chaucer's meaning as closely as is now possible. Lack of space has prevented the giving of more than a few line-references in the glossary, while the notes, when verbal, have been necessarily limited to specially hard cases. Usually students must select for themselves from the meanings offered. Nor need they always accept the rulings or the definitions of the glossator. Middle English (of which Chaucer was only one, if the most famous, user) is not known by any infallible authority apart from Middle English writings. These are a large yet very incomplete record of the English of the period, and are known by no one completely. Even in these selected texts there are passages that are our only evidence for a given sense or use, or even for the very existence of a word (as *bismotered* for example).

---

[2] This does not apply to the variations in the forms of foreign and classical proper-names, which were often distorted for convenience. It is in fact just where we should not expect it, in these bookish elements, that freedom and quaintness can be found, and not in the native English: there was in fact more certainty in polite usage of English than agreement in pedantry. See note to . . .

[3] With the exception of the modern use of final *-e* as a spelling device without etymological warrant (as in *bone*, Chaucer's *bo(o)n*, on analogy of such words as *hope*, Chaucer's *hǫpė*.

Student and glossator are in the same case, and must judge from the context—and in many a passage debate is possible as to what precisely Chaucer meant.

In some ways Chaucer offers special difficulty in this respect. Rumours of his 'debt' to this or that foreign author for material or thought need make no one afraid to recognize him principally as an original author, not only using older literary material for his own purposes, but writing the contemporary English skilfully, wittily and with point, giving a felicity or a twist to common phrases as well as striking out ones of his own. And he was a man of whimsical humour, not always content to say and mean only one thing at a time. Yet he was not always able to show this, nor by any means always careful to try. He could use hackneyed tags or devices to fill a line or help his rhyme like any minstrel or popular story-teller. It is not always easy to be sure when he is the individual and when he is handing on the common stuff of the poetry of his day. Sometimes he does the latter, but is aware of it and smiling.

That there was such a common stuff for Chaucer to use or even to make fun of must not be forgotten. The effect of Chaucer upon a contemporary ear is frequently missed, especially where he is being humorous (straightforwardly or subtly), unless the contrast and the comparison is borne in mind. Though they bear indirect testimony to his technical skill (not as matchless as is popularly supposed) and his originality, it is better to dismiss the falsehoods enshrined in 'first warbler' and 'father of English poesy' than to forget that (accomplished) English verse had been written and had developed many tricks and devices and formulas, long before Chaucer was born.

APPENDIX II

[Tolkien's Glossary proofs were date-stamped 2 MAY 1925 when sent to him from Oxford University Press, the first galley long-sheet headed with the handwritten instruction 'Please return *this* proof.' Tolkien later wrote in the upper right-hand corner: '*Corrected* but shall need check with "revise" text.' These galley pages, though indeed carefully corrected, were never returned. Three paragraphs formed an introduction, followed by a table of contents expanded from the handwritten list made by Tolkien on the title-page of his working copy of the Text's galleys, with telltale hints of his struggles with Kenneth Sisam over reducing the longer original version.]

This glossary aims at the inclusion of all the obsolete forms and meanings likely to trouble a reader used only to modern English. The following variations in spelling should be specially held in mind: (i) *ee* and *e*, as *deed, ded*; (ii) *ei, ey a'*, and *ay*, as *wey, way*; (iii) *o* and *u*, as *torne, turne* or *sodden, sudden*; (iv) *oo* and *o*, as *woot, wot*; (v) *ou* and *ow*, as *soune, sown*; (vi) *i* and *y*. Of these variations *ee, ei, o, oo, ou, i* are usually preferred and the others are not given cross-references; they are often not recorded at all.

    Note that *y* is not used in the glossary as a vowel, except initially or before *e*: *ride, eile, lik* must be sought not *ryde, eyle, lyk*; but *lye, yē, ympne* retain their textual spellings. Cross-references are not given in the case of verbal forms for which modern English provides a sufficient key to the form of their infinitives, e.g. *lay, taughte* must be sought direct under **lye, teche**.

    References to the text are only given for special reasons: where the meaning noted is not the only one in this section; where meaning or form is uncommon or important; where the passage is liable to be mistranslated, or is otherwise interpreted by other editors. The frequent references to the extracts from *Boethius* are usually cautionary, for in these pieces the language is unnatural, and the uses of words often due to clumsy translation or misunderstanding of the Latin original. The Roman numerals refer to the pieces in the order in which they appear in this book; but R, PF, LP, LC, Prol, RT, MT, NP have been used instead of I, IV, XIII, XIV, XVI, XVII, XVIII, and XIX respectively; these pieces have received special attention.

Order of Pieces Assumed in Numbering the Glossary

I.   The Romaunt of the Rose [(extracts)](R).
II.   The Compleynte unto Pite.
III.   The Book of the Duchesse (extracts).
IV.   The Parlement of Foules (PF).
V.   The Former Age.
VI.   Merciles Beaute.
VII.   To Rosemounde.
VIII.   Truth.
IX.   Gentilesse.

X. Lak of Stedfastnesse.
XI. Compleint to his Empty Purse.
XII. Boethius de Consolatione Philosophie.
    a. Book II, Metre V.
    b. Book II, Prose VII.
    c. Book II, Metre VII.
    d. Book IV, Metre VI.
XIII. The Prologue to the Legend of Good Women (LP).
XIV. The Legend of Cleopatra (LC).
XV. The Astrolabe (extract from introduction)
XVI. The Prologue to the Canterbury Tales [(extracts)] (Prol).
XVII. The Reeve's Tale (extract) (RT).
XVIII. The Monk's Tale (extract) (MT).
XIX. The Nonne Preestes Tale (NP).

Works Cited

Amendt-Raduege, Amy M. 'Dream Vision in J. R. R. Tolkien's *The Lord of the Rings*.' *Tolkien Studies* 3 (2006), 45–55.
Amis, Kingsley. *Memoirs*. New York and London: Simon and Schuster, 1991.
Anderson, Douglas A. 'Christopher Tolkien: A Bibliography.' In *Tolkien's 'Legendarium'*, ed. Flieger and Hostetter, 247–52.
Anderson, Douglas A. '"An Industrious Little Devil": E. V. Gordon as Friend and Collaborator with Tolkien.' In *Tolkien the Medievalist*, ed. Chance, 15–25.
Anderson, Douglas A. 'R. W. Chambers and *The Hobbit*.' *Tolkien Studies* 3 (2006), 137–47.
Armstrong, Helen. 'And Have an Eye to That Dwarf.' *Amon Hen: The Bulletin of the Tolkien Society* 145 (May 1997), 13–14.
Atherton, Mark. 'Old English.' In *Companion*, ed. Lee, 217–29.
Atherton, Mark. *There and Back Again: J. R. R. Tolkien and the Origins of 'The Hobbit'*. London and New York: I. B. Tauris, 2012.
Auden, W. H. 'The Quest Hero' (1961). In *Prose: Volume IV, 1956–1962*, ed. Edward Mendelson. Princeton: Princeton University Press (2010), 360–73.
Auden, W. H. 'A Short Ode for a Philologist.' In *Collected Poems*, ed. Edward Mendelson. New York: Random House (1976), 566–7.
Baker, Donald C. 'Frederick James Furnivall (1825–1910).' In *Editing Chaucer*, ed. Ruggiers, 157–69.
Bennett, J. A. W. *Chaucer at Oxford and at Cambridge*. Oxford: Clarendon Press, 1974.
Benson, Larry D. 'Chaucer's Spelling Reconsidered' (1992). In *Contradictions: From 'Beowulf' to Chaucer*, ed. Theodore M. Andersson and Stephen A. Barney. Aldershot: Scolar; Brookfield, VT: Ashgate (1995), 70–99.
Blake, N. B. 'The Northernisms in "The Reeve's Tale".' *Lore and Language* 3 (1979), 1–8.
Bloom, Harold. *The Anxiety of Influence*. New York: Oxford University Press, 1973.
Bloom, Harold. 'Chaucer: The Wife of Bath, the Pardoner, and Shakespearean Character.' In *The Western Canon: The Books and School of the Ages*. New York: Riverhead Books (1995), 99–118.
Bloom, Harold, intro. In *J. R. R. Tolkien: Modern Critical Views*. Philadelphia: Chelsea House Publishers (2000), 1–2.
Boenig, Robert. *C. S. Lewis and the Middle Ages*. Kent, OH: Kent State University Press, 2012.
Boswell's Life of Johnson. Ed. R. W. Chapman. London: Oxford University Press, 1953.
Bowers, John M., ed. *The Canterbury Tales: Fifteenth-Century Continuations and Additions*. Kalamazoo: Western Michigan University TEAMS Medieval Institute Publication, 2nd edn. rev. 1999.
Bowers, John M. 'Chaucer after Retters: The Wartime Origins of English Literature.' In *Inscribing the Hundred Years' War in French and English Cultures*, ed. Denise Baker. Albany: State University of New York Press (2000), 91–125.
Bowers, John M. *Chaucer and Langland: The Antagonistic Tradition*. Notre Dame: University of Notre Dame Press, 2007.
Bowers, John M. *The Crisis of Will in 'Piers Plowman'*. Washington, DC: Catholic University of America Press, 1986.

Bowers, John M. 'Hoccleve's Two Copies of *Lerne to Dye*: Implications for Textual Critics.' *Papers of the Bibliographical Society of America* 83 (1989), 437–72.

Bowers, John M. *An Introduction to the 'Gawain' Poet*. Gainesville: University Press of Florida, 2012.

Bowers, John M. *The Politics of 'Pearl': Court Poetry in the Age of Richard II*. Cambridge: D. S. Brewer, 2001.

Bowers, John M. 'Rival Poets: Gower's *Confessio* and Chaucer's *Legend of Good Women*.' In *John Gower, Trilingual Poet: Language, Translation, and Tradition*, ed. Elisabeth Dutton with John Hines and R. F. Yeager. Cambridge: D. S. Brewer (2010), 276–87.

Bowers, John M. '*The Tale of Beryn* and *The Siege of Thebes*: Alternative Ideas of the *Canterbury Tales*.' SAC 7 (1985), 23–50.

Bowers, John M. 'Three Readings of The Knight's Tale: Sir John Clanvowe, Geoffrey Chaucer, and James I of Scotland.' *Journal of Medieval and Early Modern Studies* 34 (2004), 279–307.

Bowers, John M. 'Tolkien's Goldberry and *The Maid of the Moor*.' *Tolkien Studies* 8 (2011), 23–36.

Brackmann, Rebecca. 'Dwarves are not Heroes: Antisemitism and the Dwarves in J. R. R. Tolkien's Writing.' *Mythlore* 28 (2010), 85–106.

Bradley, Henry. *The Goths from the Earliest Times to the End of the Gothic Dominion in Spain*. 5th edn. London: T. Fisher Unwin, 1898.

Bradley, Henry, and Kenneth Sisam. 'Textual Notes on the Old English *Epistola Alexandri*.' *Modern Language Review* 14 (1919), 202–5.

Bratman, David. 'The Literary Value of *The History of Middle-earth*.' In *Tolkien's 'Legendarium'*, ed. Flieger and Hostetter, 69–91.

Bratman, David. 'Tolkien and the Counties of England.' *Mallorn* 37 (1999), 5–13.

Brewer, Charlotte. *Editing 'Piers Plowman': The Evolution of the Text*. Cambridge: Cambridge University Press, 1996.

Brewer, Charlotte. 'Skeat, Walter William.' ODNB 50: 817–19.

Brewer, Charlotte. *Treasure-House of the Language: The Living 'OED'*. New Haven and London: Yale University Press, 2007.

Brewer, Derek. 'Introduction.' In *A Companion to the 'Gawain'-Poet*, ed. Derek Brewer and Jonathan Gibson. Cambridge: D. S. Brewer (1997), 1–21.

Brewer, Derek. 'The Tutor: A Portrait.' In *C. S. Lewis at the Breakfast Table*, ed. James T. Como. New York: Macmillan (1979), 41–67.

Burrow, J. A. 'Elvish Chaucer.' In *The Endless Knot: Essays on Old and Middle English in Honor of Marie Borroff*, ed. M. Teresa Tavormina and R. F. Yeager. Cambridge: D. S. Brewer (1995), 105–11.

Burrow, J. A. *Ricardian Poetry: Chaucer, Gower, Langland and the 'Gawain' Poet*. London: Routledge & Kegan Paul, 1971.

Burrow, J. A., and Thorlac Turville-Petre, eds. *A Book of Middle English*. Oxford: Blackwell, 1992.

Campbell, Liam. 'Nature.' In *Companion*, ed. Lee, 431–45.

Carpenter, Humphrey. *J. R. R. Tolkien: A Biography*. 1977; Boston and New York: Houghton Mifflin, 2000.

Carpenter, Humphrey. *The Inklings*. 1978; London: HarperCollins, 2006.

Chambers, R. W. 'The Lost Literature of Medieval England.' *The Library*, 4th ser., 5 (1925), 293–321.

Chambers, R. W. *Man's Unconquerable Mind: Studies of English Writers from Bede to A. E. Housman and W. P. Ker*. London: Jonathan Cape, 1939.

Chance, Jane. *J. R. R. Tolkien, Self and Other: 'That Queer Creature'*. New York: Palgrave Macmillan, 2016.
Chance, Jane, ed. *Tolkien and the Invention of Myth: A Reader*. Lexington: University Press of Kentucky, 2004.
Chance, Jane, ed. *Tolkien the Medievalist*. London: Routledge, 2003.
Chance Nitzsche, Jane. *Tolkien's Art: A 'Mythology for England'*. New York: St. Martin's Press, 1979.
Chaucer, Geoffrey. *The Canterbury Tales*. Trans. Nevill Coghill. Baltimore: Penguin Books, 1952.
Chaucer, Geoffrey. *The Canterbury Tales, Edited from the Hengwrt Manuscript*. Ed. N. F. Blake. London: Arnold, 1980.
Chaucer, Geoffrey. *The Canterbury Tales of Chaucer*. Ed. Thomas Tyrwhitt. 5 vols. London: T. Payne, 1775–8.
Chaucer, Geoffrey. *The Clerkes Tale of Oxenford*. Ed. Kenneth Sisam. Oxford: Clarendon Press, 1923.
Chaucer, Geoffrey. *The Complete Works of Geoffrey Chaucer*. Ed. Walter W. Skeat. 6 vols. Oxford: Clarendon Press, 1894.
Chaucer, Geoffrey. *The Ellesmere Chaucer Reproduced in Facsimile*. Ed. Alex Egerton. 2 vols. Manchester: Manchester University Press, 1911.
Chaucer, Geoffrey. *The Legend of Good Women*. Ed. Janet Cowen and George Kane. East Lansing: Colleagues Press, 1995.
Chaucer, Geoffrey. *The Man of Law's Tale*. Ed. Nevill Coghill and Christopher Tolkien. London: George G. Harrap, 1969.
Chaucer, Geoffrey. *The Minor Poems*. Ed. Walter W. Skeat. Oxford: Clarendon Press, 1888.
Chaucer, Geoffrey. *The Nun's Priest's Tale*. Ed. Kenneth Sisam. Oxford: Clarendon Press, 1927.
Chaucer, Geoffrey. *The Nun's Priest's Tale*. Ed. Nevill Coghill and Christopher Tolkien. London: George G. Harrap, 1959.
Chaucer, Geoffrey. *The Pardoner's Tale*. Ed. Nevill Coghill and Christopher Tolkien. London: George G. Harrap, 1958.
Chaucer, Geoffrey. *The Poetical Works of Chaucer*. Ed. F. N. Robinson. Boston: Houghton Mifflin, 1933.
Chaucer, Geoffrey. *Riverside Chaucer*. Gen. ed. Larry D. Benson. Boston: Houghton Mifflin, 1987.
Chaucer, Geoffrey. *The Student's Chaucer: Being a Complete Edition of his Works*. Ed. Walter W. Skeat. Oxford: Clarendon Press, 1895.
Chaucer, Geoffrey. *A Treatise on the Astrolabe Dedicated to his Son Lowys (A.D. 1391)*. Ed. Walter W. Skeat. EETS e.s. 16 (1872).
Chaucer, Geoffrey. *Troilus and Criseyde*. Ed. B. A. Windeatt. London and New York: Longman, 1984.
Chaucer Life-Records. Ed. Martin M. Crow and Clair C. Olson. Oxford: Clarendon Press, 1966.
Christopher, Joe R. 'Tolkien's Lyric Poetry.' In *Tolkien's 'Legendarium'*, ed. Flieger and Hostetter, 143–60.
Clouston, W. A. *On the Magical Elements in Chaucer's Squire's Tale, with Other Analogues*. London: Chaucer Society, 2nd ser., no. 26 (1890).
Clouston, W. A. 'The Three Robbers and the Treasure Trove: Buddhist Original and Asiatic and European Versions of *The Pardoner's Tale*.' In *Originals and Analogues of Some of*

Chaucer's Canterbury Tales, ed. F. J. Furnivall, Edmund Brock, and W. A. Clouston. London: Chaucer Society, 2nd ser., no. 20 (1872), 415–36.

Coghill, Nevill. *The Poet Chaucer*. 2nd. edn rev. London: Oxford University Press, 1967.

Coghill, Nevill. 'Shakespeare's Reading in Chaucer.' In *Elizabethan and Jacobean Studies Presented to F. P. Wilson*, ed. Herbert Davis and Helen Gardner. Oxford: Oxford University Press (1959), 86–99.

Coghill, Nevill. 'Two Notes on *Piers Plowman*: I. The Abbot of Abingdon and the Date of the C–Text; II. Chaucer's Debt to Langland.' *Medium Ævum* 4 (1935), 83–94.

Cole, Andrew. 'Chaucer's English Lesson.' *Speculum* 77 (2002), 1128–67.

Conrad-O'Briain, Helen, and Gerald Hynes, eds. *J. R. R. Tolkien: The Forest and the City*. Dublin: Four Courts Press, 2013.

Cook, Simon J. 'The Cauldron at the Outer Edge: Tolkien on the Oldest Fairy Tales.' *Tolkien Studies* 13 (2016), 9–29.

Croft, Janet Brennan. 'The Hen that Laid the Eggs: Tolkien and the Officers Training Corps.' *Tolkien Studies* 8 (2011), 97–106.

Croft, Janet Brennan. 'Walter E. Haigh, Author of *A Glossary of the Huddersfield Dialect*.' *Tolkien Studies* 4 (2007), 184–8.

Curry, Patrick. 'The Critical Response to Tolkien's Fiction.' In *Companion*, ed. Lee, 369–88.

Curry, Patrick. 'Iron Crown, Iron Cage: Tolkien and Weber on Modernity and Enchantment.' In *The Ring Goes Ever On*, ed. Wells, 1:128–32.

D'Ardenne, S. T. R. O. 'The Man and the Scholar.' In *Tolkien: Scholar and Storyteller*, ed. Salu and Farrell, 33–7.

D'Ardenne, S. R. T. O., ed. *Þe Liflade ant te Passiun of Seinte Iuliene*. EETS o.s. 248 (1961).

D'Ardenne, S. R. T. O., and E. J. Dobson, eds. *Seinte Katerine*. EETS s.s. 7 (1981).

Darwall-Smith, R. H. 'Gordon, George Stuart.' *ODNB*. 22:909–10.

Davis, Norman. Review of Bennett's *Chaucer at Oxford and at Cambridge*. *RES*, n.s. 27 (1976), 336–7.

Davis, Norman, with Douglas Gray, Patricia Ingham, and Anne Wallace-Hadrill. *A Chaucer Glossary*. Oxford: Clarendon Press, 1979.

De Hamel, Christopher. 'The Hengwrt Chaucer.' In *Meetings with Remarkable Manuscripts: Twelve Journeys into the Medieval World*. New York: Penguin (2017), 426–65.

Dinshaw, Carolyn. *Chaucer's Sexual Poetics*. Madison: University of Wisconsin Press, 1989.

Dinshaw, Carolyn. *Getting Medieval: Sexualities and Communities, Pre- and Postmodern*. Durham, NC: Duke University Press, 1999.

Donaldson, E. Talbot. '*Canterbury Tales*, D117: A Critical Edition' (1965). In *Speaking of Chaucer*, 119–30.

Donaldson, E. Talbot, ed. *Chaucer's Poetry: An Anthology for the Modern Reader*. New York: Ronald Press Co., 1958.

Donaldson, E. Talbot. 'The Psychology of Editors of Middle English Texts' (1966). In *Speaking of Chaucer*, 102–18.

Donaldson, E. Talbot. *Speaking of Chaucer*. New York: W. W. Norton, 1970.

Donovan, Leslie A. 'Middle-earth Mythology.' In *Companion*, ed. Lee, 92–106.

Drout, Michael D. C., ed. *J. R. R. Tolkien Encyclopedia: Scholarship and Critical Assessment*. New York and London: Routledge, 2007.

Drout, Michael D. C. 'J. R. R. Tolkien's Medieval Scholarship and its Significance.' *Tolkien Studies* 4 (2007), 113–76.

Drout, Michael D. C. '"The Tower and the Ruin": The Past in J. R. R. Tolkien's Works.' In *Tolkien: The Forest and the City*, ed. Conrad-O'Briain and Hynes, 175–90.

Dubs, Kathleen E. 'Providence, Fate, and Chance: Boethian Philosophy in *The Lord of the Rings*.' In *Tolkien and the Invention of Myth*, ed. Chance, 133–42.
Duriez, Colin. *Tolkien and C. S. Lewis: The Gift of Friendship*. Mahwah, NJ: HiddenSpring, 2003.
Eagleton, Terry. *Literary Theory: An Introduction*. Rev. edn. Minneapolis: University of Minnesota Press, 2008.
The Early South-English Legendary or Lives of Saints. Ed. Carl Horstmann. EETS o.s. 87, (1887).
Echard, Siân, ed. *A Companion to Gower*. Cambridge: D. S. Brewer, 2004.
Eco, Umberto. 'Dreaming of the Middle Ages.' In *Travels in Hyper Reality: Essays*, trans. William Weaver. San Diego, New York, and London: Harcourt Brace Jovanovich (1986), 61–72.
Eden, Bradford Lee. 'The "Music of the Spheres": Relationships between Tolkien's *The Silmarillion* and Medieval Cosmological and Religious Theory.' In *Tolkien the Medievalist*, ed. Chance, 183–93.
Edwards, A. S. G. 'Walter W. Skeat (1835–1912).' In *Editing Chaucer*, ed. Ruggiers, 171–89.
Edwards, A. S. G., and Linne R. Mooney. 'Is the *Equatorie of the Planets* a Chaucer Holograph?' *Chaucer Review* 26 (1991), 31–42.
Edwards, Raymond. *Tolkien*. London: Robert Hale, 2014.
Eilmann, Julian, and Allan Turner, eds. *Tolkien's Poetry*. Zurich and Jena: Walking Tree Publishers, 2013.
Ekman, Stefan. 'Echoes of *Pearl* in Arda's Landscape.' *Tolkien Studies* 6 (2009), 59–70.
Epstein, Robert. '"Fer in the north; I kan nat telle where": Dialect, Regionalism, and Philologism.' *SAC* 30 (2008), 95–124.
Epstein, Robert. 'London, Southwark, Westminster: Gower's Urban Context.' In *Companion to Gower*, ed. Echard, 43–60.
The 'Equatorie of the Planetis' Edited from Peterhouse MS. 75.I. Ed. Derek J. Price with linguistic analysis by R. M. Wilson. Cambridge: Cambridge University Press, 1955.
Everett, Dorothy. 'Chaucer's "Good Ear".' *RES* 23 (1947), 201–8.
Falconer, Rachel. 'Earlier Fantasy Fiction: Morris, Dunsany, and Lindsay.' In *Companion*, ed. Lee, 307–9.
Fimi, Dimitra. 'Tolkien's "Celtic Type of Legends": Merging Traditions.' *Tolkien Studies* 4 (2007), 51–71.
Fisher, Jason. 'Tolkien and Source Criticism: Remarking and Remaking.' In *Tolkien and the Study of His Sources*, ed. Fisher, 29–44.
Fisher, Jason, ed. *Tolkien and the Study of His Sources*. Jefferson, NC and London: McFarland & Co., 2011.
Fisher, John H. 'Historical and Methodological Considerations for Adopting "Best Text" or "Usus Scribendi" for Textual Criticism of Chaucer's Poems.' *Text: Transactions of the Society for Textual Scholarship* 6 (1994), 165–80.
Fisher, John H. *The Importance of Chaucer*. Carbondale and Edwardsville: Southern Illinois University Press, 1992.
Fisher, John H. *John Gower: Moral Philosopher and Friend of Chaucer*. London: Methuen, 1965.
Fitzgerald, Jill. 'A "Clerkes Compleinte": Tolkien and the Division of Lit. and Lang.' *Tolkien Studies* 6 (2009), 41–57.
Fletcher, Alan J. 'Chaucer's Norfolk Reeve.' *Medium Ævum* 52 (1983), 100–3.
Flieger, Verlyn. 'Poems by Tolkien: *The Lord of the Rings*.' In *Tolkien Encyclopedia*, 522–32.

Flieger, Verlyn. 'When Is a Fairy Story a *Faërie* Story?' In *Green Suns and Faërie: Essays on Tolkien*. Kent, OH: Kent State University Press (2012), 65–73.

Flieger, Verlyn, and Carl F. Hostetter, eds. *Tolkien's 'Legendarium': Essays on 'The History of Middle-earth'*. Westport and London: Greenwood Press, 2000.

Ford, Judy Ann. 'The White City: *The Lord of the Rings* as an Early Medieval Myth of the Restoration of the Roman Empire.' *Tolkien Studies* 2 (2005), 53–73.

Ford, Judy Ann, and Robin Anne Reid. 'Councils and Kings: Aragorn's Journey towards Kingship in J. R. R. Tolkien's *The Lord of the Rings* and Peter Jackson's *The Lord of the Rings*.' *Tolkien Studies* 6 (2009), 71–90.

Gardner, Helen. 'Clive Staples Lewis: 1898–1963.' *Proceedings of the British Academy* 51 (1965), 417–28.

Gardner, John. *The Life and Times of Chaucer*. New York: Knopf, 1977.

Garth, John. *Tolkien at Exeter College: How an Oxford Undergraduate Created Middle-earth* Oxford: Exeter College, 2014.

Garth, John. *Tolkien and the Great War: The Threshold of Middle-earth*. New York and Boston: Houghton Mifflin, 2003.

Georgianna, Linda. 'The Protestant Chaucer.' In *Chaucer's Religious Tales*, ed. C. David Benson and Elizabeth Robertson. Cambridge: D. S. Brewer (1990), 55–69.

Gilliver, Peter. *The Making of the Oxford English Dictionary*. Oxford: Oxford University Press, 2016.

Gilliver, Peter, Jeremy Marshall, and Edmund Weiner. *The Ring of Words: Tolkien and the 'Oxford English Dictionary'*. Oxford: Oxford University Press, 2006.

Gilliver, Peter, Edmund Weiner, and Jeremy Marshall. 'The Word as Leaf: Perspectives on Tolkien as Lexicographer and Philologist.' In *Tolkien's 'The Lord of the Rings': Sources of Inspiration*, ed. Stratford Caldecott and Thomas Honegger. Zollikofen, Switzerland: Walking Tree Publishers (2008), 57–83.

Glyer, Diana Pavlac. *The Company They Keep: C. S. Lewis and J. R. R. Tolkien as Writers in Community*. Kent, OH: Kent State University Press, 2007.

Glyer, Diana Pavlac, and Josh B. Long. 'Biography as Source: Niggles and Notions.' In *Tolkien and the Study of His Sources*, ed. Fisher, 193–214.

Gordon, George Stuart. *Anglo-American Literary Relations*. Intro. R. W. Chapman. Oxford: Oxford University Press, 1942.

Gordon, George. *The Discipline of Letters*. Ed. Mary Gordon. Oxford: Clarendon Press, 1946.

Gordon, George Stuart. *The Fronde: The Stanhope Essay, 1905*. Oxford: Blackwell, 1905.

Gordon, George. *The Letters of George S. Gordon, 1902–1942*. Ed. Mary Gordon. London: Oxford University Press, 1943.

Gordon, George S. *The Lives of Authors*. London: Chatto & Windus, 1950.

Gordon, George. '*Medium Aevum* and the Middle Ages.' Oxford: Clarendon Press, Society for Pure English, no. 19 (1925), 3–28.

Gordon, Capt. G. S. *Mons and the Retreat*. Preface by Field-Marshal Lord French. London: Constable and Company, 1918.

Gordon, George. *More Companionable Books*. Ed. Mary Gordon. London: Chatto & Windus, 1947.

Gordon, George. *Nine Plays of Shakespeare*. Oxford: Clarendon Press, 1928.

Gordon, George. *Shakespeare's English*. Oxford: Clarendon Press, Society for Pure English no. 29 (1928), 256–76.

Gordon, George. *Shakespearean Comedy and Other Studies*. Oxford: Oxford University Press, 1944.

Gordon, George. 'Theophrastus and His Imitators.' In *English Literature and the Classics*, ed. G. S. Gordon. Oxford: Clarendon Press (1912), 49–86.

Gordon, Mary Campbell. *The Life of George S. Gordon, 1881–1942*. London: Oxford University Press, 1945.

Gray, Douglas. 'Chaucer and *Pite*.' In *Tolkien: Scholar and Storyteller*, ed. Salu and Farrell, 173–203.

Gray, Douglas. *A Marriage of Mercury and Philology*. Oxford: Clarendon Press, 1982.

Green, Richard Firth. *Elf Queens and Holy Friars: Fairy Beliefs and the Medieval Church*. Philadelphia: University of Pennsylvania Press, 2016.

Greenblatt, Stephen. *The Swerve: How the World Became Modern*. New York and London: Norton, 2011.

Greening Lamborn, A. E. 'The Arms on the Chaucer Tomb at Ewelme.' *Oxoniensia* 5 (1940), 78–93.

Haas, Renate. 'Caroline F. E. Spurgeon (1869–1942): First Woman Professor of English in England.' In *Women Medievalists and the Academy*, ed. Jane Chance. Madison: University of Wisconsin Press (2005), 99–109.

Hall, John R. Clark. *A Concise Anglo-Saxon Dictionary*. 4th edn suppl. Herbert D. Merritt. Cambridge: Cambridge University Press, 1969.

Hammond, Eleanor Prescott. *Chaucer: A Bibliographical Manual*. London: Macmillan, 1908.

Hammond, Wayne G. '"A Continuing and Evolving Creation": Distractions in the Later History of Middle-earth.' In *Tolkien's 'Legendarium'*, ed. Flieger and Hostetter, 19–29.

Hammond, Wayne G., and Douglas A. Anderson. *J. R. R. Tolkien: A Descriptive Bibliography* Winchester: St. Paul's Bibliographies, 1993.

Hammond, Wayne G., and Christina Scull. *The Lord of the Rings: A Reader's Companion* London: HarperCollins, 2005.

Hanna, Ralph. 'Alliterative Poetry.' In *The Cambridge History of Medieval English Literature*, ed. David Wallace. Cambridge: Cambridge University Press (1999), 488–512.

Hanna, Ralph. 'The Application of Thought to Textual Criticism in All Modes—with Apologies to A. E. Housman.' *Studies in Bibliography* 53 (2000), 163–72.

Hanna III, Ralph. *Pursuing History: Middle English Manuscripts and Their Texts*. Stanford: Stanford University Press, 1996.

Hanna, Ralph, and Sarah Wood, eds. *Richard Morris's 'Prick of Conscience': A Corrected and Amplified Reading Text*. EETS o.s. 342 (2013).

Hazell, Dinah. *The Plants of Middle-earth: Botany and Sub-creation*. Kent, OH: Kent State University Press, 2006.

Hiley, Margaret. '*Lord of the Rings* and "Late Style": Tolkien, Adorno, and Said.' In *Tolkien and Modernity*, ed. Thomas Honegger and Frank Weinreich. Zurich and Jena: Walking Tree Publishers (2006), 53–73.

The History of Oxford University Press. Gen. ed. Simon Eliot. Volume II: 1780–1896, ed. Simon Eliot; Volume III: 1896–1970, ed. Wm. Roger Louis. Oxford: Oxford University Press, 2013.

The History of the University of Oxford, Volume VIII: The Twentieth Century. Ed. Brian Harrison. Oxford: Clarendon Press, 1994.

Honegger, Thomas. 'Fantasy, Escape, Recovery, and Consolation in *Sir Orfeo*: The Medieval Foundations of Tolkienian Fantasy.' *Tolkien Studies* 7 (2010), 117–36.

Honegger, Thomas. '*The Homecoming of Beorhtnoth*: Philology and the Literary Muse.' *Tolkien Studies* 4 (2007), 189–99.

Honegger, Thomas. 'The Rohirrim: "Anglo-Saxons on Horseback"? An Inquiry into Tolkien's Use of Sources.' In *Tolkien and the Study of His Sources*, ed. Fisher, 116–32.
Honegger, Thomas. 'Tolkien's "Academic Writings".' In *Companion*, ed. Lee, 27–40.
Hooper, Walter. *C. S. Lewis: A Companion and Guide*. London and New York: HarperCollins, 1996.
Horobin, Simon. 'Adam Pinkhurst, Geoffrey Chaucer, and the Hengwrt Manuscript of the *Canterbury Tales*.' *Chaucer Review* 44 (2010), 351–67.
Horobin, Simon C. P. 'Chaucer's Norfolk Reeve.' *Neophilologus* 86 (2002), 609–12.
Horobin, Simon. '"In London and Opelond": Dialect and Circulation of the C Version of *Piers Plowman*.' *Medium Ævum* 74 (2005), 248–69.
Horobin, Simon C. P. 'J. R. R. Tolkien as a Philologist: A Reconsideration of the Northernisms in Chaucer's *Reeve's Tale*.' *English Studies* 2 (2001), 97–105.
Horobin, Simon. *The Language of the Chaucer Tradition*. Cambridge: D. S. Brewer, 2003.
Hostetter, Carl F. '*Sir Orfeo*: A Middle English Version by J. R. R. Tolkien.' *Tolkien Studies* 1 (2004), 85–123.
Houghton, John Wm., and Neal K. Keesee. 'Tolkien, King Alfred, and Boethius: Platonist Views of Evil in *The Lord of the Rings*.' *Tolkien Studies* 2 (2005), 131–59.
Housman, A. E. 'The Application of Thought to Textual Criticism.' *Proceedings of the Classical Association* 18 (1922), 67–84.
Hudson, Anne. *The Premature Reformation: Wycliffite Texts and Lollard History*. Oxford: Clarendon Press, 1988.
Jackson, Leonard. *Literature, Psychoanalysis, and the New Sciences of Mind*. Harlow and New York: Longman, 2000.
Jones, Diana Wynne. 'The Shape of the Narrative in *The Lord of the Rings*' (1983). In *Reflections on the Magic of Writing*. Oxford and New York: David Fickling (2012), 5–25.
Jones, Terry. *Chaucer's Knight: The Portrait of a Medieval Mercenary*. London: Eyre Methuen, 1980.
Jones, Terry. *Who Murdered Chaucer? A Medieval Mystery*. New York: St. Martin's Press, 2003.
Kane, George. 'The Autobiographical Fallacy in Chaucer and Langland Studies' (1965). In *Chaucer and Langland: Historical and Textual Studies*. Berkeley and Los Angeles: University of California Press (1989), 1–14.
Kane, George. 'John M. Manly (1865–1940) and Edith Rickert (1871–1938).' In *Editing Chaucer*, ed. Ruggiers, 207–29.
Ker, W. P. 'The Craven Angels.' *Modern Language Review* 6 (1911), 85–7.
Ker, Neil. 'Kenneth Sisam, 1887–1971.' *Proceedings of the British Academy* 58 (1972), 409–28.
Kittredge, George Lyman. *Chaucer and His Poetry*. Cambridge, MA: Harvard University Press, 1915.
Knighton's Chronicle, 1337–1396. Ed. and trans. G. H. Martin. Oxford: Clarendon Press, 1995.
Knox, Philip. 'The "Dialect" of Chaucer's Reeve.' *Chaucer Review* 49 (2014), 102–24.
Kolve, V. A. 'From Cleopatra to Alceste: An Iconographic Study of *The Legend of Good Women*' (1981). In *Telling Images: Chaucer and the Image of Narrative II*. Stanford: Stanford University Press (2009), 28–65.
Kolve, V. A. *The Play Called Corpus Christi*. Stanford: Stanford University Press, 1966.
Kreuzer, Christopher. 'Numbers in Tolkien.' In *The Ring Goes Ever On*, ed. Wells. 2:325–38.
LaFontaine, David. 'Sex and Subtext in Tolkien's World.' *The Gay & Lesbian Review* 22/6 (2015), 14–17.

LaFontaine, David. 'The Tolkien in Bilbo Baggins.' *The Gay & Lesbian Review* 23/6 (2016), 24–8.
Larsen, Kristine. 'Myth, Milky Way, and the Mysteries of Tolkien's *Morwinyon, Telumendil,* and *Anarríma.*' *Tolkien Studies* 7 (2010), 197–210.
Larsen, Kristine. 'Sea Birds and Morning Stars: Ceyx, Alcyone, and the Many Metamorphoses of Erendil and Elwing.' In *Tolkien and the Study of his Sources*, ed. Fisher, 69–83.
Lazo, Andrew. 'Gathered round Northern Fires: The Imaginative Impact of the Kolbítar.' In *Tolkien and the Invention of Myth*, ed. Chance, 191–226.
Lazo, Andrew. 'A Kind of Mid-Wife: J. R. R. Tolkien and C. S. Lewis—Sharing Influence.' In *Tolkien the Medievalist*, ed. Chance, 36–49.
Lee, Stuart D., ed. *A Companion to J. R. R. Tolkien*. Oxford: Wiley Blackwell, 2014.
Lee, Stuart D. 'Manuscripts.' In *Companion*, ed. Lee, 56–76.
Lee, Stuart D., and Elizabeth Solopova. *The Keys of Middle-earth: Discovering Medieval Literature through the Fiction of J. R. R. Tolkien*. New York: Palgrave Macmillan, 2005.
Lewis, C. S. *The Allegory of Love*. London: Oxford University Press, 1936.
Lewis, C. S. *All My Road before Me: The Diary of C. S. Lewis, 1922–1927*. Ed. Walter Hooper. Foreword Owen Barfield. San Diego: Harcourt Brace Jovanovich, 1991.
Lewis, C. S. *C. S. Lewis's Lost 'Aeneid': Arms and the Exile*. Ed. A. T. Reyes. Foreword Walter Hooper. Preface D. O. Ross. New Haven: Yale University Press, 2011.
Lewis, C. S. *Collected Letters of C. S. Lewis*, Vol. 2: *Books, Broadcasts, and the War, 1931–1949*. Ed. Walter Hooper. New York: HarperCollins, 2004.
Lewis, C. S. *Collected Letters of C. S. Lewis*, Vol. 3: *Narnia, Cambridge, and Joy, 1950–1963*. Ed. Walter Hooper. New York: HarperCollins, 2007.
Lewis, C. S. *The Discarded Image: An Introduction to Medieval and Renaissance Literature*. Cambridge: Cambridge University Press, 1970.
Lewis, C. S. *English Literature in the Sixteenth Century Excluding Drama*. Oxford: Clarendon Press, 1954.
Lewis, C. S. *The Four Loves*. New York and London: Harcourt, 1960.
Lewis, C. S. *Letters of C. S. Lewis*. Ed. W. H. Lewis. New York: Harcourt Brace & World, 1966.
Lewis, C. S. *The Lion, the Witch, and the Wardrobe*. 1950; New York: HarperCollins, 1978.
Lewis, C. S. 'On Stories.' In *Essays Presented to Charles Williams*, ed. C. S. Lewis. London: Oxford University Press (1947), 90–105.
[Lewis, C. S.] 'Professor J. R. R. Tolkien: Creator of Hobbits and Inventor of a New Mythology.' In *Tolkien, Scholar and Storyteller*, ed. Salu and Farrell, 11–15.
Lewis, C. S. *Selected Literary Essays*. Ed. Walter Hooper. Cambridge: Cambridge University Press, 1969.
Lewis, C. S. *Studies in Medieval and Renaissance Literature*. Ed. Walter Hooper. Cambridge: Cambridge University Press, 1966.
Lewis, C. S. *Surprised by Joy: The Shape of My Early Life*. Orlando, FL: Harcourt, 1955.
Lewis, C. S. *They Stand Together: The Letters of C. S. Lewis to Arthur Greeves (1914–1963)*. Ed. Walter Hooper. New York: Macmillan, 1979.
Lewis, C. S. 'What Chaucer Really Did to *Il Filostrato*.' *Essays & Studies* 18 (1932), 56–75.
Lewis, Warren. *Brothers and Friends: The Diaries of Major Warren Hamilton Lewis*. Ed. Clyde S. Kilby and Marjorie Lamp Mead. San Francisco: Harper & Row, 1982.
Lewis, W. H. 'Memoir of C. S. Lewis.' In *Letters of C. S. Lewis*, 1–26.
Librán-Moreno, Miryam. '"Byzantium, New Rome!" Goths, Langobards, and Byzantium in *The Lord of the Rings*.' In *Tolkien and the Study of His Sources*, ed. Fisher, 84–115.

Librán-Moreno, Miryam. 'Greek and Latin Amatory Motifs in Éowyn's Portrayal.' *Tolkien Studies* 4 (2007), 73–97.
Lindsay, Sean. 'The Dream System in *The Lord of the Rings*.' *Mythlore* 13.3 (1987), 7–14.
Long, Josh. 'Clinamen, Tessera, and the Anxiety of Influence: Swerving from and Completing George MacDonald.' *Tolkien Studies* 6 (2009), 127–50.
Loomis, Laura H. 'Chaucer and the Breton Lays of the Auchinleck MS.' *Studies in Philology* 38 (1941), 14–33.
Lydgate, John. 'On the Departing of Thomas Chaucer.' In *Oxford Book of Late Medieval Verse and Prose*. Ed. Douglas Gray with Norman Davis. Oxford: Clarendon Press (1985), 60–2.
Lyman-Thomas, J. S. 'Celtic: "Celtic Things" and "Things Celtic"—Identity, Language, and Mythology.' In *Companion*, ed. Lee, 272–85.
McAlpine, Monica E. 'The Pardoner's Homosexuality and How It Matters.' *PMLA* 95 (1980), 8–22.
McCarthy, Dennis, and June Schlueter. *'A Brief Discourse of Rebellion and Rebels' by George North: A Newly Uncovered Manuscript Source for Shakespeare's Plays*. Cambridge: D. S. Brewer, 2018.
McFarlane, K. B. 'Henry V, Bishop Beaufort and the Red Hat, 1417–1421' (1945). In *England in the Fifteenth Century: Collected Essays*. Intro. G. L. Harriss. London: Hambledon Press, (1981), 79–113.
McFarlane, K. B. *Lancastrian Kings and Lollard Knights*. Oxford: Clarendon, 1972.
McGann, Jerome J. *A Critique of Modern Textual Criticism*. Chicago: University of Chicago Press, 1983.
McIlwaine, Catherine. *Tolkien: Maker of Middle-earth*. Oxford: Bodleian Library, 2018.
Manly, John M., ed. *Canterbury Tales by Geoffrey Chaucer*. New York: Holt, 1928.
Manly, John Matthews. *Some New Light on Chaucer*. New York: Henry Holt, 1926.
Manly, John M., and Edith Rickert, eds. *The Text of the Canterbury Tales Studied on the Basis of All Known Manuscripts*. 8 vols. Chicago and London: University of Chicago Press, 1940.
Manning, Jim. 'Elvish Star Lore.' *Planetarian* (December 2003), 14–22.
Masefield, John. *Letters to Reyna*. Ed. William Buchan. London: Buchan & Enright, 1983.
Mathew, Gervase. *The Court of Richard II*. New York: W. W. Norton, 1968.
Maw, Martin. 'Printing Technology, Binding, Readers, and Social Life.' In *History of Oxford University Press*. 3:277–307.
Middleton, Anne. 'Life in the Margins, or What's an Annotator to Do?" In *New Directions in Textual Studies*, ed. Dave Oliphant and Robin Bradford. Austin: University of Texas Press (1990), 167–83.
Minnis, Alastair. *Fallible Authors: Chaucer's Pardoner and Wife of Bath*. Philadelphia: University of Pennsylvania Press, 2007.
Mooney, Linne. 'Chaucer's Scribe.' *Speculum* 81 (2006), 97–138.
Mooney Linne R., and Estelle Stubbs. *Scribes and the City: London Guildhall Clerks and the Dissemination of Middle English Literature, 1375–1425*. York: York Medieval Press, 2013.
Moorhead, John. *Theoderic in Italy*. Oxford: Clarendon Press, 1992.
Morse, Robert E. *Evocation of Virgil in Tolkien's Art*. Oak Park, IL: Balchazy-Carducci Publishers, 1986.
Muir, Edwin. 'A Boy's World.' *The Observer* (27 November 1955), 11.
Murphy, Patrick J. *Medieval Studies and the Ghost Stories of M. R. James*. University Park: Pennsylvania State University Press, 2017.

Nietzsche, Friedrich. *Twilight of the Idols or How to Philosophize with a Hammer*. Trans. and intro. Duncan Large. Oxford: Oxford University Press, 1998.

Noad, Charles E. 'On the Construction of "The Silmarillion".' In *Tolkien's 'Legendarium'*, ed. Flieger and Hostetter, 31–68.

North, J. D. *Chaucer's Universe*. Oxford: Clarendon Press, 1988.

Olsen, Corey. 'The Myth of the Ent and the Entwife.' *Tolkien Studies* 5 (2008), 39–53.

Olsen, Corey. 'Poetry.' In *Companion*, ed. Lee, 173–88.

Ovid. *Tristia ex Ponto*. Ed. and trans. Arthur Leslie Wheeler. Cambridge, MA: Loeb Classics, Harvard University Press, 1965.

Palmer, D. J. *The Rise of English Studies*. London and New York: Oxford University Press, 1965.

Partridge, Stephen. 'The Vocabulary of *The Equatorie of the Planetis*.' *English Manuscript Studies, 1100–1700* 3 (1992), 29–37.

Patterson, Lee. *Chaucer and the Subject of History*. Madison, WI: University of Wisconsin Press, 1991.

Patterson, Lee. 'The Logic of Textual Criticism and the Way of Genius: The Kane–Donaldson *Piers Plowman* in Historical Perspective.' In *Negotiating the Past: The Historical Understanding of Medieval Literature*. Madison: University of Wisconsin Press (1987), 77–113.

Pearl. Ed. E. V. Gordon. Oxford: Clarendon Press, 1953.

Pearl, Cleanness, Patience, and Sir Gawain: Reproduced in Facsimile from the Unique MS. Cotton Nero A.x in the British Museum. Intro. I. Gollancz. EETS o.s. 162 (1923).

Pearsall, Derek. 'The *Canterbury Tales* and London Club Culture.' In *Chaucer and the City*, ed. Ardis Butterfield. Cambridge: D. S. Brewer (2006), 95–108.

Pearsall, Derek. *John Lydgate*. Charlottesville: University Press of Virginia, 1970.

Pearsall, Derek. *The Life of Geoffrey Chaucer: A Critical Biography*. Oxford: Blackwell, 1992.

Pearsall, Derek. 'The Literary Milieu of Charles of Orléans and the Duke of Suffolk, and the Authorship of the Fairfax Sequence.' In *Charles d'Orléans in England (1415–1440)*, ed. Mary-Jo Arn. Woodbridge and Rochester: Boydell & Brewer (2000), 145–56.

Phelpstead, Carl. 'Myth-Making and Sub-Creation.' In *Companion*, ed. Lee, 79–91.

Phelpstead, Carl. *Tolkien and Wales: Language, Literature and Identity*. Cardiff: University of Wales Press, 2011.

Plimmer, Charlotte, and Denis Plimmer. 'The Man Who Understands Hobbits.' *London Daily Telegraph Magazine* (March 1968), 32–2, 35.

Pound, Ezra. *The ABC of Reading*. London: Routledge, 1934.

Powell, L. F., and M. Clare Loughlin-Chow. 'Chapman, Robert William.' *ODNB* 11:66.

Price, Reynolds. *Ardent Spirits: Leaving Home, Coming Back*. New York: Scribner, 2009.

Putter, Ad. *'Sir Gawain and the Green Knight' and French Arthurian Romance*. Oxford: Clarendon, 1995.

Rateliff, John D. '*The Hobbit*.' In *Companion*, ed. Lee, 119–32.

Rateliff, John D. '"A Kind of Elvish Craft": Tolkien as Literary Craftsman.' *Tolkien Studies* 6 (2009), 1–21.

Rateliff, John D. 'The Missing Women: J. R. R. Tolkien's Lifelong Support for Women's Higher Education.' In *Perilous and Fair: Women in the Works and Life of J. R. R. Tolkien*, ed. Janet Brennan Croft and Leslie A. Donovan. Altadena, CA: Mythopoeic Press (2015), 41–69.

Rateliff, John D. *The Story of The Hobbit*. London: HarperCollins, 2013.

Reinecke, George F. 'F. N. Robinson (1872–1967).' In *Editing Chaucer*, ed. Ruggiers, 231–51.

Resnick, Henry. 'An Interview with Tolkien.' *Niekas* 18 (1967), 37–47.
Rex, Richard. *'The Sins of Madame Eglantyne' and Other Essays on Chaucer*. Newark: University of Delaware Press; London: Associate University Presses, 1995.
Rickert, Edith. 'Thou Vache.' *Modern Philology* 11 (1913–1914), 209–26.
Ridley, Florence H. *The Prioress and the Critics*. Berkeley and Los Angeles: University of California Press, 1965.
Rigby, Stephen H., and Alastair J. Minnis, eds. *Historians on Chaucer: The General Prologue to the 'Canterbury Tales'*. Oxford: Oxford University Press, 2014.
Risden, E. L. 'Source Criticism: Background and Applications.' In *Tolkien and the Study of His Sources*, ed. Fisher, 17–28.
Roberts, Adam. *The Riddles of the Hobbit*. London: Palgrave Macmillan, 2013.
Robinson, Pamela. 'Geoffrey Chaucer and the *Equatorie of the Planetis*.' *Chaucer Review* 26 (1991), 17–30.
Roskell, J. S. 'Thomas Chaucer of Ewelme.' In *Parliament and Politics in Late Medieval England*. London: Hambledon (1983), 151–91.
Ruggiers, Paul G., ed. *Editing Chaucer: The Great Tradition*. Norman, OK: Pilgrim Books, 1984.
Ruud, Martin R. *Thomas Chaucer*. Minneapolis: University of Minnesota Studies in Language and Literature, no. 9, 1926.
Ryan, J. S. 'J. R. R. Tolkien and the *Ancrene Riwle*, or Two Fine and Courteous Mentors to Women's Spirits.' In *In the Nameless Wood: Explorations in the Philological Hinterland of Tolkien's Literary Creations*. Zurich and Jena: Walking Tree Publishers (2013), 261–300.
Ryan, J. S. 'Tolkien and George Gordon: or, A Close Colleague and His Notion of "Mythmaker" and of Historiographic Jeux d'esprit.' In *Shaping of Middle-earth's Maker: Influences on the Life and Literature of J. R. R. Tolkien*. Highland, MI: American Tolkien Society (1992), 30–3.
Salu, Mary, and Robert T. Farrell, eds. *J. R. R. Tolkien, Scholar and Storyteller*. Ithaca and London: Cornell University Press, 1979.
Samuels, M. L. 'Chaucer's Spelling.' In *Middle English Studies Presented to Norman Davis in Honour of his Seventieth Birthday*. Ed. Douglas Gray and E. G. Stanley. Oxford: Clarendon Press (1983), 17–37.
Saul, Nigel. *Richard II*. New Haven and London: Yale University Press, 1997.
Scarf, Christopher. *The Ideal of Kingship in the Writings of Charles Williams, C. S. Lewis and J. R. R. Tolkien: Divine Kingship Is Reflected in Middle-earth*. Cambridge: James Clarke, 2013.
Scase, Wendy. 'Tolkien, Philology, and *The Reeve's Tale*: Towards the Cultural Move in Middle English Studies.' *SAC* 24 (2002), 325–34.
Scull, Christiana. 'The Influence of Archaeology and History on Tolkien's World.' In *Scholarship and Fantasy: Proceedings of the Tolkien Phenomenon*, ed. K. J. Battarbee. Turku, Finland: Anglicana Turkuensia, no. 12 (1993), 33–51.
Scull, Christina, and Wayne G. Hammond. *J. R. R. Tolkien Companion and Guide: Revised and Expanded Edition*. London: HarperCollins, 2017: Vol. 1: *Chronology*; Vol. 2: *Reader's Guide, Part I: A–M*; Vol. 3. *Reader's Guide, Part II: N–Z*.
Senior, W. A. 'Loss Eternal in J. R. R. Tolkien's Middle-earth.' In *J. R. R. Tolkien and His Literary Resonances: Views of Middle-earth*, ed. George Clark and Daniel Timmons. Westport and London: Greenwood Press (2000), 173–82.
Shippey, Tom. 'Allegory versus Bounce: (Half of) an Exchange on *Smith of Wootton Major*.' In *Roots and Branches*, 351–62.

Shippey, Tom. 'Another Road to Middle-earth: Jackson's Movie Trilogy.' In *Roots and Branches*, 365–86.
Shippey, Tom. 'Bilingualism and Betrayal in Chaucer's Summoner's Tale.' In *Speaking in the Medieval World*, ed. Jean Godsall-Myers. Leiden and Boston: Brill (2003), 125–44.
Shippey, Tom. '"A Fund of Wise Sayings": Proverbiality in Tolkien.' In *Roots and Branches*, 303–19.
Shippey, Tom. 'Goths and Romans in Tolkien's Imagination.' In *Tolkien: The Forest and the City*, ed. Conrad-O'Briain and Hynes, 19–32.
Shippey, Tom. 'History in Words: Tolkien's Ruling Passion.' In *Roots and Branches*, 157–73.
Shippey, Tom. 'Introduction: Why Source Criticism?' In *Tolkien and the Study of His Sources*, ed. Fisher, 7–16.
Shippey, T. A. *J. R. R. Tolkien: Author of the Century*. Boston and New York: Houghton Mifflin, 2001.
Shippey, Tom. *Laughing Shall I Die: Lives and Deaths of the Great Vikings*. London: Reaktion Books, 2018.
Shippey, Tom. 'A Look at *Exodus* and *Finn and Hengst*.' In *Roots and Branches*, 175–86.
Shippey, Tom. 'The Problem of the Rings: Tolkien and Wagner.' In *Roots and Branches*, 97–114.
Shippey, Tom. *The Road to Middle-earth*. Rev. edn. Boston and New York: Houghton Mifflin, 2003.
Shippey, Tom. *Roots and Branches: Selected Papers on Tolkien*. Zurich and Jena: Walking Tree Publishers, 2007.
Shippey, Tom. 'Tolkien and the Appeal of the Pagan: *Edda* and *Kalevala*.' In *Roots and Branches*, 19–38.
Shippey, Tom. 'Tolkien and the *Beowulf*-poet.' In *Roots and Branches*, 1–18.
Shippey, Tom. 'Tolkien and the *Gawain*-poet.' In *Roots and Branches*, 61–77.
Shippey, Tom. 'Tolkien and "That Noble Northern Spirit".' In McIlwaine, *Tolkien: Maker of Middle-earth*, 58–69.
Shippey, Tom. 'Tolkien as Editor.' In *Companion*, ed. Lee, 41–55.
Shippey, Tom. 'Tolkien's Academic Reputation Now.' In *Roots and Branches*, 202–12.
Shippey, Tom. 'The Versions of "The Hoard".' In *Roots and Branches*, 341–9.
Sinex, Margaret. '"Monsterized Saracens": Tolkien's Haradrim and Other "Fantasy Products".' *Tolkien Studies* 7 (2010), 175–96.
Sisam, Kenneth. 'The *Beowulf* Manuscript.' *Modern Language Review* 11 (1916), 335–7.
Sisam, Kenneth, ed. *Fourteenth Century Verse and Prose*. Oxford: Clarendon Press, 1921.
Sisam, Kenneth. 'Notes on Old English Poetry.' *RES* 22 (1946), 257–68.
Sisam, Kenneth. 'Skeat, Walter William.' *DNB*, 495–6.
Sisam, Kenneth. *The Structure of 'Beowulf'*. Oxford: Clarendon Press, 1965.
Sisam, Kenneth. *Studies in the History of Old English Literature*. Oxford: Clarendon Press, 1953.
Sisam, Kenneth, and J. R. R. Tolkien. *A Middle English Reader and Vocabulary, 1921–22*. Mineola: Dover, 2005.
Sisam, Peter J. *Roots and Branches: The Story of the Sisam Family*. Marlow: Peter J. Sisam, 1993.
Skeat, Walter W. *An Etymological Dictionary of the English Language*. Rev. edn. Oxford: Clarendon Press, 1910.
Skeat, Walter W. 'Introduction.' In *A Student's Pastime: Being a Selection of Articles Reprinted from 'Notes and Queries'*. Oxford: Clarendon Press, 1896.

Skeat, Walter W. 'Thomas, Son of Geoffrey Chaucer.' *Athenæum*, no. 3770 (27 January 1900), 116.
Smith, Jeremy J. 'Chaucer and the Invention of English.' *SAC* 24 (2002), 335–46.
Solopova, Elizabeth. 'Middle English.' In *Companion*, ed. Lee, 230–43.
Spurgeon, Caroline F. E. *Five Hundred Years of Chaucer Criticism and Allusion, 1357–1900*. 3 vols. Cambridge: Cambridge University Press, 1925.
Stallworthy, Jon. 'Davin, Daniel Marcus.' *ODNB* 15:424–6.
Steiner, George. 'Tolkien, Oxford's Eccentric Don' (1973). *Tolkien Studies* 5 (2008), 186–8.
Stenström, Anders. '*The Clerkes Compleinte* Revisited.' *Arda* 6 (1990 for 1986), 1–13.
Stevens, Martin, and Daniel Woodward, eds. *Ellesmere Chaucer: Essays in Interpretation*. San Marino, CA: Huntington Library, 1995.
Straubhaar, Sandra Ballif. 'Myth, Late Roman History, and Multiculturalism in Tolkien's Middle-earth.' In *Tolkien and the Invention of Myth*, ed. Chance, 101–17.
Strohm, Paul. *Chaucer's Tale: 1386 and the Road to Canterbury*. New York: Viking, 2014.
Strohm, Paul. 'Queens as Intercessors.' In *Huchon's Arrow: The Social Imagination of Fourteenth-Century Texts*. Princeton: Princeton University Press (1992), 95–119.
Strohm, Paul. *Social Chaucer*. Cambridge, MA: Harvard University Press, 1989.
Sudell, T. S. 'The Alliterative Verses of *The Fall of Arthur*.' *Tolkien Studies* 13 (2016), 71–100.
Sutcliffe, Peter. *The Oxford University Press: An Informal History*. Oxford: Clarendon Press, 1978.
Sutherland, John. *A Little History of Literature*. New Haven and London: Yale University Press, 2013.
Tankard, Paul. 'William Empson on C. S. Lewis's Reading and Memory.' *Notes and Queries* 61 (2014), 614–16.
Tatlock, John S. P. *The Development and Chronology of Chaucer's Works*. London: Chaucer Society, 2nd ser., no. 37 (1907).
Thomas, Mary Edith. *Medieval Skepticism and Chaucer: An Evaluation of the Skepticism of the 13th and 14th Centuries of Geoffrey Chaucer and His Immediate Predecessors—An Era That Looked Back on an Age of Faith and Forward to an Age of Reason*. 1950; rpt. New York: Cooper Square Publishers, 1971.
Tolkien, Christopher, ed. *The Saga of King Heidrek the Wise*. London: Thomas Nelson and Sons, 1960.
Tolkien, Hilary. *Black & White Ogre Country: The Lost Tales of Hilary Tolkien*. Ed. Angela Gardner. Moreton-in-Marsh: ADC Publications, 2009.
Tolkien, J. R. R. '*Ancrene Wisse* and *Hali Meiðhad*.' *Essays and Studies* 14 (1929), 104–26.
Tolkien, J. R. R., ed. *Ancrene Wisse: Edited from MS. Corpus Christi College Cambridge 402*. Intro. N. R. Ker. EETS o.s. 249 (1962).
Tolkien, J. R. R. *The Annotated Hobbit: Revised and Expanded Edition*. Ed. Douglas A. Anderson. Boston and New York: Houghton Mifflin, 2002.
Tolkien, J. R. R. *Beowulf: A Translation and Commentary*. Ed. Christopher Tolkien. Boston and New York: Houghton Mifflin, 2014.
Tolkien, J. R. R. '*Beowulf' and the Critics*. Ed. Michael D. C. Drout. Tempe: Arizona Center for Medieval and Renaissance Studies, 2002.
Tolkien, J. R. R. '*Beowulf*: The Monsters and the Critics.' Sir Israel Gollancz Memorial Lecture. *Proceedings of the British Academy* (1936), 245–95. Rpt. *Essays*, 5–48.
Tolkien, J. R. R. *Beren and Lúthien*. Ed. Christopher Tolkien. Boston and New York: Houghton Mifflin Harcourt, 2017.

Tolkien, J. R. R. *The Book of Lost Tales: Part I and II*. Ed. Christopher Tolkien. 1983-4; New York: Ballantine Books, 1992.
Tolkien, J. R. R. 'Chaucer as a Philologist: *The Reeve's Tale.*' *Transactions of the Philological Society* (1934), 1-70. Reprinted with author's corrections in *Tolkien Studies* 5 (2008), 109-71.
Tolkien, J. R. R. 'The Devil's Coach-Horses.' *RES* 1/3 (July 1925), 331-6.
Tolkien, J. R. R. 'English and Welsh' (1955). In *Essays*, 162-97.
Tolkien, J. R. R. *The Fall of Arthur*. Ed. Christopher Tolkien. Boston and New York: Houghton Mifflin Harcourt, 2013.
Tolkien, J. R. R. *The Father Christmas Letters*. Ed. Baillie Tolkien. Boston: Houghton Mifflin, 1976.
Tolkien, J. R. R. *The Fellowship of the Ring*. 1954; Boston and New York: Houghton Mifflin, 1988.
Tolkien, J. R. R. *Finn and Hengest: The Fragment and the Episode*. Ed. Alan Bliss. Boston: Houghton Mifflin, 1983.
Tolkien, J. R. R. 'Foreword.' In Walter E. Haigh, *A New Glossary of the Dialect of the Huddersfield District*. London: Oxford University Press (1928), pp. xiii-xviii.
Tolkien, J. R. R. *The History of the Lord of the Rings*. Ed. Christopher Tolkien. 4 vols. Boston and New York: Houghton Mifflin, 1988-92.
Tolkien, J. R. R. 'The Lay of Aotrou and Itroun.' *The Welsh Review* 4/4 (1945), 254-66.
Tolkien, J. R. R. *The Lay of Aotrou and Itroun together with the Corrigan Poems*. Ed. Verlyn Flieger with note on text by Christopher Tolkien. Boston and New York: Houghton Mifflin Harcourt, 2017.
Tolkien, J. R. R. *The Lays of Beleriand*. Ed. Christopher Tolkien. 1985; New York: Ballantine Books, 1994.
Tolkien, J. R. R. *Leaf by Niggle*. In *Poems and Stories*, 195-220.
Tolkien, J. R. R. *The Legend of Sigurd and Gudrún*. Ed. Christopher Tolkien. Boson and New York: Houghton Mifflin Harcourt, 2009.
Tolkien, J. R. R. *The Letters of J. R. R. Tolkien*. Ed. Humphrey Carpenter and Christopher Tolkien. 1981; Boston and New York: Houghton Mifflin, 2000.
Tolkien, J. R. R. *The Lost Road and Other Writings*. Ed. Christopher Tolkien. York York: Del Rey, 1996.
Tolkien, J. R. R. 'Middle English "Losenger": Sketch of an Etymological and Semantic Enquiry.' In *Essais de Philologie Moderne (1951)*. Paris: Société d'Édition Les Belles Lettres (1953), 63-76.
Tolkien, J. R. R. *The Monsters and the Critics, and Other Essays*. Ed. Christopher Tolkien. 1983: London: HarperCollins, 2006.
Tolkien, J. R. R. *Morgoth's Ring: The Later Silmarillion, Part I*. Ed. Cristopher Tolkien. Boston and New York: Houghton Mifflin, 1993.
Tolkien, J. R. R. *Mythopoeia. Tree and Leaf.* Intro. Christopher Tolkien. Boston: Houghton Mifflin (1989), 97-101.
Tolkien, J. R. R. 'The Name "Nodens".' Appendix I in R. E. M. Wheeler and T. V. Wheeler's *Report on the Excavation of the Prehistoric, Roman, and Post-Roman Site in Lydney Park, Gloucestershire*. London: Society of Antiquaries (1932), 132-7. Rpt. *Tolkien Studies* 4 (2007), 177-83.
Tolkien, J. R. R. *Narn I Chîn Húrin: The Tale of the Children of Húrin*. Ed. Christopher Tolkien. Boston and New York: Houghton Mifflin, 2007.
Tolkien, J. R. R. 'Nomenclature of *The Lord of the Rings*.' In *Reader's Companion*, ed. Hammond and Scull, 750-82.

Tolkien, J. R. R. *The Notion Club Papers. Sauron Defeated.* Ed. Christopher Tolkien. London: HarperCollins (1993), 145–327.

Tolkien, J. R. R. 'The Oxford English School.' *The Oxford Magazine* 48 (1930), 778–80.

Tolkien, J. R. R. *The Peoples of Middle-Earth.* Ed. Christopher Tolkien. Boston and New York: Houghton Mifflin, 1996.

Tolkien, J. R. R. 'Philology: General Works.' *Year's Work in English Studies* 4 (1924), 20–37; 5 (1926): 26–65; and 6 (1927): 32–66.

Tolkien, J. R. R. *Poems and Stories.* Boston and New York: 1980; Houghton Mifflin, 1994.

Tolkien, J. R. R. 'The Reeve's Tale: Version Prepared for Recitation at the "Summer Diversions" Oxford: 1939.' Rpt. *Tolkien Studies* 5 (2008), 173–83.

Tolkien, J. R. R. *The Return of the King.* 1955; Boston and New York: Houghton Mifflin, 1988.

Tolkien, J. R. R. *The Return of the Shadow: The History of the Lord of the Rings, Part I.* Ed. Christopher Tolkien. Boston and New York: Houghton Mifflin, 1988.

Tolkien, J. R. R. Review of *Hali Meidenhad: An Alliterative Prose Homily of the Thirteenth Century,* ed. F. J. Furnivall, EETS o.s. 18 (1922). *TLS* 26 April 1923, p. 281. Rpt. *TLS* 30 June 2017, p. 34.

Tolkien, J. R. R. 'Sigelwara Land.' *Medium Ævum* 1 (1932), 183–96, and 3 (1934), 95–111.

Tolkien, J. R. R. *The Silmarillion.* Ed. Christopher Tolkien. 1977; London: HarperCollins, 2008.

Tolkien, J. R. R. 'Sir Gawain and the Green Knight.' In *Essays,* 72–108.

Tolkien, J. R. R. *Sir Gawain and the Green Knight, Pearl, and Sir Orfeo.* Ed. Christopher Tolkien. London: George Allen & Unwin, 1975; rpt. New York: Ballantine Books, 1980.

Tolkien, J. R. R. *Smith of Wootton Major. Poems and Stories.* Illustrated by Pauline Baynes. Boston and New York: Houghton Mifflin (1994), 303–42.

Tolkien, J. R. R. 'Some Contributions to Middle-English Lexicography.' *RES* 1 (1925), 210–15.

Tolkien, J. R. R. *The Story of Kullervo.* Ed. Verlyn Flieger. Boston and New York: Houghton Mifflin Harcourt, 2016.

Tolkien, J. R. R. *The Treason of Isengard: The History of 'The Lord of the Rings': Part Two.* Ed. Christopher Tolkien. Boston and New York: Houghton Mifflin, 1989.

Tolkien, J. R. R. *The Two Towers.* 1954; Boston and New York: Houghton Mifflin, 1988.

Tolkien, J. R. R. *Unfinished Tales of Númenor and Middle-earth.* Ed. Christopher Tolkien. Boston and New York: Houghton Mifflin (1980), 228–67.

Tolkien, J. R. R. 'Valedictory Address.' In *Essays,* 224–40. A slightly different version was printed in *Tolkien, Scholar and Storyteller,* ed. Salu and Farrell, 16–32.

Tolkien, J. R. R. *The War of the Jewels.* Ed. Christopher Tolkien. Boston and New York: Houghton Mifflin, 1994.

Tolkien, J. R. R., and S. R. T. O. d'Ardenne. '"Iþþlen" in *Sawles Warde.*' *English Studies* 28 (1947), 168–70.

Tolkien, J. R. R., and E. V. Gordon, eds. *Sir Gawain and the Green Knight.* Oxford: Clarendon Press, 1925.

Tolkien, John, and Priscilla Tolkien. *The Tolkien Family Album.* Boston: Houghton Mifflin, 1992.

Unwin, Rayner. 'Early Days of Elder Days.' In *Tolkien's 'Legendarium',* ed. Flieger and Hostetter, 3–6.

Unwin, Rayner. *George Allen & Unwin: A Remembrancer.* London: Merlin Unwin Books, 1999.

Unwin, Rayner. 'Publishing Tolkien.' In *Proceedings of the J. R. R. Tolkien Centenary Conference, 1992*. Ed. Patricia Reynolds and Glen H. GoodKnight. Milton Keynes: Tolkien Society, and Altadena, CA: Mythopoeic Press (1995), 26–9.
Vink, Renée. 'Immortality and the Death of Love: J. R. R Tolkien and Simone de Beauvoir.' In *The Ring Goes Ever On: Proceedings of the Tolkien 2005 Conference*. Ed. Sarah Wells. 2 vols. Coventry: Tolkien Society (2008), 2:117–27.
Vink, Renée. '"Jewish" Dwarves: Tolkien and Anti-Semitic Stereotyping.' *Tolkien Studies* 10 (2013), 123–45.
Wain, John. 'C. S. Lewis as a Teacher.' In *Masters: Portraits of Great Teachers*, ed. Joseph Epstein. New York: Basic Books (1981), 236–52.
Wallace, David. *Chaucerian Polity: Absolutist Lineages and Associational Forms in England and Italy*. Stanford: Stanford University Press, 1992.
Warner, Lawrence. 'Scribes, Misattributed: Hoccleve and Pinkhurst.' *SAC* 37 (2015), 55–100.
Wells, Sarah, ed. *The Ring Goes Ever On: Proceedings of the Tolkien 2005 Conference: 50 Years of 'The Lord of the Rings'*. 2 vols. Coventry: The Tolkien Society, 2008.
Wenterdorf, Karl P. 'Chaucer and the Lost Tale of Wade.' *Journal of English and Germanic Philology* 65 (1966), 274–86.
Wickham-Crowley, Kelley M. '"Mind to Mind": Tolkien's Faërian Drama and the Middle English *Sir Orfeo*.' *Tolkien Studies* 12 (2015), 1–19.
Wilson, Bee. 'Querns and Curtains.' *TLS* 5842 (14 November 2014), 3–4.
Wilson, R. M. *The Lost Literature of Medieval England*. London: Methuen, 1952.
Windeatt, B. A. 'Thomas Tyrwhitt (1730–1786).' In *Editing Chaucer*, ed. Ruggiers, 117–43.
Wolf, F. A. *Prolegomena to Homer (1795)*. Trans. and intro. Anthony Grafton, Glenn W. Most, and James E. G. Zetzel. Princeton: Princeton University Press, 1985.
Woolf, Rosemary. 'Moral Chaucer and Kindly Gower.' In *Tolkien: Scholar and Storyteller*, ed. Salu and Farrell, 221–45.
Woolf, Virginia. 'The Pastons and Chaucer.' In *The Common Reader: First Series* (1925). New York: Harcourt, Brace and Co. (1953), 3–23.
Wright, Joseph. *A Grammar of the Dialect of Windhill in the West Riding of Yorkshire*. London: K. Paul, Trench, Trübner & Co., 1892.
Wynne, Patrick, and Carl F. Hostetter. 'Three Elvish Verse Modes.' In *Tolkien's 'Legendarium'*, ed. Flieger and Hostetter, 113–39.
Yeager, Robert F. 'Chaucer's "To His Purse": Begging or Begging Off?' *Viator* 36 (2005), 373–414.
Yeager, R. F. 'John Gower's French.' In *Companion to Gower*, ed. Echard, 137–51.
Zaleski, Philip, and Carol Zaleski. *The Fellowship: The Literary Lives of the Inklings: J. R. R. Tolkien, C. S. Lewis, Owen Barfield, Charles Williams*. New York: Farrar, Straus and Giroux, 2015.

Index

References to Geoffrey Chaucer, Walter W. Skeat, Kenneth Sisam, George Gordon, and C. S. Lewis—as well as characters such as Bilbo and Frodo and titles such as *Canterbury Tales* and *The Lord of the Rings*—are so numerous that no attempt has been made to include all of them in this index. Also highly selective has been the inclusion of scholars cited in the footnotes. Because assembled by paragraphs coded for the e-book version, references may actually appear on pages before or after the ones cited in this index.

Alceste 114, 149–50, 154, 243
alchemy 17, 140–1, 188, 218–19, 221, 254–5
Alfred the Great 145, 147
Alla of Northumbria 160
allegory 70, 87, 105, 111, 115, 117–18, 125, 149, 212–213
allegory of the tower 70, 122
Allen & Unwin 9, 35, 175
Alliterative tradition 6, 120, 154–60, 202
Amis, Kingsley 207–8
Ancrene Riwle/Ancrene Wisse 4, 32n61, 52, 87, 118, 175, 182, 233
Anderson, Douglas 197, 243
Anne of Bohemia 125, 138, 149
April/*Aprille* 49, 158, 168, 235, 242
Aragorn 127, 133, 137, 140, 153, 160, 167, 171–2, 175, 248
Aragorn and Arwen 122, 139, 149, 237, 244
archeology 131–2
Aristophanes 208
Aristotle 153–5
Arnold, Matthew 38, 64n100
Arwen 149, 177, 245, 251
astronomy 161, 214
Auden, W.H. 2, 18, 157, 159, 165, 207
audiences 31, 74, 155, 209, 238–9
Austen, Jane 8, 103
aventure 99, 276

Bacon, Francis, on feigned history 142–3
Baggins, Bilbo 35, 46–9, 55, 74, 111, 114, 124, 137, 140, 172, 174, 180, 185, 226, 229, 242, 252, 259, 265
Baggins, Frodo 111, 115–16, 122, 127, 165, 168, 174, 195, 196, 205, 220, 235, 242–4, 255, 259, 261–3
Ballad of Thomas Rhymer 140, 251
Barr, Helen v
Battle of the Somme 60, 125, 173, 234

Beauvoir, Simone de 117
Bennett, J.A.W. 34, 52, 118, 232
Benson, Larry 214–15
Beowulf (poem) 1, 27, 48, 59, 118, 123, 208, 220, 222, 240, 244, 254
Beren and Lúthien 3, 120–2, 149, 159–60, 175–6, 196, 244–5, 251, 253
biography as critical resource 49, 109, 140, 152, 193, 204, 217, 226, 248–9, 265, 274
birds 121, 125, 128
Bloom, Harold 5–6, 47–52, 186, 249, 262–7
Boccaccio 125, 242–3, 246, 264–5
  Decameron 165–6, 174–5, 223
  De Claris Mulieribus 154–5
  Filostrato 238, 245–6
  Teseida 126, 157
Boethius 45, 89, 90, 129, 137, 143–8, 241, 283
bookishness 152, 179, 228, 240–1
book-lovers 227–8
Bored of the Rings 9
bos/boës 51, 89, 101, 191, 201, 212
bowdlerizing 24, 58, 88, 102, 178, 210, 216–17
Bowers, John M.
  Chaucer and Langland: The Antagonistic Tradition 12
  Politics of 'Pearl': Court Poetry in the Age of Richard II 12
  'Tolkien's Goldberry and *The Maid of the Moor*' 11
Bradley, Henry 94, 179
  The Goths 145–6
Bradshaw, Henry 42, 44
Brewer, Charlotte 42n2, 44
Brewer, Derek 47, 76, 124
Brewerton, George (teacher) 148, 174, 224
Brutus (legendary founder of Britain) 142
Burchfield, R.W. 52
Burrow, J.A. 10, 36

buskes/busshes 24, 80, 84, 85
Butterbur, Barliman 183, 197, 243, 255

cadets at Oxford 3, 6–7, 55n52, 66, 188, 216–17, 245
Cambridge 41–2, 48, 170–1, 187, 189, 205, 206, 233
Cannon, Christopher 45
Carpenter, Humphrey (authorized biographer) 1, 13, 28, 52, 79, 106, 229, 239
Carr, Charlie (Merton College scout) 205
catalogues (epic lists) 123, 126, 128, 154
Catholicism (Tolkien's religion) 117–19, 139, 175, 178
Caxton, William 38–9, 273
Celeborn (Galadriel's consort) 150
Celebrimbor 132, 141, 150
Chambers, E. K. 66
Chambers, R.W. 27–8, 159–60
  Continuity of English Prose 90
  'The Lost Literature of Medieval England' 37
  Man's Unconquerable Mind 211–12
Chance, Jane 14
Chapman, R.W. 14, 32, 56, 58, 60–1, 63, 66, 103, 105, 221, 224
Chaucer, Agnes (poet's mother) 100
Chaucer, Alice (poet's granddaughter) 160, 271
Chaucer, Elizabeth (poet's sister or daughter?) 174–5
Chaucer, Geoffrey
  Adam Scriveyn 85, 143, 199, 239
  Anelida and Arcite 235, 239
  Astrolabe 45, 138, 161–3, 214–15, 232–3
  Boece 26, 45, 90–2, 97, 129, 143–8, 213, 236
  Book of the Duchess 86, 90, 119–25, 176, 193, 208, 226, 242–3
  Canon's Yeoman's Tale 140–1
  Canterbury Tales 164, 215
  Clerk of Oxford 178–80, 231–2
  Clerk's Tale 3, 22, 34, 52, 175, 236, 254
  Compleint to his Empty Purse 139–43, 153–4
  Compleinte unto Pité 84–6, 116–20
  Criseyde 39, 116–17, 246–8
  Emelye in Knight's Tale 246
  Former Age 25, 87, 89–90, 129–34
  Franklin 107, 184, 271
  Friar's Tale 252–3
  General Prologue 163–86, 196, 215, 224, 235, 242
  Gentilesse 136–7, 251
  Harry Bailey 166, 183, 185, 243–4
  House of Fame 229, 235, 239
  Knight 169–72
  Knight's Tale 108, 126, 156, 170, 202, 230, 241
  Lak of Stedfastnesse 138–9
  Legend of Cleopatra 82, 154–60, 202
  Man of Law's Tale 143, 154, 160, 204, 231, 245
  Merchant's Tale 115, 241, 275
  Merciles Beaute 69, 134–5
  Miller 7, 182, 188, 194
  Miler's Tale 22, 58, 69, 162, 179, 232
  Monk 177–8, 199
  Monk's Tale 20, 31, 48, 146, 209, 274
  Normandy Campaign (1360) 234, 271
  Nun's Priest's Tale 3, 20, 23, 57, 102, 114, 208, 243, 275
  Pardoner as a homosexual 266
  Pardoner's Tale 2–4, 35, 254–67
  Parlement of Foules 3, 20, 45, 64–5, 86, 90, 106–107, 114–15, 124–9, 141, 169, 198–9, 239–41
  Parson 159, 182, 241
  Parson's Prologue 236–7
  Physician 238
  Prioress 119, 166, 168–9, 172–7
  Prioress's French 172–4
  Prioress's Tale 23, 187
  Prologue to *Legend of Good Women* 37, 87, 90, 114, 123, 148–54, 224, 234
  Reeve 100, 183, 189, 194, 204
  Reeve's Tale 2–3, 6–7, 20, 23, 40, 49, 88–9, 177, 185–221
  Retraction 240
  Romaunt of the Rose 22, 49, 109–16, 127
  Rosemounde 22, 135
  Second Nun's Tale 119
  Shipman 180–1
  Squire 172
  Squire's Tale 172
  Summoner's Tale 174, 193, 196
  Troilus and Criseyde 7, 22, 39, 69, 116, 135, 162, 167, 193, 199, 227–8, 240, 245–8
  Truth 113, 135, 152
  Westminster Abbey residence 141, 231, 273
  Wife of Bath 181–2, 245, 249–50
  Wife of Bath's Prologue 45, 207, 249
  Wife of Bath's Tale 105–6, 137, 166, 220–1, 249–54
Chaucer, Lewis (poet's son?) 161, 230
Chaucer, Philippa (poet's wife) 230
Chaucer, Thomas (poet's son) 12, 141, 193, 230, 232, 269–74
Chaucerian incubus 32, 105–6, 121–2, 185–6, 224–5
Clarendon Chaucer (*Selections from Chaucer's Poetry and Prose*) 11, 15, 18, 36, 50, 56, 60, 67, 71–2, 226

Glossary (Tolkien's) 8–9, 20–1, 24–7, 79, 94–103
Glossary headnote (Tolkien's) 283–4
Introduction (George Gordon's) 15, 17–18, 24, 27–9, 38–9, 66
'Introduction on Language' (Tolkien's) 38, 108, 200, 209, 228, 238, 279–81
Notes (Tolkien's) 24–6, 30, 105–86
Plan for the Tales (Tolkien's) 183–5
Reeve's Tale (Tolkien's) 189–95
Testimonials (George Gordon's) 15, 29, 36, 38–40
Text (Tolkien's) 18, 24, 26, 80–94
Text Proof 1, Copy 2 89–93
Clifford, Lewis 17, 230–1
Clouston, William Alexander 172n206, 258, 264
cockney 205–6
Coghill, Nevill 57, 208, 266, 275–7
  Nun's Priest's Tale (edition) 275
  Poet Chaucer 135
Cotton, Rose 70, 112
courtly love 22, 68–9, 134, 150, 166, 245, 247n74, 276
Croft, Janet 197

D'Ardenne, S. R. T. O. (Simonne) 113, 175, 224, 228–30
daisy 82–4, 113–14, 150–1
Dante 117, 137, 147, 241, 275
Darwall-Smith, R. H. 60n83, 65n106
Davin, Dan 5, 7, 18, 34–6, 38, 60, 67, 80–1, 103, 106, 225, 275
Davis, Norman 10–11, 36, 52, 96, 189, 215
deer-hunting 123, 193
De Hamel, Christopher 40, 270, 272
Denethor 140, 169, 172
Dent, Jonathan v
Deschamps, Eustache 113, 136, 230
dogs 175–6
Donaldson, E. Talbot 46–7, 85, 203, 207, 212–13, 236–7
Drayton, Michael 249–50
dreams 114–15, 122–5
Dronke, Peter vi
Drout, Michael 4, 87
Dwarf's Hill 132
Dyson, Hugo 118

Eagle and Child 138–9, 166, 230–1
Eagles 115–17, 127–8, 234–5, 243
Eagleton, Terry 61–2
Eärendil 121, 132, 162, 171, 206
Early English Text Society (EETS) 4, 41–2, 44
Eco, Umberto 223

Edwards, A. S. G. 22n34, 44–5, 214–15
Eliot, T.S. 155, 209n60, 265
Ellesmere *Canterbury Tales* 34, 40, 44–5, 86, 89, 93, 165, 187, 199–203, 211, 213–15, 270, 273–6
Ellesmere facsimile 34, 224, 276
Ellesmere portraits 34, 39, 57, 200, 208, 223n3
elvish 127, 140–1, 143–4, 149, 174, 176–7, 238–9, 242–5, 251
Empson, William 73
Ents 114, 127–9, 188, 195, 219–20, 263
Éowyn 171–2
Epstein, Robert 192
Equatorie of the Planetis (Chaucer holograph?) 214–15, 232–3
erber/arbour 152
eucatastrophe 220, 263, 267
Everett, Dorothy 156
Ewelme (Thomas Chaucer's manor) 160, 232–3, 270–1
Exeter College (Oxford) 10, 46–7, 117–18, 180

fairies 17, 55, 105–6, 132, 249–54
Faramir 46–7, 138, 154, 165, 169, 177, 223, 246–249
Faramir and Éowyn 7, 116–17, 245–8
Felker, Kyle v
fer in the north 192, 192n11, 204, 207, 220, 252–3
Field, George 248
Fisher, John H. 214–15
Fishwick, James v–vi
Flieger, Verlyn 121n63, 157n163, 236n37, 250n82
Foden, Peter 36–7
fox, talking 243
French, dislike of 151, 155, 172–3, 229, 234
Freudian interpretation *see* Psychoanalytic criticism
Frye, Northrop 167–8
Furnivall, Frederick J. 3–5, 41–2, 44–5, 62
  Hali Meidenhad 3–5, 175
  Six-Text Edition of Chaucer's Canterbury Tales 44–5, 201–2
  Oxford English Dictionary 41–2

gaan/geen 20, 93, 198, 201–2, 205, 207
Galadriel 115–16, 150, 162–3, 172, 243, 253
Galadriel and Celeborn 254
Gamgee, Sam 70, 89, 111, 137, 170, 173, 180–1, 195, 205–6, 210, 218, 237, 243–4, 262–3, 265
Gandalf 115–16, 128–9, 146, 181, 185, 237–8, 249, 255–6, 260–2, 266
Gardner, Helen, on C. S. Lewis 34, 69, 73–4
Garth, John 46n23, 60, 176n215, 234

Gascoigne, Thomas 233
Geoffrey of Monmouth 142–3
Gibbon, Edward 147
Gilliver, Peter 15n11, 16n19, 36
Gimli 150, 181, 247
gniden/gnodded 25, 87
Gollancz, Israel 47–8
Gollum (Sméagol) 48, 99, 116, 151, 243, 255, 261–3, 267
Gordon, E.V. 4, 5, 17–18, 21, 28, 50, 79, 96, 106
Gordon, George S. 5, 7–9, 15, 18, 28–9, 31, 60–7, 92, 95, 102, 107, 112
  Anglo-American Literary Relations 66
  Companionable Books 64
  English Literature and the Classics 29–30
  '*Medium Aevum* and the Middle Ages' 65n103
  President of Magdalen College (Oxford) 30, 33, 62
  Shakespearean Comedy and Other Studies 66
  Vice Chancellor of Oxford University 33, 66, 216
Gordon, Mary (widow of George S. Gordon) 30n58, 38, 40, 66–7
Gower, John 121, 149, 153–5, 165–6, 173–4, 231, 235, 270
Gray, Douglas 10, 52, 96, 207–8
greed 180, 255, 259, 262–3, 266–7
Greenwich 100, 141, 231
grey eyes 176–7
Gunn, Steven vi

Haigh, Walter E. 50n40
  New Glossary of the Dialect of the Huddersfield District 197–8
Hali Meidenhad 3–5, 118, 175
Hammond, Eleanor Prescott 207
Hanna, Ralph 92, 276
Harris, Colin v–vi
Hatfield House (Yorkshire) 49–50, 193, 203–4, 215
hauberk 171–2
Hazell, Dinah 114
Hengwrt *Canterbury Tales* 200, 203, 270, 272–3
Henry Bolingbroke (Henry IV) 138, 140, 153–4
Henry IV 136–7, 140, 153–4, 270–1
Henry V 137, 178, 271–2
heterly 20, 82, 155–6, 202
Hobbiton 129, 188, 194–5, 220–1
Hobbler/hobbit 111
Hoccleve, Thomas 29, 38–9, 215
holly/Hollin 127
Holsinger, Bruce vi
Homer 122, 129, 155, 240
Honegger, Thomas v

horns 123, 128, 159, 169
Horobin, Simon 51n44, 100n53, 101n54
horses 171, 177–8, 180–1, 183, 192, 219
Housman, A. E. 211–12
Hudson, Anne 17, 267n125
humour/jest 54, 74, 123, 125, 131, 135, 152, 192, 194, 198, 202, 205, 208, 210, 227–9, 241, 281

incubus 105–6
Inklings 9, 34, 67, 118, 138, 166, 211, 231, 270, 276
Ioreth (old nurse) 133, 175, 182

Jackson, Leonard 46, 132n98
Jackson, Peter 11, 52, 235
James, Henry 58
James, Montague Rhodes 188
Jews 23, 118
John and Alain (students in Reeve's Tale) 180, 192, 198, 201–2, 204–5, 210, 216, 218–20
John of Gaunt, Duke of Lancaster 17, 120, 193, 270
Johnson, Dr. Samuel 43
Jones, Diana Wynne 10, 218–19, 256–7, 267
Jones, Terry 170–1
Jonson, Ben 213
Joyce, James 45, 90

Kalevala 131, 175–6, 245–6
Kent/Kentish dialect 100, 141, 152, 171, 231, 277
Ker, W. P. 47
Kittredge, George Lyman 166, 182, 254, 266
Knighton's *Chronicle* 233–4
Kolbítar 67, 71
Kolve, V.A. 10–11, 120n58, 160, 224

Lachmann, Karl 45
Lang, Andrew 114
Language versus Literature 62, 71–2, 199, 205, 223
Larkin, Philip 207n56
Late-night writing 229–30
Lavezzo, Kathy v
Lawler, Traugott 92
Lee, Stuart D. 2n9
Leeds University 8–9, 16, 28, 54, 62–3, 196–7
Legolas 171–2, 181, 209n60, 242–3
Leverhulme Research Fellowship 33, 225
Lewis, C. S. 5–6, 13, 16, 39, 67–77, 153, 213, 221, 229–31
  Allegory of Love 22, 68–71, 117–18, 213, 276
  'Alliterative Metre' 159–60
  as reader of *Hobbit* 32, 74, 236
  bad at maths 184–5

Discarded Image 74, 105–6
Dymer 74, 116
English Literature in the Sixteenth Century 73–4
first meeting with Tolkien 13n4, 62, 71–2
Four Loves 71n129, 77, 231
Great Divorce 112
lampoons annotation of Chaucer 76
Lion, the Witch, and the Wardrobe 105–6
Narnia 70
on Boethius 143
on *Canterbury Tales* 55–6
on Criseyde 247
on *Faerie Queene* 69, 71, 213
on George Gordon 63–4
on *Hobbit* 76–7
on Nun's Priest's Tale 68
on *Parlement of Foules* 243
on *Romance of the Rose* 111–12
on *Troilus and Criseyde* 69
Out of the Silent Planet 74
Preface to 'Paradise Lost' 74
Lewis, Warnie (Lewis's brother) 14–15, 34, 276
Lollards 17, 272
London 9, 15, 27–8, 32–4, 82, 89, 101, 156–7, 172, 181, 184, 193, 199, 201–3, 210, 214, 230–1, 233–4, 238, 272–3, 276, 279
Loomis, Roger Sherman 17
losenger 3, 35, 99–100, 224–5
Lydgate, John 38–9, 161, 239, 271
 On the Departing of Thomas Chaucer 271
 Siege of Thebes 183–4, 273–4
Lydney Park 131–2

Machaut, Guillaume de 151, 239–40
Macrobius 114–15, 169
Magdalen College (Oxford) 30, 62–3, 71, 75, 154
Mandevillle's *Travels* 129, 264
Manly, John M. 100n52, 185
Manly, John M. and Edith Rickert, eds. (*Text of the Canterbury Tales Studied on the Basis of All Known Manuscripts*) 45, 203, 207, 211–12
Masefield, John 3, 40, 49, 208–9, 211, 223, 252
Mathew, Gervase 138–9
Maw, Martin (OUP archivist) 36–7, 79
McCabe, Richard vi
McFarlane, Bruce 17, 65, 271–2
McGann, Jerome J. 211n65
McIlwaine, Catherine 4, 21n31, 107, 124–5
McMorris, Jenny 36
Merry and Pippin 7, 188, 192, 216, 219, 263

Merton College (Oxford) 11–12, 35, 43, 52–4, 161–2, 189, 223, 232–3, 238
Merton Professor of Language and Literature 3, 10, 15, 34, 44, 52, 72, 189
Middleton, Anne 107–8
mills/millers 7, 23–4, 88, 188, 194–5, 217–21, 241
Mooney, Linne 85n12, 214–15
Morris-Jones, John (*Welsh Grammar*) 46n24, 142
Morris, Richard (*Specimens of Early English*) 191
Morris, William 38–9, 46, 147, 165–6, 171–2, 228
Morse code 123–4
Muir, Edwin 266
music 126, 172, 239–40

Napier, A.S. 54, 72
Neave, Jane (Tolkien's aunt) 113–14, 120–1
Neolithic 130–1, 133
New Zealand 52–4, 59–60
Nichol Smith, David 25, 31–2, 64, 89, 95–6, 107
Nicholson, Jack 237
Nietzsche, Friedrich 109, 225
Nodens 132–3
Non-finishers 235–6
Norfolk 100, 183, 189, 210
North, J. D. 214–15
Northern dialect 6–7, 24, 40, 49–51, 89, 101, 190–4, 198–200, 201, 204, 210, 217
Númenóreans 129, 134, 138, 140, 170, 181, 262
nuns 174–5

OED (*Oxford English Dictionary*) 14–16, 36, 63, 94–5, 105, 134, 145, 179, 196, 197, 206, 241
Onions, C.T. 27n49, 69, 179
overthwert/overthwart 99–100, 108–9, 215
Ovid 10, 114, 121, 126–7, 129, 240
Oxford 1, 8–10, 25, 55, 59–60, 62, 64, 90, 137, 170–1, 204–5, 216, 225, 231–3, 276
Oxford Mail 209–10
Oxford University Press (OUP) 1–2, 4–6, 15–18, 20–4, 28–9, 32–5, 37–8, 40, 44, 60–1, 64–5, 80, 93, 102, 107, 121–2, 275

Patterson, Lee 7n23, 211n65
Pearsall, Derek 41, 230–1
Piers Plowman 10, 42–3, 85, 107, 118, 139, 179, 202–3
Pinkhurst, Adam (Chaucer's scribe) 85n12, 199
Poetic Edda 141
Pound, Ezra 69, 155

Prancing Pony 115, 122, 196–7, 206–7, 228, 244
Price, Derek 214
Price, Reynolds 120n58, 266n121
Prick of Conscience 203
Professor of Anglo-Saxon (Oxford) 2, 8–9, 27–8, 48, 58–9, 63, 198, 208, 254
proper names 84, 95–6, 119–20, 132, 155, 238
Prose Edda 131, 175
Psychoanalytic criticism 46–7, 60, 114, 122, 208, 221

quern 129–32
quest 7, 18, 70, 86, 111–12, 115–16, 184, 235, 251–3, 256, 263

Raleigh, Walter (Merton Professor) 2–3, 55, 62–5, 69, 87, 194
Rateliff, John v
Reid, Julian v
Revard, Carter 17n26
revision 73–4, 87–8, 106–7, 111, 111n21, 119, 148–9
Rhodes Scholar 10, 17, 52, 131
Richard II 125, 138–40, 149, 232, 271
Rickert, Edith 136 *See also* Manly, John M., and Edith Rickert
Riverside Chaucer (1933) 22–3, 35
Riverside Chaucer (1987) 45, 92, 101, 178, 203, 212, 214–15, 276
Robinson, F.N. 22–3, 156
Robinson, Pamela 214–15
Romance of the Rose 21, 69–70, 109, 112, 114, 120, 125–6, 147, 230–1
Rowling, J. K. 180

Sackville-Baggins, Lobelia 177, 181–2
Salu, Mary 175
Samuels, M. L. 215
Sandyman (Hobbiton miller) 7, 188, 195, 219–20
Sartre, Jean-Paul 117
Saruman 7, 75, 127, 172, 188, 216, 219–21, 244, 262
Sawles Warde 267
Sayers, Dorothy 181–2
Scase, Wendy 199n32
Scogan, Henry 136–7, 141
scribes 45, 84–5, 89, 135, 155, 169, 178, 198–9, 202–3, 213, 215
Scull, Christina, and Wayne G. Hammond (*J. R. R. Tolkien Companion and Guide*) see SH.
Selections from Chaucer's Poetry and Prose See Clarendon Chaucer
SH 7, 14, 18, 63, 100, 113, 120, 123, 128, 139, 159–162, 168, 174–5, 181, 209–12, 229–30, 233

Shakespeare 7–8, 29–30, 55, 63–5, 138–9, 241, 265
  Antony and Cleopatra 154, 160
  Macbeth 219, 263
  Tempest 253
  Two Noble Kinsmen 42–3
Shaw, G. B. 84, 206
Sheridan, Richard 208
Shippey, Tom 2, 16, 70, 85–6, 92, 109, 179
  Road to Middle-earth 2
Silmarils 131, 262
Simkin (miller in Reeve's Tale) 7, 188, 194, 216, 219–21
Simpson, James 45
Sir Ofreo 55, 66, 249–50
Sisam, Celia 10, 34, 54, 54n50, 67
Sisam, Kenneth 2, 6, 15, 17–18, 35, 52–60, 107, 175
  Clerk's Tale edition 22, 57
  Fourteenth Century Verse and Prose 15–16, 25, 54, 94, 192
  Structure of 'Beowulf' 59
  Nun's Priest's Tale edition 22, 57
Skeat, Walter W. 41–52, 135
  as annotator 258–9
  as editor 207, 213
  Astrolabe edition 44
  Chaucer's Minor Poems 22
  Complete Works of Geoffrey Chaucer 5–6
  discovery of Thomas Chaucer 273
  English Dialect Society 51, 191
  Etymological Dictionary 43
  Lancelot of the Laik edition 41–2
  on fairies 250
  on glossary-making 94–5
  Specimens of Early English 54
  Student's Chaucer 24, 45, 79, 87, 89–90, 106
  Student's Pastime 41, 43
Skeat Prize 46–7, 52, 142
Sméagol and Déagol 255, 259–63, 266–7
Solopova, Elizabeth 16n17
South Africa 52–3, 125–6, 168–9, 216–17, 227, 269
South English Legendary 250, 254
Southwark 166, 175, 185
Spearing, A.C. 58
Spenser, Edmund 30, 71–2, 123, 126, 213
  Faerie Queene 68–9, 72, 213
Spurgeon, Caroline 29, 38–9
Spurling, Michael v–vi
Steffensen, Peter vi
Steiner, George 131, 277n28
Stray, Christopher 59n76
Strode, Ralph 162, 232–3, 238
Strohm, Paul 136

Strother (home of John and Alain) 190, 204, 218, 220
Summer Diversions (Oxford) 6–7, 40, 187, 207–16, 275
Sutherland, John 58n67
Sweet, Henry 84

Tabard Inn 99, 119, 164, 166–7, 175, 185, 230, 237, 243
Tale of Beryn 184
Ten Brink, Bernhard 86–7
Theodoric the Great 145–7
Thomas, Mary Edith 16–17
Tolkien, Christopher (youngest son) 5, 11, 12, 13, 26, 32, 26, 36, 54, 57, 71, 106–7, 109, 112, 119, 145, 155, 161, 165, 189, 216, 236, 257, 269–70, 274–7
   Nun's Priest's Tale edition 275–7
   Saga of King Heidrek edition 276
   Silmarillion 277
Tolkien, Edith (wife) 53–4, 133, 149, 176, 196, 248, 251
Tolkien, Hilary (brother) 123, 188, 194–5, 217–19
Tolkien, John (oldest son) 37, 196–7, 205, 223–4
Tolkien, J. R. R.
   Adventures of Tom Bombadil 227–8
   affinities with Chaucer 226–41
   Akallabêth 181
   'Ancrene Wisse and Hali Meiðhad' 50, 182
   Ancrene Wisse edition 4, 30, 52, 118, 224
   Athrabeth Finrod ah Andreth (Boethian dialogue) 143–4
   believed Chaucer knew the Gawain Poet 157
   'Beowulf' and the Critics 1–2, 4, 75, 87
   Beowulf lectures 5, 208
   'Beowulf: The Monsters and the Critics' 2, 5–6, 13–14, 47, 59, 70, 75, 118, 131, 169, 209, 224–5, 257
   Beowulf translation 33, 75
   Book of Lost Tales 1, 165–6, 179, 253, 274
   Cat and the Fiddle 122, 196–7
   'Chaucer as a Philologist: The Reeve's Tale' 2, 6–7, 20, 51, 93, 107, 125–6, 187, 195–207, 217
   Children of Húrin 120
   Clerk's Compleinte 162, 196
   Cottage of Lost Play 1, 244
   'Devil's Coach Horses' 180–1
   'English and Welsh' 46, 52, 145–6
   Fall of Arthur 159–60
   Fall of Gondolin 245
   Farmer Giles of Ham 133, 142, 144, 175–6, 179, 227–8, 241
   Father Christmas Letters 59, 107, 133
   'Flotsam and Jetsam' in Two Towers 216–21
   Foreword to Second Edition of TLOR 60, 70, 117, 142–3, 188, 217–19
   Gawain edition 3–5, 9, 17, 26, 54
   Gawain lecture 249–50
   Gest of Beren and Lúthien 120
   Goblin Feet 121–2, 253
   History of Middle Earth 274
   Hoard 158, 255
   Hobbit 55, 62, 99, 105–6, 111, 114, 123, 124, 133, 151, 160, 172, 174, 185, 225, 230, 236, 252
   Homcoming of Beorhtnoth 159–60, 205–6
   Last Ship 240
   Lay of Aotrou and Itroun 120, 252
   Lay of the Children of Húrin 13–14, 151, 159–60, 253
   Lay of Leithian 30, 32, 70, 74, 76, 120, 159, 175
   Lays of Beleriand 275
   Leaf by Niggle 35, 70, 108, 240
   Legend of Sigurd and Gudrún 159–60
   legendarium 87, 148, 162–3, 165, 236, 277
   Light as Leaf on Lind 3, 122, 251, 253
   Lord of the Rings 163–4
   Lost Road 1, 74, 131, 269
   'Middle English Losenger' 224–5
   Middle English Vocabulary 16, 27–8, 54, 95
   Mr. Bliss 30, 206
   Mythopoeia 32, 88
   New Shadow 152, 241
   Notion Club Papers 37, 142
   on Chaucer's Parlement 226–7
   'On Fairy-Stories' 4, 9–10, 23, 46–7, 88, 99, 140–1, 179, 194–5, 219, 242, 251
   'Oxford English School' 72n135, 198
   Pardoner's Tale: The Story and its Form (lecture series) 2, 7, 18, 257–67
   Pearl edition 3–4, 17–18, 70, 114–15, 117–18, 120–1, 192
   Pearl translation 49, 112–13
   'Philology: General Works' (Year's Work in English Studies) 6n21, 14, 16, 26–7, 48, 113, 125, 174, 187–8
   'Prologue' to TLOR 167, 227–8, 237–8, 244
   Reeve's Tale (programme) 3, 6–7, 40, 187, 204, 209–10, 212, 216–17, 219
   Return of the Shadow 215
   Roverandom 176, 196–7
   'Scouring of the Shire' in Return of the King 220–1

Tolkien, J. R. R. (*cont.*)
  'Sigelwara Land' 1n1, 32–3, 264
  Silmarillion 1, 3, 8–9, 35, 38, 75, 126, 164–5, 170, 228–9, 274
  Smith of Wootton Major 7, 118–19, 251–3, 271
  'Steward and the King' in *Return of the King* 246
  Story of Kullervo 175–6, 236
  Tal-Elmar 182–3
  Tale of Tinúviel (Beren and Lúthien) 3, 122, 165–6, 196, 244
  Treason of Isengard 219
  Two Towers 219
  'Valedictory Address' 2, 52–3, 73, 172, 195, 223, 225
Tolkien, Michael (middle son) 118, 176, 178, 247, 247n74
Tolkien, Priscilla (daughter) 37, 156n162, 161, 168, 210, 229–30, 254
Tom Bombadil 114–15, 121–2
towers 134, 146–7
translation 112–13, 147, 227–8
Treebeard 128, 165, 216, 219, 231, 244
trees 113–14, 126–8, 195, 218–19, 241
Trevisa, John 192
Trumpington 189–90, 194, 233
Turing, Alan 266
Tyrwhitt, Thomas 8, 43, 47, 51

unfinished works 1–2, 4–5, 12–14, 35, 37–8, 66–7, 75, 162, 164, 182–5, 211–12, 235–6, 270, 274, 277

Unwin, Rayner 11, 25, 37–8, 70, 74, 109–11, 237–8, 248, 274
Unwin, Stanley 9, 217, 226, 233, 236, 269
Usher, Susan v–vi

Vache, Philip de la 136, 230–1
Vinaver, Eugene 58–9

Wagner, Richard 71, 146, 227
Walworth, Julia vi
Wanderer 160, 171–2, 207–8
Warner, Lawrence 85n12
Waugh, Evelyn 117–18
Weber, Max 253–4
Weiner, Edmund 14n8
Wells, Joseph 27–8
Wilson, R. M. 215
Wiseman, Christopher 131, 239–40
Wood, Elijah 237
Woolf, Rosemary 10
Woolf, Virginia 58, 233–4
Worcestershire 118, 139, 158, 195, 211–12
Wordsworth 23, 58, 155
Wrenn, C. L. 267
Wright, Joseph 16, 137, 196–8
  English Dialect Dictionary 51, 191
  Primer of Gothic Language 145–6, 195

Yeats, William Butler 56
Yorkshire 49–50, 62–3, 158, 176, 193, 195–8, 203–5, 217, 251